Active Directory Cookbook

Other Microsoft Windows resources from O'Reilly

Related titles

Windows XP in a Nutshell

Windows XP Annoyances

Windows XP Pro: The Missing Manual

Windows XP Home: The Missing Manual

Windows XP Pocket Guide

Windows 2000 Administration in a Nutshell

Windows 2000 Performance Guide

Windows 2000 Commands Pocket Reference

Windows Server 2003 in a Nutshell

Active Directory

ASP in a Nutshell

COM+ Programming with Visual Basic

Developing ASP Components

MCSD in a Nutshell: The Visual Basic Exams

Subclassing and Hooking with Visual Basic

VBScript in a Nutshell

VBScript Pocket Reference

Word Pocket Guide

Outlook Pocket Guide

Win32 API Programming with Visual Basic

Access Database Design and Programming

Writing Excel Macros with VBA

Windows Books Resource Center

windows.oreilly.com is a complete catalog of O'Reilly's Windows and Office books, including sample chapters and code examples.

oreillynet.com is the essential portal for developers interested in open and emerging technologies, including new platforms, programming languages, and operating systems.

Conferences

O'Reilly & Associates brings diverse innovators together to nurture the ideas that spark revolutionary industries. We specialize in documenting the latest tools and systems, translating the innovator's knowledge into useful skills for those in the trenches. Visit *conferences.oreilly.com* for our upcoming events.

Safari Bookshelf (*safari.oreilly.com*) is the premier online reference library for programmers and IT professionals. Conduct searches across more than 1,000 books. Subscribers can zero in on answers to time-critical questions in a matter of seconds. Read the books on your Bookshelf from cover to cover or simply flip to the page you need. Try it today with a free trial.

Active Directory Cookbook

Robbie Allen

O'REILLY®

Beijing · Cambridge · Farnham · Köln · Paris · Sebastopol · Taipei · Tokyo

Active Directory Cookbook
by Robbie Allen

Editor:	Andy Oram
Production Editor:	Matt Hutchinson
Production Services:	Octal Publishing, Inc.
Cover Designer:	Ellie Volckhausen
Interior Designer:	David Futato

Printing History:

September 2003:   First Edition.

ISBN: 0-596-00464-8

[C]

Table of Contents

Foreword xvii

Preface xxi

1. **Getting Started** 1
    1.1 Where to Find the Tools   2
    1.2 Getting Familiar with LDIF   4
    1.3 Programming Notes   5
    1.4 Replaceable Text   9
    1.5 Where to Find More Information   10

2. **Forests, Domains, and Trusts** 13
    2.1 Creating a Forest   17
    2.2 Removing a Forest   18
    2.3 Creating a Domain   19
    2.4 Removing a Domain   20
    2.5 Removing an Orphaned Domain   22
    2.6 Finding the Domains in a Forest   23
    2.7 Finding the NetBIOS Name of a Domain   25
    2.8 Renaming a Domain   26
    2.9 Changing the Mode of a Domain   27
    2.10 Using ADPrep to Prepare a Domain or Forest for Windows Server 2003   29
    2.11 Determining if ADPrep Has Completed   30
    2.12 Checking Whether a Windows 2000 Domain Controller Can Be Upgraded to Windows Server 2003   32
    2.13 Raising the Functional Level of a Windows Server 2003 Domain   33
    2.14 Raising the Functional Level of a Windows Server 2003 Forest   35

2.15 Creating a Trust Between a Windows NT Domain
and an AD Domain   38

2.16 Creating a Transitive Trust Between Two AD Forests   39

2.17 Creating a Shortcut Trust Between Two AD Domains   41

2.18 Creating a Trust to a Kerberos Realm   42

2.19 Viewing the Trusts for a Domain   44

2.20 Verifying a Trust   46

2.21 Resetting a Trust   48

2.22 Removing a Trust   50

2.23 Enabling SID Filtering for a Trust   51

2.24 Finding Duplicate SIDs in a Domain   51

3. Domain Controllers, Global Catalogs, and FSMOs **53**

3.1 Promoting a Domain Controller   55

3.2 Promoting a Domain Controller from Media   55

3.3 Demoting a Domain Controller   57

3.4 Automating the Promotion or Demotion of a Domain Controller 58

3.5 Troubleshooting Domain Controller Promotion or Demotion
Problems   59

3.6 Removing an Unsuccessfully Demoted Domain Controller   60

3.7 Renaming a Domain Controller   63

3.8 Finding the Domain Controllers for a Domain   64

3.9 Finding the Closest Domain Controller   65

3.10 Finding a Domain Controller's Site   67

3.11 Moving a Domain Controller to a Different Site   68

3.12 Finding the Services a Domain Controller Is Advertising   71

3.13 Configuring a Domain Controller to Use an External Time Source   72

3.14 Finding the Number of Logon Attempts Made Against
a Domain Controller   73

3.15 Enabling the /3GB Switch to Increase the LSASS Cache   74

3.16 Cleaning Up Distributed Link Tracking Objects   75

3.17 Enabling and Disabling the Global Catalog   76

3.18 Determining if Global Catalog Promotion Is Complete   78

3.19 Finding the Global Catalog Servers in a Forest   79

3.20 Finding the Domain Controllers or Global Catalog Servers in a Site   80

3.21 Finding Domain Controllers and Global Catalogs via DNS   82

3.22 Changing the Preference for a Domain Controller   83

3.23 Disabling the Global Catalog Requirement During a Windows
2000 Domain Login   85

3.24 Disabling the Global Catalog Requirement During a Windows
      2003 Domain Login   86
3.25 Finding the FSMO Role Holders   87
3.26 Transferring a FSMO Role   89
3.27 Seizing a FSMO Role   91
3.28 Finding the PDC Emulator FSMO Role Owner via DNS   92

4. Searching and Manipulating Objects **94**
4.1 Viewing the RootDSE   95
4.2 Viewing the Attributes of an Object   98
4.3 Using LDAP Controls   101
4.4 Using a Fast or Concurrent Bind   104
4.5 Searching for Objects in a Domain   105
4.6 Searching the Global Catalog   108
4.7 Searching for a Large Number of Objects   110
4.8 Searching with an Attribute-Scoped Query   112
4.9 Searching with a Bitwise Filter   114
4.10 Creating an Object   116
4.11 Modifying an Object   118
4.12 Modifying a Bit-Flag Attribute   121
4.13 Dynamically Linking an Auxiliary Class   123
4.14 Creating a Dynamic Object   125
4.15 Refreshing a Dynamic Object   126
4.16 Modifying the Default TTL Settings for Dynamic Objects   128
4.17 Moving an Object to a Different OU or Container   130
4.18 Moving an Object to a Different Domain   132
4.19 Renaming an Object   133
4.20 Deleting an Object   135
4.21 Deleting a Container That Has Child Objects   136
4.22 Viewing the Created and Last Modified Timestamp of an Object   137
4.23 Modifying the Default LDAP Query Policy   139
4.24 Exporting Objects to an LDIF File   141
4.25 Importing Objects Using an LDIF File   142
4.26 Exporting Objects to a CSV File   144
4.27 Importing Objects Using a CSV File   144

5. Organizational Units **146**
5.1 Creating an OU   147
5.2 Enumerating the OUs in a Domain   148

5.3 Enumerating the Objects in an OU   150
5.4 Deleting the Objects in an OU   151
5.5 Deleting an OU   152
5.6 Moving the Objects in an OU to a Different OU   154
5.7 Moving an OU   155
5.8 Determining How Many Child Objects an OU Has   156
5.9 Delegating Control of an OU   158
5.10 Allowing OUs to Be Created Within Containers   159
5.11 Linking a GPO to an OU   160

6. Users **163**
6.1 Creating a User   164
6.2 Creating a Large Number of Users   166
6.3 Creating an inetOrgPerson User   167
6.4 Modifying an Attribute for Several Users at Once   169
6.5 Moving a User   171
6.6 Renaming a User   172
6.7 Copying a User   173
6.8 Unlocking a User   175
6.9 Finding Locked Out Users   176
6.10 Troubleshooting Account Lockout Problems   177
6.11 Viewing the Account Lockout and Password Policies   179
6.12 Enabling and Disabling a User   182
6.13 Finding Disabled Users   184
6.14 Viewing a User's Group Membership   185
6.15 Changing a User's Primary Group   187
6.16 Transferring a User's Group Membership to Another User   189
6.17 Setting a User's Password   191
6.18 Setting a User's Password via LDAP   192
6.19 Setting a User's Password via Kerberos   193
6.20 Preventing a User from Changing His Password   193
6.21 Requiring a User to Change Her Password at Next Logon   195
6.22 Preventing a User's Password from Expiring   196
6.23 Finding Users Whose Passwords Are About to Expire   197
6.24 Setting a User's Account Options (userAccountControl)   201
6.25 Setting a User's Account to Expire in the Future   203
6.26 Finding Users Whose Accounts Are About to Expire   205
6.27 Determining a User's Last Logon Time   207
6.28 Finding Users Who Have Not Logged On Recently   209

	6.29	Setting a User's Profile Attributes	211
	6.30	Viewing a User's Managed Objects	212
	6.31	Modifying the Default Display Name Used When Creating Users in ADUC	213
	6.32	Creating a UPN Suffix for a Forest	215

7. Groups **217**

	7.1	Creating a Group	218
	7.2	Viewing the Direct Members of a Group	220
	7.3	Viewing the Nested Members of a Group	221
	7.4	Adding and Removing Members of a Group	222
	7.5	Moving a Group	224
	7.6	Changing the Scope or Type of a Group	225
	7.7	Delegating Control for Managing Membership of a Group	226
	7.8	Resolving a Primary Group ID	228
	7.9	Enabling Universal Group Membership Caching	231

8. Computers **233**

	8.1	Creating a Computer	234
	8.2	Creating a Computer for a Specific User or Group	236
	8.3	Joining a Computer to a Domain	241
	8.4	Moving a Computer	244
	8.5	Renaming a Computer	245
	8.6	Testing the Secure Channel for a Computer	247
	8.7	Resetting a Computer	248
	8.8	Finding Inactive or Unused Computers	249
	8.9	Changing the Maximum Number of Computers a User Can Join to the Domain	253
	8.10	Finding Computers with a Particular OS	254
	8.11	Binding to the Default Container for Computers	256
	8.12	Changing the Default Container for Computers	258

9. Group Policy Objects (GPOs) **261**

	9.1	Finding the GPOs in a Domain	263
	9.2	Creating a GPO	264
	9.3	Copying a GPO	265
	9.4	Deleting a GPO	268
	9.5	Viewing the Settings of a GPO	269
	9.6	Modifying the Settings of a GPO	272

	9.7	Importing Settings into a GPO	272
	9.8	Assigning Logon/Logoff and Startup/Shutdown Scripts in a GPO	275
	9.9	Installing Applications with a GPO	276
	9.10	Disabling the User or Computer Settings in a GPO	277
	9.11	Listing the Links for GPO	279
	9.12	Creating a GPO Link to an OU	281
	9.13	Blocking Inheritance of GPOs on an OU	283
	9.14	Applying a Security Filter to a GPO	285
	9.15	Creating a WMI Filter	288
	9.16	Applying a WMI Filter to a GPO	289
	9.17	Backing Up a GPO	291
	9.18	Restoring a GPO	294
	9.19	Simulating the RSoP	296
	9.20	Viewing the RSoP	297
	9.21	Refreshing GPO Settings on a Computer	299
	9.22	Restoring a Default GPO	299

10. Schema **301**

	10.1	Registering the Active Directory Schema MMC Snap-in	303
	10.2	Enabling Schema Updates	304
	10.3	Generating an OID to Use for a New Class or Attribute	306
	10.4	Generating a GUID to Use for a New Class or Attribute	307
	10.5	Extending the Schema	308
	10.6	Documenting Schema Extensions	309
	10.7	Adding a New Attribute	310
	10.8	Viewing an Attribute	313
	10.9	Adding a New Class	315
	10.10	Viewing a Class	317
	10.11	Indexing an Attribute	318
	10.12	Modifying the Attributes That Are Copied When Duplicating a User	320
	10.13	Modifying the Attributes Included with Ambiguous Name Resolution	322
	10.14	Adding or Removing an Attribute in the Global Catalog	324
	10.15	Finding the Nonreplicated and Constructed Attributes	326
	10.16	Finding the Linked Attributes	329
	10.17	Finding the Structural, Auxiliary, Abstract, and 88 Classes	330
	10.18	Finding the Mandatory and Optional Attributes of a Class	332

10.19 Modifying the Default Security of a Class 334

10.20 Deactivating Classes and Attributes 335

10.21 Redefining Classes and Attributes 336

10.22 Reloading the Schema Cache 337

11. Site Topology **340**

11.1 Creating a Site 343

11.2 Listing the Sites 345

11.3 Deleting a Site 346

11.4 Creating a Subnet 347

11.5 Listing the Subnets 349

11.6 Finding Missing Subnets 350

11.7 Creating a Site Link 352

11.8 Finding the Site Links for a Site 353

11.9 Modifying the Sites That Are Part of a Site Link 355

11.10 Modifying the Cost for a Site Link 356

11.11 Disabling Site Link Transitivity or Site Link Schedules 357

11.12 Creating a Site Link Bridge 359

11.13 Finding the Bridgehead Servers for a Site 361

11.14 Setting a Preferred Bridgehead Server for a Site 362

11.15 Listing the Servers 364

11.16 Moving a Domain Controller to a Different Site 365

11.17 Configuring a Domain Controller to Cover Multiple Sites 366

11.18 Viewing the Site Coverage for a Domain Controller 368

11.19 Disabling Automatic Site Coverage for a Domain Controller 368

11.20 Finding the Site for a Client 369

11.21 Forcing a Host to a Particular Site 370

11.22 Creating a Connection Object 372

11.23 Listing the Connection Objects for a Server 373

11.24 Load-Balancing Connection Objects 374

11.25 Finding the ISTG for a Site 375

11.26 Transferring the ISTG to Another Server 376

11.27 Triggering the KCC 378

11.28 Determining if the KCC Is Completing Successfully 379

11.29 Disabling the KCC for a Site 380

11.30 Changing the Interval at Which the KCC Runs 382

12. Replication **384**

12.1　Determining if Two Domain Controllers Are in Sync　384

12.2　Viewing the Replication Status of Several Domain Controllers　386

12.3　Viewing Unreplicated Changes Between Two Domain Controllers　386

12.4　Forcing Replication from One Domain Controller to Another　390

12.5　Changing the Intra-Site Replication Interval　391

12.6　Changing the Intersite Replication Interval　393

12.7　Disabling Inter-Site Compression of Replication Traffic　394

12.8　Checking for Potential Replication Problems　395

12.9　Enabling Enhanced Logging of Replication Events　395

12.10　Enabling Strict or Loose Replication Consistency　396

12.11　Finding Conflict Objects　397

12.12　Viewing Object Metadata　399

13. Domain Name System (DNS) **402**

13.1　Creating a Forward Lookup Zone　404

13.2　Creating a Reverse Lookup Zone　405

13.3　Viewing a Server's Zones　406

13.4　Converting a Zone to an AD-Integrated Zone　408

13.5　Moving AD-Integrated Zones into an Application Partition　409

13.6　Delegating Control of a Zone　411

13.7　Creating and Deleting Resource Records　413

13.8　Querying Resource Records　415

13.9　Modifying the DNS Server Configuration　417

13.10　Scavenging Old Resource Records　418

13.11　Clearing the DNS Cache　420

13.12　Verifying That a Domain Controller Can Register Its Resource Records　422

13.13　Registering a Domain Controller's Resource Records　423

13.14　Preventing a Domain Controller from Dynamically Registering All Resource Records　424

13.15　Preventing a Domain Controller from Dynamically Registering Certain Resource Records　426

13.16　Deregistering a Domain Controller's Resource Records　429

13.17　Allowing Computers to Use a Different Domain Suffix from Their AD Domain　429

14. Security and Authentication **432**

14.1　Enabling SSL/TLS　433

14.2　Encrypting LDAP Traffic with SSL, TLS, or Signing　434

14.3 Enabling Anonymous LDAP Access   436

14.4 Restricting Hosts from Performing LDAP Queries   438

14.5 Using the Delegation of Control Wizard   439

14.6 Customizing the Delegation of Control Wizard   440

14.7 Viewing the ACL for an Object   443

14.8 Customizing the ACL Editor   444

14.9 Viewing the Effective Permissions on an Object   445

14.10 Changing the ACL of an Object   446

14.11 Changing the Default ACL for an Object Class in the Schema   447

14.12 Comparing the ACL of an Object to the Default Defined
in the Schema   448

14.13 Resetting an Object's ACL to the Default Defined in the Schema   448

14.14 Preventing the LM Hash of a Password from Being Stored   449

14.15 Enabling List Object Access Mode   450

14.16 Modifying the ACL on Administrator Accounts   452

14.17 Viewing and Purging Your Kerberos Tickets   453

14.18 Forcing Kerberos to Use TCP   455

14.19 Modifying Kerberos Settings   456

15. Logging, Monitoring, and Quotas **458**

15.1 Enabling Extended dcpromo Logging   459

15.2 Enabling Diagnostics Logging   461

15.3 Enabling NetLogon Logging   463

15.4 Enabling GPO Client Logging   464

15.5 Enabling Kerberos Logging   465

15.6 Enabling DNS Server Debug Logging   467

15.7 Viewing DNS Server Performance Statistics   469

15.8 Enabling Inefficient and Expensive LDAP Query Logging   472

15.9 Using the STATS Control to View LDAP Query Statistics   474

15.10 Using Perfmon to Monitor AD   476

15.11 Using Perfmon Trace Logs to Monitor AD   478

15.12 Enabling Auditing of Directory Access   481

15.13 Creating a Quota   482

15.14 Finding the Quotas Assigned to a Security Principal   484

15.15 Changing How Tombstone Objects Count Against Quota Usage   485

15.16 Setting the Default Quota for All Security Principals in a Partition   487

15.17 Finding the Quota Usage for a Security Principal   488

16. Backup, Recovery, DIT Maintenance, and Deleted Objects **491**

   16.1 Backing Up Active Directory   493

   16.2 Restarting a Domain Controller in Directory Services Restore Mode   494

   16.3 Resetting the Directory Service Restore Mode Administrator Password   496

   16.4 Performing a Nonauthoritative Restore   497

   16.5 Performing an Authoritative Restore of an Object or Subtree   498

   16.6 Performing a Complete Authoritative Restore   500

   16.7 Checking the DIT File's Integrity   501

   16.8 Moving the DIT Files   502

   16.9 Repairing or Recovering the DIT   502

  16.10 Performing an Online Defrag Manually   503

  16.11 Determining How Much Whitespace Is in the DIT   505

  16.12 Performing an Offline Defrag to Reclaim Space   506

  16.13 Changing the Garbage Collection Interval   508

  16.14 Logging the Number of Expired Tombstone Objects   509

  16.15 Determining the Size of the Active Directory Database   511

  16.16 Searching for Deleted Objects   512

  16.17 Restoring a Deleted Object   513

  16.18 Modifying the Tombstone Lifetime for a Domain   515

17. Application Partitions **517**

   17.1 Creating and Deleting an Application Partition   518

   17.2 Finding the Application Partitions in a Forest   521

   17.3 Adding or Removing a Replica Server for an Application Partition   523

   17.4 Finding the Replica Servers for an Application Partition   525

   17.5 Finding the Application Partitions Hosted by a Server   527

   17.6 Verifying Application Partitions Are Instantiated on a Server Correctly   529

   17.7 Setting the Replication Notification Delay for an Application Partition   530

   17.8 Setting the Reference Domain for an Application Partition   532

   17.9 Delegating Control of Managing an Application Partition   534

18. Interoperability and Integration **539**

   18.1 Accessing AD from a Non-Windows Platform   539

   18.2 Programming with .NET   540

   18.3 Programming with DSML   542

   18.4 Programming with Perl   543

18.5 Programming with Java 544

18.6 Programming with Python 546

18.7 Integrating with MIT Kerberos 547

18.8 Integrating with Samba 548

18.9 Integrating with Apache 549

18.10 Replacing NIS 550

18.11 Using BIND for DNS 551

18.12 Authorizing a Microsoft DHCP Server 552

18.13 Using VMWare for Testing AD 553

Appendix: Tool List **557**

Index **575**

Foreword

I've been waiting for "The Year of the Directory" for 15 years, basically since "The Year of the LAN," which, if I recall correctly, occurred in 1983, 1984, 1985, and briefly again in 1988. But as I write this in 2003, there are very few enterprise networks that are not running a directory of one sort or another. While I was patiently waiting at the front door, the directory slipped in the back. I must have been napping on the couch.

The Year of the Directory never came, nor will it ever. Just as with TV, fax, LANs, cell phones, and the Internet, we've experienced another sea change in communications and information technology. But no one can point to the time when the change "happened." Ocean tides have a well-defined schedule, but watershed technology changes are more like global warming. "Look, Honey! The waves come right up to the front porch!" The IT industry has simply evolved over time to assimilate yet another new technology, making our ability to communicate and compute more seamless, more pervasive, and more affordable.

And that's sort of the point of directories: to make it possible for us to build larger, more sophisticated networks that don't collapse under the weight of their own complexity. The first commercial NOS with an integrated directory, Banyan's VINES, was a startling success in this regard. At a time when most enterprise IT executives were just dimly aware that workgroup LANs had utterly subverted their minicomputer and mainframe-based strategies, a relatively few prescient CIOs had seen the future, building centrally managed, global PC networks based on Banyan's distributed and replicated directory, StreetTalk.

I loved VINES and StreetTalk because they made it possible to operate distributed enterprise networks with extremely low administrative costs. The VINES NOS provided competent file, print, and communications on industry-standard server hardware. The StreetTalk directory service added secure, distributed naming and authentication across the entire network. VINES also came bundled with a directory-integrated email system that was a model of simplicity and scalability. VINES administrators enjoyed all this with a low level of administrative overhead that we can only appreciate in retrospect. Bringing up a new VINES server running both the directory and email service amounted to loading the OS (27 floppies worth!), configuring the NIC, and giving the server a name. Troubleshooting tools were mostly nonexistent because there were mostly no troubles to shoot. And when there was a problem that we couldn't sort out using the primitive tools we had, waving a dead chicken over the suspect server usually took care of it. StreetTalk made VINES as close to a "set it and forget it" network as the industry has ever seen, which is just what directories are supposed to do.

Banyan's 10-year lead in the enterprise network market evaporated in about 5 years, due to many factors: inept marketing, the introduction of a competitive directory from Novell (NDS, now called eDirectory), and ISV support that could only be described as hostile. Banyan's demise as a NOS company was as ugly as it was inevitable.

The NOS directory market is now left to Novell's eDirectory and Microsoft's Active Directory. eDirectory does well in many situations, but for building enterprise-scale, Windows-based networks, Active Directory's dominance seems inevitable.

Now I'll admit to being a big fan of Microsoft's Active Directory. Active Directory is a wonderfully sophisticated piece of software that performs well, scales up and scales out, and does an outstanding job of integrating computers running earlier Windows operating systems such as Windows NT 4.0 and Windows 98. I doubt that Microsoft has ever produced a piece of software as reliable as Active Directory, particularly in its 1.0 version. I'd be really surprised if there's an enterprise that can't implement Active Directory successfully.

But all that sophistication and performance requires a substantial amount of care and feeding. Running a VINES network was like driving a 60s vintage VW Beetle: push, pull, left, right, and the Bug did pretty much what you expected. Managing an Active Directory enterprise is more like piloting a Lear jet. If you don't know how to use all those knobs and dials properly, you've got a good chance of leaving a smoking crater in the ground.

A competent Active Directory administrator must have at least a passing understanding of a handful of different technologies, including DNS, WINS, Kerberos, LDAP, and the Windows operating system itself. And he must be able to perform more than a hundred different tasks using more than 30 different utilities. Even if you've read the books and taken the classes, becoming a skilled Active Directory administrator requires detailed knowledge of the ins and outs of Active Directory. Although Active Directory simplifies the management of a large network substantially, much of the administrative overhead has simply shifted to Active Directory itself.

That's where the *Active Directory Cookbook* comes in. Robbie Allen has produced an outstanding reference that spells out how to perform the hundred-plus tasks that an administrator is likely to perform during the Active Directory lifecycle. The *Active*

Directory Cookbook is essentially a book of checklists for the professional Active Directory pilot. Each administrative task includes background information, step-by-step instructions, and references to more detailed information on Microsoft's web site. If you need to do something with Active Directory, Robbie shows you how to do it with a minimum of fuss and bother.

I've known Robbie for several years, both as a first-string speaker for NetPro's Directory Experts Conference and as a frequent contributor to Tony Murray's activedir. org mailing list. Robbie brings a rare combination of skills and knowledge to the table. He has the rare ability to blend an in-depth knowledge of how Active Directory actually works, hands-on understanding of what an administrator needs to do (and not do!) to successfully deploy and run a large Active Directory installation, and a Unix administrator's inbred desire to automate everything with scripts. So not only does Robbie deliver a "how-to" for every Active Directory administrative task you're likely to perform, he shows you how to automate it using a combination of VB Script, Perl, batch files, and command-line utilities.

And that's what really excites me about this book. A catalog of step-by-step instructions for common Active Directory administrative tasks would be useful by itself. But by providing a programmatic solution for most of these tasks, Robbie has laid the groundwork for automating most of your day-to-day Active Directory management tasks. And that brings you a step closer to what you ultimately want: a network with the performance and sophistication of Windows and Active Directory, and the simplicity of administration we haven't had since VINES and StreetTalk. That would be a mighty powerful combination.

—Gil Kirkpatrick
CTO, NetPro

Gil Kirkpatrick is the Chief Technology Officer at NetPro and the founder of the Directory Experts Conference. With a strategic combination of software solutions, conferences, and web resources, NetPro is revolutionizing the way companies manage their directories and driving the availability and performance of the world's networks. NetPro delivers the only comprehensive suite of solutions designed to manage network directory services for 24 × 7 availability throughout the directory lifecycle (*http://www.netpro.com*).

Preface

In 1998 when I first became involved with the Microsoft Windows 2000 Joint Development Program (JDP), there was very little data available on Active Directory. In the following months and even after the initial release of Windows 2000, there were very few books or white papers to help early adopters of Active Directory get started. And some of the information that had been published was often inaccurate or misleading. Many early deployers had to learn by trial and error. As time passed, more and more informative books were published, which helped fill the information gap.

By the end of the second year of its release, there was an explosion of information on Active Directory. Not only were there over 50 books published, but Microsoft also cleaned up their documentation on MSDN (*http://msdn.microsoft.com*) and their AD web site (*http://www.microsoft.com/ad/*). Now those sites have numerous white papers, many of which could serve as mini booklets. Other web sites have popped up as well that contain a great deal of information on Active Directory. With Windows Server 2003, Microsoft has taken their level of documentation a step higher. Extensive information on Active Directory is available directly from any Windows Server 2003 computer in the form of the Help and Support Center (available from the Start Menu). So with all this data available on Active Directory in the form of published books, white papers, web sites, and even from within the operating system, why would you want to purchase this one?

In the summer of 2002, I was thumbing through the *Perl Cookbook* from O'Reilly, looking for help with an automation script I was writing for Active Directory. It just so happened that there was a recipe that addressed the specific task I was trying to perform. In Cookbook parlance, a recipe provides instructions on how to solve a particular problem. I thought that since Active Directory is such a task-oriented environment, the Cookbook approach might be a very good format. After a little research, I found there were books (often multiple) on nearly every facet of Active Directory, including introductory books, design guides, books that focused on migration, programming books, and reference books. The one type of book I didn't see was a task-oriented "how-to" book, which is exactly what the Cookbook format provides.

Based on my own experience, hours of research, and years of hanging out on Active Directory newsgroups and mailing lists, I've compiled over 325 recipes that should answer the majority of "How do I do X" questions one could pose about Active Directory. And just as in the Perl community where the *Perl Cookbook* was a great addition that sells well even today, I believe the *Active Directory Cookbook* will also be a great addition to any Active Directory library.

Who Should Read This Book?

As with many of the books in the Cookbook series, the *Active Directory Cookbook* can be useful to anyone who has to deploy, administer, or automate Active Directory. This book can serve as a great reference for those who have to work with Active Directory on a day-to-day basis. And because of all the programming samples, this book can be really beneficial to programmers who want to get a jumpstart on performing certain tasks in an application. For those without much programming background, the VBScript and Perl solutions are straightforward and should be pretty easy to follow and expand on.

The companion to this book, *Active Directory*, Second Edition from O'Reilly, is a great choice for those wanting a thorough description of the core concepts behind Active Directory, how to design an Active Directory infrastructure, and how to automate that infrastructure using Active Directory Service Interfaces (ADSI) and Windows Management Instrumentation (WMI). *Active Directory*, Second Edition does not describe how to accomplish every possible task within Active Directory; that is the purpose of this book. These two books, along with the supplemental information described in Recipe 1.5, should be sufficient to answer most questions you have about Active Directory.

What's in This Book?

This book consists of 18 chapters. Here is a brief overview of each chapter:

- Chapter 1, *Getting Started*, sets the stage for the book by covering where you can find the tools used in the book, VBScript and Perl issues to consider, and where to find additional information.
- Chapter 2, *Forests, Domains, and Trusts*, covers how to create and remove forests and domains, update the domain mode or functional levels, create different types of trusts, and other administrative trust tasks.
- Chapter 3, *Domain Controllers, Global Catalogs, and FSMOs*, covers promoting and demoting domain controllers, finding domain controllers, enabling the global catalog, and finding and managing Flexible Single Master Operations (FSMO) roles.

- Chapter 4, *Searching and Manipulating Objects*, covers the basics of searching Active Directory; creating, modifying, and deleting objects; using LDAP controls; and importing and exporting data using LDAP Data Interchange Format (LDIF) and comma-separated variable (CSV) files.

- Chapter 5, *Organizational Units*, covers creating, moving, and deleting Organizational Units, and managing the objects contained within them.

- Chapter 6, *Users*, covers all aspects of managing user objects, including creating, renaming, moving, resetting passwords, unlocking, modifying the profile attributes, and locating users that have certain criteria (e.g., password is about to expire).

- Chapter 7, *Groups*, covers how to create groups, modify group scope, and type and manage membership.

- Chapter 8, *Computers*, covers creating computers, joining computers to a domain, resetting computers, and locating computers that match certain criteria (e.g., have been inactive for a number of weeks).

- Chapter 9, *Group Policy Objects (GPOs)*, covers how to create, modify, link, copy, import, back up, restore, and delete GPOs using the Group Policy Management Console and scripting interface.

- Chapter 10, *Schema*, covers basic schema administration tasks, such as generating object identifiers (OIDs) and schemaIDGUIDs, how to use LDIF to extend the schema, and how to locate attributes or classes that match certain criteria (e.g., all attributes that are indexed).

- Chapter 11, *Site Topology*, covers how to manage sites, subnets, site links, and connection objects.

- Chapter 12, *Replication*, covers how to trigger and disable the Knowledge Consistency Checker (KCC), how to query metadata, force replication, and determine what changes have yet to replicate between domain controllers.

- Chapter 13, *Domain Name System (DNS)*, covers creating zones and resource records, modifying DNS server configuration, querying DNS, and customizing the resource records a domain controller dynamically registers.

- Chapter 14, *Security and Authentication*, covers how to delegate control, view and modify permissions, view effective permissions, and manage Kerberos tickets.

- Chapter 15, *Logging, Monitoring, and Quotas*, covers how to enable auditing, diagnostics, DNS, NetLogon, Kerberos and GPO logging, obtain LDAP query statistics, and manage quotas.

- Chapter 16, *Backup, Recovery, DIT Maintenance, and Deleted Objects*, covers how to back up Active Directory, perform authoritative and nonauthoritative restores, check DIT file integrity, perform online and offline defrags, and search for deleted objects.

- Chapter 17, *Application Partitions*, covers creating and managing application partitions.
- Chapter 18, *Interoperability and Integration*, covers how to integrate Active Directory with various applications, services, and programming languages.

Conventions Used in This Book

The following typographical conventions are used in this book:

Constant width
> Indicates command-line elements, computer output, and code examples.

Constant width italic
> Indicates placeholders (for which you substitute an actual name) in examples and in registry keys

Constant width bold
> Indicates user input

Italic
> Introduces new terms and URLs, commands, file extensions, filenames, directory or folder names, and UNC pathnames

 Indicates a tip, suggestion, or general note. For example, I'll tell you if you need to use a particular version or if an operation requires certain privileges.

 Indicates a warning or caution. For example, I'll tell you if Active Directory does not behave as you'd expect or if a particular operation has a negative impact on performance.

We'd Like Your Feedback!

We at O'Reilly have tested and verified the information in this book to the best of our ability, but mistakes and oversights do occur. Please let us know about errors you may find, as well as your suggestions for future editions, by writing to:

O'Reilly & Associates, Inc.
1005 Gravenstein Highway North
Sebastopol, CA 95472
(800) 998-9938 (in the U.S. or Canada)
(707) 829-0515 (international or local)
(707) 829-0104 (fax)

We have a web page for the book, where we list errata, examples, or any additional information. You can access this page at:

> *http:www.oreilly.com/catalog/activedckbk*

Examples can also be found at the author's web site:

> *http://www.rallenhome.com/books/adcookbook/code.html*

To comment or ask technical questions about this book, send email to:

> *bookquestions@oreilly.com*

For more information about our books, conferences, software, Resource Centers, and the O'Reilly Network, see our web site at:

> *http://www.oreilly.com*

Acknowledgments

The people at O'Reilly were a joy to work with. I would like to thank Robert Denn for helping me get this book off the ground. I am especially grateful for Andy Oram's insightful and thought-provoking feedback.

I was very fortunate to have an all-star group of technical reviewers. If there was ever a need to assemble a panel of the top Active Directory experts, you would be hard pressed to find a more knowledgeable group of guys. Here they are in alphabetical order:

Rick Kingslan (*rkingsla@cox.net*) is a Senior Systems Engineer and Microsoft Windows Server MVP. If you've ever posted a question to an Active Directory newsgroup or discussion forum, odds are Rick participated in the thread. His uncanny ability to provide useful feedback on just about any Active Directory problem helped ensure I covered all the angles with each recipe.

Gil Kirkpatrick (*gilk@netpro.com*) is the Executive Vice President & CTO of NetPro (*http://www.netpro.com/*). Gil is also the author of *Active Directory Programming* from MacMillan. His extensive knowledge of the underpinnings of Active Directory helped clarify several issues I did not address adequately the first time through.

Tony Murray (*tony@activedir.org*) is the maintainer of the *ActiveDir.org* web site and mailing list, which is one of the premier Active Directory discussion forums. The myriad of questions posed to the list served as inspiration for this book. Tony's comments and suggestions throughout the book helped tremendously.

Todd Myrick (*myrickt@mail.nih.gov*) has a unique perspective on Active Directory from his experience inside the government. Todd contributed several "outside the box" ideas to the book that only a creative person, such as he, could have done.

Joe Richards (*joe@joeware.net*) is the creator of the *http://www.joeware.net/* web site, which contains many must-have Active Directory tools, such as adfind, unlock, and much more. Joe is one of the most experienced Active Directory administrators and programmers I've met. He's had to do most of the tasks in this book at one point or another, so his contributions were significant.

Kevin Sullivan (*ksullivan@aelita.com*) is the Project Manager for Enterprise Directory Management at Aelita. Kevin has as much experience with Active Directory as anyone you'll find. He is a frequent contributor to Active Directory discussion forums, and he provided numerous suggestions and clarifications throughout the book.

Last, but certainly not least, I would like to thank my wife Janet. Her love, support, and bright smile are constant reminders of how lucky I am. Did I mention she cooks, too!

## CHAPTER 1

Getting Started

1.0 Approach to the Book

If you are familiar with the O'Reilly Cookbook format that can be seen in other popular books, such as the *Perl Cookbook*, *Java Cookbook*, and *DNS and BIND Cookbook*, then the layout of this book will not be anything new to you. The book is composed of 18 chapters, each containing 10–30 recipes for performing a specific Active Directory task. Within each recipe are four sections: problem, solution, discussion, and see also. The problem section briefly describes the task the recipe focuses on. The solution section contains step-by-step instructions on how to accomplish the task. The discussion section contains detailed information about the problem or solution. The see also section contains references to additional sources of information that can be useful if you still need more information after reading the discussion. The see also section may reference other recipes, MS Knowledge Base (MS KB) (*http://support.microsoft.com/*) articles, or documentation from the Microsoft Developers Network (MSDN) (*http://msdn.microsoft.com*).

At Least Three Ways to Do It!

When I first began developing the content for the book, I struggled with how to capture the fact that you can do things multiple ways with Active Directory. You may be familiar with the famous Perl motto: There Is More Than One Way To Do It; well with Active Directory, there are often At Least Three Ways To Do It. You can perform a task with a graphical user interface (GUI), such as ADSI Edit, LDP, or the Active Directory Users and Computers snap-in; you can use a command-line interface (CLI), such as the *ds* utilities (i.e., *dsadd*, *dsmod*, *dsrm*, *dsquery*, *dsget*), *nltest*, *netdom*, or *ldifde*; and, finally, you can perform the same task using a scripting language, such as VBScript or Perl.

Since people prefer different methods, and no one method is necessarily better than another, I decided to write solutions to the recipes using one of each. That means instead of just a single solution per recipe, I include up to three solutions using GUI,

CLI, and programmatic examples. That said, some recipes cannot be accomplished with one of the three methods or it is very difficult to do so. In that case, only the applicable methods are covered.

In the GUI and CLI solutions, I use standard tools that are readily accessible. There are other tools that I could have used, which would have made some of the tasks easier to accomplish, but I wanted to make this book as useful as possible without requiring you to hunt down the tools I use.

I also took this approach with the programmatic solutions; I use VBScript for the programming language, primarily because it is widely used among Windows administrators and is the most straightforward from a code perspective when using Active Directory Service Interface (ADSI) and Windows Script Host (WSH). For those familiar with other languages, such as Visual Basic, Perl and JScript, it is very easy to convert code from VBScript.

The downside to using VBScript is that it does not have all of the facilities necessary to accomplish some complicated tasks. It is for this reason that I use Perl in a few recipes that required a complicated programmatic solution. For those of you who wish that all of the solutions were written with Perl instead of VBScript, you are in luck. On the book's web site, I've posted companion Perl solutions for every recipe that had a VBScript solution. Go to *http://www.rallenhome.com/books/adcookbook/code.html* to download the code.

Windows 2000 Versus Windows Server 2003

Another challenge with writing this book is there are now two versions of Active Directory. The initial version was released with Windows 2000 and recently, Microsoft released Windows Server 2003, which provides a lot of updates and new features. Since Windows Server 2003 Active Directory is the latest and greatest version, and includes a lot of new tools that aren't present in Windows 2000, I've decided to go with the approach of making everything work under Windows Server 2003 Active Directory first, and Windows 2000 second. In fact, the majority of the solutions will work with Windows 2000 unchanged. For the recipes or solutions that are specific to a particular version, I include a note mentioning the version it is targeted for. Most GUI and programmatic solutions will work with either version unchanged, but Microsoft introduced several new CLIs with Windows Server 2003, most of which cannot be run on the Windows 2000 operating system. Typically, you can still use these newer tools on a Windows XP or Windows Server 2003 computer to manage Windows 2000 Active Directory.

1.1   Where to Find the Tools

For the GUI and CLI solutions to mean much to you, you need access to the tools that are used in the examples. For this reason, in the majority of cases and unless otherwise noted, I only used tools that are part of the default operating system or available in the Resource Kit or Support Tools. The Windows 2000 Server Resource Kit and Windows Server 2003 Resource Kit are invaluable sources of information, along with providing numerous tools that aid administrators in their daily tasks. More information on the Resource Kits can be found at the following web site: *http://www.microsoft.com/windows/reskits/*. The Windows 2000 Support Tools, which is called the Windows Support Tools in Windows Server 2003, contain many "must have" tools for people that work with Active Directory. The Microsoft installer (MSI) for the Windows Support Tools can be found on a Windows 2000 Server or Windows Server 2003 CD in the *\support\tools directory*. The Appendix contains a complete list of the tools used within this book, where they can be found, and what recipes they are used in.

Once you have the tools at your disposal, there are a couple other issues to be aware of while trying to apply the solutions in your environment, which I'll now describe.

Running Tools with Alternate Credentials

A best practice for managing Active Directory is to create separate administrator accounts that you grant elevated privileges, instead of letting administrators use their normal user account that they use to access other Network Operating System (NOS) resources. This is beneficial because an administrator who wants to use elevated privileges has to log on with his administrative account explicitly instead of having the rights implicitly, which could lead to accidental changes in Active Directory. Assuming you employ this method, then you must provide alternate credentials when using tools to administer Active Directory unless you log on to a machine, such as a domain controller, with the administrative credentials.

There are several options for specifying alternate credentials. Many GUI and CLI tools have an option to specify a user and password to authenticate with. If the tool you want to use does not have that option, you can use the runas command instead. The following command would run the enumprop command from the Resource Kit under the credentials of the administrator account in the *rallencorp.com* domain:

```
> runas /user:administrator@rallencorp.com↵
/netonly "enumprop \"LDAP://dc1/dc=rallencorp,dc=com\""
```

To run a Microsoft Management Console (MMC) console with alternate credentials, simply use mmc as the command to run from runas:

```
> runas /user:administrator@rallencorp.com /netonly "mmc"
```

This will create an empty MMC console from which you can add consoles for any snap-ins that have been installed on the local computer.

The /netonly switch is necessary if the user you are authenticating with does not have local logon rights on the machine you are running the command from.

There is another option for running MMC snap-ins with alternate credentials. Click on the Start menu and browse to the tool you want to open, hold down the Shift key, and then right-click on the tool. If you select Run As, you will be prompted to enter credentials to run the tool under.

Targeting Specific Domain Controllers

Another issue to be aware of when following the instructions in the recipes is whether you need to target a specific domain controller. In the solutions in this book, I typically do not target a specific domain controller. When you don't specify a domain controller, you are using a serverless bind and there is no guarantee what server you will be hitting. Depending on your environment and the task you need to do, you may want to target a specific domain controller so that you know where the query or change will be taking place. Also, serverless binding can work only if the DNS for the Active Directory forest is configured properly and your client can query it. If you have a standalone Active Directory environment that has no ties to your corporate DNS, you may need to target a specific domain controller for the tools to work.

1.2   Getting Familiar with LDIF

Even with the new utilities available with Windows Server 2003, support for modifying data within Active Directory using a command-line tool is relatively weak. The dsmod tool can modify attributes on a limited set of object classes, but it does not allow you to modify any object type.

One reason for the lack of command-line tools to do this is the command line is not well suited for manipulating objects, for example, that have multivalued attributes. If you want to specify more than just one or two values, a single command could get quite long. It would be easier to use a GUI editor, such as ADSI Edit, to do the task instead.

The LDAP Data Interchange Format was designed to address this issue. Defined in RFC 2849, LDIF allows you to represent directory additions, modifications, and deletions in a text-based file, which you can import into a directory using an LDIF-capable tool.

The ldifde utility has been available since Windows 2000 and it allows you to import and export Active Directory content in LDIF format. LDIF files are composed of blocks of entries. An entry can add, modify, or delete an object. The first line of an entry is the distinguished name. The second line contains a changetype, which can be add, modify, or delete. If it is an object addition, the rest of the entry contains the attributes that should be initially set on the object (one per line). For object deletions, you do not need to specify any other attributes. And for object modifications, you need to specify at least three more lines. The first should contain the type of modification you want to perform on the object. This can be add (to set a previously unset attribute or to add a new value to a multivalued attribute), replace (to replace an existing value), or delete (to remove a value). The modification type should be followed by a colon and the attribute you want to perform the modification on. The next line should contain the name of the attribute followed by a colon, and the value for the attribute. For example, to replace the last name attribute with the value Smith, you'd use the following LDIF:

```
dn: cn=jsmith,cn=users,dc=rallencorp,dc=com
changetype: modify
replace: sn
sn: Smith
-
```

Modification entries must be followed by a line that only contains a hyphen (-). You can put additional modification actions following the hyphen, each separated by another hyphen. Here is a complete LDIF example that adds a jsmith user object and then modifies the givenName and sn attributes for that object:

```
dn: cn=jsmith,cn=users,dc=rallencorp,dc=com
changetype: add
objectClass: user
samaccountname: jsmith
sn: JSmith
useraccountcontrol: 512

dn: cn=jsmith,cn=users,dc=rallencorp,dc=com
changetype: modify
add: givenName
givenName: Jim
-
replace: sn
sn: Smith
-
```

See Recipes 4.24 and 4.25 for more details on how to use the ldifde utility to import and export LDIF files.

1.3 Programming Notes

In the VBScript solutions, my intention was to provide the answer in as few lines of code as necessary. Since this book is not a pure programming book, I did not want to provide a detailed explanation of how to use ADSI or WMI. If you are looking for that, I recommend Part 3 of *Active Directory*, Second Edition. The intent of the

VBScript code is to provide you the basics for how a task can be automated and let you run with it. Most examples only take some minor tweaking to make them do something useful for you.

Just as with the GUI and CLI solutions, there are some important issues to be aware of when looking at the VBScript solutions.

Serverless Binds

I mentioned earlier that in the GUI and CLI examples I did not provide instructions for targeting a specific domain controller to perform a task. Instead, I rely on serverless binds in most cases. The same applies to the API solutions. A serverless bind for the RootDSE looks like the following in VBScript:

```
set objRootDSE = GetObject("LDAP://RootDSE")
```

That code will query the RootDSE for a domain controller in the domain of the currently logged on user. You can target a specific domain instead by simply specifying the domain name in the ADsPath:

```
set objRootDSE = GetObject("LDAP://apac.rallencorp.com/RootDSE")
```

And similarly, you can target a specific domain controller by including the server name in the ADsPath:

```
set objRootDSE = GetObject("LDAP://dc1/RootDSE")
```

So depending on how your environment is set up and what forest you want to query, you may or may not need to specify a domain or server name in the code.

Running Scripts Using Alternate Credentials

Just as you might need to run the GUI and CLI tools with alternate credentials, you may also need to run your scripts and programs with alternate credentials. One way is to use the runas method described earlier when invoking the script. A better option would be to use the Scheduled Tasks service to run the script under credentials you specify when creating the task. And yet another option is to hardcode the credentials in the script. Obviously, this is not very appealing in some scenarios because you do not want the username and password contained in the script to be easily viewable by others. Nevertheless, it is a necessary evil, especially when developing against multiple forests, and I'll describe how it can be done with ADSI and ADO.

With ADSI, you can use the IADsOpenDSObject::OpenDSObject method to specify alternate credentials. You can quickly turn any ADSI-based example in this book into one that authenticates as a particular user. For example, a solution to print out the description of a domain might look like the following:

```
set objDomain = GetObject("LDAP://dc=apac,dc=rallencorp,dc=com")
WScript.Echo "Description: " & objDomain.Get("description")
```

Using OpenDSObject, it takes only one additional statement to make the same code authenticate as the administrator in the domain:

```
set objLDAP = GetObject("LDAP:")
set objDomain = objLDAP.OpenDSObject( _
    "LDAP://dc=apac,dc=rallencorp,dc=com", _
    "administrator@apac.rallencorp.com", _
    "MyPassword", _
    0)
WScript.Echo "Description: " & objDomain.Get("description")
```

It is just as easy to authenticate in ADO code as well. Take the following example, which queries all computer objects in the *apac.rallencorp.com* domain:

```
strBase   = "<LDAP://dc=apac,dc=rallencorp,dc=com>;"
strFilter = "(&(objectclass=computer)(objectcategory=computer));"
strAttrs  = "cn;"
strScope  = "subtree"

set objConn = CreateObject("ADODB.Connection")
objConn.Provider = "ADsDSOObject"
objConn.Open "Active Directory Provider"
set objRS = objConn.Execute(strBase & strFilter & strAttrs & strScope)
objRS.MoveFirst
while Not objRS.EOF
    Wscript.Echo objRS.Fields(0).Value
    objRS.MoveNext
wend
```

Now, by adding two lines (shown in bold), we can authenticate with the administrator account:

```
strBaseDN = "<LDAP://dc=apac,dc=rallencorp,dc=com>;"
strFilter = "(&(objectclass=computer)(objectcategory=computer));"
strAttrs  = "cn;"
strScope  = "subtree"

set objConn = CreateObject("ADODB.Connection")
objConn.Provider = "ADsDSOObject"
objConn.Properties("User ID")  = "administrator@apac.rallencorp.com"
objConn.Properties("Password") = "MyPassword"
objConn.Open "Active Directory Provider"
set objRS = objConn.Execute(strBaseDN & strFilter & strAttrs & strScope)
objRS.MoveFirst
while Not objRS.EOF
    Wscript.Echo objRS.Fields(0).Value
    objRS.MoveNext
wend
```

To authenticate with ADO, you need to set the User ID and Password properties of the ADO connection object. I used the UPN of the administrator for the user ID. With ADSI and ADO, you can use a UPN, NT 4.0 style account name (e.g., APAC\Administrator), or distinguished name for the user ID.

Defining Variables and Error Checking

An important part of any script is error checking. Error checking allows your programs to gracefully identify any issues that arise during execution and take the appropriate action. Another best practice is to define variables before you use them and clean them up after you are done with them. In this book, most of the programmatic solutions do not include any error checking, predefined variables, or variable clean up. While admittedly this is not setting a good example, if I included extensive error checking and variable management, it would have made this book considerably longer with little value to the reader. Again, the goal is to provide you with a code snippet that shows you how to accomplish a task, not provide robust scripts that include all the trimmings.

Error checking with VBScript is pretty straightforward. At the beginning of the script include the following declaration:

```
On Error Resume Next
```

This tells the script interpreter to continue even if errors occur. Without that declaration, anytime an error is encountered the script will abort. When you use `On Error Resume Next`, you need to use the `Err` object to check for errors after any step where a fatal error could occur. The following example shows how to use the `Err` object.

```
On Error Resume Next
set objDomain = GetObject("LDAP://dc=rallencorp,dc=com")
if Err.Number <> 0 then
    Wscript.Echo "An error occured getting the domain object: " & Err.Description
    Wscript.Quit
end if
```

Two important properties of the `Err` object are `Number`, which if non-zero signifies an error, and `Description` which will contain the error message.

As far as variable management goes, it is always a good practice to include the following at the beginning of every script:

```
Option Explicit
```

When this is used, every variable in the script must be declared or an exception will be generated when you attempt to run the script. Variables are declared in VBScript using the `Dim` keyword. After you are done with a variable, it is a good practice to set it to `Nothing` so you release any resources bound to the variable, and don't accidentally re-use the variable with its previous value. The following code shows a complete example for printing the display name for a domain with error checking and variable management included:

```
Option Explicit
On Error Resume Next

Dim objDomain
set objDomain = GetObject("LDAP://cn=users,dc=rallencorp,dc=com")
```

```
if Err.Number <> 0 then
   Wscript.Echo "An error occured getting the domain object: " & Err.Description
   Wscript.Quit
end if

Dim strDescr
strDescr = objDomain.Get("description")
if Err.Number <> 0 then
   Wscript.Echo "An error occured getting the description: " & Err.Description
   Wscript.Quit
end if

WScript.Echo "Description: " & strDescr

objDomain = Nothing
strDescr  = Nothing
```

1.4   Replaceable Text

This book is filled with examples. Every recipe consists of one or more examples that show how to accomplish a task. Most CLI- and VBScript-based solutions use parameters that are based on the domain, forest, OU, user, etc., that is being added, modified, queried, and so on. Instead of using fictitious names, in most cases, I use replaceable text. This text should be easily recognizable because it is in italics and surrounded by angle brackets (<>). Instead of describing what each replaceable element represents every time I use it, I've included a list of some of the commonly used ones here:

<DomainDN>
> Distinguished name of domain (e.g., *dc=amer,dc=rallencorp,dc=com*)

<ForestRootDN>
> Distinguished name of the forest root domain (e.g., *dc=rallencorp,dc=com*)

<DomainDNSName>
> Fully qualified DNS name of domain (e.g., *amer.rallencorp.com*)

<ForestDNSName>
> Fully qualified DNS name of forest root domain (e.g., *rallencorp.com*)

<DomainControllerName>
> Single label or fully qualified DNS hostname of domain controller (e.g., *dc01.rallencorp.com*)

<UserDN>
> Distinguished name of user (e.g., *cn=administrator,cn=users,dc=rallencorp,dc=com*)

<GroupDN>
> Distinguished name of group (e.g., *cn=Domain Admins,cn=users,dc=rallencorp, dc=com*)

<ComputerName>
> Single label DNS hostname of computer (e.g., *rallen-xp*)

1.5   Where to Find More Information

While it is my hope that this book provides you with enough information to perform most of the tasks you need to do to maintain your Active Directory environment, it is not realistic to think every possible task has been covered. In fact, there is easily another three to four chapters I could have included in this book, but due to space and time considerations, it was not possible for this edition. Working on this book has made me realize just how must stuff Active Directory administrators need to know.

Now that Active Directory has been around for a few years, a significant user base has been built, which has led to other great resources of information. This section contains some of the useful sources of information that I use on a regular basis.

Command-Line Tools

If you have any questions about the complete syntax or usage information for any of the command-line tools I use, you should first take a look at the help information for the tools. The vast majority of CLI tools provide syntax information by simply passing /? as a parameter. For example:

```
> dsquery /?
```

Microsoft Knowledge Base

The Microsoft Support web site is a great source of information and is home of the Microsoft Knowledge Base (MS KB) articles. Throughout the book, I include references to pertinent MS KB articles where you can find more information on the topic. You can find the complete text for a KB article by searching on the KB number at the following web site: *http://support.microsoft.com/default.aspx*. You can also append the KB article number to the end of this URL to go directly to the article: *http://support.microsoft.com/?kbid=*.

Microsoft Developers Network

MSDN contains a ton of information on Active Directory and the programmatic interfaces to Active Directory, such as ADSI and LDAP. I sometimes reference MSDN pages in recipes. Unfortunately, there is no easy way to reference the exact page I'm talking about unless I provided the URL or navigation to the page, which would more than likely change by the time the book was printed. Instead I provide the name of the title of the page, which you can use to search on via the following site: *http://msdn.microsoft.com/library/*.

Web Sites

Microsoft Active Directory Home Page (http://www.microsoft.com/ad/)
> This site is the starting point for Active Directory information provided by Microsoft. It contains links to white papers, case studies, and tools.

Microsoft Webcasts (http://support.microsoft.com/default.aspx?scid=fh;EN-US;pwebcst)
> Webcasts are on-demand audio/video technical presentations that cover a wide range of Microsoft products. There are several Active Directory–related webcasts that cover such topics as disaster recovery, upgrading to Windows Server 2003 Active Directory, and Active Directory tools.

Google Search Engine (http://www.google.com/)
> Google is my primary starting point for locating information on Active Directory. It is a powerful search engine and is often quicker and easier to use to search the Microsoft web sites than using the search engines provided on Microsoft's sites.

LabMice Active Directory (http://www.labmice.net/ActiveDirectory/default.htm)
> The LabMice web site contains a large collection of links to information on Active Directory. It has links to MS KB articles, white papers, and other web sites.

Robbie Allen's Home Page (http://www.rallenhome.com/)
> This is my personal web site, which has information about the Active Directory books I've written and links to download the code contained in each (including this book).

Newsgroups

microsoft.public.win2000.active_directory
> This is a very active newsgroup where several top-notch Active Directory experts answer questions posed by users.

microsoft.public.win2000.dns
> This is another good resource if you have a DNS question you've been unable to find an answer for; odds are someone on this newsgroup will have an answer.

microsoft.public.adsi.general
> If you have questions about ADSI, this is another very active newsgroup where you can find answers.

If you have a question about a particular topic, a good starting point is to search the newsgroups using Google's Groups search engine (*http://groups.google.com/*). Just like its web search engine, the group search engine is very fast and is an invaluable resource when trying to locate information.

Mailing Lists

ActiveDir (http://www.activedir.org/)
> The ActiveDir mailing list is where the most advanced Active Directory questions can get answered. The list owner, Tony Murray, does an excellent job of not allowing topics to get out of hand as can sometimes happen on large mailing lists. The list is very active and it is rare for a question to go unanswered. Some of Microsoft's Active Directory Program Managers also participate on the list and are very helpful with the toughest questions. Keeping track of this list is a must-have for any serious Active Directory administrator.

15 Seconds (http://15seconds.com/focus/ADSI.htm)
> Just as the ActiveDir list is crucial for AD administrators, the 15 seconds list is extremely valuable for AD developers. It is also very active and the participants are good about responding to questions quickly.

Books

In addition to the Resource Kit books, the following books are good sources of information:

Active Directory, Second Edition, by Robbie Allen and Alistair Lowe-Norris (O'Reilly)
> This is a good all-purpose book on Active Directory. A few of the topics the second edition cover include new Windows Server 2003 features, designing Active Directory, upgrading from Windows 2000, and Active Directory automation.

Managing Enterprise Active Directory Services, by Robbie Allen and Richard Puckett (Addison-Wesley)
> This is a great resource for anyone who has to support a large-scale Active Directory environment. The book preaches the benefits of automation in large environments and includes over 300 sample scripts written in Perl and VBScript.

Active Directory Programming, by Gil Kirkpatrick (MacMillan)
> This is a great book for those interested in learning the details of ADSI and LDAP programming. The author, Gil Kirkpatrick, is a noted expert in the field.

Magazines

Windows & .NET Magazine (http://www.winnetmag.com/)
> This is a general-purpose monthly magazine for system administrators that support Microsoft products. The magazine isn't devoted to Active Directory, but generally there are related topics covered every month.

Windows Scripting Solutions (http://www.winscriptingsolutions.com/)
> This is a useful monthly newsletter that discusses automation scripts on a wide variety of Microsoft products including Active Directory.

## CHAPTER 2

Forests, Domains, and Trusts

2.0 Introduction

To the layperson, the title of this chapter may seem like a hodgepodge of unrelated terms. For the seasoned Active Directory administrator, however, these terms represent the most fundamental and, perhaps, most important concepts within Active Directory. In simple terms, a forest is a collection of data partitions and domains; a domain is a hierarchy of objects that is replicated between one or more domain controllers; a trust is an agreement between two domains to allow security principals (i.e., users, groups, and computers) to access resources in either domain.

Active Directory domains are named using the Domain Name Service (DNS) namespace. The domains that are part of a common DNS namespace are considered to be in the same domain tree. For example, the *amer.rallencorp.com*, *emea.rallencorp.com*, and *rallencorp.com* domains are part of the *rallencorp.com* domain tree. A single domain tree is sufficient for most implementations, but one example when multiple domain trees are necessary is with large conglomerate corporations. Conglomerates are made up of multiple individual companies. Each company typically wants to maintain its own identity and, therefore, its own namespace. Describing the conglomerate scenario is a good way to show the relationships between forests, domains, domain trees, and trusts.

Assuming each company within the conglomerate wants its Active Directory domain name to be based on its company name, you have two choices for setting up this type of environment. You could either make each company's domain(s) a domain tree within a single forest or you could implement multiple forests. One of the biggest differences between the two options is that all the domains within the forest trust each other, whereas separate forests by default do not trust each other. Without the trust relationships, users from one forest cannot access resources in the domains of the other forest. If you want users to be able to access resources within each company's domains, using separate domain trees is an easier approach than separate forests. Transitive trusts are established between the root domains of each domain tree within a forest. As a result, every domain within a forest, regardless of which domain tree they are in, is trusted. Figure 2-1 illustrates an example with three domain trees in a forest called *rallencorp.com*.

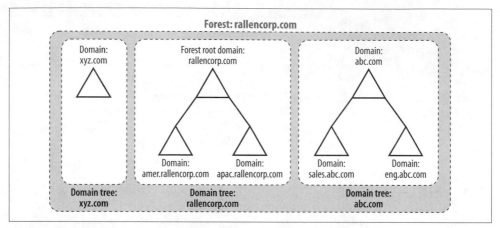

Figure 2-1. Multiple domain trees in a forest

If you implement the alternative approach and create multiple Windows 2000 Active Directory forests, to create the fully trusted model you would have to create individual trusts between the domains in every forest. This can get out of hand pretty quickly if there are numerous domains. Fortunately, with Windows Server 2003 Active Directory, you can use the new trust type called *forest trust* to create a single transitive trust between two forest root domains. This single trust causes all of the domains in both forests to trust each other.

There are many more issues to consider when deciding how many forests, domains and domain trees to implement. For a thorough explanation of Active Directory design considerations, I recommend reading Part II of *Active Directory*, Second Edition (O'Reilly).

In this chapter, I cover the most common tasks that you would need to do with forests, domains, and trusts. First, I'm going to review how each is represented in Active Directory.

The Anatomy of a Domain

Domains are represented in Active Directory by domainDNS objects. The distinguished name (DN) of a domainDNS object directly corresponds to the fully qualified DNS name of the domain. For example, the *amer.rallencorp.com* domain would have a DN of *dc=amer,dc=rallencorp,dc=com*. Table 2-1 contains a list of some of the interesting attributes that are available on domainDNS objects.

Table 2-1. Attributes of domainDNS objects

Attribute	Description
dc	Relative distinguished name of the domain (e.g., *amer*).
fSMORoleOwner	The NTDS Settings object DN of the domain controller that is the PDC Emulator FSMO role owner for the domain. See Recipe 3.25 for more information.
gPLink	List of GPOs that have been applied to the domain. By default it will contain a reference to the Domain Security Policy GPO.
lockoutDuration	A 64-bit integer representing the time an account will be locked out before being automatically unlocked. See Recipe 6.11 for more information.
lockoutObservationWindow	A 64-bit integer representing the time after a failed logon attempt that the failed logon counter for the account will be reset to 0. See Recipe 6.11 for more information.
lockoutThreshold	Number of failed logon attempts after which an account will be locked. See Recipe 6.11 for more information.
masteredBy	List of NTDS Settings objects for each domain controller in the domain.
maxPwdAge	A 64-bit integer representing the maximum number of days a password can be used before a user must change it. See Recipe 6.11 for more information.
minPwdAge	A 64-bit integer representing the minimum number of days a password must be used before it can be changed. See Recipe 6.11 for more information.
minPwdLength	Minimum number of characters allowed in a password. See Recipe 6.11 for more information.
msDS-Behavior-Version	Number that represents the functional level of the domain. This attribute is new in Windows Server 2003. See Recipe 2.13 for more information.
ms-DS-MachineAccountQuota	The number of computer accounts a non-administrator user account can join to the domain. See Recipe 8.9 for more information.
nTMixedDomain	Number that represents the mode of a domain. See Recipe 2.9 for more information.
pwdHistoryLength	Number of passwords to remember before a user can reuse a previous password. See Recipe 6.11 for more information.
pwdProperties	Bit flag that represents different options that can be configured for passwords used in the domain, including password complexity and storing passwords with reversible encryption. See Recipe 6.11 for more information.
subRefs	Multivalue attribute containing the list of subordinate naming contexts and application partitions.
wellKnownObjects	GUIDs for well-known objects, such as the default computer container. See Recipe 8.11 for more information.

In Active Directory, domains are naming contexts (NCs) and are also represented under the Partitions container in the Configuration NC as crossRef objects. In this case, the relative distinguished name (RDN) of the crossRef object is the NetBIOS name of the domain as defined by the netBIOSName attribute of the domain object. In our previous example of *amer.rallencorp.com*, the corresponding crossRef object for the domain (assuming the forest name was *rallencorp.com*) would be located at *cn=AMER,cn=Partitions,cn=Configuration,dc=rallencorp,dc=com*. Table 2-2 contains some interesting attributes of crossRef objects.

All naming contexts and application partitions have crossRef objects in the Partitions container, not just domains.

Table 2-2. Attributes of crossRef objects

Attribute	Description
cn	Relative distinguished name of the object. For domains, this will be the NetBIOS name of the domain.
dnsRoot	Fully qualified DNS name of the domain.
nCName	Distinguished name of the corresponding domainDNS object.
netBIOSName	NetBIOS name of the domain. See Recipe 2.7 for more information.
trustParent	Distinguished name of the crossRef object representing the parent domain (if applicable).

The Anatomy of a Trust

Trusts are stored as trustedDomain objects within the System container of a domain. Table 2-3 lists some of the important attributes of trustedDomain objects.

Table 2-3. Attributes of trustedDomain objects

Attribute	Description
cn	Relative distinguished name of the trust. This is the name of the target domain that is trusted. For Windows NT domains, it is the NetBIOS name. For Active Directory domains, it will be the DNS name.
trustDirection	Flag that indicates whether the trust is disabled, inbound, outbound, or both inbound and outbound. See Recipes 2.19 and 2.20 for more information.
trustType	Flag that indicates if the trust is to a down-level (NT4), up-level (Windows 2000 or above), or Kerberos (e.g., MIT) domain. See Recipe 2.19 for more information.
trustAttributes	Contain miscellaneous properties that can be enabled for a trust. See Recipe 2.19 for more information.
trustPartner	The name of the trust partner. See Recipe 2.19 for more information.

A trust also has a corresponding user object in the Users container of a domain. This is where the trust password is stored. The RDN of this user object is the same as the cn attribute for the corresponding trustedDomain object with a $ appended.

The Anatomy of a Forest

A forest is a logical structure that is a collection of domains, plus the configuration and schema naming contexts, and application partitions. Forests are considered the primary security boundary in Active Directory. By that I mean, if you need to definitively restrict access to a domain such that administrators from other domains do not have access, you need to implement a separate forest (and subsequently a domain in that forest), instead of using a domain within the current forest. This is due to the transitive trust relationship between all domains in a forest and the extensive permissions that members of the Domain Admins group have. Unlike domains and trusts, a forest is not represented by a container or any other type of object in Active Directory. At a minimum, a forest consists of three naming contexts: the forest root domain, the Configuration NC, and the Schema NC. The Partitions container in the Configuration NC contains the complete list of partitions that are associated with a forest. Here is a description of the type of partitions that can be part of a forest:

Configuration NC
> Contains data that is applicable across all of the domains and, thus, is replicated to all domain controllers in the forest. Some of this data includes the site topology, list of partitions, published services, display specifiers, and extended rights.

Schema NC
> Contains the objects that describe how data can be structured and stored in Active Directory. The classSchema objects in the Schema NC represent class definitions for objects. The attributeSchema objects describe what data can be stored with classes. The Schema NC is replicated to all domain controllers in a forest.

Domain NC
> As described earlier, a domain is a naming context that holds domain-specific data including user, group, and computer objects.

Application partitions
> Configurable partitions that can be rooted anywhere in the forest and can be replicated to any domain controller in the forest. These are not available with Windows 2000.

2.1 Creating a Forest

Problem

You want to create a new forest by creating a new forest root domain.

Solution

Using a graphical user interface

Run dcpromo from a command line or Start → Run.

On a Windows 2000 domain controller:

1. Select Domain controller for a new domain and click Next.
2. Select Create a new domain tree and click Next.

3. Select Create a new forest of domain trees and click Next.

4. Follow the rest of the configuration steps to complete the wizard.

On a Windows Server 2003 domain controller:

1. Select Domain controller for a new domain and click Next.

2. Select Domain in a new forest and click Next.

3. Follow the rest of the configuration steps to complete the wizard.

Using a command-line interface

dcpromo can also be run in unattended mode. See Recipe 3.4 for more details.

Discussion

The act of creating a forest consists of creating a forest root domain. To do this, you need to use the dcpromo executable to promote a Windows 2000 or Windows Server 2003 server to be a domain controller for a new domain. The dcpromo program has a wizard interface that requires you to answer several questions about the forest and domain you want to promote the server into. After dcpromo finishes, you will be asked to reboot the computer to complete the promotion process.

See Also

Recipe 2.3 for creating a domain, Recipe 3.1 for promoting a domain controller, Recipe 3.4 for automating the promotion of a domain controller, and MS KB 238369 (HOW TO: Promote and Demote Domain Controllers in Windows 2000)

2.2   Removing a Forest

Problem

You want to tear down a forest and decommission any domains contained within it because you no longer need it.

Solution

To remove a forest, you need to demote, using dcpromo, all the domain controllers in the forest. When you run dcpromo on an existing domain controller, you will be given the option to demote the machine to a member server. After that is completed and depending on how your environment is configured, you may need to remove WINS and DNS entries that were associated with the domain controllers and domains unless they were automatically removed via WINS deregistration and dynamic DNS

(DDNS) during demotion. The following commands can help determine if all entries have been removed:

```
> netsh wins server \\<WINSServerName> show name <ForestDNSName> 1c
> nslookup <DomainControllerDNSName>
> nslookup -type=SRV _ldap._tcp.gc._msdcs.<ForestDNSName>
> nslookup <ForestDNSName>
```

You will also want to remove any trusts that have been established for the forest (see Recipe 2.22 for more details). For more information on how to demote a domain controller, see Recipe 3.3.

Discussion

The method described in the solution is the graceful way to tear down a forest. You can also use a brute force method to remove a forest by simply reinstalling the operating system on all domain controllers in the forest. This method is not recommended except in lab or test environments. The brute force method is not a clean way to do it because the domain controllers are unaware the forest is being removed and may generate errors until they are rebuilt. You'll also need to make sure any DNS resource records for the domain controllers are removed from your DNS servers since the domain controllers will not dynamically remove them like they do during the demotion process.

See Also

Recipe 2.19 for viewing the trusts for a domain, Recipe 2.22 for removing a trust, and Recipe 3.3 for demoting a domain controller

2.3   Creating a Domain

Problem

You want to create a new domain that may be part of an existing domain tree or the root of a new domain tree.

Solution

Using a graphical user interface

Run dcpromo from a command line or Start → Run.

On a Windows 2000 domain controller, select "Domain controller for a new domain" and then you can select one of the following:

- Create a new domain tree → Place this new domain tree in an existing forest
- Create a new child domain in an existing domain tree

On a Windows Server 2003 domain controller, select "Domain controller for a new domain" and then you can select one of the following:

- Domain in a new forest
- Child domain in an existing domain tree
- Domain tree in an existing forest

Using a command-line interface

dcpromo can also be run in unattended mode. See Recipe 3.4 for more details.

Discussion

The two options dcpromo offers to create a new domain are adding the domain to an existing domain tree or starting a new domain tree. If you want to create a new domain that is a subdomain (contained within the same namespace) of a parent domain, you are creating a domain in an existing domain tree. If you are creating the first domain in a forest or a domain outside the namespace of the forest root, you are creating a domain in a new domain tree.

Each domain increases the support costs of Active Directory due to the need for maintaining additional domain controllers and time spent configuring and maintaining the domain. When designing an Active Directory forest, your goal should be to keep the number of domains that are necessary to a minimum.

See Also

Recipe 3.1 for promoting a domain controller, Recipe 3.4 for automating the promotion of a domain controller, MS KB 238369 (HOW TO: Promote and Demote Domain Controllers in Windows 2000), and MS KB 255248 (HOW TO: Create a Child Domain in Active Directory and Delegate the DNS Namespace to the Child Domain)

2.4   Removing a Domain

Problem

You want to remove a domain from a forest. You may need to remove a domain during test scenarios or if you are collapsing or reducing the number of domains in a forest.

Solution

Removing a domain consists of demoting each domain controller in the domain, which is accomplished by running dcpromo on the domain controllers and following the steps to remove them. For the last domain controller in the domain, be sure to select "This server is the last domain controller in the domain" in the dcpromo wizard so that the objects associated with the domain get removed. If you do not select that option for the last domain controller in the domain, take a look at Recipe 2.5 for how to remove an orphaned domain.

 If the domain you want to remove has subdomains, you have to remove the subdomains before proceeding.

After all domain controllers have been demoted and depending on how your environment is configured, you may need to remove WINS and DNS entries that were associated with the domain controllers and domain unless they were automatically removed via WINS deregistration and DDNS during the demotion process. The following commands can help determine if all entries have been removed:

```
> netsh wins server \\<WINSServerName> show name <DomainDNSName> 1c
> nslookup <DomainControllerName>
> nslookup -type=SRV _ldap._tcp.dc._msdcs.<DomainDNSName>
> nslookup <DomainDNSName>
```

You will also want to remove any trusts that have been established for the domain (see Recipe 2.22 for more details). For more information on how to demote a domain controller, see Recipe 3.3.

Discussion

The "brute force" method for removing a forest as described in the Discussion for Recipe 2.2 is not a good method for removing a domain. Doing so will leave all of the domain controller and server objects, along with the domain object and associated domain naming context hanging around in the forest. If you used that approach, you would eventually see a bunch of replication and file replication service (FRS) errors in the event log from failed replication events.

See Also

Recipe 2.19 for viewing the trusts for a domain, Recipe 2.22 for removing a trust, Recipe 3.3 for demoting a domain controller, MS KB 238369 (HOW TO: Promote and Demote Domain Controllers in Windows 2000), and MS KB 255229 (Dcpromo Demotion of Last Domain Controller in Child Domain Does Not Succeed)

2.5 Removing an Orphaned Domain

Problem

You want to completely remove a domain that was orphaned because "This server is the last domain controller in the domain" was not selected when demoting the last domain controller, the domain was forcibly removed, or the last domain controller in the domain was decommissioned improperly.

Solution

Using a command-line interface

The following ntdsutil commands (in bold) would forcibly remove the *emea.rallencorp.com* domain from the *rallencorp.com* forest. Replace *<DomainControllerName>* with the hostname of the Domain Naming Flexible Single Master Operation (FSMO) for the forest:

```
> ntdsutil "meta clean" "s o t" conn "con to server <DomainControllerName>" q q
metadata cleanup: "s o t" "list domains"
Found 4 domain(s)
0 - DC=rallencorp,DC=com
1 - DC=amer,DC=rallencorp,DC=com
2 - DC=emea,DC=rallencorp,DC=com
3 - DC=apac,DC=rallencorp,DC=com
select operation target: sel domain 2
No current site
Domain - DC=emea,DC=rallencorp,DC=com
No current server
No current Naming Context
select operation target: q
metadata cleanup: remove sel domain
```

You will receive a message indicating whether the removal was successful.

Discussion

Removing an orphaned domain consists of removing the domain object for the domain (e.g., *dc=emea,dc=rallencorp,dc=com*), all of its child objects, and the associated crossRef object in the Partitions container. You need to target the Domain Naming FSMO when using the ntdsutil command because that server is responsible for creation and removal of domains.

In the solution, shortcut parameters were used to reduce the amount of typing necessary. If each parameter were typed out fully, the commands would look as follows:

```
> ntdsutil "metadata cleanup" "select operation target" connections "connect toø
server <DomainControllerName>" quit quit
metadata cleanup: "select operation target" "list domains"
Found 4 domain(s)
0 - DC=rallencorp,DC=com
```

```
1 - DC=amer,DC=rallencorp,DC=com
2 - DC=emea,DC=rallencorp,DC=com
3 - DC=apac,DC=rallencorp,DC=com
select operation target: select domain 2
No current site
Domain - DC=emea,DC=rallencorp,DC=com
No current server
No current Naming Context
select operation target: quit
metadata cleanup: remove selected domain
```

See Also

Recipe 3.6 for removing an unsuccessfully demoted domain controller, MS KB 230306 (HOW TO: Remove Orphaned Domains from Active Directory), MS KB 251307 (HOW TO: Remove Orphaned Domains from Active Directory Without Demoting the Domain Controllers), and MS KB 255229 (Dcpromo Demotion of Last Domain Controller in Child Domain Does Not Succeed)

2.6   Finding the Domains in a Forest

Problem

You want a list of the domains in a forest.

Solution

Using a graphical user interface

Open the Active Directory Domains and Trusts snap-in. The list of the domains in the default forest can be browsed in the left pane.

Using a command-line interface

```
> ntdsutil "d m" "sel op tar" c "co t s <DomainControllerName>"  q "l d" q q q↵
```

Using VBScript

```
' This code gets the list of the domains contained in the
' forest that the user running the script is logged into.

set objRootDSE = GetObject("LDAP://RootDSE")
strADsPath =  "<GC://" & objRootDSE.Get("rootDomainNamingContext") & ">;"
strFilter  = "(objectcategory=domainDNS);"
strAttrs   = "name;"
strScope   = "SubTree"

set objConn = CreateObject("ADODB.Connection")
objConn.Provider = "ADsDSOObject"
```

```
objConn.Open "Active Directory Provider"
set objRS = objConn.Execute(strADsPath & strFilter & strAttrs & strScope)
objRS.MoveFirst
while Not objRS.EOF
    Wscript.Echo objRS.Fields(0).Value
    objRS.MoveNext
wend
```

Discussion

Using a graphical user interface

If you want to view the domains for an alternate forest than the one you are logged into, right-click on "Active Directory Domains and Trusts" in the left pane, and select "Connect to Domain Controller." Enter the forest name you want to browse in the Domain field. In the left pane, expand the forest root domain to see any subdomains.

Using a command-line interface

In the ntdsutil example, shortcut parameters were used to reduce the amount of typing needed. If each parameter were typed out fully, the command line would look like:

```
> ntdsutil "domain management" "select operation target" connections "connect↵
to server <DomainControllerName>" quit "List domains" quit quit quit
```

Using VBScript

In the VBScript solution, an ADO query is used to search for domainDNS objects stored in the global catalog, using the root (forest) Domain NC as the search base. This query will find all domains in the forest.

To find the list of domains for an alternate forest, include the name of the forest as part of the ADsPath used in the first line of code. The following would target the *othercorp.com* forest:

```
set objRootDSE = GetObject("LDAP://othercorp.com/" & "RootDSE")
```

See Also

Recipe 3.8 for finding the domain controllers for a domain

2.7 Finding the NetBIOS Name of a Domain

Problem

You want to find the NetBIOS name of a domain. Although Microsoft has moved to using DNS for primary name resolution, the NetBIOS name of a domain is still important, especially with down-level clients that are still based on NetBIOS instead of DNS for naming.

Solution

Using a graphical user interface

1. Open the Active Directory Domains and Trusts snap-in.
2. Right-click the domain you want to view in the left pane and select Properties.

The NetBIOS name will be shown in the "Domain name (pre-Windows 2000)" field.

Using a command-line interface

```
> dsquery * cn=partitions,cn=configuration,<ForestRootDN> -filter↵
"(&(objectcategory=crossref)(dnsroot=<DomainDNSName>)(netbiosname=*))" -attr↵
netbiosname
```

Using VBScript

```
' This code prints the NetBIOS name for the specified domain
' ------ SCRIPT CONFIGURATION ------
strDomain = "<DomainDNSName>"  ' e.g. amer.rallencorp.com
' ------ END CONFIGURATION ---------

set objRootDSE = GetObject("LDAP://" & strDomain & "/RootDSE")
strADsPath =  "<LDAP://" & strDomain & "/cn=Partitions," & _
              objRootDSE.Get("configurationNamingContext") & ">;"
strFilter = "(&(objectcategory=Crossref)" & _
              "(dnsRoot=" & strDomain & ")(netBIOSName=*));"
strAttrs = "netbiosname;"
strScope = "Onelevel"
set objConn = CreateObject("ADODB.Connection")
objConn.Provider = "ADsDSOObject"
objConn.Open "Active Directory Provider"
set objRS = objConn.Execute(strADsPath & strFilter & strAttrs & strScope)
objRS.MoveFirst
WScript.Echo "NetBIOS name for " & strDomain & " is " & objRS.Fields(0).Value
```

Discussion

Each domain has a crossRef object that is used by Active Directory to generate referrals. Referrals are necessary when a client performs a query and the directory server handling the request does not have the matching object(s) in its domain. The Net-BIOS name of a domain is stored in the domain's crossRef object in the Partitions container in the Configuration NC. Each crossRef object has a dnsRoot attribute, which is the fully qualified DNS name of the domain. The netBIOSName attribute contains the NetBIOS name for the domain.

2.8   Renaming a Domain

Problem

You want to rename a domain due to organizational changes or legal restrictions because of an acquisition. Renaming a domain is a very involved process and should be done only when absolutely necessary. Changing the name of a domain can have an impact on everything from DNS, replication, and GPOs to DFS and Certificate Services. A domain rename also requires that all domain controllers and member computers in the domain are rebooted!

Solution

Under Windows 2000, there is no supported process to rename a domain. There is one workaround for mixed-mode domains in which you revert the domain and any of its child domains back to Windows NT domains. This can be done by demoting all Windows 2000 domain controllers and leaving the Windows NT domain controllers in place. You could then reintroduce Windows 2000 domain controllers and use the new domain name when setting up Active Directory. The process is not very clean and probably won't be suitable for most situations, but you can find out more about it in MS KB 292541.

A domain rename procedure is supported if a forest is running all Windows Server 2003 domain controllers and is at the Windows Server 2003 forest functional level. Microsoft provides a rename tool (*rendom.exe*) and detailed white paper describing the process at the following location:

   http://www.microsoft.com/windowsserver2003/downloads/domainrename.mspx

Discussion

The domain rename process can accommodate very complex changes to your domain model. You can perform the following types of renames:

- Rename a domain to a new name without repositioning it in the domain tree.
- Reposition a domain within a domain tree.
- Create a new domain tree with a renamed domain.

One thing you cannot do with the domain rename procedure is reposition the forest root domain. You can rename the forest root domain, but you cannot change its status as the forest root domain. Another important limitation to note is that you cannot rename any domain in a forest that has had Exchange 2000 installed. A future service pack release of Exchange Server 2003 will reportedly handle domain renames. See the web site mentioned in the solution for more information on other limitations.

See Also

MS KB 292541 (How to: Rename the DNS name of a Windows 2000 Domain)

2.9 Changing the Mode of a Domain

Problem

You want to change the mode of a Windows 2000 Active Directory domain from mixed to native. You typically want to do this as soon as possible after installing a Windows 2000 domain to take advantage of features that aren't available with mixed-mode domains.

Solution

Using a graphical user interface

1. Open the Active Directory Domains and Trusts snap-in.
2. Browse to the domain you want to change in the left pane.
3. Right-click on the domain and select Properties. The current mode will be listed in the Domain Operation Mode box.
4. To change the mode, click the Change Mode button at the bottom.

Using a command-line interface

To retrieve the current mode, use the following command:

```
> dsquery * <DomainDN> -scope base -attr ntMixedDomain
```

Or you can use the enumprop command found in the Windows 2000 Resource Kit.

```
> enumprop /ATTR:ntMixedDomain "LDAP://<DomainDN>"
```

To change the mode to native, create an LDIF file called *change_domain_mode.ldf* with the following contents:

```
dn: <DomainDN>
changetype: modify
replace: ntMixedDomain
ntMixedDomain: 0
-
```

Then run the `ldifde` command to import the change.

```
> ldifde -i -f change_domain_mode.ldf
```

Using VBScript

```
' This code changes the mode of the specified domain to native
' ------ SCRIPT CONFIGURATION ------
strDomain = "<DomainDNSName>"  ' e.g. amer.rallencorp.com
' ------ END CONFIGURATION ---------

set objDomain = GetObject("LDAP://" & strDomain)
if objDomain.Get("nTMixedDomain") > 0 Then
   Wscript.Echo "Changing mode to native..."
   objDomain.Put "nTMixedDomain", 0
   objDomain.SetInfo
else
   Wscript.Echo "Already a native mode domain"
end if
```

Discussion

The mode of a domain restricts the operating systems the domain controllers in the domain can run. In a mixed-mode domain, you can have Windows 2000 and Windows NT domain controllers. In a native-mode domain, you can have only Windows 2000 (and Windows Server 2003) domain controllers. There are several important feature differences between mixed and native mode. Mixed mode imposes the following limitations:

- The domain cannot contain Universal security groups.
- Groups in the domain cannot have their scope or type changed.
- The domain cannot have nested groups (aside from global groups in domain local groups).
- Account modifications sent to Windows NT BDCs, including password changes, must go through PDC Emulator for the domain.
- The domain cannot use SID History.
- The domain cannot fully utilize trust transitivity.

The domain mode can be changed only from mixed to native mode. You cannot change it back from native to mixed. When a Windows 2000 domain is first created, it starts off in mixed mode even if all the domain controllers are running Windows 2000. The domain mode is stored in the `ntMixedDomain` attribute on the domain object (e.g., *dc=amer,dc=rallencorp,dc=com*). A value of 0 signifies a native-mode domain and 1 indicates a mixed-mode domain.

Windows Server 2003 Active Directory has a similar concept called functional levels. For more information on Windows Server 2003 functional levels, see Recipes 2.13 and 2.14.

See Also

Recipe 2.13 for raising the functional level of a domain, Recipe 2.14 for raising the functional level of a forest, and MS KB 186153 (Modes Supported by Windows 2000 Domain Controllers)

2.10   Using ADPrep to Prepare a Domain or Forest for Windows Server 2003

Problem

You want to upgrade your existing Windows 2000 Active Directory domain controllers to Windows Server 2003. Before doing this, you must run the ADPrep tool, which extends the schema and adds several objects in Active Directory that are necessary for new features and enhancements.

Solution

First, run the following command on the Schema FSMO with the credentials of an account that is in both the Enterprise Admins and Schema Admins groups:

```
> adprep /forestprep
```

After the updates from /forestprep have replicated throughout the forest (see Recipe 2.11), run the following command on the Infrastructure FSMO in each domain with the credentials of an account in the Domain Admins group:

```
> adprep /domainprep
```

If the updates from /forestprep have not replicated to at least the Infrastructure FSMO servers in each domain, an error will be returned when running /domainprep. To debug any problems you encounter, see the ADPrep log files located at *%SystemRoot%\System32\Debug\Adprep\Logs*.

 adprep can be found in the \i386 directory on the Windows Server 2003 CD. The tool relies on several files in that directory, so you cannot simply copy that file out to a server and run it. You must either run it from a CD or from a location where the entire directory has been copied.

Discussion

The adprep command prepares a Windows 2000 forest and domains for Windows Server 2003. Both /forestprep and /domainprep must be run before you can upgrade any domain controllers to Windows Server 2003 or install new Windows Server 2003 domain controllers.

The adprep command serves a similar function to the Exchange 2000 setup /forestprep and /domainprep commands, which prepare an Active Directory forest and domains for Exchange 2000. The adprep /forestprep command extends the schema and modifies some default security descriptors, which is why it must run on the Schema FSMO and under the credentials of someone in both the Schema Admins and Enterprise Admins groups. In addition, the adprep /forestprep and /domainprep commands add new objects throughout the forest, many of which are necessary for new features supported in Windows Server 2003 Active Directory.

If you've installed Exchange 2000 or Services For Unix 2.0 in your forest prior to running adprep, there are schema conflicts with the adprep schema extensions that you'll need to fix first. MS KB 325379 and 314649 have a detailed list of compatibility issues and resolutions.

See Also

Recipe 2.11 for determining if ADPrep has completed, Chapter 14 of *Active Directory*, Second Edition for upgrading to Windows Server 2003, MS KB 331161 (List of Fixes to Use on Windows 2000 Domain Controllers Before You Run the Adprep/Forestprep Command), MS KB 314649 (Windows Server 2003 ADPREP Command Causes Mangled Attributes in Windows 2000 Forests That Contain Exchange 2000 Servers), and MS KB 325379 (Upgrade Windows 2000 Domain Controllers to Windows Server 2003)

2.11   Determining if ADPrep Has Completed

Problem

You want to determine if the ADPrep process, described in Recipe 2.10, has successfully prepared a Windows 2000 domain or forest for Windows Server 2003. After ADPrep has completed, you will them be ready to start promoting Windows Server 2003 domain controllers.

Solution

To determine if adprep /domainprep completed, check for the existence of the following object where *<DomainDN>* is the distinguished name of the domain:

```
cn=Windows2003Update,cn=DomainUpdates,cn=System,<DomainDN>
```

To determine if adprep /forestprep completed, check for the existence of the following object where *<ForestRootDN>* is the distinguished name of the forest root domain:

```
cn=Windows2003Update,cn=ForestUpdates,cn=Configuration,<ForestRootDN>
```

Discussion

As described in Recipe 2.10, the adprep utility is used to prepare a Windows 2000 forest for the upgrade to Windows Server 2003. One of the nice features of adprep is it stores its progress in Active Directory. For /domainprep, a container with a distinguished name of *cn=DomainUpdates,cn=System,<DomainDN>* is created that has child object containers cn=Operations and cn=Windows2003Update. After adprep completes a task, such as extending the schema, it creates an object under the cn=Operations container to signify its completion. Each object has a GUID for its name, which represents some internal operation for adprep. For /domainprep, 52 of these objects are created. After all of the operations have completed successfully, the cn=Windows2003Update object is created to indicate /domainprep has completed. Figure 2-2 shows an example of the container structure created by /domainprep.

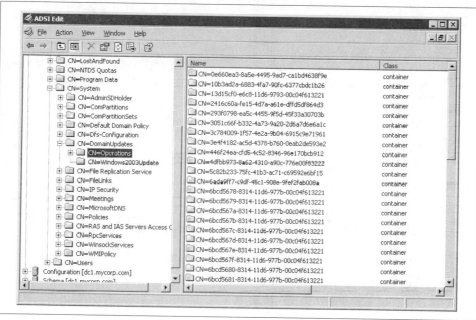

Figure 2-2. DomainPrep containers

For /forestprep, a container with the distinguished name of *cn=ForestUpdates,cn= Configuration,<ForestRootDN>*, is created with child object containers cn=Operations and cn=Windows2003Update. The same principles apply as for /domainprep except that there are 36 operation objects stored within the cn=Operations container. After /forestprep completes, the cn=Windows2003Update object will be created that marks the successful completion of /forestprep. Figure 2-3 shows an example of the container structure created by /forestprep.

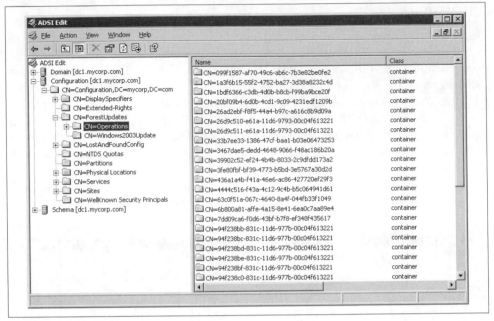

Figure 2-3. ForestPrep containers

See Also

Chapter 14 of *Active Directory*, Second Edition for upgrading to Windows Server 2003, and Recipe 2.10 for running adprep

2.12 Checking Whether a Windows 2000 Domain Controller Can Be Upgraded to Windows Server 2003

Problem

You want to determine if a domain controller is ready to be upgraded to Windows Server 2003.

Solution

Insert a Windows Server 2003 CD into the Windows 2000 domain controller or map a drive to the files contained on the CD. Run the following command from the \i386 directory:

```
> winnt32 /checkupgradeonly
```

Discussion

The /checkupgradeonly switch simulates the initial steps for upgrading a server to Windows Server 2003. It verifies, among other things, that adprep has completed and that any installed applications are compatible with the new operating system.

See Also

Recipe 2.11 for determining if adprep has completed and MS KB 331161 (List of Fixes to Use on Windows 2000 Domain Controllers Before You Run the Adprep/Forestprep Command)

2.13   Raising the Functional Level of a Windows Server 2003 Domain

Problem

You want to raise the functional level of a Windows Server 2003 domain. You should raise the functional level of a domain as soon as possible after installing a new Windows Server 2003 domain or upgrading from Windows 2000 to take advantage of the new features and enhancements.

Solution

Using a graphical user interface

1. Open the Active Directory Domains and Trusts snap-in.
2. In the left pane, browse to the domain you want to raise, right-click it, and select Raise Domain Functional Level.
3. Select the new functional level and click OK.

After a few seconds you should see a message stating whether the operation was successful.

Using a command-line interface

To retrieve the current functional level, use the following command:

```
> dsquery * <DomainDN> -scope base -attr msDS-Behavior-Version
```

Or you can use the enumprop command found in the Windows 2000 Resource Kit.

```
> enumprop /ATTR:msDS-Behavior-Version "LDAP://<DomainDN>"
```

To change the functional level to Windows Server 2003, create an LDIF file called raise_domain_func_level.ldf with the following contents:

```
dn: <DomainDN>
changetype: modify
replace: msDS-Behavior-Version
msDS-Behavior-Version: 2
-
```

Next, run the ldifde command to import the change.

```
> ldifde -i -f raise_domain_func_level.ldf
```

Using VBScript

```
' This code changes the functional level of the specified domain to
' the Windows Server 2003 domain functional level
' ------ SCRIPT CONFIGURATION ------
strDomain = "<DomainDNSName>"    ' e.g. amer.rallencorp.com
' ------ END CONFIGURATION ---------

set objDomain = GetObject("LDAP://" & strDomain)
objDomain.GetInfo
if objDomain.Get("msDS-Behavior-Version") <> 2 then
    Wscript.Echo "Changing domain to Windows Server 2003 functional level..."
    objDomain.Put "msDS-Behavior-Version", 2
    objDomain.SetInfo
else
    Wscript.Echo "Domain already at Windows Server 2003 functional level "
end if
```

Discussion

In Windows Server 2003 Active Directory, functional levels have replaced the domain mode that was used in Windows 2000 to signify what operating systems are allowed to run on the domain controllers in the domain. With Windows Server 2003, there are functional levels for both domains and forests; whereas with Windows 2000, the domain mode only applied to domains. The msDS-Behavior-Version attribute of the domainDNS object (e.g., *dc=amer,dc=rallencorp,dc=com*) holds the current domain functional level. Table 2-4 shows the three functional levels, their associated msDS-Behavior-Version value, and the operating systems that can be used on domain controllers in each.

Table 2-4. Windows Server 2003 domain functional levels

Functional level	msDS-Behavior-Version	Valid operating systems
Windows 2000	0	Windows 2000 Windows NT (when in mixed mode) Windows Server 2003
Windows Server 2003 Interim	1	Windows NT 4.0 Windows Server 2003
Windows Server 2003	2	Windows Server 2003

When a domain is at the Windows 2000 functional level, the domain can be in mixed mode or native mode, as described in Recipe 2.9. Various new features of Windows Server 2003 Active Directory are enabled with each domain functional level. See Chapter 1 of *Active Directory,* Second Edition (O'Reilly) for more details.

The value contained in msDS-Behavior-Version is mirrored in the domainFunctionality attribute of the RootDSE. That means you can perform anonymous queries against the RootDSE of a domain to quickly determine what functional level it is currently at.

 One of the benefits of the GUI solution is that if a problem is encountered, you can save and view the output log, which will contain information on any errors that were encountered.

See Also

Chapter 1 of *Active Directory,* Second Edition, Recipe 2.9 for changing domain mode, Recipe 2.10 for preparing a forest with adprep, Recipe 2.14 for raising the functional level of a forest, and MS KB 322692 (HOW TO: Raise the Domain Functional Level in Windows Server 2003)

2.14   Raising the Functional Level of a Windows Server 2003 Forest

Problem

You want to raise the functional level of a Windows Server 2003 forest. You should raise the functional level of a forest as soon as possible after installing a new Windows Server 2003 forest or upgrading from a Windows 2000 forest to take advantage of the new features and enhancements.

Solution

Using a graphical user interface

1. Open the Active Directory Domains and Trusts snap-in.

2. In the left pane, right-click on Active Directory Domains and Trusts and select Raise Forest Functional Level.

3. Select Windows Server 2003 Functional Level and click OK.

After a few seconds you should see a message stating whether the operation was successful.

Using a command-line interface

To retrieve the current forest functional level, use the following command:

```
> dsquery * <ForestRootDN> -scope base -attr msDS-Behavior-Version
```

Or you can use the enumprop command found in the Windows 2000 Resource Kit.

```
> enumprop /ATTR:msDS-Behavior-Version "LDAP://<ForestRootDN>"
```

To change the functional level to Windows Server 2003, create an LDIF file called raise_forest_func_level.ldf with the following contents:

```
dn: cn=partitions,cn=configuration,<ForestRootDN>
changetype: modify
replace: msDS-Behavior-Version
msDS-Behavior-Version: 2
-
```

Next, run the ldifde command to import the change.

```
> ldifde -i -f raise_forest_func_level.ldf
```

Using VBScript

```
' This code changes the functional level of the the forest the
' user running the script is logged into to Windows Server 2003.

set objRootDSE = GetObject("LDAP://RootDSE")
set objDomain = GetObject("LDAP://cn=partitions," & _
                         objRootDSE.Get("configurationNamingContext") )
if objDomain.Get("msDS-Behavior-Version") <> 2 then
   Wscript.Echo "Attempting to change forest to " & _
                "Windows Server 2003 functional level..."
   objDomain.Put "msDS-Behavior-Version", 2
   objDomain.SetInfo
else
   Wscript.Echo "Forest already at Windows Server 2003 functional level"
end if
```

Discussion

Windows Server 2003 forest functional levels are very similar to domain functional levels. In fact, Table 2-4 applies to forest functional levels as well, except that the list of available operating systems applies to all domain controllers in the forest not just a single domain. So even if just one of the domains in the forest is at the Windows 2000 domain functional level, you cannot raise the forest above the Windows 2000 forest functional level. If you attempt to do so you will receive an error that the operation cannot be completed. After you raise the last Windows 2000 domain functional level to Windows Server 2003, you can then raise the forest functional level as well.

You may be wondering why there is a need to differentiate between forest and domain functional levels. The primary reason is new features. Some new features of Windows Server 2003 Active Directory require that all domain controllers in the forest are running Windows Server 2003. To ensure all domain controllers are running a certain operating system throughout a forest, Microsoft had to apply the functional level concept to forests as well as domains. For more information on the new features that are available with each functional level, see Chapter 1 of *Active Directory,* Second Edition (O'Reilly).

The forest functional level is stored in the `msDS-Behavior-Version` attribute of the `Partitions` container in the Configuration NC. For example, in the *rallencorp.com* forest, it would be stored in *cn=partitions,cn=configuration,dc=rallencorp,dc=com.* The value contained in `msDS-Behavior-Version` is mirrored to the `forestFunctionality` attribute of the RootDSE, which means you can find the functional level of the forest by querying the RootDSE.

 One of the benefits of the GUI solution is that if a problem is encountered, you can save and view the output log, which will contain information on any errors that were encountered.

See Also

Chapter 1 of *Active Directory,* Second Edition, Recipe 2.9 for changing domain mode, Recipe 2.10 for preparing a forest with `adprep`, Recipe 2.13 for raising the functional level of a domain, and MS KB 322692 (HOW TO: Raise the Domain Functional Level in Windows Server 2003)

2.15 Creating a Trust Between a Windows NT Domain and an AD Domain

Problem

You want to create a one-way or two-way nontransitive trust from an AD domain to a Windows NT domain.

Solution

Using a graphical user interface

1. Open the Active Directory Domains and Trusts snap-in.
2. In the left pane, right-click the domain you want to add a trust for and select Properties.
3. Click on the Trusts tab.
4. Click the New Trust button.
5. After the New Trust Wizard opens, click Next.
6. Type the NetBIOS name of the NT domain and click Next.
7. Assuming the NT domain was resolvable via its NetBIOS name, the next screen will ask for the Direction of Trust. Select Two-way, One-way incoming, or One-way outgoing, and click Next.
8. If you selected Two-way or One-way Outgoing, you'll need to select the scope of authentication, which can be either Domain-wide or Selective, and click Next.
9. Enter and re-type the trust password and click Next.
10. Click Next twice to finish.

Using a command-line interface

```
> netdom trust <NT4DomainName> /Domain:<ADDomainName> /ADD↵
        [/UserD:<ADDomainName>\ADUser> /PasswordD:*]↵
        [/UserO:<NT4DomainName>\NT4User> /PasswordO:*]↵
        [/TWOWAY]
```

For example, to create a trust from the NT4 domain RALLENCORP_NT4 to the AD domain RALLENCORP, use the following command:

```
> netdom trust RALLENCORP_NT4 /Domain:RALLENCORP /ADD↵
        /UserD:RALLENCORP\administrator /PasswordD:*↵
        /UserO:RALLENCORP_NT4\administrator /PasswordO:*
```

You can make the trust bidirectional, i.e., two-way, by adding a /TwoWay switch to the example.

Discussion

It is common when migrating from a Windows NT environment to Active Directory to set up trusts to down-level master account domains or resource domains. This allows AD users to access resources in the NT domains without providing alternate credentials. Windows NT does not support transitive trusts and, therefore, your only option is to create a nontransitive trust. That means you'll need to set up individual trusts between the NT domain and every Active Directory domain that contains users that need to access the NT resources.

See Also

MS KB 306733 (HOW TO: Create a Trust Between a Windows 2000 Domain and a Windows NT 4.0 Domain), MS KB 308195 (HOW TO: Establish Trusts with a Windows NT-Based Domain in Windows 2000), MS KB 309682 (HOW TO: Set up a One-Way Non-Transitive Trust in Windows 2000), MS KB 325874 (HOW TO: Establish Trusts with a Windows NT-Based Domain in Windows Server 2003), and MS KB 816301 (HOW TO: Create an External Trust in Windows Server 2003)

2.16 Creating a Transitive Trust Between Two AD Forests

 This recipe requires the Windows Server 2003 forest functional level in both forests.

Problem

You want to create a transitive trust between two AD forests. This causes the domains in both forests to trust each other without the need for additional trusts.

Solution

Using a graphical user interface

1. Open the Active Directory Domains and Trusts snap-in.
2. In the left pane, right click the forest root domain and select Properties.
3. Click on the Trusts tab.
4. Click the New Trust button.
5. After the New Trust Wizard opens, click Next.
6. Type the DNS name of the AD forest and click Next.

7. Select Forest trust and click Next.

8. Complete the wizard by stepping through the rest of the configuration screens.

Using a command-line interface

```
> netdom trust <Forest1DNSName> /Domain:<Forest2DNSName> /Twoway /Transitive /ADD↵
        [/UserD:<Forest2AdminUser> /PasswordD:*]↵
        [/UserO:<Forest1AdminUser> /PasswordO:*]
```

For example, to create a two-way forest trust from the AD forest *rallencorp.com* to the AD forest *othercorp.com*, use the following command:

```
> netdom trust rallencorp.com /Domain:othercorp.com /Twoway /Transitive /ADD↵
        /UserD:administrator@othercorp.com /PasswordD:*↵
        /UserO:administrator@rallencorp.com /PasswordO:*
```

Discussion

A new type of trust called a *forest trust* was introduced in Windows Server 2003. Under Windows 2000, if you wanted to create a fully trusted environment between two forests, you would have to set up individual external two-way trusts between every domain in both forests. If you have two forests with three domains each and wanted to set up a fully trusted model, you would need nine individual trusts. Figure 2-4 illustrates how this would look.

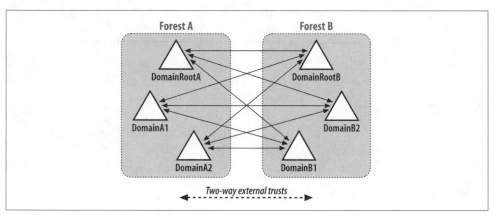

Figure 2-4. Trusts necessary for two Windows 2000 forests to trust each other

With a forest trust, you can define a single one-way or two-way transitive trust relationship that extends to all the domains in both forests. You may want to implement a forest trust if you merge or acquire a company and you want all of the new company's Active Directory resources to be accessible for users in your Active Directory environment and vice versa. Figure 2-5 shows a forest trust scenario. To create a forest trust, you need to use accounts from the Enterprise Admins group in each forest.

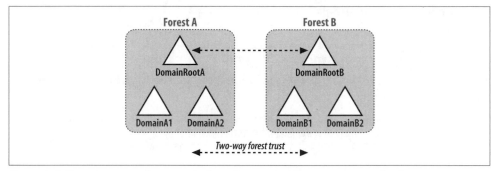

Figure 2-5. Trust necessary for two Windows Server 2003 forests to trust each other

2.17 Creating a Shortcut Trust Between Two AD Domains

Problem

You want to create a shortcut trust between two AD domains in the same forest or in different forests. Shortcut trusts can make the authentication process more efficient between two domains in a forest.

Solution

Using a graphical user interface

1. Open the Active Directory Domains and Trusts snap-in.
2. In the left pane, right-click the domain you want to add a trust for, and select Properties.
3. Click on the Trusts tab.
4. Click the New Trust button.
5. After the New Trust Wizard opens, click Next.
6. Type the DNS name of the AD domain and click Next.
7. Assuming the AD domain was resolvable via DNS, the next screen will ask for the Direction of Trust. Select Two-way and click Next.
8. For the Outgoing Trust Properties, select all resources to be authenticated and click Next.
9. Enter and retype the trust password and click Next.
10. Click Next twice.

Using a command-line interface

```
> netdom trust <Domain1DNSName> /Domain:<Domain2DNSName> /Twoway /ADD↵
        [/UserD:<Domain2AdminUser> /PasswordD:*]↵
        [/UserO:<Domain1AdminUser> /PasswordO:*]
```

To create a shortcut trust from the *emea.rallencorp.com* domain to the *apac.rallencorp.com* domain, use the following netdom command:

```
> netdom trust emea.rallencorp.com /Domain:apac.rallencorp.com /Twoway /ADD↵
        /UserD:administrator@apac.rallencorp.com /PasswordD:*↵
        /UserO:administrator@emea.rallencorp.com /PasswordO:*
```

Discussion

Consider the forest in Figure 2-6. It has five domains in a single domain tree. In order for authentication requests for Domain 3 to be processed by Domain 5, the request must traverse the path from Domain 3 to Domain 2 to Domain 1 to Domain 4 to Domain 5. If you create a shortcut trust between Domain 3 and Domain 5, the authentication path is just a single hop from Domain 3 to Domain 5. To create a shortcut trust, you must be a member of the Domain Admins group in both domains, or a member of the Enterprise Admins group.

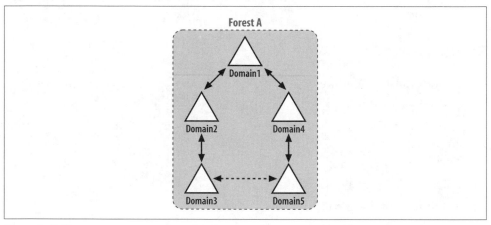

Figure 2-6. Shortcut trust

2.18   Creating a Trust to a Kerberos Realm

Problem

You want to create a trust to a Kerberos realm.

Solution

Using a graphical user interface

1. Open the Active Directory Domains and Trusts snap-in.

2. In the left pane, right-click the domain you want to add a trust for and select Properties.

3. Click on the Trusts tab.

4. Click the New Trust button.

5. After the New Trust Wizard opens, click Next.

6. Type the name of the Kerberos realm.

7. Select the radio button beside Realm Trust and click Next.

8. Select either Transitive or Nontransitive and click Next.

9. Select Two-way, One-way incoming, or One-way outgoing and click Next.

10. Enter and retype the trust password and click Next.

11. Click Next and click Finish.

Using a command-line interface

```
> netdom trust <ADDomainDNSName> /Domain:<KerberosRealmDNSName>↵
        /Realm /ADD /PasswordT:<TrustPassword>↵
        [/UserO:<ADDomainAdminUser> /PasswordO:*]
```

The *<TrustPassword>* has to match what was set on the Kerberos side. To create a realm trust from the *rallencorp.com* domain to the Kerberos realm called *kerb.rallencorp.com*, use the following command:

```
> netdom trust rallencorp.com /Domain:kerb.rallencorp.com↵
        /Realm /ADD /PasswordT:MyKerbRealmPassword↵
        /UserO:administrator@rallencorp.com /PasswordO:*
```

Discussion

You can create a Kerberos realm trust between an Active Directory domain and a non-Windows Kerberos v5 realm. A realm trust can be used to allow clients from the non-Windows Kerberos realm to access resources in Active Directory, and vice versa. See Recipe 18.7 for more information on MIT Kerberos interoperability with Active Directory.

See Also

MS KB 260123 (Information on the Transitivity of a Kerberos Realm Trust) and MS KB 266080 (Answers to Frequently Asked Kerberos Questions)

2.19   Viewing the Trusts for a Domain

Problem

You want to view the trusts for a domain.

Solution

Using a graphical user interface

1. Open the Active Directory Domains and Trusts snap-in.
2. In the left pane, right-click the domain you want to view and select Properties.
3. Click on the Trusts tab.

Using a command-line interface

```
> netdom query trust /Domain:<DomainDNSName>
```

Using VBScript

```
' This code prints the trusts for the specified domain.
' ------ SCRIPT CONFIGURATION ------
strDomain = "<DomainDNSName>"    ' e.g. rallencorp.com
' ------ END CONFIGURATION ---------

' Trust Direction Constants taken from NTSecAPI.h
set objTrustDirectionHash = CreateObject("Scripting.Dictionary")
objTrustDirectionHash.Add "DIRECTION_DISABLED", 0
objTrustDirectionHash.Add "DIRECTION_INBOUND", 1
objTrustDirectionHash.Add "DIRECTION_OUTBOUND", 2
objTrustDirectionHash.Add "DIRECTION_BIDIRECTIONAL", 3

' Trust Type Constants - taken from NTSecAPI.h
set objTrustTypeHash = CreateObject("Scripting.Dictionary")
objTrustTypeHash.Add "TYPE_DOWNLEVEL", 1
objTrustTypeHash.Add "TYPE_UPLEVEL", 2
objTrustTypeHash.Add "TYPE_MIT", 3
objTrustTypeHash.Add "TYPE_DCE", 4

' Trust Attribute Constants - taken from NTSecAPI.h
set objTrustAttrHash = CreateObject("Scripting.Dictionary")
objTrustAttrHash.Add "ATTRIBUTES_NON_TRANSITIVE", 1
objTrustAttrHash.Add "ATTRIBUTES_UPLEVEL_ONLY", 2
objTrustAttrHash.Add "ATTRIBUTES_QUARANTINED_DOMAIN", 4
objTrustAttrHash.Add "ATTRIBUTES_FOREST_TRANSITIVE", 8
objTrustAttrHash.Add "ATTRIBUTES_CROSS_ORGANIZATION", 16
objTrustAttrHash.Add "ATTRIBUTES_WITHIN_FOREST", 32
objTrustAttrHash.Add "ATTRIBUTES_TREAT_AS_EXTERNAL", 64

set objRootDSE = GetObject("LDAP://" & strDomain & "/RootDSE")
set objTrusts = GetObject("LDAP://cn=System," & _
                          objRootDSE.Get("defaultNamingContext") )
```

```
    objTrusts.Filter = Array("trustedDomain")
    Wscript.Echo "Trusts for " & strDomain & ":"

    for each objTrust in objTrusts
        for each strFlag In objTrustDirectionHash.Keys
            if objTrustDirectionHash(strFlag) = objTrust.Get("trustDirection") then
                strTrustInfo = strTrustInfo & strFlag & " "
            end If
        next

        for each strFlag In objTrustTypeHash.Keys
            if objTrustTypeHash(strFlag) = objTrust.Get("trustType") then
                strTrustInfo = strTrustInfo & strFlag & " "
            end If
        next

        for each strFlag In objTrustAttrHash.Keys
            if objTrustAttrHash(strFlag) = objTrust.Get("trustAttributes") then
                strTrustInfo = strTrustInfo & strFlag & " "
            end If
        next

        WScript.Echo " " & objTrust.Get("trustPartner") & " : " & strTrustInfo
        strTrustInfo = ""
    next
```

Discussion

Using a graphical user interface

You can view the properties of a particular trust by clicking on a trust and clicking the Properties button.

Using a command-line interface

You can include the /Direct switch if you want to view only direct-trust relationships. If you don't use /Direct, implicit trusts that occur due to transitive-trust relationships will also be listed.

Using VBScript

This script uses dictionary objects to ease the mapping of the various integer values for attributes, such as trustType and trustDirection, to descriptive names. A dictionary object in VBScript is analogous to a hash or associative array in other programming languages. The Add method accepts a key and value pair to add to the dictionary. The Keys method returns the keys of the dictionary as a collection. To access a value of the dictionary, you simply pass the key name as a parameter to the dictionary object, such as objDictionary(strKey).

Another option to query trusts programmatically is with the Trustmon WMI Provider. The Trustmon Provider is new to Windows Server 2003. See Recipe 2.20 for an example.

See Also

Recipe 2.0 for attributes of trustedDomain objects, Recipe 2.20 for another way to query trusts programmatically, MS KB 228477 (HOW TO: Determine Trust Relationship Configurations), and MSDN: TRUSTED_DOMAIN_INFORMATION_EX

2.20   Verifying a Trust

Problem

You want to verify that a trust is working correctly. This is the first diagnostics step to take if users notify you that authentication to a remote domain appears to be failing.

Solution

Using a graphical user interface

For the Windows 2000 version of the Active Directory Domains and Trusts snap-in:

1. In the left pane, right-click on the trusting domain and select Properties.
2. Click the Trusts tab.
3. Click the domain that is associated with the trust you want to verify.
4. Click the Edit button.
5. Click the Verify button.

For the Windows Server 2003 version of the Active Directory Domains and Trusts snap-in:

1. In the left pane, right-click on the trusting domain and select Properties.
2. Click the Trusts tab.
3. Click the domain that is associated with the trust you want to verify.
4. Click the Properties button.
5. Click the Validate button.

Using a command-line interface

```
> netdom trust <TrustingDomain> /Domain:<TrustedDomain> /Verify /verbose↵
  [/UserO:<TrustingDomainUser> /PasswordO:*]↵
  [/UserD:<TrustedDomainUser> /PasswordD:*]
```

Using VBScript

```
' The following code lists all of the trusts for the
' specified domain using the Trustmon WMI Provider.
' The Trustmon WMI Provider is only supported on Windows Server 2003.
' ------ SCRIPT CONFIGURATION ------
strDomain = "<DomainDNSName>"  ' e.g. amer.rallencorp.com
' ------ END CONFIGURATION ---------

set objWMI = GetObject("winmgmts:\\" & strDomain & _
                       "\root\MicrosoftActiveDirectory")
set objTrusts = objWMI.ExecQuery("Select * from Microsoft_DomainTrustStatus")
for each objTrust in objTrusts
    Wscript.Echo objTrust.TrustedDomain
    Wscript.Echo " TrustedAttributes: " & objTrust.TrustAttributes
    Wscript.Echo " TrustedDCName: "     & objTrust.TrustedDCName
    Wscript.Echo " TrustedDirection: "  & objTrust.TrustDirection
    Wscript.Echo " TrustIsOk: "         & objTrust.TrustIsOK
    Wscript.Echo " TrustStatus: "       & objTrust.TrustStatus
    Wscript.Echo " TrustStatusString: " & objTrust.TrustStatusString
    Wscript.Echo " TrustType: "         & objTrust.TrustType
    Wscript.Echo ""
next

' This code shows how to search specifically for trusts
' that have failed, which can be accomplished using a WQL query that
' contains the query: TrustIsOk = False
' ------ SCRIPT CONFIGURATION ------
strDomain = "<DomainDNSName>"  ' e.g. amer.rallencorp.com
' ------ END CONFIGURATION ---------

set objWMI = GetObject("winmgmts:\\" & strDomain & _
                       "\root\MicrosoftActiveDirectory")
set objTrusts = objWMI.ExecQuery("select * " _
                       & " from Microsoft_DomainTrustStatus " _
                       & " where TrustIsOk = False ")
if objTrusts.Count = 0 then
   Wscript.Echo "There are no trust failures"
else
   WScript.Echo "Trust Failures:"
   for each objTrust in objTrusts
      Wscript.Echo " " & objTrust.TrustedDomain & " : " & _
                       objTrust.TrustStatusString
      Wscript.Echo ""
   next
end if
```

Discussion

Verifying a trust consists of checking connectivity between the domains, and determining if the shared secrets of a trust are synchronized between the two domains.

Using a graphical user interface

The Active Directory Domains and Trusts screens have changed somewhat between Windows 2000 and Windows Server 2003. The Verify button has been renamed Validate.

Using a command-line interface

If you want to verify a Kerberos trust, use the /Kerberos switch with the netdom command.

Using VBScript

The WMI Trustmon Provider is new to Windows Server 2003. It provides a nice interface for querying and checking the health of trusts. One of the benefits of using WMI to access this kind of data is that you can use WQL, the WMI Query Language, to perform complex queries to find trusts that have certain properties. WQL is a subset of the Structured Query Language (SQL) commonly used to query databases. In the second VBScript example, I used WQL to find all trusts that have a problem. You could expand the query to include additional criteria, such as trust direction, and trust type.

See Also

MSDN: Trustmon Provider

2.21   Resetting a Trust

Problem

You want to reset a trust password. If you've determined a trust is broken, you need to reset it, which will allow users to authenticate across it again.

Solution

Using a graphical user interface

Follow the same directions as Recipe 2.20. The option to reset the trust will only be presented if the Verify/Validate did not succeed.

Using a command-line interface

```
> netdom trust <TrustingDomain> /Domain:<TrustedDomain> /Reset /verbose⏎
  [/UserO:<TrustingDomainUser> /PasswordO:*]⏎
  [/UserD:<TrustedDomainUser> /PasswordD:*]
```

Using VBScript

```
' This code resets the specified trust.
' ------ SCRIPT CONFIGURATION ------
' Set to the DNS or NetBIOS name for the Windows 2000,
' Windows NT domain or Kerberos realm you want to reset the trust for.
strTrustName = "<TrustToCheck>"

' Set to the DNS name of the source or trusting domain.
strDomain    = "<TrustingDomain>"
' ------ END CONFIGURATION ---------

' Enable SC_RESET during trust enumerations
set objTrustProv = GetObject("winmgmts:\\" & strDomain & _
             "\root\MicrosoftActiveDirectory:Microsoft_TrustProvider=@")
objTrustProv.TrustCheckLevel = 3   ' Enumerate with SC_RESET
objTrustProv.Put_

' Query the trust and print status information
set objWMI = GetObject("winmgmts:\\" & strDomain & _
                    "\root\MicrosoftActiveDirectory")
set objTrusts = objWMI.ExecQuery("Select * " _
                    & " from Microsoft_DomainTrustStatus " _
                    & " where TrustedDomain = '" & strTrustName & "'" )
for each objTrust in objTrusts
    Wscript.Echo objTrust.TrustedDomain
    Wscript.Echo " TrustedAttributes: " & objTrust.TrustAttributes
    Wscript.Echo " TrustedDCName: "     & objTrust.TrustedDCName
    Wscript.Echo " TrustedDirection: "  & objTrust.TrustDirection
    Wscript.Echo " TrustIsOk: "         & objTrust.TrustIsOK
    Wscript.Echo " TrustStatus: "       & objTrust.TrustStatus
    Wscript.Echo " TrustStatusString: " & objTrust.TrustStatusString
    Wscript.Echo " TrustType: "         & objTrust.TrustType
    Wscript.Echo ""
next
```

Discussion

Resetting a trust synchronizes the shared secrets (i.e., passwords) for the trust. The PDC in both domains is used to synchronize the password so they must be reachable.

Using a command-line interface

If you are resetting a Kerberos realm trust, you'll need to specify the /PasswordT option with netdom.

See Also

Recipe 2.20 for verifying a trust

2.22   Removing a Trust

Problem

You want to remove a trust. This is commonly done when the remote domain has been decommissioned or access to it is no longer required.

Solution

Using a graphical user interface

1. Open the Active Directory Domains and Trusts snap-in.
2. In the left pane, right-click on the trusting domain and select Properties.
3. Click the Trusts tab.
4. Click on the domain that is associated with the trust you want to remove.
5. Click the Remove button.
6. Click OK.

Using a command-line interface

```
> netdom trust <TrustingDomain> /Domain:<TrustedDomain> /Remove /verbose↵
   [/UserO:<TrustingDomainUser> /PasswordO:*]↵
   [/UserD:<TrustedDomainUser> /PasswordD:*]
```

Using VBScript

```
' This code deletes a trust in the specified domain.
' ------ SCRIPT CONFIGURATION ------
' Set to the DNS or NetBIOS name for the Windows 2000,
' Windows NT domain or Kerberos realm trust you want to delete.
strTrustName = "<TrustName>"
' Set to the DNS name of the source or trusting domain
strDomain    = "<DomainDNSName>"
' ------ END CONFIGURATION ---------

set objRootDSE = GetObject("LDAP://" & strDomain & "/RootDSE")
set objTrust = GetObject("LDAP://cn=System," & _
                        objRootDSE.Get("defaultNamingContext") )
objTrust.Delete "trustedDomain", "cn=" & strTrustName
set objTrustUser = GetObject("LDAP://cn=Users," & _
                        objRootDSE.Get("defaultNamingContext") )
objTrustUser.Delete "trustedDomain", "cn=" & strTrustName & "$"
WScript.Echo "Successfully deleted trust for " & strTrustName
```

Discussion

Trusts are stored in Active Directory as two objects; a trustedDomain object in the System container and a user object in the Users container. Both of these objects need

---

to be removed when deleting a trust. The GUI and CLI solutions take care of that in one step, but in the VBScript example both objects needed to be explicitly deleted. It is also worth noting that each solution only deleted one side of the trust. If the trust was to a remote AD forest or NT 4.0 domain, you also need to delete the trust in that domain.

2.23 Enabling SID Filtering for a Trust

Problem

You want to enable Security Identifier (SID) filtering for a trust. By enabling SID filtering you can keep a hacker from spoofing a SID across a trust.

Solution

Using a command-line interface

```
> netdom trust <TrustingDomain> /Domain:<TrustedDomain> /Quarantine Yes↵
  [/UserO:<TrustingDomainUser> /PasswordO:*]↵
  [/UserD:<TrustedDomainUser> /PasswordD:*]
```

Discussion

A security vulnerability exists with the use of SID history, which is described in detail in MS KB 289243. An administrator in a trusted domain can modify the SID history for a user, which could grant her elevated privileges in the trusting domain. The risk of this exploit is relatively low due to the complexity in forging a SID, but nevertheless, you should be aware of it. To prevent this from happening you can enable SID Filtering for a trust. When SID filtering is enabled, the only SIDs that are used as part of a user's token are from the trusted domain itself. SIDs from other trusting domains are not included. SID filtering makes things more secure, but prevents the use of SID history and can cause problems with transitive trusts.

See Also

MS KB 289243 (MS02-001: Forged SID Could Result in Elevated Privileges in Windows 2000)

2.24 Finding Duplicate SIDs in a Domain

Problem

You want to find any duplicate SIDs in a domain. Generally, you should never find duplicate SIDs in a domain, but it is possible in some situations, such as when the relative identifier (RID) FSMO role owner has to be seized or you are migrating users from Windows NT domains.

Solution

Using a command-line interface

To find duplicate SIDs run the following command, replacing *<DomainControllerName>* with a domain controller or domain name:

```
> ntdsutil "sec acc man" "co to se <DomainControllerName>" "check dup sid" q q
```

The following message will be returned:

```
Duplicate SID check completed successfully. Check dupsid.log for any duplicates
```

The *dupsid.log* file will be in the directory where you started ntdsutil.

If you want to delete any objects that have duplicate SIDs, you can use the following command:

```
> ntdsutil "sec acc man" "co to se <DomainControllerName>" "clean dup sid" q q
```

Like the check command, the clean command will generate a message like the following upon completion:

```
Duplicate SID cleanup completed successfully. Check dupsid.log for any duplicate
```

Discussion

All security principals in Active Directory have a SID, which is used to uniquely identify the object in the Windows security system. There are two parts of a SID, the domain identifier and the RID. Domain controllers are allocated a RID pool from the RID FSMO for the domain. When a new security principal (user, group, or computer) is created, the domain controller takes a RID from its pool to generate a SID for the account.

In some rare circumstances, such as when the RID master role is seized, overlapping RID pools can be allocated, which can ultimately lead to duplicate SIDs. Having duplicate SIDs is a potentially hazardous problem because a user, group, or computer could gain access to sensitive data they were never intended to have access to.

See Also

MS KB 315062 (HOW TO: Find and Clean Up Duplicate Security Identifiers with Ntdsutil in Windows 2000)

## CHAPTER 3

Domain Controllers, Global Catalogs, and FSMOs

3.0   Introduction

Domain controllers are servers that host an Active Directory domain and provide authentication and directory services to clients. A Domain controller is authoritative for a single domain, but can store partial read-only copies of objects in other domains in the forest if it is enabled as a global catalog server. All domain controllers in a forest also host the Configuration and Schema Naming Contexts, which are replicated to all domain controllers in a forest.

Active Directory is a multi-master directory, meaning that updates can be issued to any domain controller, but some tasks cannot be distributed to all servers due to concurrency issues. For example, if two different domain controllers made conflicting updates to the schema, the impact could be severe and could result in data loss. For this reason, Active Directory supports Flexible Single Master Operations (FSMO) roles. For each role there is only one domain controller that acts as the role owner and performs the tasks associated with the role. See Recipe 3.25 for more information on FSMO roles.

The Anatomy of a Domain Controller

Each domain controller is represented in Active Directory by several objects; the two main ones are a computer object and an nTDSDSA object. The computer object is necessary because a domain controller needs to be represented as a security principal like any other type of computer in Active Directory. The default location in a domain for domain controller computer objects is the Domain Controllers OU at the root of the domain. They can be moved to a different OU, but it is highly recommended that you don't unless you know what you are doing. Table 3-1 contains some useful attributes of domain controller computer objects.

Table 3-1. Attributes of domain controller computer objects

Attribute	Description
dnsHostName	Fully qualified DNS name of the DC.
msDS-AdditionalDnsHostName	Contains the old DNS name of a renamed DC. This is new in Windows Server 2003.
msDS-AdditionalSamAccountName	Contains the old NetBIOS name of a renamed DC. This is new in Windows Server 2003.
operatingSystem	Textual description of the operating system running on the DC.
operatingSystemHotFix	Currently not being used, but will hopefully be populated with the installed hotfixes at some point.
operatingSystemServicePack	Service pack version installed on the DC.
operatingSystemVersion	Numeric version of the operating system installed on the DC.
sAMAccountName	NetBIOS style name of the DC.
serverReferenceBL	DN of the DC's server object contained under the Sites container in the Configuration NC.
servicePrincipalName	List of SPNs supported by the DC.

Domain controllers are also represented by several objects under the Sites container in the Configuration NC. The Sites container stores objects that are needed to create a site topology, including site, subnet, sitelink, and server objects. The site topology is necessary so that domain controllers can replicate data efficiently around the network. See Chapter 11 for more information.

Each domain controller has an nTDSDSA object that is subordinate to the domain controller's server object in the site it is a member of. For example, if the DC1 domain controller were part of the RTP site, its nTDSDSA object would be located here:

```
cn=NTDS Settings,cn=DC1,cn=RTP,cn=sites,cn=configuration,dc=rallencorp,dc=com
```

Table 3-2 lists some of the interesting attributes that are stored with nTDSDSA objects.

Table 3-2. Attributes of domain controller nTDSDSA objects

Attribute	Description
hasMasterNCs	List of DNs for the naming contexts the DC is authoritative for. This does not include application partitions.
hasPartialReplicaNCs	List of DNs for the naming contexts the DC has a partial read-only copy of.
msDS-HasDomainNCs	The DN of the domain the DC is authoritative for. This is new in Windows Server 2003.
msDS-HasMasterNCs	List of DNs for the naming contexts (domain, configuration, and schema) and application partitions the DC is authoritative for. This is new in Windows Server 2003.
options	If the low-order bit of this attribute is set, the domain controller stores a copy of the global catalog.

3.1   Promoting a Domain Controller

Problem

You want to promote a server to a domain controller. You may need to promote a domain controller to either initially create a domain in an Active Directory forest or add additional domain controllers to the domain for load balancing and failover.

Solution

Run dcpromo.exe from a command line or via Start → Run and answer the questions according to the forest and domain you want to promote the server into.

Discussion

Promoting a server to a domain controller is the process where the server becomes authoritative for an Active Directory domain. When you run the dcpromo program, a wizard interface walks you through a series of screens that collects information about the forest and domain to promote the server into. There are several options for promoting a server:

- Promoting into a new forest (See Recipe 2.1)
- Promoting into a new domain tree or child domain (See Recipe 2.3)
- Promoting into an existing domain

You can automate the promotion process by running dcpromo during an unattended installation. See Recipe 3.4 for more details.

See Also

Recipe 2.1 for creating a new forest, Recipe 2.3 for creating a new domain, and MS KB 238369 (HOW TO: Promote and Demote Domain Controllers in Windows 2000)

3.2   Promoting a Domain Controller from Media

This recipe requires that the server being promoted run Windows Server 2003.

Problem

You want to promote a new domain controller using a backup from another domain controller as the initial source of the directory contents (DIT) instead of replicating the entire DIT over the network.

Solution

1. You first need to back up the system state of an existing domain controller in the domain the new server will go in. This can be accomplished by running the MS Backup utility found at Start → Programs → Accessories → System Tools → Backup.

2. Once you have a good backup, you then need to restore it to the new server, which can also be done using MS Backup. You should restore the files to an alternate location, not to their original location.

3. Next, run dcpromo with the /adv switch from a command line or Start → Run:

    > dcpromo /adv

4. After the dcpromo wizard starts, select Additional Domain Controller for an existing domain and click Next.

5. Under Copy Domain Information, select From these restored backup files, browse to the backup files, and click Next.

6. Enter credentials of a user in the Domain Admins group in the domain you are promoting the domain controller into and click Next.

7. Choose the folders to store the Active Directory Database and Log files and click Next.

8. Choose the folder to store SYSVOL and click Next.

9. Enter a Restore Mode password and click Next.

10. Click Next to start the promotion.

Discussion

Being able to promote a domain controller using the system-state backup of another domain controller is a new feature in Windows Server 2003. With Windows 2000, a new domain controller had to replicate the entire DIT over the network from an existing domain controller. For organizations that had either a really large Active Directory DIT file or very poor network connectivity to a remote site, replicating the full contents over the network presented challenges. Under these conditions, the promotion process could take a prohibitively long time to complete. Now with the dcpromo "install from media" option, the initial promotion process can be substantially quicker. After you've done the initial install from media (i.e., backup tape or

CD/DVD), the domain controller will replicate the changes since the backup was taken.

 Be sure that the backup files you are using are much less than 60 days old. If you install a domain controller using backup files that are older than 60 days, you could get in trouble with zombie objects getting re-injected after being purged (due to the default 60 day tombstone lifetime).

See Also

Recipe 16.1 for backing up Active Directory and MS KB 240363 (HOW TO: Use the Backup Program to Back Up and Restore the System State in Windows 2000)

3.3   Demoting a Domain Controller

Problem

You want to demote a domain controller from a domain. If you want to decommission a domain controller due to lack of use or change in architecture, you'll need to follow these demotion procedures.

Solution

Using a graphical user interface

1. Run the dcpromo command from a command line or Start → Run.
2. Click Next.
3. If the server is the last domain controller in the domain, check the box beside "This server is the last domain controller in the domain."
4. Click Next.
5. Type and confirm the password for the local Administrator account.
6. Click Next twice to begin the demotion.

Discussion

Before demoting a domain controller, ensure that all of the FSMO roles have been transferred to other servers; otherwise, they will be transferred to random domain controllers that may not be optimal for your installation. Also, if the server is a global catalog, ensure that other global catalog servers exist in the forest that can handle the load.

It is important to demote a server before decommissioning or rebuilding it so that its associated objects in Active Directory are removed, its DNS locator resource records are dynamically removed, and replication with the other domain controllers is not interrupted. If a domain controller does not successfully demote, or if you do not get the chance to demote it because of failed hardware, see Recipe 3.6 for manually removing a domain controller from Active Directory.

See Also

Recipe 3.6 for removing an unsuccessfully demoted domain controller, Recipe 3.17 for disabling the global catalog, Recipe 3.26 for transferring FSMO roles, MS KB 238369 (HOW TO: Promote and Demote Domain Controllers in Windows 2000), and MS KB 307304 (HOW TO: Remove Active Directory with the Dcpromo Tool in Windows 2000)

3.4   Automating the Promotion or Demotion of a Domain Controller

Problem

You want to automate the installation or removal of a domain controller. You can make the promotion process part of your standard build process by incorporating the necessary configuration lines in your answer file(s).

Solution

You can automate the promotion of a domain controller by using the unattended process when building the server or by manually running dcpromo after the system has been built. Pass an answer file containing the necessary lines to promote the server to dcpromo by specifying a /answer switch. Here is an example:

```
> dcpromo /answer:<path_to_answer_file>
```

If you want to run dcpromo as part of an unattended setup, you need to add a [GUIRunOnce] section in your unattended setup file that calls the dcpromo process. You can promote a domain controller only after setup has completed and someone logs in for the first time. That is why it is necessary to use a [GUIRunOnce] section, which sets the RunOnce registry key to kick off dcpromo after someone logs in. Here is an example:

```
[GUIRunOnce]
"dcpromo /answer:%systemroot%\system32\$winnt$.inf"
```

The dcpromo answer section starts with [DCInstall]. Here is an example answer file for adding a domain controller to an existing domain in the *rallencorp.com* forest:

```
[DCINSTALL]
UserName=administrator
Password=RAllencorpAdminPassword
UserDomain=rallencorp.com
DatabasePath=%systemroot%\ntds
LogPath=%systemroot%\ntds
SYSVOLPath=%systemroot%\sysvol
SafeModeAdminPassword=DSrestoreModePassword
CriticalReplicationOnly=no
ReplicaOrNewDomain=Replica
ReplicaDomainDNSName=rallencorp.com
RebootOnSuccess=yes
CreateOrJoin=Join
```

Discussion

For a complete list of Windows Server 2003 [DCInstall] settings, see the *ref.chm* help file in *support\tools\deploy.cab* that can be found on the Windows Server 2003 CD. For Windows 2000, the settings can be found in the *unattend.doc* file in *support\tools\deploy.cab* on the Windows 2000 CD.

See Also

MS KB 223757 (Unattended Promotion and Demotion of Windows 2000 Domain Controllers), and MS KB 224390 (How to Automate Windows 2000 Setup and Domain Controller Setup)

3.5   Troubleshooting Domain Controller Promotion or Demotion Problems

Problem

You are having problems promoting or demoting a domain controller and you want to troubleshoot it.

Solution

The best source of information about the status of promotion or demotion problems is the *Dcpromo.log* and *Dcpromoui.log* files contained in the *%SystemRoot%\Debug* folder on the server. The *Dcpromo.log* captures the input entered during dcpromo and logs the information that is displayed as dcpromo progresses. The *Dcpromoui.log* file is much more detailed and captures discrete actions that occur during dcpromo processing, including any user input.

Additionally, the Windows Server 2003 version of dcdiag contains two new tests that can aid in troubleshooting promotion problems. The dcpromo test reports anything it finds that could impede the promotion process. The RegisterInDNS test checks if the server can register records in DNS. Here is an example of running both commands to test against the rallencorp.com domain:

```
> dcdiag /test:dcpromo /DnsDomain:rallencorp.com /ReplicaDC /test:RegisterInDNS
```

Discussion

In most cases, the level of detail provided by *Dcpromoui.log* should be sufficient to pinpoint any problems, but you can increase logging if necessary. To enable the highest level of logging available, set the following registry value to FF0003: HKLM\Software\Microsoft\Windows\CurrentVersion\AdminDebug. You can confirm that this mask took effect by running dcpromo again, checking the *Dcpromoui.log*, and searching for "logging mask." For more information on the various logging settings, see MS KB 221254.

If you get desperate, the Network Monitor (netmon) program is very handy for getting a detailed understanding of the network traffic that is being generated and any errors that are being returned. You can identify what other servers it is talking to or if it is timing out when attempting to perform certain queries or updates.

See Also

MS KB 221254 (Registry Settings for Event Detail in the Dcpromoui.log File), and MS KB 260371 (Troubleshooting Common Active Directory Setup Issues in Windows 2000)

3.6   Removing an Unsuccessfully Demoted Domain Controller

Problem

Demotion of a domain controller was unsuccessful or you are unable to bring a domain controller back online and you want to manually remove it from Active Directory.

Solution

The first step in the removal process is to run the following ntdsutil command, where *<DomainControllerName>* is a domain controller in the same domain as the one you want to forcibly remove:

```
> ntdsutil "meta clean" conn "co to ser <DomainControllerName>" q "s o t" "l d"
Found 2 domain(s)
```

```
0 - DC=rallencorp,DC=com
1 - DC=emea,DC=rallencorp,DC=com
```

Select the domain of the domain controller you want to remove. In this case, I'll select the *emea.rallencorp.com* domain:

```
select operation target: sel domain 1
```

Now, list the sites and select the site the domain controller is in (I'll use 1 for MySite1):

```
select operation target: list sites
Found 4 site(s)
0 - CN=Default-First-Site-Name,CN=Sites,CN=Configuration,DC=rallencorp,DC=com
1 - CN=MySite1,CN=Sites,CN=Configuration,DC=rallencorp,DC=com
2 - CN=MySite2,CN=Sites,CN=Configuration,DC=rallencorp,DC=com
3 - CN=MySite3,CN=Sites,CN=Configuration,DC=rallencorp,DC=com
select operation target: sel site 1
```

Next, select the server you want to remove; in this case, I'm choosing 0 for DC5:

```
select operation target: list servers for domain in site
Found 2 server(s)
0 - CN=DC5,CN=Servers,CN=MySite1,CN=Sites,CN=Configuration,DC=rallencorp,DC=com
1 - CN=DC9,CN=Servers,CN=MySite1,CN=Sites,CN=Configuration,DC=rallencorp,DC=com
select operation target: sel server 0
```

Type quit to get back to the metadata cleanup menu.

```
select operation target: quit
metadata cleanup:
```

Finally, remove the server:

```
metadata cleanup: remove selected server
```

You should receive a message stating that the removal was complete. If you get an error, check to see if the server's nTDSDSA object (e.g., *CN=NTDS Settings,CN=DC5,CN=Servers,CN=MySite1,CN=Sites,CN=Configuration,DC=rall encorp,DC=com*) is present. If so, dcpromo may have already removed it, and it will take time for the change to replicate. If it is still present, try the ntdsutil procedure again and if that doesn't work, manually remove that object and the parent object (e.g., *CN=DC5*).

You should follow these additional steps to remove all traces of the domain controller:

1. Delete the CNAME record from DNS for *<GUID>.*_msdcs.*<RootDomainDNSName>*, where *<GUID>* is the objectGUID for the server's nTDSDSA object. If scavenging is not enabled, you'll need to manually delete all associated SRV records. Delete any A and PTR records that exist for the server. When using Microsoft DNS, you can use the DNS MMC snap-in to accomplish these tasks.

2. Delete the computer object for the server under *OU=Domain Controllers,<DomainDN>*. This can be done using the Active Directory Users and Computers snap-in.

3. Delete the FRS Member object for the computer contained under *CN=Domain System Volume (SYSVOL share),CN=file replication service,CN=system,<DomainDN>*. This can be done using the Active Directory Users and Computers snap-in when "Advanced Features" has been selected from the View menu (so the System container will be displayed).

Discussion

Forcibly removing a domain controller from a domain is not a task that should be taken lightly. If you need to replace the server quickly, consider giving it a different name just to ensure that nothing confuses the new server with the old one. If the domain controller was the last one in the domain, you'll need to manually remove the domain from the forest as well. See Recipe 2.5 for more information on removing orphaned domains.

Here are some additional issues to consider when you forcibly remove a domain controller:

- Seize any FSMO roles the DC may have had.
- If the DC was a global catalog server, ensure there is another global catalog server in the site.
- If the DC was a DNS server, ensure there is another DNS server that can handle the load.
- If the DC was the RID FSMO master, check to make sure duplicate SIDs have not been issued (see Recipe 2.24).
- Check to see if the DC hosted any application partitions and if so, consider making another server a replica server for those application partitions (see Recipe 17.5).

If the (former) domain controller that you forcibly removed is still on the network, you should strongly consider rebuilding it to avoid potential conflicts from it trying to re-inject itself back into Active Directory. If that is not an option, you can try this option to force the server to not recognize itself as a domain controller.

1. Change the ProductOptions value under the HKLM\System\CurrentControlSet\Control key from LanmanNT to ServerNT.
2. Reboot the server.
3. Delete the NTDS folder.

Alternatively, if you are running Windows Server 2003 or Windows 2000 SP4 and later you can run dcpromo /forceremoval from a command line to forcibly remove Active Directory from a server. See MS KB 332199 for more information.

See Also

Recipe 2.5 for removing an orphaned domain, Recipe 3.27 for seizing FSMO roles, MS KB 216498 (HOW TO: Remove Data in Active Directory After an Unsuccessful Domain Controller Demotion), and MS KB 332199 (Using the DCPROMO /FORCER-EMOVAL Command to Force the Demotion of Active Directory Domain Controllers)

3.7   Renaming a Domain Controller

Problem

You want to rename a domain controller.

Solution

Windows 2000 Active Directory

To rename a domain controller, you must first demote it to a member server. You can then rename it and then promote it back to a domain controller.

Windows Server 2003 Active Directory

```
> netdom computername <CurrentName> /Add:<NewName>
> netdom computername <CurrentName> /MakePrimary:<NewName>
```

Discussion

There is no supported means to rename a Windows 2000 domain controller in place. That is why you have to fake it by demoting the server before doing the rename. Before you demote the server, you should transfer any FSMO roles. Alternatively, you can let dcpromo transfer the roles during demotion, but you should check afterwards to verify which server(s) the role(s) were transferred to. Likewise if the domain controller is a global catalog server, ensure another global catalog server is available to cover for it.

Renaming a domain controller is a new feature of Windows Server 2003. A new option has been added to the netdom utility to allow an alternate computer name to be associated with a computer in Active Directory. Once you've added a new name, you can then set that name to be the primary name, thereby renaming the computer. The old name effectively remains with the domain controller until you remove it, which can be done using the netdom computername /Remove:<Name> command. You should reboot the server before removing the old name. The old names are stored in the msDS-AdditionalDnsHostName and msDS-AdditionalSamAccountName attributes on the domain controller's computer object.

See Also

MS KB 195242 (Cannot Change Computer Name of a Domain Controller), MS KB
296592 (How to Rename a Windows 2000 Domain Controller), and MS KB 814589
(HOW TO: Rename a Windows 2003 Domain Controller)

3.8   Finding the Domain Controllers
    for a Domain

Problem

You want to find the domain controllers in a domain.

Solution

Using a graphical user interface

1. Open the Active Directory Users and Computers snap-in.

2. Connect to the target domain.

3. Click on the Domain Controllers OU.

4. The list of domain controllers for the domain will be present in the right pane.

Using a command-line interface

```
> netdom query dc /Domain:<DomainDNSName>
```

Using VBScript

```
' This code displays the domain controllers for the specified domain.
' ------ SCRIPT CONFIGURATION ------
strDomain = "<DomainDNSName>"  ' e.g. emea.rallencorp.com
' ------ END CONFIGURATION ---------

set objRootDSE = GetObject("LDAP://" & strDomain & "/RootDSE")
set objDomain = GetObject("LDAP://" & objRootDSE.Get("defaultNamingContext"))
strMasteredBy = objDomain.GetEx("masteredBy")
for each strNTDSDN in strMasteredBy
   set objNTDS = GetObject("LDAP://" & strNTDSDN)
   set objServer = GetObject(objNTDS.Parent)
   Wscript.echo objServer.Get("dNSHostName")
next
```

Discussion

There are several ways to get a list of domain controllers for a domain. The GUI solution simply looks at the computer objects in the Domain Controllers OU. Whenever

---

you promote a domain controller into a domain, a computer object for the server gets placed into the Domain Controllers OU off the root of the domain. Some administrators may move their domain controller computer objects to different OUs, so this test does not guarantee accuracy in all cases.

The CLI and VBScript solutions take a slightly different approach by looking at the masteredBy attribute on the domain object (e.g., *dc=emea,dc=rallencorp,dc=com*) of the domain. The masteredBy attribute contains a list of distinguished names of the nTDSDSA objects of all the domain controllers for that domain. The parent object of the nTDSDSA object, which is the server object of the domain controller, has a dNSHostName attribute that contains the fully qualified DNS name of the server.

And for yet another solution, see Recipe 3.21 to find out how to query DNS to get the list of domain controllers for a domain.

See Also

Recipe 3.21 for finding domain controllers via DNS

3.9   Finding the Closest Domain Controller

Problem

You want to find the closest domain controller for a particular domain.

Solution

Using a command-line interface

The following command finds the closest domain controller in the specified domain (*<DomainDNSName>*). By default, it will return the closest DC for the computer nltest is being run from, but you can optionally use the /server option to target a remote host. You can also optionally specify the /site option to find a domain controller that belongs to a particular site.

```
> nltest /dsgetdc:<DomainDNSName> [/site:<SiteName>] [/server:<ClientName>]
```

Using VBScript

```
' This code finds the closest domain controller in the domain
' that the computer running the script is in.
' ------ SCRIPT CONFIGURATION ------
strDomain = "<DomainDNSName>"  ' e.g. emea.rallencorp.com
' ------ END CONFIGURATION ---------

set objIadsTools = CreateObject("IADsTools.DCFunctions")
objIadsTools.DsGetDcName( Cstr(strDomain) )
Wscript.Echo "DC: " & objIadsTools.DCName
```

```
Wscript.Echo "DC Site: " & objIadsTools.DCSiteName
Wscript.Echo "Client Site: " & objIadsTools.ClientSiteName
```

Discussion

The DC locator process as described in MS KB 314861 and MS KB 247811 defines how clients find the closest domain controller. The process uses the site topology stored in Active Directory to calculate the site a particular client is in. After the client site has been identified, then it is a matter of finding a domain controller that is either a member of that same site or that is covering for that site.

The Microsoft DsGetDcName Directory Services API method implements the DC Locator process, but unfortunately cannot be used directly from a scripting language, such as VBScript. The IADsTools interface provides a wrapper around DsGetDcName, which is what I used. The nltest /dsgetdc command is also a wrapper around the DsGetDcName method, and is a handy tool when troubleshooting client issues related to finding an optimal domain controller.

Using a command-line interface

You can use nltest to return the closest domain controller that is serving a particular function. Some of the available functions include a global catalog server (/GC switch), time server (/TIMESERV switch), KDC (/KDC switch), and PDC (/PDC switch). Run nltest /? from a command line for the complete list.

Using VBScript

Similar to nltest, you can specify additional criteria for finding a domain controller by calling the SetDsGetDcNameFlags method before calling DsGetDcName. SetDsGetDcNameFlags accepts a comma-delimited string of the following flags:

    DS_FORCE_REDISCOVERY
    DS_DIRECTORY_SERVICE_REQUIRED
    DS_DIRECTORY_SERVICE_PREFERRED
    DS_GC_SERVER_REQUIRED
    DS_PDC_REQUIRED
    DS_IP_REQUIRED
    DS_KDC_REQUIRED
    DS_TIMESERV_REQUIRED ·
    DS_WRITABLE_REQUIRED
    DS_GOOD_TIMESERV_PREFERRED
    DS_AVOID_SELF
    DS_IS_FLAT_NAME
    DS_IS_DNS_NAME
    DS_RETURN_DNS_NAME
    DS_RETURN_FLAT_NAME

See Also

For more information on the IADsTools interface see *IadsTools.doc* in the Support Tools, MS KB 247811 (How Domain Controllers Are Located in Windows), MS KB 314861 (How Domain Controllers Are Located in Windows XP), MSDN: DsGetDc-Name, and MSDN: MicrosoftDNS

3.10   Finding a Domain Controller's Site

Problem

You need to determine the site of which a domain controller is a member.

Solution

Using a graphical user interface

1. Open LDP and from the menu, select Connection → Connect.
2. For Server, enter the name of a domain controller (or leave blank to do a server-less bind).
3. For Port, enter 389.
4. Click OK.
5. From the menu select Connection → Bind.
6. Enter credentials of a domain user.
7. Click OK.
8. From the menu, select Browse → Search.
9. For BaseDN, type the distinguished name of the Sites container (e.g., *cn=sites, cn=configuration, dc=rallencorp, dc=com*).
10. For Scope, select Subtree.
11. For Filter, enter:

        (&(objectcategory=server)(dnsHostName=<DomainControllerName>))
12. Click Run.

Using a command-line interface

    > nltest /dsgetsite /server:<DomainControllerName>

Using VBScript

    ' This code prints the site the specified domain controller is in
    ' ------ SCRIPT CONFIGURATION ------
    strDC = "<DomainControllerName>" ' e.g. dc1.rallencorp.com
    ' ------ END CONFIGURATION ---------

```
set objRootDSE = GetObject("LDAP://" & strDC & "/RootDSE")
set objNTDS = GetObject("LDAP://" & objRootDSE.Get("dsServiceName"))
set objSite = GetObject(GetObject(GetObject(objNTDS.Parent).Parent).Parent)
WScript.Echo objSite.Get("cn")
```

Discussion

Domain controllers are represented in the site topology by a server object and a
child nTDSDSA object. Actually, any type of server can conceivably have a server
object; it is the nTDSDSA object that differentiates domain controllers from other types
of servers. You'll often see the nTDSDSA object of a domain controller used to refer to
that domain controller elsewhere in Active Directory. For example, the
fSMORoleOwner attribute that represents the FSMO owners contains the distinguished
name of the nTDSDSA object of the domain controller that is holding the role.

Using a command-line interface

The nltest /dsgetsite command is a wrapper around the DsGetSiteName method.

Using VBScript

Since we cannot use the DsGetSiteName method directly in VBScript, we need to take
a more indirect approach. By querying the RootDSE of the target server, we can
retrieve the dsServiceName attribute. That attribute contains the DN of the nTDSDSA
object for the domain controller; for example, *cn=NTDS Settings,cn=dc1,cn=MySite,*
cn=Sites,cn=Configuration,dc=rallencorp,dc=com. Then, by calling the Parent method
three consecutive times, we can retrieve the object for *cn=MySite,cn=Sites,*
cn=Configuration,dc=rallencorp,dc=com.

See Also

MSDN: DsGetSiteName

3.11 Moving a Domain Controller to a Different Site

Problem

You want to move a domain controller to a different site.

Solution

Using a graphical user interface

1. Open the Active Directory Sites and Services snap-in.
2. In the left pane, expand the site that contains the domain controller.

3. Expand the Servers container.

4. Right-click on the domain controller you want to move and select Move.

5. In the Move Server box, select the site to which the domain controller will be moved and click OK.

Using a command-line interface

When using the dsmove command you must specify the DN of the object you want to move. In this case, it needs to be the distinguished name of the server object for the domain controller. The value for the -newparent option is the distinguished name of the Servers container you want to move the domain controller to.

```
> dsmove "<ServerDN>" -newparent "<NewServersContainerDN>"
```

For example, the following command would move *dc2* from the Default-First-Site-Name site to the Raleigh site.

```
> dsmove "cn=dc2,cn=servers,cn=Default-First-Site-Name,cn=sites,cn=configuration,⌐
rallencorp" -newparent "cn=servers,cn=Raleigh,cn=sites,cn=configuration,rallencorp"
```

Using VBScript

```
' This code moves a domain controller to a different site
' ------ SCRIPT CONFIGURATION ------
strDCName       = "<DomainControllerName>"  ' e.g. dc2
strCurrentSite = "<CurrentSiteName>"        ' e.g. Default-First-Site-Name
strNewSite     = "<NewSiteName>"            ' e.g. Raleigh
' ------ END CONFIGURATION ---------

strConfigDN = GetObject("LDAP://RootDSE").Get("configurationNamingContext")
strServerDN = "LDAP://cn=" & strDCName & ",cn=servers,cn=" & _
                    strCurrentSite & ",cn=sites," & strConfigDN
strNewParentDN = "LDAP://cn=servers,cn=" & strNewSite & ",cn=sites," & _
                    strConfigDN

set objCont = GetObject(strNewParentDN)
objCont.MoveHere strServerDN, "cn=" & strDCName
WScript.Echo "Successfully moved " & strDCName & " to " & strNewSite
```

Discussion

When you install a new domain controller, a server object and nTDSDSA object for the domain controller get added to the site topology. The Knowledge Consistency Checker (KCC) and Intersite Topology Generator (ISTG) use these objects to determine whom the domain controller should replicate with.

A domain controller is assigned to the site that has been mapped to the subnet it is located on. If there is no subnet object that has an address range that contains the domain controller's IP address, the server object is added to the Default-First-Site-Name site. If the domain controller should be in a different site, you'll then need to manually move it. It is a good practice to ensure that a subnet object that matches the domain controller's subnet is already in Active Directory before promoting the server into the forest. That way you do not need to worry about moving it after the fact.

 When moving a server object, remember that it has to be moved to a Servers container within a site, not directly under the site itself.

Using a command-line interface

In the solution provided, you need to know the current site of the domain controller you want to move. If you do not know the site it is currently in, you can use dsquery to find it. In fact, you can use dsquery in combination with dsmove in a single command line:

```
> for /F "usebackq" %i in (`dsquery server -name "<DomainControllerName>"`) do dsmove⌐
-newparent "cn=servers,cn=Default-First-Site,cn=sites,cn=configuration,<ForestDN>" %i
```

This command is long so I'll break it up into three parts to clarify it. The first part contains the for command extension that is built into the *cmd.exe* shell. When the /F "usebackq" syntax is specified, it is typically used to iterate over output from a command and perform certain functions on the output.

```
for /F "usebackq" %i in
```

The next part of the for loop contains the data to iterate over. In this case, I use dsquery to return the distinguished name of the server object for *dc2*.

```
(`dsquery server -name "<DomainControllerName>"`)
```

The last part executes a command for each result returned from dsquery. In this case, there should only be one result, so this command will only run once.

```
do dsmove -newparent "cn=servers,cn=Default-First-
Site,cn=sites,cn=configuration,<ForestDN>" %i
```

Using VBScript

Just as with the CLI solution, in the VBScript solution you need to specify which site the server is currently in. If you prefer, you can programmatically query for the current site, as shown in Recipe 3.10.

See Also

Recipe 3.10 for finding a domain controller's site and Recipe 4.17 for moving objects to different containers

3.12 Finding the Services a Domain Controller Is Advertising

Problem

You want to find the services a domain controller is advertising.

Solution

The following command will display the list of services a domain controller is advertising:

```
> dcdiag /v /s:<DomainControllerName> /test:advertising
```

You can also use nltest to get similar information:

```
> nltest /server:<DomainControllerName> /dsgetdc:<DomainName>
```

Discussion

The dcdiag /test:advertising command is a wrapper around the DsGetDcName method. DsGetDcName returns a structure called DOMAIN_CONTROLLER_INFO that contains the list of services a domain controller provides. Table 3-3 contains the possible values returned from this call.

Table 3-3. DOMAIN_CONTROLLER_INFO flags

Value	Description
DS_DS_FLAG	Directory server for the domain
DS_GC_FLAG	Global catalog server for the forest
DS_KDC_FLAG	Kerberos Key Distribution Center for the domain
DS_PDC_FLAG	Primary domain controller of the domain
DS_TIMESERV_FLAG	Time server for the domain
DS_WRITABLE_FLAG	Hosts a writable directory service

See Also

MSDN: DsGetDcName and MSDN: DOMAIN_CONTROLLER_INFO

3.13 Configuring a Domain Controller to Use an External Time Source

Problem

You want to set the reliable time source for a domain controller.

Solution

Using a command-line interface

Run the following commands from the command line on a domain controller:

```
> net time /setsntp:<TimeServerNameOrIP>
> net stop w32time
> net start w32time
```

Using VBScript

```
' This codes configures a reliable time source on a domain controller
' ------ SCRIPT CONFIGURATION ------
strPDC = "<DomainControllerName>"        ' e.g. dc01.rallencorp.com
strTimeServer = "<TimeServerNameOrIP>"   ' e.g. ntp01.rallencorp.com
' ------ END CONFIGURATION ---------

strTimeServerReg = "SYSTEM\CurrentControlSet\Services\W32Time\Parameters"
const HKLM = &H80000002
set objReg = GetObject("winmgmts:\\" & strPDC & "\root\default:StdRegProv")
objReg.GetStringValue HKLM, strTimeServerReg, "ntpserver", strCurrentServer
WScript.Echo "Current Value: " & strCurrentServer
objReg.SetStringValue HKLM, strTimeServerReg, "ntpserver", strTimeServer
objReg.SetStringValue HKLM, strTimeServerReg, "type", "NTP"
strCurrentServer = ""
objReg.GetStringValue HKLM, strTimeServerReg, "ntpserver", strCurrentServer
WScript.Echo "New Value: " & strCurrentServer

' Restart Time Service
set objService = GetObject("winmgmts://" & strPDC & _
                          "/root/cimv2:Win32_Service='W32Time'")
WScript.Echo "Stopping " & objService.Name
objService.StopService( )

Wscript.Sleep 2000   ' Sleep for 2 seconds to give service time to stop

WScript.Echo "Starting " & objService.Name
objService.StartService( )
```

Discussion

You need to set a reliable time source on the PDC Emulator FSMO for only the forest root domain. All other domain controllers sync their time either from that server or from a PDC (or designated time server) within their own domain. The list of external time servers is stored in the registry under the W32Time Service registry key in the following location: HKLM\SYSTEM\CurrentControlSet\Services\W32Time\Parameters\ntpserver.

If you want a domain controller, such as the PDC, to use an external time source, you have to set the `ntpserver` registry value along with the `type` value. The default value for `type` on a domain controller is `Nt5DS`, which means that the domain controller will use the Active Directory domain hierarchy to find a time source. You can override this behavior and have a domain controller contact a non-DC time source by setting `type` to `NTP`. In the CLI example, the `/setsntp` switch automatically sets the `type` value to `NTP`. In the VBScript solution, I had to set it in the code.

After setting the time server, the W32Time service should be restarted for the change to take effect. You can check that the server was set properly by running the following command:

```
> net time /querysntp
```

Since the PDC Emulator is the time source for the other domain controllers, you should also make sure that it is advertising the time service, which you can do with the following command:

```
> nltest /server:<DomainControllerName> /dsgetdc:<DomainDNSName> /TIMESERV
```

See Also

MS KB 216734 (How to Configure an Authoritative Time Server in Windows 2000), MS KB 223184 (Registry Entries for the W32Time Service), MS KB 224799 (Basic Operation of the Windows Time Service), MSDN: StdRegProv, and MSDN: Win32_Service

3.14   Finding the Number of Logon Attempts Made Against a Domain Controller

Problem

You want to find the number of logon requests a domain controller has processed.

Solution

The following query returns the number of logon requests processed:

```
> nltest /server:<DomainControllerName> /LOGON_QUERY
```

Discussion

The `nltest /LOGON_QUERY` command is a wrapper around the `I_NetLogonControl2` method, and can be useful to determine how many logon requests are being processed by a server. Viewing the results of the command over a period of time and comparing them against a server in the same domain can also tell you if one server is being used significantly more or less than the others.

See Also

MSDN: I_NetLogonControl2

3.15 Enabling the /3GB Switch to Increase the LSASS Cache

Problem

You are using more than 1 GB of memory on your domain controllers and want to enable the /3GB switch so that the LSASS process can use more memory.

Solution

Edit the *boot.ini* file on the domain controller to contain the /3GB switch:

```
[boot loader]
timeout=30
default=multi(0)disk(0)rdisk(0)partition(2)\WINDOWS
[operating systems]
multi(0)disk(0)rdisk(0)partition(2)\WINDOWS="Windows Server 2003" /3GB
```

Restart the computer.

> On Windows Server 2003, you can edit the *boot.ini* file by opening the System applet in the Control Panel. Click the Startup and Recovery tab and click the Edit button.
>
> On Windows 2000, it is not so easy. You need to open an Explorer window, select Tools → Folder Options, and click the view tab. Uncheck "Hide protected operating system files (Recommended)," and check "Show hidden files and folders." Now browse to the root of your operating system partition (e.g., C:) and edit the *boot.ini* file with a text editor.

Discussion

When computers are referred to as 32 or 64-bit computers that means they support memory addresses that are 32 or 64 bits long. This is the total available memory (virtual and real) that can be processed by the system. Since the days of Windows NT, Microsoft has split memory allocation in half by giving applications up to 2 GB and the Windows kernel 2 GB of memory to use (32 bits of address space = 2^{32} = 4 GB). In many cases, administrators would rather allocate more memory to applications than to the kernel. For this reason, Microsoft developed the /3GB switch to allow applications to use up to 3 GB of memory, leaving the kernel with 1 GB.

The /3GB switch is supported only on Windows 2000 Advanced Server, Windows 2000 Datacenter Server, Windows Server 2003 Enterprise Edition, and Windows Server 2003 Data Center Edition, and should be used only if the computer has more than 1 GB of physical memory. For a good description of how LSASS uses memory, see MS KB 308356.

See Also

MS KB 99743 (Purpose of the BOOT.INI File in Windows 2000 or Windows NT), MS KB 291988 (A Description of the 4 GB RAM Tuning Feature and the Physical Address Extension Switch), and MS KB 308356 (Memory Usage By the Lsass.exe Process on Windows 2000-Based Domain Controllers)

3.16 Cleaning Up Distributed Link Tracking Objects

Problem

You want to make sure the Distributed Link Tracking (DLT) service is disabled and all DLT objects are removed from Active Directory. The Distributed Link Tracking Server service is used to track links to files on NTFS partitions. If a file that has a shortcut to it is renamed or moved, Windows uses the DLT service to find the file when the shortcut is opened. Most organizations are unaware this service even exists, but yet it can populate thousands of objects in Active Directory. Unless you are actively using the functionality of the DLT service, it is recommended that you disable it.

Solution

If you upgrade a Windows 2000 domain controller to Windows Server 2003, the DLT Server service is stopped and set to disabled. A new install of Windows Server 2003 also has the service stopped and set to disabled. But the DLT Server service on Windows 2000 domain controllers is enabled by default. Unless you need it, you should stop the service and disable it on all of your domain controllers.

Next, you'll need to remove any DLT objects (`linkTrackVolEntry` and `linkTrackOMTEntry`) from Active Directory. Since there can be hundreds of thousands of DLT objects, you will probably want to stagger the deletion of those objects. The script in MS KB 315229 (*dltpurge.vbs*) can delete DLT objects over a period of time instead of all at once. Here is an example of running the *dltpurge.vbs* script against the *dc1* domain controller in the *rallencorp.com* domain:

```
> cscript dltpurge.vbs -s dc1 -d dc=rallencorp,dc=com
```

Discussion

DLT consists of a client and server service. The server service runs on domain controllers and the client service can run on any Windows 2000 or later machine. The server service stores data in Active Directory in the form of `linkTrackVolEntry` and `linkTrackOMTEntry` objects, which are used to track the names and locations of files on NTFS partitions. The *cn=ObjectMoveTable, cn=FileLinks,cn=System,<DomainDN>* container stores `linkTrackOMTEntry` objects that contain information about files that have been moved on computers in the domain. The *cn=VolumeTable, cn=FileLinks,cn=System,<DomainDN>* container stores `linkTrackVolEntry` objects that represent NTFS volumes on computers in the domain.

Over time, the number of DLT objects can grow substantially. Even though those objects do not take up much space, if you are not actively taking advantage of this service, you should consider disabling it and removing all DLT objects from Active Directory. If you remove a lot of DLT objects, you should determine how much space you can reclaim on the disk of the domain controllers by performing an offline defrag. See Recipe 16.12 for more information.

See Also

MS KB 232122 (Performing Offline Defragmentation of the Active Directory Database), MS KB 312403 (Distributed Link Tracking on Windows-Based Domain Controllers), and MS KB 315229 (Text Version of Dltpurge.vbs for Microsoft Knowledge Base Article Q312403)

3.17   Enabling and Disabling the Global Catalog

Problem

You want to enable or disable the global catalog on a particular server.

Solution

Using a graphical user interface

1. Open the Active Directory Sites and Services snap-in.
2. Browse to the nTDSDSA object (NTDS Settings) underneath the server object for the domain controller you want to enable or disable the global catalog for.
3. Right-click on NTDS Settings and select Properties.
4. Under the General tab, check (to enable) or uncheck (to disable) the box beside Global Catalog.
5. Click OK.

Using a command-line interface

In the following command, *<ServerObjectDN>* should be the server object DN, not the DN of the nTDSDSA object.

```
> dsmod server "<ServerObjectDN>" -isgc yes|no
```

For example, the following command will enable the global catalog on *dc1* in the Raleigh site:

```
> dsmod server↵
"cn=DC1,cn=servers,cn=Raleigh,cn=sites,cn=configuration,dc=rallencorp,dc=com" -isgc↵
yes
```

Using VBScript

```
' This code enables or disables the GC for the specified DC
' ------ SCRIPT CONFIGURATION ------
strDC = "<DomainControllerName>"      ' e.g. dc01.rallencorp.com
strGCEnable = 1                       ' 1 = enable, 0 = disable
' ------ END CONFIGURATION ---------

set objRootDSE = GetObject("LDAP://" & strDC & "/RootDSE")
objNTDS = GetObject("LDAP://" & strDC & "/" & _
                    objRootDSE.Get("dSServiceName"))
objNTDS.Put "options", strGCEnable
objNTDS.SetInfo
```

Discussion

The first domain controller promoted into a forest is by default also made a global catalog server. If you want additional servers to have the global catalog, you have to enable it. The global catalog on a domain controller becomes enabled when the low-order bit on the options attribute on the nTDSDSA object under the server object for the domain controller is set to 1. The DN of this object for *dc1* in the Default-First-Site-Name site looks like this: *cn=NTDS Settings,cn=DC1,cn=Default-First-Site-Name,cn=Sites,cn=Configuration, dc=rallencorp,dc=com.*

After enabling the global catalog, it can take some time before the domain controller can start serving as a global catalog server. The length of time is based on the amount of data that needs to replicate and the type of connectivity between the domain controller's replication partners. After replication is complete, you should see Event 1119 in the Directory Services log stating the server is advertising itself as a global catalog. At that point you should also be able to perform LDAP queries against port 3268 on that server. See Recipe 3.18 for more information on how to determine if global catalog promotion is complete.

See Also

Recipe 3.18 for determining if global catalog promotion is complete, and MS KB 313994 (HOW TO: Create or Move a Global Catalog in Windows 2000)

3.18 Determining if Global Catalog Promotion Is Complete

Problem

You want to determine if a domain controller is a global catalog server. After you initially enable the global catalog on a domain controller, it can take some time for all of the read-only naming contexts to replicate to it, depending on how large your forest is.

Solution

Query the isGlobalCatalogReady attribute on the RootDSE for the domain controller. A TRUE value means the server is a global catalog and a FALSE value indicates it is not.

For more information on how to query the RootDSE, see Recipe 4.1.

Discussion

Once a server has completed initial replication of the global catalog, the isGlobalCatalogReady attribute in the RootDSE will be marked TRUE. Another way to determine if a domain controller has been at least flagged to become a global catalog is by checking if the options attribute on the nTDSDSA object for the server has been set to 1. Note that this does not necessarily mean the server is accepting requests as a global catalog. An additional query to the RootDSE as described in the Solution, or directly to port 3268 (the global catalog port) could confirm it.

See Also

Recipe 4.1 for viewing the RootDSE

3.19 Finding the Global Catalog Servers in a Forest

Problem

You want a list of the global catalog servers in a forest.

Solution

Using a graphical user interface

1. Open LDP and from the menu select Connection → Connect.
2. For Server, enter the name of a DC.
3. For Port, enter 389.
4. Click OK.
5. From the menu select Connection → Bind.
6. Enter credentials of a domain user.
7. Click OK.
8. From the menu select Browse → Search.
9. For BaseDN, type the DN of the Sites container (e.g., *cn=sites, cn=configuration, dc=rallencorp, dc=com*).
10. For Scope, select Subtree.
11. For Filter, enter (&(objectcategory=ntdsdsa)(options=1)).
12. Click Run.

Using a command-line interface

```
> dsquery server -forest -isgc
```

Using VBScript

```
' This code prints the global catalog servers for the specified forest.
' ------ SCRIPT CONFIGURATION ------
strForestName = "<ForestDNSName>"  ' e.g. rallencorp.com
' ------ END CONFIGURATION ---------

set objRootDSE = GetObject("LDAP://" & strForestName & "/" & "RootDSE")
strADsPath = "<LDAP://" & objRootDSE.Get("configurationNamingContext") & ">;"
strFilter  = "(&(objectcategory=ntdsdsa)(options=1));"
```

```
strAttrs   = "distinguishedname;"
strScope   = "SubTree"

set objConn = CreateObject("ADODB.Connection")
objConn.Provider = "ADsDSOObject"
objConn.Open "Active Directory Provider"
set objRS = objConn.Execute(strADsPath & strFilter & strAttrs & strScope)
objRS.MoveFirst
while not objRS.EOF
    set objNTDS = GetObject("LDAP://" & objRS.Fields(0).Value)
    set objServer = GetObject( objNTDS.Parent )
    Wscript.Echo objServer.Get("dNSHostName")
    objRS.MoveNext
wend
```

Discussion

To find the global catalog servers in a forest, you need to query for NTDS Settings objects that have the low-order bit of the options attribute equal to 1 under the sites container in the Configuration Naming Context. That attribute determines if a domain controller should be a global catalog server, but it does not necessarily mean it is a global catalog server yet. See Recipe 3.18 for more information on how to tell if a server marked as a global catalog is ready to accept requests as one.

Another option for locating global catalogs is DNS, which is described in Recipe 3.21.

See Also

Recipe 3.18 for determining if global catalog promotion is complete

3.20 Finding the Domain Controllers or Global Catalog Servers in a Site

Problem

You want a list of the domain controllers or global catalog servers in a specific site.

Solution

Using a graphical user interface

1. Open the Active Directory Sites and Services snap-in.
2. In the right pane, expand the site that contains the domain controller.
3. For the list of domain controllers, expand the Servers container.

---

4. To find the global catalog servers, expand each domain controller, right-click on `NTDS Settings`, and select Properties.

5. Global catalog servers will have the box checked beside Global Catalog.

Using a command-line interface

The following query finds all domain controllers in specified site.

```
> dsquery server -site <SiteName>
```

To find only the global catalog servers in a site, use the same command with the -isgc option.

```
> dsquery server -site <SiteName> -isgc
```

Using VBScript

```
' This code prints the domain controllers in a site and then
' prints the global catalog servers in the site
' ------ SCRIPT CONFIGURATION ------
strSite   = "<SiteName>"         ' e.g. Default-First-Site-Name
strForest = "<ForestDNSName>"    ' e.g. rallencorp.com
' ------ END CONFIGURATION ---------

set objRootDSE = GetObject("LDAP://" & strForest & "/RootDSE")
strADsPath = "<LDAP://cn=servers,cn=" & strSite & ",cn=sites," & _
             objRootDSE.Get("configurationNamingContext") & ">;"
strFilter = "(objectcategory=ntdsdsa);"
strAttrs  = "distinguishedName;"
strScope  = "SubTree"

WScript.Echo "Domain controllers in " & strSite & ":"
set objConn = CreateObject("ADODB.Connection")
objConn.Provider = "ADsDSOObject"
objConn.Open "Active Directory Provider"
set objRS = objConn.Execute(strADsPath & strFilter & strAttrs & strScope)
objRS.MoveFirst
while not objRS.EOF
    Set objNTDS = GetObject("LDAP://" & objRS.Fields(0).Value)
    Set objServer = GetObject( objNTDS.Parent )
    Wscript.Echo " " & objServer.Get("dNSHostName")
    objRS.MoveNext
wend

' Global Catalog filter
strFilter = "(&(objectcategory=ntdsdsa)(options=1));"
WScript.Echo ""
WScript.Echo "Global Catalogs in " & strSite & ":"
set objRS = objConn.Execute(strADsPath & strFilter & strAttrs & strScope)
objRS.MoveFirst
while not objRS.EOF
    set objNTDS = GetObject("LDAP://" & objRS.Fields(0).Value)
    set objServer = GetObject( objNTDS.Parent )
```

```
        Wscript.Echo " " & objServer.Get("dNSHostName")
        objRS.MoveNext
    wend
```

Discussion

Each domain controller has a server object within the Servers container for the site it is a member of (e.g., *cn=DC1, cn=Servers, cn=MySite, cn=site, cn=configuration, dc=rallencorp, dc=com*). Since other types of servers can have server objects in a site's Servers container, domain controllers are differentiated by the nTDSDSA object that is a child of the server object (e.g., *cn=NTDS Settings,cn=DC1,cn=Servers, cn=MySite, cn=site, cn=confiugration, dc=rallencorp, dc=com*). Querying for this nTDSDSA objects will return a list of domain controllers in the site. Locating global catalog servers consists of the same query, except where the low-order bit of the options attribute of the nTDSDSA object is equal to 1.

3.21   Finding Domain Controllers and Global Catalogs via DNS

Problem

You want to find domain controllers or global catalogs using DNS lookups.

Solution

Domain controllers and global catalog servers are represented in DNS as SRV records. You can query SRV records using nslookup by setting the type=SRV, such as the following:

```
> nslookup
Default Server:  dns01.rallencorp.com
Address:  10.1.2.3

> set type=SRV
```

You then need to issue the following query to retrieve all domain controllers for the specified domain.

```
> _ldap._tcp.<DomainDNSName>
```

You can issue a similar query to retrieve global catalogs, but since they are forest-wide, the query is based on the forest name.

```
> _gc._tcp.<ForestDNSName>
```

You can even find the domain controllers or global catalogs that are in a particular site or that *cover* a particular site by querying the following:

```
> _ldap._tcp.<SiteName>._sites.<DomainDNSName>
> _gc._tcp.<SiteName>._sites.<ForestDNSName>
```

See Recipe 11.18 for more information on site coverage.

Discussion

One of the benefits of Active Directory over its predecessor Windows NT is that it relies on DNS for name resolution. Active Directory uses DNS to locate servers that serve a particular function, such as a domain controller for a domain, global catalog server, PDC Emulator, KDC. It also uses the site topology information stored in Active Directory to populate site-specific records for domain controllers.

The DC locator process relies on this information in DNS to direct clients to the most optimal server when logging in. Reliance on DNS makes it easy to troubleshoot problems related to clients finding domain controllers. If you know the site a client is in, you can make a few DNS queries to determine which domain controller they should be authenticating with.

The resource records a domain controller registers in DNS can be restricted, so querying DNS may return only a subset of the actual domain controllers. See Recipes 13.14 and 13.15 for more information.

See Also

Recipe 3.28 for finding the PDC Emulator via DNS and MS KB 267855 (Problems with Many Domain Controllers with Active Directory Integrated DNS Zones)

3.22 Changing the Preference for a Domain Controller

Problem

You want a particular domain controller to be used less frequently for client requests or not at all. This may be necessary if a particular domain controller is overloaded, perhaps due to application requests.

Solution

You can modify the Priority or Weight fields in SRV resource records by modifying the registry on the domain controller. Open regedit or regedt32 on the domain controller and browse to the following key: HKLM\SYSTEM\CurrentControlSet\Services\Netlogon\Parameters. To configure the Priority, add a REG_DWORD with the name LdapSrvPriority. To configure the weight, add a REG_DWORD with the name LdapSrvWeight.

After you make the change, the *%SystemRoot%\System32\Config\netlogon.dns* file should be updated and the DDNS updates sent to the DNS server within an hour. You can also restart the NetLogon service to expedite the process.

Discussion

Each domain controller registers several SRV records that clients use as part of the DC locator process to find the closest domain controller. Two fields of the SRV record let clients determine which server to use when multiple possibilities are returned. The Priority field is used to dictate if a specific server or set of servers should always be contacted over others unless otherwise unavailable. A server with a higher priority (i.e., lower priority field value) will always be contacted before a server with a lower priority. For example, if DC1 has a SRV priority of 5 and DC2 has a SRV priority of 10, DC1 will always be used unless it is unavailable.

The Weight field, on the other hand, determines the percentage of time clients should use a particular server. You can easily calculate the percentage by dividing the weight by the sum of all Weights for servers with the same Priority. If server's DC1, DC2, and DC3 have Weights of 1, 2, and 3, respectively, then DC1 will be contacted one out of six times (1 / (3 + 2 + 1)), DC2 will be contacted two out of every six times or 1/3 (2 / (3 + 2 + 1)), and DC3 will be contacted three out of every six times or 1/2(3 / (3 + 2 + 1)). Here is an example of how the SRV records look with these weights:

```
C:\>nslookup -type=SRV _ldap._tcp.dc._msdcs.rallencorp.com
Server:  dns01.rallencorp.com
Address:  171.70.168.183

_ldap._tcp.dc._msdcs.rallencorp.com  SRV service location:
          priority      = 0
          weight        = 1
          port          = 389
          svr hostname  = dc1.rallencorp.com
_ldap._tcp.dc._msdcs.rallencorp.com  SRV service location:
          priority      = 0
          weight        = 2
          port          = 389
          svr hostname  = dc2.rallencorp.com
_ldap._tcp.dc._msdcs.rallencorp.com  SRV service location:
          priority      = 0
          weight        = 3
          port          = 389
          svr hostname  = dc3.rallencorp.com
```

In certain situations, having this capability can come in handy. For example, the server acting as the PDC FSMO role owner typically receives more traffic from clients simply because of the nature of tasks that the PDC FSMO has to handle. If you find a certain server like the PDC FSMO has considerably higher load than the rest of the servers, you could change the priority or weight of the SRV records so that it is

used less often during the DC locator process. You can increase the Priority to elimi-
nate its use unless all other domain controllers fail. Modify the Weight to reduce
how often it will be used.

3.23   Disabling the Global Catalog Requirement During a Windows 2000 Domain Login

Problem

You want to disable the requirement for a global catalog server to be reachable when
a user logs into a Windows 2000 domain.

Solution

Using a graphical user interface

1. Open the Registry Editor (regedit).
2. In the left pane, expand HKEY_LOCAL_MACHINE → System → Current-
   ControlSet → Control.
3. Right-click on LSA and select New → Key.
4. Enter IgnoreGCFailures for the key name and hit enter.
5. Restart the server.

Using a command-line interface

```
> reg add HKLM\SYSTEM\CurrentControlSet\Control\LSA\IgnoreGCFailures /ve
> shutdown /r
```

Using VBScript

```
' This code enables the IgnoreGCFailres registry setting and reboots
strLSA = "HKLM\SYSTEM\CurrentControlSet\Control\LSA\IgnoreGCFailures\"
Set objWSHShell = WScript.CreateObject("WScript.Shell")
objWSHShell.RegWrite strLSA, ""
WScript.Echo "Successfully created key"
WScript.Echo "Rebooting server..."
objWSHShell.Run "rundll32 shell32.dll,SHExitWindowsEx 2"
```

Discussion

With Windows 2000, a global catalog server must be contacted for every login
attempt; otherwise, the login will fail (unless there is no network connectivity, which
would result in a cached login). This is necessary to process all universal groups a
user may be a member of. When a client attempts to authenticate with a domain
controller, that domain controller contacts a global catalog server behind the scenes

to enumerate the user's universal groups. See Recipe 7.9 for more details. If you have domain controllers in remote sites and they are not enabled as global catalog servers, you may run into a situation where users cannot login if the network connection to the network with the closest global catalog server fails.

Although there is a plausible workaround in Windows Server 2003 Active Directory (see Recipe 3.24), the only option you have available with Windows 2000 is to have the domain controllers ignore GC lookup failures. You can do this by adding an IgnoreGCFailures registry key under HKLM\SYSTEM\CurrentControlSet\Control\ LSA on the domain controller(s) you want this to apply to. If you use universal groups in any capacity, having the domain controllers ignore GC failures can be very problematic because a user's token may not get updated with his universal group memberships. It may be useful, though, if you have branch-office sites where you cannot deploy domain controllers.

See Also

Recipe 3.24 for disabling the global catalog requirement for Windows Server 2003, Recipe 7.9 for enabling universal group caching, MS KB 216970 (Global Catalog Server Requirement for User and Computer Logon), and MS KB 241789 (How to Disable the Requirement that a Global Catalog Server Be Available to Validate User Logons)

3.24   Disabling the Global Catalog Requirement During a Windows 2003 Domain Login

 This recipe requires the Windows Server 2003 forest functional level.

Problem

You want to disable the requirement for a global catalog server to be reachable when a user logs into a Windows 2003 domain.

Solution

See Recipe 7.9 for information on enabling universal group caching, which effectively eliminates the need to contact a global catalog server during logon.

3.25   Finding the FSMO Role Holders

Problem

You want to find the domain controllers that are acting as one of the FSMO roles.

Solution

Using a graphical user interface

For the Schema Master:

1. Open the Active Directory Schema snap-in.
2. Right-click on Active Directory Schema in the left pane and select Operations Master.

For the Domain Naming Master:

1. Open the Active Directory Domains and Trusts snap-in.
2. Right-click on Active Directory Domains and Trusts in the left pane and select Operations Master.

For the PDC Emulator, RID Master, and Infrastructure Master:

1. Open the Active Directory Users and Computers snap-in.
2. Make sure you've targeted the correct domain.
3. Right-click on Active Directory Users and Computers in the left pane and select Operations Master.
4. There are individual tabs for the PDC, RID, and Infrastructure roles.

Using a command-line interface

In the following command, you can leave out the /Domain <DomainDNSName> option to query the domain you are currently logged on.

```
> netdom query fsmo /Domain:<DomainDNSName>
```

For some reason, this command returns a "The parameter is incorrect" error on Windows Server 2003. Until that is resolved, you can use the dsquery server command shown here, where <Role> can be schema, name, infr, pdc, or rid:

```
> dsquery server -hasfsmo <Role>
```

Using VBScript

```
' This code prints the FSMO role owners for the specified domain.
' ------ SCRIPT CONFIGURATION ------
strDomain = "<DomainDNSName>"  ' e.g. emea.rallencorp.com
' ------ END CONFIGURATION ---------
```

```
set objRootDSE = GetObject("LDAP://" & strDomain & "/RootDSE")
strDomainDN = objRootDSE.Get("defaultNamingContext")
strSchemaDN = objRootDSE.Get("schemaNamingContext")
strConfigDN = objRootDSE.Get("configurationNamingContext")

' PDC Emulator
set objPDCFsmo = GetObject("LDAP://" & strDomainDN)
Wscript.Echo "PDC Emulator: " & objPDCFsmo.fsmoroleowner

' RID Master
set objRIDFsmo = GetObject("LDAP://cn=RID Manager$,cn=system," & strDomainDN)
Wscript.Echo "RID Master: " & objRIDFsmo.fsmoroleowner

' Schema Master
set objSchemaFsmo = GetObject("LDAP://" & strSchemaDN)
Wscript.Echo "Schema Master: " & objSchemaFsmo.fsmoroleowner

' Infrastructure Master
set objInfraFsmo = GetObject("LDAP://cn=Infrastructure," & strDomainDN)
Wscript.Echo "Infrastructure Master: " & objInfraFsmo.fsmoroleowner

' Domain Naming Master
set objDNFsmo = GetObject("LDAP://cn=Partitions," & strConfigDN)
Wscript.Echo "Domain Naming Master: " & objDNFsmo.fsmoroleowner
```

Discussion

Several Active Directory operations are sensitive, such as updating the schema, and therefore, need to be done on a single domain controller. Active Directory cannot guarantee the proper evaluation of these functions in a situation where they may be invoked from more than one DC. The FSMO mechanism is used to limit these functions to a single DC.

There are five designated FSMO roles that correspond to these sensitive functions. A FSMO role can apply either to an entire forest or to a specific domain. Each role is stored in the fSMORoleOwner attribute on various objects in Active Directory depending on the role. Table 3-4 contains a list of FSMO roles.

Table 3-4. FSMO roles

Role	Description	fSMORoleOwner Location	Domain or Forest-wide?
Schema	Processes schema updates	*CN=Schema,CN=Configuration,<ForestDN>*	Forest
Domain Naming	Processes the addition, removal, and renaming of domains	*CN=Partitions,CN=Configuration,<ForestDN>*	Forest
Infrastructure	Maintains references to objects in other domains	*CN=Infrastructure,<ForestDN>*	Domain

Table 3-4. FSMO roles (continued)

Role	Description	fSMORoleOwner Location	Domain or Forest-wide?
RID	Handles RID pool allocation for the domain controllers in a domain	*CN=Rid Manager$, CN=System,<DomainDN>*	Domain
PDC Emulator	Acts as the Windows NT master browser and also as the PDC for downlevel clients and Backup Domain Controllers (BDCs)	*<DomainDN>*	Domain

Using VBScript

If you want to get the DNS name for each FSMO, you'll need to get the parent object of the nTDSDSA object and use the dNSHostName attribute, similar to Recipe 3.8. The code for getting the Schema Master could be changed to the following to retrieve the DNS name of the DC:

```
set objSchemaFsmo = GetObject("LDAP://cn=Schema,cn=Configuration," & strForestDN)
set objSchemaFsmoNTDS = GetObject("LDAP://" & objSchemaFsmo.fsmoroleowner)
set objSchemaFsmoServer = GetObject(objSchemaFsmoNTDS.Parent)
Wscript.Echo "Schema Master: " & objSchemaFsmoServer.Get("dNSHostName")
```

See Also

MS KB 197132 (Windows 2000 Active Directory FSMO Roles), MS KB 223346 (FSMO Placement and Optimization on Windows 2000 Domain Controllers), MS KB 234790 (HOW TO: Find Servers That Hold Flexible Single Master Operations Roles), and MS KB 324801 (HOW TO: View and Transfer FSMO Roles in Windows Server 2003)

3.26   Transferring a FSMO Role

Problem

You want to transfer a FSMO role to a different domain controller. This may be necessary if you need to take a current FSMO role holder down for maintenance.

Solution

Using a graphical user interface

1. Use the same directions as described in Recipe 3.25 for viewing a specific FSMO, except target (i.e., right-click and select Connect to Domain Controller) the

domain controller you want to transfer the FSMO to before selecting Operations Master.

2. Click the Change button.

3. Click OK twice.

4. You should then see a message stating whether the transfer was successful.

Using a command-line interface

The following would transfer the PDC Emulator role to <NewRoleOwner>. See the discussion to see about transferring the other roles.

```
> ntdsutil roles conn "co t s <NewRoleOwner>" q "transfer PDC" q q
```

Using VBScript

```
' This code transfers the PDC Emulator role to the specified owner.
' See the discussion to see about transferring the other roles.
' ------ SCRIPT CONFIGURATION ------
strNewOwner = "<NewRoleOwner>"  ' e.g. dc2.rallencorp.com
' ------ END CONFIGURATION ---------

Set objRootDSE = GetObject("LDAP://" & strNewOwner & "/RootDSE")
objRootDSE.Put "becomePDC", 1
objRootDSE.SetInfo
```

Discussion

The first domain controller in a new forest is assigned the two forest-wide FSMO roles (schema and domain naming). The first domain controller in a new domain gets the other three domain-wide roles. It is very likely you'll need to move the roles around to different domain controllers at some point. Also, when you need to take down a domain controller that is currently a FSMO role owner, you'll want to transfer the role beforehand. If you plan to install a hotfix or do some other type of maintenance that only necessitates a quick reboot, you may not want to go to the trouble of transferring the FSMO role.

Some FSMO roles are more time critical than others. For example, the PDC Emulator role is used extensively, but the Schema Master is needed only when extending the schema. If a FSMO role owner becomes unavailable before you can transfer it, you'll need to seize the role (see Recipe 3.27).

Using a command-line interface

Any role can be transferred using ntdsutil by replacing "transfer PDC" in the solution with one of the following:

- "transfer domain naming master"
- "transfer infrastructure master"

- "transfer RID master"
- "transfer schema master"

Using VBScript

FSMO roles can be transferred programmatically by setting the become*<FSMORole>* operational attribute on the RootDSE of the domain controller to transfer the role to. The following are the available attributes that can be set that correspond to each FSMO role:

- becomeDomainMaster
- becomeInfrastructureMaster
- becomePDC
- becomeRidMaster
- becomeSchemaMaster

See Also

Recipe 3.25 for finding FSMO role holders, Recipe 3.27 for seizing a FSMO role, MS KB 223787 (Flexible Single Master Operation Transfer and Seizure Process), MS KB 255504 (Using Ntdsutil.exe to Seize or Transfer FSMO Roles to a Domain Controller), and MS KB 324801 (HOW TO: View and Transfer FSMO Roles in Windows Server 2003)

3.27 Seizing a FSMO Role

Problem

You need to seize a FSMO role because the current role holder is down and will not be restored.

Solution

Using a command-line interface

The following would seize the PDC Emulator role to *<NewRoleOwner>*:

```
> ntdsutil roles conn "co t s <NewRoleOwner>" q "seize PDC" q q
```

Any of the other roles can be transferred as well using ntdsutil by replacing "transfer PDC" in the previous solution with one of the following:

- "seize domain naming master"
- "seize infrastructure master"
- "seize RID master"
- "seize schema master"

Using VBScript

Seizing a FSMO role is typically not something you need to do programmatically, but you can do it. All you need to do is set the `fSMORoleOwner` attribute for the object that represents the FSMO role as described in Recipe 3.25 with the distinguished name of `nTDSDSA` object of the new role owner.

Discussion

Seizing a FSMO role should not be done lightly. The general recommendation is to seize a FSMO role only when you cannot possibly bring the previous role holder back online. One reason that seizing a role is problematic is that you could possibly lose data. For example, lets say that you extended the schema, and immediately after it was extended the Schema FSMO went down. If you could not bring that server back online, those extensions may have not replicated before the server went down. You would need to determine if the any of the schema extensions replicated and, if not, re-extend the schema. A similar problem can result from losing the RID FSMO, where duplicate RID pools may be allocated. See Recipe 2.24 for more information.

See Also

Recipe 3.25 for finding FSMO role holders, Recipe 3.26 for transferring a FSMO role, MS KB 223787 (Flexible Single Master Operation Transfer and Seizure Process), and MS KB 255504 (Using Ntdsutil.exe to Seize or Transfer FSMO Roles to a Domain Controller)

3.28   Finding the PDC Emulator FSMO Role Owner via DNS

Problem

You want to find the PDC Emulator for a domain using DNS.

Solution

Using a command-line interface

```
> nslookup -type=SRV _ldap._tcp.pdc._msdcs.<DomainDNSName>
```

Discussion

The PDC Emulator FSMO role is the only FSMO role that is stored in DNS. Like many of the other Active Directory–related DNS records, the PDC record is stored as an SRV record under *_ldap._tcp.pdc._msdcs.<DomainDNSName>* where *<DomainDNSName>* is the domain the PDC is in.

See Also

Recipe 3.21 for finding domain controllers via DNS

CHAPTER 4
Searching and Manipulating Objects

4.0 Introduction

Active Directory is based on the Lightweight Directory Access Protocol (LDAP) and supports the LDAP v3 specification defined in RFC 2251. And while many of the AD tools and interfaces, such as ADSI, abstract and streamline LDAP operations to make things easier, any good AD administrator or developer must have a thorough understanding of LDAP to fully utilize Active Directory. This chapter will cover the some of the basic LDAP-related tasks you may need to do with Active Directory, along with other items related to searching and manipulating objects in the directory.

The Anatomy of an Object

The Active Directory schema is composed of a hierarchy of classes. These classes support inheritance, which enables reuse of existing class definitions. At the top of the inheritance tree is the top class, from which every class in the schema is derived. Table 4-1 contains a list of some of the attributes that are available from the top class, and subsequently are defined on every object that is created in Active Directory.

Table 4-1. Common attributes of objects

Attribute	Description
cn	Relative distinguished name (RDN) attribute for most object classes
createTimestamp	Timestamp when the object was created. See Recipe 4.22 for more information
description	Multivalued attribute that can be used as a generic field for storing a description of the object
displayName	Name of the object displayed in administrative interfaces
distinguishedName	Distinguished name of the object
modifyTimestamp	Timestamp when the object was last changed. See Recipe 4.22 for more information
name	RDN of the object. The value of this attribute will mirror the naming attribute (e.g., cn, ou, dc)
nTSecurityDescriptor	Security descriptor assigned to the object

Table 4-1. Common attributes of objects (continued)

Attribute	Description
objectCategory	Used as a grouping mechanism for objects with a similar purpose (e.g., Person)
objectClass	List of classes from which the object's class was derived
objectGUID	Globally unique identifier for the object
uSNChanged	Update sequence number (USN) assigned by the local server after the last change to the object (can include creation)
uSNCreated	USN assigned when the object was created

4.1 Viewing the RootDSE

Problem

You want to view attributes of the RootDSE, which can be useful for discovering basic information about a forest, domain, or domain controller.

Solution

Using a graphical user interface

1. Open LDP.
2. From the menu, select Connection → Connect.
3. For Server, enter a domain controller, domain name, or leave blank to do a serverless bind.
4. For Port, enter 389.
5. Click OK.
6. The contents of the RootDSE will be shown in the right pane.

Using a command-line interface

```
> enumprop "LDAP://RootDSE"
```

Using VBScript

```
' This code prints the attributes of the RootDSE
set objRootDSE = GetObject("LDAP://RootDSE")
objRootDSE.GetInfo
for i = 0 to objRootDSE.PropertyCount - 1
    set strProp = objRootDSE.Item(i)
    WScript.Echo strProp.Name & " "
    for each strPropval in strProp.Values
        WScript.Echo "  " &  strPropval.CaseIgnoreString
    next
next
```

Discussion

The RootDSE was originally defined in RFC 2251 as part of the LDAPv3 specification. It is not part of the Active Directory namespace per se. It is a synthetic object that is maintained separately by each domain controller.

The RootDSE can be accessed anonymously, and in fact, none of the three solutions used credentials. In the CLI and VBScript solutions, I used serverless binds against the RootDSE. In that case, the DC Locator process is used to find a domain controller in the domain you authenticate against. This can also be accomplished with LDP by not entering a server name from the Connect dialog box.

The RootDSE is key to writing portable AD-enabled applications. It provides a mechanism to programmatically determine the distinguished names of the various naming contexts among other things, which means you do not need to hardcode that information in scripts and programs. Here is an example from LDP when run against a Windows Server 2003–based domain controller:

```
ld = ldap_open("dc01", 389);
Established connection to dc01.
Retrieving base DSA information...
Result <0>: (null)
Matched DNs:
Getting 1 entries:
>> Dn:
1> currentTime: 05/26/2003 15:29:42 Pacific Standard Time Pacific Daylight Time;

1> subschemaSubentry:CN=Aggregate,CN=Schema,CN=Configuration,DC=rallencorp,DC=com;

1> dsServiceName: CN=NTDS Settings,CN=DC01,CN=Servers,CN=Default-First-Site-
Name,CN=Sites,CN=Configuration,DC=rallencorp,DC=com;

5> namingContexts: DC=rallencorp,DC=com; CN=Configuration,DC=rallencorp,DC=com;
CN=Schema,CN=Configuration,DC=rallencorp,DC=com;
DC=DomainDnsZones,DC=rallencorp,DC=com; DC=ForestDnsZones,DC=rallencorp,DC=com;

1> defaultNamingContext: DC=rallencorp,DC=com;

1> schemaNamingContext: CN=Schema,CN=Configuration,DC=rallencorp,DC=com;

1> configurationNamingContext: CN=Configuration,DC=rallencorp,DC=com;

1> rootDomainNamingContext: DC=rallencorp,DC=com;

21> supportedControl: 1.2.840.113556.1.4.319; 1.2.840.113556.1.4.801; 1.2.840.113556.
1.4.473; 1.2.840.113556.1.4.528; 1.2.840.113556.1.4.417; 1.2.840.113556.1.4.619; 1.2.
840.113556.1.4.841; 1.2.840.113556.1.4.529; 1.2.840.113556.1.4.805; 1.2.840.113556.1.
4.521; 1.2.840.113556.1.4.970; 1.2.840.113556.1.4.1338; 1.2.840.113556.1.4.474; 1.2.
840.113556.1.4.1339; 1.2.840.113556.1.4.1340; 1.2.840.113556.1.4.1413; 2.16.840.1.
113730.3.4.9; 2.16.840.1.113730.3.4.10; 1.2.840.113556.1.4.1504; 1.2.840.113556.1.4.
1852; 1.2.840.113556.1.4.802;
```

```
2> supportedLDAPVersion: 3; 2;

12> supportedLDAPPolicies: MaxPoolThreads; MaxDatagramRecv; MaxReceiveBuffer;
InitRecvTimeout; MaxConnections; MaxConnIdleTime; MaxPageSize; MaxQueryDuration;
MaxTempTableSize; MaxResultSetSize; MaxNotificationPerConn; MaxValRange;

1> highestCommittedUSN: 53242;

4> supportedSASLMechanisms: GSSAPI; GSS-SPNEGO; EXTERNAL; DIGEST-MD5;

1> dnsHostName: dc01.rallencorp.com;

1> ldapServiceName: rallencorp.com:dc01$@RALLENCORP.COM;

1> serverName: CN=DC01,CN=Servers,CN=Default-First-Site-
Name,CN=Sites,CN=Configuration,DC=rallencorp,DC=com;

3> supportedCapabilities: 1.2.840.113556.1.4.800; 1.2.840.113556.1.4.1670; 1.2.840.
113556.1.4.1791;

1> isSynchronized: TRUE;

1> isGlobalCatalogReady: TRUE;

1> domainFunctionality: 0 = ( DS_BEHAVIOR_WIN2000 );

1> forestFunctionality: 0 = ( DS_BEHAVIOR_WIN2000 );

1> domainControllerFunctionality: 2 = ( DS_BEHAVIOR_WIN2003 );
```

Using VBScript

All attributes of the RootDSE were retrieved and displayed. Typically, you will need only a few of the attributes; in which case, you'll want to use Get or GetEx as in the following example:

```
strDefaultNC = objRootDSE.Get("defaultNamingContext")
```

Or if want to get an object based on the distinguished name (DN) of one of the naming contexts, you can call GetObject using an ADsPath:

```
set objUser = GetObject("LDAP://cn=administrator,cn=users," & _
                        objRootDSE.Get("defaultNamingContext") )
```

See Also

RFC 2251, MS KB 219005 (Windows 2000: LDAPv3 RootDSE), MSDN: IADsPropertyEntry, MSDN: IADsPropertyValue, MSDN: IADs::Get, and MSDN: IADs::GetEx

4.2 Viewing the Attributes of an Object

Problem

You want to view one or more attributes of an object.

Solution

Using a graphical user interface

1. Open LDP.
2. From the menu, select Connection → Connect.
3. For Server, enter the name of a domain controller or domain that contains the object.
4. For Port, enter 389.
5. Click OK.
6. From the menu, select Connection → Bind.
7. Enter credentials of a user that can view the object (if necessary).
8. Click OK.
9. From the menu, select View → Tree.
10. For BaseDN, type the DN of the object you want to view.
11. For Scope, select Base.
12. Click OK.

Using a command-line interface

```
> dsquery * "<ObjectDN>" -scope base -attr *
```

For Windows 2000, use this command:

```
> enumprop "LDAP://<ObjectDN>"
```

Using VBScript

```
' This code prints all attributes for the specified object.
' ------ SCRIPT CONFIGURATION ------
strObjectDN = "<ObjectDN>" ' e.g. cn=jsmith,cn=users,dc=rallencorp,dc=com
' ------ END CONFIGURATION ---------

DisplayAttributes("LDAP://" & strObjectDN)

Function DisplayAttributes( strObjectADsPath )

    set objObject = GetObject(strObjectADsPath)
    objObject.GetInfo
```

```
'Declare the hash (dictionary), constants and variables
'Values taken from ADSTYPEENUM
set dicADsType = CreateObject("Scripting.Dictionary")
dicADsType.Add 0, "INVALID"
dicADsType.Add 1, "DN_STRING"
dicADsType.Add 2, "CASE_EXACT_STRING"
dicADsType.Add 3, "CASE_IGNORE_STRING"
dicADsType.Add 4, "PRINTABLE_STRING"
dicADsType.Add 5, "NUMERIC_STRING"
dicADsType.Add 6, "BOOLEAN"
dicADsType.Add 7, "INTEGER"
dicADsType.Add 8, "OCTET_STRING"
dicADsType.Add 9, "UTC_TIME"
dicADsType.Add 10, "LARGE_INTEGER"
dicADsType.Add 11, "PROV_SPECIFIC"
dicADsType.Add 12, "OBJECT_CLASS"
dicADsType.Add 13, "CASEIGNORE_LIST"
dicADsType.Add 14, "OCTET_LIST"
dicADsType.Add 15, "PATH"
dicADsType.Add 16, "POSTALADDRESS"
dicADsType.Add 17, "TIMESTAMP"
dicADsType.Add 18, "BACKLINK"
dicADsType.Add 19, "TYPEDNAME"
dicADsType.Add 20, "HOLD"
dicADsType.Add 21, "NETADDRESS"
dicADsType.Add 22, "REPLICAPOINTER"
dicADsType.Add 23, "FAXNUMBER"
dicADsType.Add 24, "EMAIL"
dicADsType.Add 25, "NT_SECURITY_DESCRIPTOR"
dicADsType.Add 26, "UNKNOWN"
dicADsType.Add 27, "DN_WITH_BINARY"
dicADsType.Add 28, "DN_WITH_STRING"

for intIndex = 0 To (objObject.PropertyCount - 1)
   set objPropEntry = objObject.Item(intIndex)
   for Each objPropValue In objPropEntry.Values
      value = ""

      if (dicADsType(objPropValue.ADsType) = "DN_STRING") then
         value = objPropValue.DNString

      elseIf (dicADsType(objPropValue.ADsType) = "CASE_EXACT_STRING") then
         value = objPropValue.CaseExactString

      elseIf (dicADsType(objPropValue.ADsType) = "CASE_IGNORE_STRING") then
         value = objPropValue.CaseIgnoreString

      elseIf (dicADsType(objPropValue.ADsType) = "PRINTABLE_STRING") then
         value = objPropValue.PrintableString

      elseIf (dicADsType(objPropValue.ADsType) = "NUMERIC_STRING") then
         value = objPropValue.NumericString
```

```
        elseIf (dicADsType(objPropValue.ADsType) = "BOOLEAN") then
            value = CStr(objPropValue.Boolean)

        elseIf (dicADsType(objPropValue.ADsType) = "INTEGER") then
            value = objPropValue.Integer

        elseIf (dicADsType(objPropValue.ADsType) = "LARGE_INTEGER") then
            set objLargeInt = objPropValue.LargeInteger
            value = objLargeInt.HighPart * 2^32 + objLargeInt.LowPart

        elseIf (dicADsType(objPropValue.ADsType) = "UTC_TIME") then
            value = objPropValue.UTCTime

        else
            value = "<" & dicADsType.Item(objPropEntry.ADsType) & ">"

        end if
        WScript.Echo objPropEntry.Name & " : " & value
    next
  next
End Function
```

Discussion

Objects in Active Directory are made up of a collection of attributes. Attributes can be single- or multivalued. Each attribute also has an associated syntax that is defined in the schema. See Recipe 10.7 for a complete list of syntaxes.

Using a graphical user interface

You can customize the list of attributes returned from a search with LDP by modifying the Attributes: field under Options → Search. To include all attributes enter *. For a subset enter a semicolon-separated list of attributes.

Using a command-line interface

The -attr option for the dsquery command accepts a whitespace-separated list of attributes to display. Using a * will return all attributes.

For the enumprop command, you can use the /ATTR option and a comma-separated list of attributes to return. In the following example, only the name and whenCreated attributes would be returned:

```
> enumprop /ATTR:name,whenCreated "LDAP://<ObjectDN>"
```

Using VBScript

The DisplayAttributes function prints the attributes that contain values for the object passed in. After using GetObject to bind to the object, I used the IADs::GetInfo method to populate the local property cache with all of the object's attributes from

---

AD. In order to print each value of a property, I have to know its type or syntax. The `ADsType` method returns an integer from the `ADSTYPEENUM` enumeration that corresponds with a particular syntax (e.g., boolean). Based on the syntax, I call a specific method (e.g., `Boolean`) that can properly print the value. If I didn't incorporate this logic and tried to print all values using the `CaseIgnoreString` method for example, an error would get generated when the script encountered an octet string because octet strings (i.e., binary data) do not have a `CaseIgnoreString` representation.

I stored the values from the `ADSTYPEENUM` enumeration in key/value pairs in a dictionary object (i.e., `Scripting.Dictionary`). In the dictionary object, the key for the dictionary is the `ADSTYPEENUM` integer, and the value is a textual version of the syntax. I used the dictionary object so I could print the textual syntax of each attribute. I iterated over all the properties in the property cache using `IADsPropertyList` and `IADsPropertyEntry` objects, which are instantiated with the `IADsPropertyList::Item` method.

 The `DisplayAttributes` function is used throughout the book in examples where the attributes for a given type of object are displayed.

See Also

Chapter 19, IADs and the Property Cache, from *Active Directory*, Second Edition, MSDN: IADsPropertyEntry, MSDN: IADsPropertyList, MSDN: ADSTYPEENUM, and MSDN: IADs::GetInfo

4.3   Using LDAP Controls

Problem

You want to use an LDAP control as part of an LDAP operation.

Solution

Using a graphical user interface

1. Open LDP.

2. From the menu, select Options → Controls.

3. For the Windows Server 2003 version of LDP, select the control you want to use under Load Predefined. The control should automatically be added to the list of Active Controls.

   For the Windows 2000 version of LDP, you'll need to type the object identifier (OID) of the control under Object Identifier.

4. Enter the value for the control under Value.

5. Select whether the control is server- or client-side under Control Type.

6. Check the box beside Critical if the control is critical.

7. Click the Check-in button.

8. Click OK.

9. At this point, you will need to invoke the LDAP operation (for example, Search) that will use the control. In the dialog box for any operation, be sure that the "Extended" option is checked before initiating the operation.

Using VBScript

None of the ADSI automation interfaces directly expose LDAP controls. That means they cannot be utilized from VBScript. On the other hand, many of the controls, such as paged searching or deleting a subtree, are wrapped within their own ADSI methods that can be used within VBScript.

Any LDAP-based API, such as the Perl Net::LDAP modules, can be used to set controls as part of LDAP operations.

Discussion

LDAP controls were defined in the LDAPv3 specification as a way to extend LDAP and its operations without breaking the protocol. Many controls have been implemented, some of which are used when searching the directory (e.g., paged searching, VLV, finding deleted objects, and attribute scoped query), and some are needed to do certain modifications to the directory (e.g., cross-domain object moves, tree delete, and permissive modify). Controls can be marked as *critical*, which means they must be processed with the request, or an error is returned. If an unsupported control is not flagged as critical, the server can continue to process the request and ignore the control.

The complete list of controls supported by Active Directory is included in Table 4-2.

Table 4-2. LDAP controls supported by Active Directory

Name	OID	Description
Paged Results	1.2.840.113556.1.4.319	Instructs the server to return search results in "pages."
Cross Domain Move	1.2.840.113556.1.4.521	Used to move objects between domains.
DIRSYNC	1.2.840.113556.1.4.841	Used to find objects that have changed over a period of time.
Domain Scope	1.2.840.113556.1.4.1339	Informs the server to not generate any referrals in a search response.
Extended DN	1.2.840.113556.1.4.529	Used to return an object's GUID and SID (for security principals) as part of its distinguished name.

Table 4-2. LDAP controls supported by Active Directory (continued)

Name	OID	Description
Lazy Commit	1.2.840.113556.1.4.619	Informs the server to return after directory modifications have been written to memory, but before they have been written to disk. This can speed up processing of a lot of modifications.
Change Notification	1.2.840.113556.1.4.528	Used by clients to register for notification of when changes occur in the directory.
Permissive Modify	1.2.840.113556.1.4.1413	Allows duplicate adds of the same value for an attribute or deletion of an attribute that has no values to succeed (normally, it would fail in that situation).
SD Flags	1.2.840.113556.1.4.801	Used to pass flags to the server to control certain security descriptor options.
Search Options	1.2.840.113556.1.4.1340	Used to pass flags to the server to control search options.
Show Deleted Objects	1.2.840.113556.1.4.417	Used to inform the server to return any deleted objects that matched the search criteria.
Server-side Sort Request	1.2.840.113556.1.4.473	Used to inform the server to sort the results of a search.
Server-side Sort Response	1.2.840.113556.1.4.474	Returned by the server in response to a sort request.
Tree Delete	1.2.840.113556.1.4.805	Used to delete portions of the directory tree, including any child objects.
Verify Name	1.2.840.113556.1.4.1338	Used to target a specific GC server that is used to verify DN-valued attributes that are processed during add or modification operations.
VLV Request	2.16.840.1.113730.3.4.9	Used to request a virtual list view of results from a search. This control is new to Windows Server 2003.
VLV Response	2.16.840.1.113730.3.4.10	Response from server returning a virtual list view of results from a search. This control is new to Windows Server 2003.
Attribute Scoped Query	1.2.840.113556.1.4.1504	Used to force a query to be based on a specific DN-valued attribute. This control is new to Windows Server 2003. See Recipe 4.8 for an example.
Search Stats	1.2.840.113556.1.4.970	Used to return statistics about an LDAP query. See Recipe 15.9 for an example.
Incremental Multivalue Retrieval	1.2.840.113556.1.4.802	Retrieve a range of values for a multi-valued attribute instead of all values at once. This control is new to Windows Server 2003.

See Also

RFC 2251 (Lightweight Directory Access Protocol (v3)) for a description of LDAP controls, MSDN: Extended Controls, and MSDN: Using Controls

4.4   Using a Fast or Concurrent Bind

Problem

You want to perform an LDAP bind using a concurrent bind, also known as a fast bind. Concurrent binds are typically used in situations where you need to authenticate a lot of users, but those users do not need to directly access the directory or the directory access is done with another account.

Solution

 This works only on a Windows Server 2003 domain controller.

Using a graphical user interface

1. Open LDP.
2. From the menu, select Connection → Connect.
3. For Server, enter the name of a DC.
4. For Port, enter 389.
5. Click OK.
6. From the menu, select Options → Connection Options.
7. Under Option Name: select LDAP_OPT_FAST_CONCURRENT_BIND
8. Click the Set button
9. From the menu, select Connection → Bind.
10. Enter credentials of a user.
11. Click OK.

Discussion

Concurrent binding, unlike simple binding, does not generate a security token or determine a user's group memberships during the authentication process. It only determines if the authenticating user has a valid enabled account and password, which makes it much faster than a typical bind. Concurrent binding is implemented as a session option that is set after you establish a connection to a domain controller, but before any bind attempts are made. After the option has been set, any bind attempt made with the connection will be a concurrent bind.

There are a couple of caveats when using concurrent binds. First, you cannot enable signing or encryption, which means that all data for concurrent binds will be unencrypted over the network. Secondly, because the user's security token is not generated, access to the directory is done anonymously and access restrictions are based on the ANONYMOUS LOGON principal.

It is worth mentioning that there is another type of bind that is also known as a "fast bind," which has been available since Windows 2000, but it is completely different from the procedure I just described. This fast bind is implemented within ADSI, and simply means that when you fast bind to an object, the objectClass attribute for the object is not retrieved; therefore, the object-specific IADs class interfaces are not available. For example, if you bound to a user object using an ADSI fast bind, then only the basic IADs interfaces would be available, not the IADsUser interfaces. This is the complete list of interfaces that are available for objects retrieved with fast binds: IADs, IADsContainer, IDirectoryObject, IDirectorySearch, IADsPropertyList, IADsObjectOptions, ISupportErrorInfo, and IADsDeleteOps.

You must use IADsOpenDSObject::OpenDSObject interface to enable fast binds. If you call IADsContainer::GetObject on a child object of a parent you used a fast bind with, the same fast bind behavior applies. Unlike concurrent binds, ADSI fast binds do not impose any restrictions on the authenticating user. It means that the object-specific IADs interfaces will not be available. Also, no check is done to verify the object exists when you call OpenDSObject.

ADSI fast binds are useful when you need to make a lot of updates to objects you know exist (perhaps from an ADO query that returned a list of DNs) and you do not need any IADs-specific interfaces. Instead of two trips over the network per object binding, there would only be one. Here is example code that shows how to do an ADSI fast bind:

```
const ADS_FAST_BIND = 32
set objLDAP = GetObject("LDAP:")
set objUser = objLDAP.OpenDSObject("LDAP://<ObjectDN>", _
                                   "<UserUPN>", _
                                   "<UserPassword>", _
                                   ADS_FAST_BIND)
```

See Also

MSDN: Using Concurrent Binding and MSDN: ADS_AUTHENTICATION_ENUM

4.5   Searching for Objects in a Domain

Problem

You want to find objects that match certain criteria in a domain.

Solution

Using a graphical user interface

1. Open LDP.
2. From the menu, select Connection → Connect.
3. For Server, enter the name of a domain controller (or leave blank to do a serverless bind).
4. For Port, enter 389.
5. Click OK.
6. From the menu, select Connection → Bind.
7. Enter credentials of a user.
8. Click OK.
9. From the menu, select Browse → Search.
10. For BaseDN, type the base distinguished name where the search will start.
11. For Scope, select the appropriate scope.
12. For Filter, enter an LDAP filter.
13. Click Run.

Using a command-line interface

```
> dsquery * <BaseDN> -scope <Scope> -filter "<Filter>" -attr "<AttrList>"
```

Using VBScript

```
' This code searches for objects based on the specified criteria.
' ------ SCRIPT CONFIGURATION ------
strBase   = "<LDAP://<BaseDN>>;" ' BaseDN should be the search base
strFilter = "<Filter>;"          ' Valid LDAP search filter
strAttrs  = "<AttrList>;"        ' Comma-seperated list
strScope  = "<Scope>"            ' Should be on of Subtree, Onelevel, or Base
' ------ END CONFIGURATION ---------

set objConn = CreateObject("ADODB.Connection")
objConn.Provider = "ADsDSOObject"
objConn.Open "Active Directory Provider"
set objRS = objConn.Execute(strBase & strFilter & strAttrs & strScope)
objRS.MoveFirst
While Not objRS.EOF
    Wscript.Echo objRS.Fields(0).Value
    objRS.MoveNext
Wend
```

Discussion

Most tools that can be used to search Active Directory require a basic understanding of how to perform LDAP searches using a base DN, search scope, and search filter as described in RFC 2251 and 2254. The base DN is where the search begins in the directory tree. The search scope defines how far down in the tree to search from the base DN. The search filter is a prefix notation string that contains equality comparisons of attribute and value pairs.

The scope can be base, onelevel (or one), or subtree (or sub). A base scope will only match the base DN, onelevel will only match objects that are contained directly under the base DN, and subtree will match everything below the base DN (not including the base DN).

The search filter syntax is a powerful way to represent simple and complex queries. An example filter that matches all user objects would be (&(objectclass=user)(objectcategory=Person)). For more information on filters, see RFC 2254.

Using a graphical user interface

To customize the list of attributes returned for each matching object, look at the GUI discussion in Recipe 4.2.

Using a command-line interface

<AttrList> should be a space-separated list of attributes to return. If left blank, all attributes that have a value will be returned.

Using VBScript

The VBScript solution used ADO to perform the search. When using ADO, you must first create a connection object with the following three lines:

```
set objConn = CreateObject("ADODB.Connection")
objConn.Provider = "ADsDSOObject"
objConn.Open "Active Directory Provider"
```

At this point you can pass parameters to the Execute method, which will return a ResultSet object. You can iterate over the ResultSet by using the MoveFirst and MoveNext methods.

See Recipe 4.7 for more information on specifying advanced options in ADO like the page size.

See Also

Recipe 4.2 for viewing attributes of objects, Recipe 4.7 for setting advanced ADO options, RFC 2251 (Lightweight Directory Access Protocol (v3)), RFC 2254 (Lightweight Directory Access Protocol (v3)), MSDN: Searching with ActiveX Data Objects

(ADO), and for a good white paper on performing queries with LDAP see: *http://www.microsoft.com/windows2000/techinfo/howitworks/activedirectory/ldap.asp*

4.6   Searching the Global Catalog

Problem

You want to perform a forest-wide search using the global catalog.

Solution

Using a graphical user interface

1. Open LDP.
2. From the menu, select Connection → Connect.
3. For Server, enter the name of a global catalog server.
4. For Port, enter 3268.
5. Click OK.
6. From the menu, select Connection → Bind.
7. Enter credentials of a user.
8. Click OK.
9. From the menu, select Browse → Search.
10. For BaseDN, type the base distinguished name where to start the search.
11. For Scope, select the appropriate scope.
12. For Filter, enter an LDAP filter.
13. Click Run.

Using a command-line interface

```
> dsquery * <BaseDN> -gc -scope <Scope> -filter "<Filter>" -attr "<AttrList>"
```

Using VBScript

```
' This code searches the global catalog
' ------ SCRIPT CONFIGURATION ------
strBase   = "<GC://<BaseDN>>;"
strFilter = "<Filter>;"
strAttrs  = "<AttrList>;"
strScope  = "<Scope>"
' ------ END CONFIGURATION ---------

set objConn = CreateObject("ADODB.Connection")
objConn.Provider = "ADsDSOObject"
objConn.Open "Active Directory Provider"
```

```
set objRS = objConn.Execute(strBase & strFilter & strAttrs & strScope)
objRS.MoveFirst
while Not objRS.EOF
    Wscript.Echo objRS.Fields(0).Value
    objRS.MoveNext
wend
```

Discussion

The global catalog facilitates forest-wide searches. When you perform a normal LDAP search over port 389, you are searching against a particular partition in Active Directory, whether that is the Domain naming context, Configuration naming context, Schema naming context, or application partition. If you have multiple domains in your forest, this type of search will not search against all domains.

The global catalog contains all a subset of the attributes for all objects in the forest (excluding objects in application partitions). Think of it as a subset of all the naming contexts combined. All objects will be contained in the global catalog, except for objects in application partitions, but only some of the attributes will be available. For that reason, if you perform a global catalog search and do not get values for attributes you were expecting to, make sure those attributes are included in the global catalog, also known as the partial attribute set (PAS). See Recipe 10.14 for more information.

Using a graphical user interface

The only difference between this solution and Recipe 4.5 is that the "Port" has changed to 3268, which is the standard GC port.

Using a command-line interface

The only difference between this solution and Recipe 4.5 is the addition of the -gc flag.

Using VBScript

The only difference between this solution and Recipe 4.5 is that strBase variable changed to use the GC: progID:

```
strBase = "<GC://<BaseDN>>;"
```

See Also

Recipe 4.5 for searching for objects, and MSDN: Searching with ActiveX Data Objects (ADO)

4.7 Searching for a Large Number of Objects

Problem

Your search is returning only 1,000 objects and you want it to return all matching objects.

Solution

You might notice that searches with large numbers of matches stop displaying after 1000. Domain controllers return only a maximum of 1,000 entries from a search unless paging is enabled. This is done to prevent queries from consuming a lot of resources on domain controllers by retrieving the results all at once instead of in "pages" or batches. The following examples are variations of Recipe 4.5, which will show how to enable paging and return all matching entries.

Using a graphical user interface

1. Perform the same steps as in Recipe 4.5, but before clicking OK to start the search, click the Options button.
2. For Timeout (s), enter a value such as 10.
3. For Page size, enter the number of objects to be returned with each page—e.g., 1,000.
4. Under Search Call Type, select Paged.
5. Click OK.
6. A page of results (i.e., 1,000 entries) will be displayed each time you click on Run until all results have been returned.

Using a command-line interface

```
> dsquery * <BaseDN> -limit 0 -scope <Scope> -filter "<Filter>" -attr "<AttrList>"
```

Using VBScript

```
' This code enables paged searching
' ------ SCRIPT CONFIGURATION ------
strBase   = "<LDAP://<BaseDN>>;"
strFilter = "<Filter>;"
strAttrs  = "<AttrList>;"
strScope  = "<Scope>"
' ------ END CONFIGURATION ---------

set objConn = CreateObject("ADODB.Connection")
objConn.Provider = "ADsDSOObject"
objConn.Open "Active Directory Provider"
set objComm = CreateObject("ADODB.Command")
```

```
objComm.ActiveConnection = objConn
objComm.Properties("Page Size") = 1000
objComm.CommandText = strBase & strFilter & strAttrs & strScope
set objRS = objComm.Execute
objRS.MoveFirst
while Not objRS.EOF
    Wscript.Echo objRS.Fields(0).Value
    objRS.MoveNext
wend
```

Discussion

Paged searching support is implemented via an LDAP control. LDAP controls were defined in RFC 2251 and the Paged control in RFC 2696. Controls are extensions to LDAP that were not built into the protocol, so not all directory vendors support the same ones.

 In Active Directory, you can change the default maximum page size of 1,000 by modifying the LDAP query policy. See Recipe 4.23 for more information.

If you need searches to return hundreds of thousands of entries, Active Directory will return a maximum of only 262,144 entries even when paged searching is enabled. This value is defined in the LDAP query policy and can be modified like the maximum page size (see Recipe 4.23).

Using a graphical user interface

A word of caution when using LDP to display a large number of entries—by default, only 2,048 lines will be displayed in the right pane. To change that value, go to Options → General and change the Line Value under Buffer Size to a larger number.

Using a command-line interface

The only difference between this solution and Recipe 4.5 is the addition of the *-limit 0* flag. With -limit set to 0, paging will be enabled and all matching objects will be returned. If -limit is not specified, a maximum of 100 entries.

Using VBScript

To enable paged searching in ADO, you must instantiate an ADO Command object. A Command object allows for various properties of a query to be set, including size limit, time limit, and page size, to name a few. See MSDN for the complete list.

See Also

Recipe 4.5 for searching for objects, Recipe 4.23 for viewing the default LDAP policy, RFC 2251 (Lightweight Directory Access Protocol (v3)), RFC 2696 (LDAP Control Extension for Simple Paged Results Manipulation), and MSDN: Searching with ActiveX Data Objects (ADO)

4.8   Searching with an Attribute-Scoped Query

 This recipe requires the Windows Server 2003 forest functional level.

Problem

You want to retrieve attributes of objects that have been set in a multivalued-linked attribute, such as the member attribute on group objects. An attribute-scoped query can do this in a single query, instead of the previous method, which required multiple.

Solution

Using a graphical user interface

1. Follow the steps in Recipe 4.3 to enable an LDAP control.
2. Select the Attribute Scoped Query control (you can select controls by name with the Windows Server 2003 version of LDP). For the Windows 2000 version of LDP, add a control with an OID of 1.2.840.113556.1.4.1504.
3. For Value, enter the multivalued attribute name (e.g., member).
4. Click the Check in button.
5. Click OK.
6. From the menu, select Browse → Search.
7. For BaseDN, type the DN of the object that contains the multivalued DNs.
8. For Scope, select Base.
9. For Filter, enter an LDAP filter to match against the objects that are part of the multivalued DN attribute.
10. Click Run.

Using a command-line interface

At the time of publication of this book, no CLI tools supported attribute-scoped queries.

Using VBScript

At the time of publication of this book, you cannot use attribute-scoped queries with ADSI, ADO, and VBScript. In an ADO search, you can use the `ADSI Flags` property as part of a Connection object to set the search preference, but there is no way to set the attribute that should be matched, which must be included as part of the LDAP control.

Discussion

When dealing with group objects, you may have encountered the problem where you wanted to search against the members of a group to find a subset or to retrieve certain attributes about each member. This normally involved performing a query to retrieve all of the members, and additional queries to retrieve whatever attributes you needed for each member. This was less than ideal, so an alternative was developed for Windows Server 2003.

With an attribute-scoped query, you can perform a single query against the group object and return whatever properties you need from the member's object, or return only a subset of the members based on certain criteria. Let's look at the LDAP search parameters for an attribute-scoped query:

Attribute Scoped Query Control Value
> The value to set for this control should be the multivalued DN attribute that you want to iterate over (e.g., `member`).

Base DN
> This should be the DN of the object that contains the multivalued DN attribute (e.g., *cn=Domain Admins,cn=users,dc=rallencorp,dc=com*).

Scope
> This should be set to `Base`.

Filter
> The filter will match against objects defined in the Control Value. For example, a filter of `(&(objectclass=user)(objectcategory=Person))` would match any user objects defined in the multivalued DN. You can also use any other attributes that are available with those objects. The following filter would match all user objects that have a `department` attribute equal to "Sales": `(&(objectclass=user)(objectcategory=Person)(department=Sales))`

Attributes
> This should contain the list of attributes to return for object matched in the multivalued DN.

See Also

MSDN: Performing an Attribute Scoped Query and MSDN: Searching with ActiveX Data Objects (ADO)

4.9 Searching with a Bitwise Filter

Problem

You want to search against an attribute that contains a bit flag and you need to use a bitwise filter.

Solution

Using a graphical user interface

1. Follow the directions in Recipe 4.5 for searching for objects.
2. For the Filter, enter the bitwise expression, such as the following, which will find all universal groups:

    ```
    (&(objectclass=group)(objectCategory=group)(groupType:1.2.840.113556.1.4.804:=8))
    ```

3. Click Run.

Using a command-line interface

The following query finds universal groups using a bitwise OR filter:

```
> dsquery * cn=users,dc=rallencorp,dc=com -scope subtree -attr "name" -filter↵
"(&(objectclass=group)(objectCategory=group)(groupType:1.2.840.113556.1.4.804:=8) )"
```

The following query finds disabled user accounts using a bitwise AND filter:

```
> dsquery * cn=users,dc=rallencorp,dc=com -attr name -scope subtree -filter↵
"(&(objectclass=user)(objectcategory=person)(useraccountcontrol:1.2.840.113556.1.4.↵
803:=514))"
```

Using VBScript

```
' The following query finds all disabled user accounts
strBase   = "<LDAP://cn=users,dc=rallencorp,dc=com>;"
strFilter = "(&(objectclass=user)(objectcategory=person)" & _
            "(useraccountcontrol:1.2.840.113556.1.4.803:=514));"
strAttrs  = "name;"
strScope  = "subtree"

set objConn = CreateObject("ADODB.Connection")
objConn.Provider = "ADsDSOObject"
objConn.Open "Active Directory Provider"
set objRS = objConn.Execute(strBase & strFilter & strAttrs & strScope)
objRS.MoveFirst
while Not objRS.EOF
```

```
        Wscript.Echo objRS.Fields(0).Value
        objRS.MoveNext
    wend
```

Discussion

Many attributes in Active Directory are composed of bit flags. A bit flag is often used to encode properties about an object into a single attribute. For example, the groupType attribute on group objects is a bit flag that is used to determine the group scope and type.

The userAccountControl attribute on user and computer objects is used to describe a whole series of properties, including account status (i.e., enabled or disabled), account lockout, password not required, smartcard authentication required, etc.

The searchFlags and systemFlags attributes on attributeSchema objects define, among other things, whether an attribute is constructed, indexed, and included as part of Ambiguous Name Resolution (ANR).

To search against these types of attributes, you need to use bitwise search filters. There are two types of bitwise search filters you can use, one that represents a logical OR and one that represents logical AND. This is implemented within a search filter as a *matching rule*. A matching rule is simply a way to inform the LDAP server (in this case, a domain controller) to treat part of the filter differently. Here is an example of what a matching rule looks like:

    (userAccountControl:1.2.840.113556.1.4.803:=514)

The format is (*attributename:MatchingRuleOID:=value*). As I mentioned, there are two bitwise matching rules, which are defined by OIDs. The logical AND matching rule OID is 1.2.840.113556.1.4.803 and the logical OR matching rule OID is 1.2. 840.113556.1.4.804. These OIDs instruct the server to perform special processing on the filter. A logical OR filter will return success if any bit specified by *value*, is stored in *attributename*. Alternatively, the logical AND filter will return success if all bits specified by *value*, match the value of *attributename*. Perhaps an example will help clarify this.

To create a normal user account, you have to set userAccountControl to 514. The number 514 was calculated by adding the normal user account flag of 512 together with the disabled account flag of 2 (512 + 2 = 514). If you use the following logical OR matching rule against the 514 value, as shown here:

    (useraccountcontrol:1.2.840.113556.1.4.804:=514)

then all normal user accounts (flag 512) OR disabled accounts (flag 2) would be returned. This would include enabled user accounts (from flag 512), disabled computer accounts (from flag 2), and disabled user accounts (from flag 2). In the case of userAccountControl, flag 2 can apply to both user and computer accounts and, hence, why both would be included in the returned entries.

One way to see the benefits of bitwise matching rules is that they allow you to combine a bunch of comparisons into a single filter. In fact, it may help to think that the previous OR filter I just showed could also be written using two expressions:

```
(|(useraccountcontrol:1.2.840.113556.1.4.804:=2) (useraccountcontrol:1.2.840.113556.
1.4.804:=512))
```

Just as before, this will match userAccountControl attributes that contain either the 2 or 512 flags.

For logical AND, similar principles apply. Instead of any of the bits in the flag being a possible match, ALL of the bits in the flag must match for it to return a success. If we changed our userAccountControl example to use logical AND, it would look like this:

```
(useraccountcontrol:1.2.840.113556.1.4.803:=514)
```

In this case, only normal user accounts that are also disabled would be returned. The same filter could be rewritten using the & operator instead of | as in the following:

```
(&(useraccountcontrol:1.2.840.113556.1.4.803:=2)
  (useraccountcontrol:1.2.840.113556.1.4.803:=512))
```

An important subtlety to note is that when you are comparing only a single bit-flag value, the logical OR and logical AND matching rule would return the same result. So if we wanted to find any normal user accounts we could search on the single bit flag of 512 using either of the following:

```
(useraccountcontrol:1.2.840.113556.1.4.803:=512)
```

```
(useraccountcontrol:1.2.840.113556.1.4.804:=512)
```

See Also

MSDN: Enumerating Groups by Scope or Type in a Domain, MSDN: Determining Which Properties Are Non-Replicated, Constructed, Global Catalog, and Indexed, and MS KB 305144 (How to Use the UserAccountControl Flags to Manipulate User Account Properties)

4.10 Creating an Object

Problem

You want to create an object.

Solution

In each solution below, an example of adding a user object is shown. Modify the examples as needed to include whatever class and attributes you need to create.

Using a graphical user interface

1. Open ADSI Edit.
2. If an entry for the naming context you want to browse is not already displayed, do the following:
3. Right-click on ADSI Edit in the right pane and click Connect to…
4. Fill in the information for the naming context, container, or OU you want to add an object to. Click on the Advanced button if you need to enter alternate credentials.
5. In the left pane, browse to the container or OU you want to add the object to. Once you've found the parent container, right-click on it and select New → Object.
6. Under Select a Class, select user.
7. For the cn, enter jsmith and click Next.
8. For sAMAccountName, enter jsmith and click Next.
9. Click the More Attributes button to enter additional attributes.
10. Click Finish.

Using a command-line interface

Create an LDIF file called *create_object.ldf* with the following contents:

```
dn: cn=jsmith,cn=users,dc=rallencorp,dc=com
changetype: add
objectClass: user
samaccountname: jsmith
```

then run the following command:

```
> ldifde -v -i -f create_object.ldf
```

It is also worth noting that you can add a limited number of object types with the dsadd command. Run dsadd /? from a command line for more details.

Using VBScript

```
set objUsersCont = GetObject(LDAP://cn=users,dc=rallencorp,dc=com")
set objUser = objUsersCont.Create("user", "CN=jsmith")
objUser.Put "sAMAccountName", "jsmith" ' mandatory attribute
objUser.SetInfo
```

Discussion

To create an object in Active Directory, you have to specify the objectClass, relative distinguished name (RDN) value, and any other mandatory attributes that are not automatically set by Active Directory. Some of the automatically generated attributes include objectGUID, instanceType, and objectCategory.

In the jsmith example, the objectclass was user, the RDN value was jsmith, and the only other mandatory attribute that had to be set was sAMAccountName. Admittedly, this user object is unusable in its current state because it will be disabled by default and no password was set, but it should give you an idea of how to create an object.

Using a graphical user interface

Other tools, such as AD Users and Computers, could be used to do the same thing, but ADSI Edit is useful as a generic object editor.

One attribute that you will not be able to set via ADSI Edit is the password (unicodePwd attribute). It is stored in binary form and cannot be edited directly. If you want to set the password for a user through a GUI, you can do it with the AD Users and Computers snap-in.

Using a command-line interface

For more on ldifde, see Recipe 4.25.

With dsadd, you can set numerous attributes when creating an object. The downside is that as of the publication of this book, you can create only these object types: computer, contact, group, ou, quota, and user.

Using VBScript

The first step to create an object is to call GetObject on the parent container. Then call the Create method on that object and specify the objectClass and RDN for the new object. The sAMAccountName attribute is then set by using the Put method. Finally, SetInfo commits the change. If SetInfo is not called, the creation will not get committed to the domain controller.

See Also

Recipe 4.25 for importing objects using LDIF, MSDN: IADsContainer::GetObject, MSDN: IADsContainer::Create, MSDN: IADs::Put, and MSDN: IADs::SetInfo

4.11   Modifying an Object

Problem

You want to modify one or more attributes of an object.

Solution

The following examples set the last name (sn) attribute for the jsmith user object.

Using a graphical user interface

1. Open ADSI Edit.

2. If an entry for the naming context you want to browse is not already displayed, do the following:

   a. Right-click on ADSI Edit in the right pane and click Connect to…

   b. Fill in the information for the naming context, container, or OU you want to add an object to. Click on the Advanced button if you need to enter alternate credentials.

3. In the left pane, browse to the container or OU that contains the object you want to modify. Once you've found the object, right-click on it and select Properties.

4. Edit the sn attribute.

5. Enter Smith and click OK.

6. Click Apply.

Using a command-line interface

Create an LDIF file called *modify_object.ldf* with the following contents:

```
dn: cn=jsmith,cn=users,dc=rallencorp,dc=com
changetype: modify
add: givenName
givenName: Jim
-
```

then run the following command:

```
> ldifde -v -i -f modify_object.ldf
```

You can modify a limited number of object types with the dsmod command. Run dsmod /? from a command line for more details.

Using VBScript

```
strObjectDN = "cn=jsmith,cn=users,dc=rallencorp,dc=com"
set objUser = GetObject("LDAP://" & strObjectDN)
objUser.Put "sn", "Smith"
objUser.SetInfo
```

Discussion

Using a graphical user interface

If the parent container of the object you want to modify has a lot of objects in it, you may want to add a new connection entry for the DN of the target object. This will be easier than trying to hunt through a container full of objects. You can do this by right-clicking ADSI Edit and selecting Connect to. Under Connection Point, select Distinguished Name and enter the DN of the object.

Using a command-line interface

For more on `ldifde`, see Recipe 4.25.

As of the publication of this book, the only types of objects you can modify with dsmod are computer, contact, group, ou, server, quota and user.

Using VBScript

If you need to do anything more than simple assignment or replacement of a value for an attribute, you'll need to use the `PutEx` method instead of `Put`. `PutEx` allows for greater control of assigning multiple values, deleting specific values, and appending values.

`PutEx` requires three parameters: update flag, attribute name, and an array of values to set or unset. The update flags are defined by the `ADS_PROPERTY_OPERATION_ENUM` collection and listed in Table 4-3. Finally, `SetInfo` commits the change. If `SetInfo` is not called, the creation will not get committed to the domain controller.

Table 4-3. ADS_PROPERTY_OPERATION_ENUM

Name	Value	Description
ADS_PROPERTY_CLEAR	1	Remove all value(s) of the attribute.
ADS_PROPERTY_UPDATE	2	Replace the current values of the attribute with the ones passed in. This will clear any previously set values.
ADS_PROPERTY_APPEND	3	Add the values passed into the set of existing values of the attribute.
ADS_PROPERTY_DELETE	4	Delete the values passed in.

In the following example, each update flag is used while setting the otherTelephoneNumber attribute:

```
strObjectDN = "cn=jsmith,cn=users,dc=rallencorp,dc=com"

const ADS_PROPERTY_CLEAR  = 1
const ADS_PROPERTY_UPDATE = 2
const ADS_PROPERTY_APPEND = 3
const ADS_PROPERTY_DELETE = 4

set objUser = GetObject("LDAP://" & strObjectDN)

' Add/Append two values
objUser.PutEx ADS_PROPERTY_APPEND, "otherTelephoneNumber", _
              Array("555-1212", "555-1213")
objUser.SetInfo
' Now otherTelephoneNumber = 555-1212, 555-1213

' Delete one of the values
objUser.PutEx ADS_PROPERTY_DELETE, "otherTelephoneNumber", Array("555-1213")
```

```
objUser.SetInfo
' Now otherTelephoneNumber = 555-1212

' Change values
objUser.PutEx ADS_PROPERTY_UPDATE, "otherTelephoneNumber", Array("555-1214")
objUser.SetInfo
' Now otherTelephoneNumber = 555-1214

' Clear all values
objUser.PutEx ADS_PROPERTY_CLEAR, "otherTelephoneNumber",  vbNullString
objUser.SetInfo
' Now otherTelephoneNumber = <empty>
```

See Also

MSDN: IADs::Put, MSDN: IADs::PutEx, MSDN: IADs::SetInfo, and MSDN: ADS_PROPERTY_OPERATION_ENUM

4.12   Modifying a Bit-Flag Attribute

Problem

You want to modify an attribute that contains a bit flag.

Solution

Using VBScript

```
' This code safely modifies a bit-flag attribute
' ------ SCRIPT CONFIGURATION ------
strObject = "<ObjectDN>"         ' e.g. cn=jsmith,cn=users,dc=rallencorp,dc=com
strAttr = "<AttrName>"           ' e.g. rallencorp-UserProperties
boolEnableBit = <TRUEorFALSE>    ' e.g. FALSE
intBit = <BitValue>              ' e.g. 16
' ------ END CONFIGURATION ---------

set objObject = GetObject("LDAP://" & strObject)
intBitsOrig = objObject.Get(strAttr)
intBitsCalc = CalcBit(intBitsOrig, intBit, boolEnableBit)

if intBitsOrig <> intBitsCalc then
   objObject.Put strAttr, intBitsCalc
   objObject.SetInfo
   WScript.Echo "Changed " & strAttr & " from " & intBitsOrig & " to " & intBitsCalc
else
   WScript.Echo "Did not need to change " & strAttr & " (" & intBitsOrig & ")"
end if


Function CalcBit(intValue, intBit, boolEnable)
```

```
        CalcBit = intValue

        if boolEnable = TRUE then
            CalcBit = intValue Or intBit
        else
            if intValue And intBit then
                CalcBit = intValue Xor intBit
            end if
        end if

    End Function
```

Discussion

In Recipe 4.9, I described how to search against attributes that contain a bit flag, which are used to encode various settings about an object in a single attribute. As a quick recap, you need to use a logical OR operation to match any bits being searched against, and logical AND to match a specific set of bits. If you want to set an attribute that is a bit flag, you need to take special precautions to ensure you don't overwrite an existing bit. Let's consider an example. RAllenCorp wants to secretly store some non-politically correct information about its users, including things like whether the user is really old or has big feet. They don't want to create attributes such as `rallencorp-UserHasBigFeet` so they decide to encode the properties in a single bit flag attribute. They decide to call the attribute `rallencorp-UserProperties` with the following possible bit values:

1   User is overweight

2   User is very tall

4   User has big feet

8   User is very old

After they extend the schema to include the new attribute, they need to initially populate the attribute for all their users. To do so they can simply logically OR the values together that apply to each user. So if settings 4 and 8 apply to the jsmith user, his `rallencorp-UserProperties` would be set to 12 (4 OR 8). No big deal so far. The issue comes in when they need to modify the attribute in the future.

They later find out that the jsmith user was a former basketball player and is 6'8". They need to set the 2 bit (for being tall) in his `rallencorp-UserProperties` attribute. To set the 2 bit they need to first determine if it has already been set. If it has already been set, then there is nothing to do. If the 2 bit hasn't been set, they need to logical OR 2 with the existing value of jsmith's `rallencorp-UserProperties` attribute. If they simply set the attribute to 2, it would overwrite the 4 and 8 bits that had been set previously. In the VBScript solution, they could use the `CalcBit` function to determine the new value:

```
    intBitsCalc = CalcBit(intBitsOrig, 2, TRUE)
```

The result would be 14 (12 OR 2).

The same logic applies if they want to remove a bit, except the XOR logical operator is used.

 Active Directory contains numerous bit-flag attributes, most notably options (which is used on several different object classes) and userAccountControl (which is used on user objects). I do not recommended blindly setting those attributes unless you know what you are doing. It is preferable to use a script from this recipe so that it calculates the new value based on the existing value.

See Also

Recipe 4.9 for searching with a bit-wise filter

4.13   Dynamically Linking an Auxiliary Class

 This recipe requires the Windows Server 2003 forest functional level.

Problem

You want to dynamically link an auxiliary class to an existing object instance.

Solution

In each solution below, an example of adding the custom rallencorp-SalesUser auxiliary class to the jsmith user object will be described.

Using a graphical user interface

1. Follow the directions for Recipe 4.11.
2. Edit the values for the objectClass attribute.
3. For "Value to add," enter rallencorp-SalesUser.
4. Click Add.
5. Click OK twice.

Using a command-line interface

Create an LDIF file called *dynamically_link_class.ldf* with the following contents:

```
dn: cn=jsmith,cn=users,dc=rallencorp,dc=com
changetype: modify
```

```
add: objectClass
objectClass: rallencorp-SalesUser
-
```

then run the following command:

```
> ldifde -v -i -f dynamically_link_class.ldf
```

Using VBScript

```
const ADS_PROPERTY_APPEND = 3
set objUser = GetObject("LDAP://cn=jsmith,cn=users,dc=rallencorp,dc=com")
objUser.PutEx ADS_PROPERTY_APPEND,"objectClass",Array("rallencorp-SalesUser")
objUser.SetInfo
```

Discussion

Dynamically linking an auxiliary class to an object is an easy way to use new attributes without modifying the object class definition in the schema directly. In Windows 2000, auxiliary classes could only be statically linked in the schema. With Windows Server 2003, you can dynamically link them by appending the auxiliary class name to the objectClass attribute of an object.

A situation in which it makes more sense to dynamically link auxiliary classes rather than link them statically is when several organizations or divisions within a company maintain their own user objects and want to add new attributes to the user class. Under Windows 2000, each organization would need to create their new attributes and auxiliary class in the schema, and then modify the user class to include the new auxiliary class. If you have 10 organizations that want to do the same thing, user objects in the forest could end up with a lot of attributes that would go unused. In Windows Server 2003, each division can instead create the new attributes and auxiliary class, and then dynamically link the auxiliary class with the specific objects that they want to have the new attributes. This eliminates the step of modifying the user class in the schema to contain the new auxiliary classes.

It is also worth mentioning that extensive use of dynamically linked auxiliary classes can lead to problems. If several groups are using different auxiliary classes, it might become hard to determine what attributes you can expect on your user objects. Essentially, you could end up with many variations of a user class that each group has implemented through the use of dynamic auxiliary classes. For this reason, use of dynamic auxiliary classes should be closely monitored.

See Also

Recipe 4.11 for modifying an object

4.14   Creating a Dynamic Object

 This recipe requires the Windows Server 2003 forest functional level.

Problem

You want to create an object that is automatically deleted after a period of time unless it is refreshed.

Solution

Using a graphical user interface

At the time of publication of this book, neither ADSI Edit nor LDP supported creating dynamic objects.

Using a command-line interface

Create an LDIF file called *create_dynamic_object.ldf* with the following contents:

```
dn: cn=jsmith,cn=users,dc=rallencorp,dc=com
changetype: add
objectClass: user
objectClass: dynamicObject
entryTTL: 1800
sAMAccountName: jsmith
```

then run the following command:

```
> ldifde -v -i -f create_dynamic_object.ldf
```

Using VBScript

```
' This code creates a dynamic user object with a TTL of 30 minutes (1800 secs)
set objUsersCont = GetObject("LDAP://cn=users,dc=rallencorp,dc=com")
set objUser = objUsersCont.Create("user", "CN=jsmith")
objUser.Put "objectClass", "dynamicObject"
objUser.Put "entryTTL", 1800
objUser.Put "sAMAccountName", "jsmith" ' mandatory attribute
objUser.SetInfo
```

Discussion

The ability to create dynamic objects is a new feature in Windows Server 2003. To create a dynamic object, you simply need to specify the objectClass to have a value of dynamicObject in addition to its structural objectClass (e.g., user) value when instantiating the object. The entryTTL attribute can also be set to the number of seconds before the object is automatically deleted. If entryTTL is not set, the object will use the dynamicObjectDefaultTTL attribute specified in the domain. The entryTTL cannot be lower than the dynamicObjectMinTTL for the domain. See Recipe 4.16 for more information on how to view and modify these default values.

Dynamic objects have a few special properties worth noting:

- A static object cannot be turned into a dynamic object. The object must be marked as dynamic when it is created.
- Dynamic objects cannot be created in the Configuration NC and Schema NC.
- Dynamic objects do not leave behind tombstone objects.
- Dynamic objects that are containers cannot have static child objects.

See Also

Recipe 4.15 for refreshing a dynamic object, and Recipe 4.16 for modifying the default dynamic object properties

4.15   Refreshing a Dynamic Object

 This recipe requires the Windows Server 2003 forest functional level.

Problem

You want to refresh a dynamic object to keep it from expiring and getting deleted from Active Directory.

Solution

In each solution below, an example of adding a user object is used. Modify the examples as needed to refresh whatever object is needed.

Using a graphical user interface

1. Open LDP.
2. From the menu, select Connection → Connect.
3. For Server, enter the name of a domain controller (or leave it blank to do a serverless bind).
4. For Port, enter 389.
5. Click OK.

6. From the menu, select Connection → Bind.

7. Enter credentials of a user that can modify the object.

8. Click OK.

9. Select Browse → Modify.

10. For Dn, enter the DN of the dynamic object you want to refresh.

11. For Attribute, enter entryTTL.

12. For Values, enter the new time to live (TTL) for the object in seconds.

13. Under Operation, select Replace.

14. Click Enter.

15. Click Run.

Using a command-line interface

Create an LDIF file called *refresh_dynamic_object.ldf* with the following contents:

```
dn: cn=jsmith,cn=users,dc=rallencorp,dc=com
changetype: modify
replace: entryTTL
entryTTL: 1800
-
```

then run the following command:

```
> ldifde -v -i -f refresh_dynamic_object.ldf
```

Using VBScript

```
set objUser = GetObject("LDAP://cn=jsmith,cn=users,dc=rallencorp,dc=com")
objUser.Put "entryTTL", "1800"
objUser.SetInfo
```

Discussion

Dynamic objects expire after their TTL becomes 0. You can determine when a dynamic object will expire by looking at the current value of an object's entryTTL, which contains the seconds remaining until expiration. If you've created a dynamic object and need to refresh it so that it will not get deleted, you must reset the entryTTL attribute to a new value. There is no limit to the number of times you can refresh a dynamic object. As long as the entryTTL value does not reach 0, the object will remain in Active Directory.

See Also

Recipe 4.11 for modifying an object, and Recipe 4.14 for creating a dynamic object

4.16 Modifying the Default TTL Settings for Dynamic Objects

 This recipe requires the Windows Server 2003 forest functional level.

Problem

You want to modify the minimum and default TTLs for dynamic objects.

Solution

In each solution below, I'll show how to set the DynamicObjectDefaultTTL setting to 172800. Modifying the DynamicObjectMinTTL can be done in the same manner.

Using a graphical user interface

1. Open ADSI Edit.
2. If an entry for the Configuration naming context is not already displayed, do the following:
    a. Right-click on ADSI Edit in the right pane and click Connect to...
    b. Fill in the information for the naming context for your forest. Click on the Advanced button if you need to enter alternate credentials.
3. In the left pane, browse to the following path under the Configuration naming context: Services → Windows NT → Directory Service.
4. Right-click cn=Directory Service and select Properties.
5. Edit the msDS-Other-Settings attribute.
6. Click on DynamicObjectDefaultTTL=<*xxxxx*> and click Remove.
7. The attribute/value pair should have been populated in the "Value to add" field.
8. Edit the number part of the value to be 172800.
9. Click Add.
10. Click OK twice.

Using a command-line interface

The following ntdsutil command connects to <*DomainControllerName*>, displays the current values for the dynamic object TTL settings, sets the DynamicObjectDefaultTTL to 172800, commits the change, and displays the results:

```
> ntdsutil "config settings" connections "connect to server <DomainControllerName>"↵
q "show values" "set DynamicObjectDefaultTTL to 172800" "commit changes" "show↵
values" q q
```

Using VBScript

```
' This code modifies the default TTL setting for dynamic objects in a forest
' ------ SCRIPT CONFIGURATION ------
strNewValue   = 172800

'Could be DynamicObjectMinTTL instead if you wanted to set that instead
strTTLSetting = "DynamicObjectDefaultTTL"
' ------ END CONFIGURATION ---------

const ADS_PROPERTY_APPEND = 3
const ADS_PROPERTY_DELETE = 4

set objRootDSE = GetObject("LDAP://RootDSE")
set objDS = GetObject("LDAP://CN=Directory Service,CN=Windows NT," & _
                      "CN=Services,CN=Configuration," & _
                      objRootDSE.Get("rootDomainNamingContext")
for each strVal in objDS.Get("msDS-Other-Settings")
    Set objRegEx = New RegExp
    objRegEx.Pattern = strTTLSetting & "="
    objRegEx.IgnoreCase = True
    Set colMatches = objRegEx.Execute(strVal)
    For Each objMatch in colMatches
        Wscript.Echo "Deleting " & strVal
        objDS.PutEx ADS_PROPERTY_DELETE, "msDS-Other-Settings", Array(strVal)
        objDS.SetInfo
    Next
Next

Wscript.Echo "Setting " & strTTLSetting & "=" & strNewValue
objDS.PutEx ADS_PROPERTY_APPEND, _
            "msDS-Other-Settings", _
            Array(strTTLSetting & "=" & strNewValue)
objDS.SetInfo
```

Discussion

Two configuration settings apply to dynamic objects:

dynamicObjectDefaultTTL

> Defines the default TTL that is set for a dynamic object at creation time unless another one is set via entryTTL.

dynamicObjectMinTTL

> Defines the smallest TTL that can be configured for a dynamic object.

Unfortunately, these two settings are not stored as discrete attributes. Instead, they are stored as attribute-value-assertions (AVA) in the msDS-Other-Settings attribute on the *cn=Directory Services,cn=Windows NT,cn=Configuration,<ForestRootDN>* object. AVAs are used occasionally in Active Directory on multivalued attributes, in which the values take the form of *Setting1=Value1*, *Setting2=Value2*, etc.

For this reason, you cannot simply manipulate AVA attributes as you would another attribute. You have to be sure to add or replace values with the same format, as they existed previously.

Using a command-line interface

You can use ntdsutil in interactive mode or in single-command mode. In this solution, I've included all the necessary commands on a single line. You can, of course, step through each command by simply running ntdsutil in interactive mode and entering each command one by one.

Using VBScript

Because we are dealing with AVAs, the VBScript solution is not very straightforward. Getting a pointer to the Directory Service object is easy, but then we must step through each value of the mSDS-Other-Settings attribute until we find the one we are looking for. The reason it is not straightforward is that we do not know the exact value of the setting we are looking for. All we know is that it begins with DynamicObjectDefaultTTL=. That is why it is necessary to resort to regular expressions. With a regular expression, we can compare each value against DefaultObjectDefaultTTL= and if we find a match, delete that value only. After we've iterated through all of the values and hopefully deleted the one we are looking for, we append the new setting using PutEx. Simple as that!

See Also

Recipe 4.11 for modifying an object and MSDN: Regular Expression (RegExp) Object

4.17 Moving an Object to a Different OU or Container

Problem

You want to move an object to a different container or OU.

Solution

Using a graphical user interface

1. Open ADSI Edit.
2. If an entry for the naming context you want to browse is not already displayed, do the following:

---

a. Right-click on ADSI Edit in the right pane and click Connect to.

b. Fill in the information for the naming context, container, or OU containing the object. Click on the Advanced button if you need to enter alternate credentials.

3. In the left pane, browse to the container, or OU that contains the object you want to modify. Once you've found the object, right-click on it and select Move.

4. Browse to the new parent of the object, select it, and click OK.

Using a command-line interface

```
> dsmove "<ObjectDN>" -newparent "<NewParentDN>"
```

Using VBScript

```
' This code moves an object from one location to another in the same domain.
' ------ SCRIPT CONFIGURATION ------
strNewParentDN = "LDAP://<NewParentDN>"
strObjectDN    = "LDAP://cn=jsmith,<OldParentDN>"
strObjectRDN   = "cn=jsmith"
' ------ END CONFIGURATION ---------

set objCont = GetObject(strNewParentDN)
objCont.MoveHere strObjectDN, strObjectRDN
```

Discussion

Using a graphical user interface

If the parent container of the object you want to move has a lot of objects in it, you may want to add a new connection entry for the DN of the object you want to move. This may save you time searching through the list of objects in the container. You can do this by right clicking ADSI Edit and selecting Connect to. Under Connection Point, select Distinguished Name and enter the DN of the object you want to move.

Using a command-line interface

The dsmove utility can work against any type of object (no limitations as with dsadd and dsmod). The first parameter is the DN of the object to be moved. The second parameter is the new parent container of the object. The -s parameter can additionally be used to specify a specific server to work against.

Using VBScript

The MoveHere method can be tricky, so an explanation of how to use it to move objects is in order. First, you need to call GetObject on the new parent container. Then call MoveHere on the parent container object with the ADsPath of the object to move as the first parameter and the RDN of the object to move as the second.

The reason for the apparent duplication of cn=jsmith in the MoveHere method is that the same method can also be used for renaming objects within the same container (see Recipe 4.19).

See Also

MS KB 313066 (HOW TO: Move Users, Groups, and Organizational Units Within a Domain in Windows 2000), and MSDN: IADsContainer::MoveHere

4.18   Moving an Object to a Different Domain

Problem

You want to move an object to a different domain.

Solution

Using a command-line interface

```
> movetree /start /s SourceDC /d TargetDC /sdn SourceDN /ddn TargetDN
```

In the following example, the cn=jsmith object in the *amer.rallencorp.com* domain will be moved to the *emea.rallencorp.com* domain.

```
> movetree /start /s dc-amer1 /d dc-emea1↵
   /ddn cn=jsmith,cn=users,dc=amer,dc=rallencorp,dc=com↵
   /sdn cn=jsmith,cn=users,dc=emea,dc=rallencorp,dc=com↵
```

Using VBScript

```
set objObject = GetObject("LDAP://TargetDC/TargetParentDN")
objObject.MoveHere "LDAP://SourceDC/SourceDN", vbNullString
```

In the following example, the cn=jsmith object in the *amer.rallencorp.com* domain will be moved to the *emea.rallencorp.com* domain.

```
set objObject = GetObject( _
   "LDAP://dc-amer1/cn=users,dc=amer,dc=rallencorp,dc=com")
objObject.MoveHere _
   "LDAP://dc-emea1/cn=jsmith,cn=users,dc=emea,dc=rallencorp,dc=com", _
   vbNullString
```

Discussion

You can move objects between domains assuming you follow a few guidelines:

- The user requesting the move must have permission to modify objects in the parent container of both domains.

- You need to explicitly specify the target DC (serverless binds usually do not work). This is necessary because the "Cross Domain Move" LDAP control is being used behind the scenes. For more information on controls, see Recipe 4.3.

- The move operation must be performed against the RID master for both domains.

- Both domains must be in native mode.

- When you move a user object to a different domain, its objectSID is replaced with a new SID (based on the new domain), and the old SID is added to the sIDHistory attribute.

- For group objects, you can only move universal groups. To move global or domain local groups, you must first convert them to universal.

See Also

Recipe 4.3 for more on LDAP controls, MS KB 238394 (How to Use the MoveTree Utility to Move Objects Between Domains in a Single Forest), and MSDN: IADsContainer::MoveHere

4.19   Renaming an Object

Problem

You want to rename an object and keep it in its current container or OU.

Solution

Using a graphical user interface

1. Open ADSI Edit

2. If an entry for the naming context you want to browse is not already displayed, do the following:

   a. Right-click on ADSI Edit in the right pane and click Connect to…

   b. Fill in the information for the naming context, container, or OU that contains the object you want to rename. Click on the Advanced button if you need to enter alternate credentials.

3. In the left pane, browse to the container or OU that contains the object you want to modify. Once you've found the object, right-click on it and select Rename.

4. Enter the new name and click OK.

Using a command-line interface

```
> dsmove "<ObjectDN>" -newname "<NewName>"
```

Using VBScript

```
' This code renames an object and leaves it in the same location.
' ------ SCRIPT CONFIGURATION ------
strCurrentParentDN = "<CurrentParentDN>"
strObjectOldName   = "cn=<OldName>"
strObjectNewName   = "cn=<NewName>"
' ------ END CONFIGURATION ---------

set objCont = GetObject("LDAP://" & strCurrentParentDN)
objCont.MoveHere "LDAP://" & strObjectOldName & "," & _
                 strCurrentParentDN, strObjectNewName
```

Discussion

Before you rename an object, ensure no applications reference it by name. You can make objects rename-safe by requiring all applications that must store a reference to objects to use the GUID of the object, not the name. The GUID (stored in the objectGUID attribute) is guaranteed to be unique and does not change when an object is renamed.

Using a graphical user interface

If the parent container of the object you want to rename has a lot of objects in it, you may want to add a new connection entry for the DN of the object you want to rename. This may save you time searching through the list of objects in the container. You can do this by right-clicking ADSI Edit and selecting Connect to. Under Connection Point, select Distinguished Name and enter the DN of the object you want to rename.

Using a command-line interface

The two parameters that are needed to rename an object are the original DN of the object and the new RDN (-newname). The -s option can also be used to specify a server name to work against.

Using VBScript

The MoveHere method can be tricky to use, so an explanation of how to use it to rename objects is in order. First, you need to call GetObject on the parent container of the object you want to rename. Then call MoveHere on the parent container object and specify the ADsPath of the object to rename as the first parameter. The new RDN including prefix (e.g., cn=) of the object should be the second parameter.

See Also

MSDN: IADsContainer::MoveHere

4.20 Deleting an Object

Problem

You want to delete an object.

Solution

Using a graphical user interface

1. Open ADSI Edit.
2. If an entry for the naming context you want to browse is not already displayed, do the following:
    a. Right-click on ADSI Edit in the right pane and click Connect to…
    b. Fill in the information for the naming context, container, or OU that contains the object you want to delete. Click on the Advanced button if you need to enter alternate credentials.
3. In the left pane, browse to the object you want to delete.
4. Right-click on the object and select Delete.
5. Click Yes to confirm.

Using a command-line interface

```
> dsrm "<ObjectDN>"
```

Using VBScript

```
strObjectDN = "<ObjectDN>"
set objUser = GetObject("LDAP://" & strObjectDN)
objUser.DeleteObject(0)
```

Discussion

This recipe covers deleting individual objects. If you want to delete a container or OU and all the objects in it, take a look at Recipe 4.21.

Using a graphical user interface

If the parent container of the object you want to delete has a lot of objects in it, you may want to add a new connection entry for the DN of the object you want to delete. This may save you time searching through the list of objects in the container and could help avoid accidental deletions. You can do this by right-clicking ADSI Edit and selecting Connect to. Under Connection Point, select Distinguished Name and enter the DN of the object you want to delete.

Using a command-line interface

The `dsrm` utility can be used to delete any type of object (no limitations based on object type as with `dsadd` and `dsmod`). The only required parameter is the DN of the object to delete. You can also specify -noprompt to keep it from asking for confirmation before deleting. The `-s` parameter can be used as well to specify a specific server to target.

Using VBScript

Using the `DeleteObject` method is straightforward. Passing 0 as a parameter is required, but does not have any significance at present.

An alternate and perhaps safer way to delete objects is to use the `IADsContainer::Delete` method. To use this method, you must first bind to the parent container of the object. You can then call `Delete` by passing the object class and RDN of the object you want to delete. Here is an example for deleting a user object:

```
set objCont = GetObject("LDAP://ou=Sales,dc=rallencorp,dc=com")
objCont.Delete "user", "cn=rallen"
```

`Delete` is safer than `DeleteObject` because you have to be more explicit about what you are deleting. With `DeleteObject` you only need to specify a distinguished name and it will delete it. If you happen to mis-type the DN or the user input to a web page that uses this method is mis-typed, the result could be disastrous.

See Also

Recipe 4.21 for deleting a container, MS KB 258310 (Viewing Deleted Objects in Active Directory), MSDN: IADsContainer::Delete, and MSDN: IADsDeleteOps:: DeleteObject

4.21   Deleting a Container That Has Child Objects

Problem

You want to delete a container or organizational unit and all child objects contained within.

Solution

Using a graphical user interface

Open ADSI Edit and follow the same steps as in Recipe 4.20. The only difference is that you'll be prompted to confirm twice instead of once before the deletion occurs.

Using a command-line interface

```
> dsrm "<ObjectDN>" -subtree
```

Using VBScript

The same code from Recipe 4.20 will also delete containers and objects contained within them.

Discussion

As you can see from the solutions, there is not much difference between deleting a leaf node versus deleting a container that has child objects. However, there is a distinction in what is happening in the background.

Deleting an object that has no children can be done with a simple LDAP delete operation. On the other hand, to delete a container and its children, the tree-delete LDAP control has to be used. If you were to do the deletion from an LDAP-based tool like LDP, you would first need to enable the "Subtree Delete" control, which has an OID of 1.2.840.113556.1.4.805. LDP provides another option to do a "Recursive Delete" from the client side. That will essentially iterate through all the objects in the container, deleting them one by one. The Subtree Delete is much more efficient, especially when dealing with large containers.

See Also

Recipe 4.20 for deleting objects and MSDN: IADsDeleteOps::DeleteObject

4.22 Viewing the Created and Last Modified Timestamp of an Object

Problem

You want to determine when an object was either created or last updated.

Solution

Using a graphical user interface

1. Follow the steps in Recipe 4.2.
2. Ensure that `createTimestamp` and `modifyTimestamp` are included in the list of attributes to be returned by looking at Attributes under Options → Search.

Using a command-line interface

```
> dsquery * "<ObjectDN>" -attr name createTimestamp modifyTimestamp
```

Using VBScript

```
' This code prints the created and last modified timestamp
' for the specified object.
' ------ SCRIPT CONFIGURATION ------
strObjectDN = "<ObjectDN>"
' ------ END CONFIGURATION ---------

set objEntry = GetObject("LDAP://" & strObjectDN)
Wscript.Echo "Object Name:  " & objEntry.Get("name")
Wscript.Echo " Created: " & objEntry.Get("createTimestamp")
Wscript.Echo " Changed: " & objEntry.Get("modifyTimestamp")
```

Discussion

When an object is created or modified in Active Directory, the `createTimestamp` and `modifyTimestamp` attributes get set with the current time. Those two attributes are replicated, so assuming the latest modification of the object in question has replicated to all domain controllers, they will contain the absolute create and last modified timestamps.

You may have also run across the `whenCreated` and `whenChanged` attributes. They also contain create and modify timestamps, but these values are local to the domain controller and are not replicated.

See Also

Recipe 4.2 for viewing the attributes of an object

4.23   Modifying the Default LDAP Query Policy

Problem

You want to view or modify the default LDAP query policy of a forest. The query policy contains settings that restrict search behavior, such as the maximum number of entries that can be returned from a search.

Solution

Using a graphical user interface

1. Open ADSI Edit.
2. In the Configuration partition, browse to Services → Windows NT → Directory Service → Query Policies.
3. In the left pane, click on the Query Policies container, then right-click on the Default Query Policy object in the right pane, and select Properties.
4. Double-click on the lDAPAdminLimits attribute.
5. Click on the attribute you want to modify and click Remove.
6. Modify the value in the Value to add box and click Add.
7. Click OK twice.

Using a command-line interface

To view the current settings, use the following command:

```
> ntdsutil "ldap pol" conn "con to server <DomainControllerName>" q "show values"
```

To change the MaxPageSize value to 2000, you can do the following:

```
> ntdsutil "ldap pol" conn "con to server <DomainControllerName>" q
ldap policy: set MaxPageSize to 2000
ldap policy: Commit Changes
```

Using VBScript

```
' This code modifies a setting of the default query policy for a forest
' ------ SCRIPT CONFIGURATION ------
pol_attr  = "MaxPageSize" ' Set to the name of the setting you want to modify
new_value = 1000          ' Set to the value of the setting you want modify
' ------ END CONFIGURATION ---------

Const ADS_PROPERTY_APPEND = 3
Const ADS_PROPERTY_DELETE = 4

set rootDSE = GetObject("LDAP://RootDSE")
set ldapPol = GetObject("LDAP://cn=Default Query Policy,cn=Query-Policies," & _
               "cn=Directory Service,cn=Windows NT,cn=Services," & _
               rootDSE.Get("configurationNamingContext") )
```

```
    set regex = new regexp
    regex.IgnoreCase = true
    regex.Pattern = pol_attr & "="
    for Each prop In ldapPol.GetEx("ldapAdminLimits")
        if regex.Test(prop) then
            if prop = pol_attr & "=" & new_value then
                WScript.Echo pol_attr & " already equal to " & new_value
            else
                ldapPol.PutEx ADS_PROPERTY_APPEND, "lDAPAdminLimits", _
                          Array( pol_attr & "=" & new_value )
                ldapPol.SetInfo
                ldapPol.PutEx ADS_PROPERTY_DELETE, "lDAPAdminLimits", Array(prop)
                ldapPol.SetInfo
                WScript.Echo "Set " & pol_attr & " to " & new_value
            end if
            Exit For
        end if
    next
```

Discussion

The LDAP query policy contains several settings that control how domain controllers handle searches. By default, one query policy is defined for all domain controllers in a forest, but you can create additional ones and apply them to a specific domain controller or even at the site level (so that all domain controllers in the site use that policy).

Query policies are stored in the Configuration NC as queryPolicy objects. The default query policy is located at: cn=Default Query Policy, cn=Query-Policies, cn=Directory Service, cn=Windows NT, cn=Services, <ConfigurationPartitionDN>. The lDAPAdminLimits attribute of a queryPolicy object is multivalued and contains each setting for the policy in name-value pairs. Table 4-4 contains the available settings.

Table 4-4. LDAP query policy settings

Name	Default value	Description
MaxPoolThreads	4 per proc	Maximum number of threads that are created by the DC for query execution.
MaxDatagramRecv	4096	Maximum number of datagrams that can be simultaneously processed by the DC.
MaxReceiveBuffer	10485760	Maximum size in bytes for an LDAP request that the server will attempt to process. If the server receives a request that is larger then this value, it will close the connection.
InitRecvTimeout	120 secs	Initial receive time-out.
MaxConnections	5000	Maximum number of open connections.
MaxConnIdleTime	900 secs	Maximum amount of time a connection can be idle.
MaxActiveQueries	20	Maximum number of queries that can be active at one time.

Table 4-4. LDAP query policy settings (continued)

Name	Default value	Description
MaxPageSize	1000	Maximum page size that is supported for LDAP responses.
MaxQueryDuration	120 secs	Maximum length of time the domain controller can execute a query.
MaxTempTableSize	10000	Maximum size of temporary storage that is allocated to execute queries.
MaxResultSetSize	262144	Maximum size of the LDAP Result Set.
MaxNotificationPerConn	5	Maximum number of notifications that a client can request for a given connection.

Since the settings are stored as name/value pairs inside a single attribute, also referred to as AVAs, the VBScript solution has to iterate over each value and use a regular expression to determine when the target setting has been found. It does this by matching *<SettingName>=* at the beginning of the string. See Recipe 4.16 for more on AVAs.

> You should not change the default query policy in production unless you've done plenty of testing. Changing some of the settings may result in unexpected application or domain controller behavior.

Instead of modifying the default LDAP query policy, you can create a new one. In the Query Policies container (where the default query policy object is located), create a new queryPolicy object and set the ldapAdminLimits attribute as just described based on the settings you want configured. Then modify the queryPolicyObject attribute on the nTDSDSA object of a domain controller you want to apply the new policy to. This can be done via the Active Directory Sites and Services snap-in by browsing to the nTDSDSA object of a domain controller (cn=NTDS Settings), right-clicking on it, and selecting Properties. You can then select the new policy from a drop-down menu beside Query Policy. Click OK to apply the new policy.

See Also

MS KB 315071 (HOW TO: View and Set Lightweight Directory Access Protocol Policies by Using Ntdsutil.exe in Windows 2000)

4.24   Exporting Objects to an LDIF File

Problem

You want to export objects to an LDAP Data Interchange Format (LDIF) file.

Solution

Using a graphical user interface

None of the standard Microsoft tools support exporting LDIF from a GUI.

Using a command-line interface

```
> ldifde -f output.ldf -l <AttrList> -p <Scope> -r "<Filter>" -d "<BaseDN>"
```

Using VBScript

There are no COM or VBScript-based interfaces to LDIF. With Perl you can use the Net::LDAP::LDIF module, which supports reading and writing LDIF files.

Discussion

The LDIF specification defined in RFC 2849 describes a well-defined file-based format for representing directory entries. The format is intended to be both human and machine parseable, which adds to its usefulness. LDIF is the de facto standard for importing and exporting a large number of objects in a directory and is supported by virtually every directory vendor including Microsoft.

Using a command-line interface

The -f switch specifies the name of the file to use to save the entries to, -s is the DC to query, -l is the comma-separated list of attributes to include, -p is the search scope, -r is the search filter, and -d is the base DN. If you encounter any problems using ldifde, the -v switch enables verbose mode and can help identify problems.

See Also

Recipe 4.25 for importing objects using LDIF, RFC 2849 (The LDAP Data Interchange Format (LDIF)—Technical Specification), and MS KB 237677 (Using LDIFDE to Import and Export Directory Objects to Active Directory)

4.25   Importing Objects Using an LDIF File

Problem

You want to import objects into Active Directory using an LDIF file. The file could contain object additions, modifications, and/or deletions.

Solution

Using a command-line interface

To import objects using the `ldifde` utility, you must first create an LDIF file with the objects to add, modify, or delete. Here is an example LDIF file that adds a user, modifies the user twice, and then deletes the user:

```
dn: cn=jsmith,cn=users,dc=rallencorp,dc=com
changetype: add
objectClass: user
samaccountname: jsmith
sn: JSmith
useraccountcontrol: 512

dn: cn=jsmith,cn=users,dc=rallencorp,dc=com
changetype: modify
add: givenName
givenName: Jim
-
replace: sn
sn: Smith
-

dn: cn=jsmith,cn=users,dc=rallencorp,dc=com
changetype: delete
```

Once you've created the LDIF file, you just need to run the `ldifde` command to import the new objects.

```
> ldifde -i -f input.ldf
```

Discussion

For more information on the LDIF format, check RFC 2849.

Using a command-line interface

To import with `ldifde`, simply specify the `-i` switch to turn on import mode and `-f` *<filename>* for the file. It can also be beneficial to use the `-v` switch to turn on verbose mode to get more information in case of errors.

See Also

Recipe 4.24 for information on LDIF, RFC 2849 (The LDAP Data Interchange Format (LDIF)—Technical Specification), and MS KB 237677 (Using LDIFDE to Import and Export Directory Objects to Active Directory)

4.26   Exporting Objects to a CSV File

Problem

You want to export objects to a comma-separated variable (CSV) file. The CSV file can then be opened and manipulated from a spreadsheet application or with a text editor.

Solution

Using a command-line interface

```
> csvde -f output.csv -l <AttrList> -p <Scope> -r "<Filter>" -d "<BaseDN>"
```

Discussion

Once you have a CSV file containing entries, you can use a spreadsheet application such as Excel to view, sort, and manipulate the data.

Using a command-line interface

The parameters used by cvsde are nearly identical to those used by ldifde. The -f switch specifies the name of the file to use to save the entries to, -s is the DC to query, -l is the comma-separated list of attributes to include, -p is the search scope (base, onelevel, or subtree), -r is the search filter, and -d is the base DN. If you encounter any issues, the -v switch enables verbose mode and can help identify problems.

See Also

Recipe 4.27 for importing objects using a CSV file

4.27   Importing Objects Using a CSV File

Problem

You want to import objects into Active Directory using a CSV file.

Solution

Using a command-line interface

To import objects using the csvde utility, you must first create a CSV file containing the objects to add. The first line of the file should contain a comma-separated list of attributes you want to set, with DN being the first attribute. Here is an example:

```
DN,objectClass,cn,sn,userAccountControl,sAMAccountName,userPrincipalName
```

The rest of the lines should contain entries to add. If you want to leave one of the attributes unset, then leave the value blank (followed by a comma). Here is a sample CSV file that would add two user objects:

```
DN,objectClass,sn,userAccountControl,sAMAccountName,userPrincipalName
"cn=jim,cn=users,dc=rallencorp,dc=com",user,Smith,512,jim,jim@rallencorp.com
"cn=john,cn=users,dc=rallencorp,dc=com",user,,512,john,john@rallencorp.com
```

Once you've created the CSV file, you just need to run cvsde command to import the new objects.

```
> csvde -i -f input.csv
```

Discussion

Note that each line of the CSV import file, except the header, should contain entries to add objects. You cannot modify attributes of an object or delete objects using csvde. If you have a spreadsheet containing objects you want to import, first save it as a CSV file and use csvde to import it.

Using a command-line interface

To import with csvde, simply specify the -i switch to turn on import mode and -f *<filename>* for the file. It can also be beneficial to use the -v switch to turn on verbose mode to get more information in case of errors.

See Also

Recipe 4.26 for exporting objects in CSV format, and MS KB 327620 (HOW TO: Use Csvde to Import Contacts and User Objects into Active Directory)

## CHAPTER 5

Organizational Units

5.0 Introduction

An LDAP directory, such as Active Directory, stores data in a hierarchy of containers and leaf nodes called the directory information tree (DIT). Leaf nodes are end points in the tree, while containers can store other containers and leaf nodes. In Active Directory, the two most common types of containers are organizational units (OUs) and container objects. The container objects are generic containers that do not have any special properties about them other than that they can contain objects. Organizational units, on the other hand, have some special properties, such as being able to be linked to a group policy. In most cases, when designing a hierarchy of objects in Active Directory, especially users and computers, you should use OUs instead of containers. There is nothing you can do with a container that you can't do with an OU, but the reverse is not true.

The Anatomy of an Organizational Unit

Organizational units can be created anywhere in a Domain naming context. The one exception is that by default OUs cannot be added as a child of a `container` object. See Recipe 5.10 for more on how to work around this. OUs are represented in Active Directory by `organizationalUnit` objects. Table 5-1 contains a list of some interesting attributes that are available on `organizationalUnit` objects.

Table 5-1. Attributes of organizationalUnit objects

Attribute	Description
`description`	Textual description of the OU.
`gPLink`	List of group policy objects (GPOs) that have been linked to the OU. See Recipe 5.11 for more information.
`gpOptions`	Contains 1 if GPO inheritance is blocked and 0 otherwise.
`msDS-Approx-Immed-Subordinates`	Approximate number of direct child objects in the OU. See Recipe 5.8 for more information.

Table 5-1. Attributes of organizationalUnit objects (continued)

Attribute	Description
managedBy	Distinguished name (DN) of user or group that is in charge of managing the OU.
ou	Relative distinguished name of the OU.
modifyTimestamp	Timestamp of when the OU was last modified.
createTimestamp	Timestamp of when the OU was created.

5.1   Creating an OU

Problem

You want to create an OU.

Solution

Using a graphical user interface

1. Open the Active Directory Users and Computers (ADUC) snap-in.

2. If you need to change domains, right-click on the Active Directory Users and Computers label in the left pane, select Connect to Domain, enter the domain name, and click OK.

3. In the left pane, browse to the parent container of the new OU, right-click on it, and select New → Organizational Unit.

4. Enter the name of the OU and click OK.

5. To enter a description for the new OU, right-click on the OU in the left pane and select Properties.

6. Click OK after you are done.

Using a command-line interface

```
> dsadd ou "<OrgUnitDN>" -desc "<Description>"
```

Using VBScript

```
' This code creates an OU
' ------ SCRIPT CONFIGURATION ------
strOrgUnit       = "<OUName>"       ' e.g. Tools
strOrgUnitParent = "<ParentDN>"     ' e.g. ou=Engineering,dc=rallencorp,dc=com
strOrgUnitDescr  = "<Description>"  ' e.g. Tools Users
' ------ END CONFIGURATION ---------

set objDomain = GetObject("LDAP://" & strOrgUnitParent)
set objOU = objDomain.Create("organizationalUnit", "OU=" & strOrgUnit)
objOU.Put "description", strOrgUnitDescr
```

```
objOU.SetInfo
WScript.Echo "Successfully created " & objOU.Name
```

Discussion

OUs are used to structure data within Active Directory. Typically, there are four reasons why you would need to create an OU:

Segregate objects
> It is common practice to group related data into an OU. For example, user objects and computer objects are typically stored in separate OUs (in fact, that is the default configuration with Active Directory). One reason for this is to make searching the directory easier.

Delegate administration
> Perhaps the most often used reason for creating an OU is to delegate administration. With OUs you can give a person or group of people rights to do certain functions on objects within the OU.

Apply a GPO
> An OU is the smallest unit that a GPO can be applied to. If you have different types of users within your organization that need to apply different GPOs, the easiest way to set that up is to store the users in different OUs and apply GPOs accordingly.

Controlling visibility of objects
> You can use OUs as a way to restrict what users can see in the directory.

In each solution, the `description` attribute was set. It is not a mandatory attribute, but it is good practice to set it so that others browsing the directory have a general understanding of the purpose of the OU. Also, consider setting the `managedBy` attribute to reference a user or group that is the owner of the OU.

See Also

MS KB 308194 (HOW TO: How to Create Organizational Units in a Windows 2000 Domain)

5.2   Enumerating the OUs in a Domain

Problem

You want to enumerate all containers and OUs in a domain, which effectively displays the structure of the domain.

Solution

Using a graphical user interface

1. Open the Active Directory Users and Computers snap-in.
2. If you need to change domains, right-click on "Active Directory Users and Computers" in the left pane, select Connect to Domain, enter the domain name, and click OK.
3. In the left pane, you can browse the directory structure.

Using a command-line interface

The following command will enumerate all OUs in the domain of the user running the command.

```
> dsquery ou domainroot
```

Using VBScript

```
' This code recursively displays all container and organizationalUnit
' objects under a specified base.  Using "" for the second parameter means
' that there will be no indention for the first level of objects displayed.
DisplayObjects "LDAP://<DomainDN>", ""

' DisplayObjects takes the ADsPath of the object to display
' child objects for and the number of spaces (indention) to
' use when printing the first parameter
Function DisplayObjects( strADsPath, strSpace)
   set objObject = GetObject(strADsPath)
   Wscript.Echo strSpace & strADsPath
   objObject.Filter = Array("container","organizationalUnit")
   for each objChildObject in objObject
      DisplayObjects objChildObject.ADsPath, strSpace & " "
   next
End Function
```

Discussion

Using a graphical user interface

If you want to expand all containers and OUs within an OU, you have to manually expand each one within ADUC; there is no "expand all" option.

Using a command-line interface

To enumerate both OUs and containers, you have to a use a more generic dsquery command. The following command will display all containers and OUs in the domain of the user running the command:

```
> dsquery * domainroot -filter
"(|(objectcategory=container)(objectcategory=organizationalunit))" -scope subtree
-limit 0
```

Using VBScript

When iterating over the contents of an OU using a for each loop, paging will be enabled so that all child objects will be returned (instead of only 1,000 per the administrative limit). In order to display all child container objects regardless of depth, I used a recursive function called DisplayObjects.

5.3   Enumerating the Objects in an OU

Problem

You want to enumerate all the objects in an OU.

Solution

The following solutions will enumerate all the objects directly under an OU. Look at the Discussion section for more on how to display all objects under an OU regardless of depth.

Using a graphical user interface

1. Open the Active Directory Users and Computers snap-in.
2. If you need to change domains, right-click on "Active Directory Users and Computers" in the left pane, select Connect to Domain, enter the domain name, and click OK.
3. In the left pane, browse to the OU you want to view.
4. Click on it. The contents of the OU will be displayed in the right pane.

Using a command-line interface

```
> dsquery * "<OrgUnitDN>" -limit 0 -scope onelevel
```

Using VBScript

```
set objOU = GetObject("LDAP://<OrgUnitDN>")
for each objChildObject in objOU
    Wscript.Echo objChildObject.Name
next
```

Discussion

Using a graphical user interface

By default, ADUC will display only 2,000 objects. To view more than 2000 objects, select View → Filter Options. In the box beside Maximum number of items displayed per folder:, put the maximum number of objects you want to display.

Using a command-line interface

Using `-limit 0`, all objects under the OU will be displayed. If `-limit` is not specified, 100 will be shown by default. You can also specify your own number if you want to only display a limited number of objects.

The `-scope onelevel` option causes only direct child objects of the OU to be displayed. If you want to display all objects regardless of depth, add `-scope subtree`.

Using VBScript

When a `for` each loop iterates over the contents of an OU, paging will be enabled so that all child objects will be returned regardless of how many there are. If you want to display all child objects regardless of depth, you have to implement a recursive function, such as the following:

```
' Using "" for the second parameter means that the there will be no
' indention for the first level of objects displayed.
DisplayObjects "LDAP://<OrgUnitDN>", ""

' DisplayObjects takes the ADsPath of the object to display child
' objects for and the second is the number of spaces (indention)
' to use when printing the first parameter
Function DisplayObjects( strADsPath, strSpace)
   set objObject = GetObject(strADsPath)
   Wscript.Echo strSpace & strADsPath
   for each objChildObject in objObject
      DisplayObjects objChildObject.ADsPath, strSpace & " "
   next
End Function
```

This code is nearly identical to that shown in Recipe 5.2. The only difference is that I didn't use the `Filter` method to restrict the type of objects displayed.

5.4   Deleting the Objects in an OU

Problem

You want to delete all the objects in an OU, but not the OU itself.

Solution

Using a graphical user interface

1. Open the Active Directory Users and Computers snap-in.

2. If you need to change domains, right-click on "Active Directory Users and Computers" in the left pane, select Connect to Domain, enter the domain name, and click OK.

3. In the left pane, browse to the OU that contains the objects you want to delete and click on it.

4. Highlight all the objects in the right pane and hit the Delete button.

5. Press F5 to refresh the contents of the OU. If objects still exist, repeat the previous step.

Using a command-line interface

To delete all objects within an OU, but not the OU itself, you need to use the -subtree and -exclude options with the dsrm command.

```
> dsrm "<OrgUnitDN>" -subtree -exclude
```

Using VBScript

```
' This code deletes the objects in an OU, but not the OU itself
set objOU = GetObject("LDAP://<OrgUnitDN>")
for each objChildObject in objOU
    Wscript.Echo "Deleting " & objChildObject.Name
    objChildObject.DeleteObject(0)
next
```

Discussion

If you want to delete the objects in an OU and recreate the OU, you can either delete the OU itself, which will delete all child objects, or you could just delete the child objects. The benefits to the later approach is that you do not need to reconfigure the ACL on the OU or relink GPOs.

See Also

Recipe 5.3 for enumerating objects in an OU, Recipe 5.5 for deleting an OU, and MSDN: IADsDeleteOps::DeleteObject

5.5   Deleting an OU

Problem

You want to delete an OU and all objects in it.

Solution

Using a graphical user interface

1. Open the Active Directory Users and Computers snap-in.
2. If you need to change domains, right-click on "Active Directory Users and Computers" in the left pane, select Connect to Domain, enter the domain name, and click OK.
3. In the left pane, browse to the OU you want to delete, right-click on it, and select Delete.
4. Click Yes.
5. If the OU contains child objects, you will be asked for confirmation again before deleting it. Click Yes.

Using a command-line interface

To delete an OU and all objects contained within, use the `-subtree` option with the `dsrm` command. If you don't use `-subtree` and the object you are trying to delete has child objects, the deletion will fail.

```
> dsrm "<OrgUnitDN>" -subtree
```

Using VBScript

```
' This code deletes an OU and all child objects of the OU
set objOU = GetObject("LDAP://<OrgUnitDN>")
objOU.DeleteObject(0)
```

Discussion

Deleting OUs that do not contain objects is just like deleting any other type of object. Deleting an OU that contains objects requires a special type of delete operation. The "Tree Delete" LDAP control (OID: 1.2.840.113556.1.4.805) must be used by the application or script to inform AD to delete everything contained in the OU. All three solutions in this case use the control "under the covers," but if you were going to perform the operation via an LDAP, such as LDP, you would need to enable the control first.

See Also

Recipe 4.3 for using LDAP controls and MSDN: IADsDeleteOps::DeleteObject

5.6 Moving the Objects in an OU to a Different OU

Problem

You want to move some or all of the objects in an OU to a different OU. You may need to do this as part of a domain restructuring effort.

Solution

Using a graphical user interface

1. Open the Active Directory Users and Computers snap-in.
2. If you need to change domains, right-click on "Active Directory Users and Computers" in the left pane, select Connect to Domain, enter the domain name, and click OK.
3. In the left pane, browse to the OU that contains the objects you want to move and click on it.
4. Highlight the objects in the right pane you want to move, right-click on them, and select "Move."
5. Browse to the parent container you want to move the objects to, click on it.
6. Click OK.
7. Press F5 to refresh the contents of the OU. If objects still exist, repeat the previous three steps.

Using a command-line interface

```
> for /F "usebackq delims=""" %i in (`dsquery * "<OldOrgUnitDN>" -scope onelevel`)↵
do dsmove -newparent "<NewOrgUnitDN>" %i
```

Using VBScript

```
' This code moves objects from the "old" OU to the "new" OU
' ------ SCRIPT CONFIGURATION ------
strOldOrgUnit = "<OldOrgUnitDN>" ' e.g. ou=Eng Tools,dc=rallencorp,dc=com
strNewOrgUnit = "<NewOrgUnitDN>" ' e.g. ou=Tools,dc=rallencorp,dc=com
' ------ END CONFIGURATION ---------

set objOldOU = GetObject("LDAP://" & strOldOrgUnit)
set objNewOU = GetObject("LDAP://" & strNewOrgUnit)
for each objChildObject in objOldOU
    Wscript.Echo "Moving " & objChildObject.Name
    objNewOU.MoveHere objChildObject.ADsPath, objChildObject.Name
next
```

Discussion

Using a graphical user interface

If you want to move more than 2,000 objects at one time, you will need to modify the default number of objects displayed as described in Discussion section of Recipe 5.3.

Using a command-line interface

Since dsmove can move only one object at a time, I had to use the for command to iterate over each child object returned from dsquery. Also note that if you want to move more than 100 objects, you'll need to specify the -limit xx option with dsquery, where xx is the maximum number of objects to move (use 0 for all).

Using VBScript

For more information on the MoveHere method, see Recipe 4.17.

See Also

Recipe 4.17 for moving objects, Recipe 5.3 for enumerating objects in an OU, and MSDN: IADsContainer::MoveHere

5.7   Moving an OU

Problem

You want to move an OU and all its child objects to a different location in the directory tree.

Solution

Using a graphical user interface

1. Open the Active Directory Users and Computers snap-in.
2. If you need to change domains, right-click on "Active Directory Users and Computers" in the left pane, select Connect to Domain, enter the domain name, and click OK.
3. In the left pane, browse to the OU you want to move.
4. Right-click on the OU and select Move.
5. Select the new parent container for the OU and click OK.

Using a command-line interface

```
> dsmove "<OrgUnitDN>" -newparent "<NewParentDN>"
```

Using VBScript

```
set objOU = GetObject("LDAP://<NewParentDN>")
objOU.MoveHere "LDAP://<OrgUnitDN>", "<OrgUnitRDN>"
```

Discussion

One of the benefits of Active Directory is the ability to structure and restructure data easily. Moving an OU, even one that contains a complex hierarchy of other OUs and objects, can be done without impacting the child objects.

If any applications have a dependency on the location of specific objects, you need to ensure they are either updated with the new location or preferably, reference the objects by GUID, not by distinguished name.

You should also be mindful of the impact of inherited ACLs and applied group policy on the new parent OU.

See Also

MS KB 313066 (HOW TO: Move Users, Groups, and Organizational Units Within a Domain in Windows 2000) and MSDN: IADsContainer::MoveHere

5.8   Determining How Many Child Objects an OU Has

 This recipe requires the Windows Server 2003 domain functional level.

Problem

You want to determine if an OU has any child objects or determine how many child objects it contains.

Solution

Using a graphical user interface

1. Open LDP.
2. From the Menu, select Browse → Search.
3. For Base Dn, enter `<OrgUnitDN>`.
4. For Filter, enter `(objectclass=*)`.
5. For Scope, select Base.

---

6. Click the Options button and enter `msDS-Approx-Immed-Subordinates` For Attributes.

7. Click OK and Run.

8. The results will be displayed in the right pane.

Using a command-line interface

```
> dsquery * "<OrgUnitDN>" -scope base -attr msDS-Approx-Immed-Subordinates
```

Using VBScript

```
' This code displays the approximate number of child objects for an OU
set objOU = GetObject("LDAP://<OrgUnitDN>")
objOU.GetInfoEx Array("msDS-Approx-Immed-Subordinates"), 0
WScript.Echo "Number of child objects: " & _
             objOU.Get("msDS-Approx-Immed-Subordinates")
```

Discussion

The `msDS-Approx-Immed-Subordinates` attribute is new to Windows Server 2003. It contains the approximate number of direct child objects in a container or organizational unit. Note that this is an approximation and can be off by 10% of the actual total for large containers. The main reason for adding this attribute was to give applications an idea of how many objects a container has so that it can display them accordingly.

`msDS-Approx-Immed-Subordinates` is a constructed attribute, that is, the value is not actually stored in Active Directory like other attributes. Active Directory computes the value when an application asks for it. In the VBScript solution, the `GetInfoEx` method had to be called because some constructed attributes, such as this one, are not retrieved when `GetInfo` or `Get` is called.

You can accomplish similar functionality with Windows 2000 Active Directory, but you need to perform a onelevel search against the OU and count the number of objects returned. This method is by no means as efficient as using `msDS-Approx-Immed-Subordinates` in Windows Server 2003.

See Also

MSDN: GetInfoEx

5.9 Delegating Control of an OU

Problem

You want to delegate administrative access of an OU to allow a group of users to manage objects in the OU.

Solution

Using a graphical user interface

1. Open the Active Directory Users and Computers snap-in.
2. If you need to change domains, right-click on "Active Directory Users and Computers" in the left pane, select Connect to Domain, enter the domain name, and click OK.
3. In the left pane, browse to the target OU, right-click on it, and select Delegate Control.
4. Select the users and/or groups to delegate control to by using the Add button and click Next.
5. Select the type of privilege to grant the users/groups and click Next.
6. Click Finish.

Using a command-line interface

ACLs can be set via a command-line with the `dsacls` utility from the Support Tools. See Recipe 14.10 for more information.

Discussion

Although you can delegate control of an OU to a particular user, it is generally a better practice to use a group instead. Even if there is only one user to delegate control to, you should create a group, add that user as a member, and use that group in the ACL. That way, in the future when you have to replace that user with someone else, you can make sure the new person is in the correct group instead of modifying ACLs again.

See Also

Recipe 14.10 for changing the ACL on an object

5.10   Allowing OUs to Be Created Within Containers

Problem

You want to create an OU within a container. By default, you cannot create OUs within container objects due to restrictions in the Active Directory schema.

Solution

Using a graphical user interface

1. Open the Active Directory Schema snap-in as a user that is a member of the Schema Admins group. See Recipe 10.1 for more on using the Schema snap-in.

2. Expand the Classes folder, right-click on the organizationalUnit class, and select Properties.

3. Select the Relationship tab and, next to Possible Superior, click Add Superior (Windows Server 2003) or Add (Windows 2000).

4. Select container and click OK.

5. Click OK.

Using a command-line interface

Create an LDIF file called *ou_in_container.ldf* with the following contents:

```
dn: cn=organizational-unit,cn=schema,cn=configuration,<ForestRootDN>
changetype: modify
add: possSuperiors
possSuperiors: container
-
```

then run the ldifde command to import the change:

```
> ldifde -i -f ou_in_container.ldf
```

Using VBScript

```
' This code modifies the schema so that OUs can be created within containers
Const ADS_PROPERTY_APPEND = 3
set objRootDSE = GetObject("LDAP://RootDSE")
set objOUClass = GetObject("LDAP://cn=organizational-unit," & _
                          objRootDSE.Get("schemaNamingContext") )
objOUClass.PutEx ADS_PROPERTY_APPEND, "possSuperiors", Array("container")
objOUClass.SetInfo
```

Discussion

Allowing OUs to be created within containers requires a simple modification to the schema. You have to make the container class one of the possible superiors (possSuperiors attribute) for the organizationalUnit class.

See Also

Recipe 10.1 for using the Schema snap-in and MS KB 224377 (Configuring Different Containers to Hold Organizational Units)

5.11   Linking a GPO to an OU

Problem

You want to apply the settings in a GPO to the users and/or computers within an OU, also known as linking the GPO to the OU.

Solution

Using a graphical user interface

1. Open the Group Policy Management (GPMC) snap-in.
2. Expand Forest in the left pane.
3. Expand Domain and navigate down to the OU in the domain you want to link the GPO to.
4. Right-click on the OU and select either Create and Link a GPO Here (if the GPO does not already exist) or Link an Existing GPO (if you have already created the GPO).

Using VBScript

```
' This code links a GPO to an OU in the specified domain
' ------ SCRIPT CONFIGURATION ------
strDomainDN = "<DomainDN>"    ' e.g. dc=rallencorp,dc=com
strGPO      = "<GPOName>"     ' e.g. WorkstationsGPO
strOUDN     = "<OrgUnitDN>"   ' e.g. ou=Workstations,dc=rallencorp,dc=com
' ------ END CONFIGURATION ---------

strBaseDN  =  "<LDAP://cn=policies,cn=system,dc=" & strDomainDN & ">;"
strFilter  = "(&(objectcategory=grouppolicycontainer)" & _
             "(objectclass=grouppolicycontainer)" & _
             "(displayname=" & strGPO & "));"
strAttrs   = "ADsPath;"
strScope   = "OneLevel"
```

```
set objConn = CreateObject("ADODB.Connection")
objConn.Provider = "ADsDSOObject"
objConn.Open "Active Directory Provider"
set objRS = objConn.Execute(strBaseDN & strFilter & strAttrs & strScope)
if objRS.EOF <> TRUE then
   objRS.MoveFirst
end if

if objRS.RecordCount = 1 then
   strGPOADsPath = objRS.Fields(0).Value
   WScript.Echo "GPO Found: " & strGPOADsPath
elseif objRS.RecordCount = 0 then
   WScript.Echo "Did not founding matching GPO for: " & strGPO
   Wscript.Quit
elseif objRS.RecordCount > 1 then
   WScript.Echo "More than 1 GPO found matching: " & strGPO
   Wscript.Quit
end if

set objOU = GetObject("LDAP://" & strOUDN)

on error resume next
strGPLink = objOU.Get("gpLink")
if Err.Number then
   if Err.Number <> -2147463155 then
      WScript.Echo "Fatal error while retrieving gpLink attribute: " & _
                   Err.Description
      Wscript.Quit
   end if
end if
on error goto 0

objOU.Put "gpLink", strGPLink & "[" & strGPOADsPath & ";0]"
objOU.SetInfo
WScript.Echo "GPO successfully linked"
```

Discussion

The GPOs that are linked to an OU are stored in the gpLink attribute of the OU. The format of the gpLink attribute is kind of strange, so you have to be careful when programmatically or manually setting that attribute. Since multiple GPOs can be linked to an OU, the gpLink attribute has to store multiple values; unfortunately, it does not store them as you might expect in a multivalued attribute. Instead, the links are stored as part of the single-valued gpLink attribute. The ADsPath of each linked GPO is concatenated into a string, with each enclosed in square brackets. The ADsPath for each GPO is followed by ;0 to signify the link is enabled or ;1 to signify the link is disabled. Here is an example gpLink with two GPOs linked:

```
[LDAP://cn={6491389E-C302-418C-8D9D-
BB24E65E7507},cn=policies,cn=system,DC=rallencorp,DC=com;0][LDAP://cn={6AC1786C-016F-
11D2-945F-00C04fB984F9},cn=policies,cn=system,DC=rallencorp,DC=com;0]
```

A much better VBScript solution for linking GPOs is described in Recipe 9.12, which uses the GPMC APIs.

See Also

Recipe 9.0 for more information on GPMC, and MS KB 248392 (Scripting the Addition of Group Policy Links)

## CHAPTER 6

Users

6.0   Introduction

User accounts are one of the most frequently used types of objects in Active Directory. Because Windows 2000 and Windows 2003 systems manage users through Active Directory, many key issues that system administrators have to deal with are covered in this chapter. In particular, Active Directory manages all the information regarding passwords, group membership, the disabling or expiration of accounts, and when users have logged in.

The Anatomy of a User

The default location for user objects in a domain is the `cn=Users` container directly off the domain root. You can, of course, create user objects in other containers and organizational units in a domain. Table 6-1 contains a list of some of the interesting attributes that are available on user objects. This is by no means a complete list. There are many other informational attributes that I haven't included.

Table 6-1. Attributes of user objects

Attribute	Description
accountExpires	Large integer representing when the user's account is going to expire. See Recipe 6.25 for more information.
cn	Relative distinguished name of `user` objects. This is commonly the username of the user.
displayName	Typically the full name of a user. This attribute is used in administrative tools to display a user's descriptive "name."
givenName	First name of the user.
homeDirectory	Local or UNC path of user's home directory. See Recipe 6.29 for more information.
homeDrive	Defines the drive letter to map the user's home directory to. See Recipe 6.29 for more information.
lastLogon	Last logon timestamp, which is not replicated among domain controllers.

Table 6-1. Attributes of user objects (continued)

Attribute	Description
lastLogonTimestamp	Approximate last logon timestamp, which is replicated among domain controllers. This attribute is new in Windows Server 2003. See Recipe 6.27 for more information.
managedObjects	Multivalued linked attribute (with managedBy) that contains a list of DNs of objects the user manages.
lockoutTime	Large integer representation of the timestamp for when a user was locked out. See Recipe 6.9 for more information.
memberOf	List of DNs of the groups the user is a member of. See Recipe 6.14 for more information.
objectSID	Octet string representing the SID of the user.
primaryGroupID	ID of the primary group for the user. See Recipe 6.15 for more information.
profilePath	UNC path to profile directory. See Recipe 6.29 for more information.
pwdLastSet	Large integer that can be translated into the last time the user's password was set. See Recipe 6.23 for more information.
sAMAccountName	NetBIOS style name of the user.
sidHistory	Multivalued attribute that contains a list of SIDs that is associated with the user.
scriptPath	Path to logon script. See Recipe 6.29 for more information.
sn	Last name of user.
tokenGroups	List of SIDs for the groups in the domain the user is a member of (both directly and via nesting).
unicodePwd	Octet string that contains the password for the user. This attribute cannot be directly queried.
userAccountControl	Account flags that define such things as account status and password change status.
userPrincipalName	Email-style account name for user, which a user can use to logon to a computer.
userWorkstations	Multivalued list of computers a user can logon to.

6.1   Creating a User

Problem

You want to create a user object.

Solution

Using a graphical user interface

1. Open the Active Directory Users and Computers (ADUC) snap-in.
2. If you need to change domains, right-click on "Active Directory Users and Computers" in the left pane, select Connect to Domain, enter the domain name, and click OK.
3. In the left pane, browse to the parent container of the new user, right-click on it, and select New → User.

4. Enter the values for the first name, last name, full name, and user logon name fields as appropriate and click Next.

5. Enter and confirm password, set any of the password flags, and click Next.

6. Click Finish.

Using a command-line interface

```
> dsadd user "<UserDN>" -upn <UserUPN> -fn "<UserFirstName>" -ln "<UserLastName>"↵
-display "<UserDisplayName>" -pwd <UserPasswd>
```

Using VBScript

```
' Taken from ADS_USER_FLAG_ENUM
Const ADS_UF_NORMAL_ACCOUNT = 512

set objParent = GetObject("LDAP://<ParentDN>")
set objUser   = objParent.Create("user", "cn=<UserName>") ' e.g. joes
objUser.Put "sAMAccountName", "<UserName>"   ' e.g. joes
objUser.Put "userPrincipalName", "<UserUPN>" ' e.g. joes@rallencorp.com
objUser.Put "givenName", "<UserFirstName>"   ' e.g. Joe
objUser.Put "sn", "<UserLastName>"           ' e.g. Smith
objUser.Put "displayName", "<UserFirstName> <UserLastName>" ' e.g. Joe Smith
objUser.Put "userAccountControl", ADS_UF_NORMAL_ACCOUNT
objUser.SetInfo
objUser.SetPassword("<Password>")
objUser.AccountDisabled = FALSE
objUser.SetInfo
```

Discussion

The only mandatory attribute that must be set when creating a user is sAMAccountName, which is the account name that is used to interoperate with down-level domains. To make the account immediately available for a user to use, you'll need to make sure the account is enabled, which is accomplished by setting userAccountControl to 512, and setting a password (see Recipe 6.17). If you allow UPN logons, you'll want to make sure the userPrincipalName attribute is set.

With Windows Server 2003, you can also create user accounts using the inetOrgPerson class, which is described in Recipe 6.3. inetOrgPerson objects can be used for user authentication and restricting access to resources in much the same way as user objects.

Using a graphical user interface

To set additional attributes, double-click on the user account after it has been created. There are several tabs to choose from that contain attributes that are grouped together based on function (e.g., Profile).

Using a command-line interface

Several additional attributes can be set with the dsadd user command. Run dsadd user /? for the complete list.

Using VBScript

Take a look at Recipe 6.24 for more information on the userAccountControl attribute and the various flags that can be set for it.

See Also

Recipe 6.2 for creating users in bulk, Recipe 6.3 for creating an inetOrgPerson user, and MSDN: ADS_USER_FLAG_ENUM

6.2   Creating a Large Number of Users

Problem

You want to create a large number of user objects, either for testing purposes or to initially populate Active Directory with your employee, customer, or student user accounts.

Solution

The following examples will create 1,000 users in the *rallencorp.com* domain under the Bulk OU. The password is set, but no other attributes are configured. You can modify the examples to populate whatever attributes you need.

Using a command-line interface

```
> for /L %i in (1,1,1000) do dsadd user cn=User%i,ou=bulk,dc=rallencorp,dc=com -pwd⏎
User%i
```

Using VBScript

```
' This code creates a large number of users with incremented user names
' e.g. User1, User2, User3, ....
' ------ SCRIPT CONFIGURATION ------
intNumUsers = 1000         ' Number of users to create
strParentDN = "<ParentDN>" ' e.g. ou=bulk,dc=emea,dc=rallencorp,dc=com
' ------ END CONFIGURATION ---------

' Taken from ADS_USER_FLAG_ENUM
Const ADS_UF_NORMAL_ACCOUNT = 512

set objParent = GetObject("LDAP://" & strParentDN)
for i = 1 to intNumUsers
```

```
    strUser = "User" & i
    Set objUser = objParent.Create("user", "cn=" & strUser)
    objUser.Put "sAMAccountName", strUser
    objUser.Put "userAccountControl", ADS_UF_NORMAL_ACCOUNT
    objUser.SetInfo
    objUser.SetPassword(strUser)
    objUser.AccountDisabled=FALSE
    objUser.SetInfo
    WScript.Echo "Created " & strUser
next
WScript.Echo ""
WScript.Echo "Created " & intNumUsers & " users"
```

Discussion

Using ADSI and even the new DS command line utilities on Windows Server 2003, you can create hundreds and even thousands of users easily and quickly. I ran both the CLI and VBScript solutions in a test domain, which create 1,000 user objects, on a single processor machine. The VBScript solution took less than 1.5 minutes and the CLI solution took less than 5 minutes. Admittedly, they are not populating very many attributes, but it shows that you can quickly populate Active Directory with user accounts very easily. You can also modify the examples to pull from a data source, such as an employee database, and use real data.

See Also

Recipe 6.1 for creating a user

6.3   Creating an inetOrgPerson User

Problem

You want to create an inetOrgPerson object, which is the standard LDAP object class to represent users.

Solution

Using a graphical user interface

1. Open the Active Directory Users and Computers snap-in.
2. If you need to change domains, right-click on "Active Directory Users and Computers" in the left pane, select Connect to Domain, enter the domain name, and click OK.
3. In the left pane, browse to the parent container of the new user, right-click on it, and select New → InetOrgPerson.

4. Enter first name, last name, and user logon name fields as appropriate and click Next.

5. Enter and confirm the password, set any of the password flags, and click Next.

6. Click Finish.

Using a command-line interface

The dsadd command does not support creating inetOrgPerson objects so we'll use ldifde instead. First, we need to create an LDIF file called *create_inetorgperson.ldf* with the following contents:

```
dn: <UserDN>
changetype: add
objectclass: inetorgperson
sAMAccountName: <UserName>
userAccountControl: 512
```

Be sure to replace *<UserDN>* with the distinguished name of the user you want to add and *<UserName>* with the user's username. Then run the following command:

```
> ldifde -i -f create_inetorgperson.ldf
```

Using VBScript

```
' This code creates an inetOrgPerson object

set objParent = GetObject("LDAP://<ParentDN>")
set objUser   = objParent.Create("inetorgperson", "cn=<UserName>")

' Taken from ADS_USER_FLAG_ENUM
Const ADS_UF_NORMAL_ACCOUNT = 512

objUser.Put "sAMAccountName", "<UserName>"
objUser.Put "userPrincipalName", "<UserUPN>"
objUser.Put "givenName", "<UserFirstName>"
objUser.Put "sn", "<UserLastName>"
objUser.Put "displayName", "<UserFirstName> <UserLastName>"
objUser.Put "userAccountControl", ADS_UF_NORMAL_ACCOUNT
objUser.SetInfo
objUser.SetPassword("<Password>")
objUser.AccountDisabled = FALSE
objUser.SetInfo
```

Discussion

The inetOrgPerson object class was defined in RFC 2798. It is the closest thing in the LDAP world to a standard representation of a user, and most LDAP vendors support the inetOrgPerson class. Unfortunately, Microsoft did not support inetOrgPerson with the initial release of Active Directory. Even though they provided an add-on later to extend the schema to support it, the damage had been done. Most Active

Directory implementations were already using the user object class and were unlikely to convert. This required vendors to build in support for the user class.

 You can download the InetOrgPerson Kit for Windows 2000 from the following web site: *http://msdn.microsoft.com/library/en-us/dnactdir/ html/inetopkit.asp*. This requires that you extend the schema to support an additional object class and new attributes. It also creates a schema conflict with Windows Server 2003. See MS KB 314649 for more information.

In Windows Server 2003 Active Directory, inetOrgPerson is supported natively. You can create inetOrgPerson objects for your users, who can use them to authenticate just as they would accounts of the user object class. If you haven't deployed Active Directory yet and you plan on integrating a lot of third-party LDAP-based applications that rely on inetOrgPerson, you may want to consider using it over user. You won't be losing any information or functionality because the inetOrgPerson class inherits directly from the user class. For this reason, the inetOrgPerson class has even more attributes than the Microsoft user class. The one potential downside is that some of the Microsoft tools, such as the DS utilities, do not support modifying inetOrgPerson objects.

See Also

Recipe 6.1 for creating a user and RFC 2798 (Definition of the inetOrgPerson LDAP Object Class)

6.4   Modifying an Attribute for Several Users at Once

Problem

You want to modify an attribute for several users at once.

Solution

Using a graphical user interface

 This requires the Windows Server 2003 version of the Active Directory Users and Computers snap-in.

1. Open the Active Directory Users and Computers (ADUC) snap-in.

2. If you need to change domains, right-click on "Active Directory Users and Computers" in the left pane, select Connect to Domain, enter the domain name, and click OK.

3. In the left pane, browse to the parent container of the objects you want to modify.

4. In the right pane, highlight each object you want to modify, right-click and select Properties.

5. Check the box beside the attribute(s) you want to modify and edit the fields for the attributes.

6. Click OK.

Using a command-line interface

The following command sets the home directory of all users under a parent container (<*ParentDN*>) to be on a particular file server (<*FileServer*>). The user (i.e., $username$) is automatically replaced with the sAMAccountName for the user.

```
> for /F "usebackq delims="" %i in (`dsquery user "<ParentDN>" -limit 0 -scope↵
onelevel`) do dsmod user -hmdir "\\<FileServerName>\$username$" %i
```

Using VBScript

```
' This code sets the home drive of all users under a container
' to be on a file server where the share name is the same as the user's
' sAMAccountName.
set objParent = GetObject("LDAP://<ParentDN>")
objParent.Filter = Array("user")
for each objUser in objParent
    Wscript.Echo "Modifying " & objUser.Get("sAMAccountName")
    objUser.HomeDirectory = "\\<FileServerName>\" & _
                            objUser.Get("sAMAccountName")
    objUser.SetInfo
next
```

Discussion

It is often necessary to update several users at once due to an organizational, locational or file server change. In each solution, I showed how to modify all users within a parent container, but you may need to use different criteria for locating the users.

With ADUC, you are limited to modifying multiple users that belong to the same container. You can, however, create a Saved Query with the Windows Server 2003 version of ADUC that returns users based on any criteria you specify. You can then highlight those users and modify them as described in the GUI solution.

With the CLI solution, you can modify the dsquery user command to search on whatever criteria you want. The same applies in the VBScript solution, but you'll need to use an ADO query instead of the `Filter` method if you want to do anything more complex. See Recipe 4.5 for more information on searching with ADO.

6.5   Moving a User

Problem

You want to move a user object to a different container or OU.

Solution

Using a graphical user interface

1. Open the Active Directory Users and Computers snap-in.
2. If you need to change domains, right-click on "Active Directory Users and Computers" in the left pane, select Connect to Domain, enter the domain name, and click OK.
3. In the left pane, right-click on the domain and select Find.
4. Type the name of the user and click Find Now.
5. In the Search Results, right-click on the user and select Move.
6. Browse to the new parent container or OU and click on it.
7. Click OK.

Using a command-line interface

```
> dsmove "<UserDN>" -newparent "<NewParentDN>"
```

Using VBScript

```
' This code moves a user from one container to another.
' ------ SCRIPT CONFIGURATION ------
strUserDN = "<UserDN>"       ' e.g. cn=rallen,cn=users,dc=rallencorp,dc=com
strOUDN = "<NewParentDN>"    ' e.g. ou=Sales,dc=rallencorp,dc=com
' ------ END CONFIGURATION ---------

Set objUser = GetObject("LDAP://" & strUserDN)
Set objOU = GetObject("LDAP://" & strOUDN)
objOU.MoveHere objUser.ADsPath, objUser.Name
```

Discussion

Moving a user object between OUs in the same domain has no direct impact to the actual user. The only thing to be cautious of is the impact of moving the user to a new OU that may have different security or GPOs applied to it.

See Also

Recipe 4.17 for moving objects between OUs

6.6   Renaming a User

Problem

You want to rename a user.

Solution

Using a graphical user interface

1. Open the Active Directory Users and Computers snap-in.
2. In the left pane, right-click on the domain and select Find.
3. Type the name of the user and click Find Now.
4. In the Search Results, right-click on the user and select Rename.
5. You can modify the Full Name, Last Name, First Name, Display Name, User Principal Name (logon name), and SAM Account Name (pre-Windows 2000).
6. Click OK after you are done.

Using a command-line interface

The following command will rename the RDN of the user:

```
> dsmove "<UserDN>" -newname "<NewUserName>"
```

You can modify the UPN (-upn), First Name (-fn), Last Name (-ln), and Display Name (-display) using the dsmod user command. For example, the following command would change the user's UPN and last name:

```
> dsmod user "<UserDN>" -upn "<NewUserUPN>" -ln "<NewUserLastName>"
```

Using VBScript

```
' This code renames the RDN of a user and the sAMAccountName attribute.
' ------ SCRIPT CONFIGURATION ------
strParentDN   = "<ParentDN>"     ' e.g. cn=Users,dc=rallencorp,dc=com
strUserOldName = "<OldUserName>" ' e.g. jsmith
strUserNewName = "<NewUserName>" ' e.g. jim
' ------ END CONFIGURATION --------

set objCont = GetObject("LDAP://" & strParentDN)
objCont.MoveHere "LDAP://cn=" & strUserOldName & "," & strParentDN, _
                 "cn=" & strUserNewName
set objUser = GetObject("LDAP://cn=" & strUserNewName & "," & strParentDN)
objUser.Put "sAMAccountName", strUserNewName
```

```
objUser.SetInfo
WScript.Echo "Rename successful"
```

Discussion

Renaming a user object can have a couple different meanings in Active Directory. In the generic object sense, renaming an object consists of changing the RDN for the object to something else, such as if cn=jsmith became cn=joe. Typically, you need to rename more than that with users. For example, let's say you had a username naming convention of FirstInitialLastName so Joe Smith's username would be jsmith. Let's pretend that Joe decides one day that Smith is way too common and he wants to be more unique by changing his last name to Einstein. Now his username should be jeinstein. The following attributes would need to change to complete a rename of his object:

- His RDN should change from cn=jsmith to cn=jeinstein.
- His sAMAccountName should change to jeinstein.
- His userPrincipalName (UPN) should change to jeinstein@rallencorp.com.
- His mail (email address) attribute should change to jeinstein@rallencorp.com.
- His sn (last name) attribute should change to Einstein.

While this example may be contrived, it shows that renaming Joe Smith to Joe Einstein can take up to five attribute changes in Active Directory. It is also important to note that if you change any of the first three in the bulleted list (RDN, UPN, or SAM Account Name), you should have the user log off and log back on after the changes have replicated. Since most applications and services rely on user GUID or SID, which doesn't change during a user rename, the person should not be impacted, but you want to have him log off and back on anyway just in case.

See Also

Recipe 4.19 for renaming objects

6.7   Copying a User

Problem

You want to copy an existing user account, which may be serving as a template, in order to create a new account.

Solution

Using a graphical user interface

1. Open the Active Directory Users and Computers snap-in.
2. In the left pane, browse to the parent container of the template user object.
3. In the right pane, right-click on the user and select Copy.
4. Enter the name information for the new user and click Next.
5. Enter a password, check any options you want enabled, and click Next.
6. Click Finish.

Using VBScript

```
' This code copies the attributes in the Attrs array from an
' existing object to a new one.
' ------ SCRIPT CONFIGURATION ------
arrAttrs        = Array("department","co","title","l", "c", "st")
strParentDN     = "<ParentContainer>"    ' e.g. cn=Users,dc=rallencorp,dc=com
strTemplateUser = "<TemplateUserName>"   ' e.g. template-user-sales
strNewUser      = "<NewUserName>"        ' e.g. jdoe
strPassword     = "<Password>"
' ------ END CONFIGURATION ---------

Const ADS_UF_NORMAL_ACCOUNT = 512   ' from ADS_USER_FLAG_ENUM

Set objTemplate = GetObject("LDAP://cn=" & strTemplateUser & _
                            "," & strParentDN)
Set objParent   = GetObject("LDAP://" & strParentDN)
Set objUser     = objParent.Create("user", "cn=" & strNewUser)

objUser.Put "sAMAccountName", strNewUser
objUser.Put "userAccountControl", ADS_UF_NORMAL_ACCOUNT

for each strAttr in arrAttrs
   objUser.Put strAttr, objTemplate.Get(strAttr)
next

objUser.SetInfo
objUser.SetPassword(strPassword)
objUser.AccountDisabled = FALSE
objUser.SetInfo
WScript.Echo "Successfully created user"
```

Discussion

Copying a user consists of copying the attributes that are common among a certain user base, which can include department, address, and perhaps even organizational information. ADUC actually uses attributes that are marked in the schema as "Copied when duplicating a user" to determine which attributes to copy. The VBScript solution just used a hardcoded set of attributes. If you are interested in finding the attributes that are configured in the schema to get copied, see Recipe 10.12.

Using a graphical user interface

In order to copy a user in ADUC, you have to browse to the user object. If you locate the user by using Find instead, the Copy option is not available when right-clicking a user in the search results window.

Using VBScript

ADSI has a CopyHere method, but it is available only for the NDS provider. It was not implemented for the LDAP provider and so copying a user via a single method is not supported.

See Also

Recipe 10.12 for finding the attributes that should be copied when duplicating a user

6.8   Unlocking a User

Problem

You want to unlock a locked out user.

Solution

Using a graphical user interface

1. Open the Active Directory Users and Computers snap-in.
2. In the left pane, right-click on the domain and select Find.
3. Select the appropriate domain beside In.
4. Type the name of the user beside Name and click Find Now.
5. In the Search Results, right-click on the user and select Unlock.
6. Click OK.

Using VBScript

```
' This code unlocks a locked user.
' ------ SCRIPT CONFIGURATION ------
strUsername = "<UserName>"        ' e.g. jsmith
strDomain = "<NetBiosDomainName>" ' e.g. RALLENCORP
' ------ END CONFIGURATION ---------

set objUser = GetObject("WinNT://" & strDomain & "/" & strUsername)
if objUser.IsAccountLocked = TRUE then
```

```
    objUser.IsAccountLocked = FALSE
    objUser.SetInfo
    WScript.Echo "Account unlocked"
else
    WScript.Echo "Account not locked"
end if
```

Discussion

If you've enabled account lockouts in a domain (see Recipe 6.11), users will inevitably get locked out. A user can get locked out for a number of reasons, but generally it is either because a user mistypes his password a number of times, or he changes his password and does not log off and log on again, or has mapped drives.

You can use ADSI's `IADsUser::IsAccountLocked` method to determine if a user is locked out. You can set `IsAccountLocked` to FALSE to unlock a user. Unfortunately, there is a bug with the LDAP provider version of this method so you have to use the WinNT provider instead. See MS KB 250873 for more information on this bug.

See Also

Recipe 6.9 for finding locked out users, Recipe 6.11 for viewing the account lockout policy, MS KB 250873 (Programmatically Changing the Lockout Flag in Windows 2000), and MSDN: Account Lockout

6.9   Finding Locked Out Users

Problem

You want to find users that are locked out.

Solution

Using a command-line interface

The following command finds all locked-out users in the domain of the specified domain controller:

```
> unlock <DomainControllerName> *  -view
```

 Unlock.exe was written by Joe Richards (*http://www.joeware.net/*) and can be downloaded from *http://www.joeware.net/win32/zips/Unlock.zip*.

Discussion

Finding the accounts that are currently locked out is a surprisingly complicated task. You would imagine that you could run a query similar to the one to find disabled users, but unfortunately, it is not that easy.

The lockoutTime attribute is populated with a timestamp when a user is locked. One way to find locked out users would be to find all users that have something populated in lockoutTime (i.e., lockoutTime=*). That query would definitely find all the currently locked users, but it would also find all the users that were locked, became unlocked, and have yet to log in since being unlocked. This is where the complexity comes into place.

To determine the users that are currently locked out, you have to query the lockoutDuration attribute stored on the domain object (e.g., *dc=rallencorp,dc=com*). This attribute defines the number of minutes that an account will stay locked before becoming automatically unlocked. We need to take this value and subtract it from the current time to derive a timestamp that would be the outer marker for which users could still be locked. We can then compare this timestamp with the lockoutTime attribute of user objects. The search filter to find all locked users once you've determined the locked timestamp would look something like this:

```
(&(objectcategory=Person)(objectclass=user)(lockoutTime>DerivedTimestamp))
```

For any users that have a lockoutTime that is less than the derived timestamp, their account has already been automatically unlocked per the lockoutDuration setting.

None of the current standard GUI or CLI tools incorporate this kind of logic, but fortunately, Joe Richards wrote the unlock.exe utility, which does. And as its name implies, you can also unlock locked accounts with it as well. Thanks, Joe!

See Also

MS KB 813500 (Support WebCast: Microsoft Windows 2000 Server and Windows Server 2003: Password and Account Lockout Features)

6.10 Troubleshooting Account Lockout Problems

Problem

A user is having account lockout problems and you need to determine where it is getting locked from and how it is getting locked out.

Solution

Using a graphical user interface

LockoutStatus is a new tool available for Windows 2000 or Windows Server 2003 that can help identify which domain controllers users are getting locked out. It works by querying the lockout status of a user against all domain controllers in the user's domain.

To determine the lockout status of a user

1. Open LockoutStatus and select File → Select Target from the menu.
2. Enter the target user name and the domain of the user.
3. Click OK.

At this point, each domain controller in the domain will be queried and the results will be displayed.

Discussion

The Lockoutstatus.exe tool is just one of many that are available in the new "Account Lockout and Management" tool set provided by Microsoft. These new lockout tools are intended to help administrators with account lockout problems that are very difficult to troubleshoot given the tools available under Windows 2000. Along with the tool mentioned in the Solution Section, here are a few others that are included in the set:

ALockout.dll

A script that uses this DLL called *EnableKerbLog.vbs* is included with the tool set that can be used to enable logging of application authentication. This can help identify applications using bad credentials that are causing account lockouts.

ALoInfo.exe

Displays services and shares that are using a particular account name. It can also print all the users and their password age.

NLParse.exe

Filter tool for the *netlogon.log* files. You can use it to extract just the lines that relate to account lockout information.

All of the new Account Lockout tools can be downloaded from:

http://microsoft.com/downloads/details.aspx?familyid=7AF2E69C-91F3-4E63-8629-B999ADDE0B9E&displaylang=en.

See Also

MS KB 813500 (Support WebCast: Microsoft Windows 2000 Server and Windows Server 2003: Password and Account Lockout Features)

6.11   Viewing the Account Lockout and Password Policies

Problem

You want to view the account lockout and password policies for a domain.

Solution

Using a graphical user interface

1. Open the Domain Security Policy snap-in.
2. In the left menu, expand Default Domain Policy → Computer Configuration → Windows Settings → Security Settings → Account Policies.
3. Click on Password Policy or Account Lockout Policy and double-click the property you want to set or view in the right frame.

Using a command-line interface

```
> enumprop /ATTR:↵
lockoutduration,lockoutthreshold,lockoutobservationwindow,maxpwdage,minpwdage,↵
minpwdlength,pwdhistorylength,pwdproperties "LDAP://<DomainDN>"
```

Using VBScript

```
' This code displays the current settings for the password
' and account lockout policies.
' ------ SCRIPT CONFIGURATION ------
strDomain = "<DomainDN>"   ' e.g. rallencorp.com
' ------ END CONFIGURATION ---------

set objRootDSE = GetObject("LDAP://" & strDomain & "/RootDSE")
set objDomain  = GetObject("LDAP://" & _
                           objRootDSE.Get("defaultNamingContext") )

' Hash containing the domain password and lockout policy attributes
' as keys and the units (e.g. minutes) as the values
set objDomAttrHash = CreateObject("Scripting.Dictionary")
objDomAttrHash.Add "lockoutDuration", "minutes"
objDomAttrHash.Add "lockoutThreshold", "attempts"
objDomAttrHash.Add "lockoutObservationWindow", "minutes"
objDomAttrHash.Add "maxPwdAge", "minutes"
objDomAttrHash.Add "minPwdAge", "minutes"
```

```
objDomAttrHash.Add "minPwdLength", "characters"
objDomAttrHash.Add "pwdHistoryLength", "remembered"
objDomAttrHash.Add "pwdProperties", " "

' Iterate over each attribute and print it
for each strAttr in objDomAttrHash.Keys
   if IsObject( objDomain.Get(strAttr) ) then
      set objLargeInt = objDomain.Get(strAttr)
      if objLargeInt.LowPart = 0 then
         value = 0
      else
         value = Abs(objLargeInt.HighPart * 2^32 + objLargeInt.LowPart)
         value = int ( value / 10000000 )
         value = int ( value / 60 )
      end if
   else
      value = objDomain.Get(strAttr)
   end if
   WScript.Echo strAttr & " = " & value & " " & objDomAttrHash(strAttr)
next

'Constants from DOMAIN_PASSWORD_INFORMATION
Set objDomPassHash = CreateObject("Scripting.Dictionary")
objDomPassHash.Add "DOMAIN_PASSWORD_COMPLEX", &h1
objDomPassHash.Add "DOMAIN_PASSWORD_NO_ANON_CHANGE", &h2
objDomPassHash.Add "DOMAIN_PASSWORD_NO_CLEAR_CHANGE", &h4
objDomPassHash.Add "DOMAIN_LOCKOUT_ADMINS", &h8
objDomPassHash.Add "DOMAIN_PASSWORD_STORE_CLEARTEXT", &h16
objDomPassHash.Add "DOMAIN_REFUSE_PASSWORD_CHANGE", &h32

' The PwdProperties attribute requires special processing because
' it is a flag that holds multiple settings.
for each strFlag In objDomPassHash.Keys
   if objDomPassHash(strFlag) and objDomain.Get("PwdProperties") then
     WScript.Echo "  " & strFlag & " is enabled"
   else
     WScript.Echo "  " & strFlag & " is disabled"
   end If
next
```

Discussion

Several parameters controlling account lockout and password complexity can be set on the Domain Security GPO. The properties that can be set for the "Account Lockout Policy" include:

Account lockout duration
> Number of minutes an account will be locked before being automatically unlocked. A value of 0 indicates accounts will be locked out indefinitely, i.e., until an administrator manually unlocks them.

Account lockout threshold
> Number of failed logon attempts after which an account will be locked.

Reset account lockout counter after
> Number of minutes after a failed logon attempt that the failed logon counter for an account will be reset to 0.

The properties that can be set for the "Password Policy" include:

Enforce password history
> Number of passwords to remember before a user can reuse a previous password.

Maximum password age
> Maximum number of days a password can be used before a user must change it.

Minimum password age
> Minimum number of days a password must be used before it can be changed.

Minimum password length
> Minimum number of characters a password must be.

Password must meet complexity requirements
> If enabled, passwords must meet all of the following criteria:
>
> - Not contain all or part of the user's account name
> - Be at least six characters in length
> - Contain characters from three of the following four categories:
>   — English uppercase characters (A–Z)
>   — English lowercase characters (a–z)
>   — Base 10 digits (0–9)
>   — Nonalphanumeric characters (e.g., !, $, #, %)

Store passwords using reversible encryption
> If enabled, passwords are stored in such a way that they can be retrieved and decrypted. This is essentially the same as storing passwords in plain text.

Using a graphical user interface

On a domain controller or machine that has *adminpak.msi* installed, the Domain Security Policy snap-in is present from the Start menu under Administrative Tools. On a member server, you need to open the GPO snap-in and locate the Domain Security policy. See Recipe 9.0 for more information on GPOs.

Using a command-line interface

There is no standard CLI that can be used to modify a GPO, but you can use enumprop to view each of the attributes on the domain object that make up the account lockout and password policy settings.

Using VBScript

The VBScript solution required quite a bit of code to perform a simple task; printing out the account lockout and password policy settings. First, I created a Dictionary object with each of the six attributes as the keys and the unit's designation for each key (e.g., minutes) as the value. I then iterated over each key, printing it along with the value retrieved from the domain object.

Some additional code was necessary to distinguish between the values returned from some of the attributes. In the case of the time-based attributes, such as lockoutDuration, a IADsLargeInteger object was returned from the Get method instead of a pure integer or string value. IADsLargeInteger objects represent 64-bit, also known as Integer8, numbers. 32-bit systems, which make up the majority of systems today, have to break 64-bit numbers into two parts (a high and low part) in order to store them. Unfortunately, VBScript cannot natively handle a 64-bit number and stores it as a double precision. To convert a 64-bit number into something VBScript can handle, we have to first multiply the high part by 4,294,967,296 (2^{32}) and then add the low part to the result.

```
value = Abs(objLargeInt.HighPart * 2^32 + objLargeInt.LowPart)
```

Then I divided by 10,000,000 or 10^7, which represents the number of 100 nanosecond intervals per second.

```
value = int ( value / 10000000 )
```

I then used the int function to discard any remainder and finally divided the result by 60 (number of seconds).

```
value = int ( value / 60 )
```

Note that the result is only an approximation in minutes and can be off by several minutes, hours, or even days depending on the original value.

The last part of the code iterates over another Dictionary object that contains constants representing various flags that can be set as part of the pwdProperties attribute.

See Also

MS KB 221930 (Domain Security Policy in Windows 2000), MS KB 255550 (Configuring Account Policies in Active Directory), MSDN: IADsLargeInteger, and MSDN: DOMAIN_PASSWORD_INFORMATION

6.12   Enabling and Disabling a User

Problem

You want to enable or disable a user.

Solution

Using a graphical user interface

1. Open the Active Directory Users and Computers snap-in.

2. In the left pane, right-click on the domain and select Find.

3. Select the appropriate domain beside In.

4. Type the name of the user beside Name and click Find Now.

5. In the Search Results, right-click on the user and select Enable Account to enable or Disable Account to disable.

6. Click OK.

Using a command-line interface

To enable a user, use the following command:

```
> dsmod user <UserDN> -disabled no
```

To disable a user, use the following command:

```
> dsmod user <UserDN> -disabled yes
```

Using VBScript

```
' This code will enable or disable a user.
' ------ SCRIPT CONFIGURATION ------
' Set to FALSE to disable account or TRUE to enable account
strDisableAccount = FALSE
strUserDN = "<UserDN>" ' e.g. cn=jsmith,cn=Users,dc=rallencorp,dc=com
' ------ END CONFIGURATION ---------

set objUser = GetObject("LDAP://" & strUserDN)
if objUser.AccountDisabled = TRUE then
   WScript.Echo "Account for " & objUser.Get("cn") & " currently disabled"
   if strDisableAccount = FALSE then
      objUser.AccountDisabled = strDisableAccount
      objUser.SetInfo
      WScript.Echo "Account enabled"
   end if
else
   WScript.Echo "Account currently enabled"
   if strDisableAccount = TRUE then
      objUser.AccountDisabled = strDisableAccount
      objUser.SetInfo
      WScript.Echo "Account disabled"
   end if
end if
```

Discussion

Account status is used to control if a user is allowed to log on or not. When an account is disabled, the user is not allowed to log on to her workstation with the account or access AD controlled resources. Much like the lockout status, the account status is stored as a flag in the userAccountControl attribute (see Recipe 6.24).

There is an IADsUser::AccountDisabled property that allows you to determine and change the status. Set the method FALSE to enable the account or TRUE to disable.

See Also

Recipe 6.13 for finding disabled users, and Recipe 6.24 for more on the userAccountControl attribute

6.13   Finding Disabled Users

Problem

You want to find disabled users in a domain.

Solution

Using a graphical user interface

1. Open the Active Directory Users and Computers snap-in.
2. In the left pane, connect to the domain you want to query.
3. Right-click on the domain and select Find.
4. Beside Find, select Common Queries.
5. Check the box beside "disabled accounts."
6. Click the Find Now button.

Using a command-line interface

```
> dsquery user <DomainDN> -disabled
```

Using VBScript

```
' This code finds all disabled user accounts in a domain.
' ------ SCRIPT CONFIGURATION ------
strDomainDN = "<DomainDN>"    ' e.g. dc=rallencorp,dc=com
' ------ END CONFIGURATION ---------

strBase   = "<LDAP://" & strDomainDN & ">;"
strFilter = "(&(objectclass=user)(objectcategory=person)" & _
            "(useraccountcontrol:1.2.840.113556.1.4.803:=2));"
```

```
strAttrs  = "name;"
strScope  = "subtree"

set objConn = CreateObject("ADODB.Connection")
objConn.Provider = "ADsDSOObject"
objConn.Open "Active Directory Provider"
set objRS = objConn.Execute(strBase & strFilter & strAttrs & strScope)
objRS.MoveFirst
while Not objRS.EOF
    Wscript.Echo objRS.Fields(0).Value
    objRS.MoveNext
wend
```

Discussion

Users in Active Directory can either be enabled or disabled. A disabled user cannot log in to the domain. Unlike account lockout, which is an automatic process that is based on the number of times a user incorrectly enters a password, an account has to be manually enabled or disabled.

All disabled user accounts have the bit that represents 2 (0010) set in their userAccountControl attribute. This doesn't mean that the attribute will be equal to 2, it just means that the bit that equals 2 will be enabled—other bits may also be set. See Recipes 4.9 and 4.12 for a more detailed explanation of bit flags.

See Also

Recipe 6.12 for enabling and disabling users

6.14   Viewing a User's Group Membership

Problem

You want to view the group membership of a user.

Solution

Using a graphical user interface

1. Open the Active Directory Users and Computers snap-in.
2. In the left pane, right-click on the domain and select Find.
3. Select the appropriate domain beside In.
4. Type the name of the user beside Name and click Find Now.
5. In the Search Results, double-click on the user.

6. Click the Member Of tab.

7. To view all indirect group membership (from nested groups), you'll need to double-click on each group.

Using a command-line interface

The following command displays the groups *<UserDN>* is a member of. Use the -expand switch to list nested group membership as well:

```
> dsget user <UserDN> -memberof [-expand]
```

Using VBScript

```
' This code displays the group membership of a user.
' It avoids infinite loops due to circular group nesting by
' keeping track of the groups that have already been seen.
' ------ SCRIPT CONFIGURATION ------
strUserDN = "<UserDN>"   ' e.g. cn=jsmith,cn=Users,dc=rallencorp,dc=com
' ------ END CONFIGURATION ---------

set objUser = GetObject("LDAP://" & strUserDN)
Wscript.Echo "Group membership for " & objUser.Get("cn") & ":"
strSpaces = ""
set dicSeenGroup = CreateObject("Scripting.Dictionary")
DisplayGroups "LDAP://" & strUserDN, strSpaces, dicSeenGroup

Function DisplayGroups ( strObjectADsPath, strSpaces, dicSeenGroup)

   set objObject = GetObject(strObjectADsPath)
   WScript.Echo strSpaces & objObject.Name
   on error resume next ' Doing this to avoid an error when memberOf is empty
   if IsArray( objObject.Get("memberOf") ) then
      colGroups = objObject.Get("memberOf")
   else
      colGroups = Array( objObject.Get("memberOf") )
   end if

   for each strGroupDN In colGroups
      if Not dicSeenGroup.Exists(strGroupDN) then
         dicSeenGroup.Add strGroupDN, 1
         DisplayGroups "LDAP://" & strGroupDN, strSpaces & " ", dicSeenGroup
      end if
   next

End Function
```

Discussion

The memberOf attribute on user objects is multivalued and contains the list of distinguished names for the groups the user is a member. memberOf is actually linked with the member attribute on group objects, which holds the distinguished names of its members. For this reason, you cannot directly modify the `memberOf` attribute; you must instead modify the `member` attribute on the group.

The primary group of a user, which the user is technically a member of, will not be shown in either the CLI or VBScript solutions. This is due to the fact that the primary group is not stored in the `memberOf` attribute like the rest of the groups. See Recipes 6.15 and 7.8 for more on finding the primary group of a user.

See Also

Recipe 7.3 for more on viewing the nested members of a group and Recipe 10.16 for more information on linked attributes

6.15   Changing a User's Primary Group

Problem

You want to change the primary group of a user.

Solution

Using a graphical user interface

1. Open the Active Directory Users and Computers snap-in.
2. In the left pane, right-click on the domain and select Find.
3. Select the appropriate domain beside In.
4. Type the name of the user beside Name and click Find Now.
5. In the Search Results, double-click on the user.
6. Click the Member Of tab.
7. Click on the name of the group you want to set as the primary group.
8. Click the Set Primary Group button.
9. Click OK.

Using VBScript

```
' This code first checks to see if the user's primary group is already
' set to the specified group.  If not it will a) add the user to the group
' if not already a member and b) set the primary group id to the group.
' ------ SCRIPT CONFIGURATION ------
strUserDN  = "<UserDN>"   ' e.g. cn=rallen,ou=Sales,dc=rallencorp,dc=com
strGroupDN = "<GroupDN>"  ' e.g. cn=SalesGroup,ou=Sales,dc=rallencorp,dc=com
' ------ END CONFIGURATION ---------

Const ADS_PROPERTY_APPEND = 3
```

```
    set objUser = GetObject("LDAP://" & strUserDN )
    WScript.Echo

    set objGroup = GetObject("LDAP://" & strGroupDN )
    objGroup.GetInfoEx Array("primaryGroupToken"), 0
    if objGroup.Get("primaryGroupToken") = objUser.Get("primaryGroupID") then
        WScript.Echo "Primary group for user already set to " & strGroupDN
        WScript.Quit
    end if

    intAddMember = 1
    for each strMemberDN in objUser.GetEx("memberOf")
        if LCase(strMemberDN) = LCase(strGroupDN) then
            intAddMember = 0
            Exit for
        end if
    next

    if intAddMember > 0 then
        objGroup.PutEx ADS_PROPERTY_APPEND, "member", Array(strUserDN)
        objGroup.SetInfo
        WScript.Echo "Added " & strUserDN & " as member of " & strGroupDN
    end if

    objUser.Put "primaryGroupID", objGroup.Get("primaryGroupToken")
    objUser.SetInfo
    WScript.Echo "Changed primary group id of " & strUserDN & _
                 " to " & objGroup.Get("primaryGroupToken")
```

Discussion

The primary group is a holdover from Windows NT that was used to support Macintosh and POSIX clients, but it is not used actively in Active Directory. That said, you might have some legacy applications that depend on the primary group, and therefore, you may have to change some users' primary group.

Changing the primary group is not difficult, but it is not straightforward either. The primary group is stored on user objects in the primaryGroupID attribute, which contains the RID of the primary group. You can obtain this value by querying the primaryGroupToken attribute on the target group object. Before you can set the primaryGroupID on the user object, you have to first make sure the user is a member of the group. If you try to set the primaryGroupID for a group in which the user is not a member, you will get an error.

The default primaryGroupID is set to 513 (Domain Users) for all users.

See Also

Recipe 7.8 for determining the group name given a group ID, MS KB 297951 (HOWTO: Use the PrimaryGroupID Attribute to Find the Primary Group for a

User), MS KB 321360 (How to Use Native ADSI Components to Find the Primary Group), and MS KB 243330 (Well Known Security Identifiers in Windows 2000)

6.16   Transferring a User's Group Membership to Another User

Problem

You want to transfer the group membership for one user to another.

Solution

Using a graphical user interface

1. Open the Active Directory Users and Computers snap-in.
2. In the left pane, right-click on the domain and select Find.
3. Select the appropriate domain beside In.
4. Beside Name, type the name of the user you want to transfer groups from and click Find Now.
5. In the Search Results, double-click on the user.
6. Click the Member Of tab.
7. For each group you want to add another user in, do the following:
    a. Double-click on the group.
    b. Click the Members tab.
    c. Click the Add button.
    d. Find the user you want to add in the object picker and click OK.
    e. Click OK.

Using a command-line interface

The following command line will add *<NewUserDN>* to all of the groups that *<CurrentUserDN>* is a member of:

```
> for /F "usebackq delims=""" %i in (`dsget user "<CurrentUserDN>" -memberof`) do↵
dsmod group %i -addmbr "<NewUserDN>"
```

If you want to get fancy and remove *<CurrentUserDN>* from each of the groups in the same operation, simply add an -rmmbr option on the end:

```
> for /F "usebackq delims=""" %i in (`dsget user "<CurrentUserDN>" -memberof`) do↵
dsmod group %i -addmbr "<NewUserDN>" -rmmbr "<CurrentUserDN>"
```

Using VBScript

```
' This code adds the "new" user to the groups the "current"
' user is a member of
' ------ SCRIPT CONFIGURATION ------
strCurrentUserDN = "<CurrentUserDN>"   ' e.g. cn=jsmith,ou=Sales,dc=rallencorp,dc=com
strNewUserDN     = "<NewUserDN>"       ' e.g. cn=rallen,ou=Sales,dc=rallencorp,dc=com"
' ------ SCRIPT CONFIGURATION ------

Const ADS_PROPERTY_APPEND = 3

set objCurrentUser = GetObject("LDAP://" & strCurrentUserDN )
set objNewUser = GetObject("LDAP://" & strNewUserDN )

on error resume next
WScript.Echo "Transfering groups from " & strCurrentUserDN & " to " & strNewUserDN
for each strGroupDN in objCurrentUser.GetEx("memberOf")
    set objGroup = GetObject("LDAP://" & strGroupDN)
    objGroup.PutEx ADS_PROPERTY_APPEND, "member", Array( strNewUserDN )
    objGroup.SetInfo
    if Err then
        WScript.Echo "Error adding user to group: " & strGroupDN
    else
        WScript.Echo "Added user to group: " & strGroupDN
    end if
next
```

Discussion

Employees come and go; people take on new responsibilities and move on to new jobs. It is common to have movement within an organization. When this happens, typically someone is replacing the person that is moving on. The new person needs to get up to speed as quickly as possible, including getting accounts set up and access to any necessary resources. A big part of this includes getting added to the correct groups. You can help facilitate this by using one of the processes outlined in the Solution section to help the user gain access to the exact same groups that the former employee was a member of.

One important issue to point out is that the memberOf attribute, which was used in the Solution section to determine a user's group membership, contains only the groups in the same domain as the user. Any groups the user is a member of outside of the user's domain, will not be transferred. To transfer group membership outside of a domain, you will need to perform a query against the global catalog for all group objects that have a member attribute that contains the DN of the user.

See Also

Recipe 7.4 for adding and removing members of a group

6.17   Setting a User's Password

Problem

You want to set the password for a user.

Solution

Using a graphical user interface

1. Open the Active Directory Users and Computers snap-in.
2. In the left pane, right-click on the domain and select Find.
3. Select the appropriate domain beside In.
4. Type the name of the user beside Name and click Find Now.
5. In the Search Results, right-click on the user and select Reset Password.
6. Enter and confirm the new password.
7. Click OK.

Using a command-line interface

This command changes the password for the user specified by *<UserDN>*. Using * after the -pwd option prompts you for the new password. You can replace * with the password you want to set, but it is not a good security practice since other users that are logged into the machine may be able to see it.

```
> dsmod user <UserDN> -pwd *
```

Using VBScript

```
' This code sets the password for a user.
' ------ SCRIPT CONFIGURATION ------
strUserDN = "<UserDN>"   ' e.g. cn=jsmith,cn=Users,dc=rallencorp,dc=com
strNewPasswd = "NewPasword"
' ------ END CONFIGURATION ---------

set objUser = GetObject("LDAP://" & strUserDN)
objUser.SetPassword(strNewPasswd)
Wscript.Echo "Password set for " & objUser.Get("cn")
```

Discussion

The password for a user is stored in the unicodePwd attribute. You cannot directly modify that attribute, but have to use one of the supported APIs. See Recipe 6.18 to see how to set the password using native LDAP and Recipe 6.19 for changing the password via Kerberos.

With the VBScript solution, you can use the `IADsUser::SetPassword` method or `IADsUser::ChangePassword`. The latter requires the existing password to be known before setting it. This is the method you'd want to use if you've created a web page that accepts the previous password before allowing a user to change it.

See Also

Recipe 6.18 for setting the password via LDAP, Recipe 6.19 for setting the password via Kerberos, MS KB 225511 (New Password Change and Conflict Resolution Functionality in Windows), MS KB 264480 (Description of Password-Change Protocols in Windows 2000), MSDN: IADsUser::SetPassword, and MSDN: IADsUser::ChangePassword

6.18   Setting a User's Password via LDAP

Problem

You want to set the password for a user using LDAP.

Solution

You have to first enable SSL/TLS support in your Active Directory domain. See Recipe 14.1 for more on this.

You can then set the `unicodePwd` attribute of a user object using LDAP operations over an SSL or TLS connection.

The value for the `unicodePwd` attribute must be a Unicode string that is surrounded by quotes and Base64 encoded. See Recipe 10.4 for more on encoding text with Base64.

Discussion

The `unicodePwd` attribute can be directly modified over a SSL or TLS connection, but it can never be read.

See Also

Recipe 10.4 for more on Base64 encoding, Recipe 14.1 for enabling SSL/TLS, MS KB 263991 (How to Set a User's Password with Ldifde), MS KB 264480 (Description of Password-Change Protocols in Windows 2000), and MS KB 269190 (HOWTO: Change a Windows 2000 User's Password Through LDAP)

6.19 Setting a User's Password via Kerberos

Problem

You want to change a password using Kerberos from a Unix machine.

Solution

If you have MIT Kerberos 5 client installed and configured properly, you can run the following commands, which will change your password in Active Directory:

```
$ kinit
Password for jsmith@RALLENCORP.COM: ****
$ kpasswd
Password for jsmith@RALLENCORP.COM: ****
Enter new password: ******
Enter it again: ******
Password changed.
```

Discussion

See Recipe 18.7 for more information on Kerberos.

See Also

MS KB 264480 (Description of Password-Change Protocols in Windows 2000), RFC 3244 (Microsoft Windows 2000 Kerberos Change Password and Set Password Protocols), and IETF draft-ietf-cat-kerb-chg-password-02.txt

6.20 Preventing a User from Changing His Password

Problem

You want to disable a user's ability to change his password.

Solution

Using a graphical user interface

1. Open the Active Directory Users and Computers snap-in.
2. In the left pane, right-click on the domain and select Find.
3. Select the appropriate domain beside In.
4. Beside Name, type the name of the user you want to modify and click Find Now.

5. In the Search Results, double-click on the user.

6. Click the Account tab.

7. Under Account options, check the box beside User cannot change password.

8. Click OK.

Using a command-line interface

```
> dsmod user <UserDN> -canchpwd no
```

Using VBScript

```
' This code disables a user's ability to change password
' ------ SCRIPT CONFIGURATION ------
strUserDN = "<UserDN>"    ' e.g. cn=rallen,ou=Sales,dc=rallencorp,dc=com
' ------ END CONFIGURATION ---------

Const ACETYPE_ACCESS_DENIED_OBJECT = 6
Const ACEFLAG_OBJECT_TYPE_PRESENT = 1
Const RIGHT_DS_CONTROL_ACCESS = 256
Const CHANGE_PASSWORD_GUID = "{ab721a53-1e2f-11d0-9819-00aa0040529b}"

set objUser = GetObject("LDAP://" & strUserDN)
set objSD = objUser.Get("ntSecurityDescriptor")
set objDACL = objSD.DiscretionaryAcl

' Add a deny ACE for Everyone
set objACE = CreateObject("AccessControlEntry")
objACE.Trustee = "Everyone"
objACE.AceFlags = 0
objACE.AceType = ACETYPE_ACCESS_DENIED_OBJECT
objACE.Flags = ACEFLAG_OBJECT_TYPE_PRESENT
objACE.ObjectType = CHANGE_PASSWORD_GUID
objACE.AccessMask = RIGHT_DS_CONTROL_ACCESS
objDACL.AddAce objACE

' Add a deny ACE for Self
set objACE = CreateObject("AccessControlEntry")
objACE.Trustee = "Self"
objACE.AceFlags = 0
objACE.AceType = ACETYPE_ACCESS_DENIED_OBJECT
objACE.Flags = ACEFLAG_OBJECT_TYPE_PRESENT
objACE.ObjectType = CHANGE_PASSWORD_GUID
objACE.AccessMask = RIGHT_DS_CONTROL_ACCESS
objDACL.AddAce objACE

objSD.DiscretionaryAcl = objDACL
objUser.Put "nTSecurityDescriptor", objSD
objUser.SetInfo
WScript.Echo "Enabled no password changing for " & strUserDN
```

Discussion

Even though in the GUI solution you check and uncheck the "User cannot change password" setting, actually making the change in Active Directory is a little more complicated as is evident in the VBScript solution. Not allowing a user to change her password consists of setting two deny Change Password ACEs on the target user object. One deny ACE is for the Everyone account and the other is for Self.

The VBScript solution should work as is, but it is not very robust in terms of checking to see if the ACEs already exist and making sure they are in the proper order. If you need to make the code more robust, I suggest checking out MS KB 269159 for more information on setting ACEs properly.

See Also

MS KB 269159 (HOWTO: Use Visual Basic and ADsSecurity.dll to Properly Order ACEs in an ACL)

6.21 Requiring a User to Change Her Password at Next Logon

Problem

You want to require a user to change her password the next time she logs on to the domain.

Solution

Using a graphical user interface

1. Open the Active Directory Users and Computers snap-in.
2. In the left pane, right-click on the domain and select Find.
3. Select the appropriate domain beside In.
4. Beside Name, type the name of the user you want to modify and click Find Now.
5. In the Search Results, double-click on the user.
6. Click the Account tab.
7. Under Account options, check the box beside User must change password at next logon.
8. Click OK.

Using a command-line interface

```
> dsmod user "<UserDN>" -mustchpwd yes
```

Using VBScript

```
' This code sets the flag that requires a user to change their password
' ------ SCRIPT CONFIGURATION ------
strUserDN = "<UserDN>"  ' e.g. cn=rallen,ou=Sales,dc=rallencorp,dc=com
' ------ END CONFIGURATION ---------

set objUser = GetObject("LDAP://" & strUserDN)
objUser.Put "pwdLastSet", 0
objUser.SetInfo
WScript.Echo "User must change password at next logon: " & strUserDN
```

Discussion

When a user changes her password, a timestamp is written to the pwdLastSet attribute of the user object. When the user logs in to the domain, this timestamp is compared to the maximum password age that is defined by the Domain Security Policy to determine if the password has expired. To force a user to change her password at next logon, set the pwdLastSet attribute of the target user to 0 and verify that the user's account doesn't have the never expire password option enabled.

To disable this option so that a user does not have to change her password, set pwdLastSet to −1. These two values (0 and −1) are the only ones that can be set on the pwdLastSet attribute.

6.22   Preventing a User's Password from Expiring

Problem

You want to prevent a user's password from expiring.

Solution

Using a graphical user interface

1. Open the Active Directory Users and Computers snap-in.
2. In the left pane, right-click on the domain and select Find.
3. Select the appropriate domain beside In.
4. Beside Name, type the name of the user you want to modify and click Find Now.
5. In the Search Results, double-click on the user.
6. Click the Account tab.
7. Under Account options, check the box beside Password never expires.
8. Click OK.

Using a command-line interface

```
> dsmod user "<UserDN>" -pwdneverexpires yes
```

Using VBScript

```
' This code sets a users password to never expire
' See Recipe 4.12 for the code for the CalcBit function
' ------ SCRIPT CONFIGURATION ------
strUserDN = "<UserDN>"   ' e.g. cn=rallen,ou=Sales,dc=rallencorp,dc=com
' ------ END CONFIGURATION ---------

intBit = 65536
strAttr = "userAccountControl"

set objUser = GetObject("LDAP://" & strUserDN)
intBitsOrig = objUser.Get(strAttr)
intBitsCalc = CalcBit(intBitsOrig, intBit, TRUE)
if intBitsOrig <> intBitsCalc then
   objUser.Put strAttr, intBitsCalc
   objUser.SetInfo
   WScript.Echo "Changed " & strAttr & " from " & _
                intBitsOrig & " to " & intBitsCalc
else
   WScript.Echo "Did not need to change " & strAttr & " (" & _
                intBitsOrig & ")"
end if
```

Discussion

Setting a user's password to never expire overrides any password aging policy you've defined in the domain. To disable password expiration, you need to set the bit equivalent of 65536 (i.e., 10000000000000000) in the userAccountControl attribute of the target user.

See Also

Recipe 4.12 for more on modifying a bit-flag attribute and Recipe 6.24 for more on setting the userAccountControl attribute

6.23   Finding Users Whose Passwords Are About to Expire

Problem

You want to find the users whose passwords are about to expire.

Solution

Using a command-line interface

```
> dsquery user -stalepwd <NumDaysSinceLastPwdChange>
```

Using Perl

```perl
#!perl
# This code finds the user accounts whose password is about to expire
# ------ SCRIPT CONFIGURATION ------
# Domain and container/OU to check for accounts that are about to expire
my $domain   = '<DomainDNSName>';
my $cont     = ''; # set to empty string to query entire domain
                   # Or set to a relative path in the domain, e.g. cn=Users
# Days since password change
my $days_ago = <NumDaysSinceLastPwdChange>  # e.g. 60;
# ------ END CONFIGURATION ---------

use strict;
use Win32::OLE;
   $Win32::OLE::Warn = 3;
use Math::BigInt;

# Need to convert the number of seconds from $day_ago
# to a large integer for comparison against pwdLastSet
my $past_secs = time - 60*60*24*$days_ago;
my $intObj = Math::BigInt->new($past_secs);
   $intObj = Math::BigInt->new($intObj->bmul('10 000 000'));
my $past_largeint = Math::BigInt->new(
                                   $intObj->badd('116 444 736 000 000 000'));
   $past_largeint =~ s/^[+-]//;

# Setup the ADO connections
my $connObj                             = Win32::OLE->new('ADODB.Connection');
$connObj->{Provider}                    = "ADsDSOObject";
# Set these next two if you need to authenticate
# $connObj->Properties->{'User ID'}   = '<User>';
# $connObj->Properties->{'Password'}  = '<Password>';
$connObj->Open;
my $commObj                             = Win32::OLE->new('ADODB.Command');
$commObj->{ActiveConnection}         = $connObj;
$commObj->Properties->{'Page Size'} = 1000;
# Grab the default domain naming context
my $rootDSE = Win32::OLE->GetObject("LDAP://$domain/RootDSE");
my $rootNC = $rootDSE->Get("defaultNamingContext");
# Run ADO query and print results
$cont .= "," if $cont and not $cont =~ /,$/;
my $query  = "<LDAP://$domain/$cont$rootNC>;";
$query .=  "(&(objectclass=user)";
$query .=     "(objectcategory=Person)";
$query .=     "(!useraccountcontrol:1.2.840.113556.1.4.803:=2)";
$query .=     "(pwdLastSet<=$past_largeint)";
$query .=     "(!pwdLastSet=0));";
```

```
$query .= "cn,distinguishedName;";
$query .= "subtree";
$commObj->{CommandText} = $query;
my $resObj = $commObj->Execute($query);
die "Could not query $domain: ",$Win32::OLE::LastError,"\n"
    unless ref $resObj;

print "\nUsers who haven't set their passwd in $days_ago days or longer:\n";
my $total = 0;
while (!($resObj->EOF)) {
    print "\t",$resObj->Fields("distinguishedName")->value,"\n";
    $total++;
    $resObj->MoveNext;
}
print "Total: $total\n";
```

Discussion

When a Windows-based client logs on to Active Directory, a check is done against the domain password policy and the user's pwdLastSet attribute to determine if the user's password has expired. If it has, the user is prompted to change it. In a pure Windows-based environment, this notification process may be adequate, but if you have a lot of non-Windows-based computers that are joined to an Active Directory domain (e.g., Kerberos-enabled Unix clients), or you have a lot of application and service accounts, you'll need to develop your own user password expiration notification process. Even in a pure Windows environment, cached logins present a problem because when a user logs into the domain with cached credentials (i.e., when the client is not able to reach a domain controller), this password expiration notification check is not done.

The process of finding users whose passwords are about to expire is a little complicated. Fortunately, the new dsquery user command helps by providing an option for searching for users that haven't changed their password for a number of days (-stalepwd). The downside to the dsquery user command is that it will not only find users whose password is about to expire, but also users that must change their password at next logon (i.e., pwdLastSet = 0). The Perl solution does not suffer from this limitation.

The Perl solution consists of a two-step process. First, we need to calculate a time in the past at which we would consider a password "old" or "about" to expire. The pwdLastSet attribute is a replicated attribute on user objects that contain the timestamp (as a large integer) of when the user last set her password. If today is May 31 and we want to find all users who have not set their password for 30 days, we need to query for user's who have a pwdLastSet timestamp older than May 1.

First, a brief word on timestamps stored as large integers. It may seem odd, but large integer timestamps are represented as the number of 100-nanosecond intervals since January 1, 1601. To convert the current time to a large integer, we have to find the current time in seconds since the epoch (January 1, 1970) multiply that times 10,000,000 and then add 116,444,736,000,000,000 to it. This will give you an approximate time (in 100-nanosecond intervals) as a large integer. It is only an approximate time because when dealing with big numbers like this, a degree of accuracy is lost during the arithmetic.

 I chose to use Perl over VBScript because VBScript doesn't handle computing large integers given the current time and date very well.

All right, now that you know how to calculate the current time, we need to calculate a time in the past as a large integer. Remember, we need to find the time at which passwords are considered close to expiring. In the Perl solution, you can configure the number of days since users changed their password. Once we've calculated this value, all we need is to come up with a search filter that we can use in ADO to find the matching users.

The first part of the filter will match all user objects.

```
$query .= "(&(objectclass=user)";
$query .= "(objectcategory=Person)";
```

But we really only want to find all enabled user objects (do you care if a disabled user object's password is about to expire?). This next bit-wise filter will match only enabled user objects. See Recipe 6.13 for more information on finding disabled and enabled users.

```
$query .= "(!useraccountcontrol:1.2.840.113556.1.4.803:=2)";
```

The next part of the filter is the important part. This is where we use the derived last password change timestamp to compare against pwdLastSet.

```
$query .= "(pwdLastSet<=$past_largeint)";
```

Finally, we exclude all users that are required to change their password at next logon (pwdLastSet equal to zero).

```
$query .= "(!pwdLastSet=0));";
```

See Also

Recipe 6.11 for more on the password policy for a domain, Recipe 6.17 for how to set a user's password, and Recipe 6.22 for how to set a user's password to never expire

6.24 Setting a User's Account Options (userAccountControl)

Problem

You want to view or update the userAccountControl attribute for a user. This attribute controls various account options, such as if the user must change their password at next logon and if the account is disabled.

Solution

Using a graphical user interface

1. Open the Active Directory Users and Computers snap-in.
2. In the left pane, right-click on the domain and select Find.
3. Select the appropriate domain beside In.
4. Beside Name, type the name of the user and click Find Now.
5. In the Search Results, double-click on the user.
6. Select the Account tab.
7. Many of the userAccountControl flags can be set under Account options.
8. Click OK after you're done.

Using a command-line interface

The dsmod user command has several options for setting various userAccountControl flags, as shown in Table 6-2. Each switch accepts yes or no as a parameter to either enable or disable the setting.

Table 6-2. dsmod user options for setting userAccountControl

dsmod user switch	Description
-mustchpwd	Sets whether the user must change password at next logon.
-canchpwd	Sets whether the user can change his password.
-disabled	Set account status to enabled or disabled.
-reversiblepwd	Sets whether the user's password is stored using reversible encryption.
-pwdneverexpires	Sets whether the user's password never expires.

Using VBScript

```
' This code enables or disables a bit value in the userAccountControl attr.
' See Recipe 4.12 for the code for the CalcBit function.
' ------ SCRIPT CONFIGURATION ------
strUserDN = "<UserDN>"        ' e.g. cn=rallen,ou=Sales,dc=rallencorp,dc=com
```

```
intBit = <BitValue>          ' e.g. 65536
boolEnable = <TrueOrFalse> ' e.g. TRUE
' ------ END CONFIGURATION ---------

strAttr = "userAccountControl"
set objUser = GetObject("LDAP://" & strUserDN)
intBitsOrig = objUser.Get(strAttr)
intBitsCalc = CalcBit(intBitsOrig, intBit, boolEnable)
if intBitsOrig <> intBitsCalc then
   objUser.Put strAttr, intBitsCalc
   objUser.SetInfo
   WScript.Echo "Changed " & strAttr & " from " & _
                intBitsOrig & " to " & intBitsCalc
else
   WScript.Echo "Did not need to change " & strAttr & " (" & _
                intBitsOrig & ")"
end if
```

Discussion

The userAccountControl attribute on user (and computer) objects could be considered the kitchen sink of miscellaneous and sometimes completely unrelated user account properties. If you have to work with creating and managing user objects very much, you'll need to become intimately familiar with this attribute.

The userAccountControl attribute is a bit flag, which means you have to take a couple extra steps to search against it or modify it. See Recipe 4.9 for more on searching with a bit-wise filter and Recipe 4.12 for modifying a bit-flag attribute.

The dsmod user command can be used to modify a subset of userAccountControl properties, as shown in Table 6-2. Table 6-3 contains the complete list userAccountControl properties as defined in the ADS_USER_FLAG_ENUM enumeration.

Table 6-3. ADS_USER_FLAG_ENUM values

Name	Value	Description
ADS_UF_SCRIPT	1	Logon script is executed.
ADS_UF_ACCOUNTDISABLE	2	Account is disabled.
ADS_UF_HOMEDIR_REQUIRED	8	Home Directory is required.
ADS_UF_LOCKOUT	16	Account is locked out.
ADS_UF_PASSWD_NOTREQD	32	A password is not required.
ADS_UF_PASSWD_CANT_CHANGE	64	Read-only flag that indicates if the user cannot change their password.
ADS_UF_ENCRYPTED_TEXT_PASSWORD_ALLOWED	128	Store password using reversible encryption.

Table 6-3. ADS_USER_FLAG_ENUM values (continued)

Name	Value	Description
ADS_UF_TEMP_DUPLICATE_ACCOUNT	256	Account provides access to the domain, but no other domain that trusts the domain.
ADS_UF_NORMAL_ACCOUNT	512	Enabled user account.
ADS_UF_INTERDOMAIN_TRUST_ACCOUNT	2048	A permit to trust account for a system domain that trusts other domains.
ADS_UF_WORKSTATION_TRUST_ACCOUNT	4096	Enabled computer account.
ADS_UF_SERVER_TRUST_ACCOUNT	8192	Computer account for backup domain controller.
ADS_UF_DONT_EXPIRE_PASSWD	65536	Password will not expire.
ADS_UF_MNS_LOGON_ACCOUNT	131072	MNS logon account.
ADS_UF_SMARTCARD_REQUIRED	262144	Smart card is required for logon.
ADS_UF_TRUSTED_FOR_DELEGATION	524288	Allow Kerberos delegation.
ADS_UF_NOT_DELEGATED	1048576	Do not allow Kerberos delegation even if ADS_UF_TRUSTED_FOR_DELETATION is enabled.
ADS_UF_USE_DES_KEY_ONLY	2097152	Requires DES encryption for keys.
ADS_UF_DONT_REQUIRE_PREAUTH	4194304	Account does not require Kerberos preauthentication for logon.
ADS_UF_PASSWORD_EXPIRED	8388608	Read-only flag indicating account's password has expired. Only used with the WinNT provider.
ADS_UF_TRUSTED_TO_AUTHENTICATE_FOR_DELEGATION	16777216	Account is enabled for delegation.

See Also

Recipe 4.12 for setting a bit-flag attribute and MSDN: ADS_USER_FLAG_ENUM

6.25 Setting a User's Account to Expire in the Future

Problem

You want a user's account to expire at some point in the future.

Solution

Using a graphical user interface

1. Open the Active Directory Users and Computers snap-in.
2. In the left pane, right-click on the domain and select Find.
3. Select the appropriate domain beside In.
4. Beside Name, type the name of the user you want to modify and click Find Now.
5. In the Search Results, double-click on the user.
6. Click the Account tab.
7. Under Account expires, select the radio button beside End of.
8. Select the date the account should expire.
9. Click OK.

Using a command-line interface

Valid values for the -acctexpires flag include a positive number of days in the future when the account should expire, 0 to expire the account at the end of the day, or "never" to disable account expiration.

```
> dsmod user "<UserDN>" -acctexpires <NumDays>
```

Using VBScript

```
' This code sets the account expiration date for a user.
' ------ SCRIPT CONFIGURATION ------
strExpireDate = "<Date>"   ' e.g. "07/10/2004"
strUserDN = "<UserDN>"     ' e.g. cn=rallen,ou=Sales,dc=rallencorp,dc=com
' ------ END CONFIGURATION ---------

set objUser = GetObject("LDAP://" & strUserDN)
objUser.AccountExpirationDate = strExpireDate
objUser.SetInfo
WScript.Echo "Set user " & strUserDN & " to expire on " & strExpireDate

' These two lines would disable account expiration for the user
' objUser.Put "accountExpires", 0
' objUser.SetInfo
```

Discussion

User accounts can be configured to expire on a certain date. Account expiration is stored in the accountExpires attribute on a user object. This attribute contains a large integer representation of the date in which the account expires. If you set this attribute to 0, it disables account expiration for the user (i.e., the account will never expire). Note that this is different than the dsmod user command where a value of 0 with -acctexpires will cause the account to expire at the end of the day. Why does it differ from how the accountExpires attribute works? Great question.

See Also

MS KB 318714 (HOW TO: Limit User Logon Time in a Domain in Windows 2000) and MSDN: Account Expiration

6.26 Finding Users Whose Accounts Are About to Expire

Problem

You want to find users whose accounts are about to expire.

Solution

Using Perl

```
# This code finds the user accounts that are about to expire.
# ------ SCRIPT CONFIGURATION ------
# Domain and container/OU to check for accounts that are about to expire
my $domain  = '<DomainDNSName>';  ' e.g. amer.rallencorp.com
my $cont    = ''; # set to empty string to query entire domain
                  # Or set to a relative path in the domain, e.g. cn=Users
# Number of weeks until a user will expire
my $weeks_ago = 4;
# ------ END CONFIGURATION ---------

use strict;
use Win32::OLE;
    $Win32::OLE::Warn = 3;
use Math::BigInt;

# Need to convert the number of seconds until $weeks_ago
# to a large integer for comparison against accountExpires
my $future_secs = time + 60*60*24*7*$weeks_ago;
my $intObj = Math::BigInt->new($future_secs);
    $intObj = Math::BigInt->new($intObj->bmul('10 000 000'));
my $future_largeint =
            Math::BigInt->new($intObj->badd('116 444 736 000 000 000'));
    $future_largeint =~ s/^[+-]//;

# Now need to convert the current time into a large integer
    $intObj = Math::BigInt->new( time );
    $intObj = Math::BigInt->new($intObj->bmul('10 000 000'));
my $current_largeint =
            Math::BigInt->new($intObj->badd('116 444 736 000 000 000'));
    $current_largeint =~ s/^[+-]//;
```

```
# Set up the ADO connections.
my $connObj                             = Win32::OLE->new('ADODB.Connection');
$connObj->{Provider}                    = "ADsDSOObject";
# Set these next two if you need to authenticate
# $connObj->Properties->{'User ID'}     = '<User>';
# $connObj->Properties->{'Password'}    = '<Password>';
$connObj->Open;
my $commObj                             = Win32::OLE->new('ADODB.Command');
$commObj->{ActiveConnection}            = $connObj;
$commObj->Properties->{'Page Size'} = 1000;

# Grab the default domain name.
my $rootDSE = Win32::OLE->GetObject("LDAP://$domain/RootDSE");
my $rootNC = $rootDSE->Get("defaultNamingContext");

# Run ADO query and print results.
$cont .= "," if $cont and not $cont =~ /,$/;
my $query  = "<LDAP://$domain/$cont$rootNC>;";
$query .=  "(&(objectclass=user)";
$query .=     "(objectcategory=Person)";
$query .=     "(!useraccountcontrol:1.2.840.113556.1.4.803:=2)";
$query .=     "(accountExpires<=$future_largeint)";
$query .=     "(accountExpires>=$current_largeint)";
$query .=     "(!accountExpires=0));";
$query .=  "cn,distinguishedName;";
$query .= "subtree";
$commObj->{CommandText} = $query;
my $resObj = $commObj->Execute($query);
die "Could not query $domain: ",$Win32::OLE::LastError,"\n"
   unless ref $resObj;

print "\nUsers whose account will expire in $weeks_ago weeks or less:\n";
my $total = 0;
while (!($resObj->EOF)) {
   print "\t",$resObj->Fields("distinguishedName")->value,"\n";
   $total++;
   $resObj->MoveNext;
}
print "Total: $total\n";
```

Discussion

The code to find expiring user objects is very similar to that of Recipe 6.23 for finding expiring passwords. The main difference is that instead of querying the pwdLastSet attribute, we need to query accountExpires. Also, instead of setting accountExpires to a timestamp in the past, as we did for pwdLastSet, it needs to contain a future timestamp for when accounts will expire. This makes the logic only slightly different. Let's break down the search filter and review the other differences.

This part of the filter finds all enabled user objects:

```
$query .=  "(&(objectclass=user)";
$query .=     "(objectcategory=Person)";
$query .=     "(!useraccountcontrol:1.2.840.113556.1.4.803:=2)";
```

This next part finds only the accounts that are going to expire. The second line prevents all currently expired accounts from being returned.

```
$query .=    "(accountExpires<=$future_largeint)";
$query .=    "(accountExpires>=$current_largeint)";
```

The last part of the filter excludes users that are marked to never expire:

```
$query .=    "(!accountExpires=0));";
```

See Also

Recipe 6.23 for more on large integer manipulation, Recipe 6.25 for setting a user's account to expire, and MS KB 318714 (HOW TO: Limit User Logon Time in a Domain in Windows 2000)

6.27   Determining a User's Last Logon Time

 This recipe requires the Windows Server 2003 forest functional level.

Problem

You want to determine the last time a user logged into a domain.

Solution

Using a graphical user interface

If you install the *AcctInfo.dll* extension to Active Directory Users and Computers, you can view the last logon timestamp.

1. Open the Active Directory Users and Computers snap-in.
2. In the left pane, right-click on the domain and select Find.
3. Select the appropriate domain beside In.
4. Beside Name, type the name of the user you want to modify and click Find Now.
5. In the Search Results, double-click on the user.
6. Click the Additional Account Info tab.
7. View the value for Last-Logon-Timestamp.

 AcctInfo.dll can be downloaded from the Microsoft download site:
   http://microsoft.com/downloads/details.aspx?FamilyId=7AF2E69C-91F3-4E63-8629-B999ADDE0B9E&displaylang=en

Using VBScript

```
' This code prints the last logon timestamp for a user.
' ------ SCRIPT CONFIGURATION ------
strUserDN = "<UserDN>"  ' e.g. cn=rallen,ou=Sales,dc=rallencorp,dc=com
' ------ END CONFIGURATION ---------

set objUser =  GetObject("LDAP://" & strUserDN)
set objLogon = objUser.Get("lastLogonTimestamp")
intLogonTime = objLogon.HighPart * (2^32) + objLogon.LowPart
intLogonTime = intLogonTime / (60 * 10000000)
intLogonTime = intLogonTime / 1440
WScript.Echo "Approx last logon timestamp: " & intLogonTime + #1/1/1601#
```

Discussion

Trying to determine when a user last logged on has always been a challenge in the Microsoft NOS environment. In Windows NT, you could retrieve a user's last logon timestamp from a PDC or BDC, but this timestamp was the last time the user logged on to the PDC or BDC. That means in order to determine the actual last logon, you'd have to query every domain controller in the domain. In large environments, this wasn't practical. With Windows 2000 Active Directory, things did not improve much. A lastLogon attribute is used to store the last logon timestamp, but unfortunately, this attribute isn't replicated. So again, to get an accurate picture, you'd have to query every domain controller in the domain for the user's last logon attribute and keep track of the most recent one.

Now with Windows Server 2003, we finally have a viable solution. A new attribute was added to the schema for user objects called lastLogonTimestamp. This attribute is similar to the lastLogon attribute that was available previously, with two distinct differences. First, and most importantly, this attribute is replicated. That means when a user logs in, the lastLogonTimestamp attribute will get populated and then replicate to all domain controllers in the domain.

The second difference is that since lastLogonTimestamp is replicated, special safeguards needed to be put in place so that users that logged in repeatedly over a short period of time did not cause unnecessary replication traffic. For this reason, the lastLogonTimestamp is updated only if the last update occurred a week or more ago. This means that the lastLogonTimestamp attribute could be up to a week off in terms of accuracy with a user's actual last logon. Ultimately, this shouldn't be a problem for most situations because lastLogonTimestamp is intended to address the common problem where administrators want to run a query and determine which users have not logged in over the past month or more.

See Also

Recipe 6.28 for finding users that have not logged on recently

---

6.28 Finding Users Who Have Not Logged On Recently

 This recipe requires the Windows Server 2003 domain functional level.

Problem

You want to determine which users have not logged on recently.

Solution

Using a graphical user interface

1. Open the Active Directory Users and Computers snap-in.
2. In the left pane, right-click on the domain and select Find.
3. Beside Find, select Common Queries.
4. Select the number of days beside Days since last logon.
5. Click the Find Now button.

Using a command-line interface

```
> dsquery user -inactive <NumWeeks>
```

Using Perl

```perl
# This code finds the users that have not logged in over a period of time
# ------ SCRIPT CONFIGURATION ------
# Domain and container/OU to check for inactive accounts
my $domain   = '<DomainDNSName>';  # e.g. amer.rallencorp.com
my $cont     = 'cn=Users'; # set to empty string to query entire domain
                           # Or set to a relative path in the domain:
                           #    e.g. cn=Users
# Number of weeks a user needs to be inactive to be returned
my $weeks_ago = <NumWeeks>;  # e.g. 4
# ------ END CONFIGURATION ---------

use strict;
use Win32::OLE;
   $Win32::OLE::Warn = 3;
use Math::BigInt;

# Need to convert the number of seconds since $weeks_ago
# to a large integer for comparison against lastLogonTimestamp
my $past_secs = time - 60*60*24*7*$weeks_ago;
my $intObj = Math::BigInt->new($past_secs);
```

```perl
    $intObj = Math::BigInt->new($intObj->bmul('10 000 000'));
my $past_largeint = Math::BigInt->new(
                         $intObj->badd('116 444 736 000 000 000'));
    $past_largeint =~ s/^[+-]//;

# Setup the ADO connections
my $connObj                             = Win32::OLE->new('ADODB.Connection');
$connObj->{Provider}                    = "ADsDSOObject";
# Set these next two if you need to authenticate
# $connObj->Properties->{'User ID'}    = '<UserUPNOrDN>';
# $connObj->Properties->{'Password'}   = '<Password>';
$connObj->Open;
my $commObj                             = Win32::OLE->new('ADODB.Command');
$commObj->{ActiveConnection}           = $connObj;
$commObj->Properties->{'Page Size'} = 1000;

# Grab the default domain name
my $rootDSE = Win32::OLE->GetObject("LDAP://$domain/RootDSE");
my $rootNC = $rootDSE->Get("defaultNamingContext");

# Run ADO query and print results
$cont .= "," if $cont and not $cont =~ /,$/;
my $query   = "<LDAP://$domain/$cont$rootNC>;";
$query .=  "(&(objectclass=user)";
$query .=    "(objectcategory=Person)";
$query .=    "(!useraccountcontrol:1.2.840.113556.1.4.803:=2)";
$query .=    "(lastlogontimestamp<=$past_largeint));";
$query .=  "cn,distinguishedName;";
$query .= "subtree";
$commObj->{CommandText} = $query;
my $resObj = $commObj->Execute($query);
die "Could not query $domain: ",$Win32::OLE::LastError,"\n"
   unless ref $resObj;

print "\nUsers that have been inactive for $weeks_ago weeks or more:\n";
my $total = 0;
while (!($resObj->EOF)) {
   my $cn  = $resObj->Fields(0)->value;
   print "\t",$resObj->Fields("distinguishedName")->value,"\n";
   $total++;
   $resObj->MoveNext;
}
print "Total: $total\n";
```

Discussion

As I talked about in Recipe 6.27, in Windows Server 2003 a new attribute on user objects called lastLogonTimestamp contains the approximate last time the user logged on. Using this to find the users that have not logged on in a number of weeks is much easier than the option with Windows 2000, where we would need to query every domain controller in the domain.

The GUI and CLI solutions are straightforward, but the Perl solution is a little more complicated. The code is very similar to that of Recipe 6.27, and I suggest reading that if you are curious about the large integer conversions going on.

See Also

Recipe 6.23 for more on computing large integer timestamps and Recipe 6.27 for more on finding a user's last logon timestamp

6.29 Setting a User's Profile Attributes

Problem

You want to set one or more of the user profile attributes.

Solution

Using a graphical user interface

1. Open the Active Directory Users and Computers snap-in.
2. In the left pane, right-click on the domain and select Find.
3. Select the appropriate domain beside In.
4. Beside Name, type the name of the user and click Find Now.
5. In the Search Results, double-click on the user.
6. Click the Profile tab.
7. Modify the various profile settings as necessary.
8. Click OK.

Using a command-line interface

```
> dsmod user "<UserDN>" -loscr <ScriptPath> -profile <ProfilePath> -hmdir↵
<HomeDir> -hmdrv <DriveLetter>
```

Using VBScript

```
' This code sets the various profile related attributes for a user.
strUserDN = "<UserDN>"    ' e.g. cn=jsmith,cn=Users,dc=rallencorp,dc=com
set objUser = GetObject("LDAP://" & strUserDN)
objUser.Put "homeDirectory", "\\fileserver\" & objUser.Get("sAMAccountName")
objUser.Put "homeDrive", "z:"
objUser.Put "profilePath", "\\fileserver\" & _
            objUser.Get("sAMAccountName") & "\profile"
objUser.Put "scriptPath", "login.vbs"
objUser.SetInfo
Wscript.Echo "Profile info for " & objUser.Get("sAMAccountName") & " updated"
```

Discussion

The four attributes that make up a user's profile settings include the following:

homeDirectory
: UNC path to home directory

homeDrive
: Drive letter (e.g., z:) to map home directory

profilePath
: UNC path to profile directory

scriptPath
: Path to logon script

When you set the homeDirectory attribute, the folder being referenced needs to already exist. For an example on creating shares for users, see MS KB 234746.

See Also

MS KB 234746 (How to Create User Shares for All Users in a Domain with ADSI), MS KB 271657 (Scripted Home Directory Paths Require That Folders Exist), and MS KB 320043 (HOW TO: Assign a Home Directory to a User)

6.30   Viewing a User's Managed Objects

Problem

You want to view the objects owned by a user.

Solution

Using a graphical user interface

1. Open ADSI Edit.

2. If an entry for the naming context you want to browse is not already displayed, do the following:

3. Right-click on ADSI Edit in the right pane and click Connect to.

4. Fill in the information for the naming context, container, or OU you want to add an object to. Click on the Advanced button if you need to enter alternate credentials.

5. In the left pane, browse to the naming context, container, or OU the object you want to view. Once you've found the object, right-click on it and select Properties.

6. View the managedObjects attribute.

Using a command-line interface

```
> enumprop /ATTR:managedObjects "LDAP://<UserDN>"
```

Using VBScript

```
' This code displays the managed objects for a user
' ------ SCRIPT CONFIGURATION ------
strUserDN = "<UserDN>"  ' e.g. cn=jsmith,cn=Users,dc=rallencorp,dc=com
' ------ END CONFIGURATION ---------

on error resume next
set objUser = GetObject("LDAP://" & strUserDN)
Wscript.Echo objUser.Get("cn") & "'s Managed Objects:"
colObjects =  objUser.GetEx("managedObjects")
if Err.Number = -2147463155 then
   Wscript.Echo " none"
else
   for each strObjectDN in colObjects
      Wscript.Echo " " & strObjectDN
   next
end if
```

Discussion

The managedObjects attribute is linked to the managedBy attribute that can be set on certain objects in Active Directory like computers and groups. Setting the managedBy attribute provides a quick and dirty way to define who owns an object. If you do use it, you can use the managedObjects attribute on user objects to get the list of objects the user has been configured in the managedBy attribute for.

6.31 Modifying the Default Display Name Used When Creating Users in ADUC

Problem

You want to modify how the default display name gets generated when you create a new user through the Active Directory Users and Computers snap-in.

Solution

Using a graphical user interface

1. Open ADSI Edit.
2. In the Configuration Naming Context browse to DisplaySpecifiers → <Locale> where <Locale> is the locale for your language (e.g., the US English locale is 409).
3. Double-click on cn=user-Display.

4. Edit the `createDialog` attribute with the value you want the new default to be (e.g., %<sn>, %<givenName>).

5. Click OK.

Using VBScript

```
' This code modifies the default ADUC display name.
' ------ SCRIPT CONFIGURATION ------
strNewDefault = "%<sn>, %<givenName>"
strForestName = "<ForestDNSName>"        ' e.g. rallencorp.com
' ------ END CONFIGURATION ---------

Set objRootDSE = GetObject("LDAP://" & strForestName & "/RootDSE")
Set objDispSpec = GetObject("LDAP://cn=User-Display,cn=409," & _
                            "cn=DisplaySpecifiers," & _
                            objRootDSE.Get("ConfigurationNamingContext"))
objDispSpec.Put "createDialog", strNewDefault
objDispSpec.SetInfo
WScript.Echo "New default for user's display name has been set to: " & _
             strNewDefault
```

Discussion

When you create a new user object in the Active Directory Users and Computers snap-in, it will automatically fill in the Full Name field as you type in the First Name, Initials, and Last Name fields. As a convenience, you may want to alter that behavior so that it automatically fills in a different value. To do that, you need to modify the User-Display display specifier, which has the following distinguished name:

cn=user-Display,cn=<Locale>,cn=DisplaySpecifiers,cn=Configuration,<ForestRootDN>

<Locale> should be replaced with your language specific locale and <ForestRootDN> should contain the distinguished name for your forest root domain. You need to modify the createDialog attribute, which by default has no value. Replacement variables are presented by %<attribute>, where attribute is an attribute name. For example, if you wanted to make the default be "LastName, FirstName" you would use the following value:

%<sn>, %<givenName>

See Also

MS KB 250455 (XADM: How to Change Display Names of Active Directory Users)

6.32 Creating a UPN Suffix for a Forest

Problem

You want users to have a different User Principal Name (UPN) suffix from the default provided by your forest.

Solution

Using a graphical user interface

1. Open the Active Directory Domains and Trusts snap-in.
2. In the left pane, right-click Active Directory Domains and Trusts and select Properties.
3. Under Alternate UPN suffixes, type the name of the suffix you want to add.
4. Click Add and OK.

Using VBScript

```
' This code adds a new UPN suffix.
' ------ SCRIPT CONFIGURATION ------
strNewSuffix = "<NewSuffix>"     ' e.g. othercorp.com
strDomain = "<DomainDNSName>"    ' e.g. rallencorp.com
' ------ END CONFIGURATION ---------

set objRootDSE = GetObject("LDAP://" & strDomain & "/RootDSE")
set objPartitions = GetObject("LDAP://cn=Partitions," & _
                              objRootDSE.Get("ConfigurationNamingContext"))
objPartitions.PutEx ADS_PROPERTY_APPEND, "uPNSuffixes", Array(strNewSuffix)
objPartitions.SetInfo
```

Discussion

The UPN allows users to log on with a friendly name that may even correspond to their email address. UPN logons also do not require the domain to be known so that it can be abstracted away from the user. You may need to create an additional UPN suffix (e.g., *@rallencorp.com*) if you want UPNs to map to email addresses, but your AD forest is rooted at a different domain name (e.g., *ad.rallencorp.com*) than the domain name used in email addresses (e.g., *rallencorp.com*).

Using VBScript

UPN suffixes are stored in the multivalued uPNSuffixes attribute on the Partitions container in the configuration-naming context. The default forest UPN suffix is assumed and not stored in that attribute.

See Also

MS KB 243280 (Users Can Log On Using User Name or User Principal Name), MS KB 243629 (HOW TO: Add UPN Suffixes to a Forest), and MS KB 269441 (HOWTO: Use ADSI to List the UPN Suffixes That Are Defined in Active Directory)

## CHAPTER 7

Groups

7.0   Introduction

A group is a simple concept that has been used in many different types of systems over the years. In generic terms, a group is just a collection of things. Groups are used most frequently in a security context whereby you set up a group of users and apply certain permissions or rights to that group. Using a group is much easier when applying security than using individual users because you have to apply the security only once instead of once per user.

In Active Directory, groups are flexible objects that can contain virtually any other type of object as a member. Active Directory groups can be used for many different purposes including controlling access to resources, defining a filter for the application of group policies, and as an email distribution list.

The scope and type of a group defines how the group can be used in a forest. The type of a group can be either security or distribution. Security groups can be used to restrict access to resources whereas distribution groups can be used only as a simple grouping mechanism. Both group types can be used as email lists. The scope of a group determines where members of the group can be located in the forest and where in the forest you can use the group in ACLs. The supported group scopes include universal, global, and domain local. Universal groups and domain local groups can have members that are part of any domain in the forest. Global groups can only have members that are part of the same domain the group is in.

The Anatomy of a Group

Groups are represented in Active Directory by group objects. Table 7-1 contains a list of some of the noteworthy attributes that are available on group objects.

Table 7-1. Attributes of group objects

Attribute	Description
cn	Relative distinguished name of group objects.
createTimestamp	Timestamp of when the OU was created.
description	Textual description of the group.
groupType	Flag containing the group scope and type. See Recipe 7.6 for more information.
info	Additional notes about a group.
primaryGroupToken	Local RID for the group. This matches the primaryGroupID attribute that is set on user objects.
managedBy	DN of a user or group that is the owner of the group.
managedObjects	List of DNs of objects this group is listed in the managedBy attribute for.
member	List of DNs of members of the group.
memberOf	List of DNs of the groups this group is a member of.
modifyTimestamp	Timestamp of when the OU was last modified.
sAMAccountName	Down-level account name for the group. Typically this is the same as the cn attribute.
wWWHomePage	URL of the home page for the group.

7.1   Creating a Group

Problem

You want to create a group.

Solution

Using a graphical user interface

1. Open the Active Directory Users and Computers (ADUC) snap-in.
2. If you need to change domains, right-click on Active Directory Users and Computers in the left pane, select Connect to Domain, enter the domain name and click OK.
3. In the left pane, browse to the parent container of the new group, right-click on it, and select New → Group.
4. Enter the name of the group and select the group scope (global, domain local, or universal) and group type (security or distribution).
5. Click OK.

Using a command-line interface

In the following example, <GroupDN> should be replaced with the DN of the group to create, <GroupScope> should be 1, g, or u for domain local, global, and universal groups, respectively, and -secgroup should be set to yes if the group is a security group or no otherwise. Another recommended option is to set -desc for specifying a group description.

```
> dsadd group "<GroupDN>" -scope <GroupScope> -secgrp yes|no -desc "<GroupDesc>"
```

Using VBScript

```
' The following code creates a global security group.
' ------ SCRIPT CONFIGURATION ------
strGroupParentDN = "<GroupParentDN>"   ' e.g. ou=Groups,dc=rallencorp,dc=com
strGroupName     = "<GroupName>"       ' e.g. ExecAdminsSales
strGroupDescr    = "<GroupDesc>"       ' e.g. Executive Admins for Sales group
' ------ END CONFIGURATION ---------

' Constants taken from ADS_GROUP_TYPE_ENUM
Const ADS_GROUP_TYPE_DOMAIN_LOCAL_GROUP = 1
Const ADS_GROUP_TYPE_GLOBAL_GROUP       = 2
Const ADS_GROUP_TYPE_LOCAL_GROUP        = 4
Const ADS_GROUP_TYPE_SECURITY_ENABLED   = -2147483648
Const ADS_GROUP_TYPE_UNIVERSAL_GROUP    = 8

set objOU = GetObject("LDAP://" & strGroupParentDN)
set objGroup = objDomain.Create("group","cn=" & strGroupName)
objGroup.Put "groupType", ADS_GROUP_TYPE_GLOBAL_GROUP _
                          Or ADS_GROUP_TYPE_SECURITY_ENABLED
objOU.Put "description", strGroupDescr
objOU.SetInfo
```

Discussion

In each solution, a group was created with no members. For more information on how to add and remove members, see Recipe 7.4.

The groupType attribute contains a flag indicating both group scope and type. The available flag values are defined in the ADS_GROUP_TYPE_ENUM enumeration. Recipe 7.6 contains more information on setting the group scopes and types.

See Also

Recipe 7.4 for adding and removing group members, Recipe 7.6 for setting group scope and type, MS KB 231273 (Group Type and Scope Usage in Windows), MS KB 232241 (Group Management with ADSI in Windows 2000), MS KB 320054 (HOW TO: Manage Groups in Active Directory in Windows 2000), and MSDN: ADS_GROUP_TYPE_ENUM

7.2   Viewing the Direct Members of a Group

Problem

You want to view the direct members of a group.

Solution

Using a graphical user interface

1. Open the Active Directory Users and Computers snap-in.
2. If you need to change domains, right-click on Active Directory Users and Computers in the left pane, select Connect to Domain, enter the domain name, and click OK.
3. In the left pane, right-click on the domain and select Find.
4. Enter the name of the group and click Find Now.
5. Double-click on the group in the bottom results pane.
6. Click the Members tab.

Using a command-line interface

```
> dsget group "<GroupDN>" -members
```

Using VBScript

```
' This code prints the direct members of the specified group.
' ------ SCRIPT CONFIGURATION ------
strGroupDN = "<GroupDN>" ' e.g. cn=SalesGroup,ou=Groups,dc=rallencorp,dc=com
' ------ END CONFIGURATION ---------

set objGroup = GetObject("LDAP://" & strGroupDN)
Wscript.Echo "Members of " & objGroup.Name & ":"
for each objMember in objGroup.Members
    Wscript.Echo objMember.Name
next
```

Discussion

The member attribute of a group object contains the distinguished names of the direct members of the group. By direct members, I mean the members that have been directly added to the group. This is in contrast to indirect group members, which are members of the group due to nested group membership. See Recipe 7.3 for how to find the nested membership of a group.

See Also

Recipe 7.3 for viewing nested group membership

7.3   Viewing the Nested Members of a Group

Problem

You want to view the nested members of a group.

Solution

Using a graphical user interface

1. Open the Active Directory Users and Computers snap-in.

2. If you need to change domains, right-click on Active Directory Users and Computers in the left pane, select Connect to Domain, enter the domain name, and click OK.

3. In the left pane, right-click on the domain and select Find.

4. Enter the name of the group and click Find Now.

5. Double-click on the group in the bottom results pane.

6. Click the Members tab.

7. You now have to double-click on each group member to view its membership.

Using a command-line interface

```
> dsget group "<GroupDN>" -members -expand
```

Using VBScript

```
' This code prints the nested membership of a group.
' ------ SCRIPT CONFIGURATION ------
strGroupDN = "<GroupDN>"   ' e.g. cn=SalesGroup,ou=Groups,dc=rallencorp,dc=com
' ------ END CONFIGURATION ---------

strSpaces  = " "
set dicSeenGroupMember = CreateObject("Scripting.Dictionary")
Wscript.Echo "Members of " & strGroupDN & ":"
DisplayMembers "LDAP://" & strGroupDN, strSpaces, dicSeenGroupMember

Function DisplayMembers ( strGroupADsPath, strSpaces, dicSeenGroupMember)

   set objGroup = GetObject(strGroupADsPath)
   for each objMember In objGroup.Members
      Wscript.Echo strSpaces & objMember.Name
      if objMember.Class = "group" then
         if dicSeenGroupMember.Exists(objMember.ADsPath) then
```

```
                  Wscript.Echo strSpaces & "   ^ already seen group member " & _
                                    "(stopping to avoid loop)"
               else
                  dicSeenGroupMember.Add objMember.ADsPath, 1
                  DisplayMembers objMember.ADsPath, strSpaces & " ", _
                              dicSeenGroupMember
               end if
            end if
         next

      End Function
```

Discussion

As described in Recipe 7.2, group membership is stored in the multivalued `member` attribute on group objects. But that attribute will not show the complete picture because group nesting is allowed in Active Directory after you've transitioned from mixed mode. To view the complete group membership, you have to recurse through each group's members.

In the VBScript example, I used a dictionary object (referred to as a hash or associative array in other languages) to ensure I did not get in an infinite loop. The dictionary object stores each group member; before the `DisplayMembers` function is called a check is performed to determine if the group has already been evaluated. If so, a message is displayed indicating the group will not be processed again. If this type of checking was not employed and you had a situation where group A was a member of group B, group B was a member of group C, and group C was a member of group A, the loop would repeat without terminating.

See Also

Recipe 7.2 for viewing group membership and MSDN: IADsMember

7.4   Adding and Removing Members of a Group

Problem

You want to add or remove members of a group.

Solution

Using a graphical user interface

1. Follow the same steps as in Recipe 7.2 to view the members of the group.
2. To remove a member, click on the member name, click the Remove button, click Yes, and click OK.

3. To add a member, click on the Add button, enter the name of the member, and click OK twice.

Using a command-line interface

The -addmbr option adds a member to a group:

```
> dsmod group "<GroupDN>" -addmbr "<MemberDN>"
```

The -rmmbr option removes a member from a group:

```
> dsmod group "<GroupDN>" -rmmbr "<MemberDN>"
```

The -chmbr option replaces the complete membership list:

```
> dsmod group "<GroupDN>" -chmbr "<Member1DN Member2DN ...>"
```

Using VBScript

```
' This code adds a member to a group.
' ------ SCRIPT CONFIGURATION ------
strGroupDN = "<GroupDN>"   ' e.g. cn=SalesGroup,ou=Groups,dc=rallencorp,dc=com
strMemberDN = "<MemberDN>" ' e.g. cn=jsmith,cn=users,dc=rallencorp,dc=com
' ------ END CONFIGURATION ---------

set objGroup = GetObject("LDAP://" & strGroupDN)
' Add a member
objGroup.Add("LDAP://" & strMemberDN)


' This code removes a member from a group.
' ------ SCRIPT CONFIGURATION ------
strGroupDN = "<GroupDN>"   ' e.g. cn=SalesGroup,ou=Groups,dc=rallencorp,dc=com
strMemberDN = "<MemberDN>" ' e.g. cn=jsmith,cn=users,dc=rallencorp,dc=com
' ------ END CONFIGURATION ---------

set objGroup = GetObject("LDAP://" & strGroupDN)
' Remove a member
objGroup.Remove("LDAP://" & strMemberDN)
```

Discussion

Since there are no restrictions on what distinguished names you put in the member attribute, you can essentially have any type of object as a member of a group, which makes groups very useful. While Organizational Units (OUs) are typically used to structure objects that share certain criteria, group objects can be used to create loose collections of objects.

The benefit of using group objects as a collection mechanism is that the same object can be a member of multiple groups whereas an object can only be a part of a single OU. Another key difference is that you can assign permissions on resources to groups because they are considered security principals in Active Directory, whereas

OUs are not. This is different from some other directories, such as Novel Netware, where OUs act more like security principals.

See Also

Recipe 7.2 for viewing group membership, MSDN: IADsGroup::Add, and MSDN: IADsGroup::Remove

7.5   Moving a Group

Problem

You want to move a group to a different OU or domain.

Solution

To move a group to a different OU, follow the instructions in Recipe 4.17. To move a group to a different domain, follow the instructions in Recipe 4.18.

Discussion

The only type of group that can be moved between domains are universal groups. If you want to move a global or domain local group to a different domain, first convert it to a universal group, move the group, then convert it back to a global or domain local group.

When you convert a group between types, you may encounter problems because different groups have different membership restrictions. See Recipe 7.0 for more information on group type membership restrictions.

A much easier way to accomplish inter-domain group moves is by using the Active Directory Migration Tool (ADMT). With ADMT, you can move and restructure groups without needing to go to all the trouble of converting the group to a universal and modifying the group membership. For more information on ADMT, see the following site:

    http://www.microsoft.com/windows2000/downloads/tools/admt/default.asp

See Also

Recipe 4.17 for moving an object to a different OU, Recipe 4.18 for moving an object to a different domain, and Recipe 7.6 for changing group scope and type

7.6 Changing the Scope or Type of a Group

Problem

You want to change the scope or type of a group.

Solution

Using a graphical user interface

1. Open the Active Directory Users and Computers snap-in.
2. If you need to change domains, right-click on Active Directory Users and Computers in the left pane, select Connect to Domain, enter the domain name, and click OK.
3. In the left pane, right-click on the domain and select Find.
4. Enter the name of the group you want to modify and click Find Now.
5. Double-click on the group in the results pane.
6. In the group properties dialog box, select the new scope or type and click OK.

Using a command-line interface

The following example changes the group scope for *<GroupDN>* to *<NewScope>*, which should be l for domain local group, g for global group, or u for universal group.

```
> dsmod group "<GroupDN>" -scope <NewScope>
```

The following example changes the group type for *<GroupDN>*. For the -secgrp switch, specify yes to change to a security group or no to make the group a distribution list.

```
> dsmod group "<GroupDN>" -secgrp yes|no
```

Using VBScript

```
' This code sets the scope and type of the specified group
' to a universal security group.
' ------ SCRIPT CONFIGURATION ------
strGroupDN = "<GroupDN>"   ' e.g. cn=SalesGroup,ou=Groups,dc=rallencorp,dc=com
' ------ END CONFIGURATION ---------

' Constants taken from ADS_GROUP_TYPE_ENUM
ADS_GROUP_TYPE_DOMAIN_LOCAL_GROUP = 1
ADS_GROUP_TYPE_GLOBAL_GROUP       = 2
ADS_GROUP_TYPE_LOCAL_GROUP        = 4
ADS_GROUP_TYPE_SECURITY_ENABLED   = -2147483648
ADS_GROUP_TYPE_UNIVERSAL_GROUP    = 8

set objGroup = GetObject("LDAP://" & strGroupDN )
objGroup.Put "groupType", ADS_GROUP_TYPE_UNIVERSAL_GROUP _
                    Or ADS_GROUP_TYPE_SECURITY_ENABLED
objGroup.SetInfo
```

Discussion

Group scope and type are stored as a flag in the groupType attribute on group objects. To directly update groupType, you must logically OR the values associated with each type and scope, as shown in the API solution. Note that there is no specific value for the distribution list type. If you want to create a distribution list, just do not include the ADS_GROUP_TYPE_SECURITY_ENABLED flag when setting groupType.

 For a good description of the usage scenarios for each group type, see Chapter 11 in *Active Directory*, Second Edition.

See Also

MS KB 231273 (Group Type and Scope Usage in Windows), MSDN: ADS_GROUP_TYPE_ENUM, and MSDN: What Type of Group to Use

7.7 Delegating Control for Managing Membership of a Group

Problem

You want to delegate control of managing the membership of a group.

Solution

Using a graphical user interface

 This is a new feature of Windows Server 2003 version of ADUC.

1. Open the Active Directory Users and Computers snap-in.
2. If you need to change domains, right-click on Active Directory Users and Computers in the left pane, select Connect to Domain, enter the domain name, and click OK.
3. In the left pane, right-click on the domain and select Find.
4. Enter the name of the group and click Find Now.
5. Double-click on the group in the results pane.
6. Select the Managed By tab.
7. Click the Change button.

8. Locate the group or user to delegate control to and click OK.

9. Check the box beside Manager can update membership list.

10. Click OK.

Using a command-line interface

```
> dsacls <GroupDN> /G <GroupName>@DomainName:WP;member;
```

In the following example, the SalesAdmin group will be given rights to modify membership of the PreSales group.

```
> dsacls cn=presales,ou=sales,dc=rallencorp,dc=com /G salesadmins@rallencorp.com:⏎
WP;member;
```

Using VBScript

```
' This code grants write access to the member attribute of a group.
' ------ SCRIPT CONFIGURATION ------
strGroupDN = "<GroupDN>"   ' e.g. cn=SalesGroup,ou=Sales,dc=rallencorp,dc=com"
strUserOrGroup = "<UserOrGroup>"   ' e.g. joe@rallencorp.com or RALLENCORP\joe
' ------ END CONFIGURATION ---------

set objGroup = GetObject("LDAP://" & strGroupDN)
'############################
' Constants
'############################
' ADS_ACETYPE_ENUM
Const ADS_ACETYPE_ACCESS_ALLOWED_OBJECT = &h5
Const ADS_FLAG_OBJECT_TYPE_PRESENT = &h1
Const ADS_RIGHT_DS_WRITE_PROP = &h20

' From schemaIDGUID of member attribute
Const MEMBER_ATTRIBUTE = "{bf9679c0-0de6-11d0-a285-00aa003049e2}"

'############################
' Create ACL
'############################
set objSD = objGroup.Get("ntSecurityDescriptor")
set objDACL = objSD.DiscretionaryAcl

' Set WP for member attribute
set objACE = CreateObject("AccessControlEntry")
objACE.Trustee     = strUserOrGroup
objACE.AccessMask  = ADS_RIGHT_DS_WRITE_PROP
objACE.AceFlags    = 0
objACE.Flags       = ADS_FLAG_OBJECT_TYPE_PRESENT
objACE.AceType     = ADS_ACETYPE_ACCESS_ALLOWED_OBJECT
objACE.ObjectType  = MEMBER_ATTRIBUTE

objDACL.AddAce objACE

'############################
' Set ACL
'############################
```

```
objSD.DiscretionaryAcl = objDACL
objGroup.Put "ntSecurityDescriptor", objSD
objGroup.SetInfo
WScript.Echo "Delegated control of member attribute for " & _
             strGroupDN & " to " & strUserOrGroup
```

Discussion

To grant a user or group the ability to manage group membership, you have to grant the write property (WP) permission on the member attribute of the target group. You can add this ACE directly using dsacls or more indirectly with ADUC. ADUC in Windows Server 2003 has a new feature that allows you to simply check a box to grant the ability to modify group membership to the object represented by the managedBy attribute.

If you want to configure additional permissions, such as the ability to modify the description attribute for the group, you will need to go to the Security tab in ADUC, or specify the appropriate attribute with the /G switch with dsacls. For example, this will grant write property on the description attribute:

```
/G <GroupName>@DomainDNSName:WP;description;
```

See Also

Recipe 14.10 for delegating control in Active Directory

7.8   Resolving a Primary Group ID

Problem

You want to find the name of a user's primary group.

Solution

Using a graphical user interface

1. Open the Active Directory Users and Computers snap-in.
2. If you need to change domains, right-click on Active Directory Users and Computers in the left pane, select Connect to Domain, enter the domain name, and click OK.
3. In the left pane, right-click on the domain and select Find.
4. Type the name of the user and click Find Now.
5. In the Search Results, double-click on the user.
6. Click the Member Of tab.
7. The Primary Group name is shown on the bottom half of the dialog box.

Using VBScript

```
' This code prints the group name of a user's primary group
' ------ SCRIPT CONFIGURATION ------
strNTDomain = "<DomainName>" ' NetBios Name of the AD domain, e.g. RALLENCORP
strUser     = "<UserName>"   ' e.g. Administrator
' ------ END CONFIGURATION ---------

' Iterate over the user's groups and create a search filter
' that contains each group
set objUser = GetObject("WinNT://" & strNTDomain & "/" & strUser & ",user")
strFilter = ""
for each objGroup in objUser.Groups
    strFilter = strFilter & "(samAccountName=" & objGroup.Name & ")"
next
strFilter = "(|" & strFilter & ")"

' Now need to perform a search to retrieve each group
' and their primaryGroupToken
strBase = "<LDAP://" & strNTDomain & ">;"
strFilter = "(&(objectcategory=group)" & strFilter & ");"
strAttrs = "name,primaryGroupToken,cn;"
strScope = "subtree;"
set objConn = CreateObject("ADODB.Connection")
objConn.Provider = "ADsDSOObject"
objConn.Open "Active Directory Provider"
set objComm = CreateObject("ADODB.Command")
set objComm.ActiveConnection = objConn
objComm.CommandText = strBase & strFilter & strAttrs & strScope
' Be sure to enable paging in case number of groups > 1000
objComm.Properties("Page Size") = 1000
set objRS = objComm.Execute

' Iterate over each group again and stop after a match with the user's
' primaryGroupID has been made
strPrimaryGroup = ""
while ( (not objRS.EOF) and (strPrimaryGroup = "") )
  if (objUser.PrimaryGroupID = objRS.Fields("primaryGroupToken").value) then
     strPrimaryGroup = objRS.Fields("name").Value
  end if
  objRS.moveNext
wend
objConn.Close

WScript.Echo "Primary Group for " & strUser & " is " & strPrimaryGroup & _
             " (" & objUser.PrimaryGroupID & ")"
```

Discussion

When trying to determine a user's group membership, you have to look at both user's memberOf attribute, which contains a list of DNs for each group the user is a member of, and the user's primary group. By default, all users are assigned Domain

Users as their primary group. Therefore, by default all users in a domain are implicitly members of the Domain Users group. Unfortunately, a user's primary group will not show up in the memberOf attribute unless explicitly added.

 Services for Macintosh and POSIX-based applications are the main users of primary groups. If you don't use either of those, you don't need to worry about changing a user's primary group.

The primary group is stored in the primaryGroupID attribute on user objects. Unfortunately, the RID of the group is stored in that attribute, not the DN or even sAMAccountName as you might expect. group objects have a primaryGroupToken attribute, which contains the same value, but is a constructed attribute. Because Active Directory dynamically constructs it, you cannot utilize it in search filters. So even if you have the primaryGroupID of a user, e.g., 513, you cannot do a simple query to find out which group it is associated with.

You can find the name of a user's primary group relatively easily using the Active Directory Users and Computers snap-in as I described in the GUI solution. Finding it via a script, on the other hand, is considerably more complicated. There are a few different ways to go about determining a group given a primary group ID and they are covered pretty well in MS KB 321360 and 297951. For the API solution, I use the approach I feel is the most efficient.

I first used the WinNT: provider to retrieve a user's groups. The difference between using the WinNT: provider and using the LDAP: provider is that the WinNT: provider returns the primary group as part of the IADsGroup collection whereas the LDAP: provider does not. Unfortunately, there is no indication which of the groups is the primary group. So I needed to iterate over each group and build an LDAP filter that will be used later to retrieve each group using ADO. After I execute the ADO query, I then iterate over each group and check the primaryGroupToken attribute of that group to see if it matches the user's primaryGroupID attribute. If it does, I've found the user's primary group.

See Also

MS KB 297951 (HOWTO: Use the PrimaryGroupID Attribute to Find the Primary Group for a User) and MS KB 321360 (How to Use Native ADSI Components to Find the Primary Group)

7.9 Enabling Universal Group Membership Caching

 This recipe requires the Windows Server 2003 forest functional level.

Problem

You want to enable universal group membership caching so that a global catalog server is not needed during user logins.

Solution

Using a graphical user interface

1. Open the Active Directory Sites and Services snap-in.
2. In the left pane, browse to the site you want to enable group caching for and click on it.
3. In the right pane, double-click on the NTDS Site Settings object.
4. Under Universal Group Membership Caching, check the box beside Enable Universal Group Caching.
5. If you want to force the cache refresh from a particular site, select a site or else leave the default set to <Default>.
6. Click OK.

Using a command-line interface

You can use a combination of the dsquery site and dsget site commands to find if a site has group caching enabled.

```
> dsquery site -name <SiteName> | dsget site -dn -cachegroups -prefGCSite
```

You can use ldifde to enable group caching. Create a file called *enable_univ_cache.ldf* with the following contents, but change <SiteName> to the name of the site you want to enable, and <ForestRootDN> with the distinguished name of the forest root domain:

```
dn: cn=NTDS Site Settings,cn=<SiteName>,cn=sites,cn=configuration,<ForestRootDN>
changetype: modify
replace: options
options: 32
-
```

Then use the following command to import the change:

```
> ldifde -i -f enable_univ_cache.ldf
```

Using VBScript

```
' This code enables universal group caching for the specified site.
' ------ SCRIPT CONFIGURATION ------
strSiteName = "<SiteName>"    ' e.g. Default-First-Site-Name
' ------ END CONFIGURATION ---------

set objRootDSE = GetObject("LDAP://RootDSE")
set objSite = GetObject("LDAP://cn=NTDS Site Settings,cn=" & strSiteName & _
              ",cn=sites," & objRootDSE.Get("configurationNamingContext") )
objSite.Put "options", 32
objSite.SetInfo
WScript.Echo "Successfully enabled universal group caching for " & _
             strSiteName
```

Discussion

When a client logs on to a Windows 2000 Active Directory domain controller, the domain controller must contact a global catalog server (if it is not one itself) in order to fully authenticate the client. This is necessary because of universal groups.

Universal groups can be created and used anywhere in a forest. Objects located anywhere in a forest can be added as members of a universal group. Since a universal group could be created in a domain other than where the user object resides, it is necessary to store universal group membership in the global catalog. That way, during logon, domain controllers can query a global catalog to determine all universal groups a user is a member of. Microsoft's primary reason for making this a requirement during logon is that a user could be part of a universal group that has been explicitly denied access to certain resources. If universal groups aren't evaluated, a user could gain access to resources that were previously restricted.

To remove this limitation in Windows Server 2003 Active Directory, universal group caching was introduced. Universal group caching can be enabled on a per site basis and allows domain controllers to cache universal group information locally, therefore, removing the need to query the global catalog during client logon.

You can enable universal group caching manually by enabling the 10000 bit (32 in decimal) on options attribute of the NTDS Site Settings object. The CLI and VBScript solutions blindly wrote 32 to that attribute, which is not ideal. See Recipe 4.12 for more information on properly setting a bit-flag attribute. The Sites and Services snap-in hides this logic and just requires you to check a box. Another setting can also be configured that relates to universal group caching. By default, domain controllers will use the site topology to determine what is the optimal site to query a global catalog server for universal group information. You can override this feature and explicitly set which site domain controllers should use by selecting the site in the Sites and Services snap-in or by setting the msDS-Preferred-GC-Site attribute on the NTDS Site Settings object to the DN of the target site.

## CHAPTER 8

Computers

8.0 Introduction

As far as Active Directory is concerned, computers are very similar to users. In fact, computer objects inherit directly from the user object class, which is used to represent user accounts. That means computer objects have all of the attributes of user objects and then some. Computers need to be represented in Active Directory for many of the same reasons users do, including the need to access resources securely, utilize GPOs, and have permissions granted or restricted on them.

To participate in a domain, computers need a secure channel to a domain controller. A secure channel is an authenticated connection that can transmit encrypted data. To set up the secure channel, a computer has to present a password to a domain controller. The domain controller then verifies that password against the password stored in Active Directory with the computer's account. Without the computer object, and subsequently, the password stored with it, there would be no way for the domain controller to verify a computer is what it claims to be.

The Anatomy of a Computer

The default location for computer objects in a domain is the cn=Computers container located directly off the domain root. You can, however, create computer objects anywhere in a domain. And in Windows Server 2003, you can modify the default location for computer objects as described in Recipe 8.12. Table 8-1 contains a list of some of the interesting attributes that are available on computer objects.

Table 8-1. Attributes of computer objects

Attribute	Description
cn	Relative distinguished name of computer objects.
dnsHostName	Fully qualified DNS name of the computer.

Table 8-1. Attributes of computer objects (continued)

Attribute	Description
lastLogonTimestamp	The approximate timestamp of the last time the computer logged in the domain. This is a new attribute in Windows Server 2003.
managedBy	The distinguished name (DN) of user or group that manages the computer.
memberOf	List of DNs of the groups the computer is a member of.
operatingSystem	Textual description of the operating system running on the computer. See Recipe 8.10 for more information.
operatingSystemHotFix	Currently not being used, but will hopefully be populated at some point.
operatingSystemServicePack	Service pack version installed on the computer. See Recipe 8.10 for more information.
operatingSystemVersion	Numeric version of the operating system installed on the computer. See Recipe 8.10 for more information.
pwdLastSet	Large integer that can be translated into the last time the computer's password was set. See Recipe 8.8 for more information.
sAMAccountName	NetBIOS-style name of the computer. This is typically the name of the computer with $ at the end.
userAccountControl	Account flag that defines various account properties.

8.1   Creating a Computer

Problem

You want to create a computer account.

Solution

Using a graphical user interface

1. Open the Active Directory Users and Computers snap-in.
2. If you need to change domains, right-click on Active Directory Users and Computers in the left pane, select Connect to Domain, enter the domain name and click OK.
3. In the left pane, browse to the parent container for the computer, right-click on it, and select New → Computer.
4. Enter the name of the computer and click OK.

Using a command-line interface

```
> dsadd computer "<ComputerDN>" -desc "<Description>"
```

Using VBScript

```
' This code creates a computer object.
' ------ SCRIPT CONFIGURATION ------
strBase = "<ParentComputerDN>"   ' e.g. cn=Computers,dc=rallencorp,dc=com
strComp = "<ComputerName>"       ' e.g. joe-xp
strDescr = "<Description>"        ' e.g. Joe's Windows XP workstation
' ------ END CONFIGURATION ---------

' ADS_USER_FLAG_ENUM
Const ADS_UF_WORKSTATION_TRUST_ACCOUNT = &h1000

set objCont = GetObject("LDAP://" & strBase)
set objComp = objCont.Create("computer", "cn=" & strComp)
objComp.Put "sAMAccountName", strComp & "$"
objComp.Put "description", strDesc
objComp.Put "userAccountControl", ADS_UF_WORKSTATION_TRUST_ACCOUNT
objComp.SetInfo
Wscript.Echo "Computer account for " & strComp & " created"
```

Discussion

Creating a computer object in Active Directory is not much different from creating a user object. I set the description attribute in the CLI and API solutions, but it is not a mandatory attribute. The only mandatory attribute is sAMAccountName which should be set to the name of the computer with $ appended. Also note that these solutions simply create a computer object. This does not mean any user can join a computer to the domain with that computer account. For more information creating a computer object and allowing a specific user or group to join the computer to the domain, see Recipe 8.2.

See Also

Recipe 8.2 for creating a computer for a user, MS KB 222525 (Automating the Creation of Computer Accounts), MS KB 283771 (HOW TO: Pre-stage Windows 2000 Computers in Active Directory), MS KB 315273 (Automating the Creation of Computer Accounts), MS KB 320187 (HOW TO: Manage Computer Accounts in Active Directory in Windows 2000), and MSDN: ADS_USER_FLAG_ENUM

8.2   Creating a Computer for a Specific User or Group

Problem

You want to create a computer account for a specific user or group to join to the domain. This requires setting permissions on the computer account so the user or group can modify certain attributes.

Solution

Using a graphical user interface

1. Open the Active Directory Users and Computers snap-in.
2. If you need to change domains, right-click on Active Directory Users and Computers in the left pane, select Connect to Domain, enter the domain name, and click OK.
3. In the left pane, browse to the parent container for the computer, right-click on it, and select New → Computer.
4. Enter the name of the computer.
5. Click the Change button.
6. Use the Object Picker to select a user or group to join the computer to the domain.
7. Click OK.

Using a command-line interface

In the following solution, replace *<ComputerDN>* with the distinguished name of the computer object and *<UserOrGroup>* with the user principal name or NT-style name of a user or group you want to manage the computer:

```
> dsadd computer <ComputerDN>
> dsacls <ComputerDN> /G <UserOrGroup>:CALCGRSDDTRC;;
> dsacls <ComputerDN> /G <UserOrGroup>:WP;description;
> dsacls <ComputerDN> /G <UserOrGroup>:WP;sAMAccountName;
> dsacls <ComputerDN> /G <UserOrGroup>:WP;displayName;
> dsacls <ComputerDN> /G <UserOrGroup>:WP;"Logon Information";
> dsacls <ComputerDN> /G <UserOrGroup>:WP;"Account Restrictions";
> dsacls <ComputerDN> /G <UserOrGroup>:WS;"Validated write to service principal↵
name";
> dsacls <ComputerDN> /G <UserOrGroup>:WS;"Validated write to DNS host name";
```

Using VBScript

```
' This code creates a computer object and grants a user/group rights over it
' ------ SCRIPT CONFIGURATION ------
```

```
strComputer = "<ComputerName>"   ' e.g. joe-xp
strUser     = "<UserOrGroup>"    ' e.g. joe@rallencorp.com or RALLENCORP\joe
strDescr    = "<ComputerDescr>"  ' e.g. Joe's workstation
strDomain   = "<ComputerDomain>" ' e.g. rallencorp.com
' ------ END CONFIGURATION ---------

'#############################
' Constants
'#############################

' ADS_USER_FLAG_ENUM
Const ADS_UF_PASSWD_NOTREQD            = &h0020
Const ADS_UF_WORKSTATION_TRUST_ACCOUNT = &h1000

' ADS_ACETYPE_ENUM
Const ADS_ACETYPE_ACCESS_ALLOWED        = &h0
Const ADS_ACETYPE_ACCESS_ALLOWED_OBJECT = &h5

' ADS_FLAGTYPE_ENUM
Const ADS_FLAG_OBJECT_TYPE_PRESENT = &h1

' ADS_RIGHTS_ENUM
Const ADS_RIGHT_DS_SELF          = &h8
Const ADS_RIGHT_DS_WRITE_PROP    = &h20
Const ADS_RIGHT_DS_CONTROL_ACCESS = &h100
Const ADS_RIGHT_ACTRL_DS_LIST    = &h4
Const ADS_RIGHT_GENERIC_READ     = &h80000000
Const ADS_RIGHT_DELETE           = &h10000
Const ADS_RIGHT_DS_DELETE_TREE   = &h40
Const ADS_RIGHT_READ_CONTROL     = &h20000

' schemaIDGUID values
Const DISPLAY_NAME     = "{bf967953-0de6-11d0-a285-00aa003049e2}"
Const SAM_ACCOUNT_NAME = "{3e0abfd0-126a-11d0-a060-00aa006c33ed}"
Const DESCRIPTION      = "{bf967950-0de6-11d0-a285-00aa003049e2}"

' controlAccessRight rightsGUID values
Const USER_LOGON_INFORMATION      = "{5f202010-79a5-11d0-9020-00c04fc2d4cf}"
Const USER_ACCOUNT_RESTRICTIONS   = "{4C164200-20C0-11D0-A768-00AA006E0529}"
Const VALIDATED_DNS_HOST_NAME     = "{72E39547-7B18-11D1-ADEF-00C04FD8D5CD}"
Const VALIDATED_SPN               = "{F3A64788-5306-11D1-A9C5-0000F80367C1}"

'#############################
' Create Computer
'#############################

set objRootDSE = GetObject("LDAP://" & strDomain & "/RootDSE")
set objContainer = GetObject("LDAP://cn=Computers," & _
                            objRootDSE.Get("defaultNamingContext"))
set objComputer = objContainer.Create("Computer", "cn=" & strComputer)
objComputer.Put "sAMAccountName", strComputer & "$"
objComputer.Put "userAccountControl", _
                ADS_UF_PASSWD_NOTREQD Or ADS_UF_WORKSTATION_TRUST_ACCOUNT
objComputer.Put "description", strDescr
objComputer.SetInfo
```

```
'#############################
' Create ACL
'#############################

set objSD = objComputer.Get("ntSecurityDescriptor")
set objDACL = objSD.DiscretionaryAcl

' Special: Control Rights, List Children
'          Generic Read, Delete,
'          Delete Subtree, Read Permission
set objACE1 = CreateObject("AccessControlEntry")
objACE1.Trustee    = strUser
objACE1.AccessMask = ADS_RIGHT_DS_CONTROL_ACCESS Or _
                     ADS_RIGHT_ACTRL_DS_LIST Or _
                     ADS_RIGHT_GENERIC_READ Or _
                     ADS_RIGHT_DELETE Or _
                     ADS_RIGHT_DS_DELETE_TREE Or ADS_RIGHT_READ_CONTROL
objACE1.AceFlags   = 0
objACE1.AceType    = ADS_ACETYPE_ACCESS_ALLOWED

' Write Property: description
set objACE2 = CreateObject("AccessControlEntry")
objACE2.Trustee    = strUser
objACE2.AccessMask = ADS_RIGHT_DS_WRITE_PROP
objACE2.AceFlags   = 0
objACE2.Flags      = ADS_FLAG_OBJECT_TYPE_PRESENT
objACE2.AceType    = ADS_ACETYPE_ACCESS_ALLOWED_OBJECT
objACE2.ObjectType = DESCRIPTION

' Write Property: sAMAccountName
set objACE3 = CreateObject("AccessControlEntry")
objACE3.Trustee    = strUser
objACE3.AccessMask = ADS_RIGHT_DS_WRITE_PROP
objACE3.AceFlags   = 0
objACE3.Flags      = ADS_FLAG_OBJECT_TYPE_PRESENT
objACE3.AceType    = ADS_ACETYPE_ACCESS_ALLOWED_OBJECT
objACE3.ObjectType = SAM_ACCOUNT_NAME

' Write Property: displayName
set objACE4 = CreateObject("AccessControlEntry")
objACE4.Trustee    = strUser
objACE4.AccessMask = ADS_RIGHT_DS_WRITE_PROP
objACE4.AceFlags   = 0
objACE4.Flags      = ADS_FLAG_OBJECT_TYPE_PRESENT
objACE4.AceType    = ADS_ACETYPE_ACCESS_ALLOWED_OBJECT
objACE4.ObjectType = DISPLAY_NAME

' Write Property: Logon Information
set objACE5 = CreateObject("AccessControlEntry")
objACE5.Trustee    = strUser
objACE5.AccessMask = ADS_RIGHT_DS_WRITE_PROP
objACE5.AceFlags   = 0
objACE5.AceType    = ADS_ACETYPE_ACCESS_ALLOWED_OBJECT
objACE5.Flags      = ADS_FLAG_OBJECT_TYPE_PRESENT
objACE5.ObjectType = USER_LOGON_INFORMATION
```

```
' Write Property: Account Restrictions
set objACE6 = CreateObject("AccessControlEntry")
objACE6.Trustee     = strUser
objACE6.AccessMask = ADS_RIGHT_DS_WRITE_PROP
objACE6.AceFlags    = 0
objACE6.AceType     = ADS_ACETYPE_ACCESS_ALLOWED_OBJECT
objACE6.Flags       = ADS_FLAG_OBJECT_TYPE_PRESENT
objACE6.ObjectType = USER_ACCOUNT_RESTRICTIONS

' Write Self: Validated SPN
set objACE7 = CreateObject("AccessControlEntry")
objACE7.Trustee     = strUser
objACE7.AccessMask = ADS_RIGHT_DS_SELF
objACE7.AceFlags    = 0
objACE7.AceType     = ADS_ACETYPE_ACCESS_ALLOWED_OBJECT
objACE7.Flags       = ADS_FLAG_OBJECT_TYPE_PRESENT
objACE7.ObjectType = VALIDATED_SPN

' Write Self: Validated DNS Host Name
set objACE8 = CreateObject("AccessControlEntry")
objACE8.Trustee     = strUser
objACE8.AccessMask = ADS_RIGHT_DS_SELF
objACE8.AceFlags    = 0
objACE8.AceType     = ADS_ACETYPE_ACCESS_ALLOWED_OBJECT
objACE8.Flags       = ADS_FLAG_OBJECT_TYPE_PRESENT
objACE8.ObjectType = VALIDATED_DNS_HOST_NAME

objDACL.AddAce objACE1
objDACL.AddAce objACE2
objDACL.AddAce objACE3
objDACL.AddAce objACE4
objDACL.AddAce objACE5
objDACL.AddAce objACE6
objDACL.AddAce objACE7
objDACL.AddAce objACE8

'############################
' Set ACL
'############################
objSD.DiscretionaryAcl = objDACL
objComputer.Put "ntSecurityDescriptor", objSD
objComputer.SetInfo
WScript.Echo "Successfully created " & strComputer & _
             " and gave rights to " & strUser
```

Discussion

Simply creating a computer object in Active Directory does not permit a user to join a computer to the domain. Certain permissions have to be granted so that the user has rights to modify the computer object. When you create a computer via the Active Directory Users and Computers snap-in you have the option to select a user or group to manage the computer object and join a computer to the domain using that object.

When you use that method, eight access control entries (ACEs) are added to the access control list (ACL) of the computer object. They are:

- List Contents, Read All Properties, Delete, Delete Subtree, Read Permissions, All Extended Rights (i.e., Allowed to Authenticate, Change Password, Send As, Receive As, Reset Password
- Write Property for description
- Write Property for sAMAccountName
- Write Property for displayName
- Write Property for Logon Information
- Write Property for Account Restrictions
- Validate write to DNS host name
- Validated write for service principal name

Using a graphical user interface

If you want to modify the default permissions that are applied when you select a user or group through the GUI, double-click on the computer object after you created it and go to the Security tab. For the Security tab to be visible, you have to select View → Advanced Features.

Using a command-line interface

With the dsacls utility, you can specify either a UPN (*user@domain*) or down-level style (*DOMAIN\user*) account name when applying permissions. Also, dsacls requires that the displayName of the attribute, property set, or extended right you are setting the permission on be used instead of the lDAPDisplayName, as one might expect. That is why I had to use "Validated write to service principal name," which is the displayName for the Validated-SPN controlAccessRight object with the ACE for the SPN-validated write. dsacls is also case sensitive, so be sure to specify the correct case for the words in the displayName.

Using VBScript

After creating the computer object, similar to Recipe 8.1, I create an ACE object for each of the eight ACEs I previously listed using the IADsAccessControlEntry interface. To apply the ACEs, I retrieved the current security descriptor for the computer object, which is stored in the nTSecurityDescriptor attribute, and then add the eight ACEs. Finally, I called SetInfo to commit the change to Active Directory. For more information on setting ACEs and ACLs programmatically, see the IADsAccessControlEntry documentation in MSDN.

See Also

Recipe 8.1 for creating a computer account, MS KB 238793 (Enhanced Security Joining or Resetting Machine Account in Windows 2000 Domain), MS KB 283771 (HOW TO: Prestage Windows 2000 Computers in Active Directory), MS KB 320187 (HOW TO: Manage Computer Accounts in Active Directory in Windows 2000), MSDN: IADsAccessControlEntry, MSDN: ADS_ACETYPE_ENUM, and MSDN: ADS_RIGHTS_ENUM, MSDN: ADS_FLAGTYPE_ENUM

8.3   Joining a Computer to a Domain

Problem

You want to join a computer to a domain after the computer object has already been created in Active Directory.

Solution

Using a graphical user interface

1. Log onto the computer you want to join and open the Control Panel.
2. Open the System applet.
3. Click the Computer Name tab.
4. Click the Change button.
5. Under Member of, select Domain.
6. Enter the domain you want to join and click OK.
7. You may be prompted to enter credentials that have permission to join the computer.
8. Reboot the computer.
9. Note that the tabs in the System applet vary between Windows 2000, Windows XP, and Windows Server 2003.

Using a command-line interface

```
> netdom join <ComputerName> /Domain <DomainName> /UserD <DomainUserUPN>↵
/PasswordD * /UserO <ComputerAdminUser> /PasswordO * /Reboot
```

Using VBScript

```
' This code joins a computer to a domain.
' ------ SCRIPT CONFIGURATION ------
strComputer    = "<ComputerName>"      ' e.g. joe-xp
strDomain      = "<DomainName>"        ' e.g. rallencorp.com
strDomainUser  = "<DomainUserUPN>"     ' e.g. administrator@rallencorp.com
```

```
strDomainPasswd = "<DomainUserPasswd>"
strLocalUser    = "<ComputerAdminUser>" ' e.g. administrator
strLocalPasswd  = "<ComputerUserPasswd>"
' ------ END CONFIGURATION ---------

'#######################
' Constants
'#######################
Const JOIN_DOMAIN             = 1
Const ACCT_CREATE             = 2
Const ACCT_DELETE             = 4
Const WIN9X_UPGRADE           = 16
Const DOMAIN_JOIN_IF_JOINED   = 32
Const JOIN_UNSECURE           = 64
Const MACHINE_PASSWORD_PASSED = 128
Const DEFERRED_SPN_SET        = 256
Const INSTALL_INVOCATION      = 262144

'###########################
' Connect to Computer
'###########################
set objWMILocator = CreateObject("WbemScripting.SWbemLocator")
objWMILocator.Security_.AuthenticationLevel = 6
set objWMIComputer = objWMILocator.ConnectServer(strComputer, _
                                "root\cimv2", _
                                          strLocalUser, _
                                          strLocalPasswd)
set objWMIComputerSystem = objWMIComputer.Get( _
                           "Win32_ComputerSystem.Name='" & _
                           strComputer & "'")

'###########################
' Join Computer
'###########################
rc = objWMIComputerSystem.JoinDomainOrWorkGroup(strDomain, _
                                    strDomainPasswd, _
                                    strDomainUser, _
                                    vbNullString, _
                                    JOIN_DOMAIN)
if rc <> 0 then
    WScript.Echo "Join failed with error: " & rc
else
    WScript.Echo "Successfully joined " & strComputer & " to " & strDomain
end if
```

Discussion

When trying to add a computer to Active Directory, you must first create the computer object as described in Recipes 8.1 and 8.2. Then you can join the computer to the domain.

Using a graphical user interface

If you have the correct permissions in Active Directory, you can actually create a computer object at the same time as you join it to a domain via the instructions described in the GUI solution. Since the System applet doesn't allow you to specify an OU for the computer object, if it needs to create a computer object, it will do so in the default Computers container. See Recipes 8.1 and 8.2 for more information on the default computers container and how to change it.

Using a command-line interface

The netdom command will attempt to create a computer object for the computer during a join if one does not already exist. An optional /OU switch can be added to specify the OU in which to create the computer object. To do so you'll need to have the necessary permissions to create and manage computer objects in the OU.

There are some restrictions on running the netdom join command remotely. If a Windows XP machine has the ForceGuest security policy setting enabled, you cannot join it remotely. Running the netdom command directly on the machine works regardless of the ForceGuest setting.

Using VBScript

In order for the Win32_ComputerSystem::JoinDomainOrWorkGroup method to work remotely, you have to use an AuthenticationLevel equal to 6 so that the traffic between the two machines (namely the passwords) is encrypted. You can also create computer objects using JoinDomainOrWorkGroup by using the ACCT_CREATE flag in combination with JOIN_DOMAIN.

 This function works only with Windows XP and Windows Server 2003 and is not available for Windows 2000 and earlier machines.

Just like with the netdom utility, you cannot run this script against a remote computer if that computer has the ForceGuest setting enabled.

See Also

More information on the ForceGuest setting can be found here: *http://www.microsoft.com/technet/prodtechnol/winxppro/reskit/prde_ffs_ypuh.asp*, MS KB 238793 (Enhanced Security Joining or Resetting Machine Account in Windows 2000 Domain), MS KB 251335 (Domain Users Cannot Join Workstation or Server to a Domain), MS KB 290403 (How to Set Security in Windows XP Professional That Is Installed in a Workgroup), MSDN: Win32_ComputerSystem::JoinDomainOrWorkgroup, and MSDN: NetJoinDomain

8.4   Moving a Computer

Problem

You want to move a computer object to a different container or OU.

Solution

Using a graphical user interface

1. Open the Active Directory Users and Computers snap-in.
2. If you need to change domains, right click on Active Directory Users and Computers in the left pane, select Connect to Domain, enter the domain name, and click OK.
3. In the left pane, right-click on the domain and select Find.
4. Beside Find, select Computers.
5. Type the name of the computer and click Find Now.
6. In the Search Results, right-click on the computer and select Move.
7. Browse to the new parent container or OU and click on it.
8. Click OK.

 With the Windows Server 2003 version of Active Directory Users and Computers you can also use the new drag and drop functionality to move computers and other objects.

Using a command-line interface

```
> dsmove "<ComputerDN>" -newparent "<NewParentDN>"
```

Using VBScript

```
' This code moves a computer to the specified container/OU.
' ------ SCRIPT CONFIGURATION ------
strCompDN = "<ComputerDN>"   ' e.g. cn=joe-xp,cn=Users,dc=rallencorp,dc=com
strOUDN  = "<NewParentDN>"   ' e.g. ou=workstations,dc=rallencorp,dc=com
' ------ END CONFIGURATION ---------

set objComp = GetObject("LDAP://" & strCompDN)
set objOU = GetObject("LDAP://" & strOUDN)
objOU.MoveHere objComp.ADsPath, objComp.Name
```

Discussion

You can move computer objects around a domain without much impact on the computer itself. You just need to be cautious of the security settings on the new parent

OU, which may impact a user's ability to manage the computer object in Active Directory. Also, if GPOs are used differently on the new parent, it could impact booting and logon times.

See Also

Recipe 4.17 for moving an object to a different OU, and Recipe 4.18 for moving an object to a different domain

8.5   Renaming a Computer

Problem

You want to rename a computer.

Solution

Using a graphical user interface

1. Log on to the computer either directly or with a remote console application, such as Terminal Services.
2. Open the Control Panel and double-click on the System Applet.
3. Select the Computer Name tab and click the Change button.
4. Under Computer Name, type the new name of the computer and click OK until you are out of the System applet.
5. Reboot the machine.

Using a command-line interface

```
> netdom renamecomputer <ComputerName> /NewName <NewComputerName> /UserD⌐
<DomainUserUPN> /PasswordD * /UserO <ComputerAdminUser> /PasswordO * /Reboot
```

Using VBScript

```
' This code renames a computer in AD and on the host itself.
' ------ SCRIPT CONFIGURATION ------
strComputer      = "<ComputerName>"        e.g. joe-xp
strNewComputer   = "<NewComputerName>"     e.g. joe-pc
strDomainUser    = "<DomainUserUPN>"       e.g. administrator@rallencorp.com
strDomainPasswd  = "<DomainUserPasswd>"
strLocalUser     = "<ComputerAdminUser>"   e.g. joe-xp\administrator
strLocalPasswd   = "<ComputerAdminPasswd>"
' ------ END CONFIGURATION ---------

'###########################
' Connect to Computer
'###########################
```

```
set objWMILocator = CreateObject("WbemScripting.SWbemLocator")
objWMILocator.Security_.AuthenticationLevel = 6
set objWMIComputer = objWMILocator.ConnectServer(strComputer,  _
                                                "root\cimv2", _
                                                strLocalUser, _
                                                 strLocalPasswd)
set objWMIComputerSystem = objWMIComputer.Get( _
                              "Win32_ComputerSystem.Name='" & _
                              strComputer & "'")
'###########################
' Rename Computer
'###########################
rc = objWMIComputerSystem.Rename(strNewComputer, _
                                strDomainPasswd, _
                                strDomainUser)
if rc <> 0 then
    WScript.Echo "Rename failed with error: " & rc
else
    WScript.Echo "Successfully renamed " & strComputer & " to " & _
                strNewComputer
end if

WScript.Echo "Rebooting..."
set objWSHShell = WScript.CreateObject("WScript.Shell")
objWSHShell.Run "rundll32 shell32.dll,SHExitWindowsEx 2"
```

Discussion

Renaming a computer consists of two operations: renaming the computer object in
Active Directory and renaming the hostname on the machine itself. To do it in one
step, which each of the three solutions offer, you must have permission in Active
Directory to rename the account and administrator permissions on the target
machine. For the rename operation to be complete, you must reboot the computer.

 In some cases, renaming a computer can adversely affect services running on the computer. For example, you cannot rename a machine
that is a Windows 2000 domain controller or a Windows Certificate
Authority without first removing those services.

Using a graphical user interface

After you rename the computer, you will be prompted to reboot the machine. You
can cancel out if necessary, but you'll need to reboot at some point to complete the
rename operation.

Using a command-line interface

The renamecomputer option in netdom is new to Windows Server 2003. It can run remotely and includes a /Reboot switch that allows you to automatically reboot the computer after the rename is complete.

Using VBScript

The Win32_ComputerSystem::Rename method must be run on the local machine unless the computer is a member of a domain. Unlike the GUI and CLI solutions, you cannot specify alternate credentials for the connection to the computer other than domain credentials. For this reason, the user and password you use with the Rename method must have administrative privileges on the target machine (i.e., part of the Administrators group) and on the computer object in Active Directory.

 This method is new in Windows XP and Windows Server 2003, and is not available on Windows 2000 and earlier machines.

See Also

Recipe 4.19 for renaming objects, MS KB 228544 (Changing Computer Name in Windows 2000 Requires Restart), MS KB 238793 (Enhanced Security Joining or Resetting Machine Account in Windows 2000 Domain), MS KB 260575 (HOW TO: Use Netdom.exe to Reset Machine Account Passwords of a Windows 2000 Domain Controller), MS KB 325354 (HOW TO: Use the Netdom.exe Utility to Rename a Computer in Windows Server 2003), and MSDN: Win32_ComputerSystem:: Rename

8.6   Testing the Secure Channel for a Computer

Problem

You want to test the secure channel of a computer.

Solution

Using a command-line interface

```
> nltest /server:<ComputerName> /sc_query:<DomainName>
```

Discussion

Every member computer in an Active Directory domain establishes a secure channel with a domain controller. The computer's password is stored locally in the form of an LSA secret and in Active Directory. This password is used by the NetLogon service to establish the secure channel with a domain controller. If, for some reason, the LSA secret and computer password become out of sync, the computer will no longer be able to authenticate in the domain. The `nltest /sc_query` command can query a computer to verify its secure channel is working. Here is sample output from the command when things are working:

```
Flags: 30 HAS_IP  HAS_TIMESERV
Trusted DC Name \\dc1.rallencorp.com
Trusted DC Connection Status Status = 0 0x0 NERR_Success
The command completed successfully
```

If a secure channel is failing, you'll need to reset the computer as described in Recipe 8.7. Here is sample output when things are not working:

```
Flags: 0
Trusted DC Name
Trusted DC Connection Status Status = 1311 0x51f ERROR_NO_LOGON_SERVERS
The command completed successfully
```

See Also

Recipe 8.7 for resetting a computer and MS KB 216393 (Resetting Computer Accounts in Windows 2000 and Windows XP)

8.7   Resetting a Computer

Problem

You want to reset a computer because its secure channel is failing.

Solution

Using a graphical user interface

1. Open the Active Directory Users and Computers snap-in.
2. If you need to change domains, right-click on Active Directory Users and Computers in the left pane, select Connect to Domain, enter the domain name, and click OK.
3. In the left pane, right-click on the domain and select Find.
4. Beside Find, select Computers.
5. Type the name of the computer and click Find Now.
6. In the Search Results, right-click on the computer and select Reset Account.
7. Click Yes to verify.
8. Click OK.
9. Rejoin computer to the domain.

Using a command-line interface

You can use the `dsmod` utility to reset a computer's password. You will need to rejoin the computer to the domain after doing this.

```
> dsmod computer  "<ComputerDN>" -reset
```

Another option is to use the `netdom` command, which can reset the computer so that you do not need to rejoin it to the domain:

```
> netdom reset <ComputerName> /Domain <DomainName> /UserO <UserUPN> /PasswordO *
```

Using VBScript

```
' This resets an existing computer object's password to initial default.
' You'll need to rejoin the computer after doing this.
set objComputer = GetObject("LDAP://<ComputerDN>")
objComputer.SetPassword "<ComputerName>"
```

Discussion

When you've identified that a computer's secure channel has failed, you'll need to reset the computer, which consists of setting the computer object password to the name of the computer. This is the default initial password for new computers. Every 30 days Windows 2000 and newer systems automatically change their passwords in the domain. After you've set the password, you'll need to rejoin the computer to the domain since it will no longer be able to communicate with a domain controller due to unsynchronized passwords. However, the `netdom reset` command will try to reset the password on both the computer and in Active Directory, which will not necessitate rejoining it to the domain if successful.

See Also

Recipe 8.3 for joining a computer to a domain, Recipe 8.6 for testing a secure channel, MS KB 216393 (Resetting Computer Accounts in Windows 2000 and Windows XP), and MS KB 325850 (HOW TO: Use Netdom.exe to Reset Machine Account Passwords of a Windows Server 2003 Domain Controller)

8.8   Finding Inactive or Unused Computers

Problem

You want to find inactive computer accounts in a domain.

Solution

 These solutions only apply to Windows-based machines. Other types of machines (e.g., Unix) that have accounts in Active Directory may not update their login timestamps or passwords, which are used to determine inactivity.

Using a command-line interface

The following query will locate all inactive computers in the current forest:

```
> dsquery computer forestroot -inactive <NumWeeks>
```

You can also use `domainroot` in combination with the `-d` option to query a specific domain:

```
> dsquery computer domainroot -d <DomainName> -inactive <NumWeeks>
```

or you can target your query at a specific container:

```
> dsquery computer ou=MyComputers,dc=rallencorp,dc=com -inactive <NumWeeks>
```

 This can only be run against a Windows Server 2003 domain functional level or higher domain.

Using Perl

```perl
#!perl

#-----------------------
# Script Configuration
#-----------------------
# Domain and container/OU to check for inactive computer accounts
my $domain        = 'amer.rallencorp.com';

# set to empty string to query entire domain
my $computer_cont = 'cn=Computers,';

# Number of weeks used to find inactive computers
my $weeks_ago = 30;
#-----------------------
# End Configuration
#-----------------------

use strict;
use Win32::OLE;
   $Win32::OLE::Warn = 3;
use Math::BigInt;

# Must convert the number of seconds since $weeks_ago
# to a large integer for comparison against lastLogonTimestamp
my $sixmonth_secs = time - 60*60*24*7*$weeks_ago;
```

```
my $intObj = Math::BigInt->new($sixmonth_secs);
   $intObj = Math::BigInt->new($intObj->bmul('10 000 000'));
my $sixmonth_int = Math::BigInt->new(
                       $intObj->badd('116 444 736 000 000 000'));
   $sixmonth_int =~ s/^[+-]//;

# Setup the ADO connections
my $connObj                          = Win32::OLE->new('ADODB.Connection');
$connObj->{Provider}                 = "ADsDSOObject";
$connObj->Open;
my $commObj                          = Win32::OLE->new('ADODB.Command');
$commObj->{ActiveConnection}         = $connObj;
$commObj->Properties->{'Page Size'} = 1000;

# Grab the default root domain name
my $rootDSE = Win32::OLE->GetObject("LDAP://$domain/RootDSE");
my $rootNC = $rootDSE->Get("defaultNamingContext");

# Run ADO query and print results
my $query  = "<LDAP://$domain/$computer_cont$rootNC>;";
$query .=  "(&(objectclass=computer)";
$query .=   "(objectcategory=computer)";
$query .=   "(lastlogontimestamp<=$sixmonth_int));";
$query .=  "cn,distinguishedName;";
$query .= "subtree";
$commObj->{CommandText} = $query;
my $resObj = $commObj->Execute($query);
die "Could not query $domain: ",$Win32::OLE::LastError,"\n"
  unless ref $resObj;

print "\nComputers that have been inactive for $weeks_ago weeks or more:\n";
my $total = 0;
while (!($resObj->EOF)) {
   my $cn  = $resObj->Fields(0)->value;
   print "\t",$resObj->Fields("distinguishedName")->value,"\n";
   $total++;
   $resObj->MoveNext;
}
print "Total: $total\n";
```

Discussion

Using a command-line interface

The dsquery computer command is very handy for finding inactive computers that have not logged into the domain for a number of weeks or months. You can pipe the results of the query to dsrm if you want to remove the inactive computer objects from Active Directory in a single command. Here is an example that would delete all computers in the current domain that have been inactive for 12 weeks or longer:

```
> for /F "usebackq" %i in (`dsquery computer domainroot -inactive 12`) do dsrm %i
```

Unless you have a requirement for quickly removing unused computer objects, I'd recommend allowing them to remain inactive for at least three months before removing them. If you don't really care when the objects get removed, use a year (i.e., 52 weeks) to be on the safe side.

Using Perl

With Windows 2000 Active Directory, the only way you can determine if a computer is inactive is to query either the pwdLastSet or lastLogon attributes. The pwdLastSet attribute is a 64-bit integer that translates into the date and time the computer last updated its password. Since computers are suppose to change their password every 30 days, you could run a query that finds the computers that have not changed their password in several months. This is difficult with VBScript because it does not handle 64-bit integer manipulation very well. There are third-party add-ons you can get that provide 64-bit functions, but none of the built-in VBScript functions can do it and it is non-trivial to implement without an add-on.

The lastLogin attribute can also be used to find inactive computers because that attribute contains a 64-bit integer representing the last time the computer logged into the domain. The problem with the lastLogin attribute is that it is *not replicated*. Since it is not replicated, you have to query every domain controller in the domain to find the most recent lastLogin value. As you can imagine, this is less than ideal, especially if you have a lot of domain controllers.

Fortunately, in Windows Server 2003, Microsoft added a new attribute called lastLogonTimestamp to user and computer objects. This attribute contains the approximate last logon timestamp (again in a 64-bit, large-integer format) for the user or computer and is replicated to all domain controllers. It is the "approximate" last logon because the domain controllers will update the value only if it hasn't been updated for a certain period of time (such as a week). This prevents the attribute from being updated constantly and causing a lot of unnecessary replication traffic.

Since VBScript was out of the question, I turned to my first love…Perl. It is very rare to find a problem that you can't solve with Perl and this is no exception. The biggest issue is manipulating a number to a 64-bit integer, which we can do with the Math::BigInt module.

First, I determine the time in seconds from 1970 for the date that we want to query computer inactivity against. That is, take the current time and subtract the number of weeks we want to go back. Then I have to convert that number to a big integer. The last step is simply to perform an ADO query for all computers that have a lastLogonTimestamp less than or equal to the value I just calculated.

See Also

Recipe 6.26 for finding users whose accounts are about to expire

8.9   Changing the Maximum Number of Computers a User Can Join to the Domain

Problem

You want to grant users the ability to join more or fewer than 10 computers to a domain. This limit is called the machine account quota.

Solution

Using a graphical user interface

1. Open ADSI Edit.
2. Right-click on the domainDNS object for the domain you want to change and select Properties.
3. Edit the ms-DS-MachineAccountQuota attribute and enter the new quota value.
4. Click OK twice.

Using a command-line interface

In the following LDIF code replace *<DomainDN>* with the distinguished name of the domain you want to change and replace *<Quota>* with the new machine account quota:

```
dn: <DomainDN>
changetype: modify
replace: ms-DS-MachineAccountQuota
ms-DS-MachineAccountQuota: <Quota>
-
```

If the LDIF file was named change_computer_quota.ldf, you would then run the following command:

```
> ldifde -v -i -f change_computer_quota.ldf
```

Using VBScript

```
' This code sets the machine account quota for a domain.
' ------ SCRIPT CONFIGURATION ------
intQuota  = <Quota>
strDomain = "<DomainDNSName>"  ' e.g. emea.rallencorp.com
' ------ END CONFIGURATION ---------

set objRootDSE = GetObject("LDAP://" & strDomain & "/RootDSE")
set objDomain = GetObject("LDAP://" & objRootDSE.Get("defaultNamingContext"))
objDomain.Put "ms-DS-MachineAccountQuota", intQuota
objDomain.SetInfo
WScript.Echo "Updated user quota to " & intQuota
```

Discussion

In a default Active Directory installation, members of the `Authenticated Users` group can add and join up to 10 computer accounts in the default `Computers` container. The number of computer accounts that can be created is defined in the `ms-DS-MachineAccountQuota` attribute on the `domainDNS` object for a domain. The default setting is artificially set to 10, but you can easily change that to whatever number you want, including 0, via the methods described in the Solution section. If you set it to 0, users have to be granted explicit permissions in Active Directory to join computers, such as those described in Recipe 8.3.

Another method for granting users the right to add `computer` objects, although not recommended, is via group policy. If you grant the "Add workstation to domain" right via Computer Configuration → Windows Settings → Security Settings → Local Policies → User Rights Assignment, then users will be able to create computer accounts even if they do not have create child permissions on the default `Computers` container. This is a holdover from Windows NT to maintain backwards compatibility, and should not be used unless absolutely necessary.

See Also

Recipe 8.3 for permissions needed to join computers to a domain, MS KB 251335 (Domain Users Cannot Join Workstation or Server to a Domain), and MS KB 314462 ("You Have Exceeded the Maximum Number of Computer Accounts" Error Message When You Try to Join a Windows XP Computer to a Windows 2000 Domain)

8.10   Finding Computers with a Particular OS

Problem

You want to find computers that have a certain OS version, release, or service pack in a domain.

Solution

Using a graphical user interface

1. Open LDP.
2. From the menu, select Connection → Connect.
3. For Server, enter the name of a domain controller (or leave blank to do a server-less bind).
4. For Port, enter 389.

5. Click OK.

6. From the menu, select Connection → Bind.

7. Enter credentials of a user to perform the search.

8. Click OK.

9. From the Menu, select Browse → Search.

10. For Base Dn, enter the base of where you want your search to begin.

11. For Filter, enter a filter that contains the OS attribute you want to search on. For example, a query for all computers that are running Windows XP would be the following:

```
(&(objectclass=computer)(objectcategory=computer)(operatingSystem=Windows XP
Professional))
```

12. Select the appropriate Scope based on how deep you want to search.

13. Click the Options button if you want to customize the list of attributes returned for each matching object.

14. Click Run and the results will be displayed in the right pane.

Using a command-line interface

```
> dsquery * <DomainDN> -scope subtree -attr "*" -filter "(&(objectclass=⏎
computer)(objectcategory=computer)(operatingSystem=Windows Server 2003))"
```

Using VBScript

```
' This code searches for computer objects that have Service Pack 1 installed.
' ------ SCRIPT CONFIGURATION ------
strBase    = "<LDAP://" & "<DomainDN>" & ">;"
' ------ END CONFIGURATION ---------

strFilter  = "(&(objectclass=computer)(objectcategory=computer)" & _
             "(operatingSystemServicePack=Service Pack 1));"
strAttrs   = "cn,operatingSystem,operatingSystemVersion," & _
             " operatingSystemServicePack;"
strScope   = "subtree"

set objConn = CreateObject("ADODB.Connection")
objConn.Provider = "ADsDSOObject"
objConn.Open "Active Directory Provider"
Set objRS = objConn.Execute(strBase & strFilter & strAttrs & strScope)
objRS.MoveFirst
while Not objRS.EOF
    Wscript.Echo objRS.Fields(0).Value
    Wscript.Echo objRS.Fields(1).Value
    Wscript.Echo objRS.Fields(2).Value
    Wscript.Echo objRS.Fields(3).Value
    Wscript.Echo objRS.Fields(4).Value
    WScript.Echo
    objRS.MoveNext
wend
```

Discussion

When a computer joins an Active Directory domain, the operating system attributes are updated for the computer object. There are four of these attributes, which can be used in queries to find computers that match certain OS-specific criteria, like service pack level. These attributes include the following:

operatingSystem
> Descriptive name of the installed Operating System (e.g., Windows Server 2003, Windows 2000 Server, and Windows XP Professional)

operatingSystemVersion
> Numerical representation of the operating system (e.g., 5.0 (2195) and 5.2 (3757))

operatingSystemServicePack
> Current service pack level if one is installed (e.g., Service Pack 2 and Service Pack 3)

 This recipe only applies to Windows-based machines. Other types of machines (e.g., Unix) that have accounts in Active Directory do not automatically update their OS attributes.

8.11 Binding to the Default Container for Computers

 This recipe requires the Windows Server 2003 domain functional level.

Problem

You want to bind to the default container that new computers objects are created in.

Solution

Using a graphical user interface

1. Open LDP.
2. From the menu, select Connection → Connect.
3. For Server, enter the name of a domain controller (or leave blank to do a server-less bind).
4. For Port, enter 389.
5. Click OK.
6. From the menu, select Connection → Bind.

7. Enter credentials of a domain user.

8. Click OK.

9. From the menu, select View → Tree.

10. For the DN, enter:

    `<WKGUID=aa312825768811d1aded00c04fd8d5cd,<DomainDN>>`

    where <DomainDN> is the distinguished name of a domain.

11. Click OK.

12. In the left menu, you can now browse the default computers container for the domain.

Using a command-line interface

With tools like netdom, if there is an option to only specify the name of the computer, and not its DN or parent container, the default computers container is typically used.

Using VBScript

```
' This code illustrates how to bind to the default computers container.
' ------ SCRIPT CONFIGURATION ------
strDomain = "<DomainDNSName>"   ' e.g. apac.rallencorp.com
' ------ END CONFIGURATION ---------

' Computer GUID as defined in ntdsapi.h
Const ADS_GUID_COMPUTRS_CONTAINER = "aa312825768811d1aded00c04fd8d5cd"

set objRootDSE = GetObject("LDAP://" & strDomain & "/RootDSE")
set objCompContainer = GetObject("LDAP://<WKGUID=" & _
                        ADS_GUID_COMPUTRS_CONTAINER & "," & _
                        objRootDSE.Get("defaultNamingContext") & ">" )
WScript.Echo objCompContainer.Get("distinguishedName")
```

Discussion

There are several important objects within each Active Directory domain that need to be "rename safe." By that I mean you should be able to rename the object and not impact other applications that may depend on it. It is for this reason that Microsoft created WKGUID binding. WKGUID allows you to use a well-known GUID to bind with instead of a distinguished name.

For example, the default computers container has the following WKGUID:

`aa312825768811d1aded00c04fd8d5cd`

You can use the GUID to bind to the default computers container in the domain using the following ADsPath:

`LDAP://<WKGUID=aa312825768811d1aded00c04fd8d5cd,dc=apac,dc=rallencorp,dc=com>`

The list of well-known objects for a domain is contained in the `wellKnownObjects` attribute of the `domainDNS` object for the domain. The `wellKnownObjects` attribute is multivalued with DNWithBinary syntax. The following is an example of what that attribute looks like for the *rallencorp.com* domain:

```
B:32:AA312825768811D1ADED00C04FD8D5CD:CN=Computers,DC=rallencorp,DC=com; B:32:
F4BE92A4C777485E878E9421D53087DB:CN=Microsoft,CN=Program Data,DC=rallencorp,DC=com;
B:32:09460C08AE1E4A4EA0F64AEE7DAA1E5A:CN=Program Data,DC=rallencorp,DC=com; B:32:
22B70C67D56E4EFB91E9300FCA3DC1AA:CN=ForeignSecurityPrincipals,DC=rallencorp,DC=com;
B:32:18E2EA80684F11D2B9AA00C04F79F805:CN=Deleted Objects,DC=rallencorp,DC=com; B:32:
2FBAC1870ADE11D297C400C04FD8D5CD:CN=Infrastructure,DC=rallencorp,DC=com; B:32:
AB8153B7768811D1ADED00C04FD8D5CD:CN=LostAndFound,DC=rallencorp,DC=com; B:32:
AB1D30F3768811D1ADED00C04FD8D5CD:CN=System,DC=rallencorp,DC=com; B:32:
A361B2FFFFD211D1AA4B00C04FD7D83A:OU=Domain Controllers,DC=rallencorp,DC=com; B:32:
A9D1CA15768811D1ADED00C04FD8D5CD:CN=Users,DC=rallencorp,DC=com;
```

Each value has the format of:

```
B:NumberofBytes:GUID:DistinguishedName
```

As you can see, the GUID for the first value is the same as the one we used in the ADsPath above to bind to the default computers container.

See Also

Recipe 8.12 for changing the default computers container and MSDN: Binding to Well-Known Objects Using WKGUID

8.12 Changing the Default Container for Computers

Problem

You want to change the container that computers are created in by default.

Solution

Using a graphical user interface

1. Open LDP.
2. From the menu, select Connection → Connect.
3. For Server, enter the name of a domain controller (or leave blank to do a server-less bind).
4. For Port, enter 389.
5. Click OK.
6. From the menu, select Connection → Bind.

7. Enter credentials of a domain user.

8. Click OK.

9. From the menu, select Browse → Modify.

10. For Dn, enter the distinguished name of the domainDNS object of the domain you want to modify.

11. For Attribute, enter wellKnownObjects.

12. For Values, enter the following:

    B:32:AA312825768811D1ADED00C04FD8D5CD:CN=Computers,*<DomainDN>*

    where *<DomainDN>* is the same as the DN you enter for the Dn field.

13. Select Delete for the Operation and click the Enter button.

14. Go back to the Values field and enter the following:

    B:32:AA312825768811D1ADED00C04FD8D5CD:*<NewComputersParent>*,*<DomainDN>*

    where *<NewComputersParent>* is the new parent container for new computer objects (e.g., ou=RAllenCorp Computers).

15. Select Add for the Operation and click the Enter button.

16. Click the Run button.

17. The result of the operations will be displayed in the right pane of the main LDP window.

Using a command-line interface

```
> redircmp "<NewParentDN>"
```

Using VBScript

```
' This code changes the default computers container.
' ------ SCRIPT CONFIGURATION ------
strNewComputersParent = "<NewComputersParent>" ' e.g. OU=RAllenCorp Computers
strDomain             = "<DomainDNSName>"      ' e.g. rallencorp.com
' ------ END CONFIGURATION ---------

Const COMPUTER_WKGUID = "B:32:AA312825768811D1ADED00C04FD8D5CD:"
' ADS_PROPERTY_OPERATION_ENUM
Const ADS_PROPERTY_APPEND = 3
Const ADS_PROPERTY_DELETE = 4

set objRootDSE = GetObject("LDAP://" & strDomain & "/RootDSE")
set objDomain = GetObject("LDAP://" & objRootDSE.Get("defaultNamingContext"))
set objCompWK = GetObject("LDAP://" & _
                     "<WKGUID=AA312825768811D1ADED00C04FD8D5CD," & _
                     objRootDSE.Get("defaultNamingContext") & ">")

objDomain.PutEx ADS_PROPERTY_DELETE, "wellKnownObjects", _
                Array( COMPUTER_WKGUID & objCompWK.Get("distinguishedName"))
objDomain.PutEx ADS_PROPERTY_APPEND, "wellKnownObjects", _
```

```
        Array( COMPUTER_WKGUID & strNewComputersParent & "," &
                objRootDSE.Get("defaultNamingContext") )
objDomain.SetInfo
WScript.Echo "New default Computers container set to " & _
        strNewComputersParent
```

Discussion

Most Active Directory administrators do not use the Computers container within the Domain naming context as their primary computer repository. One reason is that since it is a container and not an OU, you cannot apply a group policy to it. If you have another location where you store computer objects, you might want to consider changing the default container used to bind to the computers container by changing the well-known objects attribute, as shown in this recipe. This could be beneficial if you want to ensure computers cannot sneak into Active Directory without any group policies applied to it.

See Recipe 8.11 for more information on how well-known objects are specified in Active Directory.

See Also

MS KB 324949 (Redirecting the Users and Computers Containers in Windows Server 2003 Domains)

## CHAPTER 9

Group Policy Objects (GPOs)

9.0 Introduction

Active Directory group policy objects (GPOs) can customize virtually any aspect of a computer or user's desktop. They can also install applications, secure a computer, run logon/logoff or startup/shutdown scripts, and much more. You can assign a GPO to a specific security group, Organizational units (OU), site, or domain. This is called scope of management (SOM for short) because only the users or computers that fall under the scope of the group, OU, site, or domain will process the GPO. Assigning a GPO to a SOM is referred to as linking the GPO.

With Windows Server 2003, you can also use a WMI filter to restrict the application of a GPO. A WMI filter is simply a WMI query that can search against any information on a client's computer. If the WMI filter returns a true value (i.e., something is returned from the query), the GPO will be processed; otherwise, it will not. So not only do you have all of the SOM options for applying GPOs, you can now use any WMI information available on the client's computer to determine whether GPOs should be applied. For more on the capabilities of GPOs, I recommend reading Chapter 7 of *Active Directory*, Second Edition (O'Reilly).

GPOs consist of two parts. `groupPolicyContainer` (GPC) objects are stored in Active Directory for each GPO, which reside in the `cn=Policies,cn=System,<DomainDN>` container. These objects store information related to software deployment and are used for linking to OUs, sites, and domains. The guts of GPOs are stored on the file system of each domain controller in group policy template (GPT) files. These can be found in the *%SystemRoot%\SYSVOL\sysvol\<DomainDNSName>\Policies* directory.

So why are there two storage points for GPOs? The need for the Active Directory object is obvious: to be able to link GPOs to other types of objects, the GPOs need to be represented in Active Directory. It is necessary to store GPOs on the file system because clients currently use a file-based mechanism to process and store GPOs, and to provide legacy support for the NETLOGON share.

Managing GPOs

While the capabilities of GPOs were significant in Windows 2000 Active Directory, the one obvious thing that was lacking were good tools for managing them. The dual storage nature of GPOs creates a lot of problems. First, Microsoft did not provide a scriptable interface for accessing and manipulating GPOs. Second, there were no tools for copying or migrating GPOs from a test environment to production. In Windows 2000, the primary tool for managing GPOs was the Group Policy Editor (GPE), now known as the Group Policy Object Editor (GPOE). The main function of GPOE is to modify GPO settings; it does not provide any other management capabilities.

Microsoft realized these were major issues for group policy adoption, so they developed the Group Policy Management Console (GPMC). The GPMC is a MMC snap-in that provides the kitchen sink of GPO management capabilities. You can create, delete, import, copy, back-up, restore, and model GPOs from a single interface. Perhaps what is even better is the scriptable API that comes with the GPMC. Pretty much every function you can accomplish with the GPMC tool, you can do via a script.

 The only major feature that is still lacking is the ability to directly modify the settings of a GPO. That can be done only with the GPOE. However, the GPMC provides numerous options for migrating GPOs, which addresses the majority of the problems people face today.

You can download the GPMC from the following site: *http://www.microsoft.com/ windowsserver2003/gpmc/default.mspx*. It requires the .NET Framework on Windows Server 2003 or Windows XP SP 1 with hotfix Q326469, and cannot be run on Windows 2000. You can manage Windows 2000-based Active Directory GPOs with the GPMC as long as you run it from one of the previously mentioned platforms.

The majority of solutions presented in this chapter use GPMC. In fact, most of these recipes would not have had workable solutions were it not for the GPMC. It is for this reason that I highly recommend downloading it and becoming familiar with it. Most of the command-line solutions I provide, use one of the scripts provided in the GPMC install. A whole host of pre-canned scripts have already been written, in a mix of VBScript and JavaScript, that serve as great command-line tools and good examples to start scripting GPOs. These scripts are available, by default, in the *%ProgramFiles%\GPMC\scripts* directory. You can execute them one of two ways. You can call it using `cscript`:

```
> cscript listallgpos.wsf
```

or, if you make `cscript` your default WSH interpreter, you can execute the file directly. To make `cscript` your default interpreter, run this command:

```
> cscript //H:cscript
```

The complete documentation for the GPM API is available in the *gpmc.chm* file in the *%ProgramFiles%\GPMC\scripts* directory or from MSDN (*http://msdn.microsoft.com/*).

9.1   Finding the GPOs in a Domain

Problem

You want to find all of the GPOs that have been created in a domain.

Solution

Using a graphical user interface

1. Open the GPMC snap-in.
2. In the left pane, expand the Forest container.
3. Expand the Domains container.
4. Browse to the domain of the target GPO.
5. Expand the Group Policy Objects container. All of the GPOs in the domain will be listed under that container.

Using a command-line interface

```
> listallgpos.wsf [/domain:<DomainDNSName>] [/v]
```

You can also use the gpotool to display the GPOs:

```
> gpotool [/domain:<DomainDNSName>] [/verbose]
```

Using VBScript

```
' This code displays all of the GPOs for a domain.
' ------ SCRIPT CONFIGURATION ------
strDomain   = "<DomainDNSName>"    ' e.g. rallencorp.com
' ------ END CONFIGURATION ---------

set objGPM = CreateObject("GPMgmt.GPM")
set objGPMConstants = objGPM.GetConstants( )

' Initialize the Domain object
set objGPMDomain = objGPM.GetDomain(strDomain, "", objGPMConstants.UseAnyDC)

' Create an empty search criteria
set objGPMSearchCriteria = objGPM.CreateSearchCriteria
set objGPOList = objGPMDomain.SearchGPOs(objGPMSearchCriteria)

' Print the GPOs.
WScript.Echo "Found " & objGPOList.Count & " GPOs in " & strDomain & ":"
for each objGPO in objGPOList
   WScript.Echo "    " & objGPO.DisplayName
next
```

Discussion

See the Introduction Recipe 9.0 for more on how GPOs are stored in Active Directory.

Using VBScript

You can find the GPOs in a domain by using the `GPMDomain.SearchGPOs` method. The only parameter you need to pass to `SearchGPOs` is a `GPMSearchCriteria` object, which can be used to define criteria for your search. In this case, I created a `GPMSearchCriteria` object without additional criteria so that all GPOs are returned. The `SearchGPOs` method returns a `GPMGPOCollection` object, which is a collection of `GPMGPO` objects.

See Also

MS KB 216359 (HOW TO: Identify Group Policy Objects in the Active Directory and SYSVOL) and MSDN: GPMDomain.SearchGPOs

9.2 Creating a GPO

Problem

You want to create a GPO to force users to have a particular desktop configuration or provision configuration settings on workstations or servers.

Solution

Using a graphical user interface

1. Open the GPMC snap-in.
2. In the left pane, expand the Forest container, expand the Domains container, and browse to the domain of the target GPO.
3. Right-click on the Group Policy Objects container and select New.
4. Enter the name of the GPO and click OK.

Using a command-line interface

```
> creategpo.wsf <GPOName> [/domain:<DomainDNSName>]
```

Using VBScript

```
' This code creates an empty GPO.
' ------ SCRIPT CONFIGURATION ------
strGPO     = "<GPOName>"         ' e.g. Sales GPO
strDomain  = "<DomainDNSName>"   ' e.g. rallencorp.com
' ------ END CONFIGURATION ---------
```

```
set objGPM = CreateObject("GPMgmt.GPM")
set objGPMConstants = objGPM.GetConstants()

' Initialize the Domain object
set objGPMDomain = objGPM.GetDomain(strDomain, "", objGPMConstants.UseAnyDC)

' Create the GPO and print the results
set objGPO = objGPMDomain.CreateGPO()
WScript.Echo "Successfully created GPO"
objGPO.DisplayName = strGPO
WScript.Echo "Set GPO name to " & strGPO
```

Discussion

When you create a GPO through the GPMC, it is initially empty with no settings or links configured. See Recipe 9.6 for more on modifying GPO settings, and Recipe 9.12 for creating a link.

Using VBScript

To create a GPO, I first instantiate a GPMDomain object for the domain to add the GPO to. This is accomplished with the GPM.GetDomain method. Then it is just a matter of calling the GPMDomain.CreateGPO method (with no parameters) to create an empty GPO. A GPM.GPO object is returned from this method, which I then use to set the display name of the GPO.

See Also

MS KB 216359 (HOW TO: Identify Group Policy Objects in the Active Directory and SYSVOL) and MSDN: GPMDomain.CreateGPO

9.3   Copying a GPO

Problem

You want to copy the properties and settings of a GPO to another GPO.

Solution

Using a graphical user interface

1. Open the GPMC snap-in.
2. In the left pane, expand the Forest container, expand the Domains container, browse to the domain of the source GPO, and expand the Group Policy Objects container.
3. Right-click on the source GPO and select Copy.

4. Right-click on the Group Policy Objects container and select Paste.

5. Select whether you want to use the default permissions or preserve the existing permissions, and click OK.

6. A status window will pop up that will indicate whether the copy was successful. Click OK to close.

7. Rename the new GPO by right-clicking it in the left pane and selecting Rename.

Using a command-line interface

```
> copygpo.wsf <SourceGPOName> <TargetGPOName>
```

Using VBScript

```
' This code copies a source GPO to a new GPO
' ------ SCRIPT CONFIGURATION ------
strSourceGPO  = "<SourceGPOName>"  ' e.g. SalesGPO
strNewGPO     = "<NewGPOName>"     ' e.g. Marketing GPO
strDomain     = "<DomainDNSName>"  ' e.g. rallencorp.com
' ------ END CONFIGURATION ---------

set objGPM = CreateObject("GPMgmt.GPM")
set objGPMConstants = objGPM.GetConstants()

' Initialize the Domain object
set objGPMDomain = objGPM.GetDomain(strDomain, "", objGPMConstants.UseAnyDC)

' Find the source GPO
set objGPMSearchCriteria = objGPM.CreateSearchCriteria
objGPMSearchCriteria.Add objGPMConstants.SearchPropertyGPODisplayName, _
                         objGPMConstants.SearchOpEquals, cstr(strSourceGPO)
set objGPOList = objGPMDomain.SearchGPOs(objGPMSearchCriteria)
if objGPOList.Count = 0 then
   WScript.Echo "Did not find GPO: " & strGPO
   WScript.Echo "Exiting."
   WScript.Quit
elseif objGPOList.Count > 1 then
   WScript.Echo "Found more than one matching GPO. Count: " & _
                objGPOList.Count
   WScript.Echo "Exiting."
   WScript.Quit
else
   WScript.Echo "Found GPO: " & objGPOList.Item(1).DisplayName
End if

' Copy from source GPO to target GPO
set objGPMResult = objGPOList.Item(1).CopyTo(0, objGPMDomain, strNewGPO)

' This will throw an exception if there were any errors
' during the actual operation.
on error resume next
objGPMResult.OverallStatus()
```

```
    if objGPMResult.Status.Count > 0 then
        WScript.Echo "Status message(s): " & objGPMResult.Status.Count
        for i = 1 to objGPMResult.Status.Count
            WScript.Echo objGPMResult.Status.Item(i).Message
        next
        WScript.Echo vbCrLf
    end if

    ' Display the results
    if Err.Number <> 0 then
        WScript.Echo "Error copying GPO."
        WScript.Echo "Error: " & Err.Description
    else
        WScript.Echo "Copy successful to " & strNewGPO & "."
    end if
```

Discussion

Prior to the GPMC tool, one of the big problems with managing GPOs in large environments is migrating them from one forest to another. It is common to have a test forest where GPOs are initially created, configured, and tested before moving them into production. The problem is that once you have the GPO the way you want it in the test forest, there is no easy way to move it to the production forest.

With the GPMC you can simply copy GPOs between domains and even forests. Copying GPOs between forests requires a trust to be in place between the two target domains (or a forest trust between the two forests). If this is not possible, you can import GPOs, which is similar to a copy except that a trust is not needed. A GPO import uses a back up of the source GPO in order to create the new GPO. See Recipe 9.7 for more information on importing a GPO.

Some properties of GPOs, such as security group filters or UNC paths, may vary slightly from domain to domain. In that case, you can use a GPMC migration table to help facilitate the transfer of those types of references to the target domain. For more information on migration tables, see the GPMC help file.

Using VBScript

To copy a GPO, I have to first find the source GPO. To do this, I use a GPMSearchCriteria object to find the GPO that is equal to the display name of the GPO specified in the configuration section. I use an if elseif else conditional statement to ensure that only one GPO is returned. If zero was returned or more than one are returned, I have to abort the script.

Now that I have a GPMGPO object, I'm ready to copy the GPO using the GPMGPO.CopyTo method. The first parameter to CopyTo is a flag that indicates how permissions in the source GPO should be handled when copying them to the new GPO. I specified 0 to use the default setting (see the GPMC help file for the other values). The second parameter is a GPMDomain object of the domain the GPO should be copied to. The last parameter is the display name of the new GPO.

See Also

Recipe 9.7 for importing a GPO and MSDN: GPMGPO.CopyTo

9.4   Deleting a GPO

Problem

You want to delete a GPO.

Solution

Using a graphical user interface

1. Open the GPMC snap-in.
2. In the left pane, expand the Forest container, expand the Domains container, browse to the domain of the target GPO, and expand the Group Policy Objects container.
3. Right-click on the target GPO and select Delete.
4. Click OK to confirm.

Using a command-line interface

```
> deletegpo.wsf <GPOName> [/domain:<DomainDNSName>]
```

Using VBScript

```
' This code deletes the specified GPO.
' ------ SCRIPT CONFIGURATION ------
strGPO     = "<GPOName>"          ' e.g. My New GPO
strDomain  = "<DomainDNSName>"    ' e.g. rallencorp.com
' ------ END CONFIGURATION ---------

set objGPM = CreateObject("GPMgmt.GPM")
set objGPMConstants = objGPM.GetConstants()

' Initialize the Domain object
set objGPMDomain = objGPM.GetDomain(strDomain, "", objGPMConstants.UseAnyDC)

' Find the GPO
set objGPMSearchCriteria = objGPM.CreateSearchCriteria
objGPMSearchCriteria.Add objGPMConstants.SearchPropertyGPODisplayName, _
                         objGPMConstants.SearchOpEquals, cstr(strGPO)
set objGPOList = objGPMDomain.SearchGPOs(objGPMSearchCriteria)
if objGPOList.Count = 0 then
```

```
      WScript.Echo "Did not find GPO: " & strGPO
      WScript.Echo "Exiting."
      WScript.Quit
   elseif objGPOList.Count > 1 then
      WScript.Echo "Found more than one matching GPO. Count: " & _
                   objGPOList.Count
      WScript.Echo "Exiting."
      WScript.Quit
   else
      WScript.Echo "Found GPO: " & objGPOList.Item(1).DisplayName
   end if

   ' Delete the GPO
   objGPOList.Item(1).Delete
   WScript.Echo "Successfully deleted GPO: " & strGPO
```

Discussion

When you delete a GPO through the GPMC, it attempts to find all links to the GPO
in the domain and will delete them if the user has permissions to delete the links. If
the user does not have the necessary permissions to remove the links, the GPO will
still get deleted, but the links will remain intact. Any links external to the domain the
GPO is in are not automatically deleted. It is for this reason that it is a good practice
to view the links to the GPO before you delete it. Links to deleted GPOs show up as
"Not Found" in GPMC.

Using VBScript

I use a GPMSearchCriteria object to find the GPO that is equal to the display name of
the GPO specified in the configuration section. I use an if elseif else conditional
statement to ensure that only one GPO is returned. If zero or more than one are
returned, I abort the script. If only one is returned, I used the GPMGPO.Delete method
to delete the GPO.

See Also

Recipe 9.11 for viewing the links for a GPO and MSDN: GPMGPO.Delete

9.5   Viewing the Settings of a GPO

Problem

You want to view the settings that have been defined on a GPO.

Solution

Using a graphical user interface

1. Open the GPMC snap-in.
2. In the left pane, expand the Forest container, expand the Domains container, browse to the domain of the target GPO, and expand the Group Policy Objects container.
3. Click on the target GPO.
4. In the right pane, click on the Settings tab.
5. Click the Show All link to display all configured settings.

Using a command-line interface

```
> getreportsforgpo.wsf "<GPOName>" <ReportLocation> [/domain:<DomainDNSName>]
```

Using VBScript

```vbscript
' This code generates a HTML report of all the properties
' and settings for a GPO.
' ------ SCRIPT CONFIGURATION ------
strGPO        = "<GPOName>"           ' e.g. Sales GPO
strDomain     = "<DomainDNSName>"     ' e.g. rallencorp.com
strReportFile = "<FileNameAndPath>"   ' e.g. c:\gpo_report.html
' ------ END CONFIGURATION ---------

set objGPM = CreateObject("GPMgmt.GPM")
set objGPMConstants = objGPM.GetConstants()

' Initialize the Domain object
set objGPMDomain = objGPM.GetDomain(strDomain, "", objGPMConstants.UseAnyDC)

set objGPMSearchCriteria = objGPM.CreateSearchCriteria
objGPMSearchCriteria.Add objGPMConstants.SearchPropertyGPODisplayName, _
                  objGPMConstants.SearchOpEquals, cstr(strGPO)
set objGPOList = objGPMDomain.SearchGPOs(objGPMSearchCriteria)

if objGPOList.Count = 0 then
   WScript.Echo "Did not find GPO: " & strGPO
   WScript.Echo "Exiting."
   WScript.Quit
elseif objGPOList.Count > 1 then
   WScript.Echo "Found more than one matching GPO. Count: " & _
              objGPOList.Count
   WScript.Echo "Exiting."
   WScript.Quit
else
   WScript.Echo "Found GPO: " & objGPOList.Item(1).DisplayName
end if
```

```
set objGPMResult = objGPOList.Item(1).GenerateReportToFile( _
                        objGPMConstants.ReportHTML, _
                                      strReportFile)

' This will throw an exception if there were any errors
' during the actual operation.
on error resume next
objGPMResult.OverallStatus( )

if objGPMResult.Status.Count > 0 then
   WScript.Echo "Status message(s): " & objGPMResult.Status.Count
   for i = 1 to objGPMResult.Status.Count
      WScript.Echo objGPMResult.Status.Item(i).Message
   next
   WScript.Echo vbCrLf
end if

' Display the result
if Err.Number <> 0 then
   WScript.Echo "Error generating report."
   WScript.Echo "Error: " & Err.Description
else
   WScript.Echo "Reported saved to " & strReportFile
end if
```

Discussion

The GPMC can generate an XML or HTML report that contains all of the settings in a GPO. See Recipe 9.6 for more on how to modify GPO settings.

Using VBScript

I use a GPMSearchCriteria object to find the GPO that is equal to the display name of the GPO specified in the configuration section. I use an if elseif else conditional statement to ensure that only one GPO is returned. If zero or more than one are returned, I abort the script. If only one is returned, I used the GPMGPO. GenerateReportToFile method to generate a report of all the settings in the GPO. The first parameter for GenerateReportToFile is a constant that determines the type of report to generate (i.e., HTML or XML). The second parameter is the path of the file to store the report.

See Also

MSDN: GPMGPO.GenerateReportToFile

9.6   Modifying the Settings of a GPO

Problem

You want to modify the settings associated with a GPO.

Solution

Using a graphical user interface

1. Open the GPMC snap-in.
2. In the left pane, expand the Forest container, expand the Domains container, browse to the domain of the target GPO, and expand the Group Policy Objects container.
3. Right-click on the target GPO and select Edit. This will bring up the Group Policy Object Editor.
4. Browse through the Computer Configuration or User Configuration settings and modify them as necessary.

Using a command-line interface or VBScript

You cannot modify the settings of a GPO with any of the command-line tools or APIs, but you can copy and import settings as described in Recipes 9.3 and 9.7.

Discussion

The one function that the GPMC tool and API cannot do is modify GPO settings. This still must be done from within the GPOE. You can, however, launch GPOE from within GPMC as described in the GUI solution. Not having a scriptable way to modify GPO settings has been a big roadblock with managing GPOs, especially across multiple forests. Copying or importing GPOs can help with migrating settings across forests.

See Also

Recipe 9.3 for copying a GPO, Recipe 9.5 for viewing the settings of a GPO, and Recipe 9.7 for importing a GPO

9.7   Importing Settings into a GPO

Problem

You want to import settings from one GPO to another.

Solution

Using a graphical user interface

1. Open the GPMC snap-in.

2. In the left pane, expand the Forest container, expand the Domains container, browse to the domain of the target GPO, and expand the Group Policy Objects container.

3. Right-click on the target GPO and select Import Settings.

4. Click Next.

5. Click the Backup button if you want take a backup of the GPO you are importing into.

6. Click Next.

7. Select the backup folder location and click Next.

8. Select the backup instance you want to import from and click Next.

9. It then will scan to see if there are any security principals or UNC paths in the GPO being imported from. If there are, it will give you an option to modify those settings.

10. Click Next.

11. Click Finish.

Using a command-line interface

```
> importgpo.wsf "<GPOBackupLocation>" "<OrigGPOName>" "<NewGPOName>"
```

Using VBScript

```
' This code imports the settings from a GPO that has been backed up into
' an existing GPO.
' ------ SCRIPT CONFIGURATION ------
strGPOImportTo   = "<GPOName>"         ' e.g. Sales GPO
strDomain        = "<DomainDNSName>"   ' e.g. rallencorp.com
strBackupLocation = "<BackupLocation>" ' e.g. c:\GPMC Backups

' GUID representing specific backup
' e.g.{3E53B39B-C29B-44FF-857B-8A84528804FF}
strBackupID      = "<BackupGUID>"
' ------ END CONFIGURATION ---------

set objGPM = CreateObject("GPMgmt.GPM")
set objGPMConstants = objGPM.GetConstants()

' Initialize the Domain object
set objGPMDomain = objGPM.GetDomain(strDomain, "", objGPMConstants.UseAnyDC)

' Locate GPO backup
set objGPMBackupDir = objGPM.GetBackupDir(strBackupLocation)
```

```
set objGPMBackup = objGPMBackupDir.GetBackup(strBackupID)
WScript.Echo "Backup found:"
WScript.Echo "  ID: " & objGPMBackup.ID
WScript.Echo "  Timestamp: " & objGPMBackup.TimeStamp
WScript.Echo "  GPO ID: " & objGPMBackup.GPOID
WScript.Echo "  GPO Name: " & objGPMBackup.GPODisplayName
WScript.Echo "  Comment: " & objGPMBackup.Comment
WScript.Echo

' Find GPO to import into
set objGPMSearchCriteria = objGPM.CreateSearchCriteria
objGPMSearchCriteria.Add objGPMConstants.SearchPropertyGPODisplayName, _
                         objGPMConstants.SearchOpEquals, cstr(strGPOImportTo)
set objGPOList = objGPMDomain.SearchGPOs(objGPMSearchCriteria)
if objGPOList.Count = 0 then
   WScript.Echo "Did not find GPO: " & strGPO
   WScript.Echo "Exiting."
   WScript.Quit
elseif objGPOList.Count > 1 then
   WScript.Echo "Found more than one matching GPO. Count: " & _
                objGPOList.Count
   WScript.Echo "Exiting."
   WScript.Quit
else
   WScript.Echo "Found GPO: " & objGPOList.Item(1).DisplayName
end if

' Perform the import
set objGPMResult = objGPOList.Item(1).Import(0,objGPMBackup)

' This will throw an exception if there were any errors
' during the actual operation.
on error resume next
objGPMResult.OverallStatus() _

if objGPMResult.Status.Count > 0 then
   WScript.Echo "Status message(s): " & objGPMResult.Status.Count
   for i = 1 to objGPMResult.Status.Count
      WScript.Echo objGPMResult.Status.Item(i).Message
   next
   WScript.Echo vbCrLf
end if

' Print results
if Err.Number <> 0 then
   WScript.Echo "Error importing GPO " & objGPMBackup.GPODisplayName
   WScript.Echo "Error: " & Err.Description
else
   WScript.Echo "Import successful."
   WScript.Echo "GPO '" & objGPMBackup.GPODisplayName & _
                "' has been imported into GPO '" & _
                objGPOList.Item(1).DisplayName & "'"
end if
```

Discussion

The GPMC import function uses a back up of the source GPO to create the new "imported" GPO. This means you must first back up the source GPO using GPMC. You can then import the settings from that GPO into a new GPO, which may be in the same domain or a completely different forest. Importing a GPO is a great way to help facilitate transferring GPO settings from a test environment to production.

Some properties of GPOs, such as security group filters or UNC paths, may vary slightly from domain to domain. In this case, you can use a GPMC migration table to help facilitate the transfer of those kinds of references to the target domain. For more information on migration tables, see the GPMC help file.

Using VBScript

To import the settings of a backup, I have to first instantiate a `GPMBackup` object of the source backup by specifying the backup ID (a GUID) with the `GPMBackupDir.GetBackup` method. If you need to programmatically search for the backup ID, you can use the `GPMBackup.SearchBackups` method to find the most recent backup or a backup with a particular display name.

Next, I instantiate a `GPMGPO` object of the GPO I'm importing into. To do this, I use a `GPMSearchCriteria` object to find the GPO that is equal to the display name of the GPO specified in the configuration section. I use an `if elseif else` conditional statement to ensure that only one GPO is returned. If zero or more than one are returned, I abort the script. If only one was returned, I use the `GPMGPO.Import` method to import the settings. The first parameter to the `Import` method is a flag that determines how security principals and UNC path mapping is done. I use 0, which is the default to not copy security settings. You can also use a migration table to do mappings if necessary. The second parameter is the `GPMBackup` object I instantiated earlier. The rest of the script performs some error handling and prints the results.

See Also

Recipe 9.3 for copying a GPO, Recipe 9.17 for backing up a GPO, and MSDN: GPMGPO.Import

9.8 Assigning Logon/Logoff and Startup/Shutdown Scripts in a GPO

Problem

You want to assign either user logon/logoff scripts or computer startup/shutdown scripts in a GPO.

Solution

Using a graphical user interface

1. Open the GPMC snap-in.

2. In the left pane, expand the Forest container, expand the Domains container, browse to the domain of the target GPO, and expand the Group Policy Objects container.

3. Right-click on the target GPO and select Edit. This will bring up the Group Policy Object Editor.

4. If you want to assign a computer startup or shutdown script, browse to Computer Configuration → Windows Settings → Scripts. If you want to assign a user logon or logoff script, browse to User Computer → Windows Settings → Scripts.

5. In the right pane, double-click on the type of script you want to add.

6. Click the Add button.

7. Select the script by typing the name of it in or browsing to its location.

8. Optionally type any script parameters in the Script Parameters field.

9. Click OK twice.

Discussion

When you assign a script in a GPO, you can either reference a script that is stored locally on the domain controller somewhere under the *NETLOGON* share or a UNC path to a remote fileserver.

The logon script can also be set as an attribute of the user object (scriptPath). This is provided as legacy support for users migrated from NT 4.0 domains. You should choose either one method of specifying the logon script or the other, but not both, as this will cause the logon script to run twice.

9.9   Installing Applications with a GPO

Problem

You want to install an application on a group of computers using a GPO.

Solution

Using a graphical user interface

1. Open the GPMC snap-in.

2. In the left pane, expand the Forest container, expand the Domains container, browse to the domain of the target GPO, and expand the Group Policy Objects container.

3. Right-click on the target GPO and select Edit. This will bring up the Group Policy Object Editor.

4. Under Computer Configuration or User Configuration (depending on which you want to target the installation for), expand Software Settings.

5. Right-click on Software Installation and select New → Package.

6. Browse to the network share that has the MSI package for the application and click OK.

7. Select whether you want to Assign the application or Publish it and click OK.

Discussion

Installing applications with a GPO is a powerful feature, but you must be careful about the network and client impact it can have. If the MSI package you are installing is several megabytes in size, it will take a while for it to download to the client computer, which can result in sluggish performance on the client, especially over a slow connection. You'll also want to make sure you've thoroughly tested the application before deployment. After you've configured the GPO to install it, it will be only a short period of time before it is installed on all targeted your clients. If there is a bug in the application or the installer program is faulty, the impact could be severe to your user base.

Your two options for deploying an application are to *assign* it or *publish* it. If you assign an application, it will get automatically installed on the targeted clients. If you publish an application, it will not get automatically installed, but will be available to be installed manually from Add/Remove Programs in the Control Panel on the target computers.

9.10 Disabling the User or Computer Settings in a GPO

Problem

You want to disable either the user or computer settings of a GPO.

Solution

Using a graphical user interface

1. Open the GPMC snap-in.
2. In the left pane, expand the Forest container, expand the Domains container, browse to the domain of the target GPO, and expand the Group Policy Objects container.
3. Right-click on the target GPO and select GPO Status
4. You can either select User Configuration Settings Disabled to disable the user settings or Computer Configuration Settings Disabled to disable the computer settings.

Using VBScript

```
' This code can enable or disable the user or computer settings of a GPO.
' ------ SCRIPT CONFIGURATION ------
strGPO      = "<GPOName>"          ' e.g. Sales GPO
strDomain   = "<DomainDNSName>"    ' e.g. rallencorp.com
boolUserEnable = False
boolCompEnable = True
' ------ END CONFIGURATION ---------

set objGPM = CreateObject("GPMgmt.GPM")
set objGPMConstants = objGPM.GetConstants( )

' Initialize the Domain object
set objGPMDomain = objGPM.GetDomain(strDomain, "", objGPMConstants.UseAnyDC)

' Find the specified GPO
set objGPMSearchCriteria = objGPM.CreateSearchCriteria
objGPMSearchCriteria.Add objGPMConstants.SearchPropertyGPODisplayName, _
                         objGPMConstants.SearchOpEquals, cstr(strGPO)
set objGPOList = objGPMDomain.SearchGPOs(objGPMSearchCriteria)
if objGPOList.Count = 0 then
   WScript.Echo "Did not find GPO: " & strGPO
   WScript.Echo "Exiting."
   WScript.Quit
elseif objGPOList.Count > 1 then
   WScript.Echo "Found more than one matching GPO. Count: " & _
               objGPOList.Count
   WScript.Echo "Exiting."
   WScript.Quit
else
   WScript.Echo "Found GPO: " & objGPOList.Item(1).DisplayName
end if

' You can comment out either of these if you don't want to set one:

objGPOList.Item(1).SetUserEnabled boolUserEnable
WScript.Echo "User settings: " & boolUserEnable
```

```
objGPOList.Item(1).SetComputerEnabled boolCompEnable
WScript.Echo "Computer settings: " & boolCompEnable
```

Discussion

GPOs consist of two parts, a user and a computer section. The user section contains settings that are specific to a user that logs into a computer, while the computer section defines settings that apply to the computer regardless of which user logs in. You can enable or disable either the user configuration or computer configuration sections of a GPO, or both. By disabling both, you effectively disable the GPO. This can be useful if you want to stop a GPO from applying settings to clients, but you do not want to delete it, remove the links, or clear the settings.

Disabling the user configuration or the computer configuration is useful in environments that have separate OUs for computers and users. Typically, you would disable the computer configuration for GPOs linked to the users' OU and vice versa. Disabling half the GPO in the way makes GPO processing more efficient and can reduce logon times.

Using VBScript

First, I have to find the target GPO. To do this, I use a `GPMSearchCriteria` object to find the GPO that is equal to the display name of the GPO specified in the configuration section. I use an `if elseif else` conditional statement to ensure that only one GPO is returned. If zero or more than one are returned, I abort the script. If only one is returned, I call the `SetUserEnabled` and `SetComputerEnable` methods to either enable or disable the settings per the configuration.

See Also

MSDN: GPMGPO.SetUserEnabled and MSDN: GPMGPO.SetComputerEnabled

9.11   Listing the Links for GPO

Problem

You want to list all of the links for a particular GPO.

Solution

Using a graphical user interface

1. Open the GPMC snap-in.
2. In the left pane, expand the Forest container, expand the Domains container, browse to the domain of the target GPO, and expand the Group Policy Objects container.

3. Click on the GPO you want to view the links for.

4. In the right pane, the defined links for the GPO will be listed under Links.

Using a command-line interface

```
> dumpgpoinfo.wsf "<GPOName>"
```

Using VBScript

```
' This code lists all the sites, OUs, and domains a GPO is linked to.
' ------ SCRIPT CONFIGURATION ------
strGPO     = "<GPOName>"          ' e.g. SalesGPO
strForest  = "<ForestName>"       ' e.g. rallencorp.com
strDomain  = "<DomainDNSName>"    ' e.g. rallencorp.com
' ------ END CONFIGURATION ---------

set objGPM = CreateObject("GPMgmt.GPM")
set objGPMConstants = objGPM.GetConstants( )

' Initialize the Domain object
set objGPMDomain = objGPM.GetDomain(strDomain, "", objGPMConstants.UseAnyDC)
' Initialize the Sites Container object
set objGPMSitesContainer = objGPM.GetSitesContainer(strForest, _
                             strDomain, "", objGPMConstants.UseAnyDC)
' Find the specified GPO
set objGPMSearchCriteria = objGPM.CreateSearchCriteria
objGPMSearchCriteria.Add objGPMConstants.SearchPropertyGPODisplayName, _
                         objGPMConstants.SearchOpEquals, cstr(strGPO)
set objGPOList = objGPMDomain.SearchGPOs(objGPMSearchCriteria)
if objGPOList.Count = 0 then
   WScript.Echo "Did not find GPO: " & strGPO
   WScript.Echo "Exiting."
   WScript.Quit
elseif objGPOList.Count > 1 then
   WScript.Echo "Found more than one matching GPO. Count: " & _
                objGPOList.Count
   WScript.Echo "Exiting."
   WScript.Quit
else
   WScript.Echo "Found GPO: " & objGPOList.Item(1).DisplayName
end if

' Search for all SOM links for this GPO
set objGPMSearchCriteria = objGPM.CreateSearchCriteria
objGPMSearchCriteria.Add objGPMConstants.SearchPropertySOMLinks, _
                         objGPMConstants.SearchOpContains, objGPOList.Item(1)
set objSOMList = objGPMDomain.SearchSOMs(objGPMSearchCriteria)
set objSiteLinkList = objGPMSitesContainer.SearchSites(objGPMSearchCriteria)

if objSOMList.Count = 0 and objSiteLinkList.Count = 0 Then
   WScript.Echo "No Site, Domain, or OU links found for this GPO"
else
   WScript.Echo "Links:"
```

```
    for each objSOM in objSOMList
        select case objSOM.Type
            case objGPMConstants.SOMDomain
                strSOMType = "Domain"
            case objGPMConstants.SOMOU
                strSOMType = "OU"
        end select
        ' Print GPO Domain and OU links
        WScript.Echo "   " & objSOM.Name & " (" & strSOMType & ")"
    next

    ' Print GPO Site Links
    for each objSiteLink in objSiteLinkList
        WScript.Echo "   " & objSiteLink.Name & " (Site)"
    next
end if
```

Discussion

See Recipe 9.0 for more information on GPO linking and SOMs.

Using VBScript

First, I have to find the target GPO. To do this, I use a `GPMSearchCriteria` object to find the GPO that is equal to the display name of the GPO specified in the configuration section. I use an `if elseif else` conditional statement to ensure that only one GPO is returned. If none or more than one are returned, I abort the script. If only one is returned, I search for all SOMs (domain, OUs, and sites) that have the GPO linked using the `GPMSitesContainer.SearchSites` and `GPMDomain.SearchSOMs` methods.

See Also

Recipe 9.12 for creating a GPO link to an OU MSDN: GPMDomain.SearchSOMs, and MSDN: GPMSitesContainer.SearchSites

9.12   Creating a GPO Link to an OU

Problem

You want to apply the GPO settings to the users and/or computers in an OU. This is called linking a GPO to an OU.

Solution

Using a graphical user interface

1. Open the GPMC snap-in.

2. In the left pane, expand the Forest container, expand the Domains container, and browse to the target domain.

3. Right-click on the OU you want to link and Link an Existing GPO.

4. Select from the list of available GPOs and click OK.

Using VBScript

```
' This code links a GPO to an OU
' ------ SCRIPT CONFIGURATION ------
strGPO     = "<GPOName>"        ' e.g. Sales GPO
strDomain  = "<DomainDNSName>"  ' e.g. rallencorp.com
strOU      = "<OrgUnitDN>"      ' e.g. ou=Sales,dc=rallencorp,dc=com
intLinkPos = -1 ' set this to the position the GPO evaluated at
                ' a value of -1 signifies appending it to the end of the list
' ------ END CONFIGURATION ---------

set objGPM = CreateObject("GPMgmt.GPM")
set objGPMConstants = objGPM.GetConstants()

' Initialize the Domain object
set objGPMDomain = objGPM.GetDomain(strDomain, "", objGPMConstants.UseAnyDC)

' Find the specified GPO
set objGPMSearchCriteria = objGPM.CreateSearchCriteria
objGPMSearchCriteria.Add objGPMConstants.SearchPropertyGPODisplayName, _
objGPMConstants.SearchOpEquals, cstr(strGPO)
set objGPOList = objGPMDomain.SearchGPOs(objGPMSearchCriteria)
if objGPOList.Count = 0 then
   WScript.Echo "Did not find GPO: " & strGPO
   WScript.Echo "Exiting."
   WScript.Quit
elseif objGPOList.Count > 1 then
   WScript.Echo "Found more than one matching GPO. Count: " & _
                objGPOList.Count
   WScript.Echo "Exiting."
   WScript.Quit
else
   WScript.Echo "Found GPO: " & objGPOList.Item(1).DisplayName
end if

' Find the specified OU
set objSOM = objGPMDomain.GetSOM(strOU)
if IsNull(objSOM) then
   WScript.Echo "Did not find OU: " & strOU
   WScript.Echo "Exiting."
   WScript.Quit
```

```
else
    WScript.Echo "Found OU: " & objSOM.Name
end if

on error resume next

set objGPMLink = objSOM.CreateGPOLink( intLinkPos, objGPOList.Item(1) )

if Err.Number <> 0 then
    WScript.Echo "There was an error creating the GPO link."
    WScript.Echo "Error: " & Err.Description
else
    WScript.Echo "Sucessfully linked GPO to OU"
end if
```

Discussion

Linking a GPO is the process whereby you assign a SOM, which can be an OU, site, or domain. The solutions show how to link a GPO to an OU, but they could be easily modified to link to a site or domain.

See Recipe 5.11 for details on how to link an OU by modifying the gpLink attribute, instead of using the GPMC interface.

Using VBScript

To link a GPO, I first have to find the target GPO. I use a GPMSearchCriteria object to find the GPO that is equal to the display name of the GPO specified in the configuration section. I use an if elseif else conditional statement to ensure that only one GPO is returned. If zero or more than are are returned, I abort the script. If only one GPO was returned, I instantiate a GPMSOM object by passing the name of the OU to be linked to the GPMDomain.GetSOM method. Once I instantiate this object, I can call GPMSOM.CreateGPOLink to create a GPO link to the OU.

See Also

MS KB 248392 (Scripting the Addition of Group Policy Links) and MSDN: GPM-SOM.CreateGPOLink

9.13 Blocking Inheritance of GPOs on an OU

Problem

You want to block inheritance of GPOs on an OU.

Solution

Using a graphical user interface

1. Open the GPMC snap-in.
2. In the left pane, expand the Forest container, expand the Domains container, and browse to the target domain.
3. Right-click on the OU you want to block inheritance for and select Block Inheritance.

Using VBScript

```
' This code blocks inheritance of GPOs on the specified OU
' ------ SCRIPT CONFIGURATION ------
strDomain   = "<DomainDNSName>" ' e.g. rallencorp.com
strOU       = "<OrgUnitDN>"     ' e.g. ou=Sales,dc=rallencorp,dc=com
boolBlock   = TRUE             ' e.g. set to FALSE to not block inheritance
' ------ END CONFIGURATION ---------

set objGPM = CreateObject("GPMgmt.GPM")
set objGPMConstants = objGPM.GetConstants( )

' Initialize the Domain object
set objGPMDomain = objGPM.GetDomain(strDomain, "", objGPMConstants.UseAnyDC)

' Find the specified OU
set objSOM = objGPMDomain.GetSOM(strOU)
if IsNull(objSOM) then
   WScript.Echo "Did not find OU: " & strOU
   WScript.Echo "Exiting."
   WScript.Quit
else
   WScript.Echo "Found OU: " & objSOM.Name
end if

' on error resume next

objSOM.GPOInheritanceBlocked = boolBlock

if Err.Number <> 0 then
   WScript.Echo "There was an error blocking inheritance."
   WScript.Echo "Error: " & Err.Description
else
   WScript.Echo "Successfully set inheritance blocking on OU to " & boolBlock
end if
```

Discussion

By default, GPOs are inherited down through the directory tree. If you link a GPO to a top-level OU, that GPO will apply to any objects within the child OUs. Sometimes that may not be what you want, and you can disable inheritance as described in the solutions.

Try to avoid blocking inheritance when possible because it can make determining what settings should be applied to a user or computer difficult. If someone sees that a GPO is applied at a top-level OU, they may think it applies to any object under it. Using the Resultant Set of Policies (RSoP) snap-in can help identify what settings are applied to a user or computer (see Recipe 9.20).

Using VBScript

To block inheritance, I first have to get a GPMSOM object for the OU by calling the GPMDomain.GetSOM method. The only parameter to this method is the DN of the OU (or leave blank to reference the domain itself). Next, I call the GPMSOM.GPOInheritanceBlocked method, which should be set to either TRUE or FALSE depending if you want inheritance blocked or not.

See Also

MSDN: GPMDomain.GetSOM and MSDN: GPMSOM.GPOInheritanceBlocked

9.14 Applying a Security Filter to a GPO

Problem

You want to configure a GPO so that it applies only to members of a particular security group.

Solution

Using a graphical user interface

1. Open the GPMC snap-in.
2. In the left pane, expand the Forest container, expand the Domains container, browse to the target domain, and expand the Group Policy Objects container.
3. Click on the GPO you want to modify.
4. In the right pane under Security Filtering, click the Add button.
5. Use the Object Picker to select a group and click OK.
6. Highlight Authenticated Users and click the Remove button.
7. Click OK to confirm.

Using a command-line interface

```
> setgpopermissions.wsf "<GPOName>" "<GroupName>" /permission:Apply
> setgpopermissions.wsf "<GPOName>" "Authenticated Users" /permission:None
```

Using VBScript

```
' This code adds a security group filter permission to a GPO
' and removes the Authenticated Users filter permission.
' ------ SCRIPT CONFIGURATION ------
strGPO         = "<GPOName>"          ' e.g. Sales GPO
strDomain      = "<DomainDNSName>"    ' e.g. rallencorp.com
strGroupAdd    = "<GroupName>"        ' e.g. SalesUsers
strGroupRemove = "Authenticated Users"
' ------ END CONFIGURATION ---------

set objGPM = CreateObject("GPMgmt.GPM")
set objGPMConstants = objGPM.GetConstants( )

' Initialize the Domain object
set objGPMDomain = objGPM.GetDomain(strDomain, "", objGPMConstants.UseAnyDC)

' Find the specified GPO
set objGPMSearchCriteria = objGPM.CreateSearchCriteria
objGPMSearchCriteria.Add objGPMConstants.SearchPropertyGPODisplayName, _
                         objGPMConstants.SearchOpEquals, cstr(strGPO)
set objGPOList = objGPMDomain.SearchGPOs(objGPMSearchCriteria)
if objGPOList.Count = 0 then
   WScript.Echo "Did not find GPO: " & strGPO
   WScript.Echo "Exiting."
   WScript.Quit
elseif objGPOList.Count > 1 then
   WScript.Echo "Found more than one matching GPO. Count: " & _
                objGPOList.Count
   WScript.Echo "Exiting."
   WScript.Quit
else
   WScript.Echo "Found GPO: " & objGPOList.Item(1).DisplayName
end if

' Get permission objects to Apply GPO
set objGPMPerm1 = objGPM.CreatePermission(strGroupAdd, _
                         objGPMConstants.PermGPOApply, False)
set objGPMPerm2 = objGPM.CreatePermission(strGroupRemove, _
                         objGPMConstants.PermGPOApply, False)

' Get the existing set of permissions on the GPO
set objSecurityInfo = objGPOList.Item(1).GetSecurityInfo( )

' Add the new permission
objSecurityInfo.Add objGPMPerm1
' Remove Authenticate users
objSecurityInfo.Remove objGPMPerm2

on error resume next

' Apply the permission to the GPO
objGPOList.Item(1).SetSecurityInfo objSecurityInfo
if Err.Number <> 0 then
```

```
        WScript.Echo "There was an error setting the security filter."
        WScript.Echo "Error: " & Err.Description
    else
        WScript.Echo "Added Apply permission for group " & strGroupAdd
        WScript.Echo "Removed Apply permission for group " & strGroupRemove
    end if
```

Discussion

Creating a security filter for a GPO consists of granting a specific group the `Apply Group Policy` permission on the ACL of the GPO. By default, `Authenticated Users` are granted the Apply Group Policy right on all new GPOs, so you will also need to remove this right if you want to restrict the GPO to only be applied to members of another group.

Avoid using "Deny" as part of the security filter because it can lead to confusion with accounts that have membership of groups with conflicting filter settings. For example, if a user is a member of a group that has "Deny" set in the filter and is also a member of a group that is allowed to apply the policy, the Deny setting will always win. This can be difficult to troubleshoot.

 Be very careful when changing permissions on GPOs. If you create a very restricted GPO and apply a security filter to it, put tight controls on who can modify the GPO and how. If for some reason that security filter was removed (resulting in no security filters), the restrictive GPO could be applied to every user or computer in the domain.

Using VBScript

First, I have to find the target GPO. I use a `GPMSearchCriteria` object to find the GPO that is equal to the display name of the GPO specified in the configuration section. I use an `if elseif else` conditional statement to ensure that only one GPO is returned. If none or more than one were returned, I abort the script. If only one GPO is returned, I create two `GPM.CreatePermission` objects for the group I want to add as a security filter and for the `Authenticated Users` group. Next, I use the `GPMGPO.GetSecurityInfo` to retrieve the current ACL on the GPO. Finally, I add the permission to the ACL for group I want as the new security filter, and I remove the permission for `Authenticated Users`.

See Also

MSDN: GPM.CreatePermission and MSDN: GPMGPO.GetSecurityInfo

9.15   Creating a WMI Filter

 WMI filters can be configured only on a Windows Server 2003 domain controller, and they will apply only to Windows Server 2003- and Windows XP-based clients.

Problem

You want to create a WMI filter.

Solution

Using a graphical user interface

1. Open the GPMC snap-in.
2. In the left pane, expand the Forest container, expand the Domains container, browse to the target domain, and click the WMI Filters container.
3. Right-click on the WMI Filters container and select New.
4. Enter a name and description for the filter.
5. Click the Add button.
6. Select the appropriate namespace, enter a WQL query, and click OK.
7. Repeat steps 5 and 6 for as many queries as you need to add.
8. Click the Save button.

Using VBScript

At the time of publication of this book, there were no GPM methods available for creating WMI filters.

Discussion

WMI filters are new in Windows Server 2003 and provide another way to filter how GPOs are applied to clients. WMI filters live in Active Directory as objects under the WMIPolicy container within the System container for a domain. A WMI filter consists of a WMI Query Language (WQL) query that when linked to a GPO will be run against all clients that the GPO applies to. If the WQL returns a true value (that is returns nonempty results from the WQL query), the GPO will continue to process. If the WQL query returns false (nothing is returned from the query), the GPO will not be processed.

The great thing about WMI filters is that the vast amount of information that is available in WMI on a client becomes available to filter GPOs. You can query against

CPU, memory, disk space, hotfixes installed, service packs installed, applications installed, running processes, and the list goes on and on.

For example, if you want to create a GPO that applies only to computers that are running Windows XP Professional, it would have been really difficult to accomplish under Windows 2000. You would have either needed to create a security group that contained all of those computers as members (and apply a security filter), or move all of those workstations to a particular OU. With a WMI filter, this becomes trivial. Here is an example WQL query that would return true when run on a Windows XP Professional workstation:

```
select * from Win32_OperatingSystem
  where Caption = "Microsoft Windows XP Professional"
```

See Also

Recipe 9.16 for applying a WMI filter to a GPO and MSDN: Querying with WQL

9.16   Applying a WMI Filter to a GPO

 WMI filters can be configured only on a Windows Server 2003 domain controller, and they will apply only to Windows Server 2003- and Windows XP-based clients.

Problem

You want to apply a WMI filter to a GPO.

Solution

Using a graphical user interface

1. Open the GPMC snap-in.
2. In the left pane, expand the Forest container, expand the Domains container, browse to the domain of the GPO you want to target, and expand the Group Policy Objects container.
3. Single-click on the target GPO.
4. In the right name, at the bottom of the window you can select from the list of WMI filters.
5. After you've selected the WMI filter, click Yes to confirm.

Using VBScript

```
' This code links an existing WMI filter with a GPO
' ------ SCRIPT CONFIGURATION ------
```

```
strGPO          = "<GPOName>"            ' e.g. Sales GPO
strDomain       = "<DomainDNSName>"   ' e.g. rallencorp.com

' e.g. {D715559A-7965-45A6-864D-AEBDD9934415}
strWMIFilterID = "<WMIFilterID>"
' ------ END CONFIGURATION ---------

set objGPM = CreateObject("GPMgmt.GPM")
set objGPMConstants = objGPM.GetConstants( )

' Initialize the Domain object
set objGPMDomain = objGPM.GetDomain(strDomain, "", objGPMConstants.UseAnyDC)

' Find the GPO
set objGPMSearchCriteria = objGPM.CreateSearchCriteria
objGPMSearchCriteria.Add objGPMConstants.SearchPropertyGPODisplayName, _
                         objGPMConstants.SearchOpEquals, _
                         cstr(strGPO)
set objGPOList = objGPMDomain.SearchGPOs(objGPMSearchCriteria)
if objGPOList.Count = 0 then
   WScript.Echo "Did not find GPO: " & strGPO
   WScript.Echo "Exiting."
   WScript.Quit
elseif objGPOList.Count > 1 then
   WScript.Echo "Found more than one matching GPO. Count: " & _
                objGPOList.Count
   WScript.Echo "Exiting."
   WScript.Quit
else
   WScript.Echo "Found GPO: " & objGPOList.Item(1).DisplayName
end if

on error resume next

' Retrieve the WMI filter
strWMIFilter = "MSFT_SomFilter.Domain=""" & _
               strDomain & """,ID=""" & _
               strWMIFilterID & """"
set objWMIFilter = objGPMDomain.GetWMIFilter(strWMIFilter)
if Err.Number <> 0 then
   WScript.Echo "Did not find WMI Filter: " & strWMIFilterID
   WScript.Echo "Exiting."
   WScript.Quit
else
   WScript.Echo "Found WMI Filter: " & objWMIFilter.Name
end if

' Link the filter and print the result
objGPOList.Item(1).SetWMIFilter(objWMIFilter)
if Err.Number <> 0 then
   WScript.Echo "Failed to set WMI filter."
   WScript.Echo "Error: " & err.description
else
   WScript.Echo "Set WMI filter successfully."
end if
```

Discussion

You can link only one WMI filter to a GPO. This is not necessarily a limitation because you can still link more than one GPO to a site, domain, or OU. If you need multiple WMI filters to apply to a GPO, copy the GPO and apply a new WMI filter to it. See Recipe 9.15 for more information on WMI filters.

Using VBScript

I use a GPMSearchCriteria object to find the GPO that is equal to the display name of the GPO specified in the configuration section. I use an if elseif else conditional statement to ensure that only one GPO is returned. If none or more than one are returned, I abort the script. If only one GPO is returned, I call GPMDomain.GetWMIFilter to instantiate a GPMWMIFilter object based on the WMI filter GUID specified in the configuration section. If you need to programmatically search for the WMI filter ID, you can use the GPMDomain.SearchWMIFilters method. After I retrieve the GPMWMIFilter object, I call the GPMGPO.SetWMIFilter method to set the filter for the GPO.

See Also

MSDN: GPMDomain.GetWMIFilter and MSDN: GPMGPO.SetWMIFilter

9.17 Backing Up a GPO

Problem

You want to back up a GPO.

Solution

Using a graphical user interface

1. Open the GPMC snap-in.
2. In the left pane, expand the Forest container, expand the Domains container, browse to the domain of the GPO you want to back up, and expand the Group Policy Objects container.
3. Right-click on the GPO you want to back up, and select Back Up.
4. For Location, enter the folder path to store the backup files.
5. For Description, enter a descriptive name for the backup.
6. Click the Back Up button.
7. You will see a progress bar and status message that indicates if the back up was successful.
8. Click OK to exit.

Using a command-line interface

```
> backupgpo.wsf "<GPOName>" "<BackupFolder>" /comment:"<BackupComment>"
```

Using VBScript

```
' This code backs up a GPO to the specified backup location.
' ------ SCRIPT CONFIGURATION ------
strGPO      = "<GPOName>"        ' e.g. Default Domain Policy
strDomain   = "<DomainDNSName>"  ' e.g. rallencorp.com
strLocation = "<BackupFolder>"   ' e.g. c:\GPMC Backups
strComment  = "<BackupComment>"  ' e.g. Default Domain Policy Weekly
' ------ END CONFIGURATION ---------

set objGPM = CreateObject("GPMgmt.GPM")
set objGPMConstants = objGPM.GetConstants( )

' Initialize the Domain object
set objGPMDomain = objGPM.GetDomain(strDomain, "", objGPMConstants.UseAnyDC)

' Find the GPO you want to back up
set objGPMSearchCriteria = objGPM.CreateSearchCriteria
objGPMSearchCriteria.Add objGPMConstants.SearchPropertyGPODisplayName, _
                         objGPMConstants.SearchOpEquals, cstr(strGPO)
set objGPOList = objGPMDomain.SearchGPOs(objGPMSearchCriteria)
if objGPOList.Count = 0 then
   WScript.Echo "Did not find GPO: " & strGPO
   WScript.Echo "Exiting."
   WScript.Quit
elseif objGPOList.Count > 1 then
   WScript.Echo "Found more than one matching GPO. Count: " & _
                objGPOList.Count
   WScript.Echo "Exiting."
   WScript.Quit
else
   WScript.Echo "Found GPO: " & objGPOList.Item(1).DisplayName
End if

' Kick off the backup
On Error Resume Next
set objGPMResult = objGPOList.Item(1).Backup(strLocation, strComment)
' Call the OverallStatus method on the GPMResult.
' This will throw an exception if there were any
' errors during the actual operation.
objGPMResult.OverallStatus( )
if objGPMResult.Status.Count > 0 then
   WScript.Echo "Status messages:" & objGPMResult.Status.Count
   for i = 1 to objGPMResult.Status.Count
   WScript.Echo objGPMResult.Status.Item(i).Message
   next
   WScript.Echo vbCrLf
end if

' Print the results
if Err.Number <> 0 then
```

```
        WScript.Echo "The backup failed."
        WScript.Echo "Attempted to backup GPO '" & strGPO & "' to location " & strLocation
        WScript.Echo "Error: " & err.description
    else
        set objGPMBackup = objGPMResult.Result
        WScript.Echo "Backup completed successfully."
        WScript.Echo "GPO ID: "  & objGPMBackup.GPOID
        WScript.Echo "Timestamp: " & objGPMBackup.TimeStamp
        WScript.Echo "Backup ID: " & objGPMBackup.ID
    end if
```

Discussion

The GPMC provides a way to back up individual (or all) GPOs. A GPO backup consists of a set of folders and files that catalog the GPO settings, filters and links, and is created in the backup location you specify. You can back up a GPO to a local drive or over the network to a file server. Restoring a GPO is just as easy and is described in Recipe 9.18.

Prior to GPMC, the only way to back up GPOs was by backing up the System State on a domain controller. The System State includes Active Directory and SYSVOL (both components are needed to completely back up a GPO). To restore a GPO using this method, you'd have to boot into DS Restore mode and perform an authoritative restore of the GPO(s) you were interested in. Needless to say, the GPMC method is significantly easier.

A good practice is to back up your GPO backups. Since all the back-up information is captured in a series of files, you can back up that information to media, which provides two levels of restore capability. You could restore the last backup taken, which could be stored on a domain controller or file server, or you could go to tape and restore a previous version.

In the folder you specify to store the GPO backups is a list of folders that have GUIDs for names. This does not make it very easy to distinguish which backups are for which GPOs. A quick way to find that out is to use the querybackuplocation.wsf script. This will list each of the folder GUID names and the corresponding GPO it is for:

```
> querybackuplocation.wsf "c:\gpmc backups"
```

Using VBScript

I use a GPMSearchCriteria object to find the GPO that is equal to the display name of the GPO specified in the configuration section. I use an if elseif else conditional statement to ensure that only one GPO is returned. If none or more than one is returned, I abort the script. If only one is returned, I call the GPMGPO.Backup method to back up the GPO. The first parameter is the directory to store the GPO backup files, and the second parameter is a comment that can be stored with the back up.

This comment may come in handy later for doing searches against the backups on a server, so you may want to think about what to put for it.

See Also

Recipe 9.18 for restoring a GPO and MSDN: GPMGPO.Backup

9.18   Restoring a GPO

Problem

You want to restore a GPO.

Solution

Using a graphical user interface

1. Open the GPMC snap-in.
2. In the left pane, expand the Forest container, expand the Domains container, browse to the domain of the GPO you want to back up, and expand the Group Policy Objects container.
3. Right-click on the GPO you want to restore, and select Restore from Backup.
4. Click Next.
5. Select the backup folder location and click Next.
6. Select the backup you want to restore and click Next.
7. Click Finish.
8. You will see the restore status window. After it completes, click OK to close the window.

Using a command-line interface

```
> restoregpo.wsf "<BackupFolder>" "<GPOName>"
```

Using VBScript

```
' This code restores a GPO from a back up.
' ------ SCRIPT CONFIGURATION ------
strGPO      = "<GPOName>"        ' e.g. Sales Users GPO
strDomain   = "<DomainDNSName>" ' e.g. rallencorp.com
strLocation = "<BackupFolder>"  ' e.g. c:\GPMC Backups
strBackupID = "<BackupGUID>"     ' e.g. {85CA37AC-0DB3-442B-98E8-537291D26ED3}
' ------ END CONFIGURATION ---------

set objGPM = CreateObject("GPMgmt.GPM")
set objGPMConstants = objGPM.GetConstants()
```

```
' Initialize the Domain object
set objGPMDomain = objGPM.GetDomain(strDomain, "", objGPMConstants.UseAnyDC)

' Make sure backup location and ID are valid
set objGPMBackupDir = objGPM.GetBackupDir(strLocation)
set objGPMBackup = objGPMBackupDir.GetBackup(strBackupID)
WScript.Echo "Backup found:"
WScript.Echo "  ID: " & objGPMBackup.ID
WScript.Echo "  Timestamp: " & objGPMBackup.TimeStamp
WScript.Echo "  GPO ID: " & objGPMBackup.GPOID
WScript.Echo "  GPO Name: " & objGPMBackup.GPODisplayName
WScript.Echo "  Comment: " & objGPMBackup.Comment
WScript.Echo

' Perform restore
set objGPMResult = objGPMDomain.RestoreGPO(objGPMBackup, _
                                        objGPMConstants.DoNotValidateDC)
' This will throw an exception if there were any errors
' during the actual operation.
on error resume next
objGPMResult.OverallStatus( )
if objGPMResult.Status.Count > 0 then
   WScript.Echo "Status message(s): " & objGPMResult.Status.Count
   for i = 1 to objGPMResult.Status.Count
      WScript.Echo objGPMResult.Status.Item(i).Message
   next
   WScript.Echo vbCrLf
end if

' Print result
if Err.Number <> 0 then
   WScript.Echo "Error restoring GPO " & objGPMBackup.GPODisplayName
   WScript.Echo "Error: " & Err.Description
else
   WScript.Echo "Restore successful."
   WScript.Echo "GPO '" & objGPMBackup.GPODisplayName & _
               "' has been restored."
end if
```

Discussion

To restore a GPO using GPMC, you first need a valid backup of the GPO. The procedure for backing up a GPO is described in Recipe 9.17. You can then restore the GPO, even if the GPO has been deleted. To restore a deleted GPO, use the following steps:

1. Right-click on the Group Policy Objects container in the target domain and select Manage Backups.
2. Highlight the GPO you want to restore and click the Restore Button
3. Click Yes to confirm.
4. Click OK after the restore completes.

If you don't have a valid backup of the GPO, but you do have another GPO that is identical or similar to the one you want to restore (perhaps in another forest), you can copy that GPO to replace the one you want to restore. See Recipe 9.3 for more on copying GPOs.

Using VBScript

To restore a GPO, I have to first get a handle to the backup I am going to restore from. This is done by instantiating an object to the backup location with `GPM.GetBackupDir`, and then calling `GPMBackupDir.GetBackup` with the GUID of the backup to be restored. If you need to programmatically search for the backup ID, you can use the `GPMBackup.SearchBackups` method to find the most recent backup or a backup with a particular display name.

After I obtain a `GPMBackup` object, I call the `GPMDomain.RestoreGPO` method. The first parameter is the `GPMBackup` object that represents the backup to restore. The second parameter is a validation flag, and I use the constant that causes the restore to not be validated against a domain controller.

See Also

Recipe 9.3 for copying a GPO, Recipe 9.17 for backing up a GPO, and MSDN: GPMDomain.RestoreGPO

9.19   Simulating the RSoP

Problem

You want to simulate the RSoP based on OU, site, and security group membership. This is also referred to as Group Policy Modeling.

Solution

 This must be run against a Windows Server 2003 domain controller.

Using a graphical user interface

1. Open the GPMC snap-in.
2. In the left pane, right-click Group Policy Modeling and select Group Policy Modeling Wizard.
3. Select a domain controller to process the query and click Next.

---

4. Under User Information and/or Computer Information, select either the container you want to simulate to contain the user or computer or select a specific user or computer account, and click Next.

5. Select a site if necessary, and click Next.

6. If you selected a target user container or user account in step 4, you will be presented with an option to simulate different group membership. Click Next when you are done.

7. If you selected a target computer container or computer account in step 4, you will be presented with an option to simulate different group membership. Click Next when you are done.

8. If you selected a target user container or user account in step 4, you will be presented with an option to simulate any additional WMI filters. Click Next when you are done.

9. If you selected a target computer container or computer account in step 4, you will be presented with an option to simulate any additional WMI filters. Click Next when you are done.

10. Click Next to start the simulation.

11. Click Finish.

12. In the right pane of the GPMC window, the results of the simulation will be displayed.

Discussion

With GPMC, you can simulate the RSoP based on user-defined OU, site, group, and domain membership. This is very powerful because it allows you to create one or more GPOs, simulate it being applied to a user and computer and determine whether any changes are necessary before deployment.

See Also

Recipe 9.20 for viewing the RSoP

9.20   Viewing the RSoP

Problem

You want to view the actual RSoP for a user and computer. This is a great tool for determining if policies are being applied correctly on a client.

Solution

Using a graphical user interface

 The RSoP snap-in is available only on Windows Server 2003 and Windows XP.

Open the RSoP snap-in by running `rsop.msc` from the command line. This will cause the RSoP snap-in to evaluate the group policies for the target computer and pop open a MMC console so that you can browse the applied settings.

You can target a different computer by right-clicking the top of the tree in the left pane and selecting Change Query. You will then be prompted for the name of the computer to query.

Using a command-line interface

```
> gpresult
```

With the Windows Server 2003 version of gpresult, you can specify a /S option and the name of a computer to target, which allows you to run the command remotely. With Windows 2000, there is a /S option, but it enables super verbose mode. There is no way to target another computer with the Windows 2000 version. For a complete list of options with either version, run gpresult /? from a command line.

Discussion

If you implement more than a few GPOs, it can get confusing as to what settings will apply to users. To address this problem, you can query the resultant set of policy on a client to determine what settings have been applied.

The registry on the target computer is another source of information. You can view the list of policies that were applied to the computer by viewing the subkeys under this key:

```
HKEY_CURRENT_USER\Software\Microsoft\Windows\CurrentVersion\Group Policy\History
```

The settings that were applied are not stored in the registry, but you can obtain the GPO name, distinguished name, SYSVOL location, version, and where the GPO is linked.

See Also

Recipe 9.19 for simulating the RSoP

9.21   Refreshing GPO Settings on a Computer

Problem

You've made some changes to a GPO and want to apply them to a computer by refreshing the group policies for the computer.

Solution

Using a command-line interface

On Windows Server 2003 or Windows XP, use this command:

```
> gpupdate [/target:{Computer | User}]
```

On Windows 2000, use this command:

```
> secedit /refreshpolicy [machine_policy | user_policy]
```

Discussion

The new gpupdate command is a much-needed improvement over the older secedit utility. With gpupdate you can force all settings to be applied with the /force option (the default is only changed settings). You can apply the computer or user settings of GPOs using the /target option, and you can force a logoff or reboot after the settings have been applied using the /logoff and /boot options.

See Also

MS KB 298444 (A Description of the Group Policy Update Utility)

9.22   Restoring a Default GPO

Problem

You've made changes to the Default Domain Security Policy, Default Domain Controller Security Policy, or both, and now want to reset them to their original configuration.

Solution

 This tool can be run only from a Windows Server 2003 domain controller.

Using a command-line interface

The following command would replace both the Default Domain Security Policy and Default Domain Controller Security Policy. You can specify Domain or DC instead of Both, to only restore one or the other.

```
> dcgpofix /target:Both
```

Note that this must be run from a domain controller in the target domain where you want to reset the GPO.

Discussion

If you've ever made changes to the default GPOs and would like to revert back to the original settings, the dcgpofix utility is your solution. dcgpofix works with a particular version of the schema. If the version it expects to be current is different from what is in Active Directory, it will not restore the GPOs. You can work around this by using the /ignoreschema switch, which will restore the GPO according to the version dcgpofix thinks is current. The only time you might experience this issue is if you install a service pack on a domain controller (dc1) that extends the schema, but have not installed it yet on a second domain controller (dc2). If you try to run dcgpofix from dc2, you will receive the error since a new version of the schema and the dcgpofix utility was installed on dc1.

## CHAPTER 10

Schema

10.0 Introduction

The Active Directory schema contains the blueprint for how objects are structured and secured, what data they can contain, and even how they can be viewed. Having a thorough understanding of the schema is paramount for any Active Directory administrator. Understanding key concepts, such as class inheritance, class types, attribute syntax, and attribute indexing options, is critical to being able to adequately design an Active Directory infrastructure and should be considered mandatory for any developer that is writing applications or automation scripts that utilize Active Directory.

If you are one of the lucky few who is designated as a schema administrator (i.e., member of the Schema Admins group), then the importance of the schema is already well known to you. This chapter serves a guide to accomplishing many of the day-to-day tasks you will need to do as a schema administrator. If you feel you need more nuts and bolts information on how the schema works, I suggest reading Chapter 4 of *Active Directory*, Second Edition (O'Reilly).

The Anatomy of Schema Objects

An interesting feature of Active Directory that is not common among other LDAP implementations is that the schema is stored within Active Directory as a set of objects. This means that you can use similar interfaces and programs to manage the schema as you would any other type of object.

All schema objects are stored in the Schema container (e.g., *cn=schema, cn=configuration,<ForestRootDN>*). The schema is comprised of two classes of objects, classSchema and attributeSchema. Unsurprisingly, the classSchema objects define classes and attributeSchema objects define attributes. The Schema container contains a third type of object called subSchema, also known as the abstract schema, which is defined in the LDAP v3 specification (RFC 2251). There is only a single subSchema object in the Schema container, named *cn=Aggregate*, and it contains a summary of the entire schema.

Tables 10-1 and 10-2 contain useful attributes of classSchema objects and attributeSchema objects, respectively.

Table 10-1. Attributes of classSchema objects

Attribute	Description
adminDescription	Description of the class.
auxiliaryClass	Multivalued attribute containing any auxiliary classes defined for the class.
cn	Relative distinguished name of the class.
defaultHidingValue	Boolean that determines whether objects of this class are hidden by default in administrative GUIs.
defaultSecurityDescriptor	Default security descriptor applied to objects of this class.
governsID	Object identifier (OID) for the class.
isDefunct	Boolean that indicates whether the class is defunct (i.e., deactivated).
lDAPDisplayName	Name used when referencing the class in searches or when instantiating or modifying objects of this class.
mayContain	Multivalued attribute that contains a list of attributes that can be optionally set on the class.
mustContain	Multivalued attribute that contains a list of attributes that must be set on the class.
objectClassCategory	Integer representing the class's type. Can be one of 1 (structural), 2 (abstract), 3 (auxiliary), or 0 (88).
possibleInferiors	Multivalued list of other object classes this object can contain.
possSuperiors	Multivalued list of object classes this object can be subordinate to.
rDNAttID	Naming attribute (i.e., RDN) of instances of the class.
schemaIDGUID	GUID of the class.
showInAdvancedViewOnly	Boolean that indicates whether instances of this class should only be shown in Advanced mode in the administrative GUIs.
subClassOf	Parent class.
systemAuxiliaryClass	Multivalued attribute containing any auxiliary classes defined for the class. This can only be modified internally by Active Directory.
systemFlags	Integer representing additional properties of the class.
systemMayContain	Multivalued attribute that contains a list of attributes that can be optionally set on the class. This can only be modified internally by Active Directory.
systemMustContain	Multivalued attribute that contains a list of attributes that must be set on the class. This can only be modified internally by Active Directory.
systemPossSuperiors	Multivalued list of object classes this object can be subordinate to. This can only be modified internally by Active Directory.

Table 10-2. Attributes of attributeSchema objects

Attribute	Description
adminDescription	Description of the attribute.
attributeID	OID for the attribute.
attributeSecurityGUID	GUID to be used to apply security credentials to a set of objects.
attributeSyntax	OID representing the syntax of the attribute. This is used in conjunction with oMSyntax to define a unique syntax.
cn	Relative distinguished name of the attribute.
isDefunct	Boolean that indicates if the attribute is defunct (i.e., deactivated).
isMemberOfPartialAttributeSet	Boolean that indicates if the attribute is a member of the partial attribute set (i.e., the global catalog).
isSingleValued	Boolean that indicates whether the attribute is single valued or multivalued.
linkID	If this is populated, it will contain an integer that represents a link (either forward or backward) to another attribute.
lDAPDisplayName	Name used when referencing the attribute in searches or when populating it on objects. Note that this value may not be the same as cn.
oMSyntax	An integer representing the OM type of the attribute. This is used in conjunction with attributeSyntax to determine a unique syntax for the attribute.
schemaIDGUID	GUID of the attribute.
searchFlags	Integer representing special properties related to searching with the attribute. This includes how the attribute is indexed and if it is used in ANR searches.
systemFlags	Integer representing additional properties of the attribute.

10.1 Registering the Active Directory Schema MMC Snap-in

Problem

You want to use the Active Directory Schema snap-in for the first time on a computer.

Solution

Before you can use the Active Directory Schema snap-in, you have to register the dynamic link library (DLL) associated with it. This can be done with the regsvr32 utility using the following command:

```
> regsvr32 schmmgmt.dll
```

If the command is successful, you'll see the following message:

```
DllRegisterServer in schmmgmt.dll succeeded.
```

Discussion

Most of the Active Directory MMC snap-ins do not require that you manually register the associated DLL. Microsoft requires this with the Active Directory Schema snap-in due to the sensitive nature of modifying the schema. This doesn't actually do much to prevent users from using it, but at least it isn't available by default. And regardless, only members of the Schema Admins group have permission to modify the schema anyway, so making this snap-in available should not pose much of a risk.

The schmmgmt.dll file is installed as part of adminpak.msi or when a domain controller is promoted. If you want to use the Schema snap-in on a non-domain controller machine and you have not installed the adminpak.msi package, you'll need to specify the full path to schmmgmt.dll when using regsvr32, which can be found in the \i386 directory of a Windows Server CD.

See Also

MS KB 320337 (HOW TO: Manage the Active Directory Schema in Windows 2000), and MS KB 326310 (HOW TO: Manage the Active Directory Schema in Windows Server 2003 Enterprise Edition)

10.2   Enabling Schema Updates

 This is necessary only when the Schema FSMO role owner is running Windows 2000.

Problem

You want to enable schema modifications on the Schema FSMO. This is a necessary first step before you can extend the schema.

Solution

Using a graphical user interface

1. Open the Active Directory Schema snap-in.
2. Click on Active Directory Schema in the left pane.
3. Right-click on Active Directory Schema and select Operations Master.
4. Check the box beside Allow schema modifications.
5. Click OK.

Using a command-line interface

To enable modifications to the schema, use the following command:

```
> reg add HKEY_LOCAL_MACHINE\System\CurrentControlSet\Services\NTDS\Parameters /t↵
REG_DWORD /v "Schema Update Allowed" /d 1
```

To disable modifications to the schema, use the following command:

```
> reg delete HKEY_LOCAL_MACHINE\System\CurrentControlSet\Services\NTDS\Parameters /v↵
"Schema Update Allowed" /f
```

Using VBScript

```
' This code enables or disables schema mods on Schema FSMO.
' ------ SCRIPT CONFIGURATION ------
' TRUE to enable schema mods and FALSE to disable
boolSetReg  = TRUE

' Name of the Schema FSMO or "." to run locally
strDC = "<SchemaFSMOName>"
' ------ END CONFIGURATION ---------

const HKEY_LOCAL_MACHINE = &H80000002
set objReg = GetObject("winmgmts:\\" & strDC & "\root\default:StdRegProv")
strKeyPath   = "System\CurrentControlSet\Services\NTDS\Parameters"
strValueName = "Schema Update Allowed"

if boolSetReg = TRUE then
   strValue = 1
   intRC = objReg.SetDWORDValue(HKEY_LOCAL_MACHINE,strKeyPath, _
                                strValueName,strValue)
   if intRC > 0 then
      WScript.Echo "Error occurred: " & intRC
   else
      WScript.Echo strValueName & " value set to " & strValue
   end if
else
   intRC = objReg.DeleteValue(HKEY_LOCAL_MACHINE,strKeyPath,strValueName)
   if intRC > 0 then
      WScript.Echo "Error occurred: " & intRC
   else
      WScript.Echo strValueName & " value deleted"
   end if
end if
```

Discussion

When the Schema FSMO role owner is running Windows 2000, you must explicitly enable schema modifications on the server before extending the schema. To enable this, you need to create a key value called Schema Update Allowed with a value of 1 under the following key:

```
HKEY_LOCAL_MACHINE\System\CurrentControlSet\Services\NTDS\Parameters
```

To disable schema modifications, set the value to 0 or delete it from the registry.

 This is no longer necessary when the Schema FSMO owner is running Windows Server 2003. Microsoft removed this registry hack as a requirement for extending the schema.

See Also

MS KB 285172 (Schema Updates Require Write Access to Schema in Active Directory)

10.3 Generating an OID to Use for a New Class or Attribute

Problem

You want to generate an OID to use with a new class or attribute you intend to add to the schema.

Solution

You have two options for generating an OID. First, you can generate a base OID off of the Microsoft OID tree. This can be done with the Oidgen.exe utility from the Resource Kit:

```
> oidgen
Attribute Base OID: 1.2.840.113556.1.4.7000.233.28688.28684.8.2849.956347.1967079.
334190
    Class Base OID: 1.2.840.113556.1.5.7000.111.28688.28684.8.370553.291204.940269.
113484
```

Using Oidgen is really easy, but if you want to implement schema extensions for production use, I strongly suggest you consider using an OID from your company or organization's OID branch. To determine if your company already has an assigned OID, see these sites:

http://www.iana.org/assignments/enterprise-numbers
http://www.alvestrand.no/objectid/

If your organization does not have an assigned OID, go to your country's national registry to request one. The list of registries can be found at the following site: *http://www.iso.ch/iso/en/aboutiso/isomembers/index.html*.

Once you have a base OID, you can create branches from that OID however you want. For example, if you had a base OID of 1.2.3.4, you could start new class OIDs under 1.2.3.4.1 and new attributes under 1.2.3.4.2. In that case, the first class OID you would create would be 1.2.3.4.1.1 and the first attribute OID would be 1.2.3.4.2.1.

Discussion

An OID is nothing more than a string of numbers separated by dots (.). OIDs were initially defined by the ITU-T in X.208 and have been used to uniquely identify a variety of things including *SNMP MIB* objects and *LDAP* schema classes and attributes. OIDs are hierarchical, and the national registries are responsible for managing and assigning OID branches.

10.4 Generating a GUID to Use for a New Class or Attribute

Problem

You want to generate a GUID to use for the schemaIDGUID attribute of a new class or attribute you intend to add to the schema.

Solution

There are several ways to go about generating a GUID. If you do not specify the schemaIDGUID when initially creating a class or attribute, one will automatically be generated for you. So you could add the class or attribute to the schema of a test forest, and then use the schemaIDGUID that was generated in that forest.

You can also programmatically generate a GUID using Perl, VB, C++, or C#, but you cannot do it natively within VBScript. The Windows API supports a CoCreateGUID method that can be used to generate a GUID. If you are stuck with VBScript, you can wrap the CoCreateGUID method in an ActiveX DLL using VB and then use that DLL from within VBScript.

Finally, you can use a tool such as uuidgen.exe, which is available in the Microsoft Platform SDK to generate GUIDs. Uuidgen doesn't require any parameters (although there are a few options that can be seen by running uuidgen -h), and it can generate as many GUIDs as you need.

If you intend to use LDIF files for extending the schema (highly recommended), then you need to encode any GUIDs in base64 notation. This is necessary because GUIDs are stored as octet strings (binary data) in Active Directory. The LDIF specification requires any binary data to be encoded in base64. Again, VBScript does not support base64 encoding natively, but other languages like Perl have modules available that do. Here is an example Perl script that uses a combination of the uuidgen utility to generate a GUID, the Win32::Lanman module to convert the GUID to binary, and the MIME::Base64 module to encode it:

```perl
#!perl
use MIME::Base64;
use Win32::Lanman;
```

```
# Get the string GUID
my $str_guid = `uuidgen.exe`;
chomp $str_guid;

# Convert to a binary GUID
my $bin_guid = Win32::Lanman::StringToGuid($str_guid);

# Base64 encode binary GUID
my $b64_guid = encode_base64($bin_guid);

print "$b64_guid\n";
```

 You can avoid using uuidgen.exe altogether by using the Win32::Guidgen module or Data::UUID (for Unix), both of which can generate text-based GUIDs.

Discussion

The schemaIDGUID attribute defines the GUID or unique identifier for classes and attributes in the schema. It is a good practice to define this attribute in your schema extensions when creating new classes or attributes. This is especially true if the new class or attribute will be associated with any extended rights or property sets, which reference schema objects by GUID. If you do not explicitly set that value, the method you use for creating or modifying extended rights to use that class will have to dynamically determine the schemaIDGUID for each forest it is implemented in, which is not very clean.

10.5   Extending the Schema

Problem

You want to extend the schema to support new classes and attributes in Active Directory.

Solution

Extending the schema is a straightforward process, which consists of adding new classes or attributes, or modifying existing ones in the schema. While extending the schema is not hard, due to the sensitive nature of the schema, you should implement a schema extension process that thoroughly tests any extensions before you put them in your production forest. Here is a suggested summary of what your schema extension process should be:

1. Meet with clients and determine if there is a business justification for integrating their application with Active Directory.
2. Examine the extensions and determine what impact, if any, it will have on your Active Directory environment (e.g., adding an attribute to the global catalog).

3. Try out the extensions in a test environment. Observe any peculiarities.

4. Document the extensions.

5. Extend the schema in your production Active Directory.

For more information on defining a schema extension process, see Chapter 12 of *Active Directory*, Second Edition (O'Reilly).

Discussion

One thing to be cautious of when developing a schema extension process is not to make it an overly bureaucratic process that can require several weeks to complete. If that is the type of process you implement, you'll find that fewer people will want to integrate their applications with your Active Directory infrastructure. While some organizations may want to strictly limit schema extensions, there is nothing inherently bad about extending the schema and it is one of the core features and advantages over Active Directory's predecessor—Windows NT 4.0.

See Also

Recipe 10.7 for adding a new attribute, Recipe 10.9 for adding a new class, and MS KB 283791 (How to Modify Schema Information Using the Ldifde Utility)

10.6   Documenting Schema Extensions

Problem

You want to document your schema extensions.

Solution

There are several different ways you can document schema extensions. If you require LDIF files of the schema extensions before you extend the schema, you could use the files themselves as a simple self-documenting system. You can put comments in LDIF files by putting # at the beginning of a line. I personally prefer this option and recommend that any company that needs to extend the schema of their customer's Active Directory should include LDIF files, regardless of whether you use that method to actually extend the schema.

Another fairly easy mechanism for documenting schema extensions is with the SchemaDoc program developed by Microsoft. SchemaDoc is a simple GUI program that lets you document classes and attributes that have already been added to Active Directory. The output for SchemaDoc is XML, which you can then use to create your own management interface for viewing the contents.

SchemaDoc can be downloaded from the following site:

http://www.microsoft.com/downloads/details.aspx?FamilyId=BEF87B1D-D2F1-4795-88C5-CA66CFC3AB29&displaylang=en

More information on SchemaDoc can be found here:

http://www.microsoft.com/technet/prodtechnol/ad/windows2000/maintain/schema.asp

Discussion

There are no hard and fast rules for documenting schema extensions. Documenting schema extensions in some fashion, even if rudimentary, should be a requirement of any schema extension process you adopt. If you have the resources and time, you can even develop a much more elaborate documentation system using the web or even an object-modeling system.

See Also

RFC 2849 (The LDAP Data Interchange Format (LDIF)—Technical Specification)

10.7   Adding a New Attribute

Problem

You want to add a new attribute to the schema.

Solution

For Windows 2000 Active Directory you need to enable schema modifications before proceeding. See Recipe 10.2 for more information.

Using a graphical user interface

1. Open the Active Directory Schema snap-in.
2. In the left pane, right-click on the Attributes folder and select Create Attribute.
3. Click the Continue button to confirm that you want to extend the schema.
4. Enter the information for the new attribute.
5. Click OK.

Using a command-line interface

You can create new attributes by using ldifde and an LDIF file that contains the properties to be set on the attribute. The following text shows an example LDIF file called create_attr.ldf that creates an attribute called rallencorp-LanguagesSpoken:

```
dn: cn=rallencorp-LanguagesSpoken,cn=schema,cn=configuration,<ForestRootDN>
changetype: add
objectclass: attributeSchema
lDAPDisplayName: rallencorp-LanguagesSpoken
attributeId: 1.3.6.1.4.1.999.1.1.28.3
oMSyntax: 20
attributeSyntax: 2.5.5.4
isSingleValued: FALSE
searchFlags: 1
description: "Languages a user speaks"
```

Then run the following command:

```
> ldifde -v -i -f create_attr.ldf
```

Using VBScript

```
' This code illustrates how to create an attribute
' called rallencorp-LanguagesSpoken

set objRootDSE = GetObject("LDAP://RootDSE")
set objSchemaCont = GetObject("LDAP://" & _
                              objRootDSE.Get("schemaNamingContext") )
set objAttr = objSchemaCont.Create("attributeSchema", _
                              "cn=rallencorp-LanguagesSpoken")
objAttr.Put "lDAPDisplayName", "rallencorp-LanguagesSpoken"
objAttr.Put "attributeId", "1.3.6.1.4.1.999.1.1.28.3"
objAttr.Put "oMSyntax", 20
objAttr.Put "attributeSyntax", "2.5.5.4"
objAttr.Put "isSingleValued", FALSE
objAttr.Put "description", "Languages a user speaks"
objAttr.Put "searchFlags", 1  ' index the attribute
objAttr.SetInfo
WScript.Echo "Attribute created"
```

Discussion

To create an attribute, you need to add an attributeSchema object to the Schema container. Typically, when you extend the schema, you perform several additions or modifications at once. The order of your extensions is very important. You can't create a class, assign an attribute, and then create the attribute; you obviously need to create the attribute before it can be assigned to the class. Even if you create the attribute before you assign it to a class, you must reload the schema before doing the class assignment. Reloading the schema is described in more detail in Recipe 10.22.

Most of the attributes that can be set on attributeSchema objects are pretty straightforward, but a couple of them take a little explanation. The attributeSyntax and oMSyntax attributes together define the syntax, or the type of data that can be contained in the attribute. Table 10-3 shows the possible combinations of these two attributes and the resulting syntax.

Table 10-3. attributeSyntax and oMSyntax combinations

Name	attributeSyntax	oMSyntax	Description
AccessPointDN	2.5.5.14	127	Type of distinguished name taken from X.500.
Boolean	2.5.5.8	1	TRUE or FALSE value.
CaseExactString	2.5.5.3	27	Case-sensitive string.
CaseIgnoreString	2.5.5.4	20	Case-insensitive string.
DirectoryString	2.5.5.12	64	Case-insensitive Unicode string.
DN	2.5.5.1	127	String representing a distinguished name.
DNWithBinary	2.5.5.7	127	Octet string that has the following format: B:*CharCount*:*BinaryValue*:*ObjectDN* where *CharCount* is the number of hexadecimal digits in *BinaryValue*, *BinaryValue* is the hexadecimal representation of the binary value, and *ObjectDN* is a distinguished name.
DNWithString	2.5.5.14	127	Octet string that contains a string value and a DN. A value with this syntax has the following format: S:*CharCount*:*StringValue*:*ObjectDN* where *CharCount* is the number of characters in the *StringValue* string, and *ObjectDN* is a distinguished name of an object in Active Directory.
Enumeration	2.5.5.9	10	Defined in X.500 and treated as an integer.
GeneralizedTime	2.5.5.11	24	Time string format defined by ASN.1 standards. See ISO 8601 and X.680.
IA5String	2.5.5.5	22	Case-sensitive string containing characters from the IA5 character set.
Integer	2.5.5.9	2	32-bit integer.
Integer8	2.5.5.16	65	64-bit integer, also known as a large integer.
NTSecurityDescriptor	2.5.5.15	66	Octet string that contains a security descriptor.
NumericString	2.5.5.6	18	String that contains digits.
OctetString	2.5.5.10	4	Array of bytes used to store binary data.
OID	2.5.5.2	6	String that contains digits (0–9) and decimal points (.).
ORName	2.5.5.7	127	Taken from X.400; used for X.400 to RFC 822 mapping.
PresentationAddress	2.5.5.13	127	String that contains OSI presentation addresses.
PrintableString	2.5.5.5	19	Case-sensitive string that contains characters from the printable character set.

Table 10-3. attributeSyntax and oMSyntax combinations (continued)

Name	attributeSyntax	oMSyntax	Description
ReplicaLink	2.5.5.10	127	Used by Active Directory internally.
Sid	2.5.5.17	4	Octet string that contains a security identifier (SID).
UTCTime	2.5.5.11	23	Time string format defined by ASN.1 standards.

The searchFlags attribute is a bit flag that defines special properties related to searching with the attribute. Table 10-4 contains the values that can be set for this attribute. The values are cumulative; so in order to index an attribute and include it in ANR searches, you would set a value of 5 (1 + 4).

Table 10-4. searchFlags bit values

Value	Description
1	Index over attribute. See Recipe 10.11 for more information.
2	Index over container and attribute.
4	Include as part of Ambiguous Name Resolution (ANR). Should be used in addition to 1. See Recipe 10.13 for more information.
8	Preserve attribute in tombstone objects.
16	Copy attribute when duplicating an object. See Recipe 10.12 for more information.
32	Create a tuple index for this attribute. This improves the response time for searches that put a wildcard in front of the search string for the attribute, (e.g., givenname=*on).

See Also

Recipe 4.12 for setting a bit flag, Recipe 10.9 for adding a new class, and Recipe 10.22 for reloading the schema

10.8   Viewing an Attribute

Problem

You want to view the properties of an attribute.

Solution

Using a graphical user interface

1. Open the Active Directory Schema snap-in.
2. In the left pane, click on the Attributes folder.
3. In the right pane, double-click the attribute you want to view.
4. Click on each tab to view the available properties.

Using a command-line interface

In the following command, replace *<AttrCommonName>* with the common name (not LDAP display dame) of the attribute you want to view:

```
> dsquery * cn=schema,cn=configuration,<ForestRootDN> -scope onelevel -attr *↵
-filter "(&(objectcategory=attributeSchema)(cn=<AttrCommonName>))"
```

Using VBScript

```
' This code displays the attributes for the specified attributeSchema object
' Refer to Recipe 4.2 for the DisplayAttributes( ) function code.
' ------ SCRIPT CONFIGURATION ------
' Set to the common name (not LDAP display dame) of the attribute
strAttrName = "<AttrCommonName>"    ' e.g. surname
' ------ END CONFIGURATION ---------

set objRootDSE = GetObject("LDAP://RootDSE")
set objAttr = GetObject("LDAP://cn=" & strAttrName & "," & _
                        objRootDSE.Get("schemaNamingContext"))
objAttr.GetInfo
WScript.Echo "Properties for " & strAttrName & ":"
DisplayAttributes(objAttr.ADsPath)
```

Discussion

In the CLI and VBScript solutions, I mention that you need to specify the common name or cn of the attribute you want to view. The common name is a source of confusion for many people. For example, the surname attribute has the following distinguished name in the *rallencorp.com* forest:

```
cn=surname,cn=schema,cn=configuration,dc=rallencorp,dc=com
```

The problem is that most applications refer to attributes by their LDAP display name as defined in the lDAPDisplayName attribute for the attributeSchema object, which is typically different than the cn attribute. As an example, the surname attribute uses surname for its common name (cn), but sn for its LDAP display name (lDAPDisplayName).

In the *CLI* solution, if you want to use the LDAP display name instead of cn, simply change (cn=*<AttrCommonName>*) to (lDAPDisplayName=*<AttrLDAPName>*). In the *VBScript* solution, it is not that simple. When using cn, we can call GetObject since we know the DN of the attributeSchema object. If you want to use the lDAPDisplayName attribute instead, you'll need to do an ADO query and use the search criteria similar to that in the CLI solution.

One attribute of note that is defined on attributeSchema objects is the systemFlags bit flag, which is used to define a few miscellaneous properties about an attribute. Table 10-5 contains the bits associated with systemFlags. The values are cumulative, so a value of 17 (1 + 16) would indicate that the attribute is part of the base Active Directory installation and is not replicated.

Table 10-5. systemFlags bit values

Value	Description
1	Not replicated among domain controllers.
4	Dynamically constructed by Active Directory.
16	Part of the base Active Directory installation. This value cannot be set.

See Also

Recipe 4.2 for viewing the attributes of an object and Recipe 4.9 for searching with a bit-wise filter

10.9   Adding a New Class

Problem

You want to add a new class to the schema.

Solution

 For Windows 2000 Active Directory you need to enable schema modifications before proceeding. See Recipe 10.2 for more information.

Using a graphical user interface

1. Open the Active Directory Schema snap-in.
2. In the left pane, right-click on the Classes folder and select Create Class...
3. Click the Continue button to confirm that you want to extend the schema.
4. Enter the information for the new class and click Next.
5. Enter any mandatory and optional attributes and click Finish.

Using a command-line interface

You can create new classes by using `ldifde` and an LDIF file that contains the properties to be set on the class. The following text shows an example LDIF file called *create_class.ldf* that creates a class called `rallencorp-SalesUser`:

```
dn: cn=rallencorp-SalesUser,cn=schema,cn=configuration,<ForestRootDN>
changetype: add
objectclass: classSchema
```

```
lDAPDisplayName: rallencorp-SalesUser
governsId: 1.3.6.1.4.1.999.1.1.28.4
objectClassCategory: 3
subClassOf: top
description: Auxiliary class for Sales user attributes
adminDescription: Auxiliary class for Sales user attributes
mayContain: rallencorp-Building
mayContain: rallencorp-Theatre
```

Then run the following command:

```
> ldifde -v -i -f create_class.ldf
```

Using VBScript

```
' This code creates a class in the schema called rallencorp-SalesUser.
' It is assumed that the script is being run by a member of Schema Admins

set objRootDSE = GetObject("LDAP://RootDSE")
set objSchemaCont = GetObject("LDAP://" & _
                              objRootDSE.Get("schemaNamingContext") )
set objClass = objSchemaCont.Create("classSchema", _
                              "cn=rallencorp-SalesUser")
objClass.Put "lDAPDisplayName", "rallencorp-SalesUser"
objClass.Put "governsId", "1.3.6.1.4.1.999.1.1.28.4"
objClass.Put "objectClassCategory", 3
objClass.Put "subClassOf", "top"
objClass.Put "adminDescription", "Languages a user speaks"
objClass.Put "mayContain", Array("rallencorp-Building","rallencorp-Theatre")
objClass.SetInfo
WScript.Echo "Class created"
```

Discussion

To create a new class, you need to create a classSchema object in the Schema container. The important attributes to set include:

governsId
: Defines the OID for the class

objectClassCategory
: Defines the class type

subClassOf
: Defines the parent class

mayContain *and* mustContain
: Defines any optional and mandatory attributes for instantiated objects of the class

The lDAPDisplayName also needs to be set and should be equal to the common name (cn) as a general rule. Even though many of the default classes do not use the same name for the common name and LDAP display name, using the same name is highly recommended to avoid confusion when referencing the class. Another best practice is to set the schemaIDGUID of the class, which is especially important if you are doing anything with extended rights. The See Also section contains references to recipes that cover some of these topics in more depth.

See Also

Recipe 10.0 for attributes of classSchema objects, Recipe 10.3 for generating an OID, Recipe 10.4 for generating a GUID, Recipe 10.17 for more on object class type, Recipe 10.19 for setting the default security for a class, and Recipe 10.22 for reloading the schema cache

10.10 Viewing a Class

Problem

You want to view the attributes of a class.

Solution

Using a graphical user interface

1. Open the Active Directory Schema snap-in.
2. In the left pane, click on the Classes folder.
3. In the right pane, double-click the class you want to view.
4. Click on each tab to view the available properties.

Using a command-line interface

In the following command, replace <ClassCommonName> with the common name (not LDAP display name) of the class you want to view:

```
> dsquery * cn=<ClassCommonName>,cn=schema,cn=configuration,<ForestRootDN> -scope⏎
base -attr *
```

Using VBScript

```
' This code prints out the attributes for the specified class.
' Recipe 4.2 for the code for the DisplayAttributes() function.
' ------ SCRIPT CONFIGURATION ------
' Set to the common name (not LDAP display dame)
' of the class you want to view.
strClassName = "<ClassCommonName>"    ' e.g. user
' ------ END CONFIGURATION ---------

set objRootDSE = GetObject("LDAP://RootDSE")
```

```
set objClass = GetObject("LDAP://cn=" & strClassName & "," & _
                         objRootDSE.Get("schemaNamingContext"))
objClass.GetInfo
WScript.Echo "Properties for " & strClassName
DisplayAttributes(objClass.ADsPath)
```

Discussion

See Table 10-1 for a list of the important classSchema attributes and their descriptions.

See Also

Recipe 4.2 for viewing the attributes of an object

10.11 Indexing an Attribute

Problem

You want to index an attribute so that searches using that attribute are faster.

Solution

 For Windows 2000 Active Directory you need to enable schema modifications before proceeding. See Recipe 10.2 for more information.

Using a graphical user interface

1. Open the Active Directory Schema snap-in.

2. In the left pane, click on the Attributes folder.

3. In the right pane, double-click the attribute you want to index.

4. Check the box beside Index this attribute in the Active Directory.

5. Click OK.

Using a command-line interface

You can index an attribute by using the ldifde utility and an LDIF file that contains the following:

```
dn: cn=<AttrCommonName>,cn=schema,cn=configuration,<ForestRootDN>
changetype: modify
replace: searchFlags
searchFlags: 1
-
```

If the LDIF file were named index_attribute.ldf, you would run the following command:

```
> ldifde -v -i -f index_attribute.ldf
```

Using VBScript

```
' This code indexes an attribute.
' ------ SCRIPT CONFIGURATION ------
' Set to the common name (not LDAP display name) of the attribute
strAttrName = "<AttrCommonName>"   ' e.g. rallencorp-LanguagesSpoken
' ------ END CONFIGURATION ---------

set objRootDSE = GetObject("LDAP://RootDSE")
set objAttr = GetObject("LDAP://cn=" & strAttrName & "," &
                        objRootDSE.Get("schemaNamingContext"))
objAttr.Put "searchFlags", 1
objAttr.SetInfo
WScript.Echo "Indexed attribute: " & strAttrName
```

 The CLI and VBScript solutions assume that searchFlags wasn't previously set and just blindly overwrites whatever value is present if one was. See Recipe 4.12 for a better solution that will enable the bit you want without overwriting any previous settings.

Discussion

To index an attribute, you need to enable the 1 bit (0001) in the searchFlags attribute for the attributeSchema object.

searchFlags is a bit flag attribute that is used to set various properties related to searching with the attribute. Table 10-5 contains the various bit flags that can be set with searchFlags. When setting searchFlags, you may often need to set a couple bits together. For example, all Ambiguous Name Resolution (ANR) attributes must also be indexed, which means searchFlags should be set to 5 (1 + 4).

You can find the attributes that are indexed in the schema by using the following search criteria:

Base
> cn=Schema,cn=Configuration,<*ForestRootDN*>

Filter
> (&(objectcategory=attributeSchema)(searchFlags:1.2.840.113556.1.4.803:=1))

Scope
> onelevel

Alternatively, to find attributes that aren't indexed, change the previous search filter to the following:

> (&(objectcategory=attributeSchema)(!(searchFlags:1.2.840.113556.1.4.803:=1)))

See Also

Recipe 4.12 for modifying a bit-flag attribute, Recipe 10.7 for adding a new attribute, and MS KB 243311 (Setting an Attribute's searchFlags Property to Be Indexed for ANR)

10.12 Modifying the Attributes That Are Copied When Duplicating a User

Problem

You want to add an attribute to the list of attributes that are copied when duplicating a user with the Active Directory Users and Computers snap-in.

Solution

 For Windows 2000 Active Directory you need to enable schema modifications before proceeding. See Recipe 10.2 for more information.

Using a graphical user interface

1. Open the Active Directory Schema snap-in.
2. In the left pane, click on the Attributes folder.
3. In the right pane, double-click the attribute you want to edit.
4. Check the box beside Attribute is copied when duplicating a user.
5. Click OK.

Using a command-line interface

You can cause an attribute to get copied when duplicating a user by using the ldifde utility and an LDIF file that contains the following:

```
dn: cn=rallencorp-LanguagesSpoken,cn=schema,cn=configuration,<ForestRootDN>
changetype: modify
replace: searchFlags
searchFlags: 16
-
```

If the LDIF file were named add_dup_user_attr.ldf, you would run the following command:

```
> ldifde -v -i -f add_dup_user_attr.ldf
```

Using VBScript

```
' This code adds an attribute to the list of attributes that get
' copied when duplicating a user.
' ------ SCRIPT CONFIGURATION ------
' Set to the common name (not LDAP display dame) of the attribute
strAttrName = "<AttrCommonName>"    ' e.g. rallencorp-LanguagesSpoken
' ------ END CONFIGURATION ---------

set objRootDSE = GetObject("LDAP://RootDSE")
set objAttr = GetObject("LDAP://cn=" & strAttrName & "," & objRootDSE.
Get("schemaNamingContext"))
objAttr.Put "searchFlags", 16
objAttr.SetInfo
WScript.Echo "New copied attribute: " & strAttrName
```

 The CLI and VBScript solutions assume that searchFlags wasn't previously set and just blindly overwrites whatever value is present if one was. Check our Recipe 4.12 for a better solution that will enable the bit you want without overwriting any previous settings.

Discussion

The Active Directory Users and Computers snap-in queries the schema for the list of attributes that should be copied whenever you right-click on a user and select Copy. This flag is purely informational and does not impose any restrictions or result in any impact on the DIT, like indexing an attribute does.

To find which attributes are copied when duplicating a user, use the following search criteria:

Base
> cn=Schema,cn=Configuration,<*ForestRootDN*>

Filter
> (&(objectcategory=attributeSchema)(searchFlags:1.2.840.113556.1.4.803:=16))

Scope
> onelevel

Alternatively, to find attributes that aren't copied, change the search filter above to the following:

> (&(objectcategory=attributeSchema)(!(searchFlags:1.2.840.113556.1.4.803:=16)))

See Also

Recipe 4.12 for modifying a bit flag attribute and Recipe 10.7 for adding a new attribute

10.13 Modifying the Attributes Included with Ambiguous Name Resolution

Problem

You want to modify the attributes that are included as part of ANR.

Solution

 For Windows 2000 Active Directory, you need to enable schema modifications before proceeding. See Recipe 10.2 for more information.

Using a graphical user interface

1. In order to proceed, you must have first indexed the attribute.

2. Open the Active Directory Schema snap-in.

3. In the left pane, click on the Attributes folder.

4. In the right pane, double-click the attribute you want to edit.

5. Check the box beside ANR.

6. Click OK.

Using a command-line interface

You can include an attribute as part of ANR by using the ldifde utility and an LDIF file that contains the following:

```
dn: cn=rallencorp-LanguagesSpoken,cn=schema,cn=configuration,<ForestRootDN>
changetype: modify
replace: searchFlags
searchFlags: 5
-
```

If the LDIF file were named *add_anr_attr.ldf*, you would run the following command:

```
> ldifde -v -i -f add_anr_attr.ldf
```

Using VBScript

```
' This code will make an attribute part of the ANR set.
' ------ SCRIPT CONFIGURATION ------
' Set to the common name (not LDAP display dame) of the attribute
strAttrName = "<AttrCommonName>"    ' e.g. rallencorp-LanguagesSpoken
' ------ END CONFIGURATION ---------

set objRootDSE = GetObject("LDAP://RootDSE")
set objAttr = GetObject("LDAP://cn=" & strAttrName & "," & _
                        objRootDSE.Get("schemaNamingContext"))
```

```
objAttr.Put "searchFlags", 5
objAttr.SetInfo
WScript.Echo "New ANR attribute: " & strAttrName
```

The CLI and VBScript solutions assume that searchFlags wasn't previously set and just blindly overwrites whatever value is present if one was. Check out Recipe 4.12 for a better solution that will enable the bit you want without overwriting any previous settings.

Discussion

ANR is an efficient search algorithm that allows for a complex search filter to be written using a single comparison. For example, a search for (anr=Jim Smith) would translate into the following query:

- An OR filter with every attribute in the ANR set against Jim Smith*
- A filter for givenName = Jim* and sn = Smith*
- A filter for givenName = Smith* and sn = Jim*

These filters are ORed together and then processed by Active Directory. Since all default ANR attributes are also indexed, the query return should come back quickly.

Here is a list of the default attributes that are included as part of ANR searches. The LDAP display name of the attribute is shown first with the common name in parenthesis.

- displayName (Display-Name)
- givenName (Given-Name)
- legacyExchangeDN (Legacy-Exchange-DN)
- msDS-AdditionalSamAccountName (ms-DS-Additional-Sam-Account-Name)
- physicalDeliveryOfficeName (Physical-Delivery-Office-Name)
- name (RDN)
- sAMAccountName (SAM-Account-Name)
- sn (Surname)

msDS-AdditionalSamAccountName was added as an ANR attribute in Windows Server 2003.

It is important to make sure that any new ANR attributes are also indexed. ANR searches are intended to be very fast, and if a non-indexed attribute was added to the set, it could dramatically impact the performance of the searches.

You can find which attributes are included in the ANR set by using the following search criteria:

Base
    cn=Schema,cn=Configuration,<*ForestRootDN*>
Filter
    (&(objectcategory=attributeSchema)(searchFlags:1.2.840.113556.1.4.803:=4))
Scope
    onelevel

Alternatively, to find attributes that aren't included in ANR, change the previous search filter to the following:

    (&(objectcategory=attributeSchema)(!(searchFlags:1.2.840.113556.1.4.803:=4)))

See Also

Recipe 4.12 for modifying a bit-flag attribute, Recipe 10.7 for adding a new attribute, MS KB 243299 (Ambiguous Name Resolution for LDAP in Windows 2000), and MS KB 243311 (Setting an Attribute's searchFlags Property to Be Indexed for ANR)

10.14 Adding or Removing an Attribute in the Global Catalog

Problem

You want to add or remove an attribute in the global catalog.

Solution

 For Windows 2000 Active Directory, you need to enable schema modifications before proceeding. See Recipe 10.2 for more information.

Using a graphical user interface

1. Open the Active Directory Schema snap-in.
2. In the left pane, click on the Attributes folder.
3. In the right pane, double-click the attribute you want to edit.
4. Check the box beside Replicate this attribute to the Global Catalog to add to the global catalog, or uncheck to remove the global catalog.
5. Click OK.

Using a command-line interface

You can add an attribute to the global catalog by using the `ldifde` utility and an LDIF file that contains the following:

```
dn: cn=<AttrCommonName>,cn=schema,cn=configuration,<ForestRootDN>
changetype: modify
replace: isMemberOfPartialAttributeSet
isMemberOfPartialAttributeSet: TRUE
-
```

If the LDIF file were named add_gc_attr.ldf, you would run the following command:

```
> ldifde -v -i -f add_gc_attr.ldf
```

Using VBScript

```
' This code adds an attribute to the global catalog
' ------ SCRIPT CONFIGURATION ------
' Set to the common name (not LDAP display dame) of the attribute.
strAttrName = "<AttrCommonName>"    ' e.g. surname
' Set to TRUE to add to GC, set to FALSE to remove from GC
boolAddtoGC = TRUE
' ------ END CONFIGURATION ---------

set objRootDSE = GetObject("LDAP://RootDSE")
set objAttr = GetObject("LDAP://cn=" & strAttrName & "," & _
                        objRootDSE.Get("schemaNamingContext"))
objAttr.Put "isMemberOfPartialAttributeSet", boolAddtoGC
objAttr.SetInfo
WScript.Echo "Added attribute to GC: " & strAttrName
```

Discussion

Each domain controller in a forest replicates a copy of the Domain naming context for its own domain as well as copies of the forest-wide Configuration and Schema partitions. However, domain controllers do not replicate Domain naming contexts for other domains in the forest. When enabled as a global catalog server, a domain controller will replicate partial, read-only replicas of all the objects in other domains in the forest.

Searching against the global catalog is useful when you need to perform a single search across several naming contexts at once. The global catalog stores only a subset of each object's attributes, which is why it is considered a partial replica. Attributes stored in the global catalog are considered part of the partial attribute list (PAS). The attributes that are part of the PAS should be either ones you'd want to use as part of searches against the global catalog, or ones you would want returned after searching the global catalog.

You can add attributes that are stored in the global catalog by setting the `isMemberOfPartitalAttributeSet` attribute of an `attributeSchema` object to TRUE.

Likewise, to remove an attribute from the partial attribute set, you need to set isMemberOfPartitalAttributeSet to FALSE for the target attribute.

 With Windows 2000, anytime you added an attribute to the partial attribute set, a full sync of all of the global catalog contents was done for every global catalog server. This could have a major impact on replication in some multidomain environments, as the amount of data that needs to replicate across your forest could be significant. Fortunately, this limitation was removed in Windows Server 2003 so that a full sync is no longer performed. Removing an attribute from the partial attribute list does not force a global catalog sync, even under Windows 2000.

You can find which attributes are included in the global catalog by using a query with the following criteria:

Base
    cn=Schema,cn=Configuration,<*ForestRootDN*>

Filter
    (&(objectcategory=attributeSchema)(isMemberOfPartitalAttributeSet=TRUE))

Scope
    onelevel

Alternatively, to find attributes that aren't in the global catalog, you only need to change part of the previous filter to the following:

    (isMemberOfPartialAttributeSet=FALSE)

See Also

MS KB 229662 (How to Control What Data Is Stored in the Global Catalog), MS KB 230663 (HOW TO: Enumerate Attributes Replicated to the Global Catalog), MS KB 232517 (Global Catalog Attributes and Replication Properties), MS KB 248717 (How to Modify Attributes That Replicate to the Global Catalog), MS KB 257203 (Common Default Attributes Set for Active Directory and Global Catalog), and MS KB 313992 (HOW TO: Add an Attribute to the Global Catalog in Windows 2000)

10.15 Finding the Nonreplicated and Constructed Attributes

Problem

You want to find the attributes are not replicated or are constructed by Active Directory.

Solution

Using a graphical user interface

1. Open LDP.
2. From the menu, select Connection → Connect.
3. For Server, enter the name of a domain controller (or leave blank to do a server-less bind).
4. For Port, enter 389.
5. Click OK.
6. From the menu, select Connection → Bind.
7. Enter credentials of a domain user.
8. Click OK.
9. From the menu, select Browse → Search.
10. For BaseDN, type the Schema Container DN (e.g., *cn=schema,cn=configuration, dc=rallencorp,dc=com*).
11. For Scope, select One Level.
12. To find nonreplicated attributes, use the following for Filter:

    (&(objectcategory=attributeSchema)(systemFlags:1.2.840.113556.1.4.803:=1))
13. To find constructed attributes, use the following for Filter:

    (&(objectcategory=attributeSchema)(systemFlags:1.2.840.113556.1.4.803:=4))
14. Click Run.

Using a command-line interface

To find the nonreplicated attributes, use the following command:

```
> dsquery * cn=schema,cn=configuration,<ForestRootDN> -scope onelevel -attr "cn"↵
-filter "(&(objectcategory=attributeSchema)(systemFlags:1.2.840.113556.1.4.803:=1))"
```

To find the constructed attributes, use the following command:

```
> dsquery * cn=schema,cn=configuration,<ForestRootDN> -scope onelevel -attr "cn"↵
-filter "(&(objectcategory=attributeSchema)(systemFlags:1.2.840.113556.1.4.803:=4))"
```

Using VBScript

```
' This script will print out the nonreplicated and constructed attributes

set objRootDSE = GetObject("LDAP://RootDSE")
strBase   = "<LDAP://" & objRootDSE.Get("SchemaNamingContext") & ">;"
strFilter = "(&(objectcategory=attributeSchema)" _
          & "(systemFlags:1.2.840.113556.1.4.803:=1));"
strAttrs  = "cn;"
strScope  = "onelevel"
```

```
set objConn = CreateObject("ADODB.Connection")
objConn.Provider = "ADsDSOObject"
objConn.Open "Active Directory Provider"
set objRS = objConn.Execute(strBase & strFilter & strAttrs & strScope)
objRS.MoveFirst
WScript.Echo "Nonreplicated attributes: "
while Not objRS.EOF
    Wscript.Echo "   " & objRS.Fields(0).Value
    objRS.MoveNext
wend

strFilter = "(&(objectcategory=attributeSchema) " _
          & "(systemFlags:1.2.840.113556.1.4.803:=4));"
set objRS = objConn.Execute(strBase & strFilter & strAttrs & strScope)
objRS.MoveFirst
WScript.Echo ""
WScript.Echo "Constructed attributes: "
while Not objRS.EOF
    Wscript.Echo "   " & objRS.Fields(0).Value
    objRS.MoveNext
wend
```

Discussion

The `systemFlags` attribute of `attributeSchema` objects defines a few special attribute properties, including whether an attribute is not replicated between domain controllers and whether it is dynamically constructed by Active Directory.

Most attributes are replicated after they are updated on an object, but some never replicate between domain controllers. These attributes are considered nonreplicated. An example of a nonreplicated attribute you may be familiar with is the `lastLogon` attribute that stores the last logon timestamp for user and computer objects. Whenever a user or computer logs in to Active Directory, the authenticating domain controller updates the user or computer's `lastLogin` attribute, but the update does not get replicated out to other domain controllers.

Constructed attributes are automatically maintained by Active Directory and cannot be set manually. A good example of a constructed attribute is the new `msDS-Approx-Immed-Subordinates` that is available in Windows Server 2003. That attribute contains the approximate number of child objects within a container. Obviously this attribute wouldn't be of much value if you had to maintain it, so Active Directory does it automatically.

One of the downsides to constructed attributes is that you cannot search against them. For example, I cannot perform a search to find all containers that have more than 10 objects in them (i.e., `msDS-Approx-Immed-Subordinates>10`). This would return an operations error. Constructed attributes can only be returned as part of the attribute set for a query and not used as part of the query itself.

To find the nonreplicated or constructed attributes you have to use a bitwise LDAP filter against attributeSchema objects. A bit value of 1 indicates the attribute is non-replicated and a value of 4 indicates the attribute is constructed.

See Also

Recipe 4.9 for searching with a bitwise filter

10.16 Finding the Linked Attributes

Problem

You want to find attributes that are linked.

Solution

Using a graphical user interface

1. Open LDP.
2. From the menu, select Connection → Connect.
3. For Server, enter the name of a domain controller (or leave blank to do a server-less bind).
4. For Port, enter 389.
5. Click OK.
6. From the menu, select Connection → Bind.
7. Enter credentials of a domain user.
8. Click OK.
9. From the menu, select Browse → Search.
10. For BaseDN, type the Schema container DN (e.g., *cn=schema,cn=configuration, dc=rallencorp,dc=com*).
11. For Scope, select One Level.
12. To find linked attributes, use the following for Filter:

        (&(objectcategory=attributeSchema)(linkid=*))
13. Click Run.

Using a command-line interface

```
> dsquery * cn=schema,cn=configuration,<ForestRootDN> -scope onelevel -filter↵
"(&(objectcategory=attributeSchema)(linkid=*))" -attr cn linkID
```

Using VBScript

```
' This code prints out all of the attributes that are linked
' and their corresponding linkID values
set objRootDSE = GetObject("LDAP://RootDSE")
strBase   = "<LDAP://" & objRootDSE.Get("SchemaNamingContext") & ">;"
strFilter = "(&(objectcategory=attributeSchema)(linkid=*));"
strAttrs  = "cn,linkid;"
strScope  = "onelevel"

set objConn = CreateObject("ADODB.Connection")
objConn.Provider = "ADsDSOObject"
objConn.Open "Active Directory Provider"
set objRS = objConn.Execute(strBase & strFilter & strAttrs & strScope)
objRS.MoveFirst
while Not objRS.EOF
    Wscript.Echo objRS.Fields(1).Value & " : " & objRS.Fields(0).Value
    objRS.MoveNext
wend
```

Discussion

The values of some attributes in Active Directory are linked. For example, if you set the manager attribute on one user object to be the DN of a second user object, the reports attribute on the second user object will automatically contain the first user object's DN. In this example, the manager attribute, or the attribute that gets set, is considered the forward link and the reports attribute, or the attribute that automatically gets calculated, is called the back link. Another common example is group membership. The member attribute of the group object represents the forward link, while the memberOf attribute of the corresponding object (e.g., user) represents the back link.

You can identify which attributes are linked in the schema by searching for attributeSchema objects that have a linkID attribute that contains some value. The linkID value for a forward-link attribute will be an even, positive number. The corresponding back-link attribute will be the forward-linkID plus 1. For example, the manager attribute linkID is 42 and the back-link reports attribute has a linkID of 43.

10.17 Finding the Structural, Auxiliary, Abstract, and 88 Classes

Problem

You want to list the structural, auxiliary, abstract, and 88 classes.

Solution

Using a graphical user interface

1. Open the Active Directory Schema snap-in.
2. In the left pane, click on the Classes folder.
3. In the right pane, the list of all the classes will be displayed. The Type column contains the type of class. Even though you can click on the column header, it currently does not sort the classes by type.

Using a command-line interface

```
> dsquery * cn=schema,cn=configuration,<ForestRootDN> -limit 0 -scope onelevel↵
-filter "(objectcategory=classSchema)" -attr lDAPDisplayName objectclasscategory
```

Using VBScript

```
' This code prints out classes of a particular type
' ------ SCRIPT CONFIGURATION ------
' Set the following to TRUE or FALSE depending if you want to
' view or not view classes of the type defined by the variable
boolShowStructural = TRUE
boolShowAuxiliary  = TRUE
boolShowAbstract   = TRUE
boolShow88         = TRUE
' ------ END CONFIGURATION ---------

set objRootDSE = GetObject("LDAP://RootDSE")
set objSchemaCont = GetObject("LDAP://cn=schema," & _
                              objRootDSE.Get("configurationNamingContext"))
objSchemaCont.Filter = Array("classSchema")
WScript.Echo "Loading classes, this will take a few seconds."
for each objClass in objSchemaCont
    WScript.StdOut.Write(".")
    if objClass.Get("objectClassCategory") = 0 then
        str88 = str88 & vbTab & objClass.Get("lDAPDisplayName") & vbCrlf
    elseif objClass.Get("objectClassCategory") = 1 then
        strStruct = strStruct & vbTab & _
                    objClass.Get("lDAPDisplayName") & vbCrlf
    elseif objClass.Get("objectClassCategory") = 2 then
        strAbst = strAbst & vbTab & objClass.Get("lDAPDisplayName") & vbCrlf
    elseif objClass.Get("objectClassCategory") = 3 then
        strAux = strAux & vbTab & objClass.Get("lDAPDisplayName") & vbCrlf
    else
        WScript.Echo "Unknown class type: " & _
                     objClass.Get("lDAPDisplayName") & vbCrlf
    end if
next
WScript.Echo vbCrlf

if boolShowStructural = TRUE then
    WScript.Echo "Structural Classes: "
```

```
      WScript.Echo strStruct
      WScript.Echo
   end if

   if boolShowAbstract = TRUE then
      WScript.Echo "Abstract Classes: "
      WScript.Echo strAbst
      WScript.Echo
   end if

   if boolShowAuxiliary = TRUE then
      WScript.Echo "Auxiliary Classes: "
      WScript.Echo strAux
      WScript.Echo
   end if

   if boolShow88 = TRUE then
      WScript.Echo "88 Classes: "
      WScript.Echo str88
      WScript.Echo
   end if
```

Discussion

There are four supported class types in the Active Directory schema. The class type is defined by the objectClassCategory attribute on classSchema objects. Each class type is used for a different purpose relating to organizing and inheriting classes. Table 10-6 describes each type.

Table 10-6. Object class category values

Name	Value	Description
88	0	Legacy class type defined by the original X.500 standards. It should not be used for new classes.
Structural	1	Used for instantiating objects. Can be comprised of abstract, auxiliary, and other structural classes.
Abstract	2	Used to define a high-level grouping of attributes that can be used as part of other abstract or structural class definitions. Objects cannot be instantiated using an abstract class.
Auxiliary	3	Used as a collection of attributes that can be applied to other abstract, auxiliary, or structural classes.

10.18 Finding the Mandatory and Optional Attributes of a Class

Problem

You want to view the mandatory and optional attributes of a class.

Solution

Using a graphical user interface

1. Open the Active Directory Schema snap-in.
2. In the left pane, click on the Classes folder.
3. In the right pane, double-click the class you want to view.
4. Click on the Attributes tab.

Using a command-line interface

```
> dsquery * cn=<ClassCommonName>,cn=schema,cn=configuration,<ForestRootDN> -l↵
-scope base -attr mayContain mustContain systemMayContain systemMustContain
```

Using VBScript

```
' This code displays the mandatory and optional attributes for a class.
' ------ SCRIPT CONFIGURATION ------
' Set to common name of class to view
strClassName = "<ClassCommonName>"   ' e.g. Surname
' ------ END CONFIGURATION ---------

set objRootDSE = GetObject("LDAP://RootDSE")
set objClass = GetObject("LDAP://cn=" & strClassName & "," & _
                         objRootDSE.Get("schemaNamingContext"))

WScript.Echo "Class: " & strClassName & vbCrlf

' Need to enable this so that if an attribute is not set, it won't die
on error resume next

WScript.Echo "mayContain:"
for each strVal in objClass.Get("mayContain")
   WScript.Echo vbTab & strVal
next

WScript.Echo vbCrlf & "systemMayContain:"
for each strVal in objClass.Get("systemMayContain")
   WScript.Echo vbTab & strVal
next

WScript.Echo vbCrlf & "mustContain:"
for each strVal in objClass.Get("mustContain")
   WScript.Echo vbTab & strVal
next

WScript.Echo vbCrlf & "systemMustContain:"
for each strVal in objClass.Get("systemMustContain")
   WScript.Echo vbTab & strVal
next
```

Discussion

The mayContain and systemMayContain attributes define the optional attributes for a class while the mustContain and systemMustContain attributes contain the mandatory attributes. The systemMayContain and systemMustContain attributes are set by Active Directory and cannot be modified. You need to be careful when adding attributes to the mustContain attribute for existing classes because you can easily cause objects that use those classes to become invalid due to not having the mandatory attribute set.

It is also worth noting that each of the solutions display only the attributes defined directly on the class. It will not show any inherited attributes that are defined by inherited classes.

10.19 Modifying the Default Security of a Class

Problem

You want to modify the default security that is applied to objects instantiated from a particular structural class.

Solution

For Windows 2000 Active Directory, you need to enable schema modifications before proceeding. See Recipe 10.2 for more information.

Using a graphical user interface

1. Open the Active Directory Schema snap-in.
2. In the left pane, click on the Classes folder.
3. In the right pane, double-click the class you want to modify the security for.
4. Click the Default Security tab.
5. Modify the security as necessary.
6. Click OK.

Discussion

Whenever a new object is created in Active Directory, a default security descriptor (SD) is applied to it along with any inherited security from its parent container. The default security descriptor is stored in the defaultSecurityDescriptor attribute of the classSchema object. If you modify the default SD, every new object will get that SD, but it does not affect any existing objects.

See Also

MS KB 265399 (HOW TO: Change Default Permissions for Objects That Are Created in the Active Directory)

10.20 Deactivating Classes and Attributes

Problem

You want to deactivate a class or attribute in the schema because you no longer need it.

Solution

Using a graphical user interface

1. Open the Active Directory Schema snap-in.
2. In the left pane, click on the Classes folder.
3. In the right pane, double-click the class you want to deactivate.
4. Uncheck the box beside Class is active.
5. Click OK.

Using a command-line interface

You can deactivate a class using the `ldifde` utility and an LDIF file that contains the following lines:

```
dn: cn=<SchemaObjectCommonName>,cn=schema,cn=configuration,<ForestRootDN>
changetype: modify
replace: isDefunct
isDefunct: TRUE
-
```

If the LDIF file were named deactivate_class.ldf, you would run the following command:

```
> ldifde -v -i -f deactivate_class.ldf
```

Using VBScript

```
' This code deactivates a class or attribute.
' ------ SCRIPT CONFIGURATION ------
strName = "<SchemaObjectCommonName>"    ' e.g. rallencorp-LanguagesSpoken
' ------ END CONFIGURATION ---------

set objRootDSE = GetObject("LDAP://RootDSE")
set objSchemaObject = GetObject("LDAP://cn=" & strName & "," & _
                                objRootDSE.Get("schemaNamingContext"))
objSchemaObject.Put "isDefunct", TRUE
objSchemaObject.SetInfo
WScript.Echo "Schema object deactivated: " & strName
```

Discussion

There is no supported way to delete classes or attributes defined in the schema. You can, however, deactivate them, also known as making them defunct. Before you deactivate a class you should make sure that no instantiated objects of that class exist. If you want to deactivate an attribute, you should make sure no object classes define the attribute as mandatory. After you've verified the class or attribute is no longer being used, you can deactivate by setting the isDefunct attribute to TRUE. You can always reactivate it at a later time by simply setting isDefunct to FALSE. With Windows Server 2003 Active Directory, you can even redefine the class or attribute while it is defunct. This gives you much more flexibility over reusing classes or attributes you may have added before, but no longer want.

See Also

Recipe 10.21 for redefining classes and attributes

10.21 Redefining Classes and Attributes

 This recipe requires the Windows Server 2003 forest functional level.

Problem

You want to redefine a class or attribute that was previously created.

Solution

To redefine a class or attribute, you must first deactivate it by setting the isDefunct attribute to TRUE (see Recipe 10.20 for more details). If you are deactivating a class, make sure no objects are instantiated that use the class. If you are deactivating an attribute, make sure it isn't populated on any objects and remove it from any classes that have it defined as part of mayContain and mustContain. After the class or attribute has been deactivated, you can modify (i.e., redefine) the LDAP display name (lDAPDisplayName), the OID (governsID or attributeID), the syntax (attributeSyntax and oMSyntax), and the schemaIDGUID. The one attribute that you cannot modify is the common name.

Discussion

Redefining schema objects is a new feature of Windows Server 2003. Although you still cannot delete schema objects in Windows Server 2003,* you can work around many of the reasons that would cause you to want to delete a schema object by redefining it instead. Some examples of when redefine comes in handy includes if you accidentally mistype an OID (governsID/attributeID) or lDAPDisplayName, or no longer need an attribute you previously created. You can reuse it by renaming the attribute and giving it a different syntax.

See Also

Recipe 10.20 for deactivating classes and attributes

10.22 Reloading the Schema Cache

Problem

You want to reload the schema cache so that schema extensions take effect immediately.

Solution

Using a graphical user interface

1. Open the Active Directory Schema snap-in.
2. In the left pane, click on Active Directory Schema.
3. Right-click on the label and select Reload the Schema.

Using a command-line interface

You can reload the schema by using the ldifde utility and an LDIF file that contains the following:

```
dn:
changetype: modify
add: schemaUpdateNow
schemaUpdateNow: 1
-
```

If the LDIF file were named reload.ldf, you would run the following command:

```
> ldifde -v -i -f reload.ldf
```

---

* You could delete schema objects in W2K pre-SP3, but I won't get into that here. You find more information about that here: *http://www.winnetmag.com/Articles/Index.cfm?ArticleID=27096*

Using VBScript

```
set objRootDSE = GetObject("LDAP://dc1/RootDSE")
objRootDSE.Put "schemaUpdateNow", 1
objRootDSE.SetInfo
WScript.Echo "Schema reloaded"
```

Discussion

Each domain controller maintains a complete copy of the schema in memory to make access to the schema very fast. This is called the schema cache. When you extend the schema on the Schema FSMO role owner, the change is written to the schema cache, and not committed to disk yet. The schema automatically commits any changes to the schema every five minutes if a change has taken place, but you can also do it manually/programmatically by writing to the schemaUpdateNow operational attribute of the RootDSE on the Schema FSMO role owner. Once that is done, any changes to the schema cache are written to disk.

It is necessary to force a schema cache update if your schema extensions reference newly created attributes or classes. For example, lets say that we want to create one new auxiliary class that contains one new attribute. To do that we would first need to create the attribute and then create the auxiliary class. As part of the auxiliary class' definition, we would need to reference the new attribute, but unless we reload the schema cache, an error would be returned stating that the attribute does not exist. For this reason we need to add an additional step. First, create the attribute, then reload the schema cache, and finally, create the auxiliary class. Here is what an LDIF representation would look like:

```
dn: cn=rallencorp-TestAttr,cn=schema,cn=configuration,dc=rallencorp,dc=com
changetype: add
objectclass: attributeSchema
lDAPDisplayName: rallencorp-TestAttr
attributeId: 1.3.6.1.4.1.999.1.1.28.312
oMSyntax: 20
attributeSyntax: 2.5.5.4
isSingleValued: FALSE
searchFlags: 1

dn:
changetype: modify
add: schemaUpdateNow
schemaUpdateNow: 1
-

dn: cn=rallencorp-TestClass,cn=schema,cn=configuration,dc=rallencorp,dc=com
changetype: add
objectclass: classSchema
lDAPDisplayName: rallencorp-TestClass
```

```
governsId: 1.3.6.1.4.1.999.1.1.28.311
subClassOf: top
objectClassCategory: 3
mayContain: rallencorp-TestAttr
```

See Also

Recipe 10.7 for adding a new attribute to the schema and Recipe 10.9 for adding a new class to the schema

CHAPTER 11

Site Topology

11.0   Introduction

Active Directory needs information about the network to determine how domain controllers should replicate and what domain controller(s) are optimal for a given client to authenticate with. This network information is often referred to as the site or replication topology, and consists of numerous object types that represent various aspects of the network.

At a high level, a site is a collection of high-speed LAN segments. One or more subnets can be associated with a site, and this mapping is used to determine which site a client (based on IP address) belongs to. Sites are connected via site links, which are analogous to WAN connections. Finally, each domain controller in a site has one or more connection objects, which defines a replication connection to another domain controller.

These site topology objects are contained under the Sites container within the Configuration naming context. Figure 11-1 shows an example of the site topology hierarchy using the Active Directory Sites and Services snap-in.

Directly under the Sites container are the individual site containers, plus containers that store the site link objects (cn=Inter-site Transports) and subnets (cn=Subnets). There are three objects included within a site, an NTDS Site Settings (nTDSSiteSettings) object that contains attributes that can customize replication behavior for the whole site, a License Site Settings (licensingSiteSettings) object that can be used to direct hosts within the site to the appropriate licensing server, and a Servers container. The Servers container contains a server object for each of the domain controllers that are members of the site, along with any other servers that need to be represented in the site topology (e.g., DFS servers).

A server object can contain a NTDS Settings (nTDSDSA) object, which distinguishes domain controller server objects from other server objects. The NTDS Settings object stores several attributes that are used to customize replication behavior for a specific

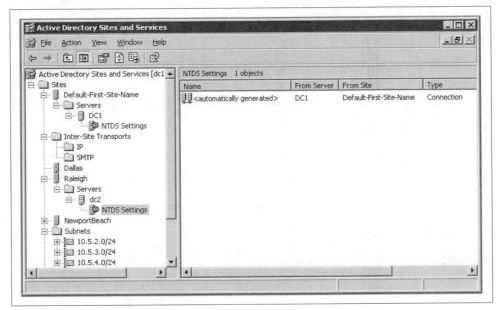

Figure 11-1. Site topology hierarchy

domain controller. The NTDS Settings object can contain one or more nTDSConnection objects, which define the replication connections between domain controllers.

The Anatomy of Site Topology Objects

Tables 11-1 through 11-7 contain some of the important attributes of the various site topology objects.

Table 11-1. Attributes of site objects

Attribute	Description
cn	RDN of the object. This is the name of the site (e.g., Raleigh).
gpLink	Contains a prioritized list of GPOs that are linked to the site.
siteObjectBL	Multivalued attribute that contains a list of distinguished names for each subnet that is associated with the site.

Table 11-2. Attributes of nTDSSiteSettings objects

Attribute	Description
cn	RDN of the object, which is always equal to NTDS Site Settings.
interSiteTopologyGenerator	Distinguished name of the NTDS Settings object of the current Inter-site Topology Generator (ISTG).
msDS-Preferred-GC-Site	If universal group caching is enabled, this contains the distinguished name of the site that domain controllers should refresh their cache from. This attribute is new to Windows Server 2003. See Recipe 7.9 for more information.

Table 11-2. Attributes of nTDSSiteSettings objects (continued)

Attribute	Description
options	Bit flag that determines if universal group caching is enabled, whether site link transitivity is disabled, and if replication schedules should be ignored. For more information see Recipe 11.11.
schedule	Octet string that represents the default replication schedule for the site.

Table 11-3. Attributes of subnet objects

Attribute	Description
cn	RDN of the object. Contains the network number and bit mask for the subnet (e.g., 10.1.3.0/24).
siteObject	Distinguished name of the site object the subnet is associated with.

Table 11-4. Attributes of siteLink objects

Attribute	Description
cn	RDN of the object. Contains the name of the link.
cost	Number that represents the site link cost. See Recipe 11.10 for more information.
replInterval	Interval in minutes that replication occurs over the site link.
schedule	Octet string that represents the replication schedule for the site link.
siteList	Multivalued list of distinguished names of each site that is associated with the site link. See Recipe 11.8 for more information.

Table 11-5. Attributes of server objects

Attribute	Description
bridgeheadTransportList	Multivalued attribute that contains the list of transports (e.g., IP or SMTP) for which the server is a preferred bridgehead server.
cn	RDN of the object. This is set to the hostname of the associated server.
dNSHostName	Fully qualified domain name of the server. This attribute is automatically maintained for domain controllers.
serverReference	Distinguished name of the corresponding computer object contained within one of the domain-naming contexts.

Table 11-6. Attributes of nTDSDSA (NTDS Settings) objects

Attribute	Description
cn	RDN of the object, which is always equal to NTDS Settings.
invocationID	GUID that represents the DIT (ntds.dit) on the domain controller.
hasMasterNCs	Multivalued attribute containing the list of writeable naming contexts (does not include application partitions) stored on the domain controller.
hasPartialReplicaNCs	Multivalued attribute containing the list of read-only naming contexts stored on the domain controller. This will be populated only if the domain controller is a global catalog server.

Table 11-6. Attributes of nTDSDSA (NTDS Settings) objects (continued)

Attribute	Description
msDS-Behavior-Version	Number that represents the functional level (i.e., operating system) of the domain controller. This attribute is new to Windows Server 2003.
msDS-HasDomainNCs	Contains the distinguished name of the writeable Domain naming context stored on the domain controller. This attribute is new to Windows Server 2003.
msDs-HasInstantiatedNCs	A combination of all available read-only and writeable naming contexts stored on the domain controller. This attribute is new to Windows Server 2003.
msDS-hasPartialReplicaNCs	Multivalued attribute that contains distinguished names of each read-only naming context stored on the domain controller. This will be populated only if the domain controller is a global catalog server. This attribute is new to Windows Server 2003.
msDS-hasMasterNCs	Multivalued attribute that contains distinguished names of each writeable naming context and application partition stored on the domain controller. This attribute is new to Windows Server 2003.
options	Bit flag that determines if domain controller is a global catalog server.
queryPolicyObject	If set, the distinguished name of LDAP query policy object to be used by the domain controller.

Table 11-7. Attributes of nTDSConnection objects

Attribute	Description
cn	RDN of the object. For Knowledge Consistency Checker (KCC) generated connections, this is a GUID.
enabledConnection	Boolean that indicates if the connection is available to be used.
fromServer	Distinguished name of the NTDS Settings object of the domain controller this connection replicates with.
ms-DS-ReplicatesNCReason	Multivalued attribute that stores reason codes for why the connection exists. There will be one entry per naming context the connection is used for.
options	Bit flag where a value of 1 indicates the connection was created by the KCC and a value of 0 means the connection was manually created. See Recipe 11.22 for more information.
schedule	Octet string that represents the replication schedule for the site link.
transportType	Distinguished name of the transport type (e.g., IP or SMTP) that is used for the connection.

11.1 Creating a Site

Problem

You want to create a site.

Solution

Using a graphical user interface

1. Open the Active Directory Sites and Services snap-in.
2. Right-click on the Sites container and select New Site.
3. Beside Name, enter the name of the new site.
4. Under Link Name, select a site link for the site.
5. Click OK twice.

Using a command-line interface

Create an LDIF file called *create_site.ldf* with the following contents:

```
dn: cn=<SiteName>,cn=sites,cn=configuration,<ForestRootDN>
changetype: add
objectclass: site

dn: cn=Licensing Site Settings,cn=<SiteName>,cn=sites,cn=configuration,
<ForestRootDN>
changetype: add
objectclass: licensingSiteSettings

dn: cn=NTDS Site Settings,cn=<SiteName>,cn=sites,cn=configuration,<ForestRootDN>
changetype: add
objectclass: nTDSSiteSettings

dn: cn=Servers,cn=<SiteName>,cn=sites,cn=configuration,<ForestRootDN>
changetype: add
objectclass: serversContainer
```

then run the following command:

```
> ldifde -v -i -f create_site.ldf
```

Using VBScript

```
' This code creates the objects that make up a site.
' ------ SCRIPT CONFIGURATION ------
strSiteName = "<SiteName>"  ' e.g. Dallas
' ------ END CONFIGURATION ---------

set objRootDSE = GetObject("LDAP://RootDSE")
set objSitesCont = GetObject("LDAP://cn=sites," & _
                             objRootDSE.Get("configurationNamingContext") )
' Create the site
set objSite = objSitesCont.Create("site","cn=" & strSiteName)
objSite.SetInfo

' Create the Licensing Site Settings object
set objLicensing = objSite.Create("licensingSiteSettings", _
                                  "cn=Licensing Site Settings")
objLicensing.SetInfo
```

```
' Create the NTDS Site Settings object
set objNTDS = objSite.Create("nTDSSiteSettings","cn=NTDS Site Settings")
objNTDS.SetInfo

' Create the Servers container
set objServersCont = objSite.Create("serversContainer","cn=Servers")
objServersCont.SetInfo

WScript.Echo "Successfully created site " & strSiteName
```

Discussion

To create a site in Active Directory, you have to create a number of objects. The first is a site object, which is the root of all the other objects. The site object contains the following:

licensingSiteSettings

> This object isn't mandatory, but is created automatically when creating a site with AD Sites and Services. It is intended to point clients to a license server for the site.

nTDSSiteSettings

> This object stores replication-related properties about a site, such as the replication schedule, current ISTG role holder, and whether universal group caching is enabled.

serversContainer

> This container is the parent of the server objects that are part of the site. All the domain controllers that are members of the site will be represented in this container.

After these objects are created, you've essentially created an empty site. If you didn't do anything else, the site would not be of much value. To make it usable, you need to assign subnet objects to it (see Recipe 11.4), and add the site to a siteLink object to link the site to other sites (see Recipe 11.7). At that point, you can promote or move domain controllers into the site, and it should be fully functional.

See Also

MS KB 318480 (HOW TO: Create and Configure an Active Directory Site in Windows 2000)

11.2   Listing the Sites

Problem

You want to obtain the list of sites.

Solution

Using a graphical user interface

1. Open the Active Directory Sites and Services snap-in.
2. Click on the Sites container.
3. The list of sites will be displayed in the right pane.
4. Double-click on a site to view its properties.

Using a command-line interface

Run the following command to list the sites:

```
> dsquery site
```

Run the following command to view the properties for a particular site:

```
> dsget site "<SiteName>"
```

Using VBScript

```
' This code lists all of the site objects.

set objRootDSE = GetObject("LDAP://RootDSE")
set objSitesCont = GetObject("LDAP://cn=sites," & _
                             objRootDSE.Get("configurationNamingContext") )
objSitesCont.Filter = Array("site")
for each objSite in objSitesCont
   Wscript.Echo "  " & objSite.Get("cn")
next
```

Discussion

Site objects are stored in the Sites container (e.g., *cn=sites,cn=configuration, dc=rallencorp,dc=com*) in the Configuration Naming Context (CNC). For more information on creating sites, see Recipe 11.1.

11.3   Deleting a Site

Problem

You want to delete a site.

Solution

Using a graphical user interface

1. Open the Active Directory Sites and Services snap-in.
2. Click on the Sites container.

---

3. In the right pane, right-click the site you want to delete and select Delete.

4. Click Yes twice.

Using a command-line interface

```
> dsrm <SiteDN> -subtree -noprompt
```

Using VBScript

```
' This code deletes a site and all child containers.
' ------ SCRIPT CONFIGURATION ------
strSiteName = "<SiteName>"    ' e.g. Dallas
' ------ END CONFIGURATION ---------

set objRootDSE = GetObject("LDAP://RootDSE")
set objSite = GetObject("LDAP://cn=" & strSiteName & ",cn=sites," & _
                         objRootDSE.Get("configurationNamingContext") )
objSite.DeleteObject(0)
WScript.Echo "Successfully deleted site " & strSiteName
```

Discussion

When deleting a site, be very careful to ensure that no active server objects exist within it. If you delete a site that contains domain controllers, it will disrupt replication for all domain controllers in that site. A more robust VBScript solution would be to first perform an ADO query for all server objects using the distinguished name of the site as the base DN. If no servers were returned, then you could safely delete the site. If server objects were found, you should move them before deleting the site.

It is also worth noting that deleting a site does not delete any of the subnets or site links that were associated with the site. This would be another good thing to add to the VBScript solution. That is, before you delete the site, delete any subnets and site links that are associated with site.

11.4   Creating a Subnet

Problem

You want to create a subnet.

Solution

Using a graphical user interface

1. Open the Active Directory Sites and Services snap-in.

2. Right-click on the Subnets container and select New Subnet.

3. Enter the Address and Mask and then select which site the subnet is part of.

4. Click OK.

Using a command-line interface

Create an LDIF file called *create_subnet.ldf* with the following contents:

```
dn: cn=<Subnet>,cn=subnets,cn=sites,cn=configuration,<ForestRootDN>
changetype: add
objectclass: subnet
siteObject: cn=<SiteName>,cn=sites,cn=configuration,<ForestRootDN>
```

then run the following command:

```
> ldifde -v -i -f create_subnet.ldf
```

Using VBScript

```
' This code creates a subnet object and associates it with a site.
' ------ SCRIPT CONFIGURATION ------
strSubnet = "<Subnet>"    ' e.g. 10.5.3.0/24
strSite   = "<SiteName>"  ' e.g. Dallas
' ------ END CONFIGURATION ---------

set objRootDSE = GetObject("LDAP://RootDSE")
set objSubnetsCont = GetObject("LDAP://cn=subnets,cn=sites," & _
                          objRootDSE.Get("configurationNamingContext") )
set objSubnet = objSubnetsCont.Create("subnet", "cn=" & strSubnet)
objSubnet.Put "siteObject", "cn=" & strSite & ",cn=sites," & _
                          objRootDSE.Get("configurationNamingContext")
objSubnet.SetInfo

WScript.Echo "Successfully created subnet " & strSubnet
```

Discussion

Subnet objects reside in the Subnets container (e.g., *cn=subnets,cn=sites, cn=configuration,dc=rallencorp,dc=com*) in the CNC. The relative distinguished name (RDN) of the subnet should be the subnet address and bit-mask combination (e.g., 10.5.3.0/24). The other important attribute to set is siteObject, which should contain the DN of the site that the subnet is associated with.

See Also

MS KB 323349 (HOW TO: Configure Subnets in Windows Server 2003 Active Directory)

11.5   Listing the Subnets

Problem

You want to list the subnet objects in Active Directory.

Solution

Using a graphical user interface

1. Open the Active Directory Sites and Services snap-in.
2. Click on the Subnets container.
3. The list of subnets will be displayed in the right pane.
4. To view the properties of a specific subnet, double-click on the one you want to view.

Using a command-line interface

The following command will list all subnets:

```
> dsquery subnet
```

The following command will display the properties for a particular subnet. Replace
<Subnet> with the subnet address and mask (e.g., 10.5.3.0/24):

```
> dsget subnet "<Subnet>"
```

Using VBScript

```
' This code lists all the subnets stored in Active Directory.
set objRootDSE = GetObject("LDAP://RootDSE")
set objSubnetsCont = GetObject("LDAP://cn=subnets,cn=sites," & _
                            objRootDSE.Get("configurationNamingContext") )
objSubnetsCont.Filter = Array("subnet")
for each objSubnet in objSubnetsCont
   Wscript.Echo "  " & objSubnet.Get("cn")
next
```

Discussion

To display the site that subnets are associated with, include the siteObject attribute
as one of the attributes to return from the query. For example, the second to last line
of the VBScript solution could be modified to return the site by using this code:

```
Wscript.Echo "  " & objSubnet.Get("cn") & " : " & objSubnet.Get("siteObject")
```

MS KB 323349 (HOW TO: Configure Subnets in Windows Server 2003 Active Directory)

11.6 Finding Missing Subnets

Problem

You want to find the subnets that are missing from your site topology. Missing subnets can result in clients not authenticating against the most optimal domain controller, which can degrade performance.

Solution

Having all of your subnets in Active Directory is important because a client that attempts to logon from a subnet that is not associated with any site may authenticate with any domain controller in the domain. This can result in the logon process taking longer to complete. Unfortunately, Microsoft has not provided an easy way to rectify this problem.

Under Windows 2000, the only source of missing subnet information was the System event 5778. Here is an example:

```
Event Type:Information
Event Source:NETLOGON
Event Category:None
Event ID:5778
Date:     1/27/2003
Time:     12:07:04 AM
User:     N/A
Computer:DC2
Description:
'JSMITH-W2K' tried to determine its site by looking up its IP address ('10.21.85.34')
in the Configuration\Sites\Subnets container in the DS.  No subnet matched the IP
address.  Consider adding a subnet object for this IP address.
```

The only way to dynamically determine missing subnets is to query each domain controller for 5778 events and map the IP addresses specified within the events to a subnet you add to the site topology.

With Windows Server 2003 things are not that much better. One of the issues with the 5778 events under Windows 2000 is that they could easily fill up your System event log if you had many missing subnets. In Windows 2003, Microsoft decided to instead display a summary event 5807 that states that some number of connection attempts have been made by clients that did not map to a subnet in the site topology. Here is an example:

```
Event Type:Warning
Event Source:NETLOGON
```

```
Event Category:None
Event ID:5807
Date:      1/10/2003
Time:      10:59:53 AM
User:      N/A
Computer:DC1
Description:
During the past 4.18 hours there have been 21 connections to this Domain Controller
from client machines whose IP addresses don't map to any of the existing sites in the
enterprise. Those clients, therefore, have undefined sites and may connect to any
Domain Controller including those that are in far distant locations from the clients.
A client's site is determined by the mapping of its subnet to one of the existing
sites. To move the above clients to one of the sites, please consider creating subnet
object(s) covering the above IP addresses with mapping to one of the existing sites.
The names and IP addresses of the clients in question have been logged on this
computer in the following log file '%SystemRoot%\debug\netlogon.log' and,
potentially, in the log file '%SystemRoot%\debug\netlogon.bak' created if the former
log becomes full. The log(s) may contain additional unrelated debugging information.
To filter out the needed information, please search for lines which contain text
'NO_CLIENT_SITE:'. The first word after this string is the client name and the second
word is the client IP address. The maximum size of the log(s) is controlled by the
following registry DWORD value 'HKEY_LOCAL_MACHINE\SYSTEM\CurrentControlSet\Services\
Netlogon\Parameters\LogFileMaxSize'; the default is 20000000 bytes.  The current
maximum size is 20000000 bytes.  To set a different maximum size, create the above
registry value and set the desired maximum size in bytes.

For more information, see Help and Support Center at http://go.microsoft.com/fwlink/
events.asp.
```

Instead of scraping the event logs on every domain controller, you can look at the
%SystemRoot%\debug\netlogon.log file on each domain controller and parse out all
the NO_CLIENT_SITE entries. This is still far from an easy process, but at least the
event logs are no longer cluttered with 5778 events.

Here is an example of some of the NO_CLIENT_SITE entries from the *netlogon.log*
file:

```
01/16 15:50:07 RALLENCORP: NO_CLIENT_SITE: RALLEN-TEST4 164.2.45.157
01/16 15:50:29 RALLENCORP: NO_CLIENT_SITE: SJC-BACKUP 44.25.26.142
01/16 16:19:58 RALLENCORP: NO_CLIENT_SITE: RALLEN-TEST4 164.2.45.157
01/16 16:20:07 RALLENCORP: NO_CLIENT_SITE: RALLEN-TEST4 164.2.45.157
01/16 16:50:07 RALLENCORP: NO_CLIENT_SITE: RALLEN-TEST4 164.2.45.157
01/16 16:57:00 RALLENCORP: NO_CLIENT_SITE: JSMITH-W2K1 10.61.80.19
01/16 17:20:08 RALLENCORP: NO_CLIENT_SITE: RALLEN-TEST4 164.2.45.157
01/16 17:50:08 RALLENCORP: NO_CLIENT_SITE: RALLEN-TEST4 164.2.45.157
```

If you wanted to get creative and automate a solution to do this, you could write a
script that goes out to each domain controller, opens the *netlogon.log* file and
retrieves NO_CLIENT_SITE entries. You can then examine all of the IP addresses
and create subnets in Active Directory that would contain them. You could associate
all of those subnets with a default site or even use the Default-First-Site-Name site.
Then once a week (or whenever), you could look at the sites that were created or that

were associated with the default site and determine what site they really should be associated with.

11.7   Creating a Site Link

Problem

You want to create a site link to connect two or more sites together.

Solution

Using a graphical user interface

1. Open the Active Directory Sites and Services snap-in.
2. Expand the Sites container.
3. Expand the Inter-Site Transports container.
4. Right-click on IP (or SMTP) and select New Site Link.
5. For Name, enter the name for the site link.
6. Under Site is not in this site link, select at least two sites and click the Add button.
7. Click OK.

Using a command-line interface

The following LDIF would create a site link connecting the SJC and Dallas sites:

```
dn: cn=Dallas-SJC,cn=IP,cn=inter-site
transports,cn=sites,cn=configuration,<ForestRootDN>
changetype: add
objectclass: siteLink
siteObject: cn=SJC,cn=sites,cn=configuration,<ForestRootDN>
siteObject: cn=Dallas,cn=sites,cn=configuration,<ForestRootDN>
```

If the LDIF file were named *create_site_link.ldf*, you'd then run the following command:

```
> ldifde -v -i -f create_site_link.ldf
```

Using VBScript

```
' This code creates a site link
' ------ SCRIPT CONFIGURATION ------
intCost  = 100          ' site link cost
intReplInterval = 180    ' replication interval in minutes
strSite1 = "<Site1>"     ' e.g. SJC
strSite2 = "<Site2>"     ' e.g. Dallas
strLinkName = strSite1 & " - " & strSite2
' ------ END CONFIGURATION ---------
```

```
' Taken from ADS_PROPERTY_OPERATION_ENUM
const ADS_PROPERTY_UPDATE = 2

set objRootDSE = GetObject("LDAP://RootDSE")
set objLinkCont = GetObject( _
                "LDAP://cn=IP,cn=Inter-site Transports,cn=sites," & _
                objRootDSE.Get("configurationNamingContext") )
set objLink = objLinkCont.Create("siteLink", "cn=" & strLinkName)
strSite1DN = "cn=" & strSite1 & ",cn=sites," & _
                objRootDSE.Get("configurationNamingContext")
strSite2DN = "cn=" & strSite2 & ",cn=sites," & _
                objRootDSE.Get("configurationNamingContext")
objLink.PutEx ADS_PROPERTY_UPDATE, "siteList", Array(strSite1DN,strSite2DN)
objLink.Put "cost", intCost
objLink.Put "replInterval", intReplInterval
objLink.SetInfo

WScript.Echo "Successfully created link: " & strLinkName
```

Discussion

Without site links, domain controllers would not be able to determine the optimal partners to replicate with. The cost that is associated with a site defines how "expensive" the link is. A lower cost is less expensive (or faster) than a higher cost. Link costs are inversely proportional to bandwidth.

See Also

MS KB 316812 (HOW TO: Create and Configure a Site Link in Active Directory in Windows 2000)

11.8   Finding the Site Links for a Site

Problem

You want to list the site links that are associated with a site.

Solution

Using a graphical user interface

1. Open LDP and from the menu, select Connection → Connect.
2. For Server, enter the name of a domain controller (or leave blank to do a server-less bind).
3. For Port, enter 389.
4. Click OK.

5. From the menu, select Connection → Bind.

6. Enter credentials of domain user.

7. Click OK.

8. From the menu, select Browse → Search.

9. For BaseDN, type the Inter-Site Transports container DN (e.g., *cn=Inter-site Transports,cn=sites,cn=configuration,dc=rallencorp,dc=com*).

10. For Scope, select Subtree.

11. For Filter, enter the following:

```
(&(objectcategory=siteLink)(siteList=cn=<SiteName>,↵
cn=sites,cn=configuration,<ForestRootDN>))
```

12. Click Run.

Using a command-line interface

```
> dsquery * "cn=inter-site transports,cn=sites,cn=configuration,<ForestRootDN>"↵
-filter "(&(objectcategory=siteLink)(siteList=cn=<SiteName>,↵
cn=sites,cn=configuration,<ForestRootDN>))" -scope subtree -attr name
```

Using VBScript

```
' This code displays the site links associated with the specified site
' ------ SCRIPT CONFIGURATION ------
strSiteName = "<SiteName>"  ' e.g. Raleigh
' ------ END CONFIGURATION ---------

set objRootDSE = GetObject("LDAP://RootDSE")
strSiteDN = "cn=" & strSiteName & ",cn=sites," & _
            objRootDSE.Get("ConfigurationNamingContext")

strBase    = "<LDAP://cn=Inter-site Transports,cn=sites," _
               & objRootDSE.Get("ConfigurationNamingContext") & ">;"
strFilter  = "(&(objectcategory=siteLink)" & _
               "(siteList=" & strSiteDN & "));"
strAttrs   = "name;"
strScope   = "subtree"

set objConn = CreateObject("ADODB.Connection")
objConn.Provider = "ADsDSOObject"
objConn.Open "Active Directory Provider"
set objRS = objConn.Execute(strBase & strFilter & strAttrs & strScope)

WScript.Echo "Total site links for " & strSiteName & ": " & objRS.RecordCount
if objRS.RecordCount > 0 then
   objRS.MoveFirst
   while Not objRS.EOF
       Wscript.Echo vbTab & objRS.Fields(0).Value
       objRS.MoveNext
   wend
end if
```

Discussion

A site can be included as part of zero or more site links. A site with no site links would be considered orphaned from the site topology, since there is no way to determine how and where it connects into the topology. Branch office sites may have only a single site link back to a hub, while a hub site may have numerous links that connect it to the rest of the world.

Finding the site links associated with a site consists of performing a query for all siteLink objects that have DN of the site included in the siteList attribute for a link. The siteList attribute is a multivalued attribute that contains all the sites that are connected via the site link.

11.9   Modifying the Sites That Are Part of a Site Link

Problem

You want to modify the sites associated with a site link.

Solution

Using a graphical user interface

1. Open the Active Directory Sites and Services snap-in.
2. In the left pane, expand Sites → Inter-Site Transports.
3. Click either the IP or SMTP folder depending where the site link is stored.
4. In the right pane, double-click on the link you want to modify.
5. Under the General tab, you can add and remove sites that are associated with the site link.
6. Click OK.

Using a command-line interface

Create an LDIF file called *modify_site_link.ldf* with the following contents. Replace *<LinkName>* with the name of the link and *<SiteName>* with the site to add to the link.

```
dn: cn=<LinkName>,cn=IP,cn=inter-site
transports,cn=sites,cn=configuration,<ForestRootDN>
changetype: modify
add: siteList
siteList: cn=<SiteName>,cn=sites,cn=configuration,<ForestRootDN>
-
```

Then run the following command:

```
> ldifde -v -i -f modify_site_link.ldf
```

Using VBScript

```
' This code adds a site to an existing site link
' ------ SCRIPT CONFIGURATION ------
strSite = "<SiteName>" ' e.g. Burlington
strLink = "<LinkName>" ' e.g. DEFAULTIPSITELINK
' ------ END CONFIGURATION ---------

' Taken from ADS_PROPERTY_OPERATION_ENUM
const ADS_PROPERTY_APPEND = 3

set objRootDSE = GetObject("LDAP://RootDSE")
set objLink = GetObject("LDAP://cn=" & strLink & _
                    ",cn=IP,cn=Inter-site Transports,cn=sites," & _
                    objRootDSE.Get("configurationNamingContext") )
strSiteDN = "cn=" & strSite & ",cn=sites," & _
            objRootDSE.Get("configurationNamingContext")
objLink.PutEx ADS_PROPERTY_APPEND, "siteList", Array(strSiteDN)
objLink.SetInfo

WScript.Echo "Successfully modified link: " & strLink
```

Discussion

To associate a site with a site link, add the DN of the site to the siteList attribute of the siteLink object that represents the link. To remove a site from a link, do the reverse. Remove the DN associated with the site from the siteList attribute.

See Also

Recipe 11.8 for finding the links associated with a site

11.10 Modifying the Cost for a Site Link

Problem

You want to modify the cost for a site link.

Solution

Using a graphical user interface

1. Open the Active Directory Sites and Services snap-in.
2. In the left pane, expand Sites → Inter-Site Transports.
3. Click either the IP or SMTP folder depending where the site link is stored.
4. In the right pane, double-click on the link you want to modify.
5. Under the General tab, you can change the cost for the site link.
6. Click OK.

Using a command-line interface

Create an LDIF file called *modify_site_link_cost.ldf* with the following contents. Replace *<LinkName>* with the name of the site you want to modify.

```
dn: cn=DEFAULTIPSITELINK,cn=IP,cn=inter-site
transports,cn=sites,cn=configuration,<ForestRootDN>
changetype: modify
replace: cost
cost: <LinkCost>
-
```

Then run the following command:

```
> ldifde -v -i -f modify_site_link_cost.ldf
```

Using VBScript

```
' This code modifies the cost attribute of a site link
' ------ SCRIPT CONFIGURATION ------
strLink = "<SiteLink>"    ' e.g. DEFAULTIPSITELINK
intCost = <LinkCost>      ' e.g. 200
' ------ END CONFIGURATION ---------

set objRootDSE = GetObject("LDAP://RootDSE")
set objLink = GetObject("LDAP://cn=" & strLink & _
                   ",cn=IP,cn=Inter-site Transports,cn=sites," & _
                   objRootDSE.Get("configurationNamingContext") )
objLink.Put "cost", intCost
objLink.SetInfo

WScript.Echo "Successfully modified link: " & strLink
```

Discussion

The cost attribute is one of the most important attributes of siteLink objects. cost is used by the KCC to determine what connection objects should be created to allow domain controllers to replicate data.

cost is inversely proportional to bandwidth. The lower the cost, the greater the bandwidth. The number you use for the cost is also arbitrary; the default is 100. You could use 100–1,000 as the range for your site link costs, or you could use 1–10. The actual number isn't important, it is relative based on the other site links.

11.11 Disabling Site Link Transitivity or Site Link Schedules

Problem

You want to disable site link transitivity to control replication.

Solution

Using a graphical user interface

1. Open the Active Directory Sites and Services snap-in.
2. In the left pane, expand Sites → Inter-Site Transports.
3. Right-click either the IP or SMTP folder depending which protocol you want to disable transitivity or ignore schedules for.
4. Select Properties.
5. To disable site link transitivity, uncheck Bridge all site links.
6. To ignore site link schedules, check Ignore schedules.
7. Click OK.

Using a command-line interface

You can modify the options attribute of a site link object using an LDIF file and ldifde, but since the attribute is a bit flag, you are better off using the GUI or VBScript solutions that look at the current value of options and modify it accordingly. ldifde doesn't handle this type of logic.

Using VBScript

```
' This code can disable site link transitivity and site
' schedules for all links of the IP transport.
' The code for the CalcBit function can be found in Recipe 4.12
' ------ SCRIPT CONFIGURATION ------
boolDisableTrans = <TrueOrFalse>    ' e.g. TRUE
boolIgnoreSchedules = <TrueOrFalse> ' e.g. FALSE
' ------ END CONFIGURATION ---------

set objRootDSE = GetObject("LDAP://RootDSE")
set objLink = GetObject( _
              "LDAP://cn=IP,cn=Inter-site Transports,cn=sites," & _
              objRootDSE.Get("configurationNamingContext") )

intBitsOrg = objLink.Get("options")
intBits = CalcBit(intBitsOrg, 2, boolDisableTrans)
intBits = CalcBit(intBitsOrg, 1, boolIgnoreSchedules)

if objLink.Get("options") <> intBits then
   objLink.Put "options", intBits
   objLink.SetInfo
   WScript.Echo "Successfully modified link transitivity for " & strLink
else
   WScript.Echo "Did not need to modify link transitivity for " & strLink
end if
```

Discussion

Active Directory site links are transitive, which means that if site A is linked to site B, and site B is linked to site C, then site A is also be linked (through site B) to site C. The Knowledge Consistency Checker (KCC) uses transitivity by default when making decisions about creating connection objects. You can disable this behavior if you want. Typically this is not something you'll want to do unless you know what you are doing. Disabling transitivity may be necessary for some Windows 2000 deployments that have a lot of sites and find that the KCC is having a hard time keeping up. With Windows Server 2003, the KCC has been greatly improved and site link transitivity should not cause problems.

The other reason you might want to disable transitivity is if you need to make replication more deterministic. Disabling transitivity makes it much easier to determine where the KCC will attempt to establish connection objects, because the KCC on a domain controller will not be able to replicate with domain controllers that are not in sites that are directly linked.

I mention site link schedules here primarily because the same attribute (i.e., options) that determines site link transitivity also determines if link schedules are enforced. If you enable the ignore schedules option for a particular transport (i.e., IP or SMTP), the KCC ignores any preconfigured link schedules. If you later disable this setting, link schedules will go back into effect.

See Also

Recipe 4.12 for more on setting a bit-flag attribute

11.12 Creating a Site Link Bridge

Problem

You want to create a site link bridge because you've disabled site link transitivity.

Solution

Using a graphical user interface

1. Open the Active Directory Sites and Services snap-in.
2. In the left pane, expand Sites → Inter-Site Transports.
3. Right-click either the IP or SMTP folder depending which protocol you want to create a site link bridge for.
4. Select New Site Link Bridge.
5. Highlight two or more sites in the left box.

6. Click the Add button.

7. Click OK.

Using a command-line interface

Create an LDIF file called *create_site_link_bridge.ldf* with the following contents, where *<Link1>* and *<Link2>* refer to the site links to be bridged:

```
dn: cn=<BridgeName>,cn=IP,cn=inter-site
transports,cn=sites,cn=configuration,<ForestRootDN>
changetype: add
objectclass: siteLinkBridge
siteLinkList: cn=<Link1>,cn=IP,cn=Inter-site Transports,cn=sites,cn=configuration,
<ForestRootDN>
siteLinkList: cn=<Link2>,cn=IP,cn=Inter-site Transports,cn=sites,cn=configuration,
<ForestRootDN>
```

Then run the following command:

```
> ldifde -v -i -f create_site_link_bridge.ldf
```

Using VBScript

```
' This code creates a site link bridge between two site links
' ------ SCRIPT CONFIGURATION ------
strLink1 = "<Link1>"        ' e.g. AMS-LON
strLink2 = "<Link2>"        ' e.g. SJC-RTP
strBridge = "<BridgeName>"  ' e.g. AMER-EUR
' ------ END CONFIGURATION ---------

set objRootDSE = GetObject("LDAP://RootDSE")
set objLinkCont = GetObject( _
                "LDAP://cn=IP,cn=Inter-site Transports,cn=sites," & _
                objRootDSE.Get("configurationNamingContext") )
set objBridge = objLinkCont.Create("siteLinkBridge", "cn=" & strBridge)
strLink1DN = "cn=" & strLink1 & _
             ",cn=IP,cn=Inter-site Transports,cn=sites," & _
             objRootDSE.Get("configurationNamingContext")
strLink2DN = "cn=" & strLink2 & _
             ",cn=IP,cn=Inter-site Transports,cn=sites," & _
             objRootDSE.Get("configurationNamingContext")
objBridge.Put "siteLinkList", Array(strLink1DN,strLink2DN)
objBridge.SetInfo

WScript.Echo "Successfully created bridge: " & strBridge
```

Discussion

If you've disabled site link transitivity or have networks that lack direct routes between sites, you will need to create site link bridges. Creating a site link bridge to link several links is analogous to creating a site link to link several sites. Lets take an example where site link transitivity is disabled and we have four sites; site A has a link to site B and site C has a link to site D. If we want domain controllers in sites A and B to replicate with sites C and D, we need to create a site link bridge to bridge the A–B link with C–D.

See Also

Recipe 11.11 for disabling site link transitivity

11.13 Finding the Bridgehead Servers for a Site

Problem

You want to find the bridgehead servers for a site.

Solution

Using a graphical user interface

1. Open the Replication Monitor from the Support Tools (replmon.exe).
2. From the menu, select View → Options.
3. In the left pane, right-click on Monitored Servers and select Add Monitored Server.
4. Use the Add Monitored Server Wizard to add a server in the site you want to find the bridgehead server(s) for.
5. In the left pane, right-click on the server and select Show BridgeHead Servers → In This Server's Site.

Using a command-line interface

```
> repadmin /bridgeheads [<ServerName>] [/verbose]
```

The /bridgeheads option is valid only with the Windows Server 2003 version of repadmin. There is no such option in the Windows 2000 version.

Using VBScript

```
' This code finds the bridgehead servers for the specified site.
' ------ SCRIPT CONFIGURATION ------
strServer = "<ServerName>" ' server to target query against, e.g. dc01
strSite = "<SiteName>"      ' name of site to query
                            ' e.g. Default-First-Site-Name
' ------ END CONFIGURATION ---------

set objIadsTools = CreateObject("IADsTools.DCFunctions")
intRes = objIadsTools.GetBridgeHeadsInSite(Cstr(strServer),Cstr(strSite),0)
```

```
   if intRes = -1 then
      Wscript.Echo "Error bridge heads: " & objIadsTools.LastErrorText
      WScript.Quit
   end if

   for count = 1 to intRes
      WScript.Echo vbTab & objIadsTools.BridgeHeadName(count)
   next
```

Discussion

Bridgehead servers are responsible for replicating data between sites. Instead of all domain controllers replicating the same naming contexts outside of the site, the bridgehead servers act as a funnel for replication into and out of a site. Any domain controller in a site can become a bridgehead server and bridgeheads are designated by the KCC for each writeable partition in the site. You can control which servers are designated as bridgehead servers by defining preferred bridgehead servers. See Recipe 11.14 for more on how to do this.

See Also

MS KB 271997 (Description of Bridgehead Servers in Windows 2000)

11.14 Setting a Preferred Bridgehead Server for a Site

Problem

You want to set a preferred bridgehead server for a site.

Solution

Using a graphical user interface

1. Open the Active Directory Sites and Services snap-in.
2. In the left pane, expand Sites, expand the site where the server you want to set as a bridgehead is contained and expand the Servers container
3. Right-click on the server you want to set as the bridgehead and select Properties.
4. Highlight IP, SMTP, or both, pertaining to the protocol(s) for which you want the server to be a bridgehead.
5. Click the Add button.
6. Click OK.

Using a command-line interface

Create an LDIF file called *set_bridgehead_server.ldf* with the following contents:

```
dn: cn=<DCName>,cn=servers,cn=<SiteName>,cn=sites,cn=configuration,<ForestRootDN>
changetype: modify
add: bridgeheadTransportList
bridgeheadTransportList: cn=IP,cn=Inter-site
Transports,cn=sites,cn=configuration,<ForestRootDN>
-
```

then run the following command:

```
> ldifde -v -i -f set_bridgehead_server.ldf
```

Using VBScript

```
' This code sets a preferred bridgehead server for a particular transport
' ------ SCRIPT CONFIGURATION ------
strServer      = "<DomainControllerName>"  ' e.g. dc1
strServerSite = "<SiteName>"               ' e.g. Default-First-Site-Name
strTransport  = "<TransportName>"          ' e.g. either IP or SMTP
' ------ END CONFIGURATION ---------

set objRootDSE = GetObject("LDAP://RootDSE")
set objServer = GetObject("LDAP://cn=" & strServer & ",cn=Servers,cn=" & _
                          strServerSite & ",cn=sites," & _
                          objRootDSE.Get("configurationNamingContext") )
objServer.Put "bridgeHeadTransportList", _
              "cn=" & strTransport & ",cn=Inter-site Transports,cn=sites," _
                  & objRootDSE.Get("configurationNamingContext")
objServer.SetInfo

WScript.Echo "Successfully set bridgehead server: " & strServer
```

Discussion

Setting a preferred bridgehead server can give you more control over which domain controllers participate in inter-site replication, but it is also limiting. The KCC typically selects bridgehead servers dynamically, but if you set preferred bridgehead servers, the KCC will not select new ones if the preferred servers become unavailable. Therefore, you should ensure that if you do select preferred bridgehead servers, you select at least two for a given partition in a site.

 As a general rule, you shouldn't set preferred bridgehead servers if at all possible.

See Also

MS KB 271997 (Description of Bridgehead Servers in Windows 2000)

11.15 Listing the Servers

Problem

You want to list the server objects in the site topology.

Solution

Using a graphical user interface

1. Open LDP.
2. From the menu, select Connection → Connect.
3. For Server, enter the name of a domain controller (or leave blank to do a server-less bind).
4. For Port, enter 389.
5. Click OK.
6. From the menu, select Connection → Bind.
7. Enter credentials of a domain user.
8. Click OK.
9. From the menu, select Browse → Search.
10. For BaseDN, type the Sites container's DN (e.g., *cn=sites,cn=configuration, dc=rallencorp,dc=com*).
11. For Scope, select Subtree.
12. For Filter, enter (objectcategory=server).
13. Click Run.

Using a command-line interface

```
> dsquery server [-site <SiteName>]
```

Using VBScript

```
' This code lists the server objects in the site topology.

set objRootDSE = GetObject("LDAP://RootDSE")
strBase     = "<LDAP://cn=sites," & _
                 objRootDSE.Get("ConfigurationNamingContext") & ">;"
strFilter   = "(objectcategory=server);"
strAttrs    = "distinguishedName;"
strScope    = "subtree"

set objConn = CreateObject("ADODB.Connection")
objConn.Provider = "ADsDSOObject"
objConn.Open "Active Directory Provider"
set objRS = objConn.Execute(strBase & strFilter & strAttrs & strScope)
```

```
objRS.MoveFirst
while Not objRS.EOF
    Wscript.Echo objRS.Fields(0).Value
    objRS.MoveNext
wend
```

Discussion

Each Active Directory domain controller is represented in the site topology by a server object that is associated with a specific site. Replication decisions are made based on links from this site to other sites that contain domain controllers.

Other types of services can also add server objects to the site topology. The way you can distinguish which ones are domain controllers is the presence of a NTDS Settings (nTDSDSA) object that is a child of the server object. Only domain controllers will have that object.

11.16 Moving a Domain Controller to a Different Site

Problem

You want to move a domain controller to a different site. This may be necessary if you promoted the domain controller without first adding its subnet to Active Directory. In that case, the domain controller will be added to the Default-First-Site-Name site.

Solution

Using a graphical user interface

1. Open the Active Directory Sites and Services snap-in.
2. In the left pane, expand Sites, expand the site where the server you want to move is contained, and expand the Servers container.
3. Right-click on the server you want to move and select Move.
4. Select the site to move the server to.
5. Click OK.

Using a command-line interface

```
> dsmove "cn=<ServerName>,cn=servers,cn=<CurrentSite>,⏎
cn=sites,cn=configuration,<ForestRootDN>" -newparent "cn=servers,cn=<NewSite>,⏎
cn=sites,cn=configuration,<ForestRootDN>"
```

Using VBScript

```
' This code moves a server to a different site.
' ------ SCRIPT CONFIGURATION ------
' Should contain the common name of the server object
strDC = "<DomainControllerName>" ' e.g. dc02
' Name of servers current site
strCurrentSite = "<CurrentSite>" ' e.g. Default-First-Site-Name
' Name of site you want to move server to
strNewSite = "<NewSite>"         ' e.g. Raleigh
' ------ END CONFIGURATION ---------

strConfigDN = GetObject("LDAP://RootDSE").Get("configurationNamingContext")
strServerDN = "LDAP://cn=" & strDC & ",cn=servers,cn=" & _
                      strCurrentSite & ",cn=sites," & strConfigDN
strNewParentDN = "LDAP://cn=servers,cn=" & strNewSite & ",cn=sites," & strConfigDN

Set objCont = GetObject(strNewParentDN)
objCont.MoveHere strServerDN, "cn=" & strDC
```

Discussion

After you move a server to a new site, you might want to monitor replication to and from that server to make sure that any new connections that are needed get created and start replicating. See Recipe 12.2 for more on viewing the replication status of a server.

See Also

MS KB 214677 (Automatic Detection of Site Membership for Domain Controllers)

11.17 Configuring a Domain Controller to Cover Multiple Sites

Problem

You want to configure a domain controller to cover multiple sites, which will cause clients in those sites to use that domain controller for authentication and directory lookups.

Solution

Using a graphical user interface

1. Run regedit.exe from the command line or Start → Run.
2. In the left pane, expand HKEY_LOCAL_MACHINE → SYSTEM → Current-ControlSet → Services → Netlogon → Parameters.

---

3. If the SiteCoverage value does not exist, right-click on Parameters in the left pane and select New → Multi-String Value. For the name, enter SiteCoverage.

4. In the right pane, double-click on the value and on a separate line, enter each site the server should cover.

5. Click OK.

Using a command-line interface

```
> reg add HKLM\System\CurrentControlSet\Services\Netlogon\Parameters /v↵
"SiteCoverage" /t REG_MULTI_SZ /d <Site1>\0<Site2>
```

Using VBScript

```
' This code configures a domain controller to cover multiple sites.
' ------ SCRIPT CONFIGURATION ------
strDC    = "<DomainControllerName>"         ' e.g. dc01
arrSites = Array("<Site1>","<Site2>") ' Array of sites to cover
' ------ END CONFIGURATION ---------

strNTDSReg = "SYSTEM\CurrentControlSet\Services\Netlogon\Parameters"
const HKLM = &H80000002
set objReg = GetObject("winmgmts:\\" & strDC & "\root\default:StdRegProv")
objReg.SetMultiStringValue HKLM, strNTDSReg, _
                  "SiteCoverage", _
                  arrSites
WScript.Echo "Site coverage set for " & strDC
```

Discussion

It is perfectly valid to have a site that does not contain its own domain controller. In fact, if you model the site topology after your real network, some sites will lack their own domain controllers unless you've deployed a branch office architecture or have very few sites. If you create sites without any domain controllers, the site links between the sites determine what domain controllers will "cover" or advertise their services to the site. When a domain controller covers for a remote site, it needs to publish site-specific DNS resource records, which clients in the site use to find the domain controller. Active Directory will select DCs to cover DC-less sites automatically, but you can hard-code the list of sites a specific domain controller should cover by modifying the Registry as described in the Solution section.

See Also

MS KB 200498 (Configure a Domain Controller for Membership in Multiple Sites)

11.18 Viewing the Site Coverage for a Domain Controller

Problem

You want to view the sites a domain controller covers.

Solution

Using a command-line interface

In the following command, replace *<DomainControllerName>* with the name of the domain controller you want to view site coverage for:

```
> nltest /server:<DomainControllerName> /DsGetSiteCov
```

Using VBScript

Although you cannot use it directly from a scripting language like VBScript, Microsoft provides a DsGetDcSiteCoverage method that can be used by languages, such as Visual Basic and C++, to retrieve site coverage information. In fact, the nltest command shown in the CLI solution is a wrapper around this method.

Discussion

Recipe 11.17 describes how to force a domain controller to cover multiple sites. Recipe 11.19 describes how you can disable a domain controller from covering for any sites other than its own.

See Also

MSDN: DsGetDcSiteCoverage

11.19 Disabling Automatic Site Coverage for a Domain Controller

Problem

You want to prevent a domain controller from covering sites outside of the one it resides in.

Solution

Using a graphical user interface

1. Run regedit.exe from the command line or Start → Run.
2. Expand HKEY_LOCAL_MACHINE → SYSTEM → CurrentControlSet → Services → Netlogon → Parameters.
3. Right-click on Parameters and select New → DWORD Value.
4. For the name, enter AutoSiteCoverage.
5. Double-click on the new value, enter 0 under Value data, and click OK.

Using a command-line interface

```
> reg add HKLM\System\CurrentControlSet\Services\Netlogon\Parameters /v↲
AutoSiteCoverage /t REG_DWORD /d 0
```

Using VBScript

```
' This code disables auto site coverage
strNetlogonReg = "SYSTEM\CurrentControlSet\Services\Netlogon\Parameters"
const HKLM = &H80000002
Set objReg = GetObject("winmgmts:root\default:StdRegProv")
objReg.SetDWORDValue HKLM, strNetlogonReg, "AutoSiteCoverage", 0
WScript.Echo "Site coverage disabled"
```

Discussion

If you want to reduce the load on a domain controller, one way is to prevent it from covering for other sites. Automatic site coverage happens when a site does not have any member domain controllers.

See Also

Recipe 11.18 for viewing the site coverage for a domain controller

11.20 Finding the Site for a Client

Problem

You want to find which site a client computer is in.

Solution

Using a command-line interface

In the following command, replace *<HostName>* with the name of the host you want to find the site for:

```
> nltest /server:<HostName> /DsGetSite
```

Using VBScript

Although you cannot use it directly from a scripting language like VBScript, Microsoft provides a DsGetSiteName method that can be used by languages, such as Visual Basic and C++, to retrieve site coverage information. In fact, the nltest command shown in the CLI solution is a wrapper around this method.

The IADsTool interface provides a wrapper around this method:

```
set objIadsTools = CreateObject("IADsTools.DCFunctions")
strSite = objIadsTools.DsGetSiteName("<HostName>")
Wscript.Echo "Site: " & strSite
```

Discussion

Each domain controller has a server object that is contained with a site. Clients are different—they are associated with a site based on their IP address and the corresponding subnet that it matches is in the Subnets container. The client site information is important because it determines the domain controller the client authenticates with. If the client's IP address does not match a subnet range of any of the subnets stored in Active Directory, it will randomly pick a site to use, which means it could authenticate against any domain controller in the domain. See Recipe 11.21 for a way to hardcode the site association for a client.

See Also

Recipe 11.21 for forcing a host to a particular site, MS KB 247811 (How Domain Controllers Are Located in Windows), and MSDN: DsGetSiteName

11.21 Forcing a Host to a Particular Site

Problem

You want to force a host to be in a particular site.

Solution

Using a graphical user interface

1. Run regedit.exe from the command line or Start → Run.

2. Expand HKEY_LOCAL_MACHINE → SYSTEM → CurrentControlSet → Services → Netlogon → Parameters.

3. Right-click on Parameters and select New → String Value.

4. Enter SiteName for the name.

5. Double-click on the new value, enter the name of the site under Value data, and click OK.

Using a command-line interface

```
> reg add HKLM\System\CurrentControlSet\Services\Netlogon\Parameters /v SiteName /t↵
REG_SZ /d <SiteName>
```

Using VBScript

```
' This code forces the host the script is run on to use a particular host
' ------ SCRIPT CONFIGURATION ------
strSite = "<SiteName>"    ' e.g. Raleigh
' ------ END CONFIGURATION ---------

strNetlogonReg = "SYSTEM\CurrentControlSet\Services\Netlogon\Parameters"
const HKLM = &H80000002
set objReg = GetObject("winmgmts:root\default:StdRegProv")
objReg.SetStringValue HKLM, strNetlogonReg, "SiteName", strSite
WScript.Echo "Set SiteName to " & strSite
```

Discussion

You can bypass the part of the DC Locator process that determines a client's site by hard-coding it in the Registry. This is generally not recommended and should primarily be used as a troubleshooting tool. If a client is experiencing authentication delays due to a misconfigured site or subnet object, you can hard-code its site so it temporarily points to a more optimal location (and domain controller).

See Also

Recipe 11.20 for finding the site of a client and MS KB 247811 (How Domain Controllers Are Located in Windows)

11.22 Creating a Connection Object

Problem

You want to create a connection object to manually set up replication between two sites.

Solution

Using a graphical user interface

1. Open the Active Directory Sites and Services snap-in.
2. In the left pane, expand Sites, expand the site that contains the connection object you want to check, expand the Servers container, and expand the server for which you want to create the connection object.
3. Right-click on the NTDS Settings object and select Create New Active Directory Connection.
4. Select the replication partner and click OK.
5. Enter the name for the connection and click OK.

Using a command-line interface

```
> repadmin /add <PartitionDN> <DC1DNSName> <DC2DNSName>
```

Discussion

Hopefully you will not need to create connection objects manually. Creating and maintaining connection objects is the job of the KCC. It can be a lot of work to keep your connection objects up to date by yourself, especially if you have a large topology. The KCC uses complex algorithms to determine the best partners for a domain controller to replicate with. The Windows 2000 KCC had problems generating very large topologies, but the Windows Server 2003 version is significantly better.

It is sometimes necessary to create connections manually if you find a replication problem and need to get replication going again between one or more sites. By creating a connection and forcing replication to occur over that connection, you can get servers back in sync quickly.

See Also

Recipe 11.23 for listing the connections for a server

11.23 Listing the Connection Objects for a Server

Problem

You want to view the connection objects associated with a domain controller.

Solution

Using a graphical user interface

1. Open the Active Directory Sites and Services snap-in.

2. In the left pane, expand Sites, expand the site that contains the connection object you want to check, expand the Servers container, expand the server that contains the connection object, and click on the NTDS Settings object.

3. In the right pane, under the name column, it will display which connection objects are automatically generated (by the KCC) and which ones were manually generated.

Using a command-line interface

```
> repadmin /showconn [<DomainControllerName>]
```

Using VBScript

```
' This code lists the connection objects for a server
' ------ SCRIPT CONFIGURATION ------
strServer = "<ServerName>"  ' e.g. dc01
strSite   = "<SiteName>"    ' e.g. MySite1
' ------ END CONFIGURATION ---------

set objRootDSE = GetObject("LDAP://RootDSE")
set objNTDSCont = GetObject("LDAP://cn=NTDS Settings,cn=" & strServer & _
                     ",cn=servers,cn=" & strSite & ",cn=sites," & _
                     objRootDSE.Get("configurationNamingContext") )
objNTDSCont.Filter = Array("ntdsConnection")
WScript.Echo "Connection objects for " & strSite & "\" & strServer
for each objConn in objNTDSCont
   if objConn.Get("options") = 0 then
      Wscript.Echo "  " & objConn.Get("cn") & " (MANUAL)"
   else
      Wscript.Echo "  " & objConn.Get("cn") & " (AUTO)"
   end if
next
```

 Another option for programmatically getting the connection objects for a server is to use the GetDSAConnections method from the IADsTool interface.

Discussion

Connection objects are used to replicate inbound changes to a domain controller. By viewing the connection objects for a server you can see what domain controllers it receives updates from. Connection objects are created automatically by the KCC, but can be created manually if necessary.

See Also

Recipe 11.22 for creating a connection object

11.24 Load-Balancing Connection Objects

Problem

You want to evenly distribute connection objects between bridgehead servers in a site.

Solution

Using a command-line interface

To see what changes the command would make, run it without the /commit option. To actually make the changes in Active Directory, use the /commit option:

```
> adlb /server:<DomainControllerName> -site:<SiteName> [/commit] [/verbose]
```

 This command is available in the Windows Server 2003 Resource Kit.

Discussion

Bridgeheads can become overloaded or end up with too many connection objects in relation to other bridgeheads in the domain. The Active Directory Load Balancing (ADLB) tool allows you to balance the load of connection objects among bridgehead servers within a site. The Windows Server 2003 algorithms are much better than Windows 2000 for load balancing connection objects across servers, but that process happens only when new connection objects are added. You can use the adlb tool to load balance the connection objects more efficiently at any time.

I recommend viewing the changes adlb would make first before using the /commit option. It is always good to do a sanity check to ensure adlb doesn't mess up your replication topology.

11.25 Finding the ISTG for a Site

Problem

You want to find the Inter-Site Topology Generator (ISTG) for a site.

Solution

Using a graphical user interface

1. Open the Active Directory Sites and Services snap-in.
2. Click on the site you are interested in.
3. In the right pane, double-click on the NTDS Site Settings object.
4. The ISTG will be displayed under Inter-Site Topology Generator if one is present.

Using a command-line interface

```
> repadmin /istg <DomainControllerName>
```

This command is available only with the Windows Server 2003 version of repadmin.

Using VBScript

```
' This code finds the ISTG for the specified site.
' ------ SCRIPT CONFIGURATION ------
strSiteName = <SiteName>   ' e.g. Raleigh
' ------ END CONFIGURATION ---------

set objRootDSE = GetObject("LDAP://RootDSE")
set objSiteSettings = GetObject("LDAP://cn=NTDS Site Settings,cn=" & _
                                strSiteName & ",cn=sites," & _
                                objRootDSE.Get("ConfigurationNamingContext"))
on error resume next
strISTGDN = objSiteSettings.Get("interSiteTopologyGenerator")
if (strISTGDN <> "") then
    set objNTDSSettings = GetObject("LDAP://" & strISTGDN)
    set objServer = GetObject( objNTDSSettings.Parent )
    WScript.Echo "ISTG for site " & strSiteName & " is " & _
                objServer.Get("dnsHostName")
else
    WScript.Echo "No ISTG found for site " & strSiteName
end if
```

Discussion

One domain controller in every site is picked as the ISTG for that site. While each domain controller is responsible for creating its own intra-site connection objects, the ISTG for a site is responsible for creating the inter-site connection objects for the bridgehead servers in the site.

The current ISTG for a site is stored in the `interSiteTopologyGenerator` attribute of the site's `NTDS Site Settings` object. The distinguished name of ISTG's `NTDS Settings` object is stored in the `interSiteTopologyGenerator` attribute.

Disabling inter-site topology generation is synonymous with disabling the KCC for a site. See Recipe 11.29 for more information on disabling the KCC.

See Also

Recipe 11.26 for moving the ISTG, MS KB 224815 (The Role of the Inter-Site Topology Generator in Active Directory Replication), and MS KB 224599 (Determining the Inter-Site Topology Generator (ISTG) of a Site in the Active Directory)

11.26 Transferring the ISTG to Another Server

Problem

You want to move the ISTG for a site to another domain controller. This happens automatically if you take the current ISTG offline, but you may want to transfer the role to a server that is more optimal in your environment.

Solution

Using a graphical user interface

1. Open ADSI Edit.
2. Connect to the CNC if it is not already displayed in the left pane.
3. In the left pane, browse the Configuration NC → Sites.
4. Click on the site you want to transfer the ISTG for.
5. In the right pane, double-click `CN=NTDS Site Settings`.
6. Modify the `interSiteTopologyGenerator` attribute to include the `NTDS Settings` object of the domain controller you want to transfer the ISTG role to.
7. Click OK.

Using VBScript

```
' This code forces a new ISTG in a site.
' ------ SCRIPT CONFIGURATION ------
' Name of site to transfer ISTG in
strSiteName = "<SiteName>"         ' e.g. Raleigh
' Site the new ISTG server is in
strNewISTGSite = "<ISTGSiteName>" ' e.g. Raleigh
```

```
' Common name of server object for new ISTG
strNewISTGName = "<DomainControllerName>"  ' e.g. dc01
' ------ END CONFIGURATION ---------

set objRootDSE = GetObject("LDAP://RootDSE")
set objSiteSettings = GetObject("LDAP://cn=NTDS Site Settings,cn=" & _
                                strSiteName & ",cn=sites," & _
                                objRootDSE.Get("ConfigurationNamingContext"))
strCurrentISTG = objSiteSettings.Get("interSiteTopologyGenerator")

objSiteSettings.Put "interSiteTopologyGenerator", _
                    "cn=NTDS Settings,cn=" & strNewISTGName & _
                    ",cn=servers,cn=" & strNewISTGSite & ",cn=sites," & _
                    objRootDSE.Get("ConfigurationNamingContext")
objSiteSettings.SetInfo
WScript.Echo "ISTG for " & strSiteName & " changed from:"
WScript.Echo "  " & strCurrentISTG
WScript.Echo "To"
WScript.Echo "  " & objSiteSettings.Get("interSiteTopologyGenerator")
```

Discussion

The current ISTG for a site is stored in the interSiteTopologyGenerator attribute of the site's NTDS Site Settings object. The distinguished name of the ISTG's NTDS Settings object is stored in that attribute.

Domain controllers communicate their presence as the ISTG by writing to the interSiteTopologyGenerator attribute at a set interval. If you want another domain controller to assume the role of the ISTG, you need to write the distinguished name of that domain controller's NTDS Settings object to the interSiteTopologyGenerator attribute of the NTDS Site Settings object for the site.

Two registry settings govern the ISTG registration process, both of which are stored under the HKEY_LOCAL_MACHINE\System\CurrentControlSet\Services\NTDS\ Parameters key. The interval (in minutes) in which the current ISTG should write to the interSiteTopologyGenerator attribute to inform the other DCs in the site that it is still the ISTG is stored in the KCC site generator renewal interval (minutes) value. The default is 30 minutes. The other value is named KCC site generator fail-over (minutes) and contains the time in minutes that each domain controller in the site should wait for the interSiteTopologyGenerator attribute to be written to before attempting to register itself as the ISTG. The default is 60 minutes.

See Also

MS KB 224815 (The Role of the Inter-Site Topology Generator in Active Directory Replication)

11.27 Triggering the KCC

Problem

You want to trigger the KCC.

Solution

Using a graphical user interface

1. Open the Active Directory Sites and Services snap-in.
2. In the left pane, browse to the NTDS Settings object for the server you want to trigger the KCC for.
3. Right-click on NTDS Settings, select All Tasks, and Check Replication Topology.
4. Click OK.

Using a command-line interface

```
> repadmin /kcc <DomainControllerName>
```

Using VBScript

```
' This code triggers the KCC on a DC.
' ------ SCRIPT CONFIGURATION ------
strDC = "<DomainControllerName>"  ' e.g. dc01
' ------ END CONFIGURATION ---------

set objIadsTools = CreateObject("IADsTools.DCFunctions")
intRes = objIadsTools.TriggerKCC(Cstr(strDC),0)

if intRes = -1 then
   Wscript.Echo objIadsTools.LastErrorText
else
   Wscript.Echo "KCC successfully triggered"
end if
```

Discussion

The KCC runs every 15 minutes by default on all domain controllers to generate the intra-site topology connections. The KCC that runs on the server that is selected as the ISTG generates inter-site topology connections to other sites from the bridge-head servers in its site. In some situations, such as when you create new site, siteLink, or subnet objects, you may want to run the KCC immediately so that any new connections between domain controllers get created.

See Also

Recipe 11.28 for determining if the KCC is completing successfully, for more information on IADsTools see *iadstools.doc* that is installed with the Support Tools, and MS KB 224815 (The Role of the Inter-Site Topology Generator in Active Directory Replication)

11.28 Determining if the KCC Is Completing Successfully

Problem

You want to determine if the KCC is completing successfully.

Solution

Using a graphical user interface

1. Open the Event Viewer of the target domain controller.
2. Click on the Directory Service log.
3. In the right pane, click on the Source heading to sort by that column.
4. Scroll down to view any events with Source: NTDS KCC.

Using a command-line interface

The following command will display any KCC errors found in the Directory Service log:

```
> dcdiag /v /test:kccevent /s:<DomainControllerName>
```

Discussion

The only way to debug issues with the KCC is by looking for NTDS KCC events in the Directory Service event log. If you suspect a problem or perhaps are seeing errors, you can increase the amount of logging in the event log by enabling diagnostics logging for the KCC. When the KCC diagnostics logging is enabled, each KCC exception logs a lot of information to the event log that may help you pinpoint the problem. See Recipe 15.2 for more information on enabling diagnostics logging.

11.29 Disabling the KCC for a Site

Problem

You want to disable the KCC for a site and generate your own replication connections between domain controllers.

Solution

Using a graphical user interface

1. Open ADSI Edit.
2. Connect to the Configuration Naming Context if it is not already displayed.
3. In the left pane, browse the Configuration Naming Context → Sites.
4. Click on the site you want to disable the KCC for.
5. In the right pane, double-click CN=NTDS Site Settings.
6. Modify the options attribute. To disable only intra-site topology generation, enable the 00001 bit (decimal 1). To disable inter-site topology generation, enable the 10000 bit (decimal 16). To disable both, enable the 10001 bits (decimal 17).
7. Click OK.

Using a command-line interface

You can disable the KCC for *<SiteName>* by using the ldifde utility and an LDIF file that contains the following:

```
dn: cn=NTDS Site Settings,<SiteName>,cn=sites,cn=configuration,<ForestRootDN>
changetype: modify
replace: options
options: <OptionsValue>
-
```

If the LDIF file were named *disable_kcc.ldf*, you would run the following command:

```
> ldifde -v -i -f disable_kcc.ldf
```

Using VBScript

```
' This code disables the KCC for a site.
' ------ SCRIPT CONFIGURATION ------
strSiteName = "<SiteName>" ' e.g. Default-First-Site-Name
boolDisableIntra = TRUE    ' set to TRUE/FALSE to disable/enable intra-site
boolDisableInter = TRUE    ' set to TRUE/FALSE to disable/enable inter-site
' ------ END CONFIGURATION ---------

strAttr = "options"
set objRootDSE = GetObject("LDAP://RootDSE")
```

```
set objObject = GetObject("LDAP://cn=NTDS Site Settings,cn=" _
                          & strSiteName & ",cn=sites," & _
                          objRootDSE.Get("configurationNamingContext") )

intBitsOrig = objObject.Get(strAttr)
intBitsCalc = CalcBit(intBitsOrig, 1, boolDisableIntra)
WScript.Echo "Checking the KCC Intra-site generation flag:"
if intBitsOrig <> intBitsCalc then
   objObject.Put strAttr, intBitsCalc
   objObject.SetInfo
   WScript.Echo "   Changed " & strAttr & " from " & _
                intBitsOrig & " to " & intBitsCalc
else
   WScript.Echo "   Did not need to change " & strAttr & _
                " (" & intBitsOrig & ")"
end if

intBitsOrig = objObject.Get(strAttr)
intBitsCalc = CalcBit(intBitsOrig, 16, boolDisableInter)
WScript.Echo "Checking the KCC Inter-site generation flag:"
if intBitsOrig <> intBitsCalc then
   objObject.Put strAttr, intBitsCalc
   objObject.SetInfo
   WScript.Echo "   Changed " & strAttr & " from " & intBitsOrig & _
                " to " & intBitsCalc
else
   WScript.Echo "   Did not need to change " & strAttr & " (" & _
                intBitsOrig & ")"
end if
```

Discussion

In some cases, you may want to disable the KCC from generating the intra-site topology connections, inter-site topology connections, or both. The connection objects
the KCC dynamically creates determines how domain controllers replicate with each
other. Disabling the KCC was sometimes necessary with Windows 2000 due to scalability issues with the KCC and very large topologies. In Windows Server 2003, the
KCC has been greatly improved and, hopefully, you will not need to disable the
KCC. I recommend against disabling the KCC unless you have really good reasons
because you will have to pay close attention to any domain controller or site topology changes and manually adjust the connection objects accordingly.

Disabling the KCC can only be done at the site level. You have to modify the NTDS
Site Settings object of the site for which you want to disable the KCC. The options
attribute (a bit flag) on this object determines whether the KCC runs. If the 00001 bit
is enabled, intra-site topology generation is disabled, if the 10000 bit is enabled (16
in decimal), inter-site topology generation is disabled. See Recipe 4.12 for more on
the proper way to set bit-flags.

See Also

Recipe 4.12 for more on setting bit flags, Recipe 11.22 for creating a connection object manually, MS KB 242780 (How to Disable the Knowledge Consistency Checker From Automatically Creating Replication Topology), and MS KB 245610 (HOW TO: Disable the Knowledge Consistency Checker Inter-Site Topology Generation for All Sites)

11.30 Changing the Interval at Which the KCC Runs

Problem

You want to change the interval at which the KCC runs.

Solution

Using a graphical user interface

1. Run regedit.exe from the command line or Start → Run.
2. Expand HKEY_LOCAL_MACHINE → SYSTEM → CurrentControlSet → Services → NTDS → Parameters.
3. Right-click on Parameters and select New → DWORD Value.
4. Enter the following for the name: Repl topology update period (secs).
5. Double-click on the new value and under Value data enter the KCC interval in number of seconds (900 is the default).
6. Click OK.

Using a command-line interface

```
> reg add HKLM\System\CurrentControlSet\Services\NTDS\Parameters /v "Repl topology↵
update period (secs)" /t REG_DWORD /d <NumSecs>
```

Using VBScript

```
' This code changes the interval in which the KCC runs.
' ------ SCRIPT CONFIGURATION ------
intNumSecs = <NumSecs>  ' Number of seconds between intervals
                        ' 900 is default
' ------ END CONFIGURATION ---------

strNetlogonReg = "SYSTEM\CurrentControlSet\Services\NTDS\Parameters"
const HKLM = &H80000002
Set objReg = GetObject("winmgmts:root\default:StdRegProv")
```

```
objReg.SetDWORDValue HKLM, strNetlogonReg, _
                    "Repl topology update period (secs)", _
                    intNumSecs
WScript.Echo "KCC interval set to " & intNumSecs
```

Discussion

By default, the KCC checks its connections ever 15 minutes and makes changes as necessary. You can modify this interval by simply modifying the registry. This was necessary with many Windows 2000 implementations that had large topologies. In that case, the KCC may have taken longer than 15 minutes to run or monopolized the CPU. Changing the KCC to run every hour instead of 15 minutes would help ensure it would complete. With Windows Server 2003, Microsoft made significant improvements to the scalability of the KCC and I recommend running the KCC at the default interval.

There is another related registry setting you should also be aware of. By default, the KCC waits 5 minutes after Active Directory starts up before it runs. You can change this delay by creating a REG_DWORD value called Repl topology update delay (secs) under the HKLM\System\CurrentControlSet\Services\NTDS\Parameters\ key. The data for the value should be the number of seconds to wait after startup before the KCC starts. The default is 300, which is 5 minutes.

See Also

MS KB 271988 (Replication Topology Updates)

## CHAPTER 12

Replication

12.0 Introduction

Replication is one of the most important and perhaps complex components of Active Directory. The infrastructure behind Active Directory replication, including the site topology, connection objects, and the KCC, was covered in Chapter 11. This chapter focuses strictly on some of the tasks and processes associated with replicating data and checking replication health. For an in-depth overview of how replication works in Active Directory, I suggest reading Chapter 5 in *Active Directory*, Second Edition (O'Reilly).

12.1 Determining if Two Domain Controllers Are in Sync

Problem

You want to determine if two domain controllers are in sync and have no objects to replicate to each other.

Solution

Using a command-line interface

By running the following two commands you can compare the up-to-dateness vector on the two DCs:

```
> repadmin /showutdvec <DC1Name> <NamingContextDN>
> repadmin /showutdvec <DC2Name> <NamingContextDN>
```

The Windows 2000 version of repadmin used a different syntax to accomplish the same thing. Here is the equivalent syntax:

```
> repadmin /showvector <NamingContextDN> <DC1Name>
> repadmin /showvector <NamingContextDN> <DC2Name>
```

Using VBScript

```
' This code prints the up-to-dateness vector for the DCs defined in
' the array arrDCList for the naming context defined by strNCDN
' ------ SCRIPT CONFIGURATION ------
' Set to the DN of the naming context you want to check the DCs against
strNCDN = "<NamingContextDN>"    ' e.g. dc=amer,dc=rallencorp,dc=com
' Enter 2 or more DCs to compare
arrDCList = Array("<DC1Name>","<DC2Name>")
' ------ END CONFIGURATION ---------

set objIadsTools = CreateObject("IADsTools.DCFunctions")

for each strDC in arrDCList
    WScript.Echo "Replication partner USNs for " & strDC & ":"
    intUSN = objIadsTools.GetHighestCommittedUSN(Cstr(strDC),0)
    if intUSN = -1 then
        Wscript.Echo "Error retrieving USN: " & objIadsTools.LastErrorText
        WScript.Quit
    end if
    WScript.Echo vbTab & strDC & " = " & intUSN

    intRes = objIadsTools.GetReplicationUSNState(Cstr(strDC), _
                                        Cstr(strNCDN),0,0)
    if intRes = -1 then
        Wscript.Echo "Error retrieving USNs: " & objIadsTools.LastErrorText
        WScript.Quit
    end if
    for count = 1 to intRes
        WScript.Echo vbTab & objIadsTools.ReplPartnerName(count) & _
                    " = " & objIadsTools.ReplPartnerUSN(count)
    next
    WScript.Echo
next
```

Discussion

To determine if two or more DCs are in sync from a replication standpoint, you need to compare their up-to-dateness vectors. Each domain controller stores what it thinks is the highest update sequence number (USN) for every DC that replicates a naming context. This is called the up-to-dateness vector. If you want to compare DC1 and DC2, you'd first want to get the up-to-dateness vector for DC1 and compare DC1's highest USN against what DC2 thinks DC1's highest USN is. If they are different, then you can deduce that DC2 has not replicated all the changes from DC1 yet. Next, compare the reverse to see if DC1 is in sync with DC2.

See Also

See *IadsTools.doc* in the Support Tools for more information on the IADsTools interface

12.2 Viewing the Replication Status of Several Domain Controllers

Problem

You want to take a quick snap-shot of replication activity for one or more domain controllers.

Solution

Using a command-line interface

The following command will show the replication status of all the domain controllers in the forest:

```
> repadmin /replsum
```

You can also use * as a wildcard character to view the status of a subset of domain controllers. The following command will display the replication status of only the servers that begin with the name dc-rtp:

```
> repadmin /replsum dc-rtp*
```

 This command is only available with the Windows Server 2003 version of repadmin.

Discussion

The new /replsum option in repadmin is a great way to quickly determine if there are any replication issues. This command should be your starting point if you suspect any replication problems. If you are running /replsum against a lot of domain controllers, you can use the /sort option to order the returned table output by any of the table columns. You can also use the /errorsonly option to display only the replication partners who are encountering errors.

12.3 Viewing Unreplicated Changes Between Two Domain Controllers

Problem

You want to find the unreplicated changes between two domain controllers.

Solution

Using a graphical user interface

1. Open the Replication Monitor from the Support Tools (`replmon.exe`).
2. From the menu, select View → Options.
3. On the General tab, check the box beside Show Transitive Replication Partners and Extended Data.
4. Click OK.
5. In the left pane, right-click on Monitored Servers and select Add Monitored Server.
6. Use the Add Monitored Server Wizard to add one of the domain controllers you want to compare (I'll call it *dc1*).
7. In the left pane, under the server you just added, expand the naming context that you want to check for unreplicated changes.
8. Right-click on the other domain controller you want to compare (I'll call it *dc2*) and select Check Current USN and Un-replicated Objects.
9. Enter credentials if necessary and click OK.
10. If some changes have not yet replicated from *dc2* to *dc1*, a box will pop up that lists the unreplicated objects.
11. To find out what changes have yet to replicate from *dc1* to *dc2*, repeat the same steps except add *dc2* as a monitored server and check for unreplicated changes against *dc1*.

Using a command-line interface

Run the following two commands to find the differences between two domain controllers. Use the `/statistics` option to view a summary of the changes:

```
> repadmin /showchanges <DC1Name> <DC2GUID> <NamingContextDN>
> repadmin /showchanges <DC2Name> <DC1GUID> <NamingContextDN>
```

The Windows 2000 version of repadmin has a different syntax to accomplish the same thing. Here is the equivalent syntax:

```
> repadmin /getchanges <NamingContextDN> <DC1Name> <DC2GUID>
> repadmin /getchanges <NamingContextDN> <DC2Name> <DC1GUID>
```

Using VBScript

```
' This code uses the IADsTools interface to print the unreplicated
' changes for the naming context defined by strNCDN for the DCs
' defined by strDC1Name and strDC2Name
' ------ SCRIPT CONFIGURATION ------
strNCDN    = "<NamingContextDN>"   ' e.g. dc=rallencorp,dc=com
strDC1Name = "<DC1Name>"           ' e.g. dc1.rallencorp.com
```

```
strDC2Name  = "<DC2Name>"            ' e.g. dc2.rallencorp.com
' ------ END CONFIGURATION ---------

set objIadsTools = CreateObject("IADsTools.DCFunctions")

' ----------------------------------
' Have to get the GUIDs of both servers in order to identify
' the correct partner in the GetReplicationUSNState call
' ----------------------------------
strDC1GUID = objIadsTools.GetGuidForServer(Cstr(strDC1Name), _
                                           Cstr(strDC1Name),0)
strDC2GUID = objIadsTools.GetGuidForServer(Cstr(strDC2Name), _
                                           Cstr(strDC2Name),0)


' ----------------------------------
' Need to get what each DC thinks is the highest USN for the other
' The USN is needed in the call to GetMetaDataDifferences to return
' the unreplicated changes
' ----------------------------------
intRes = objIadsTools.GetReplicationUSNState(Cstr(strDC1Name), _
                                             Cstr(strNCDN),0,0)
if intRes = -1 then
   Wscript.Echo objIadsTools.LastErrorText
   WScript.Quit
end if
for count = 1 to intRes
   if strDC2GUID = objIadsTools.ReplPartnerGuid(count) then
      intDC2USN = objIadsTools.ReplPartnerUSN(count)
   end if
next
if intDC2USN = "" then
   WScript.Echo strDC2Name & " is not a replication partner with " & _
                strDC1Name
end if
intRes = objIadsTools.GetReplicationUSNState(Cstr(strDC2Name), _
                                             Cstr(strNCDN),0,0)
if intRes = -1 then
   Wscript.Echo objIadsTools.LastErrorText
   WScript.Quit
end if
for count = 1 to intRes
   if strDC1GUID = objIadsTools.ReplPartnerGuid(count) then
      intDC1USN = objIadsTools.ReplPartnerUSN(count)
   end if
next
if intDC2USN = "" then
   WScript.Echo strDC1Name & " is not a replication partner with " & _
                strDC2Name
end if

' ----------------------------------
' Now that we have retrieved the highest USN for both partners,
' the GetMetaDataDifferences method will return what needs to be
' replicated
' ----------------------------------
```

```
       intRes = objIadsTools.GetMetaDataDifferences(Cstr(strDC1Name), _
                                                    Cstr(intDC1USN), _
                                                    Cstr(strNCDN),0)
   if intRes = -1 then
      Wscript.Echo objIadsTools.LastErrorText
      WScript.Quit
   end if
   WScript.Echo "Data on " & strDC1Name & " but not " & strDC2Name & ":"
   for count = 1 to intRes
      WScript.Echo count & ". " & _
                      objIadsTools.MetaDataDifferencesObjectDN(count)
      WScript.Echo vbTab & " Attribute:   " & _
                      objIadsTools.MetaDataDifferencesAttribute(count)
      WScript.Echo vbTab & " Write time:  " & _
                      objIadsTools.MetaDataDifferencesLastWriteTime(count)
      WScript.Echo vbTab & " Orig Server: " & _
                      objIadsTools.MetaDataDifferencesOrigServer(count)
      WScript.Echo vbTab & " Orig USN:    " & _
                      objIadsTools.MetaDataDifferencesOrigUSN(count)
   next
   WScript.Echo

       intRes = objIadsTools.GetMetaDataDifferences(Cstr(strDC2Name), _
                                                    Cstr(intDC2USN), _
                                                    Cstr(strNCDN), 0)
   if intRes = -1 then
      Wscript.Echo objIadsTools.LastErrorText
      WScript.Quit
   end if
   WScript.Echo "Data on " & strDC2Name & " but not " & strDC1Name & ":"
   for count = 1 to intRes
      WScript.Echo count & ". " & _
                   objIadsTools.MetaDataDifferencesObjectDN(count)
      WScript.Echo vbTab & " Attribute:   " & _
                   objIadsTools.MetaDataDifferencesAttribute(count)
      WScript.Echo vbTab & " Write time:  " & _
                   objIadsTools.MetaDataDifferencesLastWriteTime(count)
      WScript.Echo vbTab & " Orig Server: " & _
                   objIadsTools.MetaDataDifferencesOrigServer(count)
      WScript.Echo vbTab & " Orig USN:    " & _
                   objIadsTools.MetaDataDifferencesOrigUSN(count)
   next
```

Discussion

All three solutions show how to display the current unreplicated changes between
two domain controllers. The repadmin /showchanges command has several additional
options you can use to display the changes, including saving the output to a file for
later comparison. Also, with the /statistics option, you can view a summary of the
changes.

See Also

See *IadsTools.doc* in the Support Tools for more information on the IADsTools interface

12.4 Forcing Replication from One Domain Controller to Another

Problem

You want to force replication between two partners.

Solution

Using a graphical user interface

1. Open the Active Directory Sites and Services snap-in.

2. Browse to the NTDS Setting object for the domain controller you want to replicate to.

3. In the right pane, right-click on the connection object to the domain controller you want to replicate from and select Replicate Now.

Using a command-line interface

The following command will perform a replication sync of the naming context specified by *<NamingContextDN>* from *<DC2Name>* to *<DC1Name>*:

```
> repadmin /replicate <DC1Name> <DC2Name> <NamingContextDN>
```

The Windows 2000 version of repadmin has a different syntax to accomplish the same thing. Here is the equivalent syntax:

```
> repadmin /sync <NamingContextDN> <DC1Name> <DC2GUID>
```

Using VBScript

```
' This code initiates a replication event between two DCs
' for a naming context
' ------ SCRIPT CONFIGURATION ------
strDC1Name = "<DC1Name>"    ' e.g. dc1
strDC2Name = "<DC2Name>"    ' e.g. dc2
strNamingContextDN = "<NamingContextDN>"   ' e.g. dc=rallencorp,dc=com
' ------ END CONFIGURATION ---------

set objIadsTools = CreateObject("IADsTools.DCFunctions")
intRes = objIadsTools.ReplicaSync(Cstr(strDC1Name),_
                                  Cstr(strNamingContextDN),_
                                  Cstr(strDC2Name), 0, 0)
```

```
if intRes = -1 then
    Wscript.Echo "Error: " & objIadsTools.LastErrorText
else
    WScript.Echo "Replication intitiated from " & strDC2Name & _
                 " to " & strDC1Name
end if
```

Discussion

Each solution shows how to replicate all unreplicated changes from a source domain controller to a destination domain controller. This sync is one way. If you want to ensure that both domain controllers are in sync, you'll need to follow the same directions except swap the domain controllers.

> With repadmin you can replicate a single object instead of any unreplicated object in a naming context by using the /replsingleobj option. This option is only available with the Windows Server 2003 version of repadmin.

See Also

Recipe 12.3 for viewing unreplicated changes between two domain controllers, MS KB 232072 (Initiating Replication Between Active Directory Direct Replication Partners), and see *IadsTools.doc* in the Support Tools for more information on the IAds-Tools interface

12.5   Changing the Intra-Site Replication Interval

Problem

You want to change the number of seconds that a domain controller in a site waits before replicating within the site.

Solution

Using a graphical user interface

1. Run regedit.exe from the command line or Start → Run.
2. Expand HKEY_LOCAL_MACHINE → SYSTEM → CurrentControlSet → Services → NTDS → Parameters.
3. If a value entry for Replicator notify pause after modify (secs) does not exist, right-click on Parameters and select New → DWORD Value. For the name, enter: Replicator notify pause after modify (secs).

4. Double-click on the value and enter the number of seconds to wait before notifying intra-site replication partners.

5. Click OK.

Using a command-line interface

With the following command, change *<NumSeconds>* to the number of seconds to set the intra-site replication delay to:

```
> reg add HKLM\System\CurrentControlSet\Services\NTDS\Parameters /v "Replicator↵
notify pause after modify (secs)" /t REG_DWORD /d <NumSeconds>
```

Using VBScript

```
' This code sets the intra-site delay interval
' ------ SCRIPT CONFIGURATION ------
strDC       = "<DomainControllerName>" ' DC you want to configure
intNumSeconds = <NumSeconds>   ' Time in seconds to delay
' ------ END CONFIGURATION ---------

const HKLM = &H80000002
strNTDSReg = "SYSTEM\CurrentControlSet\Services\NTDS\Parameters"
set objReg = GetObject("winmgmts:\\" & strDC & _
                        "\root\default:StdRegProv")
objReg.SetDWORDValue HKLM, strNTDSReg, _
                    "Replicator notify pause after modify (secs)", _
                    intNumSeconds
WScript.Echo "Intra-site replication delay set to " & intNumSeconds
```

Discussion

After a change has been made to a domain controller's local copy of Active Directory, it waits for a period of time before sending change notification requests to its intra-site replication partners. The default delay on Windows 2000 domain controllers is five minutes. For Windows Server 2003, the default delay has been changed to 15 seconds. You can customize this notification delay by changing the registry value, Replicator notify pause after modify (secs), on the domain controllers, as described in the Solution section.

 If you are changing this setting on Windows 2000 domain controllers, Microsoft recommends removing it after upgrading to Windows Server 2003 in order to utilize the new default of 15 seconds.

See Also

MS KB 214678 (How to Modify the Default Intra-Site Domain Controller Replication Interval)

12.6 Changing the Inter-Site Replication Interval

Problem

You want to set the schedule for replication for a site link.

Solution

These solutions assume the IP transport, but the SMTP transport could be used as well.

Using a graphical user interface

1. Open the Active Directory Sites and Services snap-in.
2. Expand the Inter-Site Transport container.
3. Click on the IP container.
4. In the right pane, double-click on the site link you want to modify the replication interval for.
5. Enter the new interval beside Replicate every.
6. Click OK.

Using a command-line interface

To change the replication interval, create an LDIF file named *set_link_rep_interval.ldf* with the following contents:

```
dn: cn=<LinkName>,cn=ip,cn=Inter-Site Transports,cn=sites,
cn=configuration,<ForestRootDN>
changetype: modify
replace: replInterval
replInterval: <NewInterval>
-
```

then run the following command:

```
> ldifde -v -i -f set_link_rep_interval.ldf
```

Using VBScript

```
' This code sets the replication interval for a site link
' ------ SCRIPT CONFIGURATION ------
strLinkName    = "<LinkName>"  ' cn of the link you want to configure
intNewInterval = <NewInterval> ' replication interval in minutes
' ------ END CONFIGURATION ---------

set objRootDSE = GetObject("LDAP://RootDSE")
set objLink = GetObject("LDAP://cn=" & strLinkName & _
```

```
                        ",cn=IP,cn=Inter-site Transports,cn=sites," & _
                     objRootDSE.Get("configurationNamingContext") )
     objLink.Put "replInterval", intNewInterval
     objLink.SetInfo
     WScript.Echo "Set interval for link " & objLink.Get("cn") & _
                  " to " & intNewInterval
```

Discussion

To configure the inter-site replication interval between two sites, you need to set the `replInterval` attribute on the site-link object that connects the two sites. The value of the attribute should be the replication interval in minutes. The default value is 180 minutes (3 hours) and the minimum is 15 minutes

12.7 Disabling Inter-Site Compression of Replication Traffic

Problem

You want to disable inter-site compression of replication traffic.

Solution

You need to modify the `options` attribute of the site-link object that connects the sites you want to disable compression for. Site-link objects are stored in the following location:

```
    cn=IP,cn=Inter-site Transports,cn=Sites,cn=Configuration,<ForestRootDN>
```

The options attribute is a bit flag. In order to disable compression, you must set bit 4, or 0100 in binary. If the attribute is currently unset, you can simply set it to 4. If it contains a value, you should see Recipe 4.12 for more information on properly setting bit flags.

Discussion

By default, data replicated inter-site is compressed. By contrast, intra-site replication traffic is not compressed. It is useful to compress inter-site traffic if the traffic is going over a WAN on the assumption that the less traffic the better. The trade-off to reduce WAN traffic is increased CPU utilization on the bridgehead servers replicating the data. If CPU utilization is an issue on your bridgehead servers and you aren't as concerned about the amount of traffic being replicated, you should consider disabling inter-site compression.

See Also

Recipe 4.12 for setting bit flag attributes

12.8 Checking for Potential Replication Problems

Problem

You want to determine if replication is succeeding.

Solution

The following two commands will help identify problems with replication on a source domain controller:

```
> dcdiag /test:replications
> repadmin /showrepl /errorsonly
```

Discussion

For a more detailed report, you can use the Replication Monitor (replmon.exe). The Generate Status Report option will produce a lengthy report of site topology, replication information, and provide details on any errors encountered. The Directory Service event log can also be an invaluable source of replication and KCC problems.

See Also

Recipe 12.2 for viewing the replication status of several domain controllers

12.9 Enabling Enhanced Logging of Replication Events

Problem

You want to enable enhanced logging of replication events.

Solution

Enable diagnostics logging for 5 Replication Events. See Recipe 15.2 for more information.

See Also

MS KB 220940 (How to Enable Diagnostic Event Logging for Active Directory Services)

12.10 Enabling Strict or Loose Replication Consistency

Problem

You want to enable strict or loose replication consistency.

Solution

Using a graphical user interface

1. Run regedit.exe from the command line or Start → Run.
2. Expand HKEY_LOCAL_MACHINE → SYSTEM → CurrentControlSet → Services → NTDS → Parameters.
3. If the Strict Replication Consistency value does not exist, right-click on Parameters and select New → DWORD Value. For the name, enter Strict Replication Consistency.
4. In the right pane, double-click on the value and enter 1 to enable strict consistency or 0 to enable loose consistency.
5. Click OK.

Using a command-line interface

To enable strict consistency, run the following command:

```
> reg add HKLM\System\CurrentControlSet\Services\NTDS\Parameters /v "Strict⏎
Replication Consistency" /t REG_DWORD /d 1
```

To enable loose consistency, run the following command:

```
> reg add HKLM\System\CurrentControlSet\Services\NTDS\Parameters /v "Strict⏎
Replication Consistency" /t REG_DWORD /d 0
```

Using VBScript

```
' This code enables strict or loose consistency on the specified DC.
' ------ SCRIPT CONFIGURATION ------
intEnableStrict = 1  ' 1 = strict consistency, 0 = loose consistency
strDC = "<DomainControllerName>"
' ------ END CONFIGURATION ---------

const HKLM = &H80000002
```

```
strNTDSReg = "SYSTEM\CurrentControlSet\Services\NTDS\Parameters"
set objReg = GetObject("winmgmts:\\" & strDC & _
                        "\root\default:StdRegProv")
objReg.SetDWORDValue HKLM, strNTDSReg, "Strict Replication Consistency", _
                intEnableStrict
WScript.Echo "Strict Replication Consistency value set to " & _
            intEnableStrict
```

Discussion

Up until Windows 2000 Service Pack (SP) 3, domain controllers followed a loose replication consistency model whereby lingering objects could get reinjected into Active Directory and replicate among all the domain controllers. A lingering object is one that was previously deleted, but got reintroduced because a domain controller did not successfully replicate for the duration of the time defined by the tombStoneLifetime attribute or was restored using a backup that was older than the tombStoneLifetime. See Recipe 16.0 for more on the tombStoneLifetime attribute.

Windows 2000 SP2 and earlier domain controllers would replicate the lingering object throughout the naming context. Loose consistency has the potential to cause some security risks since an object you thought was deleted is now back in the forest again.

Some post-SP2 hotfixes and SP3 introduced strict replication consistency. Under strict replication, a domain controller will stop replicating with a destination domain controller when it determines that the source is attempting to replicate a lingering object. Event id 1084 will get logged in the Directory Service event log indicating that it couldn't replicate the lingering object. Although strict replication can halt replication, it is the preferable method and is a good check to ensure lingering objects do not infiltrate your forest. For this reason, you must monitor your domain controllers to ensure they are replicating on a regular basis and do not have any 1084 events.

See Also

Recipe 16.0 for more on the tombStoneLifetime attribute, MS KB 317097 (Lingering Objects Prevent Active Directory Replication from Occurring), and MS KB 314282 (Lingering Objects May Remain After You Bring an Out-of-Date Global Catalog Server Back Online)

12.11 Finding Conflict Objects

Problem

You want to find conflict objects that are a result of replication collisions.

Solution

Using a graphical user interface

1. Open LDP.
2. From the menu, select Connection → Connect.
3. For Server, enter the name of a domain controller (or leave blank to do a server-less bind).
4. For Port, enter 389 or 3268 for the global catalog.
5. Click OK.
6. From the menu, select Connection → Bind.
7. Enter credentials (if necessary) of a user that can view the object.
8. Click OK.
9. From the menu, select Browse → Search.
10. For BaseDN, type the base DN from where you want to start the search.
11. For Scope, select the appropriate scope.
12. For Filter, enter (|(cn=*\0ACNF:*)(ou=*\0ACNF:*)).
13. Click Run.

Using a command-line interface

The following command finds all conflict objects within the whole forest:

```
> dsquery * forestroot -gc -attr distinguishedName -scope subtree -filter↵
"(|(cn=*\0ACNF:*)(ou=*\0ACNF:*))"
```

Using VBScript

```
' This code finds any conflict objects in a forest.
' If the search times out, you may need to change strBase to
' a specific OU or container
' ------ SCRIPT CONFIGURATION ------
strBase   = "<GC://" & "<ForrestRootDN>" & ">;"
' ------ END CONFIGURATION ---------

strFilter = "(|(cn=*\0ACNF:*)(ou=*\0ACNF:*));"
strAttrs  = "distinguishedName;"
strScope  = "Subtree"

set objConn = CreateObject("ADODB.Connection")
objConn.Provider = "ADsDSOObject"
objConn.Open
Set objRS = objConn.Execute(strBase & strFilter & strAttrs & strScope)

WScript.Echo objRS.RecordCount & " conflict objects found"
while not objRS.EOF
  Wscript.Echo objRS.Fields.Item("distinguishedName").Value
```

```
    objRS.MoveNext
    wend
```

Discussion

Any distributed multi-master system has to deal with replication collisions, and Active Directory is no different. A collision can occur if an object is created on one domain controller and before that object has time to replicate out, an object with at least the same name, if not identical, is created on a different domain controller. So which object wins? With Active Directory, the last object created wins and gets to keep its name while the first object created has to be renamed. The format of the renamed object is:

    <ObjectName>\0CNF:<ObjectGUID>

where <ObjectName> is the original name of the object, followed by a null termination character, followed by CNF:, followed by the object's GUID.

It is good to periodically scan your Active Directory tree to ensure you do not have a lot of conflict objects hanging around. It is a bit problematic to find conflict objects in a single query because the filter to find them is not optimized. In all three solutions, you have to perform a leading and trailing match pattern search (with *) and this can easily timeout if you have a lot of objects. You may want to restrict your initial search to a few containers so the search is quicker. Most notably, you'll want to search against your containers that have computer objects because they can frequently generate conflict objects. This can occur when a computer account is created, joined to a domain, and then the computer reboots. After the computer starts up, if it authenticates against a domain controller that has not replicated the new computer object, the domain controller will add a new object, which eventually results in a conflict.

See MS KB 297083 for more information on how to handle conflict objects after you've identified them.

See Also

MS KB 218614 (Replication Collisions in Windows 2000) and MS KB 297083 (How to Rename an Object After a Replication Collision Has Occurred)

12.12 Viewing Object Metadata

Problem

You want to view metadata for an object. The object's `replPropertyMetaData` attribute stores metadata information about the most recent updates to every attribute that has been set on the object.

Solution

Using a graphical user interface

1. Open LDP.
2. From the menu, select Connection → Connect.
3. For Server, enter the name of a domain controller or domain that contains the object.
4. For Port, enter 389.
5. Click OK.
6. From the menu, select Connection → Bind.
7. Enter credentials (if necessary) of a user that can view the object.
8. Click OK.
9. From the menu, select Browse → Replication → View Metadata.
10. For Object DN, type the distinguished name of the object you want to view.
11. Click OK.

Using a command-line interface

In the following command, replace *<ObjectDN>* with the distinguished name of the object for which you want to view metadata:

```
> repadmin /showobjmeta <DomainControllerName> <ObjectDN>
```

This command was called /showmeta in the Windows 2000 version of repadmin. Also, the parameters are switched in that version, where *<ObjectDN>* comes before *<DomainControllerName>*.

Using VBScript

```
' This code displays the meta data for the specified object.
' ------ SCRIPT CONFIGURATION ------
strObjectDN = "<ObjectDN>"              ' e.g. dc=rallencorp,dc=com
strDC    = "<DomainControllerName>"  ' e.g. dc1
' ------ END CONFIGURATION ---------

set objIadsTools = CreateObject("IADsTools.DCFunctions")
intRes = objIadsTools.GetMetaData(Cstr(strDC),Cstr(strObjectDN),0)

if intRes = -1 then
   Wscript.Echo objIadsTools.LastErrorText
   WScript.Quit
end if

for count = 1 to intRes
   WScript.Echo count & ". " & objIadsTools.MetaDataName(count)
   WScript.Echo vbTab & " Version:    " & _
                      objIadsTools.MetaDataVersionNumber(count)
```

```
        WScript.Echo vbTab & " Last Write: " & _
                             objIadsTools.MetaDataLastWriteTime(count)
        WScript.Echo vbTab & " Local USN:   " & _
                             objIadsTools.MetaDataLocalUSN(count)
        WScript.Echo vbTab & " Source USN: " & _
                             objIadsTools.MetaDataSourceUSN(count)
        WScript.Echo vbTab & " Server:      " & _
                             objIadsTools.MetaDataServerName(count)
    next
```

Discussion

Object metadata can be an invaluable source of information when you need to troubleshoot replication problems or find out the last time an attribute was set for a particular object. In fact, a quick way to determine if two domain controllers have the same copy of an object is to look at the metadata on both servers for the object. If they both have the same metadata, then they have the same version of the object.

Unfortunately, the replPropertyMetaData attribute is stored as an octet string, so you cannot simply read the attribute to view all of the metadata information. In the VBScript solution, the IADsTool GetMetaData method is a wrapper around the DsReplicaGetInfo method call. This method understands the format of the replPropertyMetaData attribute and can return it into a readable format. The following data is stored for each attribute that has been set on the object:

Attribute ID
    Attribute that was updated.

Attribute version
    Number of originating writes to the property.

Local USN
    USN of the property on the local DC. This will be the same as the originating DC if the originating DC and local DC are the same.

Originating USN
    USN stored with the property when the update was made on the originating DC.

Originating DC
    DC that the originating write was made on.

Time/Date
    Time and date property was changed in UTC.

See Also

See *IadsTools.doc* in the Support Tools for more information on the IADsTools interface

## CHAPTER 13

Domain Name System (DNS)

13.0 Introduction

Active Directory is tightly coupled with the Domain Name System (DNS). Both clients and domain controllers use DNS to locate domain controllers in a particular site or that serve a particular function. Each domain controller requires numerous resource records to be present in DNS so it can advertise its services as a domain controller, global catalog server, PDC Emulator, etc. For a detailed description of each of these records plus much more on DNS, see Chapter 6 in *Active Directory*, Second Edition (O'Reilly).

One of the innovative uses of Active Directory is as a store of DNS data. Instead of using the antiquated primary and secondary zone transfer method or even the more recent NOTIFY method (RFC 1996) to replicate zone data between servers, AD-integrated zones store the zone data in Active Directory and use the same replication process used to replicate other data between domain controllers. The one catch with AD-integrated zones is that the DNS server must also be a domain controller. Overloading DNS server responsibilities on your domain controllers may not be something you want to do if you plan on supporting a large volume of DNS requests.

The Anatomy of a DNS Object

The only time DNS data is stored in Active Directory is if you have a zone that is AD-integrated. When using standard primary and secondary zones that are not AD-integrated, the DNS data is stored locally in the file system of each DNS server in zone files. If you have an AD-integrated zone under Windows 2000, a container is created in the following location: *cn=<ZoneName>,cn=MicrosoftDNS,cn=System,<DomainDN>*, where *<ZoneName>* is the name of the zone. For Windows Server 2003, you can use application partitions to store DNS data in an alternate location. By default, there are three options:

- Store DNS data on all domain controllers in a domain (only option for Windows 2000).
- Store DNS data on all domain controllers that are DNS servers in the domain.
- Store DNS data on all domain controllers that are DNS servers in the forest.

The default location for the second option is *dc=DomainDNSZones,<DomainDN>* and for the third option, it is *dc=ForestDNSZones,<ForestDN>*. These two locations are actually application partitions that are replicated only to the domain controllers that are DNS servers in the domain or forest, respectively.

Inside the MicrosoftDNS container, is a dnsZone object for each AD-integrated zone. Inside of the dnsZone container are dnsNode objects, which stores all resource records associated with a particular node. In the following textual representation of an A record, the *dc1.rallencorp.com* name is considered a node (generally the left side of the resource record).

```
dc1.rallencorp.com. 600 IN A 6.10.57.21
```

There could be multiple resource records associated with the *dc1.rallencorp.com* name, so Microsoft decided to implement each distinct name as a dnsNode object. The dnsNode object has a dnsRecord attribute, which is multivalued and contains all of the resource records associated with that node. Unfortunately, the contents of that attribute are stored in a binary format and are not directly readable.

Tables 13-1 and 13-2 contain some of the interesting attributes that are available on dnsZone and dnsNode objects, respectively.

Table 13-1. Attributes of dnsZone objects

Attribute	Description
dc	Relative distinguished name of the zone.
dnsProperty	Binary formatted string that stores configuration information about the zone.
msDS-Approx-Immed-Subordinates	Approximate number of nodes contained within the zone. This is new to Windows Server 2003.

Table 13-2. Attributes of dnsNode objects

Attribute	Description
dc	Relative distinguished name of the node.
dnsRecord	Binary formatted multivalued attribute that stores the resource records associated with the node.
dnsTombstoned	Boolean that indicates whether the node is marked for deletion. FALSE means it is not and TRUE means that it is.

13.1   Creating a Forward Lookup Zone

Problem

You want to create a forward lookup zone. A forward lookup zone maps names to IP addresses or other names.

Solution

Using a graphical user interface

1. Open the DNS Management snap-in.
2. If an entry for the DNS server you want to connect to does not exist, right-click on DNS in the left pane and select Connect to DNS Server. Select This computer or The following computer, enter the server you want to connect to (if applicable), and click OK.
3. Expand the server in the left pane and click on Forward Lookup Zones.
4. Right-click on Forward Lookup Zones and select New Zone.
5. Click Next.
6. Select the zone type and click Next.
7. If you selected to store the zone data in Active Directory, next you will be asked which servers you want to replicate the DNS data to. Click Next after you make your selection. (This only applies for Windows Server 2003).
8. Enter the zone name and click Next.
9. Fill out the information for the remaining screens. They will vary depending on if you are creating a primary, secondary, or stub zone.

Using a command-line interface

The following command creates an AD-Integrated zone:

```
> dnscmd <DNSServerName> /zoneadd <ZoneName> /DsPrimary
```

Using VBScript

```
' This code creates an AD-Integrated forward zone.
' ------ SCRIPT CONFIGURATION ------
strServer  = "<DNSServerName>"  ' e.g. dc1.rallencorp.com
strNewZone = "<ZoneName>"         ' e.g. othercorp.com
' ------ END CONFIGURATION ---------

set objDNS = GetObject("winMgmts:\\" & strServer & "\root\MicrosoftDNS")
set objDNSZone = objDNS.Get("MicrosoftDNS_Zone")
strNull = objDNSZone.CreateZone(strNewZone, 0 , True)
WScript.Echo "Created zone " & strNewZone
```

Discussion

Using a command-line interface

When you create an AD-integrated zone with the /DsPrimary switch, you can additionally include a /dp switch and specify an application partition to add the zone to. Here is an example:

```
> dnscmd /zoneadd <ZoneName> /DsPrimary /dp domaindnszones.rallencorp.com
```

Using VBScript

The DNS WMI Provider is Microsoft's first comprehensive DNS API. You can create and modify zones, query and manage resource records, and manipulate DNS server configuration. In the VBScript solution, the CreateZone method of the MicrosoftDNS_Zone class was used to create the forward zone.

See Also

Recipe 13.2 for creating a reverse lookup zone, MS KB 323445 (HOW TO: Create a New Zone on a DNS Server in Windows Server 2003), MSDN: DNS WMI Provider, and MSDN: CreateZone Method of the MicrosoftDNS_Zone Class

13.2   Creating a Reverse Lookup Zone

Problem

You want to create a reverse lookup zone. A reverse lookup zone maps IP addresses to names.

Solution

Using a graphical user interface

1. Open the DNS Management snap-in.
2. If an entry for the DNS server you want to connect to does not exist, right-click on DNS in the left pane and select Connect to DNS Server. Select This computer or The following computer, enter the server you want to connect to (if applicable), and click OK.
3. Expand the server in the left pane and click on Reverse Lookup Zones.
4. Right-click on Reverse Lookup Zones and select New Zone.
5. Click Next.
6. Select the zone type and click Next.

7. If you selected to store the zone data in Active Directory, next you will be asked which servers you want to replicate the DNS data to. Click Next after you make your selection. (This only applies for Windows Server 2003).

8. Type the Network ID for the reverse zone or enter a reverse zone name to use.

9. Fill out the information for the remaining screens. They will vary depending on if you are creating a primary, secondary, or stub zone.

Using a command-line interface

The following command creates an AD-integrated reverse zone:

```
> dnscmd <DNSServerName> /zoneadd <ZoneName> /DsPrimary
```

Using VBScript

```
' This code creates an AD-integrated reverse zone.
' ------ SCRIPT CONFIGURATION ------
strServer  = "<DNSServerName>"  ' e.g. dc1.rallencorp.com
strNewZone = "<ZoneName>"       ' e.g. 8.10.192.in-addr.arpa.
' ------ END CONFIGURATION ---------

set objDNS = GetObject("winMgmts:\\" & strServer & "\root\MicrosoftDNS")
set objDNSZone = objDNS.Get("MicrosoftDNS_Zone")
strNull = objDNSZone.CreateZone(strNewZone, 0 , True)
WScript.Echo "Created zone " & strNewZone
```

Discussion

Creating a reverse zone is very similar to creating a forward zone. See Recipe 13.1 for more information.

See Also

MS KB 323445 (HOW TO: Create a New Zone on a DNS Server in Windows Server 2003) and MSDN: CreateZone Method of the MicrosoftDNS_Zone Class

13.3 Viewing a Server's Zones

Problem

You want to view the zones on a server.

Solution

Using a graphical user interface

1. Open the DNS Management snap-in.
2. Right-click on DNS in the left pane and select Connect to DNS Server.

3. Enter the server you want to connect to and click Enter.

4. In the left pane, expand the server and click Forward Lookup Zones and Reverse Lookup Zones to view the supported zones.

Using a command-line interface

```
> dnscmd <DNSServerName> /enumzones
```

Using VBScript

```
' This code lists the zones that are supported by the specified server.
' ------ SCRIPT CONFIGURATION ------
strServer = "<DNSServerName>"   ' e.g. dc1.rallencorp.com
' ------ END CONFIGURATION ---------

set objDNS = GetObject("winMgmts:\\" & strServer & "\root\MicrosoftDNS")
set objDNSServer = objDNS.Get("MicrosoftDNS_Server.Name="".""")
set objZones = objDNS.ExecQuery("Select * from MicrosoftDNS_Zone " & _
                                "Where DnsServerName = '" & _
                                objDNSServer.Name & "'")
WScript.Echo "Zones on " & objDNSServer.Name
for each objZone in objZones
    WScript.Echo " " & objZOne.Name
next
```

Discussion

Using a graphical user interface

When you click on either the Forward Lookup Zones or Reverse Lookup Zones in the left pane, the right pane contains a Type column that displays the zone type for each zone.

Using a command-line interface

When using the /enumzones switch without any more parameters, it displays all zones on the server. You can specify additional filters that limit the types of zones returned. With the Windows 2000 version of dnscmd, you can specify up to two filters:

```
Filter1:
    /Primary
    /Secondary
    /Cache
    /Auto-Created
Filter2:
    /Forward
    /Reverse
```

With the Windows Server 2003 version of dnscmd, the filter behavior has changed. Instead of having two levels of criteria you can specify one or more of the following:

```
/Primary
/Secondary
```

```
/Forwarder
/Stub
/Cache
/Auto-Created
/Forward
/Reverse
/Ds
/File
/DomainDirectoryPartition
/ForestDirectoryPartition
/CustomDirectoryPartition
/LegacyDirectoryPartition
/DirectoryPartition <PartitionName>
```

Using VBScript

A WQL query was used to find all MicrosoftDNS_Zone objects. You can add additional criteria to the WQL Select statement to return a subset of zones supported on the server.

See Also

MSDN: MicrosoftDNS_Zone

13.4 Converting a Zone to an AD-Integrated Zone

Problem

You want to convert a primary zone to an AD-integrated zone. This causes the contents of the zone to be stored and replicated in Active Directory instead of in a text file.

Solution

Using a graphical user interface

1. Open the DNS Management snap-in.
2. Right-click on DNS in the left pane and select Connect to DNS Server.
3. Enter the server you want to connect to and click Enter.
4. If you want to convert a forward zone, expand the Forward Lookup Zone folder. If you want to convert a reverse zone, expand the Reverse Lookup Zone folder.
5. Click on the zone you want to convert, then right-click it and select Properties.
6. Beside Type, click the Change button.

7. Check the box beside Store the zone in Active Directory.

8. Click OK twice.

Using a command-line interface

```
> dnscmd <ServerName> /zoneresettype <ZoneName> /DsPrimary
```

Using VBScript

```
' This code converts a zone to AD-integrated.
' ------ SCRIPT CONFIGURATION ------
strZone   = "<ZoneName>"    ' e.g. rallencorp.com
strServer = "<ServerName>"  ' e.g. dc1.rallencorp.com
' ------ END CONFIGURATION ---------

set objDNS = GetObject("winMgmts:\\" & strServer & "\root\MicrosoftDNS")
set objDNSServer = objDNS.Get("MicrosoftDNS_Server.Name=""."."")
set objDNSZone = objDNS.Get("MicrosoftDNS_Zone.ContainerName=""" & _
                        strZone & """,DnsServerName=""" & _
                        objDNSServer.Name & """,Name=""" & strZone & """")
strNull = objDNSZone.ChangeZoneType(0, True)
objDNSZone.Put_
WScript.Echo "Converted " & strZone & " to AD-Integrated"
```

Discussion

See Recipes 13.0 and 13.5 for more on AD-integrated zones.

See Also

MS KB 198437 (How to Convert DNS Primary Server to Active Directory Integrated), MS KB 227844 (Primary and Active Directory Integrated Zones Differences), and MSDN: ChangeZoneType Method of the MicrosoftDNS_Zone Class

13.5 Moving AD-Integrated Zones into an Application Partition

 This recipe requires the Windows Server 2003 domain functional level.

Problem

You want to move AD-integrated zones into an application partition.

Solution

Using a graphical user interface

1. Open the DNS Management snap-in.
2. If an entry for the DNS server you want to connect to does not exist, right-click on DNS in the left pane and select Connect to DNS Server. Select This computer or The following computer, enter the server you want to connect to (if applicable), and click OK.
3. Expand the server in the left pane and expand either Forward Lookup Zones or Reverse Lookup Zones depending on the type of zone.
4. Click on the name of the zone.
5. Right-click on the zone and select Properties.
6. Click on the Change button beside Replication.
7. Select the application partition you want to move the zone into.
8. Click OK twice.

Using a command-line interface

The following command will move a zone to the default application partition that replicates across all domain controllers that are DNS servers in the domain:

```
> dnscmd <DNSServerName> /zonechangedirectorypartition <ZoneName> /domain
```

Using VBScript

At the time of publication of this book, the DNS WMI Provider did not support programmatically moving a zone into an application partition.

Discussion

With Windows 2000 Active Directory, if you had AD-integrated zones, those zones were replicated to every domain controller in the domain where they were stored. In many cases, not every domain controller also serves as a DNS server, which results in increased and unnecessary traffic to replicate changes with the zone(s).

Windows Server 2003 provides an elegant solution to this issue by using application partitions. Application partitions are user-defined partitions that can be configured to replicate with any domain controller in a forest. This provides a lot more flexibility for how you store and replicate your AD-integrated zones. You could, in fact, have a couple domain controllers from each domain act as DNS servers for all of your AD domains.

See Also

Chapter 17 for more information on application partitions

13.6 Delegating Control of a Zone

Problem

You want to delegate control of managing the resource records in a zone.

Solution

Using a graphical user interface

1. Open the DNS Management snap-in.

2. If an entry for the DNS server you want to connect to does not exist, right-click on DNS in the left pane and select Connect to DNS Server. Select This computer or The following computer, enter the server you want to connect to (if applicable), and click OK.

3. Expand the server in the left pane and expand either Forward Lookup Zones or Reverse Lookup Zones depending on the type of zone.

4. Click on the name of the zone.

5. Right-click on the zone and select Properties.

6. Click on the Security tab.

7. Click the Add button.

8. Use the Object Picker to locate the user or group to which you want to delegate control.

9. Under Permissions, check the Full Control box.

10. Click OK.

Using a command-line interface

The following command grants full control over managing the resource records in an AD-Integrated zone:

```
> dsacls dc=<ZoneName>,cn=MicrosoftDNS,<DomainOrAppPartitionDN> /G↵
<UserOrGroup>:GA;;
```

Using VBScript

```
' This code grants full control for the specified user or group over
' an AD-Integrated zone.
' ------ SCRIPT CONFIGURATION ------
strZoneDN = "dc=<ZoneName>,cn=MicrosoftDNS,<DomainOrAppPartitionDN>"
strUserOrGroup = "<UserOrGroup>"  ' e.g. joe@rallencorp.com or RALLENCORP\joe
' ------ END CONFIGURATION ---------
```

```
set objZone = GetObject("LDAP://" & strZoneDN)
'############################
' Constants
'############################

' ADS_ACETYPE_ENUM
Const ADS_ACETYPE_ACCESS_ALLOWED_OBJECT = &h5

' ADS_FLAGTYPE_ENUM
Const ADS_FLAG_OBJECT_TYPE_PRESENT = &h1

' ADS_RIGHTS_ENUM
Const ADS_RIGHT_GENERIC_ALL = &h10000000


'############################
' Create ACL
'############################

set objSD = objZone.Get("ntSecurityDescriptor")
set objDACL = objSD.DiscretionaryAcl

' Full Control
set objACE1 = CreateObject("AccessControlEntry")
objACE1.Trustee    = strUserOrGroup
objACE1.AccessMask = ADS_RIGHT_GENERIC_ALL
objACE1.AceFlags   = 0
objACE1.Flags      = ADS_FLAG_OBJECT_TYPE_PRESENT
objACE1.AceType    = ADS_ACETYPE_ACCESS_ALLOWED_OBJECT

objDACL.AddAce objACE1

'############################
' Set ACL
'############################
objSD.DiscretionaryAcl = objDACL
objZone.Put "ntSecurityDescriptor", objSD
objZone.SetInfo
WScript.Echo "Delegated control of " & strZoneDN & " to " & strUserOrGroup
```

Discussion

By default, members of the DNSAdmins group have control over DNS server and zone
configuration. You can delegate control of individual AD-integrated zones by modifying permissions on the zone object in AD. The solutions show examples for how to
grant Full Control to a user or group over a particular zone.

See Also

MS KB 256643 (Unable to Prevent DNS Zone Administrator from Creating New
Zones)

13.7 Creating and Deleting Resource Records

Problem

You want to create and delete resource records.

Solution

Using a graphical user interface

1. Open the DNS Management snap-in.
2. If an entry for the DNS server you want to connect to does not exist, right-click on DNS in the left pane and select Connect to DNS Server. Select This computer or The following computer, enter the server you want to connect to (if applicable), and click OK.
3. If you want to add or delete a record in a forward zone, expand the Forward Lookup Zone folder. If you want to add or delete a record for a reverse zone, expand the Reverse Lookup Zone folder.

   To create a resource record, do the following:

   a. In the left pane, right-click the zone and select the option that corresponds to the record type you want to create—e.g., New Host (A).

   b. Fill in all required fields.

   c. Click OK.

   To delete a resource record, do the following:

   a. In the left pane, click on the zone the record is in.

   b. In the right pane, right-click on the record you want to delete and select Delete.

   c. Click Yes to confirm.

Using a command-line interface

To add a resource record, use the following command:

```
> dnscmd <DNSServerName> /recordadd <ZoneName> <NodeName> <RecordType> <RRData>
```

The following command adds an A record in the *rallencorp.com* zone:

```
> dnscmd dc1 /recordadd rallencorp.com wins01 A 19.25.52.2.25
```

To delete a resource record, use the following command:

```
> dnscmd <DNSServerName> /recorddelete <ZoneName> <NodeName> <RecordType> <RRData>
```

The following command deletes an A record in the *rallencorp.com* zone:

```
> dnscmd dc1 /recorddelete rallencorp.com wins01 A 19.25.52.2.25
```

Using VBScript

```
' This code shows how to add an A record and PTR record using
' the DNS WMI Provider
' ------ SCRIPT CONFIGURATION ------
strForwardRRAdd = "test-xp.rallencorp.com. IN A 192.32.64.13"
strReverseRRAdd = "13.64.32.192.in-addr.arpa IN PTR test-xp.rallencorp.com"
strForwardDomain = "rallencorp.com"
strReverseDomain = "192.in-addr.arpa."
' ------ END CONFIGURATION ---------

set objDNS = GetObject("winMgmts:root\MicrosoftDNS")
set objRR = objDNS.Get("MicrosoftDNS_ResourceRecord")
set objDNSServer = objDNS.Get("MicrosoftDNS_Server.Name="".""")

' Create the A record
strNull = objRR.CreateInstanceFromTextRepresentation( _
                objDNSServer.Name, _
                strForwardDomain, _
                strForwardRRAdd, _
                objOutParam)
set objRR2 = objDNS.Get(objOutParam)
WScript.Echo "Created Record: " & objRR2.TextRepresentation

' Create the PTR record
strNull = objRR.CreateInstanceFromTextRepresentation( _
                objDNSServer.Name, _
                strReverseDomain, _
                strReverseRRAdd, _
                objOutParam)
set objRR2 = objDNS.Get(objOutParam)
WScript.Echo "Created Record: " & objRR2.TextRepresentation


' This code shows how to delete an A and PTR record for the record
' I created in the previous example.

strHostName  = "test-xp.rallencorp.com."

set objDNS = GetObject("winMgmts:root\MicrosoftDNS")
set objDNSServer = objDNS.Get("MicrosoftDNS_Server.Name="".""")

set objRRs = objDNS.ExecQuery(" select * " & _
                        " from MicrosoftDNS_ResourceRecord " & _
                        " where OwnerName = """ & strHostName & """" & _
                        " Or RecordData = """ & strHostName & """")
if objRRs.Count < 1 then
   WScript.Echo "No matches found for " & strHostName
else
   for each objRR in objRRs
      objRR.Delete_
      WScript.Echo "Deleted " & objRR.TextRepresentation
   next
end if
```

Discussion

Using a graphical user interface

The DNS Management snap-in is good for creating a small number of records, but if you need to add or delete more than a couple of dozen, then I'd recommend writing a batch file around dnscmd or preferably, use the DNS WMI Provider.

Using a command-line interface

Adding A, CNAME, and PTR resource records is pretty straightforward as far as the data you must enter, but other record types, such as SRV, require quite a bit more data. The help pages for /recordadd and /recorddelete display the required information for each record type.

Using VBScript

In the first example, I created A and PTR records using the CreateInstanceFromTextRepresentation method, which is a MicrosoftDNS_ResourceRecord method that allows you to create resource records by passing in the textual version of the record. This is the textual representation of the A record used in the example:

```
test-xp.rallencorp.com IN A 192.32.64.13
```

The first parameter to this method is the DNS server name, the second is the name of the domain to add the record to, the third is the resource record, and the last is an out parameter that returns a reference to the new resource record.

In the second example, I find all resource records that match a certain hostname and delete them. This is done by first using a WQL query to find all resource records where the OwnerName equals the target host name (this will match any A records) and where RecordData equals the target host name (this will match any PTR records). The Delete_ method is called on each matching record, removing them on the DNS server.

See Also

MSDN: MicrosoftDNS_ResourceRecord

13.8   Querying Resource Records

Problem

You want to query resource records.

Solution

Using a graphical user interface

The DNS Management snap-in does not provide an interface for searching resource records.

Using a command-line interface

In the following command, replace *<RecordType>* with the type of resource record you want to find (e.g., A, CNAME, SRV) and *<RecordName>* with the name or IP address of the record to match:

```
> nslookup -type=<RecordType> <RecordName>
```

Using VBScript

```
' This code prints the resource records that match
' the specified name
' ------ SCRIPT CONFIGURATION ------
strQuery = "<RecordName>"
' ------ END CONFIGURATION ---------

set objDNS = GetObject("winMgmts:root\MicrosoftDNS")
set objDNSServer = objDNS.Get("MicrosoftDNS_Server.Name=""."""")
set objRRs = objDNS.ExecQuery(" select * " & _
                             " from MicrosoftDNS_ResourceRecord" & _
                             " where  OwnerName = """ & strQuery & """" & _
                             " Or  DomainName = """ & strQuery & """" & _
                             " Or RecordData = """ & strQuery & """")
if objRRs.Count < 1 then
   WScript.Echo "No matches found for " & strHostName & " of " _
                & strRecordType & " type"
else
   for each objRR in objRRs
      WScript.Echo objRR.TextRepresentation
   next
end if
```

Discussion

Using a command-line interface

You can leave off the -type switch and the command will find any A, PTR, and CNAME records that match *<RecordName>*. You can also run nslookup from interactive mode, which can be entered by typing nslookup at a command prompt with no additional parameters.

Using VBScript

In the VBScript solution a WQL query was used to find all matching resource records. This is a good example of how powerful the DNS WMI Provider can be. The query attempts to find any object of the `MicrosoftDNS_ResourceRecord` class that has an `OwnerName`, `DomainName`, or `RecordData` field equal to the `<RecordName>`. This is not the most efficient query if the server supports multiple large zones, so you may want restrict it to search for specific types of records by adding criteria to match `RecordType` = `<Type>`.

See Also

MSDN: MicrosoftDNS_ResourceRecord

13.9 Modifying the DNS Server Configuration

Problem

You want to modify the DNS Server settings.

Solution

Using a graphical user interface

1. Open the DNS Management snap-in.
2. If an entry for the DNS server you want to connect to does not exist, right-click on DNS in the left pane and select Connect to DNS Server. Select This computer or The following computer, enter the server you want to connect to (if applicable), and click OK.
3. Click on the server, right-click on it, and select Properties.
4. There will be several tabs you can choose from to edit the server settings.
5. Click OK to commit the changes after you've completed your modifications.

Using a command-line interface

With the following command, replace `<Setting>` with the name of the setting to modify and `<Value>` with the value to set:

```
> dnscmd <DNSServerName> /config  /<Setting> <Value>
```

Using VBScript

```
set objDNS = GetObject("winMgmts:root\MicrosoftDNS")
set objDNSServer = objDNS.Get("MicrosoftDNS_Server.Name="".""")
objDNSServer.<Setting> = <Value>  ' e.g. objDNSServer.AllowUpdate = TRUE
objDNSServer.Put_
```

Discussion

The Microsoft DNS server supports a variety of settings to configure everything from scavenging and forwarders to logging. With the DNS Management snap-in, the settings are spread over several tabs in the Properties property page. You can get a list of these settings by simply running `dnscmd /config` from a command line. For the CLI and VBScript solutions, the setting names are nearly identical. In the VBScript solution, be sure to call the `Put_` method after you are done configuring settings in order for the changes to take effect.

See Also

MSDN: MicrosoftDNS_Server

13.10 Scavenging Old Resource Records

Problem

You want to scavenge old resource records. DNS scavenging is the process whereby resource records are automatically removed if they are not updated after a period of time. Typically, this applies to only resource records that were added via DDNS, but you can also scavenge manually added, also referred to as static, records. DNS scavenging is a recommended practice so that your DNS zones are automatically kept clean of stale resource records.

Solution

The following solutions will show how to enable automatic scavenging on all AD-integrated zones.

Using a graphical user interface

1. Open the DNS Management snap-in.
2. If an entry for the DNS server you want to connect to does not exist, right-click on DNS in the left pane and select Connect to DNS Server. Select This computer or The following computer, enter the server you want to connect to (if applicable), and click OK.
3. Click on the server, right-click on it, and select Set Aging/Scavenging for all zones.
4. Check the box beside Scavenge stale resource records.
5. Configure the No-Refresh and Refresh intervals as necessary and click OK.
6. Check the box beside Apply these settings to the existing Active Directory-integrated zones and click OK.

7. Right-click on the server again and select Properties.

8. Select the Advanced tab.

9. Check the box beside Enable automatic scavenging of stale resource records.

10. Configure the scavenging period as necessary.

11. Click OK.

Using a command-line interface

```
> dnscmd <DNSServerName> /config /ScavengingInterval <ScavengingMinutes>
> dnscmd <DNSServerName> /config /DefaultAgingState 1
> dnscmd <DNSServerName> /config /DefaultNoRefreshInterval <NoRefreshMinutes>
> dnscmd <DNSServerName> /config /DefaultRefreshInterval <RefreshMinutes>
> dnscmd <DNSServerName> /config ..AllZones /aging 1
```

Using VBScript

```
' This code enables scavenging for all AD-integrated zones
' ------ SCRIPT CONFIGURATION ------
strServer = "<DNSServerName>"
intScavengingInterval = <ScavengingMinutes>
intNoRefreshInterval  = <NoRefreshMinutes>
intRefreshInterval    = <RefreshMinutes>
' ------ END CONFIGURATION ---------

set objDNS = GetObject("winMgmts:\\" & strServer & "\root\MicrosoftDNS")
set objDNSServer = objDNS.Get("MicrosoftDNS_Server.Name="".""")

objDNSServer.ScavengingInterval        = intScavengingInterval
objDNSServer.DefaultNoRefreshInterval  = intNoRefreshInterval
objDNSServer.DefaultRefreshInterval    = intRefreshInterval
objDNSServer.DefaultAgingState         = TRUE
objDNSServer.Put_
WScript.Echo "Configured server scavenging settings"

set objZones = objDNS.ExecQuery("Select * from MicrosoftDNS_Zone " & _
                      "Where DnsServerName = '" & _
                            objDNSServer.Name & "'" & _
                      " And DsIntegrated = TRUE")
WScript.Echo "Configuring AD-integrated zones: "
for each objZone in objZones
   WScript.Echo " " & objZone.Name & " HERE: " & objZone.Aging
   objZone.Aging = 1
   objZone.Put_
next
```

Discussion

There are four settings you need to be aware of before enabling scavenging. You must use caution when enabling scavenging because an incorrect configuration could lead to resource records getting deleted by mistake.

The first setting you have to configure is the scavenging interval. This is the interval in which the DNS server will kick off the scavenging process. It is disabled by default so that scavenging does not take place unless you enable this setting. The default value is 168 hours, which is equivalent to 7 days.

The second setting is the default aging state for new zones. If you want all new zones to be configured for scavenging, set this to 1.

The next two settings control how records get scavenged. The no refresh interval determines how long before a dynamically updated record can be updated again. This setting is necessary to reduce how often a DNS server has to update its time-stamp of the resource record. The default value is 168 hours (7 days). That means that after a resource record has been dynamically updated, the server will not accept another dynamic update for the same record for another 7 days. If the IP address or some other data for the record changes, the server will accept that.

The refresh interval setting is the amount of time after the no refresh interval that a client has to update its record before it is considered old or stale. The default value for this setting is also 168 hours (7 days). If you use the default values, the combination of the no refresh interval and refresh interval would mean that a dynamically updated record would not be considered stale for up to 14 days after its last update. In actuality, it could be up to 21 days before the record is deleted if the record became stale right after the last scavenge process completed—7 days (no refresh) + 7 days (refresh) + up to 7 days (scavenge process).

13.11 Clearing the DNS Cache

Problem

You want to clear the DNS cache. The DNS cache contains resource records that are cached for a period of time in memory so that repeated requests for the same record can be returned immediately. There are two types of DNS cache. One pertains to the resolver on any Windows client (servers and workstations), and the other to the cache used by the Microsoft DNS server.

Solution

To flush the client resolver cache, use the following command:

```
> ipconfig /flushdns
```

To flush the DNS server cache, use any of the following solutions.

Using a graphical user interface

1. Open the DNS Management snap-in.
2. Right-click on DNS in the left pane and select Connect to DNS Server.
3. Enter the server you want to connect to and click Enter.
4. Right-click on the server and select Clear Cache.

Using a command-line interface

The following command will clear the cache on *<DNSServerName>*. You can leave out *<DNSServerName>* to run against the local server:

```
> dnscmd <DNSServerName> /clearcache
```

Using VBScript

```
' This code clears the DNS server cache on the specified server.
' ------ SCRIPT CONFIGURATION ------
strServer = "<DNSServerName>"  ' e.g. dc1.rallencorp.com
' ------ END CONFIGURATION ---------

set objDNS = GetObject("winmgmts:\\" & strServer & "\root\MicrosoftDNS")
set objDNSServer = objDNS.Get("MicrosoftDNS_Server.Name="".""")
set objDNSCache  = objDNS.Get("MicrosoftDNS_Cache.ContainerName=""..Cache""" & _
                              ",DnsServerName=""" & objDNSServer.Name & _
                              """,Name=""..Cache""")
objDNSCache.ClearCache
WScript.Echo "Cleared server cache"
```

Discussion

The client resolver cache is populated whenever a DNS lookup is performed on a workstation or server; for example, with the nslookup command.

```
<DeletedRepeatedText>
```

The second type of cache is only for Microsoft DNS servers. It is a cache of all DNS requests the server has made to resolve queries from clients. You can view this cache by browsing the Cached Lookups folder for a server in the DNS Management snap-in. This folder is not shown by default, so you'll need to select Advanced from the View menu.

With both the client and server cache, the records are removed from the cache after the record's TTL or Time To Live value expires. The TTL is used to age records so that clients and servers have to rerequest them at a later point and receive any changes that may have occurred.

13.12 Verifying That a Domain Controller Can Register Its Resource Records

Problem

You want to verify DNS is configured correctly so that a domain controller can register its resource records, which are needed for clients to be able to locate various AD services.

Solution

Using a command-line interface

 This test is available only with the Windows Server 2003 version of dcdiag.

With the following dcdiag command, replace *dc1* with the DNS name of the domain the domain controller is in. This command has to be run directly on the domain controller you want to test.

```
> dcdiag /test:RegisterInDNS /DnsDomain:dc1
    Starting test: RegisterInDNS
        DNS configuration is sufficient to allow this domain controller to
        dynamically register the domain controller Locator records in DNS.

        The DNS configuration is sufficient to allow this computer to dynamically
        register the A record corresponding to its DNS name.

        ........................ dc1 passed test RegisterInDNS
```

Discussion

With the default setup, domain controllers attempt to dynamically register the resource records necessary for them to be located by Active Directory clients and other domain controllers. The domain controllers must have their resource records populated in DNS in order to function. It can be very tedious and error-prone to register all of the records manually, which is why allowing the domain controllers to use dynamic DNS (DDNS) to automatically register and update their records can be much easier from a support standpoint.

The Windows Server 2003 version of the dcdiag command provides a new RegisterInDNS switch that allows you to test whether or not the DC can register its records. In the solution above, I showed the output if the domain controller passes the test.

Here is the output if an error occurs:

```
Starting test: RegisterInDNS
    This domain controller cannot register domain controller Locator DNS
    records. This is because either the DNS server with IP address
    6.10.45.14 does not support dynamic updates or the zone rallencorp.com is
    configured to prevent dynamic updates.

    In order for this domain controller to be located by other domain members
    and domain controllers, the domain controller Locator DNS records must be
    added to DNS. You have the following options:

    1. Configure the rallencorp.com zone and the DNS server with IP address
    6.10.45.14 to allow dynamic updates. If the DNS server does not
    support dynamic updates, you might need to upgrade it.

    2. Migrate the rallencorp.com zone to a DNS server that supports dynamic
    updates (for example, a Windows 2000 DNS server).

    3. Delegate the zones _msdcs.rallencorp.com, _sites.rallencorp.com,
    _tcp.rallencorp.com, and _udp.rallencorp.com to a DNS server that supports
    dynamic updates (for example, a Windows 2000 DNS server); or

    4. Manually add to the DNS records specified in the
    systemroot\system32\config\netlogon.dns file.

    DcDiag cannot reach a conclusive result because it cannot interpret the
    following message that was returned: 9501.

    ........................ dc1 failed test RegisterInDNS
```

As you can see, it offers several options for resolving the problem. The information provided will also vary depending on the error encountered.

See Also

Recipe 13.13 for registering a domain controller's resource records

13.13 Registering a Domain Controller's Resource Records

Problem

You want to manually force registration of a domain controller's resource records. This may be necessary if you've made some configuration changes on your DNS servers to allow your domain controllers to start dynamically registering resource records.

Solution

Using a command-line interface

```
> nltest /dsregdns /server:<DomainControllerName>
```

Discussion

The Windows Server 2003 version of nltest provides a /dsregdns switch that allows you to force registration of the domain controller–specific resource records. You can also force reregistration of its resource records by restarting the NetLogon service on the domain controller. The NetLogon service automatically attempts to reregister a domain controller's resource records every hour, so if you can wait that long, you do not need to use the nltest command.

See Also

Recipe 13.12 for verifying if a domain controller is registering its resource records

13.14 Preventing a Domain Controller from Dynamically Registering All Resource Records

Problem

You want to prevent a domain controller from dynamically registering its resource records using DDNS. If you manually register domain controllers' resource records, you'll want to prevent those domain controllers from attempting to dynamically register them. If you do not disable them from sending dynamic update requests, you may see annoying error messages on your DNS servers that certain DDNS updates are failing.

Solution

Using a command-line interface

```
> reg add HKLM\System\CurrentControlSet\Services\Netlogon\Parameters /v
UseDynamicDNS /t REG_DWORD /d 0
The operation completed successfully.

> net stop netlogon
The Net Logon service is stopping.
The Net Logon service was stopped successfully.

> del %SystemRoot%\system32\config\netlogon.dnb
```

```
> net start netlogon
The Net Logon service is starting.......
The Net Logon service was started successfully.
```

Using VBScript

```
' This code prevents a DC from registering resource records dynamically.
' It must be run directly on the server.

' Create Registry Value
const HKLM = &H80000002
set oReg=GetObject("winmgmts:root\default:StdRegProv")
strKeyPath = "System\CurrentControlSet\Services\Netlogon\Parameters"
if oReg.SetDWORDValue(HKLM,strKeyPath,"UseDynamicDNS",1) <> 0 then
   WScript.Echo "Error creating registry value"
else
   WScript.Echo "Created registry value successfully"
end if

' Stop Netlogon service
strService = "Netlogon"
set objService = GetObject("WinMgmts:root/cimv2:Win32_Service.Name='" & _
                           strService & "'")
if objService.StopService <> 0 then
   WScript.Echo "Error stopping " & strService & " service"
else
   WScript.Echo "Stopped " & strService & " service successfully"
end if

' Delete netlogon.dnb file
set WshShell = CreateObject("WScript.Shell")
set objFSO = CreateObject("Scripting.FileSystemObject")
set objFile = objFSO.GetFile( _
                    WshShell.ExpandEnvironmentStrings("%SystemRoot%") _
                    & "\system32\config\netlogon.dnb" )
objFile.Delete
WScript.Echo "Deleted netlogon.dnb successfully"

' Start Netlogon service
if objService.StartService <> 0 then
   WScript.Echo "Error starting " & strService & " service"
else
   WScript.Echo "Started " & strService & " service successfully"
end if

WScript.Echo
WScript.Echo "Done"
```

Discussion

By default, domain controllers attempt to dynamically register their Active Directory–
related resource records every hour via the NetLogon service. You can prevent a

domain controller from doing this by setting the UseDynamicDNS value to 0 under HKEY_LOCAL_MACHINE\System\CurrentControlSet\Services\Netlogon\Parameters. After you set that value, you should stop the NetLogon service, remove the *%SystemRoot%\system32\config\netlogon.dnb* file and then start NetLogon back up. It is necessary to remove the *netlogon.dnb* file because it maintains a cache of the resource records that are dynamically updated. This file will get recreated when the NetLogon service restarts.

See Also

Recipe 13.15 for preventing certain records from being dynamically registered, MS KB 198767 (How to Prevent Domain Controllers from Dynamically Registering DNS Names), and MS KB 246804 (How to Enable/Disable Windows 2000 Dynamic DNS Registrations)

13.15 Preventing a Domain Controller from Dynamically Registering Certain Resource Records

Problem

You want to prevent a domain controller from dynamically registering certain resource records. It is sometimes advantageous to prevent certain resource records from being dynamically registered. For example, if you want to reduce the load on the PDC Emulator for a domain, you could prevent some of its SRV records from being published, which would reduce the amount of client traffic the server receives.

Solution

Using a command-line interface

This command will disable the Ldap, Gc, and GcIpAddress resource records from being dynamically registered:

```
> reg add HKLM\System\CurrentControlSet\Services\Netlogon\Parameters /v↵
DnsAvoidRegisterRecords /t REG_MULTI_SZ /d Ldap\0Gc\0GcIpAddress
The operation completed successfully.

> net stop netlogon
The Net Logon service is stopping.
The Net Logon service was stopped successfully.

> del %SystemRoot%\system32\config\netlogon.dnb
```

```
> net start netlogon
The Net Logon service is starting.......
The Net Logon service was started successfully.
```

Using VBScript

```
' This code prevents a DC from registering the resource records
' associated with the Ldap, Gc, and GcIpAddress mnemonics and must be run
' directly on the server.

' Create Registry Value
const HKLM = &H80000002
set objReg = GetObject("winmgmts:root\default:StdRegProv")
strKeyPath = "System\CurrentControlSet\Services\Netlogon\Parameters"
' prevent Ldap, Gc, and GCIpAddress records from being registered
arrValues  = Array("Ldap","Gc","GcIpAddress")
if objReg.SetMultiStringValue(HKLM,strKeyPath,"DnsAvoidRegisterRecords", _
                             arrValues) <> 0 then
   WScript.Echo "Error creating registry value"
else
   WScript.Echo "Created registry value successfully"
end if


' Stop Netlogon service
strService = "Netlogon"
set objService = GetObject("WinMgmts:root/cimv2:Win32_Service.Name='" & _
                          strService & "'")
if objService.StopService <> 0 then
   WScript.Echo "Error stopping " & strService & " service"
else
   WScript.Echo "Stopped " & strService & " service successfully"
end if


' Delete netlogon.dnb file
On Error Resume Next
set WshShell = CreateObject("WScript.Shell")
set objFSO = CreateObject("Scripting.FileSystemObject")
set objFile = objFSO.GetFile( _
                      WshShell.ExpandEnvironmentStrings("%systemroot%") _
                      & "\system32\config\netlogon.dnb")
objFile.Delete
if (Err.Number <> 0) then
   WScript.Echo "Error deleting netlogon.dnb: " & Err.Description
else
   WScript.Echo "Deleted netlogon.dnb successfully"
end if


' Start Netlogon service
if objService.StartService <> 0 then
   WScript.Echo "Error starting " & strService & " service"
else
   WScript.Echo "Started " & strService & " service successfully"
end if
```

```
WScript.Echo
WScript.Echo "Done"
```

Discussion

The procedure to disable registration of certain resource records is very similar to that described in Recipe 13.14 for preventing all records from being dynamically registered, except in this case, you need to create a value called DnsAvoidRegister-Records under the HKEY_LOCAL_MACHINE\System\CurrentControlSet\Services\Netlogon\Parameters key. The type for DnsAvoidRegisterRecords should be *REG_MULTI_SZ* and the data should be a whitespace separated list of mnemonics. Mnemonics are used to represent various resource records that domain controllers register. The complete list of mnemonics is included in Table 13-3.

Table 13-3. Registry mnemonics for resource records

Registry mnemonic	Resource record type	Resource record name
LdapIpAddress	A	*<DnsDomainName>*
Ldap	SRV	_ldap._tcp.*<DnsDomainName>*
LdapAtSite	SRV	_ldap._tcp.*<SiteName>*._sites.*<DnsDomainName>*
Pdc	SRV	_ldap._tcp.pdc._msdcs.*<DnsDomainName>*
Gc	SRV	_ldap._tcp.gc._msdcs.*<DnsForestName>*
GcAtSite	SRV	_ldap._tcp.*<SiteName>*._sites.gc._msdcs.*<DnsForestName>*
DcByGuid	SRV	_ldap._tcp.*<DomainGuid>*.domains._msdcs.*<DnsForestName>*
GcIpAddress	A	_gc._msdcs.*<DnsForestName>*
DsaCname	CNAME	*<DsaGuid>*._msdcs.*<DnsForestName>*
Kdc	SRV	_kerberos._tcp.dc._msdcs.*<DnsDomainName>*
KdcAtSite	SRV	_kerberos._tcp.dc._msdcs.*<SiteName>*._sites.*<DnsDomainName>*
Dc	SRV	_ldap._tcp.dc._msdcs.*<DnsDomainName>*
DcAtSite	SRV	_ldap._tcp.*<SiteName>*._sites.dc._msdcs.*<DnsDomainName>*
Rfc1510Kdc	SRV	_kerberos._tcp.*<DnsDomainName>*
Rfc1510KdcAtSite	SRV	_kerberos._tcp.*<SiteName>*._sites.*<DnsDomainName>*
GenericGc	SRV	_gc._tcp.*<DnsForestName>*
GenericGcAtSite	SRV	_gc._tcp.*<SiteName>*._sites.*<DnsForestName>*
Rfc1510UdpKdc	SRV	_kerberos._udp.*<DnsDomainName>*
Rfc1510Kpwd	SRV	_kpasswd._tcp.*<DnsDomainName>*
Rfc1510UdpKpwd	SRV	_kpasswd._udp.*<DnsDomainName>*

See Also

Recipe 13.14 for preventing all records from being dynamically registered, MS KB 246804 (How to Enable/Disable Windows 2000 Dynamic DNS Registrations), and

MS KB 267855 (Problems with Many Domain Controllers with Active Directory Integrated DNS Zones)

13.16 Deregistering a Domain Controller's Resource Records

Problem

You want to manually deregister a domain controller's resource records.

Solution

Using a command-line interface

With the following `nltest` command, replace *<DomainControllerName>* with the FQDN of the domain controller you want to deregister and *<DomainDNSName>* with the FQDN of the domain of which the domain controller is a member:

```
> nltest /dsderegdns:<DomainControllerName> /Dom:<DomainDNSName>
```

Discussion

When a domain controller is demoted from a domain, it dynamically deregisters its resource records. This is a nice feature of the demotion process because it means you do not have to manually remove all of the resource records or wait for scavenging to remove them. If, however, you have a domain controller that crashes and you do not plan on bringing it back online, you'll need to remove the records manually or wait for scavenging.

You can use the DNS Mgmt MMC snap-in and even the *dnscmd.exe* utility to remove them one by one, or you can use the `nltest` command, as shown in the solution. The `/dsderegdns` switch also has `/DomGUID` and `/DsaGUID` options if you want to delete the records that are based on the domain GUID and *DSA GUID*, respectively. You need to know the actual GUIDs of the domain and domain controller to use those switches, so if you don't have them handy, it would be easier to delete them using the DNS Mgmt MMC snap-in.

13.17 Allowing Computers to Use a Different Domain Suffix from Their AD Domain

Problem

You want to allow computers to use a different domain suffix than their AD domain.

Solution

 The following solutions work only for Windows Server 2003 domains. Read the Discussion for a workaround for Windows 2000.

Using a graphical user interface

1. Open ADSI Edit.
2. Connect to the domain you want to edit.
3. Right-click on the domainDNS object and select Properties.
4. Edit the msDS-AllowedDNSSuffixes attribute and enter the DNS suffix you want to add.
5. Click OK.

Using a command-line interface

Create an LDIF file called *add_dns_suffix.ldf* with the following contents:

```
dn: <DomainDN>
changetype: modify
add: msDS-AllowedDNSSuffixes
msDS-AllowedDNSSuffixes: <DNSSuffix>
-
```

then run the following command:

```
> ldifde -v -i -f add_dns_suffix.ldf.ldf
```

Using VBScript

```
' This code adds a domain suffix that can be used by clients in the domain.
' ------ SCRIPT CONFIGURATION ------
strDNSSuffix = "<DNSSuffix>"        ' e.g. othercorp.com
strDomain    = "<DomainDNSName>"    ' e.g. amer.rallencorp.com
' ------ END CONFIGURATION ---------

set objRootDSE = GetObject("LDAP://" & strDomain & "/RootDSE")
set objDomain = GetObject("LDAP://" & objRootDSE.Get("defaultNamingContext") )
objDomain.Put "msDS-AllowedDNSSuffixes", strDNSSuffix
objDomain.SetInfo

WScript.Echo "Added " & strDNSSuffix & " to suffix list."
```

Discussion

Windows 2000, Windows XP, and Windows Server 2003 member computers dynamically maintain the dNSHostName and servicePrincipalName attributes of their corresponding computer object in Active Directory with their current host name. By default, those attributes can only contain host names that have a DNS suffix equal to the Active Directory domain the computer is a member of.

If the computer's DNS suffix is not equal to the Active Directory domain, 5788 and 5789 events will be generated in the System event log on the domain controllers the clients attempt to update. These events report that the dnsHostName and servicePrincipalName attributes could not be updated due to an incorrect domain suffix. For Windows Server 2003 domains, you can avoid this by adding the computer's DNS suffix to the msDS-AllowedDNSSuffixes attribute on the domain object (e.g., *dc=rallencorp,dc=com*).

With Windows 2000, the only workaround for this issue is to grant the Self principal the ability to write the dNSHostName and servicePrincipalName attribute for computer objects. Here are the steps:

1. Open ADSI Edit.
2. Right-click on the domain object and select Properties.
3. Click the Security tab.
4. Click the Add button.
5. Enter Self in the object picker and click OK.
6. Click the Advanced button.
7. Under the Name column, double-click on SELF.
8. Click the Properties tab.
9. Beside Apply onto, select Computer objects.
10. Under Permissions, check the Allow box for Write dNSHostName and Write servicePrincipalName.
11. Click OK until you close all the windows.

 It is worth noting that if you implement this method, it is possible for someone to cause a computer to write any name into those attributes, and, therefore, advertise itself as another computer.

See Also

MS KB 258503 (DNS Registration Errors 5788 and 5789 When DNS Domain and Active Directory Domain Name Differ)

## CHAPTER 14

Security and Authentication

14.0 Introduction

The default Windows 2000 Active Directory installation was not as secure as it could have been. It allowed anonymous queries to be executed, which could take up valuable processing resources, and it did not place any requirements on encrypting or signing traffic between clients and domain controllers. As a result, usernames, passwords, and search results could be sent over the network in clear text. Fortunately, with Windows Server 2003, things have been tightened up significantly. LDAP traffic is signed by default and anonymous queries are disabled by default. Additionally, Transport Layer Security (TLS), the more flexible cousin of Secure Sockets Layer (SSL), is supported in Windows Server 2003, which allows for end-to-end encryption of traffic between domain controllers and clients.

Active Directory's Access Control List (ACL) model provides ultimate flexibility for securing objects throughout a forest. You can restrict access down to the attribute level if you need to. With this flexibility also comes increased complexity. An object's ACL is initially generated from the default ACL for the object's class, inherited permissions, and permissions directly applied on the object.

An ACL is a collection of ACE entries (Access Control Entry), which defines the permission and properties that a security principal can use on the object on which the ACL is applied. Defining these entries and populating the ACL is the foundation of Active Directory security and delegation.

In this chapter, I will explore some of the common tasks around managing permissions in Active Directory. If you are looking for a detailed guide to Active Directory permissions, I suggest reading Chapter 11 in *Active Directory*, Second Edition (O'Reilly).

In order for ACLs to be of use, a user has to authenticate to Active Directory. Kerberos is the primary network authentication system used by Active Directory. Kerberos is a standards-based system that was originally developed at MIT, and has been widely implemented at universities. I will also be covering some Kerberos-related tasks that you likely to encounter in this chapter. For a complete review of Kerberos, I recommend *Kerberos: The Definitive Guide* (O'Reilly).

14.1   Enabling SSL/TLS

Problem

You want to enable SSL/TLS access to your domain controllers so clients can encrypt LDAP traffic to the servers.

Solution

Using a graphical user interface

1. Open the Control Panel on a domain controller.
2. Open the Add or Remove Programs applet.
3. Click on Add/Remove Windows Components.
4. Check the box beside Certificate Services and click Yes to verify.
5. Click Next.
6. Select the type of authority you want the domain controller to be (select Enterprise root CA if you are unsure) and click Next.
7. Type the common name for the CA, select a validity period, and click Next.
8. Enter the location for certificate database and logs and click Next.
9. After the installation completes, click Finish.
10. Now open the Domain Controller Security Policy GPO.
11. Navigate to Computer Configuration → Windows Settings → Security Settings → Public Key Policies.
12. Right-click on Automatic Certificate Request Settings and select New → Automatic Certificate Request.
13. Click Next.
14. Under Certificate Templates, click on Domain Controller and click Next.
15. Click Finish.
16. Right-click on Automatic Certificate Request Settings select New → Automatic Certificate Request.
17. Click Next.
18. Under Certificate Templates, click on Computer and click Next.
19. Click Finish.

Discussion

After domain controllers obtain certificates, they open up ports 636 and 3289. Port 636 is for LDAP over SSL/TLS and port 3289 is used for the global catalog over SSL/TLS. See Recipe 14.2 for more information on how to query a domain controller using SSL/TLS.

See Also

MS KB 247078 (HOW TO: Enable Secure Socket Layer (SSL) Communication Over LDAP For Windows 2000 Domain Controllers), MS KB 281271 (Windows 2000 Certification Authority Configuration to Publish Certificates in Active Directory of Trusted Domain), and MS KB 321051 (How to Enable LDAP over SSL with a Third-Party Certification Authority)

14.2   Encrypting LDAP Traffic with SSL, TLS, or Signing

Problem

You want to encrypt LDAP traffic using SSL, TLS, or signing.

Solution

Using a graphical user interface

Most of the GUI-based tools on a Windows Server 2003, Windows XP, or Windows 2000 SP 3 machine automatically sign and encrypt traffic between the server and client. This includes the following tools:

- Active Directory Domains and Trusts
- Active Directory Sites and Services
- Active Directory Schema
- Active Directory Users and Computers
- ADSI Edit
- Group Policy Management Console
- Object Picker

Also with ADSI Edit, you can specify the port number to use when browsing a partition. View the Settings for a connection by right-clicking on the partition and selecting Settings. Click the Advanced button and enter 636 for LDAP over SSL or 3269 for the global catalog over SSL.

The Windows Server 2003 version of LDP supports encryption using the StartTLS and StopTLS operations, which are available from the Options → TLS menu. With the Windows 2000 version, you can use SSL by going to Connection → Connect and entering 636 or 3269 for the port.

Using a command-line interface

The DS command-line tools support LDAP signing and encryption when run from Windows Server 2003 or Windows XP against a Windows 2000 SP3 or Windows Server 2003 domain controller. This includes dsadd, dsmod, dsrm, dsmove, dsget, and dsquery.

Using VBScript

```
' This code shows how to enable SSL and secure authentication using ADSI

ADS_SECURE_AUTHENTICATION = 1
ADS_USE_SSL = 2

set objLDAP = GetObject("LDAP:")
set objOU = objLDAP.OpenDSObject("LDAP://ou=Sales,dc=rallencorp,dc=com", _
                                 "administrator@rallencorp.com", _
                                 "MyAdminPassword", _
                                 ADS_SECURE_AUTHENTICATION + ADS_USE_SSL)
WScript.Echo objOU.Get("ou")


' This code shows how to enable SSL and secure authentication using ADO:

' Constants taken from ADS_AUTHENTICATION_ENUM
ADS_SECURE_AUTHENTICATION = 1
ADS_USE_SSL = 2

set objConn = CreateObject("ADODB.Connection")
objConn.Provider = "ADsDSOObject"
objConn.Properties("User ID") = "administrator@rallencorp.com"
objConn.Properties("Password") = "MyAdminPassword"
objConn.Properties("Encrypt Password") = True
objConn.Properties("ADSI Flag") = ADS_SECURE_AUTHENTICATION + ADS_USE_SSL
objConn.Open "Active Directory Provider"
set objRS = objConn.Execute("<LDAP://cn=users,dc=rallencorp,dc=com>;" & _
                            "(cn=*);" & "cn;" & "onelevel")
objRS.MoveFirst
while Not objRS.EOF
    Wscript.Echo objRS.Fields(0).Value
    objRS.MoveNext
wend
```

Discussion

The out-of-the-box install of Windows 2000 Active Directory did not provide any default data encryption over the network between clients and domain controllers with most of the standard tools. If you run Network Monitor (*netmon.exe*) while using tools that perform simple LDAP binds, you'll see LDAP requests, usernames, and passwords going over the network in plain text. Obviously this is not the most secure configuration, so with Windows Server 2003 most of the AD tools sign and encrypt traffic from the clients to the domain controllers by default.

To use the more secure Windows Server 2003 tools against Windows 2000 domain controllers, you need to install SP 3 on the Windows 2000 domain controllers. The new versions of the tools cannot be run directly on Windows 2000, so you must use a Windows XP or Windows Server 2003 machine to host them.

If you want to take advantage of some of the new features of the tools, but have not installed SP 3 yet, you can disable signing on the Windows XP or Windows Server 2003 machine. It is worth stating the obvious that this is insecure and defeats one of the major benefits of the new tools, but you may have no other choice. To disable signing, set the following registry value to 0x03:

```
HKLM\SOFTWARE\Microsoft\Windows\CurrentVersion\AdminDebug\ADsOpenObjectFlags
```

See Also

Recipe 14.1 for enabling SSL/TLS, MS KB 325465 (Windows 2000 Domain Controllers Require SP3 or Later When Using Windows Server 2003 Administration Tools), MS KB 304718 (Administering Windows Server-Based Computers Using Windows XP Professional-Based Clients), and MSDN: ADS_AUTHENTICATION_ENUM

14.3   Enabling Anonymous LDAP Access

Problem

You want to enable anonymous LDAP access for clients. In Windows 2000 Active Directory, anonymous queries were enabled by default, although restricted. With Windows Server 2003 Active Directory, anonymous queries are disabled except for querying the RootDSE.

Solution

Using a graphical user interface

1. Open ADSI Edit.
2. In the Configuration partition, browse to cn=Services → cn=Windows NT → cn=Directory Service.

---

3. In the left pane, right-click on the Directory Service object and select Properties.

4. Double-click on the dSHeuristics attribute.

5. If the attribute is empty, set it with the value: 0000002.

6. If the attribute has an existing value, make sure the seventh digit is set to 2.

7. Click OK twice.

Using VBScript

```
' This code enables or disables anonymous query mode for a forest.
' ------ SCRIPT CONFIGURATION ------
boolEnableAnonQuery = 2  ' e.g. 2 to enable, 0 to disable
' ------ END CONFIGURATION ---------

set objRootDSE = GetObject("LDAP://RootDSE")
set objDS = GetObject( _
            "LDAP://cn=Directory Service,cn=Windows NT,cn=Services," _
            & objRootDSE.Get("configurationNamingContext") )
strDSH = objDS.Get("dSHeuristics")

for i = len(strDSH) to 6
    strDSH = strDSH & "0"
next

strNewDSH = Left(strDSH,6) & boolEnableAnonQuery
strNewDSH = strNewDSH & Right(strDSH, len(strDSH) - 7 )

WScript.Echo "Old value: " & strDSH
WScript.Echo "New value: " & strNewDSH

if strDSH <> strNewDSH then
    objDS.Put "dSHeuristics", strNewDSH
    objDS.SetInfo
    WScript.Echo "Successfully set anon query mode to " & boolEnableAnonQuery
else
    WScript.Echo "Anon query mode already set to " & boolEnableAnonQuery
end if
```

Discussion

To enable anonymous access, you have to modify the dSHeuristics attribute of the *cn=Directory Service,cn=Windows NT,cn=Services,ConfigurationDN* object. The dSHeuristics attribute is an interesting attribute used to control certain behavior in Active Directory. For example, you can enable "List Object Mode" (see Recipe 14.15) by setting the dSHeuristics flag.

The dSHeuristics attribute consists of a series of digits that when set enable certain functionality. To enable anonymous access, the seventh bit must be set to 2. By default, dSHeuristics does not have a value. If you set it to enable anonymous access, the value would be the following: 0000002.

After enabling anonymous access, the assumption is you'll want to grant access for anonymous users to retrieve some data from Active Directory. To do that, grant the ANONYMOUS LOGON user access to the parts of the directory you want anonymous users to search. You must grant the access from the root of the directory down to the object of interest. See MS KB 320528 for an example of how to enable the anonymous user to query email addresses of user objects.

See Also

MS KB 320528 (How to Configure Active Directory to Allow Anonymous Queries), and MS KB 326690 (Anonymous LDAP Operations to Active Directory Are Disabled on Windows Server 2003 Domain Controllers)

14.4 Restricting Hosts from Performing LDAP Queries

Problem

You want domain controllers to reject LDAP queries from certain IP addresses. This can be useful if you want to prohibit domain controllers from responding to LDAP queries for certain applications or hosts.

Solution

Using a command-line interface

This option is not present in the Windows Server 2003 version of ntdsutil.

The following adds network 10.0.0.0 with mask 255.255.255.0 to the IP deny list:

```
> ntdsutil "ipdeny list" conn "co t s <DomainControllerName>" q
IP Deny List: Add 10.0.0.0 255.255.255.0
*[1] 10.0.0.0 GROUP MASK      255.255.255.0

NOTE: * | D - uncommitted addition | deletion
IP Deny List: Commit
 [1] 10.10.10.0 GROUP MASK      255.255.255.0

NOTE: * | D - uncommitted addition | deletion
```

Discussion

The IP deny list is stored as an octet string in the `lDAPIPDenyList` attribute of a query policy. See Recipe 4.23 for more information on the LDAP query policy.

When the IP deny list is set, domain controllers that are using the default query policy will not respond to LDAP queries from any IP address specified in the deny list address range. To test whether a certain IP address would be denied, run Test *x.x.x.x*, where *x.x.x.x* is an IP address, from the IP Deny List: subcommand in `ntdsutil`.

By setting the IP deny list on the default query policy, you would effectively restrict the IP address range from querying any domain controller in the forest. If you need to only restrict queries for a specific domain controller, you'll need to create a new LDAP query policy and apply it to the domain controller.

See Also

Recipe 4.23 for more information on the LDAP query policy, and MS KB 314976 (HOW TO: Use the Ntdsutil Utility to Deny Access to IP Addresses in Windows 2000)

14.5   Using the Delegation of Control Wizard

Problem

You want to delegate control over objects in Active Directory to a user or group.

Solution

Using a graphical user interface

1. Open the Active Directory Users and Computers or Active Directory Sites and Services snap-in depending on the type of object you want to delegate.
2. In the left pane, browse to the object you want to delegate control on.
3. Right-click on the object and select Delegate Control. Only certain objects support the Delegation of Control Wizard, so this option will not show up for every type of object.
4. Click Next.
5. Click the Add button and use the Object Picker to select the users or groups you want to delegate control to.
6. Click Next.
7. If the task you want to delegate is an option under Delegate the following common tasks, check it and click Next. If the task is not present, select Create a custom task

to delegate and click Next. If you selected the latter option, you will need to go perform two additional steps:

    a. Select the object type you want to delegate.

    b. Click Next.

    c. Select the permissions you want to delegate.

    d. Click Next.

8. Click Finish.

Discussion

The Delegation of Control Wizard is Microsoft's attempt to ease the pain of trying to set permissions for common tasks. Because Active Directory permissions are so granular, they can also be cumbersome to configure. The Delegation of Control Wizard helps in this regard, but it is limited. The default tasks that can be delegated are fairly minimal, although you can add more tasks as described in Recipe 14.6. Another limitation is that you can only add new permissions; you cannot undo or remove permissions that you set with the wizard. To do that, you have to use the ACL Editor directly as described in Recipe 14.10.

See Also

Recipe 14.6 for customizing the Delegation of Control wizard

14.6 Customizing the Delegation of Control Wizard

Problem

You want to add or remove new delegation options in the Delegation of Control Wizard.

Solution

Open the Delegation of Control Wizard INF file *(%SystemRoot%\Inf\Delegwiz.inf)* on the computer you want to modify the wizard for.

Under the [DelegationTemplates] section, you'll see a line like the following:

```
Templates = template1, template2, template3, template4, template5, template6,
template7, template8, template9,template10, template11, template12, template13
```

You need to append a new template name. In this case I'll follow the same naming convention and create a template named `template14`. The line now looks like this:

```
Templates = template1, template2, template3, template4, template5, template6,
template7, template8, template9,template10, template11, template12, template13,
template14
```

Scroll to the end of the file and append a new template section. You can use the other template sections as examples. Here is the generic format:

```
[<TemplateName>]
AppliesToClasses = <CommaSeparatedOfObjectClassesInvokedFrom>

Description = "<DescriptionShownInWizard>"

ObjectTypes = <CommaSeparatedListOfObjectClassesThatAreSet>

[<TemplateName>.SCOPE]
<Permission entries for Scope>

[<TemplateName>.<ObjectClass1>]
<Permission entries for ObjectClass1>

[<TemplateName>.<ObjectClass2>]
<Permission entries for ObjectClass2>

...
```

`<TemplateName>` is the same as what we used in the [DelegationTemplates] section, e.g., `template14`.

In the `AppliesToClasses` line, replace `<CommaSeparatedObjectClassesInvokedFrom>` with a comma-separated list of LDAP display names of the classes that can be delegated. This delegation action will show up on the classes listed here only when you select Delegate Control from a snap-in. To make our new template entry apply to domain objects, OUs, and containers, we would use this:

```
AppliesToClasses = domainDNS,organizationalUnit,container
```

In the `Description` line, replace `<DescriptionShownInWizard>` with the text you want shown in the wizard that describes the permissions being delegated. Here is an example description for delegating full control over `inetOrgPerson` objects:

```
Description = "Create, delete, and manage user and inetOrgPerson accounts"
```

In the `ObjectTypes` line, replace `<CommaSeparatedListOfObjectClassesThatAreSet>` with a comma-separated list of object classes that be delegated. In this example, permissions will be modified for `user` and `inetOrgPerson` objects:

```
ObjectTypes = user,inetOrgPerson
```

Next, define the actual permissions to set when this action is selected. You can define two different types of permissions. You can use a [`<TemplateName>.SCOPE`] section to define permissions that are set on the object that is used to start the wizard.

This will be one of the object classes defined in the `AppliesToClass` line. This is commonly used in the context of containers and organizational units to specify create, modify, or delete child objects of a particular type. For example, to grant the ability to create (CC) or delete (DC) user and `inetOrgPerson` objects, you would use the following:

```
[template14.SCOPE]
user=CC,DC
inetOrgPerson=CC,DC
```

As you can see, each permission (e.g., create child) is abbreviated to a two-letter code. Here are the valid codes:

RP Read Property

WP Write Property

CC Create Child

DC Delete Child

GA Full Control

It is perfectly valid to leave out a `SCOPE` section if it is not needed. The rest of the lines are used to specify permissions that should be set on the object classes defined by the `ObjectTypes` line.

To grant full control over all existing user and `inetOrgPerson` objects, I'll use these entries:

```
[template14.user]
@=GA

[template14.inetOrgPerson]
@=GA
```

This is very similar to the previous example except that `SCOPE` was replaced with the names of the object classes the permissions apply to. The @ symbol is used to indicate that the permission applies to all attributes on the object. You can get more granular by replacing @ with the name of attribute the permission applies to. For example, this would grant read and write permissions on the department attribute for inetOrgPerson objects:

```
[template14.inetOrgPerson]
department=RP,WP
```

You can also enable control access rights using the `CONTROLRIGHT` designator instead of @ or an attribute name. You need to specify the LDAP display name of the control access right you want to enable. This next section enables the Reset Password right on inetOrgPerson objects and enables read and write access to the pwdLastSet attribute:

```
[template14.inetOrgPerson]
CONTROLRIGHT="Reset Password"
pwdLastSet=RP,WP
```

Discussion

You can completely customize the tasks that can be delegated with the Delegation of Control Wizard, but you still have the problem of getting the *delegwiz.inf* file on all the clients that need to use the new settings. You can manually copy it to the computers that need it or use group policy to automate the distribution of it.

See Also

Recipe 14.5 for more on using the Delegation of Control wizard

14.7   Viewing the ACL for an Object

Problem

You want to view the ACL for an object.

Solution

Using a graphical user interface

1. Open the ACL Editor. You can do this by viewing the properties of an object (right-click on the object and select Properties) with a tool, such as Active Directory Users and Computers (ADUC) or ADSI Edit. Select the Security tab. To see the Security tab with ADUC, you must select View → Advanced Features from the menu.

2. Click the Advanced button to view a list of the individual ACEs.

Using a command-line interface

```
> dsacls <ObjectDN>
```

Using VBScript

Unfortunately, the code to view the ACEs in an ACL is quite messy and long. This will be included as part of the code on the web site for the book (*http://www.oreilly.com/catalog/activedckbk/*).

Discussion

Viewing an object's ACL is a common task and should already be familiar to most administrators. The ACL editor is useful for checking the permissions that have been set on objects, especially after running the Delegation of Control Wizard. In addition to viewing permissions, the options available in the GUI include, viewing Auditing settings and the Owner of the object. Knowing the owner of and object is important because ownership confers certain inherent rights.

Because the ACL Editor is the same for NTFS permissions and properties as it is for Active Directory objects, you should feel comfortable with the look and feel of the interface—it is exactly the same as File and Folder permissions. I also highly recommend getting familiar with the Advanced View of the ACL Editor, as this is truly the view in which you can determine what is going on with permissions. The Basic view presents a list of security principals that have permissions configured, but it will not always show every ACE entry. The Advanced view will show the complete picture including the scope of permissions for ACEs down to the object and even attribute level.

See Also

Recipe 14.10 for changing an ACL and Recipe 15.12 for auditing of object access

14.8   Customizing the ACL Editor

Problem

You want to set permissions on attributes that do not show up in the default ACL Editor.

Solution

The ACL Editor shows only a subset of the object's attributes that permissions can be set on. These can be seen in the ACL Editor by clicking the Advanced button, adding or editing a permission entry, and selecting the Properties tab.

An attribute can have a read permission, write permission, or both, either of which can be set to Allow or Deny. If the attribute you want to secure is not in the list, you will need to modify the *%SystemRoot%\system32\dssec.dat* file on the computer running the ACL Editor.

There are sections for each object class, represented in square brackets—e.g., [user]. Underneath that heading is a list of attributes that you can configure to display or not display in the ACL Editor. These are the first few lines for the [user] section:

```
[user]
aCSPolicyName=7
adminCount=7
allowedAttributes=7
```

The value to the right of the attribute determines whether it is shown in the ACL Editor. The valid values include the following:

0   Both Read Property and Write Property are displayed for attribute.

1   Write property is displayed for the attribute.

2   Read property is displayed for the attribute.

7   No entries are displayed for the attribute.

If the attribute is not defined, then the default value (specified by @, if present) is used.

Discussion

Much like the Delegation of Control Wizard, you can customize the attributes that are shown in the ACL Editor, but you still need to distribute the *dssec.dat* file to all computers that need to see the change.

A good example of when this recipe is needed is for delegating the ability to unlock accounts. This is common in larger organizations where you want to assign this task to the help desk without giving them additional rights on user objects. In this case, you need to set the lockoutTime in the [user] section of the *dssec.dat* file to 0.

See Also

MS KB 296490 (How to Modify the Filtered Properties of an Object) and MS KB 294952 (How To Delegate the Unlock Account Right)

14.9 Viewing the Effective Permissions on an Object

Problem

You want to view the effective permissions for a user or group on a particular object.

Solution

Using a graphical user interface

1. Open the ACL Editor. You can do this by viewing the properties of an object (right-click on the object and select Properties) with a tool, such as Active Directory Users and Computers (ADUC) or ADSI Edit. Select the Security tab. To see the Security tab with ADUC, you must select View → Advanced Features from the menu.

2. Click the Advanced button.

3. Select the Effective Permissions tab.

4. Click the Select button to bring up the Object Editor.

5. Find the user or group you for which want to see the effective permissions.

6. The results will be shown under Effective Permissions.

 The Effective Permissions tab is available only in the Windows Server 2003 version of the ACL Editor. For Windows 2000, you'll need to use the acldiag solution.

Using a command-line interface

```
> acldiag <ObjectDN> /geteffective:<UserOrGroup>
```

Discussion

Viewing the permissions on an object does not tell the whole story as to what the actual translated permissions are for a user or group on that object. The *effective permissions* of an object take into account all group membership and any inherited permissions that may have been applied further up the tree.

14.10 Changing the ACL of an Object

Problem

You want to change the ACL on an object to grant or restrict access to it for a user or group.

Solution

Using a graphical user interface

1. Open the ACL Editor. You can do this by viewing the properties of an object (right-click on the object and select Properties) with a tool, such as Active Directory Users and Computers (ADUC) or ADSI Edit. Select the Security tab. To see the Security tab with ADUC, you must select View → Advanced Features from the menu.

2. Click the Advanced button to view a list of the individual ACEs.

Using a command-line interface

```
> dsacls <ObjectDN>
```

Using VBScript

See Recipes 7.7, 8.2, 13.6, and 17.9 for several examples of modifying an ACL with VBScript.

Discussion

Changing the ACL of an object is a common task for administrators in any but the most basic AD implementations because, as shown in Recipes 14.5 and 14.6, the Delegation of Control Wizard is limited and cumbersome to extend and deploy. The GUI and command-line methods are useful for one-off changes to permissions, but for making global changes to a number of objects you should consider using a script.

See Also

MS KB 281146 (How to Use Dsacls.exe in Windows 2000)

14.11 Changing the Default ACL for an Object Class in the Schema

Problem

You want to change the default ACL for an object class in the schema.

Solution

Using a graphical user interface

1. Open the Active Directory Schema snap-in.
2. In the left pane, browse to the class you want to modify.
3. Right-click on it and select Properties.
4. Select the Default Security tab.
5. Use the ACL Editor to change the ACL.
6. Click OK.

 The Default Security tab is available only in the Windows Server 2003 version of the Active Directory Schema snap-in. See MS KB 265399 for the manual approach that is needed with Windows 2000.

Discussion

Each instantiated object in Active Directory has an associated structural class that defines a default security descriptor (defaultSecurityDescriptor attribute). When an object is created, the default security descriptor is applied to it. This, along with inheritable permissions from the parent container, determines how an object's security descriptor is initially defined.

See Also

Recipe 14.12 for comparing the ACL of an object to the default defined in the schema, Recipe 14.13 for resetting the ACL of an object to that defined in the schema, and MS KB 265399 (HOW TO: Change Default Permissions for Objects That Are Created in the Active Directory)

14.12 Comparing the ACL of an Object to the Default Defined in the Schema

Problem

You want to determine if an object has the permissions defined in the schema for its object class as part of its ACL.

Solution

Using a command-line interface

```
> acldiag <ObjectDN> /schema
```

Discussion

For more on the default security descriptor, see Recipe 14.11.

See Also

Recipe 14.13 for resetting an object's ACL to the default defined in the schema

14.13 Resetting an Object's ACL to the Default Defined in the Schema

Problem

You want to reset an object's ACL to the one defined in the schema for the object's object class.

Solution

Using a graphical user interface

 This is available only in the Windows Server 2003 version of the ACL Editor.

1. Open the ACL Editor. You can do this by viewing the properties of an object (right-click on the object and select Properties) with a tool, such as Active Directory Users and Computers (ADUC) or ADSI Edit. Select the Security tab. To see the Security tab with ADUC, you must select View → Advanced Features from the menu.
2. Click the Advanced button.
3. Click the Default button.
4. Click OK twice.

Using a command-line interface

```
> dsacls <ObjectDN> /s
```

Discussion

For more on the default security descriptor, see Recipe 14.11.

14.14 Preventing the LM Hash of a Password from Being Stored

Problem

You want to prevent the LM hash for new passwords from being stored in Active Directory. The LM hash is primarily used for backwards compatibility with Windows 95 and 98 clients. The LM hash is susceptible to brute force attacks.

Solution

For Windows 2000, you need to create the following Registry key on all domain controllers: HKLM\SYSTEM\CurrentControlSet\Control\Lsa\NoLMHash. Note that this is a key and not a value entry. Also, this is only supported on W2K SP2 and later domain controllers.

For Windows Server 2003, the NoLMHash key has turned into a DWORD value entry under the HKLM\SYSTEM\CurrentControlSet\Control\Lsa key. This value should be set to 1. You can accomplish this by modifying the Default Domain Controller Security Policy as described next.

Using a graphical user interface

1. Open the Default Domain Controller Security Policy snap-in.
2. In the left pane, expand Local Policies → Security Options.
3. In the right pane, double-click on Network security: Do not store LAN Manager hash value on next password change.
4. Check the box beside Define this policy setting.
5. Click the Enabled radio button.

Discussion

If you do not have Windows 98 or older clients in your domain, you should consider disabling the storage of the LM password hash for users. The LM hash uses an old algorithm (pre-Windows NT 4.0) and is considered to be relatively weak compared to the NT hash that is also stored.

 The LM hash is generated only for passwords that are shorter than 15 characters. So if you are one of the few people who have a password longer than this, the LM hash is not stored for you.

See Also

MS KB 299656 (How to Prevent Windows from Storing a LAN Manager Hash of Your Password in Active Directory and Local SAM Databases)

14.15 Enabling List Object Access Mode

Problem

You want to prevent any authenticated user from being able to browse the contents of Active Directory by default. Enabling List Object Access mode means users will need explicit permissions to see directory listings of containers.

Solution

Using a graphical user interface

1. Open ADSI Edit.
2. In the Configuration partition, browse to cn=Services → cn=Windows NT → cn=Directory Service.

3. In the left pane, right-click on the Directory Service object and select Properties.

4. Double-click on the dSHeuristics attribute.

5. If the attribute is empty, set it with the value: 001. If the attribute has an existing value, make sure the third bit (from the left) is set to 1.

6. Click OK twice.

Using VBScript

```
' This code enables or disables list object mode for a forest.
' ------ SCRIPT CONFIGURATION ------
boolEnableListObject = 1  ' e.g. 1 to enable, 0 to disable
' ------ END CONFIGURATION ---------

set objRootDSE = GetObject("LDAP://RootDSE")
set objDS = GetObject( _
               "LDAP://cn=Directory Service,cn=Windows NT,cn=Services," _
               & objRootDSE.Get("configurationNamingContext") )
strDSH = objDS.Get("dSHeuristics")
if len(strDSH) = 1 then
   strDSH = strDSH & "0"
end if
strNewDSH = Left(strDSH,2) & boolEnableListObject
if len(strDSH) > 3 then
   strNewDSH = strNewDSH & Right(strDSH, len(strDSH) - 3)
end if

WScript.Echo "Old value: " & strDSH
WScript.Echo "New value: " & strNewDSH

if strDSH <> strNewDSH then
   objDS.Put "dSHeuristics", strNewDSH
   objDS.SetInfo
   WScript.Echo "Successfully set list object mode to " & _
               boolEnableListObject
else
   WScript.Echo "List object mode already set to " & boolEnableListObject
end if
```

Discussion

List Object Access mode is useful if you want your users to only view a subset of objects when doing a directory listing of a particular container or you do not want them to be able to list the objects in a container at all. By default, the Authenticated Users group is granted the List Contents access control right over objects in a domain. If you remove or deny this right on a container by modifying the ACL, users will not be able to get a listing of the objects in that container in tools, such as Active Directory Users and Computers or ADSI Edit.

To limit the objects' users can see when they do a listing, you first need to enable List Object Access mode as described in the solution. You should then remove the List Contents access control right on the target container. Lastly, you'll need to grant the List Object right to the objects the users or groups should be able to list.

 Enabling List Object Access mode can significantly increase the administration overhead for configuring ACLs in Active Directory.

See Also

MSDN: Controlling Object Visibility and Microsoft's High-Volume Hosting Site at *http://www.microsoft.com/serviceproviders/deployment/hvh_ad_deploy.asp*

14.16 Modifying the ACL on Administrator Accounts

Problem

You want to modify the ACL for user accounts that are members of one of the administrative groups.

Solution

Using one of the methods described in Recipe 14.10, modify the ACL on the *cn=AdminSDHolder,cn=Systems,<DomainDN>* object in the domain the administrator accounts reside in. The ACL on this object gets applied every hour to all user accounts that are members of the administrative groups.

Discussion

If you've ever tried to directly modify the ACL on a user account that was a member of one of the administrative groups in Active Directory, or you modified the ACL on the OU containing an administrative account and wondered why the account's ACL was overwritten later, you've come to the right place. The Admin SD Holder feature of Active Directory is one that many administrators stumble upon after much grinding of teeth. However, after you realize the purpose for it, you'll understand it is a necessary feature.

Once an hour, a process on the PDC Emulator, which I'll refer to as the Admin SD Holder process, compares the ACL on the AdminSDHolder object to the ACL on the accounts that are in administrative groups in the domain. If it detects a difference, it will overwrite the account ACL and disable inheritance. If you later remove a user from an administrative group, you will need to reapply any inherited permissions and enable inheritance if necessary. The Admin SD Holder process will not take care of this for you.

The Admin SD Holder process is intended to subvert any malicious activity by a user that has been delegated rights over an OU or container that contains an account that is in one of the administrative groups. The malicious user could, for example, reset the password of the account and log in to the domain using that account, which would give him elevated privileges to do even more malicious things.

These are the groups included as part of the Admin SD Holder processing:

- Administrators
- Account Operators
- Cert Publishers
- Backup Operators
- Domain Admins
- Enterprise Admins
- Print Operators
- Schema Admins
- Server Operators

The Administrator and Krbtgt user accounts are also specifically checked during the Admin SD Holder process.

See Also

MS KB 232199 (Description and Update of the Active Directory AdminSDHolder Object), MS KB 306398 (AdminSDHolder Object Affects Delegation of Control for Past Administrator Accounts), and MS KB 817433 (Delegated Permissions Are Not Available and Inheritance Is Automatically Disabled)

14.17 Viewing and Purging Your Kerberos Tickets

Problem

You want to view and possibly purge your Kerberos tickets.

Solution

Both the kerbtray and klist utilities can be found in the Resource Kit.

Using a graphical user interface

1. Run kerbtray.exe from the command line or Start → Run.

2. A new icon (green) should show up in the system tray (where the system time is located). Double-click on that icon. This will allow you to view your current tickets.

3. To purge your tickets, right-click on the kerbtray icon in the system tray and select Purge Tickets.

4. Close the kerbtray window and reopen it by right-clicking on the kerbtray icon and selecting List Tickets.

Using a command-line interface

Run the following command to list your current tickets:

```
> klist tickets
```

Run the following command to purge your tickets:

```
> klist purge
```

Discussion

Active Directory uses Kerberos as its preferred network authentication system. When you authenticate to a Kerberos Key Distribution Center (KDC), which in Active Directory terms is a domain controller, you are issued one or more tickets. These tickets identify you as a certain principal in Active Directory and can be used to authenticate you to other Kerberized services. This type of ticket is known as a ticket-granting-ticket, or TGT. Once you've obtained a TGT, the client can pass that to a Kerberized service and if the service accepts the ticket, it will issue a service ticket that represents the client for the particular service.

Kerberos is a fairly complicated system that cannot be done justice in a single paragraph. If you want more information on tickets and how the Kerberos authentication system works, see *Kerberos: The Definitive Guide* (O'Reilly).

See Also

RFC 1510 (The Kerberos Network Authentication Service V5), and MS KB 232179 (Kerberos Administration in Windows 2000)

14.18 Forcing Kerberos to Use TCP

Problem

Clients are experiencing authentication problems and you've determined it is due to UDP fragmentation of Kerberos traffic. You want to force Kerberos traffic to go over TCP instead.

Solution

Using a graphical user interface

1. Run regedit.exe from the command line or Start → Run.
2. In the left pane, expand HKEY_LOCAL_MACHINE → System → Current-ControlSet → Control → Lsa → Kerberos → Parameters.
3. Right-click on Parameters and select New → DWORD value. Enter MaxPacket-Size for the value name.
4. In the right pane, double-click on MaxPacketSize and enter 1.
5. Click OK.

Using a command-line interface

```
> reg add "HKLM\SYSTEM\CurrentControlSet\Control\Lsa\Kerberos\Parameters" /v↵
"MaxPacketSize" /t REG_DWORD /d 1
```

Using VBScript

```
' This code forces Kerberos to use TCP
' ------ SCRIPT CONFIGURATION ------
strComputer = "<ComputerName>"  ' e.g. rallen-w2k3
' ------ END CONFIGURATION ---------

const HKLM = &H80000002
strRegKey = "SYSTEM\CurrentControlSet\Control\Lsa\Kerberos\Parameters"
set objReg = GetObject("winmgmts:\\" & strComputer & _
                       "\root\default:StdRegProv")
objReg.SetDwordValue HKLM, strRegKey, "MaxPacketSize", 1
WScript.Echo "Kerberos forced to use TCP for " & strComputer
```

Discussion

If you have users that are experiencing extremely slow logon times (especially over VPN) or they are seeing the infamous "There are currently no logon servers available to service the logon request," then they may be experiencing UDP fragmentation of Kerberos traffic. One way to help identify if there is a problem with Kerberos is to have the users run the following command:

```
> netdiag /test:kerberos
```

Another source of information is the System event log on the clients. Various Kerberos-related events are logged there if problems with authentication occur.

For more information about Kerberos and UDP, see MS KB 244474 (How to Force Kerberos to Use TCP Instead of UDP).

14.19 Modifying Kerberos Settings

Problem

You want to modify the default Kerberos settings that define things, such as maximum ticket lifetime.

Solution

Using a graphical user interface

1. Open the Domain Security Policy snap-in.
2. In the left pane, expand Account Policies → Kerberos Policy.
3. In the right pane, double-click on the setting you want to modify.
4. Enter the new value and click OK.

Discussion

There are several Kerberos-related settings you can customize. In most environments, the default settings are sufficient, but the ones you can modify are listed in Table 14-1.

 Change the default settings with caution as it could cause operational problems and compromise security if done incorrectly.

Table 14-1. Kerberos policy settings

Setting	Default value
Enforce user logon restrictions	Enabled
Maximum lifetime for service ticket	600 minutes
Maximum lifetime for user ticket	10 hours
Maximum lifetime for user ticket renewal	7 days
Maximum tolerance for computer clock synchronization	5 minutes

See Also

MS KB 231849 (Description of Kerberos Policies in Windows 2000) and MS KB 232179 (Kerberos Administration in Windows 2000)

## CHAPTER 15

Logging, Monitoring, and Quotas

15.0 Introduction

This chapter deals with tracking the activity and usage of various Active Directory components. Whenever you need to troubleshoot a problem, often the first place you look is log files. With Active Directory, there are several different log files, and each have different ways to increase or decrease the verbosity of information that is logged. Viewing log messages can be useful, but you may also want to look at performance metrics to determine if the system is being over-utilized. I'll review a couple of ways you can view performance metrics and monitor Active Directory performance. For more extensive monitoring, I suggest looking at NetPro's (*http://www.netpro.com/*) Active Directory monitoring tools or Microsoft Operations Manager (*http://microsoft.com/mom/*).

I'll also cover a somewhat-related topic in this chapter called quotas, which allow you to monitor and limit the number of objects a security principal (user, group, or computer) can create in a partition. This feature, introduced in Windows Server 2003, closes a hole that existed in Windows 2000 where users that had access to create objects in Active Directory could create as many as they wanted. These users could even cause a denial of service by creating objects until the disk filled on the domain controllers. This kind of attack is not likely to happen in most environments, but the possibility should still be considered.

The Anatomy of a Quota Object Container

Quota objects are stored in the NTDS Quotas container in all Windows Server 2003-based naming contexts and application partitions except the schema-naming context (quotas cannot be associated with the schema-naming context). By default, this container is hidden from view within tools, such as Active Directory Users and Computers, but can be seen by selecting View → Advanced Features from the menu. The quota object container has an objectClass of msDS-QuotaContainer, and contains several attributes that define default quota behavior. Table 15-1 lists some of the important attributes of msDS-QuotaContainer objects.

Table 15-1. Attributes of msDS-QuotaContainer objects

Attribute	Description
cn	RDN of quota container objects. By default, this is equal to NTDS Quotas.
msDS-DefaultQuota	The default quota applied to all security principals that do not have another quota specification applied. See Recipe 15.16 for more details.
msDS-QuotaEffective	A constructed attribute that contains the effective quota of the security principal that is viewing the attribute. See Recipe 15.17 for more details.
msDS-QuotaUsed	A constructed attribute that contains the quota usage of the security principal that is viewing the attribute. See Recipe 15.17 for more details.
msDS-TombstoneQuotaFactor	Percentage that tombstone objects count against a quota. The default is 100, which means a tombstone object has equal weighting to a normal object. See Recipe 15.15 for more details.
msDS-TopQuotaUsage	Multivalued attribute that contains information about the security principals with the top quota usage. See Recipe 15.17 for more details.

The Anatomy of a Quota Object

Quota objects have an objectClass of msDS-QuotaControl, which defines three attributes that relate to quotas. Table 15-2 contains these attributes and provides a description for each.

Table 15-2. Attributes of msDS-QuotaControl objects

Attribute	Description
cn	RDN of the quota object.
msDS-QuotaAmount	Number of objects that can be created by the security principals that the quota applies to. See Recipe 15.13 for more information.
msDS-QuotaTrustee	SID of the security principal that the quota applies to. This can be a user, group, or computer SID. See Recipe 15.13 for more information.

15.1 Enabling Extended dcpromo Logging

Problem

You want to enable extended dcpromo logging. This can be useful if you are experiencing problems during the promotion or demotion process and the dcpromo log files are not providing enough information to indicate the problem.

Solution

These solutions are slightly different on Windows 2000. See the Discussion section for more information. To enable the maximum amount of logging, use 16711683 (FF0003 in hexadecimal) as the flag value. For a complete description of the possible bit values, see MS KB 221254.

Using a graphical user interface

1. Run regedit.exe from the command line or Start → Run.

2. In the left pane, expand HKEY_LOCAL_MACHINE → Software → Microsoft → Windows → CurrentVersion → AdminDebug → dcpromoui.

3. If the LogFlags value does not exist, right-click on dcpromoui in the left pane and select New → DWORD Value. For the name, enter LogFlags.

4. In the right pane, double-click on the LogFlags value and enter the flag value you want to set.

5. Click OK.

Using a command-line interface

With the following command, *<FlagValue>* needs to the decimal version (not hexidecimal) of the flag value:

```
> reg add HKLM\Software\Microsoft\Windows\CurrentVersion\AdminDebug\dcpromoui /v↵
"LogFlags" /t REG_DWORD /d <FlagValue>
```

Using VBScript

```
' This code sets the dcpromoui logging flag (for Windows Server 2003 only)
' ------ SCRIPT CONFIGURATION ------
strDC   = "<DomainControllerName>"  ' e.g. dc01
intFlag = <FlagValue>               ' Flag value in decimal, e.g. 16711683
' ------ END CONFIGURATION ---------

const HKLM = &H80000002
strDcpromoReg = "Software\Microsoft\Windows\CurrentVersion\AdminDebug\dcpromoui"
set objReg = GetObject("winmgmts:\\" & strDC & "\root\default:StdRegProv")
objReg.SetDwordValue HKLM, strDcpromoReg, "LogFlags", intFlag
WScript.Echo "Dcpromoui flag set to " & intFlag
```

Discussion

As described in Recipe 3.5, the dcpromo wizard creates a couple of log files in *%SystemRoot%\debug* when it is executed, which can be useful in troubleshooting promotion or demotion problems. Typically, the default amount of logging that is done in the *dcpromoui.log* file is sufficient to identify most problems, but you can increase it as described in the Solution section.

The location of the log flags registry value changed from Windows 2000 to Windows Server 2003. In Windows 2000, the value is located here:

```
HKLM\Software\Microsoft\Windows\CurrentVersion\AdminDebug\dcpromoui
```

In Windows Server 2003, the value is located here (which was used in the Solutions section):

```
HKLM\Software\Microsoft\Windows\CurrentVersion\AdminDebug\dcpromoui\LogFlags
```

See Also

Recipe 3.5 for more on troubleshooting dcpromo problems, and MS KB 221254 (Registry Settings for Event Detail in the Dcpromoui.log File)

15.2   Enabling Diagnostics Logging

Problem

You want to enable diagnostics event logging because the current level of logging is not providing enough information to help pinpoint the problem you are troubleshooting.

Solution

Using a graphical user interface

1. Run regedit.exe from the command line or Start → Run.
2. In the left pane, expand HKEY_LOCAL_MACHINE → System → Current-ControlSet → Services → NTDS → Diagnostics.
3. In the right pane, double-click on the diagnostics logging entry you want to increase, and enter a number (0–5) based on how much you want logged.
4. Click OK.

Using a command-line interface

```
> reg add HKLM\SYSTEM\CurrentControlSet\Services\NTDS\Diagnostics /v⏎
"<LoggingSetting>" /t REG_DWORD /d <0-5>
```

Using VBScript

```
' This code sets the specified diagnostics logging level
' ------ SCRIPT CONFIGURATION ------
strDC    = "<DomainControllerName>"  ' e.g. dc01
strLogSetting = "<LoggingSetting>"   ' e.g. 1 Knowledge Consistency Checker
intFlag = <FlagValue>                ' Flag value in decimal, e.g. 5
' ------ END CONFIGURATION ---------

const HKLM = &H80000002
strRegKey = "SYSTEM\CurrentControlSet\Services\NTDS\Diagnostics"
set objReg = GetObject("winmgmts:\\" & strDC & "\root\default:StdRegProv")
objReg.SetDwordValue HKLM, strRegKey, "LogFlags", intFlag
WScript.Echo "Diagnostics logging for " & strLogSetting _
             & " set to " & intFlag
```

Discussion

A useful way to troubleshoot specific problems you are encountering with Active Directory is to increase the diagnostics logging level. Diagnostics logging can be enabled by component. For example, if you determine the Knowledge Consistency Checker (KCC) is not completing every 15 minutes, you can enable diagnostics logging for the "1 Knowledge Consistency Checker" setting.

These settings are stored under HKLM\SYSTEM\CurrentControlSet\Services\NTDS\ Diagnostics. By default, all settings are set to 0, which disables diagnostic logging, but you can increase it by setting it to a number from 1 through 5. As a general rule, a value of 1 is used for minimum logging, 3 for medium logging, and 5 for maximum logging. It is a good practice to ease your way up to 5 because some diagnostics logging settings can generate a bunch of events in the event log, which may make it difficult to read, along with increasing resource utilization on the domain controller.

Here is the complete list of diagnostics logging settings for Windows Server 2003. Note that settings 20–24 are not available on Windows 2000-based domain controllers.

```
 1 Knowledge Consistency Checker
 2 Security Events
 3 ExDS Interface Events
 4 MAPI Interface Events
 5 Replication Events
 6 Garbage Collection
 7 Internal Configuration
 8 Directory Access
 9 Internal Processing
10 Performance Counters
11 Initialization/Termination
12 Service Control
13 Name Resolution
14 Backup
15 Field Engineering
16 LDAP Interface Events
17 Setup
18 Global Catalog
19 Inter-site Messaging
20 Group Caching
21 Linked-Value Replication
22 DS RPC Client
23 DS RPC Server
24 DS Schema
```

See Also

MS KB 220940 (How to Enable Diagnostic Event Logging for Active Directory Services)

15.3 Enabling NetLogon Logging

Problem

You want to enable NetLogon logging to help with troubleshooting client account logon, lockout, or domain controller location issues.

Solution

Using a command-line interface

To enable Netlogon logging, use the following command:

```
> nltest /dbflag:0x2080ffff
```

To disable Netlogon logging, use the following command:

```
> nltest /dbflag:0x0
```

Discussion

The *netlogon.log* file located in *%SystemRoot%\Debug* can be invaluable for troubleshooting client logon and related issues. When enabled at the highest setting (0x2000ffff), it logs useful information, such as the site the client is in, the domain controller the client authenticated against, additional information related to the DC Locator process, account password expiration information, account lockout information, and even Kerberos failures.

The NetLogon logging level is stored in the following registry value:

```
HKLM\System\CurrentControlSet\Services\Netlogon Parameters\DBFlag
```

If you set that registry value manually, instead of using `nltest`, you'll need to restart the NetLogon service for it to take effect.

One of the issues with the *netlogon.log* file is that it can quickly grow to several megabytes, which makes it difficult to peruse. A new tool available for Windows XP and Windows Server 2003 called `nlparse` can filter the contents of the *netlogon.log* file so that you'll only see certain type of log entries. The `nlparse` tool is part of the Account Lockout and Management Tools that Microsoft made available from the following web site (assuming the tools haven't moved):

http://www.microsoft.com/downloads/details.aspx?FamilyID=7af2e69c-91f3-4e63-8629-b999adde0b9e&DisplayLang=en

See Also

MS KB 109626 (Enabling Debug Logging for the Netlogon Service), MS KB 247811 (How Domain Controllers Are Located in Windows), and MS KB 273499 (Description of Security Event 681)

15.4   Enabling GPO Client Logging

Problem

You want to troubleshoot GPO processing issues on a client or server by enabling additional logging in the Application event log.

Solution

Using a graphical user interface

1. Run regedit.exe from the command line or Start → Run.
2. In the left pane, expand HKEY_LOCAL_MACHINE → Software → Microsoft → Windows NT → CurrentVersion.
3. If the Diagnostics key doesn't exist, right-click on CurrentVersion and select New → Key. Enter Diagnostics for the name and hit enter.
4. Right-click on Diagnostics and select New → DWORD value. Enter RunDiagnosticLoggingGroupPolicy for the value name.
5. In the right pane, double-click on RunDiagnosticLoggingGroupPolicy and enter 1.
6. Click OK.

Using a command-line interface

```
> reg add "HKLM\SOFTWARE\Microsoft\Windows NT\CurrentVersion\Diagnostics" /v↵
"RunDiagnosticLoggingGroupPolicy" /t REG_DWORD /d 1
```

Using VBScript

```
' This code enables GPO logging on a target computer
' ------ SCRIPT CONFIGURATION ------
strComputer = "<ComputerName>"  ' e.g. rallen-w2k3
' ------ END CONFIGURATION ---------

const HKLM = &H80000002
strRegKey = "SOFTWARE\Microsoft\Windows NT\CurrentVersion\Diagnostics"
set objReg = GetObject("winmgmts:\\" & strComputer _
                       & "\root\default:StdRegProv")
objReg.SetDwordValue HKLM, strRegKey, "RunDiagnosticLoggingGroupPolicy", 1
WScript.Echo "Enabled GPO logging for " & strComputer
```

Discussion

If you experience problems with client GPO processing, such as a GPO not getting applied even though you think it should, there aren't many tools that can help you troubleshoot the problem. One way to get detailed information about what GPOs are applied on a client is by enabling additional GPO event logging. If you set the RunDiagnosticLoggingGroupPolicy Registry value to 1, extensive logging will be done in the Application event log. Events detailing the beginning of the GPO processing cycle, what GPOs are applied, and any errors encountered will all be logged. Here is an example of a log message that shows which GPOs are going to be applied on the host DC1. To disable this logging, either delete RunDiagnosticLoggingGroupPolicy or set the value to 0.

Here is a sample event log message:

```
Event Type:Error
Event Source:Userenv
Event Category:None
Event ID:1031
Date:    5/26/2003
Time:    5:52:13 PM
User:    NT AUTHORITY\SYSTEM
Computer:DC1
Description:
Group Policy objects to be applied: "Default Domain Policy" "Default Domain
Controllers Policy" .
```

See Also

MS KB 186454 (How to Enable User Environment Event Logging in Windows 2000)

15.5   Enabling Kerberos Logging

Problem

You want to enable Kerberos logging on a domain controller to troubleshoot authentication problems.

Solution

Using a graphical user interface

1. Run regedit.exe from the command line or Start → Run.
2. In the left pane, expand HKEY_LOCAL_MACHINE → System → Current-ControlSet → Control → Lsa → Kerberos → Parameters.
3. If the LogLevel value doesn't already exist, right-click on Parameters and select New → DWORD value. Enter LogLevel for the value name and click OK.

4. In the right pane, double-click on LogLevel and enter 1.

5. Click OK.

Using a command-line interface

```
> reg add HKLM\SYSTEM\CurrentControlSet\Control\Lsa\Kerberos\Parameters /v "LogLevel"↵
/t REG_DWORD /d 1
```

Using VBScript

```
' This code enables Kerberos logging for the specified domain controller
' ------ SCRIPT CONFIGURATION ------
strDC = "<DomainControllerName>"  ' e.g. dc01
' ------ END CONFIGURATION ---------

const HKLM = &H80000002
strRegKey = "SYSTEM\CurrentControlSet\Control\Lsa\Kerberos\Parameters"
set objReg = GetObject("winmgmts:\\" & strDC & "\root\default:StdRegProv")
objReg.SetDwordValue HKLM, strRegKey, "LogLevel", 1
WScript.Echo "Enable Kerberos logging for " & strDC
```

Discussion

If you are experiencing authentication problems or would like to determine whether you are experiencing any Kerberos-related issues, enabling Kerberos logging will cause Kerberos errors to be logged in the System event log. The Kerberos events can point out if the problem is related to clock skew, an expired ticket, expired password, etc. For a good overview of some of the Kerberos error messages, see MS KB 230476.

Here is an example event:

```
Event Type:Error
Event Source:Kerberos
Event Category:None
Event ID:3
Date:     5/26/2003
Time:     5:53:43 PM
User:     N/A
Computer:DC01
Description:
A Kerberos Error Message was received:
        on logon session
 Client Time:
 Server Time: 0:53:43.0000 5/27/2003 Z
 Error Code: 0xd KDC_ERR_BADOPTION
 Extended Error: 0xc00000bb KLIN(0)
 Client Realm:
 Client Name:
 Server Realm: RALLENCORP.COM
 Server Name: host/ dc01.rallencorp.com
 Target Name: host/dc01.rallencorp.com@RALLENCORP.COM
```

```
Error Text:
File: 9
Line: ab8
Error Data is in record data.
```

See Also

MS KB 230476 (Description of Common Kerberos-Related Errors in Windows 2000) and MS KB 262177 (HOW TO: Enable Kerberos Event Logging)

15.6   Enabling DNS Server Debug Logging

Problem

You want to enable DNS debug logging to troubleshoot issues related to DNS queries or updates.

Solution

Using a graphical user interface

1. Open the DNS Management snap-in.
2. Right-click on DNS in the left pane and select Connect to DNS Server.
3. Enter the server you want to connect to and click Enter.
4. Right-click on the server and select Properties.
5. Click on the Debug Logging tab (or the Logging tab for Windows 2000).
6. Select what you want to log and the location of the log file (the log file location is hardcoded to *%systemroot%\system32\dns\dns.log* on Windows 2000).
7. Click OK.

Using a command-line interface

Use the following command to enable debug logging. You have to add together the event codes you want logged and specify the result in hex for the log level. The available event codes can be found in Table 15-3.

```
> dnscmd <DNSServerName> /Config /LogLevel <EventFlagSumInHex>
```

Use the following command to specify the location of the log file:

```
> dnscmd <DNSServerName> /Config /LogFilePath <DirectoryAndFilePath>
```

Use the following command to log only entries that pertain to certain IP addresses:

```
> dnscmd <DNSServerName> /Config /LogIPFilterList <IPAddress1>[,<IPAddress2>...]
```

Use the following command to specify the maximum log file size:

```
> dnscmd <DNSServerName> /Config /LogFileMaxSize <NumberOfBytesInHex>
```

Using VBScript

```
' This code enables DNS debug logging.
' ------ SCRIPT CONFIGURATION ------
strServer    = "<DNSServerName>"           ' e.g. dc1
' The log level must be in decimal, not hex like dnscmd
intLogLevel  = <EventFlagSumInDecimal>     ' e.g. 65535
arrFilterList = Array("<IPAddress1>")      ' e.g. 192.168.1.12
strFilePath  = <DirectoryAndFilePath>      ' e.g. c:\dnslog.txt
intFileSize  = <NumberOfBytesInDecimal>    ' e.g. 50000000
' ------ END CONFIGURATION ---------

set objDNS = GetObject("winMgmts:\\" & strServer & "\root\MicrosoftDNS")
set objDNSServer = objDNS.Get("MicrosoftDNS_Server.Name="".""")
objDNSServer.LogLevel = intLogLevel
objDNSServer.LogIPFilterList = arrFilterList
objDNSServer.LogFilePath = strFilePath
objDNSServer.LogFileMaxSize = intFileSize
objDNSServer.Put_
WScript.Echo "Enabled DNS Debug Logging on " & strServer
```

Discussion

With the DNS Server debug log, you can record all DNS operations received and initiated by the server, including queries, updates, zone transfers, etc. If you need to troubleshoot a particular host, you can use the `LogIPFilterList` setting in dnscmd or the WMI DNS Provider to restrict the log to operations performed only for or by that host.

The most important debug log setting is the log level. With the DNS Console, you can select from a list of available options. With Windows Server 2003, the DNS Console provides an intuitive interface for selecting the required options. On Windows 2000, you are presented with a list of check boxes and you have to figure out which ones need to be used in conjunction with one another. You have a similar issue with CLI and VBScript solutions, where you need to determine what log level you want to set.

Table 15-3 contains all of the event codes with their hexadecimal and decimal values.

Table 15-3. DNS debug logging event codes

Hexadecimal value	Decimal value	Description
0x0	0	No logging. This is the default.
0x1	1	Queries transactions.
0x10	16	Notifications transactions.
0x20	32	Updates transactions.
0xFE	254	Non-queries transactions.
0x100	256	Question packets.

Table 15-3. DNS debug logging event codes (continued)

Hexadecimal value	Decimal value	Description
0x200	512	Answer packets.
0x1000	4096	Send packets.
0x2000	8192	Receive packets.
0x4000	16384	UDP packets.
0x8000	32768	TCP packets.
0xFFFF	65535	All packets.
0x10000	65536	AD write transactions.
0x20000	131072	AD update transactions.
0x1000000	16777216	Full packets.
0x80000000	2147483648	Write-through transactions.

DNS debug logging can come in handy if you want to look at the dynamic update requests a particular DNS server is processing. For example, if a client or DHCP server is attempting to dynamically register records, you can enable the Update Transactions log category on the DNS server you think should be processing the updates. If you don't see any update transactions, that can indicate another server is processing the dynamic update requests.

 Transactions are not immediately written to the debug log file as they occur. They are buffered and written to the file after a certain number of requests are processed.

See Also

MSDN: MicrosoftDNS_Server

15.7   Viewing DNS Server Performance Statistics

Problem

You want to view DNS Server performance statistics.

Solution

Using a graphical user interface

1. Open the Performance Monitor.
2. Click on System Monitor in the left pane.
3. In the right pane, click the + button. This will bring up the page to add counters.

4. Under Select counters from computer, enter the DNS server you want to target.

5. Select the DNS performance object.

6. Select the counters you want to add and click the Add button.

7. Click Close.

Using a command-line interface

```
> dnscmd <DNSServerName> /statistics
```

Using VBScript

```
' This code displays all statistics for the specified DNS server
' ------ SCRIPT CONFIGURATION ------
strServer = "<DNSServerName>"    ' e.g. dc1.rallencorp.com
' ------ END CONFIGURATION ---------

set objDNS = GetObject("winmgmts:\\" & strServer & "\root\MicrosoftDNS")
set objDNSServer = objDNS.Get("MicrosoftDNS_Server.Name=""."""")
set objStats = objDNS.ExecQuery("Select * from MicrosoftDNS_Statistic ")
for each objStat in objStats
   WScript.Echo " " & objStat.Name & " : " & objStat.Value
next
```

Discussion

The Microsoft DNS Server keeps track of dozens of performance metrics. These metrics include the number of queries, updates, transfers, directory reads, and directory writes processed by the server. If you can pump these metrics into an enterprise management system, you can track DNS usage and growth over time.

These statistics can also be useful to troubleshoot load-related issues. If you suspect a DNS Server is being overwhelmed with DNS update requests, you can look at the Dynamic Update Received/sec counter and see if it is processing an unusually high number of updates.

Using a command-line interface

You can obtain a subset of the statistics by providing a "statid" after the /statistics option. Each statistics category has an associated number (i.e., statid). For a complete list of categories and their statid, run the following command:

```
> dnscmd /statistics /?
```

Here is an example of viewing the Query (statid = 2) and Query2 (statid = 4) statistics:

```
> dnscmd /statistics 6
DNS Server . statistics:
```

```
Queries and Responses:
----------------------
Total:
    Queries Received =      14902
    Responses Sent   =      12900
UDP:
    Queries Recvd    =      14718
    Responses Sent   =      12716
    Queries Sent     =      23762
    Responses Recvd  =          0
TCP:
    Client Connects  =        184
    Queries Recvd    =        184
    Responses Sent   =        184
    Queries Sent     =          0
    Responses Recvd  =          0

Queries:
--------
Total         =      14902
    Notify    =          0
    Update    =       2207
    TKeyNego  =        184
    Standard  =      12511
      A       =       1286
      NS      =         29
      SOA     =       2263
      MX      =          0
      PTR     =          1
      SRV     =       8909
      ALL     =          0
      IXFR    =          0
      AXFR    =          0
      OTHER   =         23

Command completed successfully.
```

Using VBScript

You can obtain a subset of statistics by adding a where clause to the WQL query.
The following query would match only counters that start with "Records":

```
select * from MicrosoftDNS_Statistic where Name like 'Records%'
```

See Also

MSDN: MicrosoftDNS_Statistic

15.8 Enabling Inefficient and Expensive LDAP Query Logging

Problem

You want to log inefficient and expensive LDAP queries to the Directory Services event log.

Solution

To log a summary report about the total number of searches, total expensive searches, and total inefficient searches to the Directory Services event log, set the 15 Field Engineering diagnostics logging setting to 4. This summary is generated every 12 hours during the garbage collection cycle.

To log an event to the Directory Services event log every time an expensive or inefficient search occurs, set the 15 Field Engineering diagnostics logging setting to 5.

See Recipe 15.2 for more on enabling diagnostics logging.

Discussion

A search is considered *expensive* if it has to visit a large number of objects in Active Directory. A search is considered *inefficient* if it returns less than 10% of the total objects it visits. The default threshold for an expensive query is 10,000. That means any search that visits 10,000 or more objects would be considered expensive. The default bottom limit for an inefficient query is 1,000. If a query visited 1,000 objects and only returned 99 of them (less than 10%), it would be considered inefficient. If it returned 900 instead, it would not be considered inefficient. To summarize, with 1,000 being the default bottom threshold, no search that visits less than 1,000 entries (even if it visited 999 and returned 0) would be considered inefficient.

Here is an example summary report event that is logged when 15 Field Engineering is set to 4:

```
Event Type:Information
Event Source:NTDS General
Event Category:Field Engineering
Event ID:1643
Date:    5/24/2003
Time:    7:24:24 PM
User:    NT AUTHORITY\ANONYMOUS LOGON
Computer:DC1
Description:
Internal event: Active Directory performed the following number of search operations
within this time interval.
```

```
Time interval (hours):
9
Number of search operations:
24679

During this time interval, the following number of search operations were
characterized as either expensive or inefficient.

Expensive search operations:
7
Inefficient search operations:
22
```

If you set 15 Field Engineering to 5, the summary event is logged during the garbage
collection cycle, and event 1644 every time an expensive or inefficient search occurs.
Notice that this event provides details on all aspects of the search including the client IP, authenticating user, search base DN, search filter, attributes, controls, number of entries visited, and number of entries returned. This was taken from a
Windows Server 2003 domain controller. Windows 2000 does not provide quite as
much detail.

```
Event Type:Information
Event Source:NTDS General
Event Category:Field Engineering
Event ID:1644
Date:     5/24/2003
Time:     7:50:40 PM
User:     RALLENCORP\rallen
Computer:DC1
Description:
Internal event: A client issued a search operation with the following options.

Client:
192.168.4.14
Starting node:
DC=rallencorp,DC=com
Filter:
 (description=*)
Search scope:
subtree
Attribute selection:
cn
Server controls:

Visited entries:
10340
Returned entries:
1000
```

With the default settings, the query shown in the above event is considered both
expensive and inefficient. It is expensive because it visited more than 10,000 entries.
It is inefficient because it returned less than 10% of those entries.

You can customize what a domain controller considers *expensive* and *inefficient* by creating a couple registry values under the HKLM\SYSTEM\CurrentControlSet\ Services\NTDS\Parameters key. You can create a value named Expensive Search Results Threshold of type DWORD, and specify the number of entries a search would need to visit to be considered expensive. Similarly, you can create a value named Inefficient Search Results Threshold of type DWORD, and specify the minimum number of entries visited where a match returning less than 10% would be considered inefficient.

 If you want to see all the LDAP queries that are being sent to a domain controller, a quick way to do that would be to set the 15 Field Engineering setting to 5 and Expensive Search Results Threshold to 0. This would cause the domain controller to consider every search as expensive and log all the LDAP searches. While this can be very useful, you should use it with care as it could quickly fill your event log.

See Also

Recipe 15.2 for enabling diagnostics logging

15.9 Using the STATS Control to View LDAP Query Statistics

Problem

You want to use the STATS LDAP control to test the efficiency of a query.

Solution

Using a graphical user interface

1. Open LDP.
2. From the menu, select Connection → Connect.
3. For Server, enter the name of a domain controller (or leave blank to do a server-less bind).
4. For Port, enter 389.
5. Click OK.
6. From the menu, select Connection → Bind.
7. Enter credentials of a user to perform the search.
8. Click OK.
9. From the menu, select Options → Control.

---

10. For the Windows Server 2003 version of LDP, you can select Search Stats from the Load Predefined selection. For Windows 2000, add a control with the OID 1.2.840.113556.1.4.970.

11. Click OK.

12. From the menu, select Browse → Search.

13. Enter your search criteria and then click the Options button.

14. Under Search Call Type, be sure that Extended is selected.

15. Click OK and Click Run.

Discussion

The STATS control is a useful way to obtain statistics about the performance of an LDAP query. With the STATS control, you can find out information, such as the amount of time it took the server to process the query, how many entries were visited versus returned, what the search filter expanded to, and if any indexes were used. Here is an example of what the STATS control returns for a search for all group objects in the cn=Users container:

```
***Searching...
ldap_search_ext_s(ld, "cn=users,DC=rallencorp,DC=com", 2, "(objectcategory=group)",
attrList,  0, svrCtrls, ClntCtrls, 20, 1000 ,&msg)
Result <0>:
Matched DNs:
Stats:
     Call Time:10 (ms)
     Entries Returned:17
     Entries Visited:17
     Used Filter:
(objectCategory=CN=Group,CN=Schema,CN=Configuration,DC=rallencorp,DC=com) ⏎
     Used Indexes:INTERSECT_INDEX:17:I;
```

A couple things are worth noting here. First, the search visited only 17 entries and ended up returning all 17. In terms of the definitions defined in Recipe 15.8, this query is both *inexpensive* and *efficient*. You can also see that the filter that I used, (objectcategory=group), was expanded to (objectCategory=CN=Group,CN=Schema, CN=Configuration,DC=rallencorp,DC=com). The syntax of the objectCategory attribute is a distinguished name, but Active Directory provides a shortcut so that you need to use only the LDAP display name of the class instead. Internally, Active Directory converts the display name to the distinguished name, as shown here. Finally, we can see that our search used an index INTERSECT_INDEX:17:I.

Let's look at another example, except this time I'll perform an ANR search for "Jim Smith":

```
***Searching...
ldap_search_ext_s(ld, "ou=Sales,DC=rallencorp,DC=com", 2, "(anr=Jim Smith)",
attrList,  0, svrCtrls, ClntCtrls, 20, 1000 ,&msg)
```

```
Result <0>:
Matched DNs:
Stats:
    Call Time:20 (ms)
    Entries Returned:1
    Entries Visited:2
    Used Filter: ( | (displayName=Jim Smith*) (givenName=Jim Smith*)
(legacyExchangeDN=Jim Smith) (msDS-AdditionalSamAccountName=Jim Smith*)
(physicalDeliveryOfficeName=Jim Smith*) (proxyAddresses=Jim Smith*) (name=Jim
Smith*) (sAMAccountName=Jim Smith*) (sn=Jim Smith*) ( & (givenName=Jim*)
(sn=Smith*) ) ( & (givenName=Smith*) (sn=Jim*) ) )
    Used Indexes:idx_givenName:10:N;idx_givenName:10:N;idx_sn:9:N;idx_
sAMAccountName:8:N;idx_name:7:N;idx_proxyAddresses:6:N;idx_
physicalDeliveryOfficeName:5:N;idx_msDS-AdditionalSamAccountName:4:N;idx_
legacyExchangeDN:3:N;idx_givenName:2:N;idx_displayName:1:N;
```

You can see from the second line that I used a very simple filter (anr=Jim Smith). If you look down a little farther at "Used Filter:" you can see a better example of search filter expansion. Like the objectCategory example earlier, ANR is a shorthand way to do something complex. A simple one-term search filter expands into a multiterm filter that searches across numerous attributes. For more on the behavior of ANR, see Recipe 10.13. The point of showing this is that the STATS control is very powerful and can be an invaluable tool when trying to troubleshoot or optimize LDAP queries.

See Also

Recipe 4.3 for using a LDAP controls, Recipe 4.5 for searching for objects, Recipe 10.13 for more on ANR, and Recipe 15.8 for more on expensive and inefficient searches

15.10 Using Perfmon to Monitor AD

Problem

You want to use Perfmon to monitor the performance of Active Directory.

Solution

Using a graphical user interface

1. Open the Performance Monitor.
2. Click on System Monitor in the left pane.
3. Type Ctrl + I. This will bring up the page to add counters.
4. Under Select counters from computer, enter the name of the domain controller you want to target.
5. Select the NTDS performance object.

6. Select the counters you want to monitor.

7. After you done with your selections, click Close.

Discussion

There are several Perfmon counters that can be very valuable for monitoring and troubleshooting Active Directory. The NTDS performance object has counters for address book lookups, inbound and outbound replication, LDAP reads, writes and searches, Kerberos authentication, and the Security Account Manager (SAM).

Here is a list of some of the most useful NTDS counters. I've also included their Perfmon explanation, which you can view by clicking on the Explain button in the Add Counters dialog box.

DRA Inbound Bytes Total/sec
> Shows the total number of bytes replicated in. It is the sum of the number of uncompressed bytes (never compressed) and the number of compressed bytes (after compression).

DRA Inbound Objects/sec
> Shows the number of objects received from neighbors through inbound replication. A neighbor is a domain controller from which the local domain controller replicates locally.

DRA Inbound Values Total/sec
> Shows the total number of object property values received from inbound replication partners. Each inbound object has one or more properties, and each property has zero or more values. Zero values indicates property removal.

DRA Outbound Bytes Total/sec
> Shows the total number of bytes replicated out. It is the sum of the number of uncompressed bytes (never compressed) and the number of compressed bytes (after compression).

DRA Outbound Objects/sec
> Shows the number of objects replicated out.

DRA Outbound Values Total/sec
> Shows the number of object property values sent to outbound replication partners.

DRA Pending Replication Synchronizations
> Shows the number of directory synchronizations that are queued for this server, but not yet processed.

DS Client Binds/sec
> Shows the number of Ntdsapi.dll binds per second serviced by this DC.

DS Directory Reads/sec
> Shows the number of directory reads per second.

DS Directory Searches/sec
> Shows the number of directory searches per second.

DS Directory Writes/sec
> Shows the number of directory writes per second.

KDC AS Requests
> Shows the number of Authentication Server (AS) requests serviced by the Kerberos Key Distribution Center (KDC) per second. AS requests are used by client to obtain a ticket-granting ticket.

KDC TGS Requests
> Shows the number of Ticket Granting Server (TGS) requests serviced by the KDC per second. TGS requests are used by the client to obtain a ticket to a resource.

Kerberos Authentications
> Shows the number of times per second that clients use a ticket to this DC to authenticate to this DC.

LDAP Bind Time
> Shows the time, in milliseconds, taken for the last successful LDAP bind.

LDAP Client Sessions
> Shows the number of currently connected LDAP client sessions.

LDAP Searches
> Shows the percentage of directory searches coming from LDAP.

LDAP Searches/sec
> Shows the rate at which LDAP clients perform search operations.

LDAP Successful Binds
> Shows the percentage of LDAP bind attempts that are successful.

LDAP Successful Binds/sec
> Shows the number of LDAP binds per second.

LDAP Writes
> Shows the percentage of directory writes coming from LDAP.

LDAP Writes/sec
> Shows the rate at which LDAP clients perform write operations.

15.11 Using Perfmon Trace Logs to Monitor AD

Problem

You want to enable Perfmon Trace Logs to view system level calls related to Active Directory.

Solution

1. Open the Performance Monitor.
2. In the left pane, expand Performance Logs and Alerts.
3. Right-click on Trace Logs and select New Log Settings.
4. Enter a name for the log and click OK.
5. Click the Add button.
6. Highlight one or more of the Active Directory providers and click OK.
7. Use the tabs to configure additional settings about the log.
8. When you are done, click OK.
9. Unless you've scheduled it to run at a different time, the trace log you created should show up in the right pane next to a green icon, which indicates it is running.
10. To stop the Trace Log, right-click on it in the right pane and select Stop.
11. Now open up a command shell (cmd.exe).
12. Use cd to change into the directory where the trace log files are stored (*c:\perflogs* by default).
13. Run the following command:

    > tracerpt <LogFileName>

This command is available by default with Windows Server 2003. On Windows 2000, you'll need to use the Resource Kit utility called tracedmp.exe.

The tracerpt command generates a *summary.txt* file that summarizes all of the events by total. A second file called *dumpfile.csv* is created that can be imported into Excel or viewed with a text viewer to show the details of each event.

Discussion

Trace Logs capture detailed system and application level events. Applications support Trace Log capability by developing a Trace Log Provider. Active Directory supports several providers that log low-level system calls related to Kerberos, LDAP, and DNS, to name a few. This can be an extremely valuable tool for debugging and even figuring out the inner-workings of Active Directory. Trace Logs can be resource intensive, so you should enable them with care.

Here is an example of what the *summary.txt* file looks like on a domain controller that had all of the Active Directory–related Trace Log Providers enabled:

```
Files Processed:
    AD_000001.etl
Total Buffers Processed 5
Total Events  Processed 193
Total Events  Lost      0
```

```
Start Time              Friday, May 23, 2003
End Time                Friday, May 23, 2003
Elapsed Time            24 sec
+-----------------------------------------------------------------------+
|Event Count Event Name          Event Type  Guid                       |
+-----------------------------------------------------------------------+
|   1        EventTrace                Header      {68fdd900-4a3e-11d1-84f4-0000f80464e3}|
|  69        SamNameById              Start       {25059476-899f-11d2-819e-0000f875a064}|
|  69        SamNameById              End         {25059476-899f-11d2-819e-0000f875a064}|
|   2        KerbInitSecurityContext End         {52e82f1a-7cd4-47ed-b5e5-fde7bf64cea6}|
|   2        KerbInitSecurityContext Start       {52e82f1a-7cd4-47ed-b5e5-fde7bf64cea6}|
|   1        KerbAcceptSecurityContext Start     {94acefe3-9e56-49e3-9895-7240a231c371}|
|   1        KerbAcceptSecurityContext End       {94acefe3-9e56-49e3-9895-7240a231c371}|
|   1        SamGetAliasMem           Start       {1cf5fd19-1ac1-4324-84f7-970a634a91ee}|
|   1        SamGetAliasMem           End         {1cf5fd19-1ac1-4324-84f7-970a634a91ee}|
|  14        LdapRequest              End         {b9d4702a-6a98-11d2-b710-00c04fb998a2}|
|  14        LdapRequest              Start       {b9d4702a-6a98-11d2-b710-00c04fb998a2}|
|   1        DsLdapBind               Start       {05acd009-daeb-11d1-be80-00c04fadfff5}|
|   1        DsLdapBind               End         {05acd009-daeb-11d1-be80-00c04fadfff5}|
|   8        DsDirSearch              End         {05acd000-daeb-11d1-be80-00c04fadfff5}|
|   8        DsDirSearch              Start       {05acd000-daeb-11d1-be80-00c04fadfff5}|
+-----------------------------------------------------------------------+
```

Here you can see that over a 24-second period there was 1 LDAP bind request (DsLdapBind), 8 directory searches (DsDirSearch), and 14 total LDAP requests (LdapRequest).

The *dumpfile.csv* contains entries for every event that was generated during the time period. Here is an example of an entry for one of the DsDirSearch requests (note that the lines will wrap due to their length so I've added a blank line in between for separation):

```
DsDirSearch, Start, 0x000003F4, 126982224636242128, 61350, 440530, "DS", 3, 3,
1141178432, 2694848000, "192.168.5.26", "deep", "OU=Sales,DC=rallencorp,DC=com", "0,
0

DsDirSearch, End, 0x000003F4, 126982224636342271, 61350, 440540, "DS", 3, 5,
1157955648, 2694848000, "0", "
(&(objectCategory=CN=Person,CN=Schema,CN=Configuration,DC=rallencorp,DC=com)
(objectClass=user)) 0, 0
```

Based on just those two lines (disregarding most of the numeric values), we can deduce that a user on the host with IP address 192.168.5.26 performed an LDAP query for user objects in the Sales OU. Pretty neat, huh?

See Also

MS KB 302552 (HOW TO: Create and Configure Performance Monitor Trace Logs in Windows 2000)

15.12 Enabling Auditing of Directory Access

Problem

You want to enable auditing of directory access and modifications. Audit events are logged to the Security event log.

Solution

Using a graphical user interface

1. Open the Domain Controller Security Policy snap-in.
2. In the left pane, expand Local Policies and click on Audit Policy
3. In the right pane, double-click Audit directory service access.
4. Make sure the box is checked beside Define these policy settings.
5. Check the box beside Success and/or Failure.
6. Click OK.

Using a command-line interface

```
> auditpol \\<DomainControlerName> /enable /directory:all
```

Discussion

You can log events to the Security event log for every successful and/or failed attempt to access or modify the directory, which is referred to as auditing. Auditing is enabled via the Domain Controller Security GPO with the Audit directory service access setting. Once this is enabled, you need to use the ACL Editor to define auditing in the SACL of the objects and containers you want to monitor.

By default, the domain object has an inherited audit entry for the Everyone security principal for all object access and modifications. That means once you enable auditing in the Domain Controller Security Policy and it replicates out, domain controllers will log events for any directory access or modification to any part of the directory. As you can imagine, auditing every access to Active Directory can generate a lot of events, so you'll either want to disable the Everyone auditing and apply more specific auditing, or keep a close eye on your domain controllers to ensure they are not adversely affected while auditing is enabled.

Here is an example event that was logged after the Administrator account created a contact object called foobar in the Sales OU:

```
Event Type:Success Audit
Event Source:Security
Event Category:Directory Service Access
Event ID:566
```

```
Date:     5/26/2003
Time:     7:24:10 PM
User:     RALLENCORP\administrator
Computer:DC1
Description:
Object Operation:
    Object Server:DS
    Operation Type:Object Access
    Object Type:organizationalUnit
    Object Name:OU=Sales,DC=rallencorp,DC=com
    Handle ID:-
    Primary User Name:DC1$
    Primary Domain:RALLENCORP
    Primary Logon ID:(0x0,0x3E7)
    Client User Name:administrator
    Client Domain:RALLENCORP
    Client Logon ID:(0x0,0x3B4BE)
    Accesses:Create Child

    Properties:
    Create Child
    contact

    Additional Info:CN=foobar,OU=Sales,DC=rallencorp,DC=com
    Additional Info2:CN=foobar,OU=Sales,DC=rallencorp,DC=com
    Access Mask:0x1
```

It can also be useful to enable Audit Account Management in the Domain Controller Security GPO. This provides additional information about account management operations, for example, finding what account deleted a certain object.

See Also

MS KB 232714 (HOW TO: How to Enable Auditing of Directory Service Access), MS KB 314955 (HOW TO: Audit Active Directory Objects in Windows 2000), MS KB 314977 (HOW TO: Enable Active Directory Access Auditing in Windows 2000), and MS KB 814595 (HOW TO: Audit Active Directory Objects in Windows Server 2003)

15.13 Creating a Quota

This recipe requires a Windows Server 2003 domain controller.

Problem

You want to limit the number of objects a security principal can create in a partition by creating a quota.

Solution

Using a command-line interface

```
> dsadd quota -part <PartitionDN> -qlimit <QuotaLimit> -acct <PrincipalName>↵
  [-rdn <QuotaName>]
```

The following command creates a quota specification that allows the RALLENCORP\
rallen user to create only 5 objects in the *dc=rallencorp,dc=com* partition:

```
> dsadd quota -part dc=rallencorp,dc=com -qlimit 5 -acct RALLENCORP\rallen
```

Discussion

Quotas are a new feature in Windows Server 2003 that allow an administrator to limit the number of objects that a user (or group of users) can create. This is similar in nature to the quota for creating computer objects found in Windows 2000 (see Recipe 8.9 for more details), except the quotas in Windows Server 2003 apply to the creation of all object types.

There are three things that need to be set when creating a quota specification, including:

Partition

> Currently, quotas can apply only to an entire partition. You cannot create a quota that pertains only to a subtree in a partition. You can create quotas for any partition, including application partitions, except for the schema-naming context. The reasoning behind this restriction is that the schema is a highly protected area of the directory and you shouldn't need to restrict how many objects get created there.

Target security principal

> A quota can be defined for any type of security principal. The msDS-QuotaTrustee attribute on the quota object stores the target principal in the form of a SID.

Limit

> This determines how many objects the target security principal can create.

The quota limit is a combination of the new objects that a user creates plus any tombstone objects that are created by that user. If a user creates an object and then deletes another object, that would count as 2 toward any quotas that apply to the user. This is because when an object is deleted, a tombstone object is created in its place, which counts as another object creation. If a user creates an object and later deletes the same object, this would count as only 1 object against their quota. After the tombstone object is removed from Active Directory (60 days by default), the user's quota would be decremented. By default, a tombstone object counts as 1 object, but that is configurable. See Recipe 15.15 for more on changing the tombstone quota factor.

Since quotas can be assigned to users, groups, or computers, it is conceivable that multiple quotas may apply to a user. In this case, the quota with the highest limit will be in force for the user. You can also create a default quota for a partition that applies to all security principals. See Recipe 15.16 for more information on configuring the default quota.

 Quotas do not apply to members of the Enterprise Admins and Domain Admins groups. Even if you've configured a default quota for all users, members of those administrative groups will not have any restrictions.

See Also

Recipe 8.9 for more on the computer object quota, Recipe 15.0 for more on the attributes of quota objects, Recipe 15.14 for finding the quotas assigned to a security principal, Recipe 15.15 for changing the tombstone quota factor, and Recipe 15.16 for setting a default quota

15.14 Finding the Quotas Assigned to a Security Principal

 This recipe requires a Windows Server 2003 domain controller.

Problem

You want to find the quotas that have been configured for a security principal (i.e., user, group, or computer).

Solution

Using a command-line interface

```
> dsquery quota -part <PartitionDN> -acct <PrincipalName>
```

The following command searches for quotas that have been assigned to the RALLENCORP\rallen user in the *dc=rallencorp,dc=com* partition:

```
> dsquery quota -part dc=rallencorp,dc=com -acct RALLENCORP\rallen
```

Discussion

The dsquery solution will find only quotas that have been directly assigned to a security principal. The msDS-QuotaTrustee attribute on quota objects defines a SID that the quota applies to. The dsquery quota command will look up the SID for the specified account and match that against quota objects that reference that SID. Unfortunately, this doesn't quite show the whole picture. A user could have a quota assigned directly, which the dsquery command would show, but the user could also be part of one or more groups that have quotas assigned. These won't show up using dsquery.

A more robust solution would entail retrieving the tokenGroups attribute of the user, which contains a list of SIDs for all expanded group memberships, and then querying each of those groups to determine whether any of them have quotas assigned. This is actually the type of algorithm that is used to determine a user's effective quota, as shown in Recipe 15.17.

See Also

Recipe 15.13 for creating a quota

15.15 Changing How Tombstone Objects Count Against Quota Usage

 This recipe requires a Windows Server 2003 domain controller.

Problem

You want to change the relative weight of tombstone objects in quota calculations.

Solution

Using a graphical user interface

1. Open ADSI Edit.
2. Connect to the partition on which you want to modify this setting (has to be done on a per partition basis).
3. In the left pane, expand the root of the partition.
4. Right-click on cn=NTDS Quotas and select Properties.
5. Set the msDS-TombstoneQuotaFactor attribute to a value between 0 and 100.
6. Click OK.

Using a command-line interface

Create an LDIF file called *change_tombstone_quota.ldf* with the following contents:

```
dn: cn=NTDS Quotas,<PartitionDN>
changetype: modify
replace: msDs-TombstoneQuotaFactor
msDs-TombstoneQuotaFactor: <0-100>
-
```

then run the following command:

```
> ldifde -v -i -f change_tombstone_quota.ldf
```

Using VBScript

```
' This code modifies the tombstone quota factor for the specified partition
' ------ SCRIPT CONFIGURATION ------
strPartitionDN = "<PartitionDN>"  ' e.g. dc=rallencorp,dc=com
intTombstoneFactor = <0-100>      ' e.g. 50
' ------ END CONFIGURATION ---------

set objPart = GetObject("LDAP://cn=NTDS Quotas," & strPartitionDN )
objPart.Put "msDs-TombstoneQuotaFactor", intTombstoneLifetime
objPart.SetInfo
WScript.Echo "Set the tombstone quota factor for " & _
             strPartitionDN & " to " & intTombstoneFactor
```

Discussion

The tombstone quota factor is a percentage that determines how much each tombstone object counts against a security principal's quota usage. By default, tombstone objects count as one object. This means if a user's quota is set to 10, and the user deletes 10 objects, that user will not be able to create or delete any other objects until those tombstone objects have been purged from Active Directory.

The msDs-TombstoneQuotaFactor attribute on the NTDS Quota container for each partition defines the tombstone quota factor. As mentioned previously, the default is that tombstone objects count 100% of a normal object, and thus, the msDs-TombstoneQuotaFactor attribute contains 100 by default. If you modify that attribute to contain 50, and a user has a quota limit of 10, then that user could delete 20 objects (i.e., create 20 tombstone objects) because 20 × 50% = 10. You may not care about how many objects your users delete; in which case, you'd want to set the tombstone quota factor to 0.

15.16 Setting the Default Quota for All Security Principals in a Partition

 This recipe requires a Windows Server 2003 domain controller.

Problem

You want to set a default quota for all security principals.

Solution

Using a graphical user interface

1. Open ADSI Edit.
2. Connect to the partition you want to modify (has to be done on a per partition basis).
3. In the left pane, expand the root of the partition.
4. Right-click on cn=NTDS Quotas and select Properties.
5. Set the msDS-DefaultQuota attribute to the number objects that security principals should be allowed to create if they are not assigned another quota.
6. Click OK.

Using a command-line interface

Create an LDIF file called *set_default_quota.ldf* with the following contents:

```
dn: cn=NTDS Quotas,<PartitionDN>
changetype: modify
replace: msDs-DefaultQuota
msDs-DefaultQuota: <NumberOfObjects>
-
```

then run the following command:

```
> ldifde -v -i -f set_default_quota.ldf
```

Using VBScript

```
' This code sets the default quota for the specified partition
' ------ SCRIPT CONFIGURATION ------
strPartitionDN = "<PartitionDN>"        ' e.g. dc=rallencorp,dc=com
intDefaultQuota = <NumberOfObjects>     ' e.g. 10
' ------ END CONFIGURATION ---------
```

```
set objPart = GetObject("LDAP://cn=NTDS Quotas," & strPartitionDN )
objPart.Put "msDs-DefaultQuota", intDefaultQuota
objPart.SetInfo
WScript.Echo "Set the default quota for " & _
             strPartitionDN & " to " & intDefaultQuota
```

Discussion

The easiest way to apply a default quota to all of your users is to modify the msDS-DefaultQuota attribute on the NTDS Quotas container for the target partition. This attribute contains the default quota limit that is used if no other quotas have been assigned to a security principal.

You should be careful when setting the default quota because it applies to every non-administrator security principal. If you set the default to 0, for example, computers would not be able to dynamically update their DNS records in an AD–integrated zone because that creates an object. This may not be applicable in your environment, but the point is that you need to consider the impact of the default quota and test it thoroughly before implementing it.

15.17 Finding the Quota Usage for a Security Principal

 This recipe requires a Windows Server 2003 domain controller.

Problem

You want to find the quota usage for a certain security principal.

Solution

The quota usage of a security principal can be determined a few different ways. First, you can use the dsget command. Here is an example:

```
> dsget user "<UserDN>" -part <PartitionDN> -qlimit -qused
```

This displays the effective quota limit and how much quota has been used for a particular user. You can use similar parameters with dsget computer and dsget group to find the quota usage for those types of objects.

Users can find their own quota usage by querying the msDs-QuotaUsed and msDs-QuotaEffective attributes on the cn=NTDS Quotas container for a partition. These two attributes are constructed, which means they are dynamically calculated based on the user that is accessing them (see Recipe 10.15 for more on constructed attributes). The msDs-QuotaUsed attribute returns how much of the quota has been used by the user and the msDs-QuotaEffective attribute contains the quota limit.

Alternatively, view the msDs-TopQuotaUsage attribute on a partition's cn=NTDS Quotas container, which contains the user's with the top quota usage. This attribute is multi-valued, with each value being XML-like text that contains the SID and how much of the quota the principal has used. See the Discussion section for an example.

Discussion

If you implement quotas, you'll certainly need to tell users what their quotas are (or provide instructions on how they can find out for themselves). Currently, there are a few ways to determine quota usage as outlined in the Solution section.

Perhaps the most interesting is obtaining the top-quota usage. Each value of the msDs-TopQuotaUsage attribute contains an entry that details someone that has high-quota usage (at the time of publication of this book, it was unknown exactly what "high" constituted). Each value of the msDs-TopQuotaUsage attribute contains blocks of data formatted in XML-like language. Each block has the SID of the security principal (<ownerSID>), quota used (<quotaUsed>), number of tombstone objects created (<tombstonedCount>) and the number of objects that are still active (<liveCount>) (i.e., not tombstoned). Here is an example of what the attribute can contain:

```
>> Dn: CN=NTDS Quotas,DC=rallencorp,DC=com
    3> msDS-TopQuotaUsage:
<MS_DS_TOP_QUOTA_USAGE>
    <partitionDN> DC=rallencorp,DC=com </partitionDN>
    <ownerSID> S-1-5-21-1422208173-2062366415-1864960452-512 </ownerSID>
    <quotaUsed> 152 </quotaUsed>
    <tombstonedCount> 2 </tombstonedCount>
    <liveCount> 150 </liveCount>
</MS_DS_TOP_QUOTA_USAGE>
;
<MS_DS_TOP_QUOTA_USAGE>
    <partitionDN> DC=rallencorp,DC=com </partitionDN>
    <ownerSID> S-1-5-18 </ownerSID>
    <quotaUsed> 43 </quotaUsed>
    <tombstonedCount> 32 </tombstonedCount>
    <liveCount> 11 </liveCount>
</MS_DS_TOP_QUOTA_USAGE>
;
<MS_DS_TOP_QUOTA_USAGE>
    <partitionDN> DC=rallencorp,DC=com </partitionDN>
    <ownerSID> S-1-5-32-544 </ownerSID>
```

```
        <quotaUsed> 14 </quotaUsed>
        <tombstonedCount> 0 </tombstonedCount>
        <liveCount> 14 </liveCount>
</MS_DS_TOP_QUOTA_USAGE>
```

See Also

Recipe 15.14 for more on finding the quotas assigned to a security principal

## CHAPTER 16

Backup, Recovery, DIT Maintenance, and Deleted Objects

16.0 Introduction

The AD Directory Information Tree (DIT) is implemented as a transactional database using the Extensible Storage Engine (ESE). The primary database file is named *ntds.dit* and by default is stored in *%SystemRoot%\NTDS*, but can be relocated during the initial promotion process or manually via the `ntdsutil` command (see Recipe 16.8 for more details).

Each database write transaction is initially stored in a log file called *edb.log*, which is stored in the same directory as *ntds.dit*. That log file can grow to 10 MB in size after which additional log files are created (e.g., *edb00001.log*), each growing to up to 10 MB. After the transactions in the log files are committed to the database, the files are rotated. These log files are useful when a domain controller is shut down unexpectedly. When the DC comes back online, Active Directory can replay the log files and apply any transactions that may have not previously been written to disk. The *edb.chk* file stores the last committed transaction, which can be used to determine the transactions in the log files that have yet to be committed. Two 10 MB placeholder files called *res1.log* and *res2.log* are used if the disk runs out of space and Active Directory needs to commit changes.

In order to recover portions of Active Directory, or the entire directory itself, you need to have a solid backup strategy in place. You can back up Active Directory while it is online, which means you do not need to worry about having regular downtime just to do backups. Restoring Active Directory is also easy. To do any type of restore, you have to boot into offline mode, more commonly referred to as Directory Services (DS) Restore Mode, where the Active Directory database is not active. You can then restore a single object, an entire subtree, or the complete database if necessary. For a detailed discussion on backing up and restoring Active Directory, see Chapter 13 in *Active Directory*, Second Edition (O'Reilly).

You need to be familiar with how deleted objects are treated in Active Directory, which can affect your backup procedures. When an object is deleted, the original object is removed, but a tombstone object is created in its place that contains a small subset of the original object's attributes. These objects are stored in the cn=Deleted Objects container in the naming context the original object was located in.

The deleted object is named using the following format: *<OrigName>*\0ADEL: *<ObjectGUID>*, where *<OrigName>* was the original RDN of the object, *<ObjectGUID>* is the GUID of the original object, and \0 is a null-terminated character. For example, if I deleted the jsmith user object, its tombstone object would have a distinguished name, such as the following:

```
CN=jsmith\0ADEL:fce1ca8e-a5ec-4a29-96e1-c8013e533d2c,CN=Deleted↵
Objects,DC=rallencorp,DC=com
```

After a period of time known as the tombstone lifetime (60 days is the default), the tombstone object is finally removed from Active Directory. At that point, no remnants of the former object exist in Active Directory.

Tombstone objects are important to understand in regard to your backup strategy because you should not keep backups longer than the tombstone lifetime. If you attempt to restore a backup that is older than the tombstone lifetime, it may introduce objects that were deleted, but the tombstone object no longer exists. Under normal conditions, if you do a nonauthoritative restore from backup, objects that were valid when the backup was taken, but were deleted afterward will not be re-added. A check is done before injecting new objects via the nonauthoritative restore to determine if a tombstone object exists for it. If a tombstone object exists for it, Active Directory knows the object was deleted after the backup. If the tombstone object has already expired (e.g., the backup is older than 60 days), Active Directory has no way to determine if the object was previously deleted and will happily re-add it. Reinjected deleted objects are referred to as lingering or zombie objects.

The tombstone lifetime value is stored in the tombStoneLifetime attribute on the following object: cn=Directory Service,cn=Windows NT, cn=Services, cn=Configuration, *<ForestRootDN>*.

The Anatomy of a Deleted Object

Deleted objects are stored in the Deleted Objects container of a naming context. You cannot browse that container by default. You need to enable an LDAP control, as explained in Recipe 16.16, to view deleted objects. Table 16-1 contains some of the attributes that are stored with deleted objects.

 The attributes that are preserved in tombstone objects are determined by attributeSchema objects that have the 01000 bit enabled (8 in decimal) in the searchFlags attribute.

Table 16-1. Useful attributes of deleted objects

Attribute	Description
isDeleted	The value for this attribute is TRUE for deleted objects.
lastKnownParent	Distinguished name of container the object was contained in. This is new in Windows Server 2003.
name	RDN of the object original object.
userAccountControl	This attribute is copied from the original object after it is deleted. This only applies to user and computer objects.
objectSID	This attribute is copied from the original object after it is deleted. This only applies to user and computer objects.
sAMAccountName	This attribute is copied from the original object after it is deleted. This only applies to user and computer objects.

16.1 Backing Up Active Directory

Problem

You want to back up Active Directory to tape or disk.

Solution

Back up the System State, which includes the Active Directory–related files on the domain controller. Here are the directions for backing up the System State using the NtBackup utility that comes installed on Windows 2000 and Windows Server 2003 computers:

Using a graphical user interface

1. Go to Start → All Programs (or Programs for Windows 2000) → Accessories → System Tools → Backup.

2. Click the Advanced Mode link.

3. Click the Backup tab.

4. Check the box beside System State.

5. Check the box beside any other files, directories, or drives you would also like to back up.

6. For Backup destination, select either File or Tape depending on where you want to back up the data to.

7. For Backup media or file name, type either the name of a file or select the tape to save the backup to.

8. Click the Start Backup button twice.

Using a command-line interface

The NtBackup utility supports several command-line parameters that you can use to initiate backups without ever bringing up the GUI.

For the complete list of supported commands on Windows 2000, see MS KB 300439 (How to Use Command Line Parameters With the "Ntbackup" Command).

For the complete list of supported commands on Windows Server 2003, see MS KB 814583 (HOW TO: Use Command Line Parameters with the Ntbackup Command in Windows Server 2003).

Discussion

Fortunately, domain controllers can be backed up while online. Having the ability to do live backups makes the process very easy. And since Active Directory is included as part of the System State on domain controllers, you are required to back up only the System State, although you can back up other folders and drives as necessary. On a domain controller, the System State includes the following:

- Boot files
- Registry
- COM+ class registration database
- Active Directory files
- System Volume (SYSVOL)
- Certificates database (if running Certificate Server)

See Also

Recipe 16.18 for modifying the tombstone lifetime, MS KB 216993 (Backup of the Active Directory Has 60-Day Useful Life), MS KB 240363 (HOW TO: Use the Backup Program to Back Up and Restore the System State in Windows 2000), MS KB 300439 (How to Use Command Line Parameters With the "Ntbackup" Command), MS KB 326216 (HOW TO: Use the Backup Feature to Back Up and Restore Data in Windows Server 2003), and MS KB 814583 (HOW TO: Use Command Line Parameters with the Ntbackup Command in Windows Server 2003)

16.2 Restarting a Domain Controller in Directory Services Restore Mode

Problem

You want to restart a domain controller in DS Restore Mode.

Solution

To enter DS Restore Mode, you must reboot the server at the console. Press F8 after the power-on self test (POST), which will bring up a menu, as shown in Figure 16-1. From the menu, select Directory Services Restore Mode.

```
Windows Advanced Options Menu
Please select an option:

    Safe Mode
    Safe Mode with Networking
    Safe Mode with Command Prompt

    Enable Boot Logging
    Enable VGA Mode
    Last Known Good Configuration (your most recent settings that worked)
    Directory Services Restore Mode (Windows domain controllers only)
    Debugging Mode

    Start Windows Normally
    Reboot
    Return to OS Choices Menu

Use the up and down arrow keys to move the highlight to your choice.
```

Figure 16-1. Boot options

Discussion

The Active Directory database is live and locked by the system when a domain controller is booted into normal mode. If you want to perform integrity checks, manipulate the Active Directory database in some way or restore part of the database, you have to reboot into DS Restore Mode. In this mode, Active Directory does not start up and the database files *(ntds.dit)* are not locked.

It is not always practical to be logged into the console of the server when you need to reboot it into DS Restore Mode. You can work around this by modifying the *boot.ini* file for the server to automatically boot into DS Restore Mode after reboot. You can then use Terminal Services to log on to the machine remotely while it is in that mode. See MS KB 256588 for more information on how to enable this capability. Be careful if you try to access DS Restore Mode via Terminal Services. Unless you have configured everything properly, you may end up with the domain controller booted into DS Restore Mode and not be able to access it via Terminal Services.

See Also

MS KB 256588 (Using Terminal Services for Remote Administration of Windows 2000 DCs in Directory Service Restore Mode)

16.3 Resetting the Directory Service Restore Mode Administrator Password

Problem

You want to reset the DS Restore Mode administrator password. This password is set individually (i.e., not replicated) on each domain controller, and is initially configured when you promote the domain controller into a domain.

Solution

Using a graphical user interface

1. For this to work you must be booted into DS Restore Mode (see Recipe 16.2 for more information).

2. Go to Start → Run.

3. Type compmgmt.msc and press Enter.

4. In the left pane, expand System Tools → Local Users and Computers.

5. Click on the Users folder.

6. In the right pane, right-click on the Administrator user and select Set Password.

7. Enter the new password and confirm, then click OK.

Using a command-line interface

With the Windows Server 2003 version of ntdsutil, you can change the DS Restore Mode administrator password of a domain controller while it is live (i.e., not in DS Restore Mode). Another benefit of this new option is that you can run it against a remote domain controller. Here is the sample output when run against domain controller DC1.

```
> ntdsutil "set dsrm password" "reset password on server DC1"
ntdsutil: set dsrm password
Reset DSRM Administrator Password: reset password on server DC1
Please type password for DS Restore Mode Administrator Account: **********
Please confirm new password: **********
Password has been set successfully.
```

Microsoft added a new command in Windows 2000 Service Pack 2 and later called setpwd. It works similarly to the Windows Server 2003 version of ntdsutil by allowing you to reset the DS Restore Mode password while a domain controller is live. It can also be used remotely.

Discussion

You may be thinking that having a separate DS Restore Mode administrator password can be quite a pain. Yet another thing you have to maintain and update on a regular basis, right? But if you think about it, you'll see that it is quite necessary.

Generally, you boot a domain controller into DS Restore Mode when you need to perform some type of maintenance on the Active Directory database. To do this, the database needs to be offline. If the database is offline, then there is no way to authenticate against it. The system has to use another user repository, so it reverts back to the legacy SAM database. The DS Restore Mode administrator account and password are stored in the SAM database just like with standalone Windows clients.

See Also

Recipe 16.2 for booting into Directory Services Restore Mode, MS KB 239803 (How to Change the Recovery Console Administrator Password on a Domain Controller), and MS KB 322672 (HOW TO: Reset the Directory Services Restore Mode Administrator Account Password in Windows Server 2003)

16.4   Performing a Nonauthoritative Restore

Problem

You want to perform a nonauthoritative restore of a domain controller. This can be useful if you want to quickly restore a domain controller that failed due to a hardware problem.

Solution

Using a graphical user interface

1. You must first reboot into Directory Services Restore Mode (see Recipe 16.2 for more information).
2. Open the NT Backup utility; go to Start → All Programs (or Programs for Windows 2000) → Accessories → System Tools → Backup.
3. Click the Advanced Mode link.
4. Under the Welcome tab, click the Restore Wizard button and click Next.
5. Check the box beside System State and any other drives you want to restore and click Next.
6. Click the Advanced button.
7. Select Original location for Restore files to.
8. For the How to Restore option, select Replace existing files and click Next.

9. For the Advanced Restore Options, be sure that the following are checked: Restore Security Settings, Restore junction points, and Preserve existing mount volume points. Then click Next.

10. Click Finish.

11. Restart the computer.

Discussion

If you encounter a failed domain controller that you cannot bring back up (e.g., multiple hard disks fail), you have two options for restoring it. One option is to remove the domain controller completely from Active Directory (as outlined in Recipe 3.6) and then repromote it back in. This is known as the restore from replication method, because you are essentially bringing up a brand new domain controller and letting replication restore all the data on the server. On Windows Server 2003 domain controllers, you can also use the Install From Media option described in Recipe 3.2 to expedite this process.

The other option is described in the Solution section. You can restore the domain controller from a good backup. This method involves getting into DS Restore Mode, restoring the system state and any necessary system drive(s) and then rebooting. As long as the domain controller comes up clean, it should start participating in Active Directory replication once again and sync any changes that have occurred since the backup was taken.

For a detailed discussion of the advantages and disadvantages of each option, see Chapter 13 in *Active Directory*, Second Edition (O'Reilly).

See Also

Recipe 16.2 for getting into Directory Services Restore Mode and MS KB 240363 (HOW TO: Use the Backup Program to Back Up and Restore the System State in Windows 2000)

16.5   Performing an Authoritative Restore of an Object or Subtree

Problem

You want to perform an authoritative restore of one or more objects, but not the entire Active Directory database.

Solution

Follow the same steps as Recipe 16.4, except after the restore has completed, do not restart the computer.

To restore a single object, run the following:

```
> ntdsutil "auth restore" "restore object cn=jsmith,ou=Sales,dc=rallencorp,dc=com" q
```

To restore an entire subtree, run the following:

```
> ntdsutil "auth restore" "restore subtree ou=Sales,dc=rallencorp,dc=com" q
```

Restart the computer.

There are some issues related to restoring user, group, computer, and trust objects that you should be aware of. See MS KB 216243 and MS KB 280079 for more information.

Discussion

If an administrator or user accidentally deletes an important object or entire subtree from Active Directory, you can restore it. Fortunately, the process isn't very painful. The key is having a good backup that contains the objects you want to restore. If you don't have a backup with the objects in it, you are out of luck. Well, that is not completely true with Windows Server 2003. See Recipe 16.17 for another option to restore deleted objects.

To restore one or more objects, you need to follow the same steps as performing a nonauthoritative restore. The only difference is that after you do the restore, you need to use the ntdsutil command to mark the objects in question as authoritative on the restored domain controller. After you reboot the domain controller, it will replicate any changed objects since the backup that was restored on the machine, except for the objects or subtree that were marked as authoritative. For those objects, Active Directory increments the USN in such a way that they will become authoritative and replicate out to the other domain controllers.

You can also use ntdsutil without first doing a restore in situations where an object has been deleted accidentally, but the change has not yet replicated to all domain controllers. The trick here is that you need to find a domain controller that has not had the deletion replicated yet and either stop it from replicating or make the object authoritative before it receives the replication update.

See Also

Recipe 16.2 for booting into Directory Services Restore Mode, Recipe 16.17 for restoring a deleted object, MS KB 216243 (Authoritative Restore of Active Directory and Impact on Trusts and Computer Accounts), and MS KB 280079 (Authoritative

Restore of Groups Can Result in Inconsistent Membership Information Across Domain Controllers)

16.6 Performing a Complete Authoritative Restore

Problem

You want to perform a complete authoritative restore of the Active Directory database because something very bad has happened.

Solution

Follow the same steps as Recipe 16.4, except after the restore has completed, do not restart the computer.

Run the following command to restore the entire database:

```
> ntdsutil "auth restore" "restore database" q
```

Restart the computer.

Discussion

In a production environment, you should never have to perform a complete authoritative restore. It is a drastic measure and you will inevitably lose data as a result. Before you even attempt such a restore, you may want to contact Microsoft Support to make sure all options have been exhausted. That said, you should test the authoritative restore process in a lab environment, and make sure you have the steps properly documented in case you ever do need to use it.

See Also

Recipe 16.2 for getting into Directory Services Restore Mode, MB KB 216243 (Authoritative Restore of Active Directory and Impact on Trusts and Computer Accounts), MS KB 241594 (HOW TO: Perform an Authoritative Restore to a Domain Controller in Windows 2000), and MS KB 280079 (Authoritative Restore of Groups Can Result in Inconsistent Membership Information Across Domain Controllers)

16.7 Checking the DIT File's Integrity

Problem

You want to check the integrity and semantics of the DIT file to verify there is no corruption or bad entries.

Solution

Using a command-line interface

First, reboot into Directory Services Restore Mode. Then run the following commands:

```
> ntdsutil files integrity q q
> ntdsutil "semantic database analysis" "verbose on" go
```

Discussion

The Active Directory DIT file (*ntds.dit*) is implemented as a transactional database. Microsoft uses the ESE database (formerly called Jet) for Active Directory, which has been used for years in other products, such as Microsoft Exchange.

Since the Active Directory DIT ultimately is a database, it can suffer from many of the same issues that traditional databases do. The ntdsutil integrity command checks for any low-level database corruption and ensures that the database headers are correct and the tables are in a consistent state. It reads every byte of the database and can take quite a while to complete depending on how large your DIT file is. The time it takes is also greatly dependent on your hardware, but some early estimates from Microsoft for Windows 2000 put the rate at 2 GB an hour.

Whereas the ntdsutil integrity command verifies the overall structure and health of the database, the ntdsutil semantics command looks at the contents of the database. It will verify, among other things, reference counts, replication metadata, and security descriptors. If any errors are reported back, you can run go fixup to attempt to correct them. You should have a recent backup handy before doing this because in the worst case the corruption cannot be fixed or may become worse after the go fixup command completes.

See Also

Recipe 16.2 for booting into Directory Services Restore Mode and MS KB 315136 (HOW TO: Complete a Semantic Database Analysis for the Active Directory Database by Using Ntdsutil.exe)

16.8 Moving the DIT Files

Problem

You want to move the Active Directory DIT files to a new drive to improve performance or capacity.

Solution

Using a command-line interface

First, reboot into DS Restore Mode. Then, run the following commands, in which `<DriveAndFolder>` is the new location where you want to move the files (e.g., *d:\NTDS*):

```
> ntdsutil files "move db to <DriveAndFolder>" q q
> ntdsutil files "move logs to <DriveAndFolder>" q q
```

Discussion

You can move the Active Directory database file *(ntds.dit)* independently of the log files. The first command in the solution moves the database and the second moves the logs. You may also want to consider running an integrity check against the database after you've moved it to ensure everything checks out. See Recipe 16.7 for more details.

See Also

Recipe 16.2 for booting into Directory Services Restore Mode, Recipe 16.7 for checking DIT file integrity, MS KB 257420 (HOW TO: Move the Ntds.dit File or Log Files), and MS KB 315131 (HOW TO: Use Ntdsutil to Manage Active Directory Files from the Command Line in Windows 2000)

16.9 Repairing or Recovering the DIT

Problem

You need to repair or perform a soft recovery of the Active Directory DIT because a power failure or some other failure caused the domain controller to enter an unstable state.

Solution

Using a command-line interface

First, reboot into DS Restore Mode.

Run the following command to perform a soft recovery of the transaction log files:

```
> ntdsutil files recover q q
```

If you continue to experience errors, you may need to run a repair, which does a low level repair of the database, but can result in loss of data:

```
> ntdsutil files repair q q
```

If either the recover or repair are successful, you should then check the integrity (see Recipe 16.7).

Discussion

You should (hopefully) never need to recover or repair your Active Directory database. A recovery may be needed after a domain controller unexpectedly shuts down, perhaps due to a power loss, and certain changes were never committed to the database. When it boots back up, a soft recovery is automatically done in an attempt to reapply any changes contained in the transaction log files. Since Active Directory does this automatically, it is unlikely that running the ntdsutil recover command will be of much help. The ntdsutil repair, on the other hand, can fix low-level problems, but it can also result in a loss of data, which cannot be predicted. USE AT YOUR OWN PERIL!

I recommend you use extreme caution when performing a repair, and you may want to engage Microsoft Support first in case something really bad goes wrong. If you try the repair and it makes things worse, you should consider rebuilding the domain controller from scratch. See Recipe 3.6 for forcibly removing a domain controller.

See Also

Recipe 16.2 for booting into Directory Services Restore Mode, Recipe 16.7 for checking the integrity of the DIT, and MS KB 315131 (HOW TO: Use Ntdsutil to Manage Active Directory Files from the Command Line in Windows 2000)

16.10 Performing an Online Defrag Manually

 This recipe must be run against a Windows Server 2003 domain controller.

Problem

You want to initiate an online defragmentation. This can be useful if you want to expedite the defrag process after deleting a bunch of objects.

Solution

Using a graphical user interface

1. Open LDP.
2. From the menu, select Connection → Connect.
3. For Server, enter the name of the target domain controller.
4. For Port, enter 389.
5. Click OK.
6. From the menu, select Connection → Bind.
7. Enter credentials of a user from one of the administrator groups.
8. Click OK.
9. From the menu, select Browse → Modify.
10. Leave the Dn blank.
11. For Attribute, enter DoOnlineDefrag.
12. For Values, enter 180.
13. For Operation, select Add.
14. Click Enter.
15. Click Run.

Using a command-line interface

Create an LDIF file called *online_defrag.ldf* with the following contents:

```
dn:
changetype: modify
replace: DoOnlineDefrag
DoOnlineDefrag: 180
-
```

then run the following command:

```
> ldifde -v -i -f online_defrag.ldf
```

Using VBScript

```
' This code kicks off an online defrag to run for up to 180 seconds
' ------ SCRIPT CONFIGURATION ------
strDC = "<DomainControllerName>"  ' e.g. dc01
' ------ END CONFIGURATION ---------

set objRootDSE = GetObject("LDAP://" & strDC & "/RootDSE")
objRootDSE.Put "DoOnlineDefrag", 180
objRootDSE.SetInfo
WScript.Echo "Successfully initiated an online defrag"
```

Discussion

New to Windows Server 2003 is the ability to initiate an online defragmentation. By default, the online defrag process runs every 12 hours on each domain controller. This process defrags the Active Directory database (*ntds.dit*) by combining whitespace generated from deleted objects, but does not reduce the size of the database file.

To kick off an online defrag, simply write the `DoOnlineDefrag` attribute to the RootDSE with a value equal to the maximum time the defrag process should run (in seconds). You must be a member of one of the administrator groups in the domain controller's domain in order to write to this attribute.

See Also

Recipe 16.12 for performing an offline defrag and MS KB 198793 (The Active Directory Database Garbage Collection Process)

16.11 Determining How Much Whitespace Is in the DIT

Problem

You want to find the amount of whitespace in your DIT. A lot of whitespace in the DIT may mean that you could regain enough space on the disk to warrant performing an offline defrag.

Solution

Using a graphical user interface

1. Run regedit.exe from the command line or Start → Run.
2. Expand HKEY_LOCAL_MACHINE → SYSTEM → CurrentControlSet → Services → NTDS → Diagnostics.
3. In the right pane, double-click on 6 Garbage Collection.
4. For Value data, enter 1.
5. Click OK.

Using a command-line interface

```
> reg add HKLM\System\CurrentControlSet\Services\NTDS\Diagnostics /v "6 Garbage⏎
Collection" /t REG_DWORD /d 1
```

Using VBScript

```
' This code enables logging of DIT whitespace information in the event log.
' ------ SCRIPT CONFIGURATION ------
strDCName = "<DomainControllerName>"  ' e.g. dc1
' ------ END CONFIGURATION ---------

const HKLM = &H80000002
strNTDSReg = "SYSTEM\CurrentControlSet\Services\NTDS\Diagnostics"
set objReg = GetObject("winmgmts:\\" & strDCName & "\root\default:StdRegProv")
objReg.SetDWORDValue HKLM, strNTDSReg, "6 Garbage Collection", 1
WScript.Echo "Garbage Collection logging set to 1"
```

Discussion

By setting the 6 Garbage Collection diagnostics logging option, event 1646 will get generated after the garbage collection process runs. Here is an example 1646 event:

```
Event Type:Information
Event Source:NTDS Database
Event Category:Garbage Collection
Event ID:1646
Date:     5/25/2003
Time:     9:52:46 AM
User:     NT AUTHORITY\ANONYMOUS LOGON
Computer:DC1
Description:
Internal event: The Active Directory database has the following amount of free hard
disk space remaining.

Free hard disk space (megabytes):
100
Total allocated hard disk space (megabytes):
1024
```

This shows that domain controller *dc1* has a 1 GB DIT file with 100 MB that is free (i.e., whitespace).

See Also

Recipe 16.12 for performing an offline defrag

16.12 Performing an Offline Defrag to Reclaim Space

Problem

You want to perform an offline defrag of the Active Directory DIT to reclaim whitespace in the DIT file.

Solution

Using a command-line interface

1. First, reboot into Directory Services Restore Mode.

2. Next, check the integrity of the DIT, as outlined in Recipe 16.7.

3. Now, you are ready to perform the defrag. Run the following command to create a compacted copy of the DIT file. You should check to make sure the drive on which, you create the copy has plenty of space. A rule of thumb is that it should have at least 115% of the size of the current DIT available.

    ```
    > ntdsutil files "compact to <TempDriveAndFolder>" q q
    ```

4. Next, you need to delete the transaction log files in the current NTDS directory.

    ```
    > del <CurrentDriveAndFolder>\*.log
    ```

5. You may want to keep a copy of the original DIT file for a short period of time to ensure nothing catastrophic happens to the compacted DIT. If you are going to copy or move the original version, be sure you have enough space in its new location.

    ```
    > move <CurrentDriveAndFolder>\ntds.dit <TempDriveAndFolder>\ntds_orig.dit
    > move <TempDriveAndFolder>\ntds.dit <CurrentDriveAndFolder>\ntds.dit
    ```

6. Repeat the steps in Recipe 16.7 to ensure the new DIT is not corrupted. If it is clean, reboot into normal mode and monitor the event log. If no errors are reported in the event log, make sure the domain controller is backed up as soon as possible.

Discussion

Performing an offline defragmentation of your domain controllers can reclaim disk space if you've deleted a large number of objects from Active Directory. You should only perform an offline defrag when (and if) this occurs, e.g., following a spin-off. The database will reuse whitespace and grow organically as required. Typically, the database grows year over year as more objects are added, so the offline defrag should be seldom required. An offline defrag always carries a small element of risk, so it should not be done unnecessarily.

You might want to consider doing an offline defrag after the upgrade to Windows Server 2003. A new feature called *single instance storage for security descriptors* can greatly reduce the amount of space your DIT requires. With this new feature, unique security descriptors are stored once regardless of how many times they are used, whereas in Windows 2000 the same security descriptor would be stored individually on each object that uses it.

The key thing to plan ahead of time is your disk space requirements. If you plan on creating the compacted copy of the DIT on the same drive as the current DIT, you need to make sure that drive has 115% of the size of the DIT available. If you plan on storing the original DIT on the same drive, you'll need to make sure you have at least that much space available.

See Also

Recipe 16.2 for booting into Directory Services Restore Mode, Recipe 16.7 for checking the integrity of the DIT, MS KB 198793 (The Active Directory Database Garbage Collection Process), MS KB 229602 (Defragmentation of the Active Directory Database), and MS KB 232122 (Performing Offline Defragmentation of the Active Directory Database)

16.13 Changing the Garbage Collection Interval

Problem

You want to change the default garbage collection interval.

Solution

Using a graphical user interface

1. Open ADSI Edit.
2. In the left pane, expand cn=Configuration → cn=Services → cn=Windows NT.
3. Right-click on cn=Directory Service and select Properties.
4. Edit the garbageColPeriod attribute and set it to the interval in hours that the garbage collection process should run (the default is 12 hours).
5. Click OK.

Using a command-line interface

Create an LDIF file called *change_garbage_period.ldf* with the following contents:

```
dn: cn=Directory Service,cn=Windows NT,cn=Services,cn=Configuration,<ForestRootDN>
changetype: modify
replace: garbageCollPeriod
garbageCollPeriod: <IntervalInHours>
-
```

then run the following command:

```
> ldifde -v -i -f change_garbage_period.ldf
```

Using VBScript

```
' This code changes the default garbage collection interval
' ------ SCRIPT CONFIGURATION ------
intGarbageColl = <IntervalInHours>
' ------ END CONFIGURATION ---------
```

```
set objRootDSE = GetObject("LDAP://RootDSE")
set objDSCont = GetObject("LDAP://cn=Directory Service,cn=Windows NT," & _
             "cn=Services," & objRootDSE.Get("configurationNamingContext") )
objDSCont.Put "garbageCollPeriod", intGarbageColl
objDSCont.SetInfo
WScript.Echo "Successfully set the garbage collection interval to " & _
             intGarbageColl
```

Discussion

When an object is deleted from the Configuration naming context, a Domain naming context, or an application partition, the original object is removed from Active Directory, and a tombstone object is created that contains a small subset of the object's original attributes. This tombstone object remains in Active Directory for the duration of the tombstone lifetime (default is 60 days) before it gets completely removed. See Recipe 16.18 for more information on the tombstone lifetime.

A garbage collection process runs on each domain controller that automatically removes expired tombstone objects. This process runs every 12 hours by default, but you can change it to run more or less frequently by setting the garbageCollPeriod attribute on the *cn=Directory Service,cn=Windows NT,cn=Services,cn=Configuration, <RootDomainDN>* object to the frequency in hours.

See Also

Recipe 16.18 for modifying the tombstone lifetime, Recipe 16.14 for logging the number of tombstones that get garbage collected, and MS KB 198793 (The Active Directory Database Garbage Collection Process)

16.14 Logging the Number of Expired Tombstone Objects

Problem

You want to log the number of expired tombstone objects that are removed from Active Directory during each garbage-collection cycle.

Solution

Using a graphical user interface

1. Run regedit.exe from the command line or Start → Run.
2. Expand HKEY_LOCAL_MACHINE → SYSTEM → CurrentControlSet → Services → NTDS → Diagnostics.

3. In the right pane, double-click on 6 Garbage Collection.

4. For Value data, enter 3.

5. Click OK.

Using a command-line interface

```
> reg add HKLM\System\CurrentControlSet\Services\NTDS\Diagnostics /v "6 Garbage↵
Collection" /t REG_DWORD /d 3
```

Using VBScript

```
' This code enables garbage collection logging.
' ------ SCRIPT CONFIGURATION ------
strDCName = "<DomainControllerName>"
intValue = 3
' ------ END CONFIGURATION ---------

const HKLM = &H80000002
strNTDSReg = "SYSTEM\CurrentControlSet\Services\NTDS\Diagnostics"
set objReg = GetObject("winmgmts:\\" & strDCName & "\root\default:StdRegProv")
objReg.SetDWORDValue HKLM, strNTDSReg, "6 Garbage Collection," intValue
WScript.Echo "Garbage Collection logging enabled"
```

Discussion

Here is a sample event that is logged when the 6 Garbage Collection diagnostics logging level is set to 3 or higher:

```
Event Type:Information
Event Source:NTDS General
Event Category:Garbage Collection
Event ID:1006
Date:      6/24/2003
Time:      11:29:31 AM
User:      NT AUTHORITY\ANONYMOUS LOGON
Computer:DC1
Description:
Internal event: Finished removing deleted objects that have expired (garbage
collection). Number of expired deleted objects that have been removed: 229.
```

See Also

Recipe 15.2 for more on diagnostics logging and Recipe 16.13 for more on the garbage-collection process

16.15 Determining the Size of the Active Directory Database

Problem

You want to determine the size of the Active Directory database.

Solution

Using a command-line interface

If you are in DS Restore Mode, you can use ntdsutil to report the size of the Active Directory database:

```
> ntdsutil files info
```

If you are not in DS Restore Mode and run this command, you will receive the following error message:

```
*** Error: Operation only allowed when booted in DS restore mode
        "set SAFEBOOT_OPTION=DSREPAIR" to override - NOT RECOMMENDED!
```

As you can see, it is possible to override this failure by setting the SAFEBOOT_OPTION environment variable to DSREPAIR, but I do not recommend this unless you know what you are doing. By setting that environment variable, the ntdsutil command will not stop you from performing other commands. This can be very dangerous.

Another method, which is safer and easier, is to bring up a command shell by going to Start → Run, typing cmd.exe, and pressing Enter. Then type cd <NTDSDir>, where <NTDSDir> is the full path to the *ntds.dit* file. Finally, run the dir command; the output will show the size of the files.

Discussion

The size of the Active Directory database on a domain controller is effectively the size of the *ntds.dit* file. This file can vary slightly in size between domain controllers even within the same domain due to unreplicated changes or differences with nonreplicated data.

You should monitor the size of this file on one or more domain controllers in each domain to ensure you have adequate disk space. Also, by knowing the average size of your DIT, you can recognize if it spikes dramatically, perhaps due to a new application that is writing data to the directory.

If you find that you are running out of disk space, you have a couple of options. You could move the Active Directory files to a new drive with more capacity. Alternatively, you can perform an offline defragmentation if the DIT file contains a lot of whitespace.

See Also

Recipe 16.8 for moving the DIT files, Recipe 16.11 for determining how much whitespace is in the DIT, and Recipe 16.12 for performing an offline defragmentation of the Active Directory database

16.16 Searching for Deleted Objects

Problem

You want to search for deleted objects.

Solution

Using a graphical user interface

1. Open LDP.
2. From the menu, select Connection → Connect.
3. For Server, enter the name of a domain controller you want to target (or leave blank to do a serverless bind).
4. For Port, enter 389.
5. Click OK.
6. From the menu, select Connection → Connect.
7. Enter credentials of a user that is an administrator for the domain.
8. Click OK.
9. From the menu, select Options → Controls.
10. For Windows Server 2003, select the Return Deleted Objects control under Load Predefined.
11. For Windows 2000, type 1.2.840.113556.1.4.417 for the Object Identifier and click the Check In button.
12. Click OK.
13. From the menu, select Browse → Search.
14. For BaseDN, enter: cn=Deleted Objects,<DomainDN>.
15. For Scope, select One Level.
16. For Filter, enter: (isDeleted=TRUE).
17. Click the Options button.
18. Under Search Call Type, select Extended.
19. Click OK.
20. Click Run.

Using a command-line interface

As of this writing, none of the standard command-line tools provide a way to search for deleted objects.

Using VBScript

It is currently not possible to search for deleted objects with ADSI or ADO.

Discussion

When an object is deleted in Active Directory, it is not completely deleted. The original object is removed, but a tombstone (deleted) object takes its place in the Deleted Objects container within the naming context it was deleted in. See Recipe 16.0 for more on tombstone objects.

Both the Deleted Objects container and tombstone objects themselves are hidden by default in tools, such as Active Directory Users and Computers and ADSI Edit. To query tombstone objects you have to enable the Return Deleted Objects LDAP control, which has an OID of 1.2.840.113556.1.4.417. When that control is enabled, you can perform searches for tombstone objects by specifying a search filter that contains (isDeleted=TRUE) in it. Only members of the administrator groups can perform searches for tombstone objects.

See Also

MSDN: Retrieving Deleted Objects

16.17 Restoring a Deleted Object

This recipe must be run against a Windows Server 2003 domain controller.

Problem

You want to restore an object that was previously deleted.

Solution

Using a graphical user interface

1. Open LDP.
2. From the menu, select Connection → Connect.

3. For Server, enter the name of a domain controller (or leave blank to do a server-less bind).

4. For Port, enter 389.

5. Click OK.

6. From the menu, select Connection → Bind.

7. Enter credentials of a user that can restore the deleted object (only administrators for the domain by default).

8. Click OK.

9. From the menu, select Options → Controls.

10. Select `Return deleted objects` from the Load Predefined selection.

11. Click OK.

12. From the menu, select Browse → Modify.

13. For Dn, enter the distinguished name of the deleted object you want to restore.

14. For Attribute, enter `distinguishedName`.

15. For Values, enter the original DN of the object.

16. For Operation, select Replace.

17. Click Enter.

18. For Attribute, enter `isDeleted`.

19. For Values, remove any text.

20. For Operation, select Delete.

21. Click Enter.

22. Add mandatory attributes as necessary:

23. For Attribute, enter `<ManadatoryAttribute>`.

24. For Values, enter `<MandatoryAttributeValue>`.

25. For Operation, select Add.

26. Check the box beside Extended.

27. Click Run.

28. The results will be displayed in the right pane.

Discussion

Windows Server 2003 supports restoring tombstone (deleted) objects, which have not expired. This is an alternative to performing an authoritative restore for an object that was accidentally deleted. The downside to this approach is that since most attributes that you care about (excluding those in Table 16-1) are not populated on tombstone objects, the restored deleted object will only be a shadow of its former self.

Here are the basic steps to restore a deleted object:

1. Enable the Return Deleted Objects control (1.2.840.113556.1.4.417).
2. Remove the isDeleted attribute of the object (do not simply set to FALSE).
3. Replace the distinguishedName attribute with its new location in the tree.
4. Restore any mandatory attributes.

This should all be done in a single LDAP operation.

After the object has been restored, you can repopulate any optional attributes that were set previously. By default only members of the administrator groups can restore deleted objects. You can delegate control over restoring deleted objects by granting the Reanimate Tombstone extended right to a user or group. The user or group will also need rights to modify attributes of the restored object including the ability to create child objects in the container the object is restored to.

 Granting the privilege to restore objects should be done with caution. A user could restore a user object and after setting the password, login with the account. This could give the user access to resources he was not suppose to have.

See Also

Recipe 16.16 for searching for deleted objects and MSDN: Restoring Deleted Objects

16.18 Modifying the Tombstone Lifetime for a Domain

Problem

You want to change the default tombstone lifetime for a domain.

Solution

Using a graphical user interface

1. Open ADSI Edit.
2. In the left pane, expand cn=Configuration → cn=Services → cn=Windows NT.
3. Right-click on cn=Directory Service and select Properties.
4. Set the tombstoneLifetime attribute to the number of days that tombstone objects should remain in Active Directory before getting removed completely (the default is 60 days).
5. Click OK.

Using a command-line interface

Create an LDIF file called *change_tombstone_lifetime.ldf* with the following contents:

```
dn: cn=Directory Service,cn=Windows NT,cn=Services,cn=Configuration,<ForestRootDN>
changetype: modify
replace: tombstoneLifetime
tombstoneLifetime: <NumberOfDays>
-
```

then run the following command:

```
> ldifde -v -i -f change_tombstone_lifetime.ldf
```

Using VBScript

```
' This code modifies the default tombstone lifetime
' ------ SCRIPT CONFIGURATION ------
intTombstoneLifetime = <NumberOfDays>
' ------ END CONFIGURATION ---------

set objRootDSE = GetObject("LDAP://RootDSE")
set objDSCont = GetObject("LDAP://cn=Directory Service,cn=Windows NT," & _
                "cn=Services," & objRootDSE.Get("configurationNamingContext") )
objDSCont.Put "tombstoneLifetime", intTombstoneLifetime
objDSCont.SetInfo
WScript.Echo "Successfully set the tombstone lifetime to " & _
             intTombstoneLifetime
```

Discussion

It is not recommended that you change this setting unless you have a very good reason. Lowering this value below the 60-day default, also lowers the length of time a backup of Active Directory is good for. See Recipes 16.0 and 16.16 for more information on tombstone (deleted) objects and the tombstone lifetime.

See Also

Recipe 16.13 for more on the garbage collection process, MS KB 198793 (The Active Directory Database Garbage Collection Process), MS KB 216993 (Backup of the Active Directory Has 60-Day Useful Life), and MS KB 314282 (Lingering Objects May Remain After You Bring an Out-of-Date Global Catalog Server Back Online)

## CHAPTER 17

Application Partitions

17.0 Introduction

Active Directory domain controllers host exactly three predefined partitions. The configuration naming context is replicated to all domain controllers in the forest and contains information that is forest-wide, such as the site topology and LDAP query policies. The schema-naming context is also replicated forest-wide and contains all of the schema objects that define how data is stored and structured in Active Directory. The third partition is the domain naming context, which is replicated to all of the domain controllers that host a particular domain.

Windows Server 2003 introduces a new type of partition called an application partition, which is very similar to the other naming contexts except you can configure which domain controllers in the forest replicate the data contained within it. This capability gives administrators much more flexibility over how they can store and replicate data contained in Active Directory. If you need to replicate a certain set of data to only two different sites, you can create an application partition that will only replicate the data to the domain controllers in those two sites.

For more details on application partitions, see Chapter 3 in *Active Directory*, Second Edition (O'Reilly).

Application Partitions are new to Windows Server 2003, so this entire chapter applies only to Windows Server 2003 domain controllers. Windows 2000 domain controllers cannot host application partitions.

The Anatomy of an Application Partition

Application partitions are stored in Active Directory similar to domains. In fact, they consist of the same two objects as domains, a domainDNS object and a crossRef object that resides under the Partitions container in the Configuration Naming Context (CNC). Application partitions are named like domains and can be virtually anything you want. You can create an application partition that uses the current namespace within the forest. For example, in the *rallencorp.com* (*dc=rallencorp,dc=com*) forest, you could create an *apps.rallencorp.com* (*dc=apps,dc=rallencorp,dc=com*) application partition. Alternatively, a name that is part of a new tree can also be used, for example, *apps.local* (*dc=apps,dc=local*). Application partitions can also be subordinate to other application partitions.

Tables 17-1 and 17-2 contain some of the interesting attributes of `domainDNS` and `crossRef` objects as they apply to application partitions.

Table 17-1. Attributes of domainDNS objects

Attribute	Description
dc	Relative distinguished name of the application partition.
instanceType	This attribute must be set to 5 when creating an application partition. See Recipe 17.1 for more information.
msDs-masteredBy	List of nTDSDSA object DNs of the domain controllers that replicate the application partition. See Recipe 17.4 for more information.

Table 17-2. Attributes of crossRef objects

Attribute	Description
cn	Relative distinguished name of the `crossRef` object. This value is generally a GUID for application partitions.
dnsRoot	Fully qualified DNS name of the application partition.
msDS-NC-Replica-Locations	List of nTDSDSA object DNs of the domain controllers that replicate the application partition. See Recipe 17.4 for more information.
msDS-SDReferenceDomain	Domain used for security descriptor translation. See Recipe 17.8 for more information.
nCName	Distinguished name of the application partition's corresponding `domainDNS` object.
systemFlags	Bit flag that identifies if the `crossRef` represents an application. See Recipe 17.2 for more information.

17.1 Creating and Deleting an Application Partition

Problem

You want to create or delete an application partition. Application partitions are useful if you need to replicate data to a subset of locations where you have domain controllers. Instead of replicating the application data to all domain controllers in a domain, you can use an application partition to only replicate the data to the domain controllers of your choosing.

Solution

Using a graphical user interface

To create an application partition, do the following:

1. Open ADSI Edit.
2. Connect to the domain of which the new application partition will be a child.
3. In the left pane, right-click on the domain and select New → Object.
4. Select domainDNS and click Next.
5. For Value, enter the name of the application partition and click Next.
6. Click on More Attributes.
7. Select Both for which properties to view.
8. Select instanceType for property to view.
9. For the Edit Attribute field, enter 5.
10. Click the Set button.
11. Click OK.
12. Click Finish.

To delete an application, do the following:

1. Open ADSI Edit.
2. Connect to the configuration naming context of the forest the application partition is in, if it is not already present in the left pane.
3. Expand the configuration naming context and click on the Partitions container.
4. In the right pane, right-click on the crossRef object that represents the application partition and select Delete.
5. Click Yes to confirm.

Using a command-line interface

Use the following command to create an application partition on a domain controller:

```
> ntdsutil "dom man" conn "co to se <DomainControllerName>" q "create nc⏎
<AppPartitionDN> NULL" q q
```

Use the following command to delete an application partition:

```
> ntdsutil "dom man" conn "co to se <DomainControllerName>" q "delete nc⏎
<AppPartitionFQDN>" q q
```

Using VBScript

```
' This code creates an application partition off of the
' root of the default forest.
```

```
' ------ SCRIPT CONFIGURATION ------
strAppPart = "<AppPartitionName>" ' DN of the app partition to delete
strServer  = "<DomainControllerName>" ' DNS name of DC to host app partition
strDescr   = "<Description>"  ' Descriptive text about the app partition
' ------ END CONFIGURATION ---------

set objRootDSE = GetObject("LDAP://" & strServer & "/RootDSE")
set objLDAP = GetObject("LDAP://" & strServer & "/" & _
                        objRootDSE.Get("rootDomainNamingContext") )
set objAppPart = objLDAP.Create("domainDNS", "dc=" & strAppPart)
objAppPart.Put "instancetype", 5
objAppPart.Put "description", strDescr
objAppPart.SetInfo
WScript.Echo "Created application partition: " & strAppPart


' This code deletes the specified application partition
' ------ SCRIPT CONFIGURATION ------
strAppPart = "<AppPartitionDN>"  ' DN of the app partition to delete
' ------ END CONFIGURATION ---------

set objRootDSE = GetObject("LDAP://RootDSE")
strBase = "<LDAP://cn=Partitions," & _
            objRootDSE.Get("ConfigurationNamingContext") & ">;"
strFilter = "(&(objectcategory=crossRef)(nCName=" & _
              strAppPart & "));"
strAttrs  = "cn,distinguishedName;"
strScope  = "onelevel"

set objConn = CreateObject("ADODB.Connection")
objConn.Provider = "ADsDSOObject"
objConn.Open "Active Directory Provider"
set objRS = objConn.Execute(strBase & strFilter & strAttrs & strScope)

if objRS.RecordCount <> 1 then
   WScript.Echo "Did not find a match for " & strAppPart
else
   objRS.MoveLast
   set objAppPart = GetObject("LDAP://" & _
                             objRS.Fields("distinguishedName").Value )
   objAppPart.DeleteObject(0)
   Wscript.Echo "Deleted " & objRS.Fields("distinguishedName").Value
end if
```

Discussion

To create an application partition, you need to create a domainDNS object that serves as
the root container for the partition. A crossRef object is automatically created in the
Partitions container in the CNC. Conversely, when removing an application partition, you only need to remove the crossRef object and the domainDNS is automatically
deleted. When you delete an application partition, all objects within the partition also

---

get deleted. Tombstone objects are not created for any of the objects within the application partition or for the application partition itself.

See Also

MS KB 322669 (HOW TO: Manage the Application Directory Partition and Replicas in Windows Server 2003), and MSDN: Creating an Application Directory Partition, and MSDN: Deleting an Application Directory Partition

17.2 Finding the Application Partitions in a Forest

Problem

You want to find the application partitions that have been created in a forest.

Solution

Using a graphical user interface

1. Open LDP.
2. From the menu, select Connection → Connect.
3. For Server, enter the name of a DC.
4. For Port, enter 389.
5. Click OK.
6. From the menu, select Connection → Bind.
7. Enter a user and password with the necessary credentials.
8. Click OK.
9. From the menu, select Browse → Search.
10. For BaseDN, type the DN of the Partitions container (e.g., *cn=partitions, cn=configuration, dc=rallencorp, dc=com*).
11. For Filter, enter:

    (&(objectcategory=crossRef)(systemFlags:1.2.840.113556.1.4.803:=5))

12. For Scope, select One Level.
13. Click the Options button.
14. For Attributes, type dnsRoot.
15. Click OK.
16. Click Run.

Using a command-line interface

Use the following command to find all of the application partitions in a forest:

```
> dsquery * cn=partitions,cn=configuration,<ForestDN> -filter↵
"(&(objectcategory=crossRef)(systemFlags:1.2.840.113556.1.4.803:=5))"↵
-scope onelevel -attr dnsRoot
```

Using VBScript

```
' This code displays the application partitions contained in the
' default forest

set objRootDSE = GetObject("LDAP://RootDSE")
strBase    = "<LDAP://cn=Partitions," & _
                objRootDSE.Get("ConfigurationNamingContext") & ">;"
strFilter  = "(&(objectcategory=crossRef)" & _
                "(systemFlags:1.2.840.113556.1.4.803:=5));"
strAttrs   = "cn,ncName;"
strScope   = "onelevel"

set objConn = CreateObject("ADODB.Connection")
objConn.Provider = "ADsDSOObject"
objConn.Open "Active Directory Provider"
set objRS = objConn.Execute(strBase & strFilter & strAttrs & strScope)

objRS.MoveFirst
while not objRS.EOF
    Wscript.Echo objRS.Fields("nCName").Value
    objRS.MoveNext
wend
```

Discussion

The method I used in the Solution to get the list of application partitions was to query all crossRef objects in the Partitions container that have the systemFlags attribute with the 0101 bits set (5 in decimal). To do this, I used a logical AND bitwise filter. See Recipe 4.9 for more on searching with a bitwise filter.

You can take a shortcut by not including the bitwise OID in the search filter, and changing it to systemFlags=5. This currently produces the same results in my test forest as with the bitwise filter, but there are no guarantees since it is a bit-flag attribute. There may exist special circumstances when an application partition would have another bit set in systemFlags that would yield a different value.

In each solution, I printed the dnsRoot attribute for each application partition, which contains the DNS name of the application partition. You can also retrieve the nCName attribute, which contains the distinguished name of the application partition.

17.3 Adding or Removing a Replica Server for an Application Partition

Problem

You want to add or remove a replica server for an application partition. After you've created an application partition, you should make at least one other server a replica server in case the first server fails.

Solution

Using a command-line interface

Use the following command to add a replica server for an application partition:

```
> ntdsutil "dom man" conn "co to se <DomainControllerName>" q "add nc replica↵
<AppPartitionDN> <DomainControllerName>" q q
```

Use the following command to remove a replica server for an application partition:

```
> ntdsutil "dom man" conn "co to se <DomainControllerName>" q "remove nc replica↵
<AppPartitionDN> <DomainControllerName>" q q
```

Using VBScript

```
' This code adds or removes a replica server for the
' specified application partition
' ------ SCRIPT CONFIGURATION ------
strAppPart = "<AppPartitionFQDN>" ' DNS name of the application partition

' Hostname of server to add as replica for app partition.
' This needs to match the common name for the DC's server object.
strServer  = "<DomainControllerName>"  ' e.g. dc01

' Set to True to add server as new replica or False to remove
boolAdd    = True
' ------ END CONFIGURATION ---------

' Constants taken from ADS_PROPERTY_OPERATION_ENUM
const ADS_PROPERTY_APPEND = 3
const ADS_PROPERTY_DELETE = 4

set objRootDSE = GetObject("LDAP://RootDSE")

' ----------------------------------------------------------
' First find the NTDS Settings object for the server
' ----------------------------------------------------------
strBase    = "<LDAP://cn=Sites," & _
             objRootDSE.Get("ConfigurationNamingContext") & ">;"
strFilter  = "(&(objectcategory=server)(cn=" & strServer & "));"
strAttrs   = "cn,distinguishedName;"
```

```
strScope    = "subtree"
set objConn = CreateObject("ADODB.Connection")
objConn.Provider = "ADsDSOObject"
objConn.Open "Active Directory Provider"
set objRS = objConn.Execute(strBase & strFilter & strAttrs & strScope)
if objRS.RecordCount <> 1 then
   WScript.Echo "Did not find a match for server " & strServer
   WScript.Quit
else
   objRS.MoveLast
   strServerDN = "cn=NTDS Settings," & _
                 objRS.Fields("distinguishedName").Value
   ' Make sure the NTDS Settings object actually exists
   set objNTDSDSA = GetObject("LDAP://" & strServerDN)
   Wscript.Echo "Found server: "
   WScript.Echo strServerDN
   Wscript.Echo
end if


' ---------------------------------------------------------------------
' Now need to find the crossRef object for the application partition
' ---------------------------------------------------------------------
strBase = "<LDAP://cn=Partitions," & _
          objRootDSE.Get("ConfigurationNamingContext") & ">;"
strFilter  = "(&(objectcategory=crossRef)" & _
             "(dnsRoot=" & strAppPart & "));"
strAttrs   = "cn,distinguishedName;"
strScope   = "onelevel"
set objRS = objConn.Execute(strBase & strFilter & strAttrs & strScope)
if objRS.RecordCount <> 1 then
   WScript.Echo "Did not find a match for application partition " & _
                strAppPart
   WScript.Quit
else
   objRS.MoveLast
   set objAppPart = GetObject("LDAP://" & _
                    objRS.Fields("distinguishedName").Value )
   Wscript.Echo "Found app partition: "
   WScript.Echo objRS.Fields("distinguishedName").Value
   WScript.Echo
end if


' -----------------------------------------------
' Lastly, either add or remove the replica server
' -----------------------------------------------
if boolAdd = TRUE then
   objAppPart.PutEx ADS_PROPERTY_APPEND, "msDS-NC-Replica-Locations", _
                    Array(strServerDN)
   objAppPart.SetInfo
   WScript.Echo "Added server to replica set"
else
   objAppPart.PutEx ADS_PROPERTY_DELETE, "msDS-NC-Replica-Locations", _
                    Array(strServerDN)
```

```
    objAppPart.SetInfo
    WScript.Echo "Removed server from replica set"
end if
```

Discussion

When you initially create an application partition, there is only one domain controller that hosts the application partition, namely the one you created the application partition on. You can add any other domain controllers in the forest as replica servers assuming the domain controllers are running Windows Server 2003. The list of replica servers is stored in the msDS-NC-Replica-Locations attribute on the crossRef object for the application partition in the Partitions container. That attribute contains the distinguished name of each replica server's nTDSDSA object. To add a replica server, simply add the DN of the new replica server. To remove a replica server, remove the DN corresponding to the server you want to remove. Behind the scene, the Knowledge Consistency Checker (KCC) gets triggered anytime there is a change to that attribute and will either cause the application partition to get replicated to the target domain controller or will remove it from the target domain controller. When a domain controller is demoted, it will automatically remove itself as a replica server for any application partitions it replicated.

See Also

Recipe 17.4 for finding the replica servers for an application partition and MS KB 322669 (HOW TO: Manage the Application Directory Partition and Replicas in Windows Server 2003)

17.4 Finding the Replica Servers for an Application Partition

Problem

You want to find the replica servers for an application partition.

Solution

Using a graphical user interface

1. Open ADSI Edit.
2. Connect to the configuration naming context of the forest the application partition is in, if it is not already present in the left pane.
3. Expand the configuration naming context and click on the Partitions container.

4. In the right pane, right-click on the crossRef object that represents the application partition and select Properties.

5. Under Attributes, select the msDS-NC-Replica-Locations attribute.

Using a command-line interface

```
> ntdsutil "dom man" conn "co to se <DomainControllerName>" q "list nc replicas↵
<AppPartitionDN>" q q
```

Using VBScript

```
' This code displays the DN of each domain controller's
' nTDSDSA object that is a replica server for the
' specified app partition
' ------ SCRIPT CONFIGURATION ------
' Fully qualified DNS name of app partition
strAppPart = "<AppPartitionFQDN>"    ' e.g. apps.rallencorp.com
' ------ END CONFIGURATION ---------

set objRootDSE = GetObject("LDAP://RootDSE")
strBase    = "<LDAP://cn=Partitions," & _
               objRootDSE.Get("ConfigurationNamingContext") & ">;"
strFilter  = "(&(objectcategory=crossRef)(dnsRoot=" & strAppPart & "));"
strAttrs   = "msDS-NC-Replica-Locations;"
strScope   = "onelevel"
set objConn = CreateObject("ADODB.Connection")
objConn.Provider = "ADsDSOObject"
objConn.Open "Active Directory Provider"
set objRS = objConn.Execute(strBase & strFilter & strAttrs & strScope)
if objRS.RecordCount <> 1 then
   WScript.Echo "Did not find a match for application partition " & _
                strAppPart
   WScript.Quit
else
   objRS.MoveLast
   if objRS.Fields("msDS-NC-Replica-Locations").Properties.Count > 0 then
      Wscript.Echo "There are no replica servers for app partition " & _
                   strAppPart
   else
      Wscript.Echo "Replica servers for app partition " & strAppPart & ":"
      for each strNTDS in objRS.Fields("msDS-NC-Replica-Locations").Value
         WScript.Echo " " & strNTDS
      next
   end if
end if
```

Discussion

The list of replica servers for an application partition is stored in the multivalued msDS-NC-Replica-Locations attribute on the crossRef object for the application partition. This object is located in the Partitions container in the configuration naming context.

See Also

Recipe 17.3 for adding and removing replica servers

17.5 Finding the Application Partitions Hosted by a Server

Problem

You want to find the application partitions that a particular server replicates. Before you decommission a server, it is good to check to see if it hosts any application partitions and if so, add another replica server to replace it.

Solution

Using a graphical user interface

1. Open LDP.
2. From the menu, select Connection → Connect.
3. For Server, enter the name of a DC.
4. For Port, enter 389.
5. Click OK.
6. From the menu, select Connection → Bind.
7. Enter a user and password with the necessary credentials.
8. Click OK.
9. From the menu, select Browse → Search.
10. For BaseDN, type the DN of the Partitions container (e.g., *cn=partitions, cn=configuration, dc=rallencorp, dc=com*).
11. For Filter, enter:

    ```
    (&(objectcategory=crossRef)(systemFlags:1.2.840.113556.1.4.803:=5)
    (msDS-NC-Replica-Locations=cn=NTDS Settings,cn=<DomainControllerName>,
    cn=servers,cn=<SiteName>,cn=sites, cn=configuration,<ForestDN>))
    ```

12. For Scope, select One Level.
13. Click the Options button.
14. For Attributes, type dnsRoot.
15. Click OK.
16. Click Run.

Using a command-line interface

Use the following command to find all of the application partitions hosted by a domain controller. To run this command, you need the distinguished name of the forest root domain (*<ForestDN>*), the common name of the DC's server object (*<DomainControllerName>*), and the common name of the site object the server is in (*<SiteName>*).

```
> dsquery * "cn=partitions,cn=configuration,<ForestDN>" -scope onelevel -attr↵
dnsRoot -filter "(&(objectcategory=crossRef)(systemFlags:1.2.840.113556.1.4.803:=5)↵
(msDS-NC-Replica-Locations=cn=NTDS Settings,cn=<DomainControllerName>,↵
cn=servers,cn=<SiteName>,cn=sites, cn=configuration,<ForestDN>))"
```

Using VBScript

```
' This code finds the application partitions hosted by the specified server.
' ------ SCRIPT CONFIGURATION ------
' Hostname of server to add as replica for app partition.
' This needs to match the common name for the DC's server object.
strServer  = "<DomainControllerName>"  ' e.g. dc01
' ------ END CONFIGURATION ---------


' -----------------------------------------------------------
' First need to find the NTDS Settings object for the server
' -----------------------------------------------------------
set objRootDSE = GetObject("LDAP://RootDSE")
strBase     = "<LDAP://cn=Sites," & _
                  objRootDSE.Get("ConfigurationNamingContext") & ">;"
strFilter   = "(&(objectcategory=server)(cn=" & strServer & "));"
strAttrs    = "cn,distinguishedName;"
strScope    = "subtree"
set objConn = CreateObject("ADODB.Connection")
objConn.Provider = "ADsDSOObject"
objConn.Open "Active Directory Provider"
set objRS = objConn.Execute(strBase & strFilter & strAttrs & strScope)
if objRS.RecordCount <> 1 then
   WScript.Echo "Did not find a match for server " & strServer
   WScript.Quit
else
   objRS.MoveLast
   strServerDN = "cn=NTDS Settings," & _
                 objRS.Fields("distinguishedName").Value
   Wscript.Echo "Found server object: "
   WScript.Echo strServerDN
   Wscript.Echo
end if


' -------------------------------------------------------------------
' Find the crossRef objects that are hosted by the server
' -------------------------------------------------------------------
strBase = "<LDAP://cn=Partitions," & _
          objRootDSE.Get("ConfigurationNamingContext") & ">;"
strFilter   = "(&(objectcategory=crossRef)" & _
              "(msDS-NC-Replica-Locations=" & strServerDN & "));"
```

```
strAttrs    = "nCName;"
strScope    = "onelevel"
set objRS = objConn.Execute(strBase & strFilter & strAttrs & strScope)
if objRS.RecordCount = 0 then
   WScript.Echo "Server " & strServer & _
                 " does not host any application partitions"
   WScript.Quit
else
   Wscript.Echo "App partitions hosted by server " & strServer & ": "
   objRS.MoveFirst
   while not objRS.EOF
      WScript.Echo " " & objRS.Fields("nCName").Value
      objRS.MoveNext
   wend
end if
```

Discussion

As described in Recipes 17.3 and 17.4, the msDS-NC-Replica-Locations attribute on crossRef objects contains the list of replica servers for a given application partition. Each of the solutions illustrates how to perform a query using this attribute to locate all of the application partitions a particular domain controller is a replica server for. For the GUI and CLI solutions, you need to know the distinguished name of the nTDSDSA object for the target domain controller. The VBScript solution tries to dynamically determine the distinguished name given a server name.

See Also

Recipe 17.4 for finding the replica servers for an application partition

17.6   Verifying Application Partitions Are Instantiated on a Server Correctly

Problem

You want to verify that an application partition is instantiated on a replica server. After you add a domain controller as a replica server for an application partition, the data in the application partition needs to fully replicate to that domain controller before it can be used on that domain controller.

Solution

Using a command-line interface

Use the following command to determine if there are any problems with application partitions on a domain controller:

```
> dcdiag /test:checksdrefdom /test:verifyreplicas /test:crossrefvalidation /s:↵
<DomainControllerName>
```

 These tests are valid only with the Windows Server 2003 version of dcdiag.

Discussion

The dcdiag CheckDSRefDom, VerifyReplicas, and CrossRefValidation tests can help determine if an application partition has been instantiated on a server and if there are any problems with it. Here is the dcdiag help information for those three tests:

CrossRefValidation
> This test looks for cross-referencess that are in some way invalid.

CheckSDRefDom
> This test checks that all application directory partitions have appropriate security descriptor reference domains.

VerifyReplicas
> This test verifies that all application directory partitions are fully instantiated on all replica servers.

Another way you can check to see if a certain application partition has been instantiated on a domain controller yet is to look at the msDS-HasInstantiatedNCs attribute for the server's nTDSDSA object. That attribute has DN with Binary syntax and contains a list of all the application partitions that have been successfully instantiated on the server. Unfortunately, tools such as ADSI Edit and dsquery do not interpret DN with Binary attributes correctly, but it can be viewed with LDP.

17.7 Setting the Replication Notification Delay for an Application Partition

Problem

Two replication-related settings that you can customize for application partitions (or any naming context for that matter) include the first and subsequent replication delay after a change to the partition has been detected. The first replication delay is the time that a domain controller waits before it notifies its first replication partner that there has been a change. The subsequent replication delay is the time that the domain controller waits after it has notified its first replication partner before it will notify its next partner. You may need to customize these settings so that replication happens as quickly as you need it to for data in the application partition.

Solution

Using a graphical user interface

1. Open ADSI Edit.
2. Connect to the configuration naming context of the forest the application partition is in if it is not already present in the left pane.
3. Expand the configuration naming context and click on the Partitions container.
4. In the right pane, right-click on the crossRef object that represents the application partition and select Properties.
5. Set the msDS-Replication-Notify-First-DSA-Delay and msDS-Replication-Notify-Subsequent-DSA-Delay attributes to the number of seconds you want for each delay (see the Discussion section for more details).
6. Click OK.

Using a command-line interface

The Windows Server 2003 version of repadmin supports setting the notification delays:

```
> repadmin /notifyopt <AppPartitionDN> /first:<FirstDelayInSeconds> /subs:⏎
<NextDelayInSeconds>
```

For Windows 2000, you can create an LDIF file with the following contents:

```
dn: <AppPartitionCrossRefDN>
changetype: modify
replace: msDS-Replication-Notify-First-DSA-Delay
msDS-Replication-Notify-First-DSA-Delay: <FirstDelayInSeconds>
-
replace: msDS-Replication-Notify-Subsequent-DSA-Delay
msDS-Replication-Notify-Subsequent-DSA-Delay: <NextDelayInSeconds>
-
```

If the file were named *change_replication_delays.ldf*, you'd run the following command:

```
> ldifde -v -i -f change_replication_delays.ldf
```

Using VBScript

```
' This code sets the replication delay for an application partition
' ------ SCRIPT CONFIGURATION ------
strAppPartDN = "<AppPartitionDN>"   ' e.g. dc=apps,dc=rallencorp,dc=com
```

```
intFirstDelay = <FirstDelayInSeconds>
intNextDelay  = <NextDelayInSeconds>
' ------ END CONFIGURATION ---------

set objRootDSE = GetObject("LDAP://RootDSE")
strBase   = "<LDAP://cn=Partitions," & _
              objRootDSE.Get("ConfigurationNamingContext") & ">;"
strFilter = "(&(objectcategory=crossRef)(nCName=" & strAppPartDN & "));"
strAttrs  = "cn,distinguishedName;"
strScope  = "onelevel"
set objConn = CreateObject("ADODB.Connection")
objConn.Provider = "ADsDSOObject"
objConn.Open "Active Directory Provider"
set objRS = objConn.Execute(strBase & strFilter & strAttrs & strScope)

if objRS.RecordCount <> 1 then
   WScript.Echo "Did not find a match for " & strAppPartDN
else
   objRS.MoveLast
   set objAppPart = GetObject("LDAP://" & _
                    objRS.Fields("distinguishedName").Value )
   objAppPart.Put "msDS-Replication-Notify-First-DSA-Delay", intFirstDelay
   objAppPart.Put "msDS-Replication-Notify-Subsequent-DSA-Delay", intNextDelay
   objAppPart.SetInfo
   Wscript.Echo "Modified " & objRS.Fields("distinguishedName").Value
end if
```

Discussion

The settings that control the notification delay are stored in the msDS-Replication-Notify-First-DSA-Delay and msDS-Replication-Notify-Subsequent-DSA-Delay attributes on the application partition's crossRef object in the Partitions container. The time values are stored as seconds. The default for application partitions is 60 seconds for the first delay and 60 seconds for the subsequent delay.

17.8   Setting the Reference Domain for an Application Partition

Problem

Whenever you create an object in Active Directory, the default security descriptor defined in the schema for the object's class is applied to the object. This default security descriptor may reference specific groups, such as Domain Admins, but it is not specific to a domain. This makes a lot of sense for domain-naming contexts, where the Domain Admins group in question would be the one defined in the domain. For application partitions, which don't contain a Domain Admins group, it is not so straightforward. Which domain's Domain Admins group do you use? To work around this issue, you can set a default security descriptor reference domain for an application partition by setting the msDS-SDReferenceDomain attribute of the partition's crossRef object.

Solution

Using a graphical user interface

1. Open ADSI Edit.
2. Connect to the Configuration naming context of the forest the application partition is in if it is not already present in the left pane.
3. Expand the Configuration naming context and click on the Partitions container.
4. In the right pane, right-click on the crossRef object that represents the application partition and select Properties.
5. Under Attributes, select the msDS-SDReferenceDomain attribute.

Using a command-line interface

```
> ntdsutil "dom man" conn "co to se <DomainControllerName>" q "set nc ref domain↵
<AppPartitionDN> <DomainDN>" q q
```

Using VBScript

```
' This code sets the SD reference domain for the specified app partition
' ------ SCRIPT CONFIGURATION ------
' DN of reference domain
strRefDomainDN = "<DomainDN>"          ' e.g. dc=emea,dc=rallencorp,dc=com
' Fully qualified DNS name of app partition
strAppPart = "<AppPartitionFQDN>"      ' e.g. app.rallencorp.com
' ------ END CONFIGURATION ---------

set objRootDSE = GetObject("LDAP://RootDSE")
strBase = "<LDAP://cn=Partitions," & _
            objRootDSE.Get("ConfigurationNamingContext") & ">;"
strFilter  = "(&(objectcategory=crossRef)(dnsRoot=" & _
              strAppPart & "));"
strAttrs   = "nCName,msDS-SDReferenceDomain,distinguishedName;"
strScope   = "onelevel"
set objConn = CreateObject("ADODB.Connection")
objConn.Provider = "ADsDSOObject"
objConn.Open "Active Directory Provider"
set objRS = objConn.Execute(strBase & strFilter & strAttrs & strScope)
if objRS.RecordCount <> 1 then
   WScript.Echo "Did not find a match for application partition " & _
                strAppPart
   WScript.Quit
else
   objRS.MoveLast
   WScript.Echo "Current Reference Domain: " & _
                objRS.Fields("msDS-SDReferenceDomain").Value
```

```
    set objCrossRef = GetObject("LDAP://" & _
                      objRS.Fields("distinguishedName").Value )
    objCrossRef.Put "msDS-SDReferenceDomain", strRefDomainDN
    objCrossRef.SetInfo
    WScript.Echo "New Reference Domain: " & _
              objCrossRef.Get("msDS-SDReferenceDomain")
end if
```

Discussion

If you don't set the `msDS-SDReferenceDomain` attribute for an application partition, then a certain hierarchy is followed to determine the default security descriptor domain. These are the guidelines:

- If the application partition is created as part of a new tree, the forest root domain is used as the default domain.
- If the application partition is a child of a domain, the parent domain is the default domain.
- If the application partition is a child of another application partition, the parent application partition's default domain is used.

See Also

Recipe 10.19 for more on setting the default security descriptor for a class, Recipe 17.1 for creating an application partition, and MS KB 322669 (HOW TO: Manage the Application Directory Partition and Replicas in Windows Server 2003)

17.9 Delegating Control of Managing an Application Partition

Problem

You want to delegate control over the management of an application partition.

Solution

Using a graphical user interface

1. Open ADSI Edit.
2. Connect to the Configuration naming context of the forest the application partition is in if it is not already present in the left pane.
3. Expand the Configuration naming context and click on the Partitions container.

4. In the right pane, right-click on the crossRef object that represents the application partition and select Properties.

5. Click the Security tab.

6. Click the Advanced button.

7. Click the Add button.

8. Use the object picker to find the user or group you want to delegate control to and click OK.

9. Click the Properties tab.

10. Under Allow, check the boxes beside Write msDS-NC-Replica-Locations, Write msDS-SDReferenceDomain, Write msDS-Replication-Notify-First-DSA-Delay, and Write msDS-Replication-Notify-Subsequent-DSA-Delay.

11. Click OK.

Using a command-line interface

```
> dsacls <AppPartitionCrossRefDN> /G <UserOrGroup>:RPWP;msDS-NC-Replica-Locations
> dsacls <AppPartitionCrossRefDN> /G <UserOrGroup>:RPWP;msDS-SDReferenceDomain
> dsacls <AppPartitionCrossRefDN> /G <UserOrGroup>:RPWP;msDS-Replication-Notify-↵
First-DSA-Delay
> dsacls <AppPartitionCrossRefDN> /G <UserOrGroup>:RPWP;msDS-Replication-Notify-↵
Subsequent-DSA-Delay
```

Using VBScript

```
' This script delegates control over the four key attributes
' of an app partition to the specified user or group.
' ------ SCRIPT CONFIGURATION ------
' Fully qualified DNS name of app partition
strAppPart = "<AppPartitionFQDN>"  ' e.g. apps.rallencorp.com
' User or group to delegate control to
strUser = "<UserOrGroup>"  ' e.g. joe@rallencorp.com or RALLENCORP\joe
' ------ END CONFIGURATION ---------

'############################
' Constants
'############################

' ADS_ACETYPE_ENUM
Const ADS_ACETYPE_ACCESS_ALLOWED        = &h0
Const ADS_ACETYPE_ACCESS_ALLOWED_OBJECT = &h5

' ADS_FLAGTYPE_ENUM
Const ADS_FLAG_OBJECT_TYPE_PRESENT = &h1

' ADS_RIGHTS_ENUM
Const ADS_RIGHT_DS_WRITE_PROP = &h20
Const ADS_RIGHT_DS_READ_PROP  = &h10
```

```
' schemaIDGUID values
Const REPLICA_LOCATIONS              = "{97de9615-b537-46bc-ac0f-10720f3909f3}"
Const SDREFERENCEDOMAIN              = "{4c51e316-f628-43a5-b06b-ffb695fcb4f3}"
Const NOTIFY_FIRST_DSA_DELAY         = "{85abd4f4-0a89-4e49-bdec-6f35bb2562ba}"
Const NOTIFY_SUBSEQUENT_DSA_DELAY = "{d63db385-dd92-4b52-b1d8-0d3ecc0e86b6}"

'############################
' Find App Partition
'############################

set objRootDSE = GetObject("LDAP://RootDSE")
strBase = "<LDAP://cn=Partitions," & _
          objRootDSE.Get("ConfigurationNamingContext") & ">;"
strFilter  = "(&(objectcategory=crossRef)(dnsRoot=" & _
             strAppPart & "));"
strAttrs   = "cn,distinguishedName;"
strScope   = "onelevel"
set objConn = CreateObject("ADODB.Connection")
objConn.Provider = "ADsDSOObject"
objConn.Open "Active Directory Provider"
Set objRS = objConn.Execute(strBase & strFilter & strAttrs & strScope)
if objRS.RecordCount <> 1 then
   WScript.Echo "Did not find a match for " & strAppPart
else
   objRS.MoveLast
   set objAppPart = GetObject("LDAP://" & _
                    objRS.Fields("distinguishedName").Value )
end if

'############################
' Create ACL
'############################

set objSD = objAppPart.Get("ntSecurityDescriptor")
set objDACL = objSD.DiscretionaryAcl

' Read/Write Property: msDS-NC-Replica-Locations
set objACE1 = CreateObject("AccessControlEntry")
objACE1.Trustee    = strUser
objACE1.AccessMask = ADS_RIGHT_DS_WRITE_PROP Or ADS_RIGHT_DS_READ_PROP
objACE1.AceFlags   = 0
objACE1.Flags      = ADS_FLAG_OBJECT_TYPE_PRESENT
objACE1.AceType    = ADS_ACETYPE_ACCESS_ALLOWED_OBJECT
objACE1.ObjectType = REPLICA_LOCATIONS    '

' Read/Write Property: msDS-SDReferenceDomain
set objACE2 = CreateObject("AccessControlEntry")
objACE2.Trustee    = strUser
objACE2.AccessMask = ADS_RIGHT_DS_WRITE_PROP Or ADS_RIGHT_DS_READ_PROP
objACE2.AceFlags   = 0
objACE2.Flags      = ADS_FLAG_OBJECT_TYPE_PRESENT
objACE2.AceType    = ADS_ACETYPE_ACCESS_ALLOWED_OBJECT
objACE2.ObjectType = SDREFERENCEDOMAIN
```

```
' Read/Write Property: msDS-Replication-Notify-First-DSA-Delay
set objACE3 = CreateObject("AccessControlEntry")
objACE3.Trustee    = strUser
objACE3.AccessMask = ADS_RIGHT_DS_WRITE_PROP Or ADS_RIGHT_DS_READ_PROP
objACE3.AceFlags   = 0
objACE3.Flags      = ADS_FLAG_OBJECT_TYPE_PRESENT
objACE3.AceType    = ADS_ACETYPE_ACCESS_ALLOWED_OBJECT
objACE3.ObjectType = NOTIFY_FIRST_DSA_DELAY

' Read/Write Property: msDS-Replication-Notify-Subsequent-DSA-Delay
set objACE4 = CreateObject("AccessControlEntry")
objACE4.Trustee    = strUser
objACE4.AccessMask = ADS_RIGHT_DS_WRITE_PROP Or ADS_RIGHT_DS_READ_PROP
objACE4.AceFlags   = 0
objACE4.Flags      = ADS_FLAG_OBJECT_TYPE_PRESENT
objACE4.AceType    = ADS_ACETYPE_ACCESS_ALLOWED_OBJECT
objACE4.ObjectType = NOTIFY_SUBSEQUENT_DSA_DELAY

objDACL.AddAce objACE1
objDACL.AddAce objACE2
objDACL.AddAce objACE3
objDACL.AddAce objACE4

'############################
' Set ACL
'############################
objSD.DiscretionaryAcl = objDACL
objAppPart.Put "ntSecurityDescriptor", objSD
objAppPart.SetInfo
WScript.Echo "Delegated control of " & strAppPart & " to " & strUser
```

Discussion

If you want to delegate control of management of application partitions, you must
grant control over four key attributes. Here is a description of each attribute and
what can be accomplished by having control over it:

msDS-NC-Replica-Locations
    By having write access to this attribute, a user can add replica servers for the
    application partition. See Recipe 17.3 for more information.

msDS-SDReferenceDomain
    By having write access to this attribute, a user can define the default security
    descriptor domain for the application partition. See Recipe 17.8 for more
    information.

msDS-Replication-Notify-First-DSA-Delay
    See Recipe 17.7 for more information.

msDS-Replication-Notify-Subsequent-DSA-Delay
    See Recipe 17.7 for more information.

If you want to delegate control over managing objects within the application partition, you need to follow the same procedures you would when delegating control
over objects in a domain naming context. See Recipe 14.5 for more information on
delegating control.

See Also

Recipe 14.5 for delegating control, Recipe 17.3 for more on adding and removing
replica servers, Recipe 17.7 for more on the replication delay attributes, and Recipe
17.8 for more on the default security descriptor domain

## CHAPTER 18

Interoperability and Integration

18.0 Introduction

Active Directory supports several important industry standards, which allow other services and platforms to interoperate and integrate with it. The Lightweight Directory Access Protocol (LDAP) is the standards-based protocol used by all major directory service vendors for directory access and management. LDAP is platform neutral, which means you can access and manage data in Active Directory from a variety of platforms. Active Directory uses the Domain Name System (DNS) for its name resolution services so you can use tools, such as nslookup, to locate domain controllers by making DNS queries. Kerberos is the most widely used network authentication protocol and is supported by Active Directory, so even non-Windows-based Kerberos-enabled clients can authenticate. These are just a few of the standards Active Directory supports. Throughout this chapter I will cover how you can access, manage, and integrate Active Directory in ways that are not typically documented.

18.1 Accessing AD from a Non-Windows Platform

Problem

You want to access or manage AD from a non-Windows platform.

Solution

Using a graphical user interface

One of the best platform-neutral graphical user interfaces for managing an LDAP directory, such as Active Directory, is the LDAP Browser/Editor. It was written in Java and can run on virtually any machine that has Java 1.2.2 or greater installed. It can be downloaded from the following site: *http://www.iit.edu/~gawojar/ldap/*.

Using a command-line interface

The original LDAP server produced at the University of Michigan included a set of command-line utilities that can query and update an LDAP directory. Over time these tools have become very popular on the UNIX platforms, and they can even be used to query and update Active Directory. The OpenLDAP project took over maintenance of the University of Michigan's LDAP server and also the command-line tools. To download the latest version of the tools, go to the following site: *http://www.openldap.org/*.

Using a programming language

Any programming language that supports LDAP can be used to programmatically access and manage Active Directory. See the other recipes in this chapter for using Perl, Python, Java, and PHP.

Discussion

Due to the fact that LDAP is an open standard, it has been adopted on many platforms and programming languages. While you can perform 90% of the things you would need to do from a non-Windows platform, some tasks do still require a Windows GUI, CLI, or API. For example, there is no easy way to manage ACLs in Active Directory from a non-Windows platform. You can, however, do virtually anything you need to do as far as adding, modifying, and removing objects in Active Directory with the basic LDAP-enabled tools.

See Also

Recipes 18.4, 18.5, and 18.6 for more on how to programmatically query and update Active Directory using Perl, Java, and Python

18.2   Programming with .NET

Problem

You want to programmatically access Active Directory using the .NET Framework.

Solution

The System.DirectoryServices namespace can be used to interface with Active Directory using the .NET Framework. The following code is a simple VB.NET program that prints the attributes of the RootDSE:

```
Imports System.DirectoryServices

Module Module1
```

```
    Sub Main( )

        Dim objRootDSE As New DirectoryEntry("LDAP://RootDSE")

        Dim strAttrName As String
        Dim objValue As Object

        For Each strAttrName In objRootDSE.Properties.PropertyNames
            For Each objValue In objRootDSE.Properties(strAttrName)
                Console.WriteLine(strAttrName & " : " & objValue.ToString)
            Next objValue
        Next strAttrName

    End Sub

End Module
```

Discussion

The System.DirectoryServices namespace is a generic directory service interface that is intended to replace ADSI. It provides a rich set of properties and methods for accessing, querying, and manipulating objects in Active Directory. Currently, there is no native support for scripting languages, such as VBScript and Perl, but you can use Microsoft's version of JavaScript (i.e., JScript) with .NET to utilize System.DirectoryServices.

The System.DirectoryServices DirectorySearcher class is a simple interface for making LDAP queries. The DirectoryEntry class is used for instantiating existing objects or creating new ones. In the Solution section, I used the DirectoryEntry class to access the RootDSE. DirectorySearcher and DirectoryEntry are the two main classes to become familiar with if you want to do Active Directory programming with .NET. For more information and examples on using System.DirectoryServices, see Chapter 28 of *Active Directory*, Second Edition (O'Reilly).

System.DirectoryServices does not currently provide interfaces for everything that could be done with ADSI. Instead, you can use the NativeObject property on an instantiated object to return an ADSI object, which you can then use to access any ADSI properties or methods for the object.

See Also

Chapter 28 in *Active Directory*, Second Edition (O'Reilly) and System.DirectoryServices reference information can be found at *http://msdn.microsoft.com/library/en-us/cpref/html/frlrfSystemDirectoryServices.asp*

18.3   Programming with DSML

Problem

You want to programmatically access Active Directory using the Directory Services Markup Language (DSML). DSML is the answer for all programmers who have been longing for an XML-based interface to query and access a directory.

Solution

To use DSML with Active Directory, you have to install the Windows DSML client (DSFW) on a Windows 2000 or Windows Server 2003 computer that is running IIS. The DSML client can be downloaded from the following site: *http://www.microsoft.com/windows2000/server/evaluation/news/bulletins/dsml.asp*. If you are installing the client on a Windows 2000 machine, you will also need to make sure MSXML 3.0 SP2 is installed.

After the client is installed, you can perform DSML queries against that server, which will translate the calls into LDAP queries to Active Directory. No additional software needs to be installed on domain controllers to support DSML.

The following code shows a DSML request for the RootDSE:

```
<se:Envelope xmlns:se="http://schemas.xmlsoap.org/soap/envelope/">
    <se:Body xmlns="urn:oasis:names:tc:DSML:2:0:core">
        <batchRequest>
            <searchRequest dn="" scope="baseObject">
                <filter>
                    <present name="objectclass"/>
                </filter>
            </searchRequest>
        </batchRequest>
    </se:Body>
</se:Envelope>
```

Discussion

DSML is an XML alternative to using LDAP to access and manage a directory server. The Oasis standards body has driven the development of DSML *(http://www.oasis-open.org/committees/dsml/)* and now most directory vendors support it as of Version 2 (DSMLv2).

DSML encodes LDAP-like functions in XML messages and transmits them to a SOAP client that can sit directly on the directory server or a separate server. Currently, Active Directory domain controllers do not support DSML directly and, thus, a separate client must be installed. For more information including the DSML specification, see the Oasis web site.

See Also

DSMLfW home page: *http://www.microsoft.com/windows2000/server/evaluation/news/bulletins/dsml.asp*

18.4   Programming with Perl

Problem

You want to programmatically access Active Directory using Perl.

Solution

There are two options for accessing Active Directory with Perl. You can use the Net:: LDAP modules that are cross platform and use the LDAP protocol, or you can use the Win32::OLE module that gives you access to ADSI and must be run on a Windows machine. Both modules can be downloaded from the Comprehensive Perl Archive Network (CPAN) web site, *http://www.cpan.org/*.

The following example shows how to use the Net::LDAP modules to query the RootDSE:

```
#!/usr/SD/perl/bin/perl

use strict;
use Net::LDAP;

my $ldap_server  = $ARGV[0] || 'dc1';
my $ldapobj = Net::LDAP->new($ldap_server) or die " Could not connect: $@";
my $rootdse = $ldapobj->search(
                  base   => '',
                  filter => '(objectclass=*)',
                  scope  => 'base',
);
die $rootdse->error if $rootdse->code;
foreach $entry($rootdse->entries) {
   foreach $attr(sort $entry->attributes) {
      foreach ($entry->get($attr)) {
         print "$attr: $_\n";
      }
   }
}
```

This next example uses the Win32::OLE module and ADSI to display the attributes of the RootDSE:

```
use strict;
use Win32::OLE 'in';

my $rootdse = Win32::OLE->GetObject("LDAP://RootDSE");
$rootdse->GetInfo;
```

```
for my $i ( 0 .. $rootdse->PropertyCount - 1) {
    my $prop = $rootdse->Item($i);
    print $prop->Name,"\n";
    foreach my $val (in $prop->Values) {
        print "   ",$val->CaseIgnoreString,"\n";
    }
}
```

It is worth noting that with Net::LDAP, you generally need to bind to the target domain controller before performing a search or any other operation. In the Net::LDAP example above, I didn't need to do that because I queried the RootDSE, which allows anonymous (i.e., unauthenticated) connections. A bind can be done using the following code:

```
$ldapobj->bind('administrator@rallencorp.com', password => 'galt');
```

In the second code sample where I used ADSI with Win32::OLE, the credentials of the user running the script are used by default, so you only need to do an explicit bind if you need to authenticate as a different user.

Discussion

The Net::LDAP modules are a robust set of modules for querying and modifying an LDAP directory. Net::LDAP also supports DSML, the abstract schema, and LDIF. Net::LDAP is a native Perl implementation, which means that it does not rely on an external LDAP SDK. Since it is a pure Perl implementation, you can write Net::LDAP-based scripts on a variety of platforms to interface with Active Directory or other LDAP-based directories. Graham Barr initially developed the Net::LDAP modules and more information can be found about the modules on the following web site: *http://perl-ldap.sourceforge.net/*.

The Win32::OLE modules provide an interface into Microsoft's Component Object Model (COM). Most of the ADSI classes and methods are available from the COM automation interface, known as IDispatch. This allows you to combine the flexibility of Perl with the robustness of ADSI. Documentation for the Win32::OLE module can be found at *http://aspn.activestate.com/ASPN/Perl/Products/ActivePerl/site/lib/Win32/OLE.html*.

See Also

http://www.cpan.org/ to download Perl modules

18.5   Programming with Java

Problem

You want to programmatically access Active Directory using Java.

Solution

The Java Naming and Directory Interface (JNDI) is a standard extension to Java that can be used to access a variety of naming and directory services including DNS and LDAP. JNDI is part of the Java Enterprise API set and is documented on the following site: *http://java.sun.com/products/jndi/*. JNDI provides an object-oriented interface to programming with LDAP, and is not based on the LDAP C API, which many other LDAP API's are based on.

The following code uses JNDI to print out the RootDSE for the host DC1:

```java
/**
 * Print the RootDSE for DC1
 * usage: java RootDSE
 */

import javax.naming.*;
import javax.naming.directory.*;

class RootDSE {
    public static void main(String[] args) {

        try {
            // Create initial context.
            DirContext ctx = new InitialDirContext();

            // Read attributes from root DSE.
            Attributes attrs = ctx.getAttributes(
                "ldap://DC1", new String[]{"*"});

            // Get a list of the attributes.
            NamingEnumeration enums = attrs.getIDs();

            // Print out each attribute and its values.
            while (enums != null && enums.hasMore()) {
                String nextattr = (String)enums.next();
                System.out.println( attrs.get(nextattr) );
            }

            // Close the context.
            ctx.close();

        } catch (NamingException e) {
            e.printStackTrace();
        }
    }
}
```

Discussion

Any serious Java programmer should be familiar with JNDI. It is a generic interface that can be used with a variety of services, not least of which includes Active Directory. A good tutorial on JNDI is available on Sun's web site: *http://java.sun.com/products/jndi/tutorial/*.

See Also

Sun's JNDI home page: *http://java.sun.com/products/jndi/*

18.6 Programming with Python

Problem

You want to programmatically access Active Directory using Python.

Solution

As with Perl, you have two options for programming Active Directory with Python: the native LDAP-based approach, and a COM interface, which allows you to use ADSI. The LDAP module can be downloaded from *http://python-ldap.sourceforge.net/*. The COM interface is part of the standard ActivePython install available from ActiveState (*http://www.activestate.com/ActivePython/*).

The following Python code sample prints out the RootDSE of DC1 using the LDAP interface:

```
import ldap

try:
    l = ldap.open("dc1")
except ldap.LDAPError, e:
    print e

baseDN = ""
searchScope = ldap.SCOPE_BASE
retrieveAttributes = None
searchFilter = "objectclass=*"

try:
    ldap_result_id = l.search(baseDN, searchScope, searchFilter,
                              retrieveAttributes)
    result_type, result_data = l.result(ldap_result_id, 0)
    if result_type == ldap.RES_SEARCH_ENTRY:
        print result_data

except ldap.LDAPError, e:
    print e
```

This next code sample uses the win32com.client module to access the RootDSE with ADSI:

```
import win32com.client

objRootDSE = win32com.client.GetObject('LDAP://RootDSE')
objRootDSE.GetInfo()

for i in range( 0, objRootDSE.PropertyCount - 1):
    prop = objRootDSE.Item(i)
    print prop.Name
    for val in prop.Values:
        print "   ",val.CaseIgnoreString
```

Discussion

More information is available on Python by going to the Python home page: *http://www.python.org/*.

18.7   Integrating with MIT Kerberos

Problem

You want to integrate your existing MIT Kerberos infrastructure with Active Directory.

Solution

Integrating MIT Kerberos with Active Directory typically means setting up a trust between an Active Directory domain and your MIT Kerberos realm. Creating a trust between a domain and realm is the first step toward Kerberos interoperability. It will allow users to access resources in either the AD domain or Kerberos realm. Here are the steps to create the trust:

1. Create a trust to the Kerberos realm on a domain controller:

   ```
   > netdom trust AD.RALLENCORP.COM /Domain:MIT.RALLENCORP.COM /Add /Realm /↵
   PasswordT:"Password"
   ```

2. Make the trust transitive (if necessary):

   ```
   > netdom trust AD.RALLENCORP.COM /Domain:MIT.RALLENCORP.COM /Transitive:yes
   ```

3. Add a KDC for the Kerberos realm on the domain controller(s):

   ```
   > ksetup /addkdc MIT.RALLENCORP.COM kdc01.mit.rallencorp.com
   ```

4. Add the AD domain principal to the Kerberos realm (on the Unix host):

   ```
   kadmin: addprinc -e des-cbc-crc:normal krbtgt/ad.rallencorp.com
   ```

Discussion

What I've shown here is just the tip of the iceberg. You may need to configure service principals, create account mappings, create host principals, and tweak the *krb5.conf* configuration file on your MIT KDCs to accomplish full integration in your environment. Providing details on how to do all of that is beyond the scope of this book, but a great resource on Kerberos is O'Reilly's *Kerberos: The Definiteive Guide*, which covers all the ins and outs of the Kerberos protocol and interoperability with Active Directory. Also, there are some good resources on the Web, which I've listed here:

- MIT Kerberos home page (*http://web.mit.edu/kerberos/www/*)
- Microsoft's Step-by-Step Guide to MIT Kerberos Interoperability (*http://www.microsoft.com/windows2000/techinfo/planning/security/kerbsteps.asp*)
- Windows 2000-MIT Kerberos Interop Trip-ups (*http://calnetad.berkeley.edu/documentation/test_environment/kerb_interop_trip-ups.html*)

See Also

MS KB 217098 (Basic Overview of Kerberos User Authentication Protocol in Windows 2000), MS KB 230476 (Description of Common Kerberos-Related Errors in Windows 2000), MS KB 248758 (Information About the Windows 2000 Kerberos Implementation), MS KB 324143 (HOW TO: Use the Kerberos Setup Tool (Ksetup.exe)), and MS KB 810755 (White Paper: Windows 2000 Kerberos Interoperability and Authentication)

18.8   Integrating with Samba

Problem

You want your Samba clients to authenticate against Active Directory and access Active Directory resources.

Solution

Samba 2.2 currently does not provide Active Directory support. The next release, Samba 3.0, which is in Beta at the time of this writing, will provide client-side support of Active Directory. OpenLDAP and MIT Kerberos must also be installed on the client to provide full LDAP and Kerberos functionality.

Discussion

Samba has a rich history of providing Unix integration and interoperability solutions for the Windows network operating system (NOS) under Windows NT. Samba is typically deployed so that Windows-based clients can use Unix-based file and print services seamlessly. A Samba server can also act as a PDC in a Windows NT 4.0 environment. Do not expect this level of server emulation for Active Directory domain controllers any time soon.

See Also

For more information on the Samba project, see *http://www.samba.org/*.

18.9   Integrating with Apache

Problem

If your organization has Active Directory and Apache deployed, one way to reduce logins is to integrate the two by having HTTP authentication on Apache use Active Directory.

Solution

There are several Apache modules that support authentication to an LDAP store, and with the release of Apache 2.0, it is supported natively with the mod_auth_ldap module. The documentation for mod_auth_ldap can be found at the following site: *http://httpd.apache.org/docs-2.0/mod/mod_auth_ldap.html*.

The mod_auth_ldap module works in the following way:

1. Binds using preconfigured bind DN and bind password.
2. Searches the directory with the preconfigured search filter and username of the user that is authenticating.
3. If a match was found, performs a bind attempt with the matching user's DN and password.

If you are still running Apache 1.x, the auth_ldap module is widely used and works in much the same way as mod_auth_ldap. For more information, visit the following site: *http://www.rudedog.org/auth_ldap/*.

Discussion

The mod_auth_ldap module isn't ideal from an Active Directory perspective. Typically, the second step (search for the user's DN) is completely unnecessary. If you have been configuring a user principal name (UPN) for all of your users, the search could be eliminated by attempting to authenticate the user with its UPN instead of the DN. Active Directory supports binding with either. That means mod_auth_ldap could instead just take the user name entered in the user name/password prompt and prepend it to a preconfigured UPN suffix (e.g., @rallencorp.com). Hopefully, the developers of mod_auth_ldap will take this into consideration for a future enhancement.

Another issue to be aware of when using this module is that you will need to hard-code a domain controller name to query and bind against in the mod_auth_ldap configuration. Unless you are using some type of load balancing software or hardware, you will be placing a dependency on that domain controller.

Both mod_auth_ldap and auth_ldap support SSL and TLS, and I highly recommend enabling that if you plan on using either of these modules. If you don't enable SSL/TLS support, passwords sent from the Apache server to a domain controller will be sent in clear text.

See Also

For more information on Apache, see *http://www.apache.org/*.

18.10 Replacing NIS

Problem

You want to replace all or part of your NIS infrastructure with Active Directory. NIS serves many of the same functions as Active Directory and you can reduce costs by integrating both infrastructures.

Solution

The Microsoft Services for Unix (SFU) suite provides numerous tools that can aid in integrating your Unix and Windows systems. SFU has a NIS server that can be used as a replacement for existing NIS servers and uses Active Directory as its data store. SFU comes with a set of schema extensions that the NIS server uses to structure the user, group, and host information that NIS clients require. SFU also includes a NFS server and client software if you are trying to interoperate with NFS. All of the SFU software runs on Windows operating systems. More information on SFU can be found on the following site: *http://www.microsoft.com/windows/sfu/default.asp*.

If you'd rather not use SFU, another option is the NIS/LDAP Gateway from PADL Software *(http://www.padl.com/)*. The PADL NIS/LDAP Gateway utilizes the SFU schema extensions to provide NIS services with an Active Directory backend. NIS clients can use the gateway to resolve user, group, and host information and works with SunONE Directory Server as well as Active Directory. The NIS/LDAP Gateway is supported on a host of Unix-based platforms including Solaris, FreeBSD, and Linux.

See Also

LDAP System Administration (O'Reilly), MS KB 324083 (HOW TO: Install Server for NIS on Windows for Unix-to-Windows Migration), MS KB 324541 (HOW TO: Configure Server for NIS for a Unix-to-Windows Migration), and MS KB 324543 (HOW TO: Migrate Existing NIS Maps to Server for NIS in a Unix-to-Windows Migration)

18.11 Using BIND for DNS

Problem

You've decided that you do not want to use Microsoft DNS for Active Directory and instead prefer to use BIND.

Solution

The two main requirements for supporting Active Directory DNS are SRV records and Dynamic DNS support. The first version of BIND to support SRV records was 8.2.2 patch 7. Hopefully you are running a much more recent version since that was released in 2000. You technically don't have to use DDNS with Active Directory DNS records, but if you don't, you end up doing a lot of work to manually maintain the Active Directory–related resource records.

Here is an example BIND 8 configuration to support the *ad.rallencorp.com* domain:

```
Options {
directory "/etc/namedb";
};
Zone "ad.rallencorp.com" IN {
type master;
file "db.ad.rallencorp.com";
allow-update { dc1.; dc2.; dc3.; };
check-names ignore;
};
```

The directory directive specifies where the zone files are stored. The type should be master, and the file directive is the name of the file to store the contents of the zone in. The allow-update directive indicates which servers (either by name or IP address) can dynamically update the zone. Finally, the check-names ignore directive tells BIND not to be restrictive about the names used in resource records. Without this setting, BIND would fail to respond to queries for records containing underscores used by Active Directory.

The BIND 9 configuration for the same zone would look exactly the same, except the `check-names ignore` line is not necessary. By default, BIND 9 allows underscores in resource records.

After your BIND servers are properly configured, be sure the resolver on your domain controllers points to at least one of the BIND name servers. This can be done by going into the Network Connections for each domain controller and right-clicking the active connection. Click on Properties, highlight Internet Protocol (TCP/IP), and select Properties. You can configure the resolvers under the General tab. This setting can also be configured through DHCP or Group Policy.

Discussion

See Recipe 13.13 for forcing a domain controller to reregister its records and Recipe 13.12 for verifying a domain controller can register its records.

BIND documentation and source can be downloaded from the following ISC site: *http://www.isc.org/products/BIND/*.

See Also

MS KB 255913 (Integrating Windows 2000 DNS into an Existing BIND or Windows NT 4.0-Based DNS Namespace), and MS KB 323419 (HOW TO: Migrate an Existing DNS Infrastructure from a BIND-Based Server to a Windows Server 2003-Based DNS)

18.12 Authorizing a Microsoft DHCP Server

Problem

You want to authorize a Microsoft DHCP server in Active Directory so that clients can use it.

Solution

Using a graphical user interface

1. Open the DHCP snap-in.
2. In the left pane, right-click on DHCP and select New Server.
3. Type in the name of the new DHCP server and click OK.
4. Click on the server entry in the left pane.
5. Right-click on the server and select Authorize.

Discussion

Windows 2000- and Windows Server 2003-based DHCP servers must be authorized before they can give out leases to clients. This feature helps reduce the occurrence of rogue DHCP servers that an end-user sets up, perhaps even unintentionally. A rogue DHCP server can provide incorrect lease information or deny lease requests altogether, ultimately causing a denial of service for clients on your network.

If the DHCP Server service is enabled on a domain controller, it is automatically authorized. A DHCP server that is a member server of an Active Directory domain performs a query in Active Directory to determine whether it is authorized. If it is, it will respond to DHCP requests, if not, it will not respond to requests. A standalone DHCP server that is not a member of an Active Directory domain sends out a DHCPINFORM message when it first initializes. If an authorized DHCP server responds to the message, the standalone server will not respond to any further DHCP requests. If it does not receive a response from any DHCP servers, it will respond to client requests and give out leases.

Authorized DHCP servers are represented in Active Directory as objects of the dhcpClass class, which can be found in the *cn=NetServices,cn=Services, cn=Configuratation,<ForestRootDN>* container. The RDN for each authorized DHCP server is the IP address of the server.

 Windows 2000 DHCP servers cannot be authorized with the Windows Server 2003 version of the DHCP snap-in unless the DHCP server has Service Pack 2 installed.

See Also

MS KB 279908 (Unexpected Results in the DHCP Service Snap-In After Using NETSH to Authorize DHCP), MS KB 300429 (HOW TO: Install and Configure a DHCP Server in an Active Directory Domain in Windows 2000), and MS KB 303351 (How to Use Netsh.exe to Authorize, Unauthorize, and List DHCP Servers in Active Directory), MS KB *306925* (Cannot Authorize New DHCP Server in Active Directory), and MS KB 323360 (HOW TO: Install and Configure a DHCP Server in an Active Directory Domain in Windows Server 2003)

18.13 Using VMWare for Testing AD

Problem

One of the issues that developers and administrators commonly face when trying to do Active Directory testing is the limitation of being able to host only a single domain on a server. You can use VMWare to work around this issue and host multiple domains on a single server.

Solution

VMWare, Inc. (*http://www.vmware.com/*) develops a very popular virtual machine technology that allows you to run multiple operating systems, even of different varieties, on a single machine. Their VMWare Workstation product can be used on laptops and desktop servers and is great for running simulations. Their VMWare GSX Server is oriented for enterprise solutions so that you could even run production-grade services from VMWare virtual machines.

As far as Active Directory goes, you can create several virtual machines on a single host using either the Workstation or GSX Server products to simulate a forest. I've personally used VMWare to help facilitate schema extension testing. Since there is no supported schema deletion process, once you've extended the schema, you cannot extend the schema again with the same extensions (if you wanted to test the extension process again). VMWare stores each virtual machine as a collection of files. Once you've created a baseline domain controller virtual machine, you can copy the files that make up that virtual machine and create as many domain controllers as needed.

If you support multiple domains in a forest, it can be expensive in terms of both hardware and people to support multiple test environments that are similar to your production environment. For each domain in a forest, you need a separate server. If you have a four-domain forest and want to create three test environments, you'd need 12 servers total. With VMWare, you could use three servers and host all four domains on each server. I suppose if you had a big enough server, you could even host all four test environments on the same server!

The new snapshot capability with VMWare 4.0 can make testing even easier. With it you can take a snapshot of a virtual machine and preserve its state at a specific moment in time. You can then revert to the saved snapshot at any time, irrespective of whether the machine is powered on or off. This is ideal for testing schema changes.

Discussion

One of the caveats with using VMWare is that Microsoft will not support any issues that arise while running Active Directory or any other product for that matter under VMWare. In my experience, Microsoft support will make a best effort to try and troubleshoot problems with VMWare, but they will not guarantee a resolution.

Speaking of Microsoft, they have plans of their own for developing virtual server technology. In February 2003, Microsoft purchased rights to the Virtual PC software developed by Connectix, a privately held company. By mid-2003 Microsoft released a customer preview of the newly packaged Microsoft Virtual Server for Windows Server 2003. This will be a direct competitor to VMWare and provides many of the same capabilities. For more information on the Virtual Server, see *http://www.microsoft.com/ windowsserver2003/evaluation/news/bulletins/vmnews.mspx*.

See Also

MS KB 273508 (VMWare Support Policy and Support Boundaries)

Tool List

There are more Active Directory tools than you can shake a domain controller at! There are over 50 tools used in this book alone. In this appendix, I've listed each tool I used in the book along with the tasks that can be accomplished with it, what kind of tool it is, where it can be found, and the recipes in which it was used.

ACL Diagnostics Command (acldiag.exe)

Tasks that can be accomplished:
    View the ACL (permission and audit entries) for an object, check an object's ACL against the default in the schema, get effective permissions for a user or group, and check and fix delegations performed through the Delegation of Control wizard

Type of tool:
    Command line

Where to find it:
    Support Tools for Windows 2000 and Windows Server 2003

Recipes in which it is used:
    14.9, 14.12

Active Directory Domains and Trusts Snap-in (domain.msc)

Tasks that can be accomplished:
    Raise domain mode (Windows 2000) or functional level (Windows Server 2003) of a domain or forest, manage trusts, and view and modify the description and managedBy attributes for a domain

Type of tool:
    MMC snap-in

Where to find it:
   adminpak.msi for Windows 2000 and Windows Server 2003

Recipes in which it is used:
   2.6, 2.7, 2.9, 2.13, 2.14, 2.15, 2.16, 2.17, 2.18, 2.19, 2.20, 2.21, 2.22, 3.25

Active Directory Installation Wizard (dcpromo.exe)

Tasks that can be accomplished:
   Promote and demote a domain controller

Type of tool:
   Wizard

Where to find it:
   %SystemRoot%\System32 on Windows 2000 and Windows Server 2003

Recipes in which it is used:
   2.1, 2.2, 2.3, 2.4, 3.1, 3.2, 3.3, 3.4

Active Directory Load Balancer Command (adlb.exe)

Tasks that can be accomplished:
   Balance the load among connection objects within a site

Type of tool:
   Command line

Where to find it:
   Windows Server 2003 Resource Kit

Recipes in which it is used:
   11.24

Active Directory Schema Snap-in (schmmgmt.msc)

Tasks that can be accomplished:
   Browse, create, and modify classes and attributes

Type of tool:
   MMC snap-in

Where to find it:
   adminpak.msi for Windows 2000 and Windows Server 2003

Recipes in which it is used:
   3.25, 5.10, 10.1, 10.2, 10.7, 10.8, 10.9, 10.10, 10.11, 10.12, 10.13, 10.14, 10.19, 10.20, 10.21, 14.11

Active Directory Sites and Services (dssite.msc)

Tasks that can be accomplished:
Browse and manipulate site topology objects (sites, subnets, links, servers, etc.), manage connection objects, schedule replication, force replication from a partner, trigger the KCC, enable the global catalog, specify an alternate LDAP query policy for a domain controller, and enable universal group caching

Type of tool:
MMC snap-in

Where to find it:
adminpak.msi for Windows 2000 and Windows Server 2003

Recipes in which it is used:
3.11, 3.17, 3.20, 7.9, 11.1, 11.2, 11.3, 11.4, 11.5, 11.7, 11.9, 11.10, 11.11, 11.12, 11.14, 11.16, 11.22, 11.23, 11.25, 11.27, 12.4, 12.6

Active Directory Users and Computers Snap-in (dsa.msc)

Tasks that can be accomplished:
Browse, create, and manipulate users, groups, computers, OUs, and other domain specific objects. Create and save queries to find objects, raise the functional level of a domain, view and transfer the FSMOs for a domain, delegate control, and much more

Type of tool:
MMC snap-in

Where to find it:
adminpak.msi for Windows 2000 and Windows Server 2003

Recipes in which it is used:
3.8, 3.25, 5.1, 5.2, 5.3, 5.4, 5.5, 5.6, 5.7, 5.9, 6.1, 6.3, 6.4, 6.5, 6.6, 6.7, 6.8, 6.12, 6.13, 6.14, 6.15, 6.16, 6.17, 6.20, 6.21, 6.22, 6.24, 6.25, 6.27, 6.28, 6.29, 7.1, 7.2, 7.3, 7.4, 7.6, 7.7, 7.8, 8.1, 8.2, 8.4, 8.7

AD Prep Utility (adprep.exe)

Tasks that can be accomplished:
Prepare a Windows 2000 domain and forest for update to Windows Server 2003

Type of tool:
Command

Where to find it:
\i386 on Windows Server 2003 CD

Recipes in which it is used:
2.10, 2.11

ADSI Edit (adsiedit.msc)

Tasks that can be accomplished:
Generic Active Directory editor that can be used to search, browse, create, and manipulate objects throughout a forest

Type of tool:
MMC snap-in

Where to find it:
Support Tools for Windows 2000 and Windows Server 2003

Recipes in which it is used:
4.10, 4.11, 4.13, 4.16, 4.17, 4.18, 4.20, 4.21, 4.23, 6.30, 6.31, 8.9, 11.26, 11.29, 13.17, 14.3, 14.15, 15.15, 15.16, 16.13, 16.18, 17.1, 17.4, 17.7, 17.8, 17.9

Audit Policy Command (auditpol.exe)

Tasks that can be accomplished:
Enable or disable auditing on a computer

Type of tool:
Command line

Where to find it:
Resource Kit for Windows 2000

Recipes in which it is used:
15.12

Backup Wizard (ntbackup.exe)

Tasks that can be accomplished:
Back up and restore a domain controller, including Active Directory

Type of tool:
Wizard

Where to find it:
%SystemRoot%\System32 on Windows 2000 and Windows Server 2003

Recipes in which it is used:
3.2, 16.1, 16.4, 16.5, 16.6

CSVDE Command (csvde.exe)

Tasks that can be accomplished:
Import and export objects using a comma-separated value (CSV) formatted file

Type of tool:
   Command line

Where to find it:
   %SystemRoot%\System32 on Windows 2000 and Windows Server 2003

Recipes in which it is used:
   4.26, 4.27

Default Domain Controller Security Policy Snap-in (dcpol.msc)

Tasks that can be accomplished:
   Modify the settings of the Domain Controller Security GPO

Type of tool:
   MMC snap-in

Where to find it:
   %SystemRoot%\System32 on Windows 2000 and Windows Server 2003

Recipes in which it is used:
   14.1, 14.14, 15.12

Default Domain Security Policy Snap-in (dompol.msc)

Tasks that can be accomplished:
    Modify the settings of the Domain Security GPO

Type of tool:
   MMC snap-in

Where to find it:
   %SystemRoot%\System32 on Windows 2000 and Windows Server 2003

Recipes in which it is used:
   6.11, 14.19

Default Group Policy Restore Command (dcgpofix.exe)

Tasks that can be accomplished:
   Restore the Domain Controllers Security Policy and Domain Security Policy to the default

Type of tool:
   Command line

Where to find it:
   %SystemRoot%\System32 on Windows Server 2003

Recipes in which it is used:
   9.22

DNS Snap-in (dnsmgmt.msc)

Tasks that can be accomplished:
Browse and manipulate DNS server configuration; and browse, create, and modify zones and resource records. Enable debug logging, perform DNS test queries, restart the DNS service, modify permissions, and modify application partition configuration

Type of tool:
MMC snap-in

Where to find it:
adminpak.msi for Windows 2000 and Windows Server 2003

Recipes in which it is used:
13.1, 13.2, 13.3, 13.4, 13.5, 13.6, 13.7, 13.9, 13.10, 13.11, 15.6

DNSCmd Command (dnscmd.exe)

Tasks that can be accomplished:
Manipulate DNS server configuration; query, create, and modify zones; and resource records. View server statistics, enable debug logging, and modify application partition configuration

Type of tool:
Command line

Where to find it:
Support Tools for Windows 2000 and Windows Server 2003

Recipes in which it is used:
13.1, 13.2, 13.3, 13.4, 13.5, 13.7, 13.9, 13.10, 13.11, 15.6, 15.7

Domain Controller Diagnosis Command (dcdiag.exe)

Tasks that can be accomplished:
Run a variety of diagnostics tests against a domain controller

Type of tool:
Command line

Where to find it:
Support Tools for Windows 2000 and Windows Server 2003

Recipes in which it is used:
3.5, 3.12, 11.28, 12.8, 13.12, 17.6

DS ACL Command (dsacls.exe)

Tasks that can be accomplished:
   View and set ACLs on objects

Type of tool:
   Command line

Where to find it:
   Support Tools for Windows 2000 and Windows Server 2003

Recipes in which it is used:
   7.7, 8.2, 13.6, 14.7, 14.10, 14.13, 17.9

DS Add Command (dsadd.exe)

Tasks that can be accomplished:
   Add computer, contact, group, OU, user, and quota objects

Type of tool:
   Command line

Where to find it:
   %SystemRoot%\System32 on Windows Server 2003

Recipes in which it is used:
   5.1, 6.1, 6.2, 7.1, 8.1, 8.2, 15.13

DS Get Command (dsget.exe)

Tasks that can be accomplished:
   Retrieve the properties of computer, contact, subnet, group, OU, server, site, user, quota, and partition objects

Type of tool:
   Command line

Where to find it:
   %SystemRoot%\System32 on Windows Server 2003

Recipes in which it is used:
   7.2, 7.3, 6.14, 6.16, 11.2, 11.5, 15.17

DS Modify Command (dsmodify.exe)

Tasks that can be accomplished:
   Modify properties of computer, contact, group, OU, server, user, quota, and partition objects

Type of tool:
    Command line

Where to find it:
    %SystemRoot%\System32 on Windows Server 2003

Recipes in which it is used:
    3.17, 6.3, 6.6, 6.12, 6.16, 6.17, 6.20, 6.21, 6.22, 6.24, 6.25, 6.29, 7.4, 7.6, 8.7

DS Move Command (dsmove.exe)

Tasks that can be accomplished:
    Move and rename objects

Type of tool:
    Command line

Where to find it:
    %SystemRoot%\System32 on Windows Server 2003

Recipes in which it is used:
    3.11, 4.17, 4.19, 5.6, 5.7, 6.5, 6.6, 8.4, 11.16

DS Query Command (dsquery.exe)

Tasks that can be accomplished:
    Perform queries for computer, contact, group, OU, server, site, subnet, user, quota, and partition objects. Perform generic queries to retrieve any type of object

Type of tool:
    Command line

Where to find it:
    %SystemRoot%\System32 on Windows Server 2003

Recipes in which it is used:
    2.7, 2.9, 2.13, 2.14, 3.19, 3.20, 3.25, 4.2, 4.5, 4.6, 4.7, 4.9, 4.22, 5.2, 5.3, 5.6, 5.8, 6.4, 6.13, 6.23, 6.28, 7.9, 8.8, 10.8, 10.10, 10.15, 10.16, 10.17, 10.18, 11.2, 11.3, 11.5, 11.8, 11.15, 12.11, 15.14, 17.2, 17.5

DS Remove Command (dsrm.exe)

Tasks that can be accomplished:
    Remove leaf nodes and subtrees

Type of tool:
    Command line

Where to find it:
    %SystemRoot%\System32 on Windows Server 2003

Recipes in which it is used:
    4.20, 4.21, 5.4, 5.5

Enumprop Command (enumprop.exe)

Tasks that can be accomplished:
    View the attributes of an object

Type of tool:
    Command line

Where to find it:
    Windows 2000 Resource Kit

Recipes in which it is used:
    2.9, 2.13, 2.14, 4.1, 4.2, 6.11, 6.30

Group Policy Management Console (gpmc.msc)

Tasks that can be accomplished:
    One-stop shopping for all your GPO management needs. You can perform just about any GPO management task from this tool. A variety of scripts are also provided with the GPMC install that can be used to manage GPOs from a command line. The GPMC scripts used in this book include: *BackupGpo.wsf, CopyGpo.wsf, CreateGpo.wsf, DeleteGpo.wsf, DumpGpoInfo.wsf, GetReportsForGpo.wsf, ImportGpo.wsf, ListAllGpos.wsf, QueryBackupLocation.wsf, RestoreGpo.wsf,* and *SetGpoPermissions.wsf*

Type of tool:
    MMC snap-in

Where to find it:
    http://www.microsoft.com/downloads/details.aspx?FamilyId=F39E9D60-7E41-4947-82F5-3330F37ADFEB&displaylang=en

Recipes in which it is used:
    5.11, 9.1, 9.2, 9.3, 9.4, 9.5, 9.6, 9.7, 9.8, 9.9, 9.10, 9.11, 9.12, 9.13, 9.14, 9.15, 9.16, 9.17, 9.18, 9.19

Group Policy Object Editor (gpedit.msc)

Tasks that can be accomplished:
    Modify the settings of a GPO

Type of tool:
    MMC snap-in

Where to find it:
    %SystemRoot%\System32 on Windows 2000 and Windows Server 2003

Recipes in which it is used:
    9.6

Group Policy Verification Tool (gpotool.exe)

Tasks that can be accomplished:
    Verify consistency of a GPO across domain controllers, view properties of GPOs, such as display name, when created and changed, version number, GUID, and flags

Type of tool:
    Command line

Where to find it:
    Resource Kit for Windows 2000 and Windows Server 2003

Recipes in which it is used:
    9.1

Group Policy Results Command (gpresult.exe)

Tasks that can be accomplished:
    Display the resultant set of policy (RSoP) for a user and computer

Type of tool:
    Command line

Where to find it:
    %SystemRoot%\System32 on Windows Server 2003

Recipes in which it is used:
    9.20

Group Policy Refresh Command (gpupdate.exe)

Tasks that can be accomplished:
    Apply the changed settings of a GPO, apply all settings of a GPO, and reboot or logoff user after GPO processing completes

Type of tool:
    Command line

Where to find it:
%SystemRoot%\System32 on Windows Server 2003

Recipes in which it is used:
9.21

IP Configuration (ipconfig.exe)

Tasks that can be accomplished:
Request, release, renew an IP address, flush the local DNS cache, display the local DNS cache, and register resource records in DNS

Type of tool:
Command line

Where to find it:
%SystemRoot%\System32 on Windows 2000 and Windows Server 2003

Recipes in which it is used:
13.11

Kerberos List (klist.exe)

Tasks that can be accomplished:
View and purge Kerberos tickets

Type of tool:
Command line

Where to find it:
Resource Kit for Windows 2000 and Windows Server 2003

Recipes in which it is used:
14.9

Kerberos Tray (kerbtray.exe)

Tasks that can be accomplished:
View and purge Kerberos tickets

Type of tool:
Graphical User Interface

Where to find it:
Resource Kit for Windows 2000 and Windows Server 2003

Recipes in which it is used:
14.17

LDIFDE Command (ldifde.exe)

Tasks that can be accomplished:
Import and export objects using the LDAP Interchange Format (LDIF)

Type of tool:
Command line

Where to find it:
%SystemRoot%\System32 on Windows 2000 and Windows Server 2003

Recipes in which it is used:
2.11, 2.13, 2.14, 4.10, 4.11, 4.13, 4.14, 4.15, 4.24, 4.25, 5.10, 6.3, 7.9, 8.9, 8.10, 10.7, 10.9, 10.11, 10.12, 10.13, 10.14, 10.20, 10.22, 11.1, 11.4, 11.7, 11.9, 11.10, 11.12, 11.14, 11.29, 12.6, 13.17, 15.15, 15.16, 16.10, 16.13, 16.18, 17.7

LDP (ldp.exe)

Tasks that can be accomplished:
Generic LDAP object editor and browser

Type of tool:
Graphical User Interface

Where to find it:
Support Tools for Windows 2000 and Windows Server 2003

Recipes in which it is used:
3.10, 3.19, 4.1, 4.2, 4.2, 4.3, 4.5, 4.6, 4.7, 4.8, 4.9, 4.15, 4.22, 5.8, 8.10, 8.11, 8.12, 10.15, 10.16, 10.17, 10.18, 11.8, 11.15, 12.11, 12.12, 15.9, 16.10, 16.16, 16.17, 17.2, 17.3

Move Tree Command (movetree.exe)

Tasks that can be accomplished:
Move objects within and between a domain

Type of tool:
Command line

Where to find it:
Support Tools for Windows 2000 and Windows Server 2003

Recipes in which it is used:
4.18

Netdom Command (netdom.exe)

Tasks that can be accomplished:
Add a computer to the domain, rename a computer, join a computer to the domain, move a computer to a new domain, query computers, trusts, and FSMOs in a domain, remove a computer from a domain, reset a computer, and manage and verify trusts

Type of tool:
Command line

Where to find it:
Support Tools for Windows 2000 and Windows Server 2003

Recipes in which it is used:
2.15, 2.16, 2.17, 2.18, 2.20, 2.20, 2.21, 2.22, 2.23, 3.7, 3.8, 3.25, 8.3, 8.5, 8.7, 18.7

Network Connectivity Tester (netdiag.exe)

Tasks that can be accomplished:
Run a variety of network-based diagnostics tests

Type of tool:
Command line

Where to find it:
Support Tools for Windows 2000 and Windows Server 2003

Recipes in which it is used:
14.18

NLTest Command (nltest.exe)

Tasks that can be accomplished:
Query, verify, and reset the secure channel of a computer; obtain a list of domain controllers for a domain; find a domain controller; find a client's site; display the site coverage for a domain controller; register and deregister a domain controller's resource records; display the parent domain; query trusts; view the number of logon attempts processed by a domain controller; and perform a shutdown

Type of tool:
Command line

Where to find it:
Support Tools for Windows 2000 and Windows Server 2003

Recipes in which it is used:
3.9, 3.10, 3.12, 3.14, 8.6, 11.18, 11.20, 13.13, 13.16, 15.3

Nslookup Command (nslookup.exe)

Tasks that can be accomplished:
Perform DNS lookups for any resource record type

Type of tool:
Command line

Where to find it:
%SystemRoot%\System32 on Windows 2000 and Windows Server 2003

Recipes in which it is used:
2.2, 2.4, 3.21, 3.28, 13.8

NTDS Util Command (ntdsutil.exe)

Tasks that can be accomplished:
Perform a variety of DIT maintenance functions, such as checking DIT file integrity and semantics, perform a soft recovery, perform restores, view FSMO role holders, manages LDAP query policies, find and remove duplicate SIDs, clean-up metadata from a failed domain controller, and set the DS Restore mode administrator password

Type of tool:
Command line

Where to find it:
%SystemRoot%\System32 on Windows 2000 and Windows Server 2003

Recipes in which it is used:
2.5, 2.6, 2.24, 3.6, 3.26, 3.27, 4.16, 4.23, 14.4, 16.3, 16.5, 16.6, 16.7, 16.8, 16.9, 16.12, 16.15, 17.1, 17.3, 17.4, 17.8

OID Generator Command (oidgen.exe)

Tasks that can be accomplished:
Generate an object identifier to be used when creating new classes or attributes in the schema

Type of tool:
Command line

Where to find it:
Windows 2000 Resource Kit

Recipes in which it is used:
10.3

Redirect Default Computers Command (redircmp.exe)

Tasks that can be accomplished:
Redirect the default computers container to another location in the directory tree

Type of tool:
Command line

Where to find it:
%SystemRoot%\System32 on Windows Server 2003

Recipes in which it is used:
8.12

Redirect Default Users Command (redirusr.exe)

Tasks that can be accomplished:
Redirect the default users container to another location in the directory tree

Type of tool:
Command line

Where to find it:
%SystemRoot%\System32 on Windows Server 2003

Recipes in which it is used:
8.12

Reg Command (reg.exe)

Tasks that can be accomplished:
Query, add, delete, copy, save, restore, load, unload, compare, export, and import registry keys and values

Type of tool:
Command line

Where to find it:
Support Tools for Windows 2000 and Windows Server 2003

Recipes in which it is used:
3.23, 10.1, 11.16, 11.18, 11.20, 11.29, 12.4, 12.9, 13.13, 13.14, 14.17, 15.0, 15.1, 15.3, 15.4, 16.9, 16.13

Registry Editor (regedit.exe)

Tasks that can be accomplished:
Browse, query, add, delete, rename, export, import, and copy registry keys and values

Type of tool:
  Graphical User Interface
Where to find it:
  %SystemRoot%\System32 on Windows 2000 and Windows Server 2003
Recipes in which it is used:
  3.22, 3.23, 11.17, 11.19, 11.21, 11.30, 12.5, 12.10, 14.18, 15.1, 15.2, 15.4, 15.5, 16.11, 16.14

Rename Domain Command (rendom.exe)

Tasks that can be accomplished:
  Rename a domain (requires the Windows Server 2003 forest functional level)
Type of tool:
  Command line
Where to find it:
  http://www.microsoft.com/windowsserver2003/downloads/domainrename.mspx
Recipes in which it is used:
  2.8

Replication Diagnostics Command (repadmin.exe)

Tasks that can be accomplished:
  Display the bridgeheads for a site, find the ISTG for a site, trigger the KCC, force replication to a partner, replicate a single object, force synchronization of a naming context, view the replication status of several domain controllers, show the differences between two domain controllers, view object metadata, obtain the up-to-dateness vector, and a variety of other replication management functions
Type of tool:
  Command line
Where to find it:
  Support Tools for Windows 2000 and Windows Server 2003
Recipes in which it is used:
  11.13, 11.22, 11.23, 11.25, 11.27, 12.1, 12.2, 12.3, 12.4, 12.8, 12.12, 17.7

Replication Monitor (replmon.exe)

Tasks that can be accomplished:
  View the replication status of the naming contexts supported by a domain controller, force replication to a partner, force synchronization of a naming context,

get the current USN, search a domain for replication errors, generate a detailed status report, and much more

Type of tool:
Graphical User Interface

Where to find it:
Support Tools for Windows 2000 and Windows Server 2003

Recipes in which it is used:
11.13, 12.3

Resultant Set of Policy Snap-in (rsop.msc)

Tasks that can be accomplished:
View the RSoP for a user and computer

Type of tool:
MMC snap-in

Where to find it:
%SystemRoot%\System32 on Windows Server 2003

Recipes in which it is used:
9.20

SecEdit Command (secedit.exe)

Tasks that can be accomplished:
Refresh group policy settings, and analyze, configure, export and validate security settings

Type of tool:
Command line

Where to find it:
%SystemRoot%\System32 on Windows 2000 and Windows Server 2003

Recipes in which it is used:
9.21

Time Service (w32tm.exe)

Tasks that can be accomplished:
Configure and monitor the Windows Time Service

Type of tool:
Command line

Where to find it:
%SystemRoot%\System32 on Windows 2000 and Windows Server 2003

Recipes in which it is used:
3.13

Unlock (unlock.exe)

Tasks that can be accomplished:
Find users that are locked out and unlock them

Type of tool:
Command line

Where to find it:
http://www.joeware.net/win32/zips/Unlock.zip

Recipes in which it is used:
6.9

UUID Generator Command (uuidgen.exe)

Tasks that can be accomplished:
Generate a UUID/GUID that can be used when creating new classes and attributes

Type of tool:
Command line

Where to find it:
Windows 2000 Platform SDK

Recipes in which it is used:
10.4

WinNT32 Command (winnt32.exe)

Tasks that can be accomplished:
Upgrade a computer to Windows 2000 or Windows Server 2003; can also perform checks to determine if an upgrade is possible

Type of tool:
Wizard

Where to find it:
\i386 on Windows 2000 and Windows Server 2003 CD

Recipes in which it is used:
2.12

Index

A

abstract classes, searching, 330–334
access
    auditing, 481–482
    from non-Windows, 539–540
Access Control Entry (ACE), 432
Access Control List (see ACL)
accounts
    ACLs, modifying, 452–453
    policies, viewing, 179–182
    user
        configuring expiration, 203–207
        updating, 201–203
ACE (Access Control Entry), 432
ACL (Access Control List), 432
    modifying, 446–448, 452–453
    schemas
        comparing, 448
        resetting, 448–449
    viewing, 443–444
ACL Diagnostics Command
        (acldiag.exe), 557
ACL Editor, customizing, 444–445
Active Directory Domains and Trusts Snap-in
        (domain.msc), 557
Active Directory Installation Wizard
        (dcpromo.exe), 558
Active Directory Load Balancer Command
        (adlb.exe), 558
Active Directory Schema Snap-in
        (schmmgmt.msc), 558
Active Directory Sites and Services
        (dssite.msc), 559

Active Directory Users and Computers
        (ADUC), 164
Active Directory Users and Computers
        Snap-in (dsa.msc), 559
AD Prep Utility (adprep.exe), 559
adding
    application partitions, replicas, 523–525
    attributes to schemas, 306–308, 310–313,
        324–326
    classes to schemas, 315–317
    members to groups, 222–224
    resource records, 413–415
administration
    Active Directory, 3
    (see also management)
administrator accounts, modifying
        ACLs, 452–453
ADPrep tool, 29–30
    domain controllers, promoting, 30–32
ADSI Edit (adsiedit.msc), 560
ADUC (Active Directory Users and
        Computers), 164
advertisements, 71
ambiguous name resolution (ANR), 322–324
anonymous access, LDAP, 436–438
ANR (ambiguous name resolution), 322–324
Apache, 549–550
application partitions
    creating, 518–521
    delegating, 534–538
    overview of, 517–518
    references, setting, 532–534
    replicas
        modifying, 523–525
        searching, 525–527

We'd like to hear your suggestions for improving our indexes. Send email to *index@oreilly.com*.

application partitions *(continued)*
    replication, resetting, 530–532
    searching, 521–522
    servers
        searching, 527–529
        verifying, 529–530
applications, installing GPOs, 276–277
applying Delegation of Control
              Wizard, 439–440
assignment of scripts, 275–276
attributes
    application partitions, 518
    bit-flag, modifying, 121–123
    computer objects, 233
    crossRef objects, 15
    deleted objects, 493
    DNS object, 403
    domain controller objects, 54
    domainDNS objects, 14
    objects, 94
        viewing, 98–101
    OU, 146
    quota object container, 459
    RootDSE, 95–97
    schemas, 302
        adding, 306–308, 310–313
        adding/deleting, 324–326
        deactivating, 335–336
        extending, 308–309
        indexing, 318–320
        modifying, 320–321
        modifying ANR, 322–324
        redefining, 336–337
        searching, 326–330
        viewing, 313–315
    site objects, 341
    trustedDomain objects, 16
    user objects, 163
        configuring profiles, 211–212
        modifying, 169–171
attribute-scoped queries, searching, 112–114
Audit Policy Command (auditpol.exe), 560
auditing, 481–482
authoritative restores, 498–500
authorization, DHCP servers, 552–553
automation of domain controllers, 58–59
auxiliary classes
    dynamically linking, 123–124
    searching, 330–334

B

backing up, 493–494
    GPOs, 291–294
Backup Domain Controllers (BDCs), 89
Backup Wizard (ntbackup.exe), 560
BDCs (Backup Domain Controllers), 89
BIND, 551–552
binds
    computer objects, 256–258
    LDAP, 104–105
    serverless, 6
bit-flag attributes, modifying, 121–123
bitwise filters, searching, 114–116
blocking GPOs, 283–285
bridgehead servers
    configuring, 362–363
    searching, 361–362
bridging site objects, 359–361

C

caching
    DNS, clearing, 420–421
    group membership, 231–232
    schemas, 337–339
channels
    resetting, 248–249
    testing, 247–248
Checking, 32
child objects
    deleting, 136–137
    OU, 156–157
classes
    auxiliary, 123–124
    schemas
        adding, 306–308, 315–317
        deactivating, 335–336
        extending, 308–309
        modifying security, 334
        redefining, 336–337
        searching, 330–334
        viewing, 317–318
clearing DNS caches, 420–421
clients, site objects, 369–370
code, 5
    error checking, 8–9
    executing scripts, 6–7
    serverless binds, 6
command-line interface
    ANR, 322
    attribute-scoped queries, 112
    auxiliary classes, 123

bitwise filter, 114
computer objects, 253
    binding, 257
    joining, 241
    modifying containers, 259
    moving, 244
    renaming, 245
    resetting, 249
    searching, 250, 255
    testing, 247
computer objects, creating, 234
containers, deleting, 137
domain controllers
    configuring, 72
    enabling/disabling global catalog, 77
    forcing replication, 390
    moving, 68
    searching, 64
    searching FSMO role holders, 87
    searching unreplicated changes, 387
    synchronizing, 384
    transferring FSMO role holders, 89
    viewing synchronization status, 386
domains
    creating, 20
    deleting orphans, 22
    finding duplicate SIDs, 52
    functional levels, 33
    modifying modes, 27
    searching forests, 23
    searching NetBIOS names, 25
forests
    creating, 17–18
    functional levels, 36
global catalogs
    disabling, 85
    searching, 79, 108
GPOs
    backing up, 291
    copying, 266
    creating, 264
    deleting, 268
    filtering security, 286
    importing, 273
    listing links, 280
    modifying, 272
    refreshing, 299, 300
    restoring, 294
    searching, 263
    viewing, 270
    viewing RSoP, 298

groups, 225
    adding/deleting members, 223
    caching, 231
    creating, 218
    creating computer objects, 236
    managing, 227
    searching, 228
    viewing, 220
    viewing nested members, 221
LDAP query policy, 139
objects
    creating, 117
    creating dynamic, 125
    deleting, 135
    exporting, 142, 144
    importing, 143, 144
    modifying, 119
    modifying TTL settings, 128
    moving, 131, 132
    refreshing dynamic objects, 127
    renaming, 133
    searching, 106, 110
    viewing attributes, 98
OU
    child objects, 156–157
    creating, 147–148, 159–160
    delegating, 158
    deleting, 151
    enumerating, 148, 152–153
    linking GPOs, 160–162
    moving, 154–156
replication
    enabling consistency, 396
    modifying intervals, 392
    scheduling, 393
    searching conflict objects, 398
    viewing metadata, 400
RootDSE, 95
schemas, 315
    adding attributes, 311, 324
    deactivating, 335
    deleting attributes, 324
    enabling, 304
    indexing attributes, 318
    linking, 329
    modifying, 320
    reloading caches, 337
    searching, 327
    searching classes, 331
    viewing attributes, 313
    viewing classes, 317

command-line interface *(continued)*
  SID filtering, 51
  site objects
    bridging, 359
    completing KCC, 379
    configuring bridgehead servers, 362
    configuring domain controllers, 366
    creating, 344
    creating connection objects, 372
    creating subnets, 347
    deleting, 347
    disabling, 358, 369
    disabling KCC, 380
    forcing hosts, 371
    linking, 352
    listing, 346
    listing connection objects, 373
    listing servers, 364
    listing subnets, 349
    load-balancing connection
      objects, 374
    modifying, 355
    modifying KCC, 382
    moving, 365
    searching, 370
    searching bridgehead servers, 361
    triggering KCC, 378
    troubleshooting, 375
    viewing domain controllers, 368
  timestamps, 138
  trusts
    creating between Windows NT and
      AD domains, 38
    creating transitive trusts, 40
    deleting, 50
    Kerberos realm, 43
    resetting, 48
    shortcut trusts, 42
    verifying, 46
    viewing, 44
  user objects
    configuring account expiration, 204
    configuring passwords, 191
    configuring profiles, 211
    creating, 165
    creating large number of, 166
    enabling, 183
    inetOrgPerson, 167
    locking passwords, 193
    modifying, 170
    modifying passwords, 195
    moving, 171
    preventing password expiration, 196
    renaming, 172
    searching, 176
    searching disabled users, 184
    searching login, 209
    transferring groups, 189
    updating accounts, 201
    viewing, 179, 212
    viewing groups, 186
command-line tools, 10
comma-separated variable (see CSV)
completing KCC, 379
compression, disabling, 394
computer objects
  binding, 256–258
  creating, 234–241
  joining, 241–243
  modifying, 253–254
  modifying containers, 258–260
  moving, 244–245
  overview of, 233–234
  renaming, 245–247
  resetting, 248–249
  searching, 249–252, 254–256
  testing, 247–248
concurrent binds, 104–105
configuration
  application partitions, 518–521
    references, 532–534
  connection objects, 372
  domain controllers, 72–73
    multiple sites, 366–367
  domains, 19–20
  forests, 17–18
  GPOs, 264–265
  groups, 218–219
  objects, 116–118, 125–126
  OU, 147–148, 159–160
  quota object, 483–484
  shortcut trusts, 41–42
  site objects, 343–345
    bridgehead servers, 362–363
    subnets, 347–348
  transitive trusts, 39–41
  trusts
    Kerbero realm, 42–43
    Windows NT, 38–39
  user objects, 164–166
    account expiration, 203–207
    copying, 173–175

determining logon, 207–208
enabling, 182–184
formatting UPN suffixes, 215
inetOrgPerson, 167–169
large number of, 166–167
locking passwords, 193–195
modifying, 169–171
modifying groups, 187–189
modifying names, 213–214
modifying passwords, 195–196
moving, 171–172
passwords, 191–193
preventing password
    expiration, 196–200
profiles, 211–212
renaming, 172–173
searching, 176–177
searching disabled users, 184–185
searching logon, 209–211
transferring groups, 189–190
troubleshooting, 177–179
unlocking, 175–176
updating accounts, 201–203
viewing, 179–182, 212–213
viewing groups, 185–187
WMI filters, 288–289
applying, 289–291
conflict objects, searching, 397–399
connection objects
creating, 372
load-balancing, 374, 376
viewing, 373–374
consistency, enabling, 396–397
constructed attributes, searching, 326–330
containers
computer objects, modifying, 258–260
objects
    deleting, 136–137
    moving, 130
    renaming, 133
user objects, moving, 171–172
(see also quota object containers)
controls, LDAP, 101–103
converting zones, 408–409
copying
GPOs, 265–268
user objects, 173–175
credentials
executing tools with, 3–4
scripts, 6–7
crossRef objects, 15

CSV (comma-separated variable)
exporting, 144
importing, 144
CSVDE Command (csvde.exe), 560
customization
ACL Editor, 444–445
application partitions, 530
Delegation of Control Wizard, 440–443

D

databases, sizing, 511–512
deactivating
attributes, 335–336
classes, 335–336
Default Domain Controller Security Policy
    Snap-in (dcpol.msc), 561
Default Domain Security Policy Snap-in
    (dompol.msc), 561
Default Group Policy Restore Command
    (dcgpofix.exe), 561
default TTL settings, modifying, 128–130
defining variables, 8–9
defragmentation
reclaiming whitespace, 506–508
repairing manually, 503–505
delegation
application partitions, 534–538
control of group membership, 226–228
OU, 158
zones, 411–412
Delegation of Control Wizard
applying, 439–440
customizing, 440–443
deleted objects
overview of, 492–493
restoring, 513–515
searching, 512–513
deleting
application partitions, 518–521
    replicas, 523–525
attributes, 324–326
domain controllers, 60–63
domains, 20–21
    orphans, 22–23
forests, 18–19
GPOs, 268–269
members, 222–224
objects, 135–136
    containers, 136–137
OU, 151
resource records, 413–415

deleting (continued)
    site objects, 346–347
    trusts, 50–51
demoting domain controllers, 57–58
    automating, 58–59
    deleting, 60–63
    troubleshooting, 59–60
deregistering resource records, 429
DHCP (Dynamic Handshake Challenge
    Protocol), 552–553
diagnostics logging, enabling, 461–462
Directory Information Tree (see DIT)
Directory Services Markup Language
    (DSML), 542–543
disabled users, 184–185
disabling
    compression, 394
    domain controllers, 368–369
    global catalog, 76–78, 85–86
    GPOs, 277–279
    KCC, 380–382
    site object, 357–359
    user objects, 182–184
        searching, 184–185
    (see also enabling)
Distributed Link Tracking (DLT), 75–76
DIT (Directory Information Tree)
    integrity, 501
    moving, 502
    recovery, 502–503
    whitespace, 505–506
DLT (Distributed Link Tracking), 75–76
DNS (Domain Name Service), 13
    BIND, 551–552
    global catalogs, searching, 82
DNS object
    caches, clearing, 420–421
    overview of, 402–403
    resource records
        deregistering, 429
        managing, 413–415
        querying, 415–417
        registering, 422–429
        scavenging, 418–420
    servers, modifying, 417–418
    suffixes, allowing, 429–431
    zones
        converting, 408–409
        creating forward lookup
            zones, 404–405

        creating reverse lookup
            zones, 405–406
        delegating, 411–412
        moving, 409–411
        viewing, 406–408
DNS Snap-in (dnsmgmt.msc), 562
DNSCmd Command (dnscmd.exe), 562
documentation, extensions, 309–310
Domain Controller Diagnosis Command
    (dcdiag.exe), 562
domain controllers
    authoritative restores, 498–500
    configuring, 72–73
    demoting, 57–58
        automating, 58–59
        deleting, 60–63
        troubleshooting, 59–60
    disabling, 368–369
    DLT, 75–76
    FSMO role holders, 87–91
        seizing, 91–92
    global catalog, 76–78
        disabling, 85–86
        promoting, 78
        searching, 79–83
    logon attempts, 73–74
    media, promoting, 56–57
    memory, optimizing, 74–75
    modifying, 83–85
    moving, 68–70, 365–366
    multiple sites, configuring to
        cover, 366–367
    nonauthoritative restores, 497–498
    overview of, 53–54
    promoting, 30–32
        automating, 58–59
        troubleshooting, 59–60
    renaming, 63–64
    replication
        disabling compression, 394
        enabling consistency, 396–397
        enabling logging, 395
        forcing, 390–391
        modifying intervals, 391–392
        scheduling, 392–394
        searching conflict objects, 397–399
        searching unreplicated
            changes, 386–390
        troubleshooting, 395
        viewing metadata, 399–401

restarting, 494–495
searching, 64–68
servers, promoting, 55
services, searching, 71
synchronizing, 384–385
    viewing status, 386
targeting, 4
upgrading, 29–30, 32–33
viewing, 368
Domain Name Service (see DNS)
domainDNS objects, 14
domains, 14
    ADPrep tool, 29–30
        promoting domain controllers, 30–32
    computer objects, joining, 241–243
    creating, 19–20
    deleting, 20–21
        orphans, 22–23
    forests, searching, 23–24
    functional levels, 33–35
    modes, modifying, 27–29
    NetBIOS, searching names, 25–26
    objects, moving, 132
    overview of, 14–16
    PDC Emulator, searching, 92
    renaming, 26–27
    SID, finding duplicates, 51–52
    tombstone objects, modifying, 515–516
    trees, 14
    trusts
        deleting, 50–51
        resetting, 48–49
        verifying, 46–48
        viewing, 44–46
    Windows NT, creating trusts, 38–39
    (see also forests)
DS ACL Command (dsacls.exe), 563
DS Add Command (dsadd.exe), 563
DS Get Command (dsget.exe), 563
DS Modify Command (dsmodify.exe), 563
DS Move Command (dsmove.exe), 564
DS Query Command (dsquery.exe), 564
DS Remove Command (dsrm.exe), 564
DS Restore Mode, 494–495
    resetting, 496–497
DSML (Directory Services Markup
        Language), 542–543
duplicates
    finding SIDs, 51–52
    users, 320–321

dynamic objects
    creating, 125–126
    modifying, 128–130
    refreshing, 126–127
dynamically linking auxiliary
        classes, 123–124

E

effective permissions, viewing, 445–446
enabling
    anonymous LDAP access, 436–438
    consistency, 396–397
    diagnostics logging, 461–462
    DNS logging, 467–469
    extended dcpromo logging, 459–461
    global catalog, 76–78
    GPO client logging, 464–465
    Kerberos logging, 465–467
    LDAP logging, 472–474
    List Object Access mode, 450–452
    logging, 395
    NetLogon logging, 463–464
    schemas, 304–306
    SSL/TLS, 433–434
    user objects, 182–184
encryption, SSL/TLS, 434–436
enumeration, OU, 148–153
Enumprop Command (enumprop.exe), 565
error checking
    (see also troubleshooting)
ESE (Extensible Storage Engine), 491
executing with alternate credentials, 3–4
exporting objects, 141–142, 144
extended dcpromo logging,
        enabling, 459–461
extending attributes, 308–309
Extensible Storage Engine (see ESE)
extensions, documenting, 309–310
external time sources, configuring, 72–73

F

fast binds, 104–105
files, DIT, 501
    moving, 502
    recovering, 502–503
    whitespace, 505–506
filtering
    bitwise filters, 114–116
    security, 285–287

filtering *(continued)*
  SID, 51
  WMI filters
    applying, 289–291
    creating, 288–289
finding
  domain controllers, 64
  FSMO role holders, 87–89
  global catalog, 79–83
  number of logon attempts, 73–74
  services, 71
  (see also searching)
forcing
  Kerberos traffic, 455–456
  replication, 390–391
forcing hosts, 370–371
forests, 14, 16–17
  creating, 17–18
  deleting, 18–19
  domains
    deleting, 20–21
    deleting orphans, 22–23
    searching, 23–24
  functional levels, 35–37
  global catalogs, searching, 79–83,
      108–109
  overview of, 16–17
  shortcut trusts, 41–42
  transitive trusts, 39–41
  trusts, 40
  UPN suffixes, creating, 215
formatting suffixes, 215
forward lookup zones, creating, 404–405
FSMO role holders
  searching, 87–89
  seizing, 91–92
  transferring, 89–91
functional levels
  Windows 2003 Server domains, 33–35
  Windows 2003 Server forests, 35–37

G

garbage collection, modifying, 508–509
global catalogs, 76–78
  attributes, adding/deleting, 324–326
  searching, 108–109
GPOs (group policy objects)
  backing up, 291–294
  blocking, 283–285
  copying, 265–268
  creating, 264–265
  deleting, 268–269

  disabling, 277–279
  importing, 272–275
  installing, 276–277
  linking, 160, 281–283
  listing links, 279–281
  managing, 262–263
  modifying, 272
  refreshing, 299
  restoring, 294–296, 299–300
  RSoP
    simulating, 296–297
    viewing, 297–298
  scripts, assigning, 275–276
  searching, 263–264
  security, filtering, 285–287
  viewing, 269–271
  WMI filters
    applying, 289–291
    creating, 288–289
graphical user interface (see GUI)
Group Policy Management Console
      (gpmc.msc), 565
Group Policy Object Editor
      (gpedit.msc), 565
group policy objects (see GPOs)
Group Policy Refresh Command
      (gpupdate.exe), 566
Group Policy Results Command
      (gpresult.exe), 566
Group Policy Verification Tool
      (gpotool.exe), 566
groups
  computer objects, creating, 236
  creating, 218–219
  Delegation of Control Wizard, 439–440
    customizing, 440–443
  effective permissions, 445–446
  members
    adding/deleting, 222–224
    caching, 231–232
    managing, 226–228
  modifying, 187–189, 225–226
  moving, 224
  overview of, 217–218
  searching, 228–230
  transferring, 189–190
  viewing, 185–187, 220–221
    nesting, 221–222
GUI (graphical user interface), 365
  attributes
    customizing, 100, 107
    queries, 112

auxiliary classes, linking, 123
binds, 104
bitwise filters, 114
computer objects
    binding, 256
    creating, 234
    joining, 241
    modifying, 253
    modifying containers, 258
    moving, 244
    renaming, 245
    resetting, 248
    searching, 254
containers, 137
domain controllers
    demoting, 57
    enabling/disabling global catalog, 77
    forcing replication, 390
    moving, 68
    searching, 64
    searching FSMO role holders, 87
    searching unreplicated changes, 387
    transferring FSMO role holders, 89
domains
    creating, 19
    functional levels, 33
    modifying modes, 27
    searching forests, 23
    searching NetBIOS names, 25
forests
    creating, 17–18
    functional levels, 36
global catalogs
    disabling, 85
    searching, 79, 108
GPOs
    applying WMI filters, 289
    assigning scripts, 276
    backing up, 291
    blocking, 284
    copying, 265
    creating, 264
    creating WMI filters, 288
    deleting, 268
    disabling, 278
    filtering security, 285
    importing, 273
    installing applications, 277
    linking, 282
    listing links, 279
    modifying, 272
    restoring, 294

searching, 263
    simulating RSoP, 296
    viewing, 270
    viewing RSoP, 298
groups
    adding/deleting members, 223
    caching, 231
    creating, 218
    creating computer objects, 236
    managing, 226
    modifying, 225
    searching, 228
    viewing, 220
    viewing nested members, 221
LDAP controls, 101
    modifying query policies, 139
objects
    creating, 117
    creating dynamic objects, 125
    deleting, 135
    exporting, 142
    modifying, 119, 128
    moving, 130
    refreshing, 126
    renaming, 133
    searching, 106
    searching large number of, 110
    viewing attributes, 98
OU
    child objects, 156–157
    creating, 147–148, 159–160
    delegating, 158
    deleting, 151
    enumerating, 148–153
    linking GPOs, 160–162
    moving, 154–156
replication
    modifying intervals, 392
    scheduling, 393
    searching conflict objects, 398
    viewing metadata, 400
RootDSE, 95
schemas
    adding attributes, 311, 324
    adding classes, 315
    ANR, 322
    deactivating, 335
    deleting attributes, 324
    enabling, 304
    indexing attributes, 318
    linking, 329
    modifying, 320

GUI (graphical user interface), schemas
    (*continued*)
    modifying security, 334
    reloading caches, 337
    searching, 327
    searching classes, 331
    viewing attributes, 313
    viewing classes, 317
site objects
    bridging, 359
    completing KCC, 379
    configuring bridgehead servers, 362
    configuring domain controllers, 366
    creating, 344
    creating connection objects, 372
    creating subnets, 347
    deleting, 347
    disabling, 358, 369
    disabling KCC, 380
    forcing hosts, 371
    linking, 352
    listing, 346
    listing connection objects, 373
    listing servers, 364
    listing subnets, 349
    modifying, 355
    modifying KCC, 382
    searching bridgehead servers, 361
    transferring, 376
    triggering KCC, 378
    troubleshooting, 375
timestamps, 138
trusts
    creating between Windows NT and
      AD domains, 38
    creating transitive trusts, 39
    deleting, 50
    Kerberos realm, 43
    resetting, 48
    shortcut trusts, 41
    verifying, 46
    viewing, 44
user objects
    configuring account expiration, 204
    configuring passwords, 191
    configuring profiles, 211
    copying, 174
    creating, 164
    determining logon, 207
    enabling, 183
    formatting UPN suffixes, 215
    inetOrgPerson, 167
    locking passwords, 193
    modifying, 170
    modifying groups, 187
    modifying names, 213
    modifying passwords, 195
    moving, 171
    preventing password expiration, 196
    renaming, 172
    searching disabled users, 184
    searching logon, 209
    transferring groups, 189
    troubleshooting, 178
    unlocking, 175
    updating accounts, 201
    viewing, 212
    viewing groups, 185

H

hosts, forcing, 370–371

I

importing
    GPOs, 272–275
    objects, 142–144
inactive computer objects,
    searching, 249–252
indexing attributes, 318–320
inetOrgPerson object, creating, 167–169
installing GPOs, 276–277
integration
    access from non-Windows, 539–540
    Apache, 549–550
    MIT Kerberos, 547–548
    Samba, 548–549
integrity, DIT files, 501
interoperability, access from
    non-Windows, 539–540
Inter-Site Topology Generator (ISTG), 375
intervals, garbage collection,
    modifying, 508–509
IP Configuration (ipconfig.exe), 567
ISTG (Inter-Site Topology Generator), 375

J

Java, programming, 544–546
joining computer objects, 241–243

K

Kerberos
  logging, enabling, 465–467
  passwords, configuring, 193
  realms, 42–43
  tickets, viewing, 453–454
  traffic
    forcing, 455–456
    modifying, 456–457
Kerberos List (klist.exe), 567
Kerberos Tray (kerbtray.exe), 567

L

large numbers of objects, searching, 110–112
LDAP Data Interchange Format (see LDIF)
LDAP (Lightweight Directory Access
      Protocol), 94
  anonymous access, 436–438
  binds, 104–105
  controls, 101–103
  passwords, 192
  queries, 438–439
  query policy, modifying, 139–141
  SSL/TLS, 434–436
LDIF (LDAP Data Interchange Format), 4–5
  exporting, 141–142
  importing, 142–143
LDIFDE Command (ldifde.exe), 568
ldifde utility, 4
LDP (ldp.exe), 568
Lightweight Directory Access Protocol (see
      LDAP)
linking
  attributes, 329
  auxiliary classes, 123–124
  GPOs, 281–283
    listing, 279–281
  OU, 160–162
  site objects, 352–355
    bridging, 359–361
    modifying, 355–357
List Object Access, enabling, 450–452
listing
  connection objects, 373–374
  domains in forests, 23–24
  links, 279–281
  servers, 364–365
  site objects, 345–346
    subnets, 349–350
LM hash, preventing password
      storage, 449–450

load-balancing connection objects, 374, 376
locked users
  searching, 176–177
  troubleshooting, 177–179
  viewing, 179–182
locking passwords, 193–195
logging
  diagnostics, 461–462
  DNS, enabling, 467–469
  enabling, 395
  extended dcpromo, 459–461
  GPO client, enabling, 464–465
  Kerberos, enabling, 465–467
  LDAP, enabling, 472–474
  NetLogon, enabling, 463–464
  tombstone objects, 509–510
login
  global catalogs, disabling, 85–86
  scripts, assigning, 275–276
logoff, 275–276
logon
  attempts, finding number of, 73–74
  determining, 207–208
  NetLogon logging, enabling, 463–464
  passwords, 195–196
  searching, 209–211
loose consistency, 396

M

mailing lists, 12
maintenance, backing up, 493–494
  (see also troubleshooting)
management
  Active Directory, 3
  application partitions, 534–538
  GPOs, 262–263
  groups, 226–228
  user objects, 212–213
mandatory attributes, searching, 332
margins
  DIT files, 505–506
  reclaiming, 506–508
media, promoting domain controllers, 56–57
members
  adding/deleting, 222–224
  caching, 231–232
  managing, 226–228
memory, optimizing, 74–75
metadata, viewing, 399–401
Microsoft Developers Network (MSDN), 10
Microsoft Knowledge Base (MS KB), 10
MIT Kerberos, 547–548

mixed mode, modifying, 27–29
modification
    ACLs, 446–448, 452–453
    application partitions, 523–525
    attributes
        ANR, 322–324
        schemas, 320–321
    bit-flag attributes, 121–123
    classes, 334
    computer objects, 253–254, 258–260
    DNS server, 417–418
    domain controllers, 83–85
    domain modes, 27–29
    garbage collection, 508–509
    GPOs, 272
    groups, 225–226
    KCC, 382–383
    Kerberos traffic, 456–457
    LDIF, 5
    objects, 118–121, 128–130
    passwords, 195–196
    query policies, 139–141
    quota object, 485–486
    replication intervals, 391–392
    schemas, 320
        enabling, 304–306
    site objects, 355–357
    tombstone objects, 515–516
    user objects, 169–171
        groups, 187–189
        names, 213–214
monitoring Active Directory, 476–480
Move Tree Command (movetree.exe), 568
moving
    computer objects, 244–245
    DIT files, 502
    domain controllers, 68–70
    FSMO role holders, 89–91
    groups, 224
    objects, 130–133
    OU, 154–156
    site objects, 365–366
    zones, 409–411
MS KB (Microsoft Knowledge Base), 10
MSDN (Microsoft Developers Network), 10

N

names
    ANR, 322–324
    domains, renaming, 26–27
    NetBIOS, searching domains, 25–26
    user objects

formatting UPN suffixes, 215
        modifying, 213–214
naming contexts (NCs), 15
native mode, modifying, 27–29
NCs (naming contexts), 15
nested group members, viewing, 221–222
.NET, programming, 540–541
NetBIOS, searching names, 25–26
Netdom Command (netdom.exe), 569
NetLogon logging, enabling, 463–464
Network Connectivity Tester
        (netdiag.exe), 569
Network Information System (NIS),
        replacing, 550–551
Network Operating System (NOS), 3
newsgroups, 11
NIS (Network Information System),
        replacing, 550–551
NLTest Command (nltest.exe), 569
nonauthoritative restores, 497–498
NOS (Network Operating System), 3
Nslookup Command (nslookup.exe), 570
NTDS Util Command (ntdsutil.exe), 570
nTDSDSA object, 54

O

objects
    ACLs, viewing, 443–444
    attributes, 94
        viewing, 98–101
    creating, 116–118, 125–126
    deleting, 135–136
        OU, 151
    DLT, 75–76
    exporting, 141–142, 144
    importing, 142–144
    modifying, 118–121, 128–130
    moving, 130–133
    nTDSDSA, 54
    OU
        delegating, 158
        enumerating, 150
        moving, 156
    overview of, 94–95
    refreshing, 126–127
    renaming, 133–134
    searching, 105–108
        large numbers of, 110–112
    user, 163–164
        configuring account
            expiration, 203–207
        configuring passwords, 191–193

configuring profiles, 211–212
copying, 173–175
creating, 164–166
creating large number of, 166–167
determining logon, 207–208
enabling, 182–184
formatting UPN suffixes, 215
inetOrgPerson, 167–169
locking passwords, 193–195
modifying, 169–171
modifying groups, 187–189
modifying names, 213–214
modifying passwords, 195–196
moving, 171–172
preventing password
    expiration, 196–200
renaming, 172–173
searching, 176–177
searching disabled users, 184–185
searching logon, 209–211
transferring groups, 189–190
troubleshooting, 177–179
unlocking, 175–176
updating accounts, 201–203
viewing, 179–182, 212–213
viewing groups, 185–187
offline defrag, repairing manually, 506–508
OID Generator Command (oidgen.exe), 570
online defrag, repairing manually, 503–505
operating systems, NOS, 3
optimizing memory, 74–75
optional attributes, searching, 332
organizational unit (see OU), 156
orphans, deleting, 22–23
OU (organizational unit)
    child objects, 156–157
    creating, 147–148, 159–160
    delegating, 158
    deleting, 151
    enumerating, 148–153
    GPOs
        blocking, 283–285
        linking, 281–283
    linking GPOs, 160–162
    moving, 154–156
    objects
        moving, 130, 171–172
        renaming, 133
    overview of, 146–147

P

partitions
    forests, 17
    (see also application partitions)
passwords
    DS Restore Mode, 496–497
    LM hash, preventing storage, 449–450
    policies, viewing, 179–182
    user objects
        configuring, 191–193
        locking, 193–195
        modifying, 195–196
        preventing expiration, 196–200
PDC Emulator, 92
Perfmon, 476–480
Perl
    computer objects, 250
    programming, 543–544
    user objects, 209
permissions
    schemas, comparing to ACLs, 448
    viewing, 445–446
policies, queries, 139–141
preferences, modifying, 83–85
profiles, 211–212
programming
    DSML, 542–543
    Java, 544–546
    .NET, 540–541
    Perl, 543–544
    Python, 546–547
    VBScript, 5
        error checking, 8–9
        executing scripts, 6–7
        serverless binds, 6
promoting
    domain controllers, 30–32
        automating, 58–59
        media, 56–57
        servers, 55
        troubleshooting, 59–60
    global catalog, 78
purging Kerberos tickets, 453–454
Python, programming, 546–547

Q

queries
    attribute-scoped, searching, 112–114
    LDAP, restricting, 438–439
    policies, modifying, 139–141

queries *(continued)*
    resource records, 415–417
    testing, 474–476
quota object
    auditing, 481–482
    containers, 458
    creating, 483–484
    diagnostics, 461–462
    DNS logging, enabling, 467–469
    DNS Server performance,
        viewing, 469–471
    extended dcpromo logging,
        enabling, 459–461
    GPO client logging, 464–465
    Kerberos logging, enabling, 465–467
    LDAP logging, enabling, 472–474
    modifying, 485–486
    NetLogon logging, enabling, 463–464
    overview of, 459
    Perfmon, 476–480
    queries, testing, 474–476
    searching, 484–485
    security, 487–488
        searching, 488–490

R

RDN (relative distinguished name), 15
recovery, DIT files, 502–503
redefining
    attributes, 336–337
    classes, 336–337
Redirect Default Computers Command
    (redircmp.exe), 571
Redirect Default Users Command
    (redirusr.exe), 571
references, application partitions, 532–534
refreshing
    GPOs, 299
    objects, 126–127
Reg Command (reg.exe), 571
registration
    resource records, 422–429
    schema, 303–304
Registry Editor (regedit.exe), 571
relative distinguished name (RDN), 15
reloading schema caches, 337–339
Rename Domain Command
    (rendom.exe), 572
renaming
    computer objects, 245–247
    domain controllers, 63–64

    domains, 26–27
    objects, 133–134
    user objects, 172–173
replaceable text, 9
replacing NIS, 550–551
replication
    application partitions, 530–532
    attributes, 326–330
    domain controllers
        disabling compression, 394
        enabling consistency, 396–397
        enabling logging, 395
        forcing, 390–391
        modifying intervals, 391–392
        scheduling, 392–394
        searching conflict objects, 397–399
        searching unreplicated
            changes, 386–390
        synchronizing, 384–385
        troubleshooting, 395
        viewing metadata, 399–401
        viewing synchronization status, 386
    site objects, controlling, 357–359
Replication Diagnostics Command
    (repadmin.exe), 572
Replication Monitor (replmon.exe), 572
resetting
    ACLs, 448–449
    application partitions, 530–532
    computer objects, 248–249
    DS Restore Mode, 496–497
    trusts, 48–49
resource records
    deregistering, 429
    managing, 413–415
    querying, 415–417
    registering, 422–429
    scavenging, 418–420
resources
    books, 12
    magazines, 12
    mailing lists, 12
    newsgroups, 11
    web sites, 11
restarting domain controllers, 494–495
restoring
    authoritative restores, 498–500
    deleted objects, 513–515
    GPOs, 294–296, 299–300
    nonauthoritative restores, 497–498
restricting LDAP queries, 438–439

Resultant Set of Policy Snap-in
        (rsop.msc), 573
reverse lookup zones, creating, 405–406
RootDSE, viewing, 95–97
RSoP
    simulating, 296–297
    viewing, 297–298

S

Samba, 548–549
saving GPOs, 291–296
scavenging resource records, 418–420
scheduling replication, 392–394
schemas
    ACLs
        comparing, 448
        resetting, 448–449
    attributes
        adding, 306–308, 310–313, 324–326
        deactivating, 335–336
        deleting, 324–326
        extending, 308–309
        indexing, 318–320
        modifying, 320–321
        modifying ANR, 322–324
        redefining, 336–337
        searching, 326–330
        viewing, 313–315
    caches, reloading, 337–339
    classes
        adding, 315–317
        deactivating, 335–336
        modifying security, 334
        redefining, 336–337
        searching, 330–334
        viewing, 317–318
    enabling, 304–306
    extensions, documenting, 309–310
    overview of, 301–303
    registering, 303–304
scope, modifying, 225–226
scripts
    error checking, 8–9
    executing, 6–7
    GPOs, 275–276
searching, 92
    application partitions, 521–522
        replicas, 525–527
        servers, 527–529
    attributes, schemas, 326–330

attribute-scoped queries, 112–114
    with bitwise filters, 114–116
    classes, 330–334
    computer objects, 249–252, 254–256
    conflict objects, 397–399
    deleted objects, 512–513
    domain controllers, 64–68
        unreplicated changes, 386–390
    domains
        forests, 23–24
        NetBIOS names, 25–26
    FSMO role holders, 87–89
    global catalog, 79–83, 108–109
    GPOs, 263–264
    groups, 228–230
    logon attempts, 73–74
    objects, 105–108
        large numbers of, 110–112
    quota object, 484–485
    security, 488–490
    services, 71
    site objects, 369–370
        bridgehead servers, 361–362
        subnets, 350–352
    user objects, 176–177, 184–185
Secure Sockets Layer (see SSL)
security, 16–18
    classes, 334
    computer objects, 247–248
        resetting, 248–249
    GPOs, 285–287
    quota objects, 487–488
        searching, 488–490
Security Identifier (see SID)
seizing FSMO role holders, 91–92
Server, 572
serverless binds, 6
servers
    application partitions, 529–530
    bridgehead
        configuring, 362–363
        searching, 361–362
    DHCP, authorizing, 552–553
    DNS object, modifying, 417–418
    domain controllers, 55
    listing, 364–365
services, searching, 71
shortcut trusts, 41–42
SID (Security Identifier)
    duplicates, 51–52
    filtering, 51

simulating RSoP, 296–297
site objects, 341–343
    bridgehead servers, 362–363
    bridging, 359–361
    completing KCC, 379
    connection objects, 372
        load-balancing, 374, 376
        viewing, 373–374
    creating, 343–345
    deleting, 346–347
    disabling, 357–359
    disabling KCC, 380–382
    domain controllers
        configuring multiple sites, 366–367
        disabling, 368–369
        viewing, 368
    forcing hosts, 370–371
    linking, 352–355
    listing, 345–346
        servers, 364–365
    modifying, 355–357
    modifying KCC, 382–383
    moving, 365–366
    searching, 369–370
        bridgehead servers, 361–362
    subnets
        creating, 347–348
        listing, 349–350
        searching, 350–352
    transferring, 376–377
    triggering KCC, 378–379
    troubleshooting, 375
sites
    domain controllers
        moving, 68–70
        searching, 67
    global catalogs, searching, 80
sizing databases, 511–512
SSL (Secure Sockets Layer), 432
    enabling, 433–434
    encrypting, 434–436
strict consistency, 396
structural classes, searching, 330–334
subnets
    creating, 347–348
    listing, 349–350
    searching, 350–352
suffixes
    allowing, 429–431
    UPN, 215

synchronization
    domain controllers, 384–385
    status, viewing, 386

T

targeting domain controllers, 4
testing
    computer objects, 247–248
    queries, 474–476
    VMWare, 553–555
text, replaceable, 9
Time Service (w32tm.exe), 573
timestamps, viewing, 137–138
time-to-live (TTL), modifying, 128–130
TLS (Transport Layer Security), 432
    enabling, 433–434
    encrypting, 434–436
tombstone objects
    logging, 509–510
    modifying, 485–486, 515–516
tools, 2–4
    ADPrep, 29–30
        promoting domain controllers, 30–32
    command-line, 10
    ldifde utility, 4
traffic
    forcing, 455–456
    modifying, 456–457
transferring
    FSMO role holders, 89–91
    site objects, 376–377
    user objects, 189–190
transitive trusts, creating, 39–41
transitivity, disabling site links, 357–359
Transport Layer Security (see TLS)
trees, 14
    creating, 19–20
    deleting, 20–21
    deleting orphans, 22–23
triggering KCC, 378–379
troubleshooting
    DIT files, 502–503
    domain controller
        promotion/demotion, 59–60
    error checking, 8–9
    offline defrag, reclaiming
        whitespace, 506–508
    online defrag, repairing
        manually, 503–505

replication, 395
site objects, 375
user objects, 177–179
(see also quota object)
trustedDomain objects, 16
trusts, 14
    deleting, 50–51
    Kerberos realm, 42–43
    overview of, 16
    resetting, 48–49
    shortcuts, 41–42
    SID filtering, 51
    transitive, 39–41
    verifying, 46–48
    viewing, 44–46
    Windows NT, 38–39
TTL (time-to-live), modifying, 128–130
types of groups, 225–226

U

Unlock (unlock.exe), 574
unlocking user objects, 175–176
unused computer objects,
        searching, 249–252
updating
    schemas, 304–306
    user accounts, 201–203
upgrading domain controllers, 29–30, 32–33
UPN (User Principal Name), 215
user objects, 163–164
    accounts
        configuring expiration, 203–207
        updating, 201–203
    computer objects, 236
    copying, 173–175
    creating, 164–166
        inetOrgPerson, 167–169
        large number of, 166–167
        modifying, 169–171
    Delegation of Control Wizard, 439–440
        customizing, 440–443
    duplicating, 320–321
    effective permissions, 445–446
    enabling, 182–184
    logon
        determing, 207–208
        searching, 209–211
    modifying groups, 187–189

moving, 171–172
names
    formatting UPN suffixes, 215
    modifying, 213–214
passwords
    configuring, 191–193
    locking, 193–195
    modifying, 195–196
    preventing expiration, 196–200
profiles, 211–212
renaming, 172–173
searching, 176–177
searching disabled users, 184–185
transferring groups, 189–190
troubleshooting, 177–179
unlocking, 175–176
viewing, 179–182, 212–213
viewing groups, 185–187
User Principal Name (UPN), 215
UUID Generator Command
        (uuidgen.exe), 574

V

variables, defining, 8–9
VBScript, 5
    attribute-scoped queries, 112
    auxiliary classes, 123
    bitwise filter, 114
    computer objects
        binding, 257
        creating, 235
        joining, 241
        modifying, 253
        modifying containers, 259
        moving, 244
        renaming, 245
        resetting, 249
        searching, 255
    containers, 137
    domain controllers
        configuring, 72
        forcing replication, 390
        moving, 68
        searching, 64
        searching FSMO role holders, 87
        searching unreplicated changes, 387
        synchronizing, 385
        transferring FSMO role holders, 89

VBScript *(continued)*
  domains
    functional levels, 34
    modifying modes, 28
    searching forests, 23
    searching NetBIOS names, 25
  forests, 36
  global catalogs
    disabling, 85
    searching, 79, 108
  GPOs
    applying WMI filters, 289
    backing up, 292
    blocking, 284
    copying, 266
    creating, 264
    creating WMI filters, 288
    deleting, 268
    disabling, 278
    filtering security, 286
    importing, 273
    linking, 282
    listing links, 280
    modifying, 272
    restoring, 294
    searching, 263
    viewing, 270
  groups
    adding/deleting members, 223
    caching, 231
    creating, 218
    creating computer objects, 236
    managing, 227
    modifying, 225
    searching, 228
    viewing, 220
    viewing nested members, 221
  LDAP
    controls, 102
    query policy, 139
  objects
    creating, 117
    creating dynamic, 125
    deleting, 135
    exporting, 142
    importing, 143
    modifying, 119
    modifying TTL settings, 128
    moving, 131, 132
    refreshing dynamic objects, 127
    renaming, 133

    searching, 106, 110
    viewing attributes, 98
OU
  child objects, 156–157
  creating, 147–148, 159–160
  delegating, 158
  deleting, 151
  enumerating, 148–153
  linking GPOs, 160–162
  moving, 154–156
replication
  enabling consistency, 396
  modifying intervals, 392
  scheduling, 393
  searching conflict objects, 398
  viewing metadata, 400
RootDSE, 95
schemas
  adding attributes, 311
  adding classes, 316
  adding/deleting attributes, 324
  ANR, 322
  deactivating, 335
  enabling, 304
  indexing attributes, 318
  linking, 329
  reloading caches, 338
  searching, 327
  searching classes, 331
  viewing attributes, 313
  viewing classes, 317
scripts
  error checking, 8–9
  executing, 6–7
serverless binds, 6
site objects
  bridging, 359
  completing KCC, 379
  configuring bridgehead servers, 362
  configuring domain controllers, 366
  creating, 344
  creating subnets, 347
  deleting, 347
  disabling, 358, 369
  disabling KCC, 380
  forcing hosts, 371
  linking, 352
  listing, 346
  listing connection objects, 373
  listing servers, 364
  listing subnets, 349

modifying, 355
modifying KCC, 382
moving, 365
searching, 370
searching bridgehead servers, 361
transferring, 376
triggering KCC, 378
troubleshooting, 375
viewing domain controllers, 368
timestamps, 138
trusts
deleting, 50
resetting, 49
verifying, 47
viewing, 44
user objects
configuring account expiration, 204
configuring passwords, 191
configuring profiles, 211
copying, 174
creating, 165
creating large number of, 166
determining logon, 207
enabling, 183
formatting UPN suffixes, 215
inetOrgPerson, 167
locking passwords, 193
modifying, 170
modifying groups, 187
modifying names, 214
modifying passwords, 195
moving, 171
preventing password expiration, 196
renaming, 172
searching disabled users, 184
transferring groups, 189
unlocking, 175
updating accounts, 201
viewing, 179, 212
viewing groups, 186
verification
application partitions, 529–530
trusts, 46–48
viewing
ACLs, 443–444
attributes
objects, 98–101
schemas, 313–315

classes, 317–318
connection objects, 373–374
DNS Server performance, 469–471
domain controllers, 368
effective permissions, 445–446
GPOs, 269–271
groups, 220–221
nesting, 221–222
Kerberos tickets, 453–454
metadata, 399–401
objects, 137–138
RootDSE, 95–97
RSoP, 297–298
trusts, 44–46
user accounts, 201–203
user objects, 179–182, 212–213
groups, 185–187
zones, 406–408
VMWare, 553–555

W

web sites, 11
whitespace
DIT files, 505–506
reclaiming, 506–508
Windows 2000
comparing to Windows Server 2003, 2
domain controllers, 63
domains, 27–29
forests, 40
global catalog, 85–86
Windows 2003 Server
comparing to Windows 2000, 2
domain controllers, 63
promoting, 30–32
upgrading, 29–30, 32–33
domains, 33–35
forests, 35–37
global catalog, 86
Windows NT
Backup Domain Controllers, 89
trusts, 38–39
WinNT32 Command (winnt32.exe), 574
WMI filters
applying, 289–291
creating, 288–289

About the Author

Robbie Allen (*www.rallenhome.com*) is a Member of Technical Staff at Cisco Systems, where he has been working since 1997. He has been involved with Active Directory since the Windows 2000 JDP and is the author of several articles and books, including O'Reilly's best-selling *Windows 2000 Active Directory*, Second Edition.

Colophon

Our look is the result of reader comments, our own experimentation, and feedback from distribution channels. Distinctive covers complement our distinctive approach to technical topics, breathing personality and life into potentially dry subjects.

The animal on the cover of *Active Directory Cookbook* is a bluefin tuna (*Thunnus thynnus*), also known as a horse mackerel. It inhabits both the Atlantic and Pacific Oceans in temperate and subtropical waters. The body of a bluefin tuna is a metallic, deep blue on top, while the undersides and belly are silvery white. The first dorsal fin is yellow or blue; the second is red or brown. The rear fin and finlets are yellow, edged with black. The central caudal keel is black.

The bluefin tuna is one of the largest and fastest species of marine fish. An adult can weigh as much as 1,500 pounds (680 kilograms), and can swim up to speeds of 55 miles per hour (88.5 kilometers per hour). A bluefin tuna can swim across the Atlantic Ocean in 40 days. Recent pop-up satellite tracking has revealed that the bluefin tuna can dive to depths greater than 3,000 feet in a matter of minutes and still maintain a body temperature of 77 degrees Fahrenheit (25 degrees Celsius), even in near-freezing water.

Commercial fishing has reduced the stock of bluefin tuna to the extent that a single fish, once caught, can be worth up to $40,000 (U.S.). However, the situation is reversible, and the numbers of tuna could increase if the guidelines of the International Commission for the Conservation of Atlantic Tuna (ICCAT), an intergovernmental fishing organization that oversees tuna, are followed.

Matt Hutchinson was the production editor for *Active Directory Cookbook*. Genevieve d'Entremont, Marlowe Shaeffer, and Darren Kelly provided quality control. Octal Publishing, Inc. provided production services.

Ellie Volckhausen designed the cover of this book, based on a series design by Edie Freedman. The cover image is a 19th-century engraving from the Dover Pictorial Archive. Emma Colby produced the cover layout with QuarkXPress 4.1 using Adobe's ITC Garamond font.

David Futato designed the interior layout. This book was converted by Julie Hawks to FrameMaker 5.5.6 with a format conversion tool created by Erik Ray, Jason McIntosh, Neil Walls, and Mike Sierra that uses Perl and XML technologies. The text font is Linotype Birka; the heading font is Adobe Myriad Condensed; and the code font is LucasFont's TheSans Mono Condensed. The illustrations that appear in the book were produced by Robert Romano and Jessamyn Read using Macromedia FreeHand 9 and Adobe Photoshop 6. The tip and warning icons were drawn by Christopher Bing. This colophon was written by Reg Aubry.

Other Titles Available from O'Reilly

Visual Basic 6.0 Programming

Access Cookbook

By Ken Getz, Paul Litwin
& Andy Baron
1st Edition February 2002
718 pages, ISBN 0-596-00084-7,

Access Cookbook provides solutions to practical user interface and programming problems for the Microsoft Access power user or programmer who is running up against some of the apparent limits of the software. The book contains a comprehensive collection of problems, solutions, and practical examples for Access power users and programmers at all levels, from the relatively inexperienced to the most sophisticated.

COM+ Programming with Visual Basic

By Jose Mojica
1st Edition June 2001
304 pages, ISBN 1-56592-840-7

There's simply no other documentation available for much of what's in *COM+ Programming with Visual Basic*; this book draws from the author's wide experience as a COM+ developer and instructor. The first part delivers information that's indispensable for creating robust, efficient, high-performance COM+ applications. The second focuses on incorporating individual COM+ services, like transaction support, security, and asynchronous operations, into applications.

VB & VBA in a Nutshell: The Language

By Paul Lomax
1st Edition October 1998
656 pages, ISBN 1-56592-358-8

For Visual Basic and VBA programmers, this book boils down the essentials of the VB and VBA languages into a single volume, including undocumented and little-documented areas essential to everyday programming. The convenient alphabetical reference to all functions, procedures, statements, and keywords allows programmers to use this book both as a standard reference guide and as a tool for troubleshooting and identifying programming problems.

VBScript in a Nutshell, 2nd Edition

By Paul Lomax, Matt Childs
& Ron Petrusha
2nd Edition March 2003
512 pages, ISBN 0-596-00488-5

Lightweight yet powerful, VBScript from Microsoft is used in four main areas: server-side web applications using Active Server Pages (ASP), client-side web scripts using Internet Explorer, code behind Outlook forms, and automating repetitive tasks using Windows Script Host (WSH). *VBScript in a Nutshell*, Second Edition delivers current and complete documentation for programmers and system administrators who want to develop effective scripts.

Access Database Design & Programming, 3rd Edition

By Steven Roman
3rd Edition January 2002
448 pages, ISBN 0-59600-273-4

When using GUI-based software, we often focus so much on the interface that we forget about the general concepts required to use the software effectively. *Access Database Design & Programming* takes you behind the details of the interface, focusing on the general knowledge necessary for Access power users or developers to create effective database applications. The main sections of this book include: database design, queries, and programming.

MCSD in a Nutshell: The Visual Basic Exams

By James Foxall, MCSD
1st Edition October 2000
632 pages, ISBN 1-56592-752-4

Programmers tend to be specialists—they often do the same kind of programming over and over. The MCSD exam is targeted at technical generalists—developers familiar with a broad array of Microsoft technologies and development approaches. With its comprehensive overview of core technology areas, *MCSD in a Nutshell* is the perfect study guide and resource to help developers master the technologies that are less familiar to them.

How to stay in touch with O'Reilly

1. Visit our award-winning web site

http://www.oreilly.com/

★ "Top 100 Sites on the Web"—PC Magazine
★ CIO Magazine's Web Business 50 Awards

Our web site contains a library of comprehensive product information (including book excerpts and tables of contents), downloadable software, background articles, interviews with technology leaders, links to relevant sites, book cover art, and more. File us in your bookmarks or favorites!

2. Join our email mailing lists

Sign up to get email announcements of new books and conferences, special offers, and O'Reilly Network technology newsletters at:

http://elists.oreilly.com

It's easy to customize your free elists subscription so you'll get exactly the O'Reilly news you want.

3. Get examples from our books

To find example files for a book, go to:

http://www.oreilly.com/catalog

select the book, and follow the "Examples" link.

4. Work with us

Check out our web site for current employment opportunities:

http://jobs.oreilly.com/

5. Register your book

Register your book at:

http://register.oreilly.com

6. Contact us

O'Reilly & Associates, Inc.
1005 Gravenstein Hwy North
Sebastopol, CA 95472 USA
TEL: 707-827-7000 or 800-998-9938
          (6am to 5pm PST)
FAX: 707-829-0104

order@oreilly.com
For answers to problems regarding your order or our products. To place a book order online visit:

http://www.oreilly.com/order_new/

catalog@oreilly.com
To request a copy of our latest catalog.

booktech@oreilly.com
For book content technical questions or corrections.

corporate@oreilly.com
For educational, library, government, and corporate sales.

proposals@oreilly.com
To submit new book proposals to our editors and product managers.

international@oreilly.com
For information about our international distributors or translation queries. For a list of our distributors outside of North America check out:

http://international.oreilly.com/distributors.html

adoption@oreilly.com
For information about academic use of O'Reilly books, visit:

http://academic.oreilly.com

O'REILLY®

To order: *800-998-9938* • *order@oreilly.com* • *www.oreilly.com*
Online editions of most O'Reilly titles are available by subscription at *safari.oreilly.com*
Also available at most retail and online bookstores.